THE BICENTENNIAL EDITION
OF THE
WORKS OF JOHN WESLEY

General Editor: Randy L. Maddox

THE WORKS OF
JOHN WESLEY

Volume 27

Letters
III
1756–1765

EDITED BY
TED A. CAMPBELL

Abingdon Press
Nashville

THE WORKS OF JOHN WESLEY, VOLUME 27
LETTERS III, 1756–1765

Copyright © 2015 by Abingdon Press

This book is printed on acid-free paper.

Library of Congress Cataloging-in-Publication Data has been requested.

ISBN: 978-1-5018-0622-3

Scripture quotations from The Authorized (King James) Version. Rights in the Authorized Version in the United Kingdom are vested in the Crown. Reproduced by permission of the Crown's patentee, Cambridge University Press.

This project uses the SBL Greek font, which is available from the Society of Biblical Literature at www.sbl-site.org.

15 16 17 18 19 20 21 22 23 24—10 9 8 7 6 5 4 3 2 1
MANUFACTURED IN THE UNITED STATES OF AMERICA

THE BICENTENNIAL EDITION OF
THE WORKS OF JOHN WESLEY

THIS edition of the works of John Wesley reflects the quickened interest in the heritage of Christian thought that has become evident during the last half century. A fully critical presentation of Wesley's writings had long been a desideratum in order to furnish documentary sources illustrating his contribution to both catholic and evangelical Christianity.

Several scholars, notably Professor Albert C. Outler, Professor Franz Hildebrandt, Dean Merrimon Cuninggim, and Dean Robert E. Cushman, discussed the possibility of such an edition. Under the leadership of Dean Cushman, a board of directors was formed in 1960 comprising the deans of four sponsoring theological schools of Methodist-related universities in the United States: Drew, Duke, Emory, and Southern Methodist. They appointed an Editorial Committee to formulate plans and enlisted an international and interdenominational team of scholars for the Wesley Works Editorial Project.

The works were divided into units of cognate material, with a separate editor (or joint editors) responsible for each unit. Dr. Frank Baker was appointed textual editor for the whole project, with responsibility for supplying each unit editor with a critically developed, accurate Wesley text. The text seeks to represent Wesley's thought in its fullest and most deliberate expression insofar as this can be determined from the available evidence. Substantive variant readings in any British edition published during Wesley's lifetime are shown in appendices to the units, preceded by a summary of the problems faced and the solutions reached in the complex task of securing and presenting Wesley's text. The aim throughout is to enable Wesley to be read with maximum ease and understanding, and with minimal intrusion by the editors.

This edition includes all of Wesley's original or mainly original prose works, some select examples of his extensive work as editor and publisher of extracts from the writings of others, and one volume devoted to his *Collection of Hymns* (1780). An essential feature of the project is a bibliography outlining the historical settings of the works published by Wesley and his brother Charles, sometimes

v

jointly, sometimes separately. The bibliography also offers full analytical data for identifying each of the two thousand editions of these 450 items that were published during the lifetime of John Wesley, and notes the location of copies. An index is supplied for each unit and a general index for the whole edition.

The Delegates of the Oxford University Press agreed to undertake publication, but announced in June 1982 that because of severe economic problems they would regretfully be compelled to withdraw from the enterprise with the completion in 1983 of volume 7, the *Collection of Hymns*. Abingdon Press offered its services, beginning with the publication of the first volume of the *Sermons* in 1984, the bicentennial year of the formation of American Methodism as an autonomous church. The new title now assumed, however, refers in general to the bicentennial of Wesley's total activities as author, editor, and publisher, from 1733 to 1791, especially as summarized in the first edition of his collected works in thirty-two volumes, 1771–74.

Dean Robert E. Cushman of Duke University undertook general administration and promotion of the project until 1971, when he was succeeded as president by Dean Joseph D. Quillian Jr., of Southern Methodist University, these two universities having furnished the major support and guidance for the enterprise. During the decade 1961–70, the Editorial Committee supervised the task of setting editorial principles and procedures, and general editorship was shared by Dr. Eric W. Baker, Dean William R. Cannon, and Dean Cushman. In 1969 the directors appointed Dr. Frank Baker, early attached to the project as bibliographer and textual editor for Wesley's text, as editor-in-chief also. Upon Dean Quillian's retirement in 1981, he was succeeded as president of the project by Dean James E. Kirby Jr., also of Southern Methodist University. In 1986 the Directors appointed Richard P. Heitzenrater as general editor to begin the chief editorship of the project with the *Journal and Diaries* unit, with Dr. Baker continuing as textual editor. Dean Dennis M. Campbell of Duke University was elected president of the project in 1990. Dean Russell E. Richey of Emory University succeeded Dr. Campbell in 2003. At that same point the directors named Randy L. Maddox as associate general editor, to work alongside Dr. Heitzenrater in completing the project. Dean William B. Lawrence of Southern Methodist University assumed the role of president in 2006. And most recently, in 2014, Randy L. Maddox stepped into the role of General Editor, upon Dr. Heitzenrater's retirement from that capacity.

Other sponsoring bodies have been successively added to the original four: Boston University School of Theology, the Conference of the Methodist Church of Great Britain, The General Commission on Archives and History of The United Methodist Church, The United Methodist Board of Higher Education and Ministry, and the World Methodist Council. For the continuing support of the sponsoring institutions the Directors express their profound thanks. They gratefully acknowledge also the encouragement and financial support that have come from the Historical Societies and Commissions on Archives and History of many Annual Conferences, as well as the donations of private individuals and foundations.

On June 9, 1976, The Wesley Works Editorial Project was incorporated in the State of North Carolina as a nonprofit corporation. In 1977 by-laws were approved governing the appointment and duties of the Directors, their officers, and their Executive Committee.

The Board of Directors

President: William B. Lawrence, Dean of Perkins School of Theology, Southern Methodist University, Dallas, Texas

Vice-President: Russell Richey (at large member), Candler School of Theology (emeritus), Emory University, Atlanta, Georgia

Treasurer: Richard B. Hays, Dean of The Divinity School, Duke University, Durham, North Carolina

General Editor and Secretary: Randy L. Maddox, The Divinity School, Duke University, Durham, North Carolina

Ivan Abrahams, General Secretary of The World Methodist Council, Lake Junaluska, North Carolina

Dennis M. Campbell (at large member), Woodberry Forest School, Woodberry Forest, Virginia

Richard P. Heitzenrater (General Editor emeritus), The Divinity School (emeritus), Duke University, Durham, North Carolina

PREFACE AND ACKNOWLEDGMENTS

Professor Frank Baker (1910–99) served as editor for the first two volumes of this edition of John Wesley's letters, covering the periods 1721–39 (vol. 25, published in 1980) and 1740–55 (vol. 26, published in 1982). In the late 1980s he took me on as an assistant when beginning work on the present volume. But other aspects of the Wesley Works Editorial Project, such as the *Bibliography*, increasingly consumed Dr. Baker's attention, resulting in this volume being set aside until I could take it up again in earnest some twenty years later. A few of the early annotations in this volume are Dr. Baker's, though I have reviewed and am happy to take responsibility for those he authored.

Technological advances over the three decades since the first two volumes appeared help explain some differences in this third installment. For example, more repositories containing Wesley manuscript letters have produced and made public catalogues of their holdings. This has not only helped in finding a few letters that escaped Dr. Baker's extensive pre-internet sleuthing, but frequently makes possible including shelf references or accession numbers for items. It has also eliminated the need for providing sample images of manuscript letters, because there are nice collections available online, such as the collection at the Bridwell Library of Southern Methodist University (http://digitalcollections.smu.edu/all/bridwell/jwl/index.asp) or the collection at Drew University (https://www2.atla.com/digitalresources/#drew).

The most significant difference that readers will note in this third volume is the absence of 'in-letters', or surviving letters that were addressed to John Wesley. This decision was made by the Board of the Wesley Works Editorial Project—in order to provide readers with *more* access to in-letters. To keep the first two volumes within a manageable size, Dr. Baker included only select in-letters, and frequently abridged them. The Board decided to make *all* of the known in-letters available *in their entirety*, but to do so *online*, on an internet site dedicated to the project: www.wesley-works.org. This is where readers will find the letters addressed to Wesley that are mentioned in footnotes or appear in the cumulative correspondence list in the Appendix.

I am especially grateful to William B. Lawrence, who has served both as my Dean at Perkins School of Theology, Southern Methodist University, and as President of the Board of the Wesley Works Editorial Project. He helped me obtain grants for the employment of a student assistant 2008–10, and for funding travel to consult the originals of letters that are included in this volume. I am also deeply grateful for the work of that student assistant, Dr. Kevin Watson. I have worked most directly with Dr. Richard Heitzenrater and Dr. Randy Maddox, the general editors of the Wesley Works Project, in preparing this volume, and I want to express my deep gratitude to both of them.

Ted A. Campbell
All Saints Day, 2013

CONTENTS

EDITORIAL GUIDELINES

Readers of this volume are strongly encouraged to read Dr. Frank Baker's excellent introductory essay in vol. 25, which places John Wesley's correspondence in historical context, describes previous editions of Wesley's letters, and elaborates the editorial principles adopted for this edition. But it may be helpful to distill the most important principles here, including a couple of slight changes adopted in this volume.

One set of principles concerns the sources privileged in preparing the text of Wesley's letters. We present the text of the actual letter that Wesley sent (the holograph) whenever it has survived. In the absence of a surviving holograph, on a few occasions we have either Wesley's working draft or a final copy that he made and retained for his records. Typically, no manuscript version survives for letters that Wesley sent to newspapers and journals for publication, or those that he published in the *Arminian Magazine*, because the manuscripts were discarded after publication. In such cases the original published transcription must serve as source. Finally, there are several instances where previous editors and researchers had access to holographs that no longer survive or are in undiscovered private hands. In this situation we are dependent upon either the earliest (or most complete and detailed) published transcription, or on a manuscript transcription in surviving records. In every case we identify the type of item that is serving as our source.

A second set of principles relates to the presentation of Wesley's text. After describing problems with previous editions in this regard (25:120–23), Baker depicted the approach of this edition of Wesley's letters as a careful balance between historical accuracy, showing Wesley 'warts and all', and modern readability (25:123–28). We continue Baker's practice of retaining Wesley's colloquialisms, contractions, and outdated grammatical usages. But, like Baker, we routinely expand Wesley's abbreviations (whenever clear), including abbreviated names and his frequent use of the ampersand. We also silently update archaic spellings (though retaining typical British spellings). Likewise we have followed Baker's precedent in imposing modern practices of capitalisation and punctuation. We keep editorial additions to Wesley's text at a minimum, and clearly identify them with [square brackets]. A few of the manuscript sources have been damaged or have obscured text. In these cases we have reconstructed the missing text as much as possible, placing the reconstructed text within ‹angled brackets›.

Instances of emphasis deserve special notice. In manuscript materials Wesley usually showed emphasis by <u>underlining</u>. We have generally rendered such material in *italics* (as the modern parallel). But, as was typical in the eighteenth century, Wesley also often used <u>underlining</u> in his manuscripts to identify direct quotations from Scripture. We have rendered these instances within quotation marks, unless there was some ambiguity about whether he was intending *emphasis* as well. These principles have their parallel in cases where the source is a published transcription of a Wesley letter. Eighteenth-century printing conventionally placed direct quotations of Scripture in *italics*, which we have altered in all clear instances to standard font and quotation marks. Similarly, printed works of this period typically italicise proper names of people, places, languages, and the like; all of which we render in standard font, unless there is reason to assume that emphasis was intended.

The most noticeable changes in presentation of Wesley's text adopted in this volume (in comparison to the prior two volumes) involve standardising the format of letters. For example, Wesley fluctuated some in where he positioned on his letters the current date and the place from where he was writing. He also occasionally omitted one or the other of these details. We present this material consistently at the top of the letter, listing place of origin on one line and date on the next. We also reconstruct missing place or date information, placing it in [square brackets], drawing in particular on Wesley's *Journal*. Another change from Baker's practice is that the header line for female recipients now identifies them by maiden and married names (if known). Thus, for example, 'To Mrs. Mary Wesley' becomes 'To Mary (Goldhawk/Vazeille) Wesley'. Finally, while limitations of page size and other factors often led Wesley to vary the format of his closing line and signature, we render them in a uniform format.

The third set of editorial principles guiding this edition of Wesley's letters focus on the information given at the end of holograph letters. Five types of information are potentially listed:

Address:	*Giving the address exactly as written (usually by Wesley), without expanding abbreviations or correcting spelling.*

Seal:	*Most holographs have the remnants of a wax seal, but details are provided only when the symbol or inscription in the seal remains legible.*
Postmark:	*Some holographs have only the 'Bishop Mark' indicating the month and date of posting. Others have as well a stamp of the town where the letter was posted. A few contain more than one listing because the letter was redirected. All marks that are legible are indicated.*
Charge:	*This mark records the charge to be paid when the letter was collected or delivered (it became common only near the end of the eighteenth century for the sender to pay the charge).*
Endorsement:	*Many of the holographs have annotations of when they were received, and sometimes short summaries of their contents or the recipient's response. There are also later cataloguing remarks on some letters. We generally present here only annotations that appear to be contemporary to when the letter was received. These can usually be presumed to be in the hand of the recipient. We note this as the case only when it is in a hand that we could verify (such as that of Charles Wesley).*

The final set of principles for this edition relates to annotation of the letters. Our goal is to aid in understanding the letters. We privilege original sources in documenting quoted material in Wesley's letters and in providing background information, in part because these older sources are increasingly available over the web. For example, transcriptions of the original editions of the various collections of hymns and poems published by John or Charles Wesley (from which John frequently quotes in his letters) are available through the Center for Studies in the Wesleyan Tradition, Duke Divinity School (http://divinity.duke.edu/initiatives-centers/cswt/wesley-texts). We identity whenever possible both Wesley's correspondents and other persons mentioned in the letters. More detailed biographical information is given on the first occasion a name appears, and can be located through use of the name index. Finally, we identify all quotations from Scripture, as well as significant allusions to Scripture, using 'cf.' and 'see' in the specific manner described under 'Signs, Special Usages, and Abbreviations'.

SIGNS, SPECIAL USAGES, ABBREVIATIONS

[ ]	Square brackets enclose editorial insertions or substitutions in the original text, or (with a query) doubtful readings.
‹ ›	Angle brackets enclose conjectural readings where the original text is defective or obscured.
…	An ellipsis indicates a passage omitted by the preparer of the original source—for this purpose Wesley generally employed a dash.
[…]	An ellipsis within square brackets indicates a passage omitted silently by Wesley from a text he was quoting, to which the present editor is drawing attention.
(())	Double parentheses enclose words that have been struck through by the author in the original manuscript (particularly drafts), to indicate their omission.
[[ ]]	Double square brackets enclose passages supplied from shorthand or cipher, from an abstract or similar document in the third person, or reconstructed from secondary evidence.
/	A solidus or slant line marks the division between two lines of text in the original manuscript.
a,b,c	Small superscript letters indicate footnotes supplied by Wesley.
1,2,3	Small superscript numbers indicate footnotes supplied by the editor.
Cf.	Before a scriptural or other citation by Wesley, indicates that he was quoting with more than minimal inexactness, yet nevertheless displaying the passage as a quotation.
See	Before a scriptural citation indicates an undoubted allusion or a quotation that was not displayed as such by Wesley, and that is more than minimally inexact.

Wesley's publications. Where a work by Wesley was first published separately, its title is italicised; where it first appeared within a different work such as a collected volume, the title appears within quotation marks.

Book titles in Wesley's text are italicised if accurate, and given in roman type with capitals if inaccurate. If a title consists of only one generic word that forms a major part of the original title, it is italicised; but if it is inaccurate (such as 'Sermons' for a volume entitled *Discourses*), it is printed in lower case roman.

Abbreviations. In addition to common abbreviations like c[irca], ed[itio]n, n[ote], orig[inal], and st[anza], the footnotes in this volume utilise the following abbreviated forms for items referred to repeatedly:

AM	*Arminian Magazine* (London, 1778–97).
Atmore, *Memorial*	Charles Atmore, *The Methodist Memorial; being an Impartial Sketch of the Lives and Characters of the Preachers* (Bristol: Edwards, 1801).
BCP	The Book of Common Prayer, London, 1662.

xvii

Bennis, *Correspondence*	Thomas Bennis (ed.), *Christian Correspondence; being a Collection of Letters written by the late Rev. John Wesley, the late Mrs. Eliza Bennis, and others* (Philadelphia: B. Graves, 1809).
Benson, *Works*	Joseph Benson (ed.), *The Works of the Rev. John Wesley*, 2nd edn. 16 vols. (London: Cordeux, 1813).
Bibliography	Forthcoming bibliography in this edition (vols. 33–34), which has a different numbering system from Richard Green's *Wesley Bibliography*.
Bridwell Library (SMU)	Bridwell Library, Perkins School of Theology, Southern Methodist University, Dallas, Texas, Special Collections.
CPH (1743)	John and Charles Wesley, *A Collection of Psalms and Hymns* (London, Strahan, 1743; 2nd edn. of 1741, with additions).
Crookshank, *Ireland*	Charles H. Crookshank, *History of Methodism in Ireland*, Vol. 1 (Belfast: Allen, 1885).
CW	Charles Wesley.
Dale, *Letters*	Helen Pelham Dale (ed.), *The Life and Letters of Thomas Pelham Dale*, 2 vols. (London: G. Allen, 1894), 1:1–26.
Drew, Methodist Archives	Drew University (Madison, New Jersey), Methodist Library, Archives.
Duke, Rubenstein	Duke University (Durham, North Carolina), David M. Rubenstein Rare Book and Manuscript Library.
Emory, MARBL	Emory University (Atlanta, Georgia), Manuscript, Archives, and Rare Book Library.
EMP	Thomas Jackson (ed.), *Lives of Early Methodist Preachers*, 4th edn., 6 vols. (London: Wesleyan Conference Office, 1871).
Everett, *Sheffield*	James Everett, *Historical Sketches of Wesleyan Methodism, in Sheffield and Its Vicinity*, 2 vols. (Sheffield: James Montgomery, 1823).
Garrett-Evangelical	Evanston, Illinois, Garrett-Evangelical Theological Seminary, Library, Special Collections.
Hastling et al., *Kingswood*	A. H. L. Hastling, W. A. Willis, and W. P. Workman, *The History of Kingswood School* (London: Charles Kelly, 1898).
HSP (1739)	John and Charles Wesley, *Hymns and Sacred Poems* (London: Strahan, 1739).
HSP (1740)	John and Charles Wesley, *Hymns and Sacred Poems* (London: Strahan, 1740).
HSP (1742)	John and Charles Wesley, *Hymns and Sacred Poems* (Bristol: Farley, 1742).
HSP (1749)	Charles Wesley, *Hymns and Sacred Poems* (Bristol: Farley, 1749).
Huntington Library	San Marino, California, The Huntington Library, Manuscripts Collection.

Jackson, *Works* (3rd)	Thomas Jackson (ed.), *The Works of the Rev. John Wesley, A.M.*, 3rd edn., 14 vols. (London: Nichols for Mason, 1829–31).
JW	John Wesley.
MARC	Methodist Archives and Research Centre, The John Rylands Library, The University of Manchester, Manchester, England.
Melbourne, Queen's College	Queen's College Library, University of Melbourne (Australia), Sugden Collection.
MM	*The Methodist Magazine* (1798–1821).
MSP (1744)	John Wesley (ed.), *Collection of Moral and Sacred Poems*, 3 vols. (Bristol: Farley, 1744).
NT Notes	John Wesley, *Explanatory Notes Upon the New Testament*, 3rd corrected edn. (Bristol: Graham and Pine, 1760–62).
ODNB	*Oxford Dictionary of National Biography* (2003).
OED (1989)	*The Oxford English Dictionary*, 2nd edn. (New York: Oxford University Press, 1989).
Redemption Hymns (1747)	Charles Wesley, *Hymns for Those That Seek and Those That Have Redemption in the Blood of Jesus Christ* (London: Strahan, 1747).
Seymour, *Huntingdon*	Aaron Crossley Hobart Seymour, *The Life and Times of Selina, Countess of Huntingdon*, 2 vols. (London: W. E. Painter, 1839).
Telford, *Letters*	John Telford (ed.), *The Letters of the Rev. John Wesley, A.M.*, 8 vols. (London: Epworth, 1931).
Tompson, *Original Letters*	Richard Tompson, *Original Letters between the Rev. Mr. John Wesley and Mr. Richard Tompson* (London: Davis & Reymers, 1760).
Tyerman, *John Wesley*	Luke Tyerman, *Life and Times of the Rev. John Wesley*, 3 vols. (2nd edn.; New York: Harper and Brothers, 1872).
Upper Room Museum	Nashville, Tennessee, The Upper Room, Museum of Christian Art.
Vickers, *Dictionary*	John Vickers (ed.), *A Dictionary of Methodism in Britain and Ireland* (London: Epworth, 2000).
Wesley's Chapel (London)	London, England, Wesley's Chapel & Leysian Mission, Museum of Methodism, Archival Material.
Whitehead, *Life*	John Whitehead, *The Life of the Rev. John Wesley*, 2 vols. (London: Couchman, 1793–96).
WHS	*The Proceedings of the Wesley Historical Society* (England, 1898–present).
WHS Ireland Archives	Belfast, Edgehill College, Wesley Historical Society of Ireland Archives.
WHS Library	Library of the Wesley Historical Society, Oxford Centre for Methodism and Church History, Oxford Brookes University.
WMC Museum	Lake Junaluska, North Carolina, World Methodist Council, Museum.
WMM	*The Wesleyan Methodist Magazine* (London, 1822–1913).

1756

To Mary (Goldhawk/Vazeille) Wesley

[LEWISHAM]
WEDNESDAY AFTERNOON [JANUARY 7, 1756]

When I saw you, my dear, I did not expect to have so large a demand made so suddenly upon me. I shall be puzzled to answer it, without coming to town on purpose, which I am unwilling to do, 5 before I have finished the *Address*.[1] I desire you would give John Spenser[2] (taking his receipt) or brother Atkinson[3] (unless you choose to pay Mr. Davenport[4] yourself) what note-money remains in your hands. Unless you can help me out for a month or two, I must borrow some more in town. If you can, you will do it with 10 pleasure.

My dear,

Adieu.

Address: 'To / Mrs Wesley'.

No *postmark* or indications of postal *charge*; apparently delivered by hand.

Endorsement: (on attached page, 'Rec'd Jan. 9. [1]756 of Mrs Wesley Twenty pounds on Acc. of Paying for the press. Materials etc., by Will Atkinson.' There follows in a different hand a list of accounted items.

Source: holograph; Bridwell Library (SMU).

---

[1] JW was apparently staying at the home of Ebenezer and Elizabeth Blackwell, in Lewisham, to have concentrated time to write *An Address to the Clergy* (1756); see *Bibliography*, No. 216, and vol. 14 of this edn.

[2] John Spenser (or Spencer) was one of JW's publishing assistants at the Foundery; see letters to Mary Wesley, May 7 and June 18, 1756.

[3] William Atkinson of Plymouth Dock (Devonport) was another of JW's assistants at the Foundery (see his letter to JW, Nov. 20, 1753, 26:531–32 in this edn.).

[4] This does not appear to be JW's correspondent Richard Davenport (see 26:390). More likely is B. Davenport, a partner of Joseph Johnson in London in book-selling, who are listed in 1756 among the publishers of Alexander Pope's *Works*.

To Joseph Cownley[5]

LONDON
JANUARY 10, 1756

My Dear Brother,

I have no objection to anything but the blister.[6] If it does good,
5   well. But if I had been at Cork,[7] all the physicians in Ireland should
not have put it upon your head. Remember poor Bishop Pearson.
An apothecary, to cure a pain in his head, covered it with a large
blister. In an hour he cried out, 'Oh! my head, my head!' and was
a fool ever after, to the day of his death.[8] I believe cooling things
10   (if anything under heaven) would remove that violent irritation of
your nerves, which probably occasions the pain. Moderate riding
may be of use; I believe of more [use] than the blister. Only do not
take more labour upon you than you can bear. Do as much as you
can, and no more. Let us make use of the present time. Every day is
15   of importance. We know not how few days of peace remain. We join
in love to you and yours.

    I am, dear Joseph,

        Your affectionate friend and brother,

20   John Wesley

Source: published transcription; *Arminian Magazine* 17 (1794): 527–28.

---

[5] Joseph Cownley (1723–92) was one of the early itinerant preachers; see *EMP*, 2:1–47.
John Gaulter, Cownley's biographer, prefaces this letter thus: 'The fever which Mr. Cownley
had in 1755 so relaxed his nerves that his labours were considerably interrupted. A pain settled
in his head, which no medicine could ever remove. After consulting the most able physicians
in Ireland, he stated his case to Mr. Wesley, and received the following answer' (*AM* 17 [1794]:
527; *EMP*, 2:18).

[6] An irritating substance or plaster used to raise blisters on the skin—a favourite remedy
of eighteenth-century physicians. Although Wesley included one recommendation of a blister
in his *Primitive Physick* from 1781 onwards (for involuntary urine), his general rule was, 'No
bleeding, no blistering.' See letter of Nov. 5, 1762, and JW, *Journal* for June 17, 1742 (19:279
in this edn.).

[7] Spelled here, as often by Wesley, 'Corke'.

[8] John Pearson, Bishop of Chester (1613–86). The anecdote seems to be apocryphal.

To [Jonathan Pritchard][9]

LONDON
JANUARY 16, 1756

My Dear Brother,

If our brethren at Chester purpose ever to prosecute, they cannot have a fairer opportunity, provided they have a sufficient number 5 of witnesses whose depositions will come home to the point, particularly with regard to those words, 'You shall have no justice from me'. Those depositions might be drawn up in the country, and sent up to Mr. I'Anson,[10] in New Palace Yard, Westminster. The sooner the better, for term will begin shortly.[11] Delay does much hurt in 10 cases of this kind. Do you hear how the Manchester mob is now?

I am,
    Your affectionate brother,

J. Wesley 15

Is brother Moss gone yet into the Birstall circuit?[12]

Source: holograph; MARC, MAM JW 4/42 (address portion missing).

---

[9] For Jonathan Pritchard, the steward of the Chester society, see JW's letter to him of Jan. 16, 1753 (26:499–500 in this edn.). In July 1752 a mob had pulled down the Methodist preaching-house in Chester, and the magistrates had been of no help. Similar outbreaks continued to occur sporadically (cf. Wesley's letter of Oct. 11, 1753; 26:525 in this edn.), and from this letter it appears that once more the Chester Methodists were being denied justice by a local magistrate.

[10] For Bryan I'Anson (d. 1775), a solicitor at New Palace Yard, Westminster, whom JW had consulted for legal advice since at least 1760, see *WHS* 5 (1906): 230–37.

[11] Hilary Term for hearing cases began on Jan. 23 or 24, and ended Feb. 12 or 13.

[12] The reference may be to Richard Moss, an itinerant listed in the Minutes from at least 1745 (see 10:147 in this edn.).

To Samuel Furly

LONDON
FEBRUARY 3, 1756

Dear Sammy,

The *Serious Thoughts*[13] will be sent as soon as they are reprinted.
5 I shall make an addition of eight or ten pages, consisting chiefly of a
correct and regular account of the earthquakes at Lisbon and other
places.

Now is the time to arise and shake yourself from the dust. Now
assert your liberty. When you are on the field, you can't make head
10 against the enemy. But now you may secure armour of proof. You
may be stronger every day than the other. Only be instant in prayer.

I have an extremely pretty letter from Mr. Dodd.[14] It is wonderfully civil and peremptory. I purpose to answer him this week, and
perhaps P. V.[15] too.

15 I am,

Your affectionate brother,

J. Wesley

Address: 'To / Mr Samuel Furly / In Queen's College / Cambridge'.
Postmark: missing. *Charge*: '3'.
Source: holograph; privately held (current owner unknown, Wesley Works
Editorial Project Archive includes a copy).

---

[13] JW, *Serious Thoughts occasioned by the late Earthquake at Lisbon*, of which four edns.
were published in Dec. 1755; see *Bibliography*, No. 213, and vol. 15 of this edn.

[14] On Dodd, see JW's letter of Feb. 5, 1756. Dodd had written to JW on Jan. 26.

[15] I.e., Richard Tompson; see the letters of Feb. 12 & 18, 1756.

To the Rev. William Dodd[16]

Rev. Sir,

I am favoured with yours of January 26,[17] for which I return you my sincere thanks. Your frank and open manner of writing is far 5 from needing any apology, and I hope will never occasion your receiving such treatment from me as I did from Mr. [William] Law, who, after some very keen expressions in answer to the second private letter I sent him, plainly told me he desired to 'hear no more on that head'.[18] I do desire to hear, and am very willing to consider, 10 whatever you have to advance on the head of 'Christian perfection'.

When I began to make the Scriptures my chief study (about seven and twenty years ago),[19] I began to see that Christians are called to 'love God with all' their 'heart', and to 'serve him with all' their 'strength',[20] which is precisely what I apprehend to be meant 15 by the scriptural term 'perfection'. After weighing this for some years, I openly declared my sentiments before the university, in the sermon on 'The Circumcision of the Heart', now printed in the second volume.[21] About six years after, in consequence of an advice I received from Bishop Gibson,[22] 'Tell all the world what you mean 20 by perfection', I published my coolest and latest thoughts in the sermon on that subject.[23] You easily observe, I therein build on no authority, ancient or modern, but the Scripture. If this supports any doctrine, it will stand; if not, the sooner it falls the better. Neither the

---

[16] William Dodd (1729–77), ordained deacon in 1751, became a popular preacher in London, especially from the pulpit of Magdalen House, and in 1763 was appointed chaplain to the king. He graduated D.D. in 1766. He was known as the 'macaroni parson' because of his worldly style of living, became deeply involved in debt, was arrested for forging a bond, was convicted and sentenced to death. The execution was carried out on June 27, 1777. He attacked JW's views in the *Christian Magazine* (1760–67) and Wesley defended himself. At Dodd's request JW visited him in prison. See *ODNB*.

[17] This letter does not appear to have survived.

[18] This phrase does not occur in Law's letter of May 19 or that of [May 22?], 1738, but seems to be Wesley's summary of the correspondence, as expressed in the closing sentence of the second letter: 'Pray, sir, be at peace with me.' See 25:543–46, 548–50 in this edn.

[19] Wesley consistently dated the origins of the Methodist movement to the year 1729. In response to the question 'What was the rise of Methodism, so called?' in the Large Minutes, Wesley wrote, 'In 1729, two young men, reading the Bible, saw they could not be saved without holiness, followed after it and incited others so to do' (10:875 in this edn.).

[20] Cf. Deut. 6:5, Luke 10:27, and parallels.

[21] I.e., of JW's *Sermons on Several Occasions*, published in 1748 (1:398–414 in this edn.).

[22] Edmund Gibson (1669–1748), Bishop of London.

[23] JW, *Christian Perfection*, published in 1741 (2:97–124 in this edn.).

doctrine in question, nor any other, is anything to me, unless it be the doctrine of Christ and his apostles. If, therefore, you will please to point out to me any passages in that sermon which are either contrary to Scripture, or not supported by it, and to show that they
5   are not, I shall be full as willing to oppose as ever I was to defend them. I search for truth: plain, Bible truth, without any regard to the praise or dispraise of men.

If you will assist me in this search, more especially by showing me where I have mistaken my way, it will be gratefully acknowledged
10   by, rev. sir,

> Your affectionate brother and servant,

> John Wesley

Source: published transcription; *Arminian Magazine* 2 (1779): 434–35. The letter is entitled 'On Christian Perfection'; at the end Wesley adds the note: 'N. B. I had at this time no acquaintance with Dr. Dodd; nor did I ever see him till I saw him in prison.'

To Richard Tompson ('P. V.')[24]

[LONDON]
FEBRUARY 5, 1756

15   Sir,

I was in Cornwall when your last was brought to the Foundery and delivered to my brother. When I returned it was mislaid, and could not be found; so that I did not receive it till some months after the date.
20   You judge right with regard to the tract enclosed to you. It was sent to you by mistake, for another that bears the same name.[25]

'Christian perfection', we agree, may stand aside for the present. The point now to be considered is 'Christian faith'. This, I apprehend, implies a *divine evidence* or *conviction* of our *acceptance*; you
25   apprehend it does not.

[24] Replying to Tompson's of Aug. 15, 1755, 26:576–80 in this edn. For the introduction to the correspondence see 26:566–67.
[25] Wesley had sent his Disciplinary *Minutes* instead of his Doctrinal *Minutes*—both published in 1749, with indistinguishable title pages; see 26:574, 576 in this edn.

In debating this (or indeed any) point with you I lie under a great disadvantage. *First*, you know *me*, whereas I do not know *you*. *Secondly*, I am a very slow, you seem to be a very swift, writer. *Thirdly*, my time is so taken up, from day to day and from week to week, that I can spare very little from my stated employments, so that I can neither write so largely nor so accurately as I might otherwise do. All, therefore, which you can expect from me is (not a close-wrought chain of connected arguments, but) a short sketch of what I should deduce more at large if I had more leisure.

I believe the ancient fathers are far from being silent on our question, though none that I know has treated it *ex professo*.[26] But I have not leisure to wade through that sea. Only to the argument from the baptism of heretics I reply.[27] If any had averred, during that warm controversy, 'I received a sense of pardon when I was baptised by such an heretic', those on the other side would in no wise have believed him; so that the dispute would have remained as warm as ever. I know this from plain fact: many have received a sense of pardon when I baptised them. But who will believe them when they assert it? Who will put any dispute on this issue?

I know, likewise, that Luther, Melanchthon, and many other (if not all) of the Reformers frequently and strongly assert that every believer is conscious of *his own* acceptance with God; and that by a *supernatural evidence*, which if any choose to term 'immediate revelation' he may.[28] But neither have I leisure to re-examine this cloud of witnesses. Nor indeed (as you justly observe) would the testimony of them all together be sufficient to establish an unscriptural doctrine. Therefore, after all, we must be determined by higher evidence. And herein we are clearly agreed. We both appeal to the 'law and to the testimony'.[29] May God enable us to understand it aright.

But first, that you may not beat the air[30] by disproving what I never attempted to prove, I will show you, as distinctly as I can, what my sentiments are upon the question; and the rather because I plainly perceive you do not yet understand them. You seem to think I allow *no degrees* in grace, and that I make no distinction between the *full assurance* of faith and a low or common *measure* of it.

---

[26] 'Professedly' or 'explicitly'.
[27] See Tompson's letter, ¶3.
[28] Ibid., ¶5.
[29] Isa. 8:20.
[30] See 1 Cor. 9:26.

Several years ago some clergymen and other gentlemen with whom we had a free conversation proposed the following questions to my brother and me, to which we gave the answers subjoined.

5   June 25, 1744[31]

Ques. [4]. What is faith?

Answ. Faith, in general, is a divine, supernatural *elenchos*[32] of things not seen, i.e., of past, future, or spiritual: it is a spiritual

10 sight of God and the things of God. [...] Justifying faith is a divine *elenchos* that Christ loved me, and gave himself for me.[33] [...]

Ques. [5]. Have all Christians this faith? And may not a man have it, and not know it?

15 Answ. That all Christians have such a faith as implies a consciousness of God's love appears from Rom. 8:15, Eph. 4:32, 2 Cor. 13:5, Heb. 8:10, 1 John 4:10, 5:1, etc. And that no man can have it, and not know that he has, appears from the nature of the thing. For faith after repentance is ease after pain, rest after toil,

20 light after darkness. It appears also from its immediate fruits, which are peace, joy, love, and power over sin. [...]

Ques. [8]. Does anyone believe any longer than he sees, loves, obeys God?

25 Answ. We apprehend not, seeing God being the very essence of faith; love and obedience the inseparable properties of it.

                              August 2, 1745[34]

30 Ques. [1]. Is an assurance of God's pardoning love absolutely necessary to our being in his favour? Or may there possibly be some exempt cases?

Answ. We dare not positively say there are not. [...]

Ques. [3]. Is it necessary to final salvation in those (as

35 Papists) who never heard it preached?

---

[31] Wesley quotes somewhat freely from the Minutes of the 1744 Conference, which were incorporated into the Doctrinal Minutes of 1749 (see 10:126–27, 778–79 in this edn.).

[32] Transliterated from the Greek; i.e., 'proof' or 'evidence' (see Heb. 11:1).

[33] See Gal. 2:20.

[34] Wesley quotes somewhat freely from the Minutes of the 1745 Conference, which were incorporated into the Doctrinal Minutes of 1749 (see 10:149–50, 876–79 in this edn.).

Answ. We know not how far invincible ignorance may excuse: love hopeth all things.

Ques. [4]. But what if one who does hear it preached should die without it?

Answ. We determine nothing: we leave his soul in the hands   5
of him that made it.

Ques. [5]. Does a man believe any longer than he sees a reconciled God?

Answ. We conceive not: but we allow there may be very many degrees in seeing God, even as many as are between seeing   10
the sun with the eyelids closed, and with the eyes open.

The doctrine which I espouse, till I receive farther light, being thus explained and limited, I observe:

First, a *divine conviction* of my being reconciled to God is (I think)   15
directly implied (not in a *divine evidence* or *conviction* of *something else*, but) in a *divine conviction* that Christ loved *me*, and gave himself for *me*; and still more clearly in 'the Spirit's bearing witness with my spirit, that I am a child of God'.[35]

Secondly, I see no reason either to retract or soften the expres-   20
sion, 'God's mercy, in some cases, obliges him to act thus and thus.'[36] Certainly as his *own nature obliges* him (in a very clear and sound sense) to act according to truth and justice in all things, so, in some sense, his love *obliged* him to give his only Son, that whosoever believeth in him might not perish.[37] So much for the phrase.   25
My meaning is, the same compassion which moves God to pardon a mourning, broken-hearted sinner, moves him to comfort that mourner by witnessing to his spirit that his sins are pardoned.

Thirdly, you think, '*Full assurance* excludes all doubt.'[38] I think so too. But there may be faith without *full assurance*. And these lower   30
degrees of faith do not exclude doubts, which frequently mingle therewith more or less. But this you cannot allow. You say it cannot be[39] *shaken* without being *overthrown*, and trust I shall be 'convinced upon reflection that the distinction between "shaken" and "destroyed" is *absolutely* without a difference'. Hark! The wind   35
rises! The house *shakes!* But it is not *overthrown*. It *totters*, but it

---

[35] See Rom. 8:16, and Tompson's letter, ¶7.

[36] See Tompson's letter, ¶¶15–16, referring back to JW's letter of July 25, 1755, 26:575 in this edn.

[37] See John 3:16.

[38] See Tompson's letter, ¶¶17–18.

[39] The word 'be' is doubled in the original publication, an apparent typographical error.

is not *destroyed*. You add: '*Assurance* is quite a distinct thing from *faith*; neither does it depend on the same agent. *Faith* is an act of my mind; *assurance* an act of the Holy Ghost.'[40] I answer, *First*, the 'assurance' in question is no other than 'the full assurance of
5   faith'; therefore it cannot be a distinct thing from *faith*, but only so high a degree of *faith* as excludes all doubt and fear. *Secondly*, this *plerophory*,[41] or 'full assurance', is doubtless wrought in us by the Holy Ghost. But so is every degree of true *faith*. Yet the *mind of man* is the subject of both: *I* believe feebly;[42] *I* believe without all doubt.
10   Your next remark is, 'The Spirit's witnessing that we are accepted cannot be the faith whereby we are accepted.'[43] I allow it. A conviction of our being *justified* cannot be implied in *justifying faith*.

You subjoin, 'A *sure trust* that God hath accepted me is not the same thing with *knowing* that God has accepted me.'[44] I think it is
15   the same thing with *some degree* of that knowledge. But it matters not whether it be so or no. I will not contend for a term. I contend only for this, that every true Christian believer has a 'sure trust and confidence in God, that through the merits of Christ, he is reconciled to God';[45] and that in consequence of this he is able to
20   say, 'The life which I now live I live by faith in the Son of God, who loved me, and gave himself for me.'[46]

It is a very little thing to excuse a warm expression (if you need any such excuse) while I am convinced of your real goodwill to, sir,

Your servant, for Christ's sake,

25   J. Wesley

Source: published transcription; Tompson, *Original Letters*, 34–40.

---

[40] See Tompson's letter, ¶19.

[41] Another transliteration from the Greek (see Heb. 10:22).

[42] Orig., 'freely', corrected in the errata.

[43] See Tompson, ¶19.

[44] See ibid., ¶¶20–21.

[45] Wesley's consistent definition of Christian faith—taken from *Homilies* (1683), 'Of Salvation', Pt. III; included in JW's published abridgement, *The Doctrine of Salvation, Faith, and Good Works*, I.15, 12:37 in this edn.

[46] Gal. 2:20.

To Mrs. Burgoyne[47]

LONDON
FEBRUARY 7, 1756

If the estate is in the hands of an attorney it is not likely that you should recover anything of it. You have then only to say, 'The Lord gave, and the Lord hath taken away.'[48] It seems God is now teaching you the great lesson of giving yourself up, soul and body, into his hands. And he has never failed and never will fail them that put their trust in him.[49]

Acquaint yourself with him, and you will be at peace,[50] even when the waves and storms go over you.[51] Suffer all things for his sake who suffered more for you. And whenever you want help, ask and it shall be given you.[52]

I am,

    Your affectionate brother,

        John Wesley

Source: secondary transcription of holograph; MARC, MA/1977/609 (another transcription in the National Register of Archives, No. 0279, which states that the ms. is endorsed 'Methodist Westley's letter to the widow Burgoine').

To Samuel Furly

LONDON
FEBRUARY 18, 1756

Dear Sammy,

You are a very complaisant person. I know, in my little circle of acquaintance, more than twenty who have all the natural qualifications mentioned in the *Address to the Clergy*,[53] and several others who have all the acquired ones, either by education or by grace. And I would engage to take any person of fourteen years of age,

---

[47] No details about Mrs. Burgoyne have been discovered.
[48] Job 1:21.
[49] See Ps. 18:30 (BCP), etc.
[50] See Job 22:21.
[51] See Ps. 42:9 (BCP).
[52] Matt. 7:7.
[53] JW, *An Address to the Clergy* (1756); see *Bibliography*, No. 216, and vol. 14 of this edn.

who has good natural abilities, and to teach him in seven years everything which is there required, to a good degree of perfection. *Ex pede Herculem.*[54] You may easily see what Latin I write by one of the *Dissertationes in Jobum;*[55] or even by the short conversation with Count Zinzendorf which is printed in the *Journal.*[56] I do not know that I have any theme or declamation left.[57] But why do you not talk Latin when you are with me? Do this, and you will see the excellence of Terence's language; whereas Tully [i.e., Cicero] would make you talk like a mere stiff pedant.

Randal's Geographical Grammar[58] is the best compendium of geography which I have seen; and you need nothing more on that subject, adding only the *terrestrial globe.*

If you are master of Hutcheson's Metaphysics[59] and Clerc's *Ontologia,*[60] I advise you to look no farther that way; unless you would add Malebranche's *Search after Truth,*[61] or the Bishop of Cork's two books[62] again.

The main point is, with all and above all, study the Greek and Hebrew Bible, and the love of Christ.

I am,

Yours affectionately,

J. Wesley

Address: 'To / Mr Sam. Furley / In Queen's College / Cambridg.'.
Postmark: '19/FE'. *Charge:* '3'.
Source: holograph; MARC, MAM JW 3/15.

---

[54] A Latin proverb: '[You can tell it is] Hercules from his foot'.

[55] Samuel Wesley Sr.'s *magnum opus* on Job, to which JW contributed much both in research and by translations into Latin; see *Bibliography*, No. 7.

[56] JW, *Journal*, Sept. 3, 1741, 19:211–15 in this edn.

[57] I.e., exercises in Latin that JW would have prepared while a student at Oxford.

[58] Wesley is likely referring to Joseph Randall's *A System of Geography* (1744), which he placed on the reading list for Kingswood School (the fifth class) in 1748; see *Minutes*, June 4, 1748, Q. 11, 10:217 in this edn.

[59] [Francis Hutcheson,] *Synopsis Metaphysicae Ontologiam et Pneumatologiam complectans* (1742); see also JW's letter to Furly of Mar. 14, 1756.

[60] One of the early works of the prolific Dutch scholar, Jean Le Clerc (1657–1736). It formed the second of three parts of a Latin work on logic, ontology, and pneumatology, first published in 1692 and dedicated to John Locke.

[61] Wesley read Nicholas Malebranche's *De la Recherche de la Verité* (1674) in French in 1733; he frequently recommended the translated form, *Father Malebranche's Treatise concerning the Search After Truth*, translated by Thomas Taylor (1694).

[62] For Peter Browne, Bishop of Cork, see 25:251 in this edn., where Wesley recommended Browne's *Procedure, Extent, and Limits of Human Understanding* (1728) to Mary Pendarves. The second book would be Browne's *Things Supernatural and Divine conceived by Analogy with Things Natural and Human* (1733); see JW, *A Letter to the Reverend Mr. Law* (1756), §II.7, vol. 14 in this edn.

To Richard Tompson ('P. V.')[63]

[LONDON]
FEBRUARY 18, 1756

Sir,

You ask, [1.] 'Can a man who has not a *clear assurance* that his sins are forgiven be in a state of justification?' 5
I believe there are some instances of it.

2. 'Can a person be in a state of justification, who being asked "Do you know your sins are forgiven?" answers, "I am not *certainly sure*; but I do not entertain the *least doubt* of it."'
I believe he may. 10

3. 'Can he who answers, "I *trust* they are"?'
'Tis very possible he may be in that state.

[4.] 'Can anyone *know* that his sins are forgiven while he *doubts* thereof?'
Not at that instant when he doubts of it. But he may *generally* 15 know it, though he doubts at some *particular* time.

I answer as plainly and as simply as I can, that if I am in a mistake I may the more easily be convinced of it.

Source: published transcription; Tompson, *Original Letters*, 43–44.

To Samuel Furly

LONDON 20
FEBRUARY 21, 1756

Dear Sammy,

There is but one possible way to gain the victory—conquer desire, and you will conquer fear. But as long as you are a slave you must be a coward. Be free, therefore, or you can't be bold. Never 25 write to that person at all, nor of her,[64] and continue instant in prayer. Cut off the right hand and cast it from you, otherwise you will be a poor dastardly wretch all your days, and one sin will punish another till the day of grace is at an end.

---

[63] Replying to the four queries in Tompson's letter of Feb. 12, 1756.
[64] Wesley is attempting to guide Furly in his love affairs; cf. his letter of Mar. 14, 1756.

I am,
　　Your affectionate brother,

J. Wesley

Source: published transcription; *United Methodist Free Church Magazine* 9
　(1866): 174–75. Part of a series of letters from Wesley to Furly about
　which Jonathan Couch states he 'copied the whole of them from the
　originals, with his own hand' (p. 173).

To Ebenezer Blackwell[65]

MARLBOROUGH
MARCH 1, 1756

Dear Sir,
　I hope the enclosed will do,[66] for I have not leisure to alter it any
more.
　To make professions does not belong to me. It is quite foreign to my
character. Let those who mean nothing *talk*, like Goneril[67] and Regan
in *King Lear*.[68] By God's help, I will *do* what a good subject ought.
　Wishing Mrs. [Elizabeth] Blackwell and you all health of soul and
body, I am, dear sir,
　　Your affectionate servant,

John Wesley

Address: 'To / Mr Blackwell, Banker / in / London'.
Postmarks: 'MARLBO/ROUGH', '3 MR'. *Charge*: '6'.

---

[65] Blackwell was apparently the friend with whom Wesley had discussed his idea of a
company of volunteers in the event of a French invasion, and who had agreed to handle the
proposal for him.

[66] Wesley enclosed a fair copy of his letter to James West (see the following), which is why
the charge to be paid by Blackwell was sixpence instead of the threepence which would have
been normal for a letter from Marlborough to London, under eighty miles.

[67] Orig., 'Gonorill'.

[68] See Shakespeare, *King Lear*, I.i.57–73.

Endorsement: 'Revd Mr John Wesley, Marlborough, 1 March 1756.' Blackwell also transcribed (before passing it on) Wesley's enclosed letter to West.

Source: holograph; Drew, Methodist Archives.

To James West[69]

MARLBOROUGH
MARCH 1, 1756

Sir,

A few days since Mr. [George] Whitefield and I desired a friend to ask your advice to whom it would be proper to make an offer   5 of raising a company of volunteers for his Majesty's service. We apprehended the number would be about five hundred. Finding Mr. Whitefield has since been persuaded that such an offer is premature, I am constrained to make the following independently on him.[70]   10

To raise, for his Majesty's service, at least two hundred volunteers to be supported by contributions among themselves, and to be ready in case of an invasion to act for a year (if needed so long) at his Majesty's pleasure, only within ____[71] miles of London.

---

[69] Although the English part of the Seven Years' War (1756–63) began only with its declaration of war on May 15, 1756, tensions with France had been brewing throughout 1755. Rumors of an invasion were rife. By the beginning of December (perhaps earlier), JW had begun to 'discipline' some London Methodists 'for soldiers, and they'd begun exercising at the Foundery' (Thomas Illingworth diary, Dec. 14, 1755, at Duke University). Charles Wesley wrote to his wife on Dec. 7, 1755: 'My brother tells me the French are expected every hour by General Hawley, in battle array, etc.; that the Government have not the least doubt of the invasion, but will do their best to repel force by force.' He continued, 'I question whether my brother's soldiers, with all his pains and haste to train them up, will not be too tardy to rescue us.' About Jan. 31, 1756 he wrote that he planned to return to Bristol a week later—'unless Jack Frenchman snaps me up'. On Dec. 20 the Privy Counsel issued a royal proclamation appointing Friday, Feb. 6, as a national Fast Day when prayers should be offered for God's help in 'the present situation of public affairs'.

This letter contains JW's official offer of Methodist military support to the government, via James West (c. 1704–72), a Member of Parliament for St. Albans who had been at Balliol College, Oxford at roughly the same time as JW was at Christ Church and then Lincoln, and who at the time of this letter was serving as Joint Secretary to the Treasury. See *ODNB*.

[70] It is possible that Charles Wesley's scepticism infected George Whitefield, with whom CW informed his wife on Dec. 22, 1755 that he had 'talked largely'.

[71] A blank was left in the ms., obviously subject to discussion.

If this be acceptable to his Majesty, they beg to have arms out of the Tower, giving the usual security for their return, and some of his Majesty's sergeants to instruct them in the military exercise.

5   I am now hastening to Bristol on account of the election,[72] concerning which I wrote to my brother last week. But if my return to London would be of any service, you may command, sir,

Your obedient servant,

John Wesley

10
Address: none; because hand delivered to West by Ebenezer Blackwell (whose transcription noted previously included the address, 'To The Honourable James West, Esq.').
Source: holograph; British Library, Department of Manuscripts, Add. MS. 32685, f. 64.

To Ebenezer Blackwell

BRISTOL
MARCH 4, 1756

Dear Sir,
    If the election of Mr. Spenser be a thing of any consequence,[73]
15   then it was extremely ill-judged to prevent his coming down. He ought to have been here at all hazards, if he was not very dangerously ill. His absence will probably turn the scale. And if the

---

[72] See JW's letter to Blackwell of Mar. 4, 1756.

[73] This was a by-election to fill the vacancy in Parliament created by the death of the Tory member, Richard Beckford. The Tory candidate was Sir Jarrit Smyth (or Smith, 1692-1783), a Bristol lawyer and entrepreneur in mining activities. In this case, Wesley favoured the moderate Whig John Spencer (or Spenser, 1734-1783), apparently fearing that Smyth's election would be worse for the Tory cause that Wesley elsewhere supported. Smyth was a member of the Steadfast Society of Bristol, the main Tory group in Bristol, which was sometimes represented as harbouring Jacobite tendencies (see W. E. Minchinton, ed., *Politics and the Port of Bristol in the Eighteenth Century* [Bristol: Bristol Record Society, 1963], p. 78, n. 2, and p. 80, n. 1). The vote was indeed close: 2418 for Smyth, 2347 for Spencer. Later in the same year Spencer was elected Member of Parliament for Warwick, and in 1765 was named First Earl Spencer. On Spencer, see *ODNB*, 51:864–65. I am grateful to Dr. William Gibson and to Professor J. C. D. Clark for assistance in identifying the political affiliations of Smyth and Spencer.

Jacobites[74] gain one member now, they will have two the next time. Whereas, there is all reason to believe, had Mr. Spenser appeared, there would have been no opposition.

Last night I desired all the Freemen of our society to meet me after preaching, and enlarged a little upon his Majesty's character, 5 and the reasons we had to spare no pains in his service. I believe all who had been wavering were fully convinced. But some had absolutely promised to vote for Mr. Smith, it having been confidently reported that both the candidates were equally acceptable to his Majesty. 10

The whole city is in confusion. O what pity there could not be some way of managing elections of every sort without this embittering Englishmen against Englishmen, and kindling fires which cannot be quenched in many years?

Wishing Mrs. [Elizabeth] Blackwell and you the peace which the 15 world cannot give,[75] I remain, dear sir,
     Yours most affectionately,

                         John Wesley

Address: 'To / Mrs [*sic*] Blackwell, Banker / in / London'.
Postmarks: stylised 'B/RIS/TOL' and '8/MR'. *Charge*: '4'.
Endorsement: 'Revd Mr John Wesley / Bristol, 4 March, 1756'.
Source: holograph; MARC, MAM JW 1/62.

---

[74] Wesley indicates his fear that 'Jacobites', i.e., those who had supported James II and conversely did not support the House of Orange and the Hanoverian monarchs, would gain influence by the election of Smyth.

[75] See John 14:27.

To the Editor of *The Gentleman's Magazine*[76]

BRISTOL

MARCH 8, [1756]

Mr. Urban,

5   I have met with many persons in my life who did not abound with modesty, but I never yet met with one who had less of it than your anonymous correspondent, whose letter is inserted p. 56 of your *Magazine* for February.

    The whole account of Whiston Cliff, near Black Hamilton in Yorkshire, inserted in one of your *Magazines*, I aver to be punctu-

10 ally true, having been an eye-witness of every particular of it. And if F. D. will set his name and aver the contrary, I will make him ashamed, unless shame and he have shook hands and parted.

        Yours, etc.,

15   John Wesley

Source: published transcription; *Gentleman's Magazine* 26 (March 1756): 103. Reprinted in *Felix Farley's Bristol Journal* (Mar. 6–13, 1756), p. 3; and *Scots Magazine* (1756): 432.

---

[76] Wesley published a report of some earth tremors that occurred Mar. 25–30, 1755 in *Felix Farley's Bristol Journal* on Sept. 27 of that year (see 26:597–600 in this edn.), and incorporated this report in his *Serious Thoughts occasioned by the late Earthquake at Lisbon*, published in December. In November 1755—following news about the Lisbon earthquake on Nov. 1—the *Gentleman's Magazine* (p. 514) published an abridged account of this Yorkshire earthquake, reprinted from the *Public Advertiser*. This account was challenged by 'F. D.' in the *Gentleman's Magazine* for Feb. 1756 (p. 56), where he characterised it as a lie that was 'deliberately invented and propagated', though he hints that Wesley may have been taken in by the lie. This letter is JW's response.

In a preamble to Wesley's response the editor of *Gentleman's Magazine* gave some justification for printing the letter by 'F. D.', citing the anonymity of Wesley's pamphlet on earthquakes and the lack of signed verification of the Yorkshire account. He then stated that if 'F. D.' is unable or unwilling to make good his assertion, then Wesley's response treats him 'with less severity than he deserves.'

The April issue of *Gentleman's Magazine* capped this exchange with an 'Authentic account of the phenomenon at Blackhamilton Cliffs' (p. 159), signed 'J. Langhorne, Thirsk, April 20.' Needless to say, nothing more was heard from 'F. D.'

To the Rev. William Dodd[77]

KINGSWOOD
MARCH 12, 1756

Rev. Sir,

1. You and I the more easily bear with each other because we are both of us *rapid* writers and therefore the more liable to mistake. I will thank you for showing me any mistake I am in, being not so tenacious of my opinions now as I was twenty or thirty years ago. Indeed, I am not fond of any opinion as such. I read the Bible with what attention I can, and regulate all my opinions thereby to the best of my understanding. But I am always willing to receive more light; particularly with regard to any less common opinions, because the explaining and defending them takes up much time, which I can ill spare from other employments. Whoever, therefore, will give me more light with regard to Christian perfection will do me a singular favour. The opinion I have concerning it at present I espouse merely because I think it is scriptural. If, therefore, I am convinced it is not scriptural, I shall willingly relinquish it.

2. I have no particular fondness for the term. It seldom occurs either in my preaching or writings. It is my opponents who thrust it upon me continually, and ask me what I mean by it. So did Bishop Gibson, till by his advice I publicly declared what I *did not* mean by it and what I *did*. This I supposed might be best done in the form of a sermon, having a text prefixed wherein that term occurred.[78] But that text is there used only as an occasion or introduction to the subject. I do not build any doctrine thereon, nor undertake critically to explain it.

3. What is the meaning of the term 'perfection' is another question; but that it is a *scriptural term* is undeniable. Therefore none ought to object to the use of the *term*, whatever they may do to this or that *explication* of it. I am very willing to consider whatever you have to object to what is advanced under the first head of that sermon. But I still think that *perfection* is only another term for *holiness*, or the image of God in man. God *made man perfect*, I think, is just the same as, he made him *holy*, or 'in his own image'.[79] And you are the very first person I ever read of or spoke with who made

---

[77] JW's reply of Feb. 5 to Dodd's opening letter of the correspondence was brief, a request that Dodd should make comments on JW, *Christian Perfection*. Both the substance and specific passages in Dodd's second letter can be gathered from Wesley's lengthy reply.

[78] Sermon 40, *Christian Perfection*, 2:96–124 in this edn.

[79] Cf. Gen. 1:26.

any doubt of it. Now *this perfection* does certainly admit of degrees.
Therefore I readily allow the propriety of that distinction, perfection of kinds and perfection of degrees. Nor do I remember one
writer ancient or modern who excepts against it.

5   4. In the sermon on Salvation by Faith I say, 'He that is born
of God sinneth not' (a proposition explained at large in another
sermon,[80] and there and[81] everywhere either explicitly or virtually
connected with, 'while he keepeth himself') 'by any sinful desire;
for any unholy desire he stifleth in the birth.'[82] Assuredly he does

10   *while he keepeth himself.* 'Nor doth he sin by infirmities; for his infirmities have no concurrence of his will, and without this they are
not properly sins.'[83] Taking the words as they lie in connection thus
(and taken otherwise they are not *my* words, but *yours*), I must still
aver they speak both my own experience and that of many hun-

15   dred children of God whom I personally know. And all this, with
abundantly more than this, is contained in that single expression,
'the loving God with all our heart, and serving him with all our
strength'.[84] Nor did I ever say or mean any *more* by perfection than
the *thus* loving and serving God. But I dare not say *less* than this; for

20   it might be attended with worse consequences than you seem to be
aware of. If there be a mistake, it is far more dangerous on the one
side than on the other. If I set the mark too high, I drive men into
needless fears; if you set it too low, you drive them into hell-fire.

      5. We agree that true 'Christianity implies a destruction of the

25   kingdom of sin and a renewal of the soul in righteousness; which
even babes in Christ do in a measure experience, though not in so
large a measure as young men and fathers'.[85] But here we divide. I
believe even babes in Christ (*while they keep themselves*) *do not commit sin.*[86] By 'sin' I mean outward sin; and the word 'commit' I take

30   in its plain, literal meaning. And this I think is fully proved by all
the texts cited (Sect. 3) from the 6th chapter to the Romans.[87] Nor
do I conceive there is any material difference between *committing sin*
and *continuing therein.* I tell my neighbour here, 'William, you are a
child of the devil, for you *commit sin*; you was drunk yesterday.' 'No,

[80] Sermon 19, 'The Great Privilege of those that are Born of God', 1:431–43 in this edn.

[81] The second 'and' is missing in the printed text, but added in the errata and in manuscript by JW in his personal copy.

[82] Sermon 1, *Salvation by Faith*, II.6, 1:124 in this edn.

[83] Ibid.

[84] Cf. Deut. 6:5, Luke 10:27, and parallels.

[85] Wesley is apparently quoting Dodd's letter.

[86] Cf. Sermon 40, *Christian Perfection*, II.2, 2:105 in this edn.

[87] I.e., ibid., II.3, 2:106 in this edn.

sir,' says the man, 'I do not *live* or *continue in sin*' (which Mr. Dodd says is the true meaning of the text), 'I am not drunk *continually*, but only now and then, once in a fortnight or in a month.' Now, sir, how shall I deal with this man? Shall I tell him he is in the way to heaven or to hell? I think he is in the high road to destruction, and that if I tell him otherwise his blood will be upon my head; and all that you say of 'living', 'continuing in', 'serving sin', as different from 'committing it', and of its not *reigning*, not having *dominion* over him who still frequently *commits* it, is making so many *loopholes* whereby any impenitent sinner may escape from all the terrors of the Lord. I dare not, therefore, give up the plain, literal meaning either of St. Paul's or St. Peter's words.

6. As to those of St. John (cited sect. 5), I do not think you have proved they are not to be taken literally. In every single act of obedience, as well as in a continued course of it, ποιῶ δικαιοσύνην; and in either an act or a course of sin ποιῶ ἁμαρτίαν.[88] Therefore, that I may give no countenance to any kind or degree of sin, I still interpret these words by those in the 5th chapter, and believe 'he that is born of God' (while he keepeth himself) 'sinneth not',[89] doth not commit outward sin.

7. But 'it is absolutely necessary', as you observe, 'to add sometimes explanatory words to those of the sacred penmen.' It is so—to add words *explanatory* of their sense, but not subversive of it. The words added to that text, 'Ye know all things', are such.[90] And you yourself allow them so to be. But I do not allow the words 'wilfully' and 'habitually' to be such.[91] These do not explain but overthrow the text. That the first Fathers thus explained it I deny; as also that I ever spoke lightly of them.

8. You proceed, 'You allow in another sermon, in evident contradiction to yourself, that the true children of God *could* and *did* commit sin.'[92] This is no contradiction to anything I ever advanced. I everywhere allow that a child of God *can* and *will* commit sin, *if he does not keep himself*. But this, you say, is nothing to the present argument. Yes, it is the whole thing. If they *keep themselves* they do not; otherwise they *can* and *do* commit sin. I say nothing contrary

[88] Ibid., II.5, varying the Greek of 1 John 3:7–8 (ὁ ποιῶν, 'the one practising'), to read 'I practise'; changed in 1782 to ποιεῖ (no accent mark given),'he practises'.

[89] 1 John 5:18.

[90] Sermon 40, *Christian Perfection*, I.6, 2:102–3 in this edn.

[91] See ibid., II.6, 2:107 in this edn.; including Wesley's qualifications noted in note 66.

[92] Dodd is referring to Sermon 19, *The Great Privilege of those that are Born of God*, section II (1:435–42 in this edn.).

to this in either sermon. But, 'hence, you say, we conclude *that he who is* born of God *may possibly commit sin.*' An idle conclusion as ever was formed. For who ever denied it? I flatly affirm it in both the sermons and in the very paragraph now before us. The only
5   conclusion which I deny is that 'all Christians *do and must commit sin as long as they live*'. Now, this you yourself (though you seem to start at it) maintain from the beginning of your letter to the end— viz., that all Christians *do sin,* and *cannot but sin,* more or less to their lives' end. Therefore I do not '*artfully put* this conclusion';
10 but it is your own conclusion from your own premises.[93] Indeed, were I *artfully* to *put* in anything in expounding the Word of God, I must be an errant knave. But I do not. My conscience bears me witness that I speak the very truth, so far as I know it, in simplicity and godly sincerity.
15   9. I think that all this time you are directly pleading for *looseness of manners*, and that everything you advance naturally tends thereto. This is my grand objection to that doctrine of the *necessity of sinning*; not only that it is false, but that it is directly subversive of all holiness. The doctrine of the Gnostics was not that a child of
20 God *does not commit sin* (i.e., act the things which are forbidden in Scripture), but that they are *not sin* in him, that he is a child of God still. So they contended not for *sinless* but *sinful perfection*—just as different from what I contend for as heaven is from hell. What the Donatists were I do not know. But I suspect they were the real
25 Christians of that age, and were therefore served by St. Augustine and his warm adherents as the Methodists are now by their zealous adversaries. It is extremely easy to blacken; and could I give myself leave, I could paint the consequences of your doctrine in at least as dark and odious colours as you could paint mine.
30   10. The passage of St. Peter (mentioned sect. 12[94]) I still think proves all which I brought it to prove. 'But you allow' (sect. 14[95]) 'that Paul and Barnabas did commit sin; and these were without all controversy fathers in Christ.' That is not without controversy— that either Barnabas when he left Paul, or Peter when he dissem-
35 bled at Antioch, was at that time a father in Christ in St. John's sense—though *by office* undoubtedly they were. Their example, therefore, only proves what no one denies—viz., that if a believer

---

[93] The conclusion to *Great Privilege*, section II (II.10, 1:441 in this edn.) reads: 'Thus it is unquestionably true that he who is born of God, keeping himself, doth not, cannot commit sin, and yet if he keepeth not himself he may commit all manner of sin with greediness.'
[94] Sermon 40, *Christian Perfection*, II.12, 2:111 in this edn.
[95] Ibid., II.14, 2:112–13 in this edn.

keep not himself, *he may sin*. Would the conclusion there drawn 'be made only by a very weak opponent'? You are the man who make them all,[96] either from these or other premises; for you believe and maintain: 1) that *all the other apostles committed sin sometimes*; 2) that *all the other Christians* of the apostolic age sometimes committed sin; 3) that *all other Christians in all ages* do and will commit sin as long as they live; and 4) that every man *must* commit sin, *cannot help* it, as long as he is in the body. You cannot deny one of these propositions, if you understand your own doctrine.[97] It is *you*, therefore, who 'cast dust in people's eyes' if you dissemble your real sentiments. I declare mine with all the plainness I can, that if I err I may be sooner convinced of it. Neither does it appear that St. Paul was 'an aged father in Christ' when he had that thorn in the flesh. I doubt whether he was above thirty years of age, fourteen years before he mentioned it to the Corinthians. 'You conclude' (these are your words) 'a Christian is so far perfect as not to commit sin—as to be free from all *possibility* of sinning. That this is your meaning is evident from your whole discourse.' Not so. The contrary is glaringly evident from that whole discourse to which you before referred, as well as from many parts of this. I conclude just this much: *While he keepeth himself*, a Christian *doth not* commit sin.

11. With regard to fathers in Christ, before you enter on the subject, you say I 'set aside the experience of the best of Christians'. I did not tell you so. I say nothing about them. In a sermon of a single sheet (such it is, printed single[98]) I had no room for anything but plain arguments from Scripture. I have somewhat to say, if need should be, from the head of authority likewise—yea, and abundantly more than you seem to apprehend. *Sed nunc non erat his locus.*[99]

12. I think section 23 very closely and directly concerns the present subject.[100] For if you have sinful thoughts still, then certainly *every thought* is not brought into captivity to the obedience of Christ. With regard to the 24th, you give one interpretation of

---

[96] *AM* (1782) reads, 'Then you are a weak opponent; for you make them all'.

[97] *AM* (1782) ends here, thus: 'You cannot deny one of these propositions, if you understand your own premises. I am, rev. sir, your affectionate brother, J. Wesley.'

[98] The first edition, of 1741, printed by William Strahan of London, was printed in two sheets (48 pages); but the second, printed by John Gooding of Newcastle in 1743, was indeed completed in one sheet (24 pages). See *Bibliography*, No. 53.

[99] Horace, *Ars Poetica* ('The Art of Poetry'), 19; 'For such things there is a place, but not now.'

[100] Sermon 40, *Christian Perfection*, II.23, 2:117–18 in this edn.; quoting 2 Cor. 10:5.

those words, 'Everyone that is perfect shall be as his Master'; I
another.[101] You likewise appeal to the context; so do I. *Et adhuc sub
judice lis est.*[102] But I must observe, whether one interpretation or
the other be true, to assert God *can* or *does* so renew his children
5   as to save them from all evil tempers has no more alliance with
blasphemy than with adultery. You make a little mistake as to section 26. I do not cite 'is purified' as St. John's words.[103] You say on
section 27: 'As is he, so are we' refers to our being conformed to
his patient long-suffering. It may; but it directly refers to our be-
10 ing 'made perfect in love'. You do not answer or attempt to answer
either of the arguments whereby I have proved that the 'cleansing
from all unrighteousness' does not mean justification only. Hitherto, therefore, the conclusion stands good—that it relates chiefly,
if not wholly, to sanctification.
15   13. In your last paragraph you say, 'You set aside all authority,
ancient and modern.' Sir, who told you so? I never did; it never
entered my thoughts. Who it was gave you that rule I know not. But
my father gave it me thirty years ago (I mean concerning reverence
to the ancient Church and our own), and I have endeavoured to
20 walk by it to this day.[104] But I try every Church and every doctrine
by the Bible. This is the word by which we are to be judged in that
day. O that we may then give up our account with joy![105]
     Whatever further thoughts you are pleased to communicate will
be seriously considered by, rev. dear sir,
25   Your affectionate brother and fellow-labourer,

John Wesley

Source: published transcription; *Arminian Magazine* 2 (1779): 475–81, en-
     titled 'On Christian Perfection'. Wesley also published an extended
     extract of this letter in *Arminian Magazine* 5 (1782): 429–34, entitled

[101] Ibid., II.24 (2:118); quoting Luke 6:40—for which see notes on 2:117.

[102] Horace, *Ars Poetica* ('The Art of Poetry'), 78; 'and the case is still before the court'.
Wesley's original has '*Sed adhuc*' ('but'), which is corrected to Horace's text, '*Et adhuc*', in the
printed errata and in Wesley's hand in his personal copy.

[103] See Sermon 40, *Christian Perfection*, II.26, 2:119 in this edn. Wesley's direct quote of
1 John 3:3 reads 'purifieth himself even as he is pure'; but he begins the next sentence 'He is
purified'.

[104] In his *Advice to a Young Clergyman* (originally a personal letter to his curate, but published with the help of JW in 1735; see *Bibliography*, No. 5) Samuel Wesley Sr. urges study of
the more important early Fathers (pp. 30–34) and the Nicene Fathers (38–52), supported by the
scholars of the Church of England.

[105] See Matt. 12:36; Acts 20:24.

'An Answer to Mr. Dodd' (adding 'Revd.' in the errata). There are several minor alterations in the second setting—those of major importance are noted.

To Samuel Furly

KINGSWOOD
MARCH 14, 1756

Dear Sammy,

You are sick of two diseases: that affection for a poor silly worm like yourself, which only absence (through the grace of God) will cure;[106] and that evil disease which Marcus Antonius complains of—the δίψαν βιβλίων.[107] That you are far gone in the latter plainly appears from your not loving and admiring that masterpiece of reason and religion, the *Reflections [up]on the Conduct of Human Life, with Reference to Knowledge and Learning*,[108] every paragraph of which must stand unshaken (with or without the Bible) till we are no longer mortal.

If your French book is *The Art of Thinking*, the author is a very poor tool.[109] But there is none like Aldrich.[110] I scarce know one Latin writer who says so much in so few words. Certainly I shall not write much in metaphysics or natural philosophy. My life is

---

[106] See letters of Feb. 21 and Apr. 16, 1756.

[107] Marcus Aurelius Antoninus, *Meditations*, ii.3; 'thirst after books'. The printed text in the *United Methodist Free Church Magazine* has the apparently incorrect δίχα βιβλίων. See Wesley's letters of Apr. 16, 1756, to Furly, and of Nov. 30, 1770, to Joseph Benson, where he issues a similar warning.

[108] Published by John Norris (1657–1711) in 1690; JW published an abridgement in 1734 (see *Bibliography*, No. 3). In the conclusion of his abridgment Wesley quoted a reference to Marcus Antoninus, giving a fuller Greek quotation, translated as 'Rid thyself of the thirst after books' while dealing with 'this bookish humour, which … is one of the spiritual diseases … of mankind' (p. 53). Thus a 'bookish humour' and the 'thirst after books' were clearly linked in his mind as he addressed Furly.

[109] Antoine Arnauld (1612–94) and Pierre Nichole (1625–95), *La Logique ou L'Art de Penser* (1662), translated into English in 1685 as *Logic, or the Art of Thinking*. Wesley had a copy of this in the library of Kingswood School.

[110] Henry Aldrich (1647–1710), who published his *Artis Logicae Compendium* in 1691. It was revised several times; JW's signed copy of the 1771 edition remains in the Kingswood School library. Wesley's own *Compendium of Logic* (1750, *Bibliography*, No. 186) depended heavily on an edition with an Appendix by Bishop Robert Sanderson.

too far spent. But if you can tell me of anything (not stuffed with mathematics) which is worth abridging, well.[111]

Hutcheson's compendium is entitled *Synopsis Metaphysicae Ontologiam et Pneumatologiam Complectens*.[112] It is a masterly thing. I believe there is nothing yet extant in natural philosophy like the abridgement of the *Philosophical Transactions*.[113] But an abridgement of that abridgement would be far better.

Fight, Sammy, fight. If you do not conquer soon, probably God may send a French army to help you. I am,

    Yours affectionately,

                        J. Wesley

Address: 'To Mr Samuel Furly, In Queen's College, Cambridge'.

Source: published transcription; *United Methodist Free Churches Magazine* 9 (1866): 175; part of a series of letters from Wesley to Furly about which Jonathan Couch states he 'copied the whole of them from the originals, with his own hand' (p. 173).

To Richard Tompson ('P.V.')[114]

[COLEFORD]
MARCH 16, 1756

My Dear Brother,

My belief in general is this, that every Christian believer has a divine conviction of his reconciliation with God. The sum of those concessions is, 'I am inclined to think there may be some exceptions'.

---

[111] It was apparently after this that Wesley discovered Johann Franciscus Buddeus's *Elementa Philosophiae Theoretica* (1706), which he translated and abridged as the core of the first edition of *A Survey of the Wisdom of God in the Creation: or, A Compendium of Natural Philosophy* (1763, see *Bibliography*, No. 259). This grew into a five-volume work.

[112] See JW's early letter to Furly, of Feb. 18.

[113] Royal Society, The Philosophical Transactions ... abridged and disposed under general heads, 10 vols. (London: W. Innys, 1720–50).

[114] Replying to Tompson's of Feb. 12, 1756.

Faith implies both the *perceptive faculty* itself and the *act of perceiving* God and the things of God. And the expression, 'seeing God' may include both: the *act* and the *faculty* of seeing him.

Bishop Pearson's definition is abundantly too wide for the faith of which we are speaking.[115] Neither does he give that definition either of *justifying* or *saving faith*. But if he did, I should prefer the definition of Bishop Paul.[116]

A clear conviction of the love of God cannot remain in any who do not walk closely with God. And I know no one person who has lost this without some *voluntary defect* in his conduct, though perhaps at the time he was not conscious of it; but upon prayer, it was revealed to him.

Your reasons for concealing your name were good. We cannot too carefully guard against prejudice. You have no need of any excuse at all. For you have done no wrong, but rather a pleasure to
    Your affectionate brother,

J. Wesley

Source: published transcription; Tompson, *Original Letters*, 51–52.

To Howell Harris[117]

HOLYHEAD

SATURDAY, MARCH 27, 1756

My Dear Brother,

After some difficulties, out of all which our good Lord delivered us, we came hither on Thursday evening. The packet had sailed the night before, but was driven back again in the morning. Today an

---

[115] Bishop John Pearson, *An Exposition of the Creed* (1659), 12th edn., 1741, p. 4: 'Human faith is an assent unto anything credible merely upon the testimony of man.'

[116] Wesley consistently defined 'faith' by reference to Heb. 11:1 (which he assumed was authored by Paul): 'Now faith is the substance of things hoped for, the evidence of things not seen.'

[117] Howell Harris's health was deteriorating, and he was gradually being superseded in leadership by his Welsh Calvinistic colleagues. His preaching itineraries were more restricted and his Christian community at Trevecka became increasingly the focal point of his activities. During his brief twentieth tour in Wales Wesley visited Harris at Trevecka March 19–21, when Harris told him that 'he preached till he could preach no longer, his constitution being entirely broken'. From there Wesley went on to Brecon and Holyhead en route to Ireland.

honest man is to carry our horses to William Roberts's.[118] And when God pleases, he will carry us to Ireland. We willingly wait his leisure.

Self-will, which suffers not Christ to reign over us, self-righteousness, which renounces the righteousness of God our
5   Saviour, and our own fleshly wisdom, which will not be taught by the eternal wisdom of the Father, are undoubtedly the great enemies we have to contend with, and assault us in a thousand shapes. But I find (though they are closely connected together) self-will the hardest of all to conquer. O Howell, let us be more and more
10   aware of this deadly enemy. It contains passion, stubbornness, unpersuadableness, and what not? O let us give it no quarter! The Lord make us mild, quiet, loving, patient of reproof, advice, contradiction, contempt, willing to suffer all things for his name's sake!
I am,
15   Your very affectionate brother,

J. Wesley

When you write, have patience. For sometimes you write so hastily that I can't read it.[119]

20
Address: 'To / Mr Howell Harris / At Trevecka / Near the Hay / Brecknockshire / turn at Gloster'.
Charge: '4'.
Source: holograph; New Room (Bristol).

To Samuel Furly

Dublin
Good Friday [April 16], 1756

How? Going up to town? Are you stark, staring mad? Will you leap into the fire with your eyes open?[120] Keep off. What else have

---

[118] William Roberts of Plas Bach (d. 1760) was a Calvinistic Methodist who had been converted in 1748 and had long supported Harris. He welcomed Wesley on his return from Ireland, Aug. 13, 1756 (21:75 in this edn.).

[119] This footnote is written vertically on the back of the letter page.

[120] This apparently refers to Furly's love affair. See JW's letters of Feb. 21 and Mar. 14, 1756, and also the reference on Nov. 20 [1756]—'when you resolved to quit your trifling companion'.

you to do? Fly for your life, for your salvation. If you thus tempt the Spirit of God any more, who knows what may be the consequence? I should not wonder at all to hear you was confined in St. Luke's Hospital.[121] And then farewell study! Farewell all hope, either of intellectual or moral improvement, for after this poor machine has received a shock of that kind, it is never more capable of close thinking.

If you have either sense or religion enough to keep you close to the College, it is well. If not, I see but one possible way to save you from destruction, temporal and eternal. Quit the College at once. Think of it no more. And come away to me. You can take a little advice from me, from other people none at all. You are on the brink of the pit. Fly away, or you perish. There is no disagreement at all between the *Reflections*[122] and the *Address to the Clergy*.[123] I have followed Mr. [John] Norris's advice these thirty years, and so must every man that is well in his senses. But whether *you* study more or less does not signify a pin's point. You are taking all this pains in a sinking ship. Stop the leak, stop the leak the first thing you do. Else what signifies it to adorn the ship?

As to the qualifications[124] of a gospel minister, grace is necessary; learning is expedient. Grace and supernatural gifts are ninety-nine parts in an hundred. Acquired learning may then have its place.

I am, dear Sammy,

Yours affectionately,

J. Wesley

Address: 'To / Mr Sam: Furly / At Queen's College / Cambridge'.
Postmarks: 'DUBLIN' and the London date stamp, '26/AP'.
Charge: what appears to be an elaborate 'No', and '6' struck through with '4', possibly the Dublin-London charge (6d) together with the London-Cambridge '3'.
Endorsement: 'Good friday / 1756'.
Source: holograph; Bridwell Library (SMU).

---

[121] An overflow institution for the insane asylum in Moorfields, Bethlehem (corrupted to 'Bedlam'). See JW, *Journal*, Dec. 21, 1762, 21:400 in this edn.

[122] See letter of Mar. 14, 1756.

[123] See letters of Jan. 7 and Feb. 18, 1756.

[124] Wesley originally wrote, 'If we could divide the qualifications', and later struck through the first four words, supplying 'As to' above.

To Ebenezer Blackwell

DUBLIN
APRIL 19, 1756

Dear Sir,

While you in England are under I know not what apprehensions,
5   all here are as safe as if they were already in paradise. We have no
fortifying of seaports, no military preparations, but all is in absolute
peace and safety. Both high and low seem fully persuaded that the
whole talk of an invasion is only a trick to get money.[125]

I dined at Mrs. Moreland's[126] last week, and promised to drink tea
10   with her this evening. She has been at the preaching several times,
and desires much to be remembered to Mrs. [Elizabeth] Blackwell
and you. She seems to have a liking to the gospel. It may sink deeper.
There is nothing too hard for God.

I hope Mrs. Blackwell and you are improving to the utmost these
15   days of tranquillity. I purpose going to Cork directly, and after
two or three weeks turning back toward the north of Ireland. If it
please God that troublous times come between the design and the
execution, I shall go as far as I can go, and no farther. But I take no
thought for the morrow. Today I am determined by his grace to do
20   the work of him that sent me. I find encouragement so to do; for all
the people here are athirst for the word of life.

I am, dear sir,
    Your affectionate servant,

[John Wesley]

25

Do you at London believe that the danger of an invasion is over?

Source: published transcription; Jackson, *Works* (3rd), 12:169–70.

[125] Wesley refers to the fears of the French invasion, which had led to his offer of a company of volunteers in case of such an event (see his letter of Mar. 1, 1756). When he arrived in Dublin, however, he was 'surprised to find that all Ireland is in perfect safety. None here has any more apprehension of an invasion than of being swallowed up in the sea, everyone being absolutely assured that the French dare not attempt any such thing' (*Journal* for Mar. 31, 1756; 21:47–48 in this edn.). Later he wrote: 'The sleepers here began to open their eyes, it being rumoured that an express was come to the Lord Lieutenant to inform him that the French were hastening their preparation, being determined to land in Ireland.' This, however, was supposed to be 'a mere trick of State', and the Lord Lieutenant was ignoring the 'express orders from his Majesty to put this kingdom in a posture of defence' (*Journal* for Apr. 6, 9; 21:49 in this edn.).

[126] There is no Mrs. Moreland listed as a member of the Dublin society in JW's manuscript list dated July 20, 1769 (held at MARC).

To Mary (Goldhawk/Vazeille) Wesley

WATERFORD
MAY 7, 1756

My Dear Molly,

From Portarlington we rode (twenty miles, as they call it) in about eight hours to Kilkenny.[127] There our brethren in the army received 5 us gladly, and opened a door which none were able to shut. Yesterday in the afternoon (through heavy rain; but it was nothing to me) we came hither. Here is a poor, shattered society, who have been for these seven years tearing one another in pieces. What I shall be able to do with them I know not, but it is enough if I can deliver my own 10 soul.[128] On Monday I hope to be in Clonmel, and on Wednesday evening in Cork.

From time to time, my love, you should tell me all you know concerning public affairs: for it is hard to depend on the authority of the newspapers for the truth of anything. If King George recovers,[129] I 15 trust there will be a lengthening of our tranquillity. If God should take him away, for anything I see yet, I should quit this kingdom as soon as possible. In the meantime, let you and I improve today. The morrow shall take thought for the things of itself.[130]

Sister Cownley[131] sends her kindest love to you and Jenny.[132] Is 20 there something extremely remarkable in her dream? I have heard of several other uncommon notices which have been given to others in this kingdom. But I stay till I can see the persons concerned, and take the accounts from their own mouths.

I dreamed last night that I was carried to execution, and had but a 25 few minutes to live. We had not been talking of anything of the kind overnight. What I gather hence is, while we live, let us live; that if we do not meet again here, we may in a better place.

My dear Molly,

Adieu!   30

---

[127] Orig., 'Killkenny'.

[128] On the expression 'deliver my own soul', see 2:36, n. 23 in this edn.

[129] George II (1683–1760) suffered from gout in his later years and was irritable (perhaps on that account), but he continued to be interested in ceremony and in public affairs until his death. It appears, however, that some rumours of a royal illness had reached Wesley.

[130] See Matt. 6:34.

[131] His preacher, Joseph Cownley, now stationed in Dublin, had the previous October married Martha Susannah Massiot of Cork, and they were now expecting a child.

[132] Jeanne Vazeille, Wesley's step-daughter (1737–1820); see 26:451, n. 2 in this edn.

I have now yours of April 20. It is all in all, to keep the issues of our heart. And by his strength we are able so to do. Draw us, and we will run after thee![133]

Pay the printers yourself; that is the sure way, unless John Spen-
5 cer[134] gives you his account, as I have written.

I hope H. Brown will do everything you bid him. Else you must send him home. I have wrote to Mr. Blackwell from Dublin. Peace be with your spirit![135]

Address: 'To / Mrs Mary Wesley'.
No *postmark* or indications of postal *charge*; apparently delivered by hand.
Source: holograph; MARC, MAM JW 5/55.

To Unidentified Preacher (Thomas Walsh?)[136]

10   CORK
                                                              MAY 14, 1756

My Dear Brother,

I have consulted the preachers that are with me here, and they have no objection to your proposal, only it might be well if you
15 delayed the putting it in execution till there is another travelling preacher in the round, because otherwise many of the other societ-ies will suffer great loss.

You should wherever you are take care of one thing—do not puz-zle people about the Church. Those that are there, let them con-

---

[133] See Song of Songs, 1:4.

[134] See the letter to Mary Wesley of Jan. 7, 1756.

[135] These postscript lines appear on the third page of the ms.

[136] Telford does not identify the recipient of this letter, probably because the address por-tion of the manuscript was missing. Perhaps the best possibility is Thomas Walsh, who was serving as JW's General Assistant in Ireland at the time (on Walsh, see 26:430 in this edn.). JW had held a conference with his preachers in Dublin during Easter week 1756 (April 19ff), and likely on that occasion announced his intention of a subsidiary consultation in Cork around May 11–13. Walsh surely attended the Dublin conference (though there are no minutes to verify this; cf. 10:276 in this edn.). He may have been urged there to fulfill his earlier charge of spying out the land in the north, and wrote to Wesley about the situation in time for the Cork consultation. He had written to Wesley on Sept. 23, 1755, 'You desire I would go into the north', although at that time he was too weak, but that after remaining in Limerick a little he would 'then, if possible … visit either Castlebar, the Athlone circuit, or the north'. JW's brief 1750 letter to Walsh began with exactly the same salutation that is used here (see 26:430).

tinue there, else the gain will not countervail the damage. Take care
likewise that you do not buy the favour of the world too dear.[137]
   I am,
       Your affectionate brother,

                               [J. Wesley]   5

Source: published transcription; Telford, *Letters*, 3:178.

To Mary (Goldhawk/Vazeille) Wesley[138]

CORK[139]
MAY 21, 1756

My Dear Love,

   I can easily remove that difficulty of your not knowing which of   10
your letters I answer, by writing just letter for letter. Then there can
be no mistake. There could never have been any, if I had not wrote
two or three letters to your one.

   The money in Ireland is just as safe as that in London. All the
first subscription-money[140] (but a few pounds which I have received   15
here) you received at the Foundery long ago. And if the books
come into this kingdom while I am in it, I will be answerable for

---

[137] Cf. the proverb, 'Do not buy gold too dear', as used in JW, 'The Use of Money', 2:269 in this edn.

[138] Wesley is apparently replying to a letter from his wife written about May 14, to whose contents his reply affords some clues, such as her complaint that it is difficult to keep pace with their correspondence, and inquiring whether Irish money subscribed for his publications is as safe as English money.

[139] Orig., 'Corke' as earlier, though the last appearance of this spelling in his letters is on July 21, 1758.

[140] Several of Wesley's works were published by subscription, whereby subscribers advanced a certain amount before publication, and a further amount (or amounts) after receiving the work. In this instance it seems clear that the work in question was *Explanatory Notes upon the New Testament* (*Bibliography*, No. 209). Proposals for this were first published in August 1754, then again in September, and once more in April 1755. The second condition ran: 'The price to subscribers is twelve shillings, six to be paid at the time of subscribing, and six on the delivery of the book in quires.' Although the title-page gave the date as 1755, and although JW's *Journal* for Sept. 23, 1755 claimed that he then had 'a little leisure to sit still, and finish' the *NT Notes*, in fact William Bowyer's ledgers show that his first deliveries were not made until May 14, 1756, so that the Irish copies might indeed have been received while he was there.

the second subscription-money, which I can then receive and (if it please God) bring over with me.

There is the prospect of a glorious harvest here. Such times were never seen in Cork before. If I could stay here some weeks,[141] I think this society would bid fair for outrunning that in Dublin.[142] But my journeys are fixed.[143] I found last night a particular blessing to my own soul. Today I am free from every human creature. And I trust God for tomorrow.

Dear Molly,

      Adieu!

Source: holograph; Wesley's Chapel (London), LDWMM 1994/2068 (address portion missing).

To Mary (Goldhawk/Vazeille) Wesley[144]

LIMERICK
JUNE 18, 1756

My Dear Love,

At Newmarket on Wednesday night and last night at Ballingrane[145] our lodging was not very warm or elegant. But I do not perceive that I have taken any cold. Rather, I am better than when I set out. A week or two ago I was not very strong; but I have now no reason to complain. I preach no more than twice a day. And not once abroad since my coming to Limerick. Let the wind be east, west, or north, we have rain every day; so that I keep to the Abbey,[146] whether I will or no.

[141] Wesley did indeed remain in Cork (apart from a few days' interlude in Bandon) for four weeks.

[142] Probably thinking about his forthcoming visit, JW originally wrote 'Bandon', and then immediately replaced it by 'Dublin'.

[143] This did not mean that they were never subject to alteration, of course, but in general Wesley did plan ahead very carefully, and inform his Assistants and often the society stewards of his planned itinerary. In later years this was sometimes done by means of a printed leaflet.

[144] Some clues to Mary Wesley's letter that this answers, probably written about June 4, are present.

[145] For this Irish town that had been settled by German Palentines, which became an important center of Methodist converts like Philip Embury and Barbara Heck who took Methodism with them when they subsequently moved to New York and elsewhere, see JW, *Journal*, June 16, 1756 (21:60–61 in this edn.). Wesley spells it 'Ballygarrane'.

[146] Orig., 'Abby'. Wesley describes the Methodist leasing of the shell of Limerick Abbey in JW, *Journal*, May 12, 1749 (20:272 in this edn.).

I think the paper was to be fifteen shillings a ream. I shall not be sorry if an hundred people will return the subscription money. Let not one copy unsubscribed for go under fifteen shillings. Many will be glad of them at any price. They may have the picture (and the errata) or let it alone.[147] It is well done. I saw it before I left London. I am afraid there have not copies enough been sent to Ireland. The money remitted from hence, at four payments, was between fifty and sixty pounds. Brother Atkinson[148] can easily compute how many subscribers this implies. I hear nothing of any books come to Dublin yet. I hope they were directed to Mr. Powell.[149]

'Tis not unlikely poor sister Atkinson[150] may talk so. But (unless you heard them with your own ears) do not believe a word of it concerning John Downes[151] or Robert Windsor.[152] You did well to send George Whitefield and my brother the *Notes*.[153] I will trust you; give a copy to any preacher or any other person you judge proper. Pray pay Mr. Wyat and brother Buhet as soon as you can. The next money should pay our printing debts. If John Spencer[154] can spare you for three weeks, go to Bristol by all means. It is an excellent thought. Now, my Molly, overcome evil with good.

Indeed, I fear our fleets are bought and sold. Poor King George! Where will he find an honest man? If I hear of the French landing or beating our fleet on the 14th of July (the day those sights appeared in the air over Cornwall[155]), I shall endeavour to come into England directly; otherwise, to go on my way.

My brother does not oppose field preaching in general. But he does not like preaching in Smithfield. Though I know not why any should oppose it, unless they are apprehensive of the mob.

---

[147] *NT Notes* was delivered unbound, in 'quires' or gatherings of four quarto leaves (eight pages). The portrait was issued separately, an engraving of John Williams's portrait of Wesley. Wesley here states that he approved the engraving before he left London on Mar. 1. The general text and notes of the work were completed in gathering '5D', and the last, '5E', was devoted to a summary of Revelation, a brief index, and three pages of errata.

[148] William Atkinson; see JW to Mary Wesley, Jan. 7, 1756.

[149] Samuel Powell (d. 1792), Wesley's main Dublin printer.

[150] The wife of William Atkinson.

[151] John Downes (c. 1723–74) was one of Wesley's itinerant preachers, who did the engraving of Wesley's portrait for *NT Notes*. Wesley considered him a natural genius (JW, *Journal*, Nov. 4, 1774, 22:435–36 in this edn.). See Atmore, *Memorial*, 109–10; Vickers, *Dictionary*, 99.

[152] Orig., 'Winsor'. Robert Windsor of London, one of the founding members and a steward of the Foundery society, whose funeral sermon Wesley preached on Feb. 7, 1790; see 26:566 in this edn.

[153] I.e., *NT Notes*.

[154] See letter of May 7, 1756.

[155] Apparently a supposed portent in the Cornish sky on July 14 of an earlier year.

I am now writing on Original Sin, so the papers come in good time.[156] John Haughton is in Dublin.[157] Michael, with his little wit, does much good.[158] Watch over John Spencer. It will do him a solid kindness. You may perhaps convince him it is his interest to be honest, and to save me all the money he can. Should not one preacher go to Norwich immediately, and another to Portsmouth?

Molly, let us make the best of life. O for zeal! I want to be on the full stretch for God!

My dear love,

Adieu!

Pray put brother Norton's into the post.[159]

Address: 'To / Mrs Mary Wesley'.
No *postmark* or indications of postal *charge*; apparently delivered by hand.
Source: holograph; MARC, MAM JW 5/56.

To the Rev. James Clark[160]

CASTLEBAR
JULY 3, 1756

Rev. Sir,

I am obliged to you for the openness and candour with which you write, and will endeavour to follow the pattern which you have set me.

---

[156] Wesley had begun his response to John Taylor's *Scripture Doctrine of Original Sin* (1740), which would be published as *The Doctrine of Original Sin* (1757, *Bibliography*, No. 222; 12:117–481 in this edn.).

[157] John Haughton (d. 1781) had been an itinerant from 1741 and was one of Wesley's pioneer preachers in Ireland. He secured episcopal ordination, and became rector of Kilrea, near Londonderry, where he entertained Wesley on June 4, 1778 (JW, *Journal*, 23:90 in this edn.).

[158] Michael Fenwick (d. 1797), an eccentric follower who was removed after a few years of service as an itinerant. He idolised JW and was presently accompanying him as a valet and groom (see Atmore, *Memorial*, 123).

[159] This postscript appears on the first page of the ms. It seems that Wesley had made up a small packet of letters—at least two—to send by courier to his wife in London, including one to Nicholas Norton; for whom, see JW's letter of Sept. 3, 1756.

[160] James Clark was the rector of Hollymount, 4 miles SSE of Castlebar, Co. Mayo in 1756. On May 10 of that year he preached a sermon on 1 John 4:1, 'Beloved, believe not every spirit, but try the spirits whether they be of God, because many false prophets are gone out into the world.' He used the text to exhort Methodist sympathisers in his parish. A few weeks later, on June 26, Clark welcomed Wesley to his pulpit, from which Wesley referred to the Methodist society as 'his little church' (p. 26). Within a couple of days Clark fired off a letter to Wesley, who had moved on to Castlebar. This is Wesley's reply. Clark answered on July 9, and Wesley wrote again on Sept. 18. Clark closed their correspondence on Sept. 30, 1756. In 1760 he published the sermon, their correspondence, and other material as *Montanus Redivivus*.

I did not know of John Langston's affair till you gave me an account of it. He is no preacher allowed of by me. I do not believe that God ever called him to it. Neither do I approve his conduct with regard to you. I fear he is, or at least was, a real enthusiast. The same character, I fear, may be justly given to poor Mr. Bermingham.[161]

I sent you that sermon with no particular view, but as a testimony of love to a fellow-labourer in the gospel.[162]

From the text of that sermon I do not *infer* that Christians should not inquire[163] into each other's opinions. Indeed, from the text I infer nothing;[164] I use it to *illustrate*, not to *prove*. I am very sensible 'Jehu had more regard to state policy than to religion' (p. 5[165]); and have no objection [at all] to the very fair explication you have made[166] of his words. Accordingly I say (p. 13), '[What is implied in the question?] *I do not mean* what Jehu implied therein,[167] but what a follower of Christ should understand by it[168] when he proposes it to any of his brethren.'

Of these only I speak. My general proposition, you may please to remember, was this (p. 5):[169] 'All the children of God may unite in love, notwithstanding differences in opinion or modes of worship.'

From this persuasion, when[170] I meet with any whom I have reason to believe to be children of God,[171] I do not ask of him [with whom I would unite in love] (never at our first meeting,[172] seldom till we are better[173] acquainted), 'Do you agree with me in opinion or modes[174] of worship, particularly with regard to church government, baptism, and the Lord's Supper?' I let [all] these stand by till we begin to know and confirm[175] our love to each other. Then may

---

[161] Clark singles out Mr. Langston and Mr. Bermingham in his letter of June 28, 1756. *AM* omits this paragraph.

[162] Wesley had sent Clark a copy of his sermon titled 'Catholic Spirit', which first appeared in *Sermons on Several Occasions* in 1750, and was published as a separate pamphlet in 1755. The page references that follow are to this pamphlet edition.

[163] *AM*, 'are not to inquire'.

[164] *AM*, 'that text I do not infer anything'.

[165] Orig., 'p. 15'; corrected in *AM*.

[166] *AM*, 'given'.

[167] *AM*, 'What did Jehu imply therein?'

[168] *AM*, 'But what should a follower of Christ understand thereby'.

[169] *AM*, 'is this', with no page reference, which is to JW's *Catholic Spirit*, I.4, 2:82 of this edn.

[170] *AM*, 'whenever'.

[171] *AM*, 'believe "children of God"'

[172] *AM*, 'never at the entrance upon our conversation'.

[173] *AM*, 'a little'.

[174] *AM*, 'with my opinions, and mode'.

[175] *AM*, 'have confirmed'.

come a more convenient season for [entering into] controversy. My only question at *present* is, 'Is thy heart right with my heart, etc.?' [(p. 13[176])]

5　*At present*, I say, Keep your own opinion, I mine (p. 17[177]). I do not desire you to dispute these points. Whether we shall dispute them hereafter is another question; perhaps we may, perhaps we may not. This will depend on a great variety of circumstances—particularly on a probability of success; for I am determined never to dispute at all if I have no hopes of convincing my opponent.

10　As to my own judgment, I still believe the episcopal form of Church government to be both scriptural and apostolical, I mean, well agreeing with the practice and writings of the apostles. But that it is *prescribed* in Scripture I do not believe. This opinion, which I once heartily espoused, I have been heartily ashamed of ever since

15　I read Dr. Stillingfleet's *Irenicum*.[178] I think he has unanswerably proved that neither Christ [n]or his apostles *prescribed* any particular form of church government, and that the plea for the divine right of episcopacy[179] was never heard of in the primitive Church.

But were it otherwise, I would[180] still call these smaller matters than

20　the love of God and mankind (p. 18).[181] And could any man answer these questions: 'Dost thou believe in the Lord Jesus Christ, God over all, blessed for evermore?' (which, indeed, no Arian, semi-Arian, or[182] Socinian can do); 'Is God the centre of thy soul? [The sum of all thy desires?] Art thou more afraid of offending God than of death

25　or hell?'[183] (p. 15) (which no wicked man can possibly do, none that is not a real child of God). If, I say, any man could answer these questions in the affirmative, I would [then] gladly give him my hand.

This is certainly a principle held by those that are in derision called[184] Methodists, and to whom a Popish priest in Dublin gave

30　the still more unmeaning title of 'swaddlers'. They all desire to be of a catholic spirit; meaning thereby not an indifference to all opin-

---

[176] Sermon 39, *Catholic Spirit*, I.11, 2:87 in this edn.

[177] Orig., 'p. 13'; confusing with the prior quotation. The quotation is from *Catholic Spirit*, II.1 (2:89 in this edn.), which appears on p. 17 of the pamphlet.

[178] *AM*, 'Bishop Stillingfleet's *Irenicon*'. See JW's letter of July 16, 1755, to his brother Charles.

[179] *AM*, 'plea of *divine right* for diocesan episcopacy'.

[180] *AM*, 'should'.

[181] *AM*, 'smaller points', as in p. 18 of *Catholic Spirit*, II.2 (2:90 in this edn.).

[182] *AM*, 'and much less'.

[183] *AM*, 'of displeasing God than either of death', which is, in fact, the reading of p. 15 of *Catholic Spirit*, I.16 (2:88 in this edn.).

[184] *AM*, 'those who are ... termed'.

ions, not an indifference as to modes of worship.[185] This they know to be quite another thing. 'Love, they judge, gives a title [to] this character.[186] Catholic love is [a] catholic spirit' (p. 25[187]).

As to *heresy* and *schism*, I cannot find one text in Scripture[188] where they are taken in the modern sense. I remember no one scripture where[189] *heresy* signifies 'error in opinion', whether fundamental or not; nor any where[190] *schism* signifies [a] 'separation from the Church', either with or without cause.[191] I wish, sir, you would reconsider this point, and review the scriptures where[192] these terms occur.

But[193] I would take some pains to recover a man[194] from error and[195] reconcile him to our Church. I mean, [to] the Church of England, from which I do not separate yet, and probably never shall. The little church, in the vulgar sense [of the word], which I occasionally mentioned at Hollymount is that wherein I read prayers, preach, and administer the sacrament every Sunday when I am in London.[196]

But I would take much more pains to recover a man[197] from sin. A man[198] who lives and dies in error or in dissent from our Church may yet be saved; but a man[199] who lives and dies in sin must perish. O sir, let us lend[200] our main force against this, against all sin, both in ourselves and those[201] that hear us! I would to God we could all agree [both] in opinion[s] and outward worship. But if that cannot be, may we not agree in holiness? May we not all agree in being holy, as he that hath called us is holy, [both] in heart and [in all manner of] conversation? This is the great desire of, reverend sir,

Your [very humble servant],

J. W.

---

[185] *AM*, 'as to the manner of public worship'.

[186] *AM*, 'Love, they judge, alone gives …'.

[187] I.e., *Catholic Spirit*, III.4, 2:94 in this edn.

[188] *AM*, 'the Bible'.

[189] *AM*, 'wherein'.

[190] *AM*, 'wherein'.

[191] *AM*, 'either with cause or without'.

[192] *AM*, 'wherein'.

[193] *AM*, 'Yet'.

[194] *AM*, 'anyone'.

[195] *AM*, 'or to'.

[196] I.e., West Street Chapel, a consecrated building that had been made available to John and Charles Wesley starting May 29, 1743 (see JW, *Journal*, 19:326 in this edn.).

[197] *AM*, 'anyone'.

[198] *AM*, 'One'.

[199] *AM*, 'One'.

[200] *AM*, 'bend'.

[201] *AM*, 'them'.

PS.—Perhaps I have not spoke distinctly enough on one point. Orthodoxy, I say, or right opinion, is but a slender part of religion at best, and sometimes no part at all. I mean, if a man be a child of God, holy in heart and life, his right opinions are but the small-
5   est part of his religion. If a man be a child of the devil, his right opinions are no part of religion, they cannot be; for he that does the works of the devil has no religion at all.[202]

Source: published transcription; Clark, *Montanus Redivivus*, 36–39; compared to Wesley's heavily edited version in *Arminian Magazine* 2 (1779): 598–601. While Wesley may be editing Clark's published version, he more likely drew on his personal fair copy of the original. The transcription above follows Clark, with Wesley's additions in *AM* inserted within square brackets and other significant variants annotated. The italicising of emphasised words comes from Wesley's version. In *AM* Wesley prefixed the title, 'Of a Catholic Spirit'.

To Thomas Olivers[203]

ATHLONE
10   JULY 10, 1756

Dear Tommy,
    I cannot imagine how a letter of yours written March 9 should come to me on the ninth of July. Certainly you should write to me a little oftener, once a month at least.
15   Now there are several preachers in town, you should take care to supply Portsmouth, Bedford, Norwich, Leigh, and Canterbury

---

[202] The postscript is omitted from *AM*. On this statement about orthodoxy see Wesley's Sermon 7, 'The Way to the Kingdom', I.6, 1:220 in this edn.

[203] Thomas Olivers (1725–99), a Welshman awakened under the preaching of George Whitefield in Bristol around 1750. Some months later he moved to Bradford-on-Avon where he became a committed Christian and later a member of the Methodist society and an authorised lay preacher. After a round of preaching while paying his debts in various cities, he was diverted from setting up in his own business (he was a shoemaker) by a call from JW to become an official Methodist itinerant preacher. Accordingly he set out for Cornwall on Oct. 24, 1753, and served faithfully throughout Great Britain and Ireland until 1776, when JW appointed him to superintend his printing operation in London. At this he was only moderately successful, so that eventually Wesley replaced him. Nevertheless, he was a prodigious worker and a prolific writer in defence of Methodism. His most lasting memorial is probably his hymn, 'The God of Abraham Praise'. See *EMP*, 2:48–106.

by turns.[204] O Tommy, how precious are these days! We must not always have this sunshine. But make the best of the present calm. And then, if a storm comes,[205] you are ready.

I am,

Your affectionate brother,

J. Wesley

Source: holograph; MARC, WCB, D6/3/1/2 (the manuscript is affixed to a page and thus the address side cannot be read).

To Mary (Goldhawk/Vazeille) Wesley

ATHLONE
JULY 10, 1756

Two or three of your letters, my dear love, I have just received all together, together with the eight or ten letters from various parts dated in March. Where they have stuck these four months I cannot imagine.

You did well to pay brother Staines. I can receive it of brother Martin in Dublin. If there is a preacher to spare in London, let him go to Norwich, Bedford, or Portsmouth.[206]

All books should be sent to Bristol by land. ⟨I[207]⟩ hear nothing of any *Notes* come to Ireland. But I will ⟨tell⟩ you more when I hear from Dublin next. To booksellers you may let them go for 12s. They should be advertised over and over, at 15s. I am glad you was at London now, but shall be more glad when I am by your side. Shall not you too?

Why do not you immediately consult Dr. Turner?[208] O make no delay. Why does not my Jenny[209] write? Has she forgot how?

---

[204] Olivers was one of four itinerant preachers in addition to Wesley charged with serving both the London societies and smaller pockets in the whole of the south-east. Norwich was inserted later, over the line of writing.

[205] Wesley refers to the fears of a French invasion.

[206] Each of these cities was large, and had first been visited by JW within the last three years, but as yet had no strongly established Methodist society or preaching-house.

[207] A small portion of the manuscript is torn away, but the missing text is fairly clear.

[208] A London physician who was friendly to the Methodist leaders. Wesley consulted Turner about his preacher Joseph Cownley, writing Cownley, 'Ted Perronet says Dr. Turner expects no fee at all, but will do you all the service he can' (Apr. 23, 1757).

[209] Jeanne Vazeille, Wesley's step-daughter.

My love, your advice is good and seasonable. Nobody sees your letters. I burn them all as soon as I have answered them.[210] I will write to my brother about commending George Whitefield,[211] and to Bristol about the *Library*.[212]

5   My dear Molly, if you write to me more than once a day, perhaps I may say it is too often. But I shall not say so till then.

My dear,
    Adieu!

Address: 'To/ Mrs Mary Wesley'.
No *postmark* or indications of postal *charge*; apparently delivered by hand.
Source: holograph; Wesley's Chapel (London), LDWMM 1994/2069.

To an Unidentified Clergyman[213]

SUNDAY MORNING [JULY 18, 1756?]

10   Rev. Sir,

A flying report[214] which I heard last night occasions you this trouble. That I may not put you to any inconvenience, which I should be sorry to do (it would not be doing as I would be done to[215]), I beg to

---

[210] This is confirmed by the fact that not one seems to have survived, and only a scrap or two in her very poor hand from any source.

[211] This likely related to a fracas with Dr. Zachary Pearce, who seems to have been trying to undermine Whitefield's status as a clergyman.

[212] JW's *Christian Library* (32 volumes, 1749–55).

[213] One of JW's shortest letters, its unique importance as a demonstration of his sacramental dedication and his clerical sensitivity has entailed far more research than hundreds of longer ones. Even so we remain with no definitive clues to the date and place of its writing. We do have, however, strong impressions about its probable background. Wesley seems to be engaged in one of the summer preaching itineraries of his middle years, after his name had become a household word, and his reputation somewhat formidable. He has arrived on a Saturday where he has no close clerical acquaintance, but probably a few friendly hearers. It might have been almost any rural area in the British Isles. Monmouthsire in Wales, for example, is surely a possibility, for W.H.V. Bythway (from whom John Telford secured a transcription) was a long-time solicitor in Pontypool, where his grandfather had been Wesleyan Superintendent minister from 1854 to 1857. But lacking conclusive evidence for any option, we have chosen to relate this letter to an occasion when Wesley heard Rev. Moore Booker of Rosmead, in County Westmeath, Ireland preach a 'useful sermon' on July 18, 1756; because Booker had been episcopally reprimanded five years earlier for offering communion to local Methodists (see JW, *Journal* of that date; and Crookshank, *Ireland*, 1:80–82).

[214] *OED* (1989), 'circulating without definite authority'.

[215] See Matt. 7:12.

know whether you have any scruple as to administering the Lord's Supper to, rev. sir,

Your brother and servant,

John Wesley[216]

Source: holograph; Bridwell Library (SMU) (identified as 'J. Wesley, 4 October 1741').

To Robert Marsden[217]

BRISTOL
AUGUST 31, 1756

A careless reader of the *Address* may possibly think 'I make it necessary for a minister to have much learning', and thence imagine I act inconsistently, seeing many of our preachers have no learning at all. But the answer is easy. First, I do not make any learning *necessary* even for a *minister* (the minister of a parish, who, as such, undertakes *single* to guide and feed, to instruct ⟨and[218]⟩ govern that whole flock) but the knowledge of the Scriptures; although many branches of learning are highly *expedient* for him. Secondly, These preachers are not *ministers*: none of them undertakes *single* the care of a whole flock, but ten, twenty, or thirty, one following and helping another; and all, under the direction of my brother and me, undertake jointly what (as I judge) no man in England is equal to alone.

[216] Wesley used his full signature only in more formal letters. The handwriting in this letter is typical of his middle years, with two bold loops for 'W', and neat regular lines 1 cm. apart rather than the 7–8mm. more normal for longer letters.

[217] JWs *Address to the Clergy* (*Bibliography*, No. 216) was published in February 1756, and soon garnered several attacks in print, mainly by clergy who felt that he was challenging their fitness for this task—as he almost certainly was. Robert Marsden seems to have been an inquirer rather than an opponent.

Almost nothing is known of Robert Marsden, though Everett, *Sheffield* (1:106) tells us that in 1756 one of this name subscribed with William Green, the book agent for the Sheffield area, for a copy of Wesley's *NT Notes*. It is at least possible that this Robert Marsden was the one who wrote to Wesley claiming that in his *Address to the Clergy* he was making such heavy demands on preachers in general that he was setting an impossible task for the lay preachers of Methodism.

[218] The ms. is torn at this point.

Fight your way through all. God is on your side. And what then can man do to you? Make known all your wants to him, and you shall have the petitions you ask of him. I am,
Your affectionate brother,

John Wesley

5

Address: 'To / Mr Rob. Marsden / At Mr Frith's, Grocer / in / Sheffield'.
Postmark: '4/SE'. *Charge*: '4'.
Source: holograph; Bridwell Library (SMU).

To an Unidentified Man

[KINGSWOOD]
[SEPTEMBER 3, 1756[219]]

You give five reasons why the Reverend Mr. P—— will come no
10 more amongst us:

1) 'Because we despise the ministers of the Church of England.'
This I flatly deny. I am answering letters this very post which bitterly blame me for just the contrary.

2) 'Because so much backbiting and err-speaking is suffered
15 amongst our people.' It is not suffered; all possible means are used both to prevent and remove it.

3) 'Because I, who have written so much against hoarding up money, have put out seven hundred pounds to interest.' I never put sixpence out to interest since I was born; nor had I ever an hundred pounds together my own since I came into the world.

20 4) 'Because our lay preachers have told many stories of my brother and me.' If they did, I am sorry for them; when I hear the particulars, I can answer, and perhaps make those ashamed who believed them.

5) 'Because we did not help a friend in distress.' We did help him
25 as far as we were able. 'But we might have made his case known to Mr. G——, Lady Huntingdon, etc.' So we did more than once. But we could not pull money from them whether they would or no.

---

[219] This letter is undated in Whitehead; Telford assigned it the tentative date of Sept. 3, 1756, apparently due to similarities with the letter to Nicholas Norton that follows.

Therefore these reasons are of no weight. You conclude with praying that God would remove pride and malice from amongst us. Of pride I have too much; of malice I have none. However, the prayer is good and I thank you for it.

Source: published transcription; Whitehead, *Life*, 2:274–75.

To Nicholas Norton[220]

Kingswood
September 3, 1756

My Dear Brother,

In your letters of July and August 27, you charge me 1) with *self-inconsistency*, in tolerating *lay-preaching* and not *lay-administering*; and 2) with showing a spirit of *persecution*, in denying my brethren the liberty of *acting* (as well as *thinking*) according to their own *conscience*.

As to the former charge, the fact alleged is true. I do *tolerate unordained persons* in *preaching* the gospel, whereas I do not tolerate them in *administering* the sacraments. But it is not true I am *self-inconsistent* in so doing. I act on one and the same principle still. My principle (frequently declared) is this: 'I submit to every ordinance of man wherever I do not conceive there is an absolute necessity for acting contrary to it.' Consistently with this I do tolerate *lay-preaching*, because I conceive there is an absolute necessity for it; inasmuch as, were it not, thousands of souls would perish everlastingly. Yet I do not tolerate *lay-administering*, because I do not conceive there is any such necessity for it; seeing it does not appear that, if this is not at all, one soul will perish for want of it.

I am therefore so far from self-inconsistency in tolerating the former and not the latter that I readily should be self-inconsistent were I to act otherwise. Were I to break, or allow others to break, an

---

[220] This letter illustrates a growing rift in the Wesleyan movement over lay administration of the Lord's Supper. JW at this point had allowed lay preaching. Some of his lay preachers, including Edward and Charles Perronet, were urging their peers to take authority to administer the sacrament of the Lord's Supper. Almost two years earlier Charles Wesley had asked John, 'Is not Nicholas Norton under the influence of Charles Perronet?' (letter of Feb. 4, 1755). Norton cared for the bookroom at JW's Chapel in Bristol in the early 1750s and assisted in reading over proofs of books that JW published at Bristol printers; see *WHS* 28 (1932): 122.

ordinance of man where there is no necessity, I should contradict my own principle as much as if I did not allow it to be broken where there is.

5 As to the latter charge, that 'I deny my brethren the *liberty* of *acting* according to their own *conscience*, and therefore show a spirit of *persecution*', I again allow the fact, but deny the consequence. I mean, I allow the fact thus far. Some of our preachers who are not ordained think it quite right to administer the Lord's Supper, and believe it would do much good. I think it quite wrong, and believe 10 it would do much hurt. Hereupon I say, 'I have no right over your conscience, nor you over mine; therefore both you and I must follow our own conscience. You believe it is a duty to administer; do so, and therein follow your own conscience. I verily believe it is a sin, which consequentially I dare not *tolerate*; and herein I follow mine.' 15 Yet this is no *persecution*, were I to separate from our society (which I have not done yet) those who practice what I believe is contrary to the Word and destructive of the work of God.

Last week I had a long letter from William Darney,[221] who likewise wonders we should be of 'so *persecuting* a spirit as to deny him the 20 *liberty* of *thinking* and *speaking* in our societies according to his own *conscience*.' How will you answer him, and excuse Ted and Charles Perronet from the charge of persecuting their brother? They then said (as did all), 'Let him preach Calvinism elsewhere (we have no right to hinder him); but not among us, because we are persuaded 25 it would do much hurt.' Take the answer back: if it was good in one case, so was it in the other likewise.

If John Jones,[222] my brother, or any other preacher has preached sharply on this head, I certainly 'am a stranger' to it, and therefore not answerable for it. I persecute no man on this account, or any 30 other. And yet I cannot *consent* that any of our lay preachers should either preach predestination or administer the sacraments to those who are under my care.

---

[221] This letter has apparently not survived. On William Darney, see 26:537, n. 20 in this edn.

[222] On John Jones (1721–85), see 26:310, n. 14, in this edn. During this decade he was JW's right-hand man in Bristol, and the amanuensis who preserved JW's important correspondence with 'John Smith' (now at Drew University). In late 1763 or early 1764 Jones was ordained by the Greek church leader Gerasimos Avlonites (Erasmus Aulonita), who described himself as Bishop of Arcadia. Although other ordinations performed by Avlonites were disavowed by JW, he helped arrange Jones's ordination. See A. B. Sackett, *John Jones – First After the Wesleys* (1972).

But is it immoral? It is *immoral* to think, speak, or act contrary to the love which 'thinketh no evil'.[223] Now, of this both Charles and you are palpably guilty in thinking the body of the Methodists (either preachers or people) are fallen from the *simplicity* and *uprightness* of the gospel. Whatever seven or eight of the preachers may be who have warmly debated this point with you, whatever two or three hundred of the people may be who have been hurt by the disputants on either side, the main body of the Methodists never were more *simple* or *upright* than at this day. Therefore your *thinking* so *ill* of both preachers and people is a manifest breach of the law of love. And whoever is or is not fallen from the spirit of the gospel, it is certain *you* are for one.

But after all this pother, what is this *persecution* concerning which you make so loud an outcry? Why, some of our lay preachers did what we thought was both ill in itself and likely to do much harm among the people. Of this, complaint was made to me. And what did I do? Did I expel those preachers out of our community? Not so. Did I forbid them to preach any more? Not so neither. Did I degrade them from itinerant to local preachers? Not so much as this. 'I told them I thought the thing was wrong and would do hurt, and therefore *advised* them to do it no more.' Certainly this is a new species of *persecution*! I cannot but think you might as well call it *murder*.

'Oh, but you would have done more if they had persisted.' That is, I would have *persecuted*. Whatever I *would have done* if things had been which were not, I have not done it yet. I have used no *arbitrary*, no *coercive* power—nay, no power at all in this matter but that of love. I have given no man an ill word or an ill look on the account. I have not withdrawn my confidence or my conversation from any. I have dealt with every man as, if the tables were turned, I should desire he would deal with me.

'But I would not dispute with you.' Not for a time; not till your spirits were a little evaporated. But you argue too fast when you infer from hence that 'I myself *cannot confute* your favourite notion.' You are not sure of that. But, come what will, you are resolved to try. Well, then, move fair and softly. You and Charles Perronet aver that you have a right to administer the Lord's Supper, and that therefore you ought to administer it among the Methodists or to separate from them. If the assertion were proved, I should deny the consequence. But first, I desire proof of the assertion.

[223] 1 Cor. 13:5.

Let him or you give the proof, only without any flourish or rhetorical amplifications (which exceedingly abound in all Charles Perronet's letters to my brother on this subject), and I will give you an answer—though we are not on even ground; for you have no business, and I have no leisure. And if you continue instant in prayer, particularly for a lowly and teachable spirit, I do not despair of your finding both that light and love which you have not lately enjoyed.

I am,
    Your affectionate brother,

                                                   J. W.

I shall add a few remarks on Charles Perronet's letters, though the substance of them is contained in yours. 'Some of the fundamentals of your constitution are wrong.' Our fundamentals are laid down in the *Plain Account*.[224] Which of these is wrong, and yet 'borne by you for eight years'?

'Oh inconsistency! Oh excuseless tyranny!' etc. Flourish. Set that down for nothing. '*These very men* who themselves break *the* laws of the state deny us liberty of conscience.' In plain terms, *these very men* who preach the gospel contrary to law *do not approve of* our administering the sacraments. They do not. They greatly disapprove of it; and that without any inconsistency at all, because the case is not parallel. The one is absolutely necessary to the salvation of thousands; the other not.

'Your brother has to the last refused me liberty of conscience.' Under what penalty? This heavy charge amounts in reality to this: I still think you have no right to administer the Lord's Supper; in consequence of which I *advise* you not to do it. Can I do less? Or have I done more?

'I wish I could say that anything of *wicked lewdness* would have met with the same opposition'! Is not this pretty, brother Norton? Do you subscribe to this? I think you know us better. Do we not so much as *advise* our preachers and people to abstain from *wicked lewdness*? 'Can it be denied that known wantonness, that deceit and knavery have been among us, and that little notice has been taken of it?' I totally deny it. Much notice has been taken, by *me* in particular, of what evil has been done by any preacher. I have constantly examined all the parties, and have in every instance so far animadverted on the delinquent as justice joined with mercy required.

---

[224] JW, *Plain Account of the People Called Methodists* (1749), 9:254–80 in this edn.

'My crime is that I would worship Christ as his word, his Spirit, and my own conscience teach me. Let God and man be witness that we part *for this* and nothing else.' Namely, because I am of a different judgment, and cannot *approve* of what I judge to be wrong. So says William Darney, 'My crime is that I would *preach* Christ as his word, his Spirit, and my own conscience teach me.' But he has far more ground for complaint than you. For we ourselves separated him from us, whereas you call God and man to witness that you *separate yourself* for this and nothing else—that I cannot *approve* what I judge to be wrong.

But this is not all your crime. You have also drank into the spirit of James Wheatley, and you have adopted his very language. You are become, like him, an accuser of your brethren. O Charles, it was time you should *separate* from them, for your heart was gone from them before!

'Whatever motives of another kind might be blended with those that really belonged to *your* conscience, in your rejecting what I laid before you' (not *consenting* that I should administer), 'God knows.' I know of none. I have no other motive of acting than the glory of God and the good of souls. Here again you are become not only an accuser but a false accuser and an unjust judge of your brother.

'You grant more to others. To my certain knowledge both of you have been told for more than two years that James Morris[225] administered.' You may as well say, 'To my certain knowledge black is white.' I never was told it to this day, unless by Charles Perronet. But whether he does or no, it is nothing to me. He never was in close connexion with us; he is now in no connexion at all. We have totally renounced him. So here is another instance of accusing, yea falsely accusing, your brethren.

'A man may be circumcised, count his beads, or adore a cross, and still be a member of your society.' That is, may be a Papist or a Jew. I know no such instance in England or Ireland. We have many members in Ireland that *were* Papists, but not one that continues so.

'Other reasons than those that could possibly relate to conscience have borne too much share in the late affair.' I say as before, I am not conscious of it. And who art thou that judgest another's servant?

'You have allowed, we are called to this by the Holy Ghost and that God was with us in what we did.' I allow? No more than I allow you to be archangels. I allow neither the one nor the other. I believe you felt joy or power, so called. But I do not know that it was

---

[225] JW later referred to the Irish itinerant James Morris's 'false step' in his *Journal* for July 12, 1769 (22:194 in this edn.).

from God, and I said, 'Supposing you were called of God to this' (which is exceeding far from granting it), 'still you ought to waive that privilege out of tenderness to your brethren.' I do not grant either that God *calls* you to do this or that he ever *blessed* you in it.

5   That Methodism (so called)—that is, vital religion, loving faith, in the hearts of those who are vulgarly termed Methodists—should seem to you 'sitting snug' at London or Bristol, to be 'very much in its decline', is no wonder. But I, who see things in every place with my own eyes, know it is very much in its increase. Many are daily
10 added to them that believe. Many more are continually awakened. So that the societies from east to west, from north to south, in both kingdoms, increase in grace as well as number.

'I wish the argument' (which is no argument at all, as being grounded on a palpable mistake) 'be not too home to bear a dispute
15 among *honest* men.' Very well! Another clear proof of the *love* that *thinketh* no evil.

'If you had *consented*.' This is the very point. I could not *consent* (which implies some degree of approbation) to what I judged to be totally wrong. Yet nether did I *persecute*. I inflicted no penalty of any
20 kind on those whom I judged to have done wrong, because I believed they acted from conscience though erroneous. I only mildly *advised* them to desist.

'I never will be again united with any who *will* not *let* others choose their own religion.' Then you will never unite with any but
25 *knaves*; for no honest men who preside over any community *will let* the members of it do what they judge to be wrong and hurtful to that community without endeavouring to prevent it, at least by mild, loving friendly *advice*.

'I go away, not of choice but of necessity.' So you *must* think, till
30 God opens your eyes. 'Your kindness at our first acquaintance, the providence that brought us together, and the keeping up that acquaintance after so many snares of the enemy to destroy it, make it sacred as well as dear to me.' And yet for such a reason as this— 'because I *advise* you to abstain from doing what I think you have no
35 right to do, what I judge to be both evil in itself and productive of ill consequences'—for *this reason* you burst all the bonds asunder and cast away the cords from you.

The Lord God enlighten the eyes of your understanding and soften and enlarge your heart![226]

Source: published transcription; *Arminian Magazine* 2 (1779): 648–55.

[226] See Eph. 1:17–18.

To the Rev. Samuel Walker[227]

KINGSWOOD
SEPTEMBER 3, 1756

Rev. and Dear Sir,

I have one point in view, to promote, so far as I am able, vital, practical religion; by the grace of God to beget, preserve, and increase the life of God in the souls of men. On this single principle I have hitherto proceeded, and taken no step but in subserviency to it. With this view, when I found it absolutely necessary, for the continuance of the work God had begun in many souls (which their *regular pastors* generally used all possible means to destroy) I permitted several of their brethren whom I believed God had called thereto, and qualified for the work, to comfort, exhort, and instruct those who were athirst for God, or who walked in the light of his countenance. But, as the persons so qualified were few, and those who wanted their assistance very many, it followed that most of these were obliged to travel continually from place to place. And this occasioned several regulations from time to time, which were chiefly made in our Conferences.

So great a blessing has from the beginning attended the labours of these itinerants that we have been more and more convinced every year of the more than lawfulness of this proceeding. And the inconveniences, most of which we foresaw from the very first, have been both fewer and smaller than were expected. Rarely two in one year, out of the whole number of preachers, have either separated themselves or been rejected by us. A great majority have all along behaved as becometh the gospel of Christ, and I am clearly persuaded still desire nothing more than to spend and be spent for their brethren.[228]

But the question is, 'How may these be settled on such a footing as one would wish they might be after my death?' It is a weighty point, and has taken up many of my thoughts for several years. But I know nothing yet. The steps I am now to take are plain. I see broad light shining upon them. But the other part of the prospect I cannot see, clouds and darkness rest upon it.[229]

---

[227] Answering Walker's of Aug. 16. On Walker and the start of this conversation, see 26:582 in this edn.

[228] See 2 Cor. 12:15.

[229] Cf. Addison, *Cato*, V.i.13–14:

> The wide, th'unbounded prospect lies before me,
> But shadows, clouds, and darkness rest upon it.

Your *general* advice on this head, 'to follow my own conscience, without any regard to consequences, or prudence, so called', is unquestionably right. And it is a rule which I have closely followed[230] for many years, and hope to follow to my life's end. The first of your
5   *particular* advices is, 'To keep full in view the interests of Christ's church in general and of practical religion, not considering the Church of England or the cause of Methodism but as subordinate thereto.' This advice I have punctually observed from the beginning, as well as at our late Conference. You advise, 2. 'to keep in
10 view also the unlawfulness of a separation from the Church of England.' To this likewise I agree. It cannot be lawful to separate from it, unless it be unlawful to continue in it.[231] You advise, 3. 'Fully to declare myself on this head, and to suffer no dispute concerning it.' The very same thing I wrote to my brother from Ireland.[232] And
15 we have declared ourselves without reserve. Nor was there any at the Conference otherwise minded. Those who would have aimed at dispute had left us before. 4. All our preachers, as well as ourselves, purpose to continue in the Church of England.[233] Nor did they ever before so freely and explicitly declare themselves on this subject.
20 Your last advice is, 'That as many of our preachers as are fit for it be ordained, and that the others be fixed to certain societies, not as preachers, *but* readers or inspectors.'

    You oblige me by speaking your sentiments so freely.[234] With the same plainness I will answer. So far as I know myself, I have no
25 more concern for the reputation of Methodism or my own than for the reputation of Prester John.[235] I have the same point in view as

---

[230] Orig., 'pursued'; changed by JW in *AM*.

[231] JW seems to indicate at this point an important reservation, namely, that if it should become 'unlawful to continue in' the Church of England, then it might be lawful to separate from it. That is, if he were forced out of the national Church, then it might be 'lawful' to separate.

[232] No letter of 1756 from JW in Ireland to his brother has survived. That John had not yet made himself sufficiently clear to his brother prompted Charles to write to Walker on Aug. 7, 1756: 'To this end my brother ought (in my judgment), 1. To declare and avow in the strongest and most explicit manner his resolution to live and die in the communion of the Church of England.'

[233] As Charles Wesley mentioned to Walker in his letter of Aug. 7, 1756, the two brothers had subscribed to an agreement on Mar.10, 1752, and most preachers thereafter, 'never to leave the communion of the Church of England without the consent of all whose names are subjoined'.

[234] *AM*, 'plainly'.

[235] 'Prester': an Anglo-Saxon variation on the word 'presbyter' (Lat. *presbyterus*; Gk. πρεσβύτερος). Prester John was a legendary eastern Christian ruler who aroused hopes during the Crusades.

when I set out, the promoting, as I am able, vital, practical religion. And in all our discipline I still aim at the continuance of the work which God has already begun in so many souls. With this view, and this only, I permitted those whom I believed God had called thereto to comfort, exhort, and instruct their brethren. And if this end can 5 be better answered some other way, I shall subscribe to it without delay.

But is that which you propose a better way? This should be coolly and calmly considered. If I mistake not, there are now in the County of Cornwall about four-and-thirty of these little societies, part of 10 whom now experience the love of God, part are more or less earnestly seeking it. Four preachers—Peter Jaco,[236] Thomas Johnson,[237] William Crabb,[238] and William Allwood[239]—design for the ensuing year partly to call other sinners to repentance, but chiefly to feed and guide these few feeble sheep; to forward them, as of the ability 15 which God giveth, in vital, practical religion. Now suppose we can effect that Peter Jaco and Thomas Johnson be ordained, and settled in the curacies of St. Buryan[240] and St. Just. And suppose William Crabb and William Allwood fix at Launceston and the Dock[241] as readers and exhorters.[242] Will this answer the end which I have in 20 view so well as their travelling through the county?

It will not answer it so well, even with regard to those societies with whom Peter Jaco and Thomas Johnson have settled. Be their talents ever so great, they will ere long grow dead themselves, and so will most of those that hear them. I know, were I myself to preach 25 one whole year in one place I should preach both myself and most of my congregation asleep. Nor can I believe it was ever the will of our Lord that any congregation should have one teacher only. We

---

[236] Peter Jaco (d. 1781) was converted by Methodist preachers in 1747 and given his first assignment as an itinerant preacher in 1754 (see Atmore, *Memorial*, 215–17; and *EMP* 1:260–68).

[237] Thomas Johnson (1720–97) was born in Wakefield, Yorkshire, converted by Methodist preachers in 1748, and entered the roll of itinerant preachers in 1752 (see Atmore, *Memorial*, 220–24).

[238] William Crabb (d. 1764) was a pious but temperamentally weak preacher who laboured intermittently between 1754 and 1759 (see Atmore, *Memorial*, 94–95).

[239] William Allwood appears first in the Minutes of the 1753 Conference as an itinerant preacher (see 10:260 in this edn.).

[240] Orig., 'Burrian'; corrected in *AM*.

[241] Plymouth Dock, now Devonport.

[242] Walker had used the phrase 'inspectors and readers' rather than 'preachers'. This JW (or his amanuensis) changed to 'readers and inspectors' (para. 4), but here altered 'inspectors' to 'exhorters'. Wesley had favoured this latter term for a decade for the less able men (especially in Cornwall) who might simply be called on to 'give an exhortation'.

have found by long and constant experience that a frequent change of preachers[243] is best. This preacher has one talent; that, another. No one whom I ever yet knew has all the talents which are needful for beginning, continuing, and perfecting the work of grace in a whole congregation.

But suppose this would better answer the end with regard to those two societies, would it answer in those where William Alwood and William Crabb were settled as inspectors and readers? First, who shall feed them with the milk of the Word?[244] The ministers of their parishes? Alas, they cannot, they neither know,[245] nor live, nor teach the gospel. These readers? Can then either they, or I, or you always find something to read to our congregations which will be exactly adapted to their wants, and as much blessed to them as our preaching? And here is another difficulty still. What authority have I to forbid their doing what I believe God has called them to do? I apprehend, indeed, that there ought if possible to be both an outward and an inward call to this work. Yet if one be supposed wanting, I had rather want the outward than the inward call. I rejoice that I am called to preach the gospel both by God and man. Yet I acknowledge I had rather have the divine without the human than the human without the divine call.

But waiving this, and supposing these four societies to be better provided for than they were before, what becomes of the other thirty? Will they prosper as well when they are left as sheep without a shepherd? The experiment has been tried again and again, and always with the same event. Even the strong in faith grew weak and faint. Many of the weak made shipwreck of the faith.[246] The awakened fell asleep. Sinners, changed for a while, returned as a dog to the vomit.[247] And so by our lack of service many of the souls perished for whom Christ died. Now had we willingly withdrawn our service from them by voluntarily settling in one place, what account of these could we have given to the great Shepherd of all our souls?

I cannot therefore see how any of those four preachers, or any others in like circumstances, can ever, while they have health and strength, ordained or unordained, fix in one place without a grievous wound to their own conscience, and damage to the *general*

---

[243] *AM*, 'teachers'.
[244] See 1 Pet. 2:2.
[245] Orig., 'neither know themselves'.
[246] See 1 Tim. 1:19 (*NT Notes*).
[247] See 2 Pet. 2:22.

work of God. Yet I trust I am open to conviction, and your farther thoughts on this or any subject will be always acceptable to,
    Your very affectionate brother and fellow-labourer,

John Wesley

Address: 'To/ the Revd Mr Walker / In Truro / Cornwall / single sheet'.
Postmark: 'B/RIS/TOL'. *Charge*: '4'.
Endorsement: 'JW to SW Sepr. 3d 56'.
Source: manuscript in hand of John Jones, with JW signature; Drew, Methodist Archives. Compared with version that JW published in *Arminian Magazine* 2 (1779): 644–48.

To the Monthly Reviewers[248]

[LONDON]
SEPTEMBER 9, 1756

Gentlemen,

For a considerable time I have had a desire to trouble you with a few lines, but have been prevented, partly by a variety of other business, partly by the small probability of your impartially considering what was said. I will, however, make the trial. If you can read candidly, well; if not, it is but a little labour lost.

The question I would propose is this: Is it prudent, is it just, is it humane, to jumble whole bodies of people together and condemn them by the lump? Is it not a maxim now almost universally received that there are good and bad in every society? Why, then, do you continually jumble together and condemn by the lump the whole body of people called 'Methodists'? Is it prudent (just to touch even on so low a consideration) to be constantly insulting and provoking those who do you

---

[248] JW's *Journal* indicates that he devoted Sept. 8–9, 1756 to matters related to his publications. In this context he wrote to the *Monthly Review*, apparently protesting a single sentence in a review of *Poems Sacred to Religion and Virtue* by Thomas Drummond: 'How far the Doctor has done this' [offered an attractive and positive depiction of religion and virtue] 'in the present work, better than his predecessors, Herbert and Norris, or his contemporaries, the gentlemen who write hymns and spiritual songs for the Methodists and Moravians, the reader will be presently enabled to judge' (*Monthly Review* 15 [Aug. 1756], 129). Although Wesley's letter does not appear to have been published in the *Monthly Review*, a subsequent letter (Oct. 5, 1756) refers to some notice of it that had been taken by the publication.

no wrong, and had far rather be your friends than your enemies? Is it
consistent with humanity to strike again one who gives no provocation and makes no resistance? Is it common justice to treat with such
contempt as you have done in the last month's *Review* those who are
5   by no means contemptible writers? Be persuaded, gentlemen, to give
yourselves the pains of reading either Mr. Herbert's 'Providence',[249]
or the verses which Norris entitles 'The Meditation',[250] and you will
find them scarce inferior either in sense or language to most com-
positions of the present age. To speak more freely still, where is the
10 justice of coupling the hymns of Methodists and Moravians together?
Lay prejudice aside and read with candour but the very first hymn
in our first hymn book; and then say whether your prose is not as
nearly allied to John Bunyan's as our verse to Count Zinzendorf's.

As probably you have never seen the books which you condemn,
15 I will transcribe a few lines.

> Thee, when morning greets the skies
> With rosy cheeks and humid eyes;
> Thee when sweet declining day
20 > Sinks in purple waves away;
> Thee will I sing, O Parent Jove!
> And teach the world to praise and love.
>
> Yonder azure vault on high,
25 > Yonder blue, low, liquid sky,
> Earth, on its firm basis placed,
> And with circling waves embraced,
> All creating power confess,
> All their mighty Maker bless.
30 > Thou shak'st all nature with thy nod,
> Sea, earth, and air confess thee God:
> Yet does thy powerful hand sustain
> Both earth and heaven, both firm and main.
>
35 > The feathered souls that swim the air,
> And bathe in liquid ether there;

---

[249] 'Providence' was poem #92 in George Herbert's *The Temple* (Cambridge, 1633). John
Wesley valued it, including a copy in a ms. poetry miscellany that he compiled during his college years and publishing it in *MSP* (1744), 1:32–33. Wesley included over 50 of Herbert's
poems from *The Temple* in various collections he published.
   [250] 'The Meditation' was from John Norris's best-known book, *A Collection of Miscel-
lanies* (Oxford, 1687), 30–31. Wesley reprinted the poem in *MSP* (1744), 1:74.

The lark, precentor of their choir,
Leading them higher still and higher,
Listen and learn; th' angelic notes
Repeating in their warbling throats:
And, ere[251] to soft repose they go,   5
Teach them to their lords below.
On the green turf, their mossy nest,
The evening anthem swells their breast.
Thus, like thy golden chain from high,
Thy praise unites the earth and sky.   10

O ye nurses of soft dreams,
Reedy brooks, and winding streams;
Or murmuring o'er the pebbles sheen,
Or sliding through the meadows green,   15
Or where through matted sedge you creep,
Travelling to your parent deep;
Sound his praise by whom you rose,
That sea which neither ebbs nor flows.
                                                                           20
O y' immortal woods and groves,
Which the enamour'd student loves;
Beneath whose venerable shade,
For thought and friendly converse made,
Fam'd Hecadem, old hero, lies,   25
Whose shrine is shaded from the skies
And, through the gloom of silent night
Projects from far its trembling light;
You, whose roots descend as low
As high in air your branches grow,   30
Your leafy arms to heaven extend,
Bend your heads, in homage bend;
Cedars, and pines that wave above,
And the oak belov'd of Jove![252]

                                                                           35
Now gentlemen, can you say, between God and your own souls,
that these verses deserve the treatment you have given them? I

---

[251] Orig., 'e're'; but used in sense of 'before'.

[252] Samuel Wesley Sr., 'Eupolis's Hymn to the Creator'. JW included an earlier version
of this hymn in his first *Collection of Psalms and Hymns* (Charleston, 1737), 71–74; and this
revised version as the opening entry in *HSP* (1739), 1–5 (which Wesley here rightly calls the
'first hymn book' of the Methodist revival).

think you cannot. You are men of more understanding. You know they are not contemptible. If any of you will strike a real blot, if you will point out even in public (though that is not the most obliging way) anything justly reproveable in our writings, probably we
5　shall acknowledge and correct what is amiss; at least, we shall not blame you. But every impartial man must blame that method of proceeding which neither consists with justice nor humanity.

Perhaps you may say you have been provoked. By whom? 'By Mr. Romaine.'[253] I answer, I am not Mr. Romaine; neither am I accountable
10　for his behaviour. And what equity is this? One man has offended you, therefore you fall upon another. Will it excuse you to say, 'But he is called by the same name'? Especially when neither is this his own name, but a term of derision. Gentlemen, do to others as you would have them do to you. Then you will no more injure one who
15　never offended you (unless this offend you, that he does ready believe Jesus Christ to be God over all, blessed for ever[254]); then you will not return hatred for goodwill, even to so insignificant a person as,

John Wesley

Source: published transcription; *Arminian Magazine* 3 (1780): 217–20.

To Martha (Wesley) Hall[255]

20　　　　　　　　　　　　　　　　　　　　LONDON
SEPTEMBER 15, 1756

Dear Sister,

In what path it is best for us to tread, God knows better than man. And we are well assured he orders all things for our profit, that we
25　may be partakers of his holiness. Probably he withheld you from

---

[253] William Romaine (1714–95) graduated B.A. from Christ Church, Oxford, in 1734. By the mid 1750s he had abandoned his earlier Arminian views, becoming an ardent follower of George Whitefield and the most prominent Evangelical priest of the Church of England in London. See *ODNB*.

[254] See Rom. 9:5.

[255] JW had helped Martha move to London from Salisbury the previous year (see his letter of May 9, 1755, 26:556 in this edn.), after the final desertion by her husband Westley Hall, who had left for the West Indies. She was apparently in Salisbury to pick up some items left behind.

prosperity to save you from pride; certainly to rescue you from your own will, and from that legion of foolish and hurtful desires which so naturally attend abundance. Be good and do good to the utmost of your present power, and then happy are you.

I have ordered Betty Duchesne[256] to get the things you spoke of, which probably by this time she has done. Therefore you need not delay your return to London. I purposed to have come through Salisbury, but I was so ill that it was judged not safe for me to ride. O make the best of a few days. I am,
        Your affectionate friend and brother,

                                 J. Wesley

Address: 'To / Mrs Martha Hall / At Mr Marsh / in / Salisbury'.
Postmark: '18/SE'. *Charge*: '3' [?].
Source: holograph, MARC, DDWes 5/1.

To the Rev. James Clark[257]

LONDON
SEPTEMBER 18, 1756

Rev. Sir,

Yesterday I received your favour of July 9. As you therein speak freely and openly, I will endeavour to do the same, at which I am persuaded you will not be displeased.

1. Of the words imputed to Mr. Langston[258] I said nothing because he denied the charge, and I had not an opportunity of having the accuser and the accused face to face.

2. That there are enthusiasts among the Methodists I doubt not, and among most other people under heaven; but that they are made such by our doctrine and discipline still remains to be proved. If they are such in spite of our doctrine and discipline, their madness will not be laid to our charge.

---

[256] Elizabeth Duchesne was a friend and coadjutor of both John and Charles Wesley during this period. JW presided at her burial on Dec. 22, 1776 (see JW, *Journal*, 23:39 in this edn.).

[257] Responding to Clark's letter dated July 9, 1756.

[258] Possibly John Langston, whom JW visited in Castlebar on May 20, 1785; see JW, Diary, 23:524 in this edn.

I know nothing about the anonymous pamphlet on inspiration. How does it appear to be wrote by one of my disciples? Be it good, bad or indifferent, I am not concerned or any way accountable for it.

5   3. I believe several who are not episcopally ordained are nevertheless called of God to preach the gospel. Yet I have no exception to the Twenty-third Article, though I judge there are exempt cases. That the seven deacons were outwardly ordained even to that low office cannot be denied. But when Paul and Barnabas were sepa-
10   rated from the work to which they were called, this was not ordaining them. St. Paul was ordained long before, and that not of man or by men. It was inducting him into the province for which our Lord had appointed him from the beginning. For this end the prophets and teachers fasted and prayed and laid their hand upon them—
15   a rite which was used, not in ordination only, but in blessing and many other occasions.

4. Concerning diocesan episcopacy, there are several questions which I should be glad to have answered, as: 1) Where is it prescribed in scripture? 2) How does it appear that the apostles settled
20   it in all the churches which they planted? 3) How does it appear they settled it in any so as to make it of perpetual obligation? It is allowed that Christ and his apostles settled the church under some form of government. But 1) did they put all churches under the same precise form? If they did, 2) can we prove this to be the pre-
25   cise form and the very same which now obtains in England?

5. How Phavorinus or many more may define heresy or schism I am not concerned to know.[259] I well know heresy is vulgarly defined 'a false opinion touching some necessary article of faith, and schism a causeless separation from a true church'. But I keep to my Bible,
30   as our Church in her Sixth Article teaches me. Therefore I cannot take schism for a separation from a church, because I cannot find it so taken in Scripture. The first time I meet the term there is 1 Corinthians 1:10. I meet with it again, chap. 11, v.18. But it is plain in both places by schism is meant not any separation from the church
35   but uncharitable divisions in it. For the Corinthians continued to be one church, notwithstanding their strife and contention; there was no separation of one part from the other with regard to external communion. It is in the same sense the word is used chap. 12, v. 25. And these are the only places in the New Testament where the

---

[259] Varinus Camers (variant: Varinus Phavorinus; d. 1537), a Benedictine monk, Bishop of Nocera, and the compiler of a Greek lexicon whose definition of 'heresy' Clark had cited.

term occurs. Therefore the indulging any unkind temper towards our fellow Christians is the true scriptural schism.

Indeed, both heresy and schism (which are works of the flesh, and consequently damnable if not repented) are here mentioned by the apostle in very near the same sense; unless by schisms be meant rather those inward animosities which occasioned heresies—that is, outward divisions and parties. So that while one said, I am of Paul; another, I am of Apollos; this implied both heresy and schism. So wonderfully have latter ages distorted the words 'heresies' and 'schisms' from their scriptural meaning! Heresy is not in all the Bible taken for an error in fundamentals, nor in anything else; nor schism for any separation from the communion of others. Therefore heresy and schism in the modern sense of the words are sins that the Scriptures know nothing of.

6. But though I aver this, am I quite indifferent as to any man's principles in religion? Far from it, as I have declared again and again in the very sermon under present consideration.[260] In *The Character of a Methodist*,[261] in the *Plain Account*,[262] and twenty tracts besides, I have written severally against deists, papists, mystics, etc. An odd way to ingratiate myself with them, to strike at the apple of their eye! Nevertheless, in all things indifferent (but not at the expense of truth) I rejoice to please all men for their good to edification, if happily I may gain the more proselytes to genuine scriptural Christianity, if I may prevail on the more to love God and their neighbour and to walk as Christ walked. So far as I find them obstructive of these, I oppose opinions with my might; though even then rather by guarding those that are free than by disputing with those that are deeply infected. I need not dispute with many of them to know there is no probability of success or of convincing them. A thousand times I have found my father's words true: 'You may have peace with the Dissenters, if you do not so humour them as to dispute with them. If you do, they will out-face and out-lung you, and at the end you will be just where you were in the beginning.'

I have now, sir, humoured you so as to dispute a little with you. But with what probability of success? Suppose you have a single eye in this debate, suppose you aim not at victory but at the truth, yet what man of threescore (unless perchance one in an age) was ever convinced? Is not an old man's motto, '*Non persuadebis etiamsi*

[260] I.e., Sermon 39, 'Catholic Spirit', 2:81–95 in this edn.
[261] See 9:32–46 in this edn.
[262] *Plain Account of the People Called Methodists* (1749), 9:254–80 in this edn.

persuaseris'?[263] When we are past middle age, do we not find a kind of stiffness and inflexibility stealing upon the mind as well as on the body? And does not this bar the gate against all conviction? Even before the eye of the soul grows dim, and so less and less capable of
5 discerning things which we are not already well acquainted with.

7. Yet on one point I must add a few words, because it is of the last importance. I said orthodoxy, or right opinion, was never more than a slender part of religion, and sometimes no part at all. And this I explained thus: 'In a child of God it is but a slender part, in
10 a child of the devil it is no part at all of religion.' The religion of a child of God is righteousness, peace, and joy in the Holy Ghost. Now, if orthodoxy be any part of this (which in itself might admit of a question), it is certainly a very slender part; though it is a considerable help of love, peace, and joy. Religion, in other words, is
15 the love of God and man, producing all holiness of conversation. Now, are right opinions any more than a slender part (if they be so much) of this? Once more, religion is the mind that was in Christ and walking as Christ walked. Now, how slender a part of this are opinions, how right soever!

20 By a child of the devil I mean one that neither loves, fears, or serves God, and has no true religion at all. But it is certain such a man may be still orthodox, may entertain right opinions; and yet it is equally certain these are no parts of religion in him that has no religion at all.

25 Permit me, sir, to speak exceeding plainly. Are you not an orthodox man? Perhaps there is none more so in the diocese. Yet possibly you may have no religion at all. If it be true that you frequently drink to excess, you may have orthodoxy, but you can have no religion. If, when you are in a passion, you call your brother 'Thou
30 fool',[264] you have no religion at all. If you then even curse and swear by taking God's name in vain, you can have no other religion but orthodoxy, a religion of which the devil and his angels have as much as you.

O sir, what an idle thing it is for you to dispute about lay preachers!
35 Is not a lay preacher preferable to a drunken preacher, to a cursing, swearing preacher? 'To the ungodly saith God, Why takest thou my covenant in thy mouth,' whereas thou hatest to be reformed, 'and cast

---

[263] Robert Burton, *Anatomy of Melancholy* (1621), 734. JW translated this, 'Thou shalt not persuade me, though thou dost persuade me' in his sermon 'On Patience', §11, 3:177 in this edn.
[264] Matt. 5:22.

my words behind thee'?[265] In tender compassion I speak this. May God apply it to your heart! And then you will not receive this as an affront but as the truest instance of brotherly love from, reverend sir, Yours, etc.,

J. W. 5

Source: published transcription; Clark, *Montanus Redivivus*, 54–58.

To the Monthly Reviewers[266]

[LONDON]
OCTOBER 5, 1756

Really, gentlemen, you do me too much honour. I could scarce expect so favourable a regard from those who are professed admirers 10 of Mr. Aaron Hill's verse and Mr. Caleb Fleming's prose.[267] Nevertheless I cannot but observe a few small mistakes in the eight lines with which you favour me. You say, 'We suppose the specimen of Mr. Wesley's hymns' (the false spelling is of little consequence) '*was sent us for this purpose*'—namely, to publish. Truly it 15 was not. It never entered my thought, as I apprehend may appear from the whole tenor of the letter wherein those lines were inserted. 'And if the Moravians please to *select* a like sample of what has been done by them, they may expect from us the same justice.' Another little mistake. Those lines are not *selected*, but are found in the very 20 first hymn (as I observed in my last) that occurs in the first verses which my brother and I have ever published.[268] We have received a letter 'complaining of our having *jumbled* the poetry of the Methodists and Moravians in an indiscriminate censure'. Not so. The thing chiefly complained of was: 1) Your 'jumbling whole bodies 25

---

[265] Ps. 50:6.

[266] The editor or editors of *The Monthly Review* had replied to JW's letter of Sept. 9. While Wesley's excerpts sound like a public response, no published version has been located.

[267] *The Monthly Review* for January 1754 (pp. 16–30) had carried an extremely laudatory excerpt on the life of the poet Aaron Hill (1685–1750) from Theophilus Cibber's *Lives of the Poets of Great Britain and Ireland* (1753). And the current issue carried a positive review of Caleb Fleming (1698–1779), as we shall see.

[268] JW had published two earlier *Collections of Psalms and Hymns* (1737, 1738), but *HSP* (1739) was the first collection containing original verse by the Wesley brothers.

of people together and of condemning them by the lump without
any regard either to prudence, justice or humanity'. 2) Your 'treat-
ing with such contempt those who are by no means contemptible
writers—Mr. Norris and Mr. Herbert'. The last and least thing was
5   your 'coupling the hymns of Moravians and Methodists together'.
It was here I added, 'As probably you have never seen the books
which you condemn, I will transcribe a few lines'. But neither did I
give the least intimation of 'appealing hereby to the public in proof
of our superiority over the Moravians'. This is another mistake.
10   At first I was a little inclined to fear a want of integrity had occasioned this misrepresentation. But upon reflection I would put a
milder construction upon it, and only impute it to want of understanding. Even bodies of men do not see all things, and are then especially liable to err when they imagine themselves hugely superior
15   to their opponents, and so pronounce *ex cathedra*.
Another instance of this is just now before me. A week or two ago
one put a tract into my hands in which I could discern nothing of the
Christian, gentleman, or scholar, but much of low, dull, ill-natured
scurrility and blasphemy.[269] How was I surprised when I read in your
20   350th page, 'We have read this little piece with great pleasure'! When
I found you so smitten with the author's '*spirit, sense,* and *freedom,*'
his '*smart animadversions*' and '*becoming* severity'! O gentlemen! Do
not you speak too plain? Do not you discover too much at once? Especially when you so keenly ridicule Mr. Pike's supposition that 'the
25   Son and Spirit are truly divine'? May I ask, if the Son of God is not
truly divine, is he divine at all? Is he a little God, or no God at all? If
no God at all, how came he to say, 'I and the Father are one'?[270] Did
any prophet before, from the beginning of the world, use any one
expression which could possibly be so interpreted as this and other
30   expressions were by all that heard Jesus speak? And did he ever attempt to undeceive them? Be pleased, then, to let me know, if he was
not God, how do you clear him from being the vilest of men?
I am, gentlemen,
Your well-wisher, though not admirer,

35

John Wesley

Source: published transcription; *Arminian Magazine* 3 (1780): 221–22.

[269] JW refers to Caleb Fleming's *No Protestant Popery*, which was critical of the orthodox
trinitarian theology of Samuel Pike. *The Monthly Review* for September 1756 carried a positive
review of Fleming's work on p. 315.
[270] John 10:30.

To an Unidentified Person

[LONDON]
NOVEMBER 6, 1756

I was glad when I saw your name. If no other end be answered by your writing, it may be an ease to your own mind. And we know not but God may apply to your heart a word written as well as a word spoken. Indeed my time seldom allows me to write long letters. But we can tell our mind without a multitude of words.

The wilderness state[271] of which you complain is nothing strange or uncommon. It may be partly owing to temptation, or bodily distemper. Probably these are mixed in your case. But the chief cause is either inward or outward unfaithfulness to the grace of God. Your first point then is to know wherein you have grieved his Spirit, that you may do it no more. For it avails not to apply balm to the wound while the dart is sticking in the flesh. But even when it is drawn out, pain and soreness may remain. Time is required before there will be a perfect cure. And meantime, why doth a living man complain? A man for the punishment of his sin? This is God's ordinary method—to leave the smart of sin even after the power is taken away. But not always. Perhaps he will thoroughly heal in one moment. It may be you will find it so. Be ready. Do not lose time in thinking you have not *repented* enough. Nay, you have not *believed* enough. It is high time you should begin. Look unto Jesus. Hang upon him alone. Let reasoning be swallowed up in love. Love alone will do the deed.

The God of love and peace be with you![272] I am,
Your affectionate brother and servant,

J. Wesley

Source: holograph; Madison, New Jersey, General Commission on Archives and History, The United Methodist Church (the address and postage information do not survive).

---

[271] The 'wilderness state' was JW's term for a time of temptation and distress into which new believers frequently fell; see his later sermon on the topic, Sermon 46, 'The Wilderness State', 2:205–21 in this edn.
[272] See 2 Cor. 13:11.

To the Rev. John Gillies[273]

LONDON
NOVEMBER 12, 1756

There is a wonderful increase of the work of God in London.
Many are daily convinced of sin, and many converted. Mr. [Thomas]
5 Walsh (one of our preachers, who is critically skilled in Hebrew)
has once or twice disputed openly with the Jews in their synagogue.
All were patient; one of them is convinced of the truth. He hopes to
visit them there, again and again.

Source: published transcription; John Gillies, ed., *Appendix to the Historical Collections Relating to Remarkable Periods of the Success of the Gospel* (Glasgow: John Orr, 1761), 101–2.

To Richard Williams[274]

10 LONDON
NOVEMBER 16, 1756

My Dear Brother,
You do me too much honour. Yet I do not think you flatter, for you
speak out of the sincerity of your heart. But love is apt to make us
15 a little blind, so that we cannot see clearly. However, I am obliged
to you for your good intention. I wish you may be more and more
zealous for God; and am, dear Richard,
Your affectionate brother,

[John Wesley]

20
Address: 'To Capt. R. Williams, Camborne, Cornwall'.
Source: published transcription; Telford, *Letters*, 3:205–6.

---

[273] On Gillies, see 26:504 in this edn.
[274] Captain Richard Williams was a strong lay supporter of Methodism in Cornwall,
eventually serving as circuit steward.

To Samuel Furly

LONDON
NOVEMBER 20, 1756

My Dear Brother,

Just at the time when you resolved to quit your trifling companion, God gave you a serious one—a plain token that he will with-   5
hold from you no good thing, if you will yet turn to him. Do you
now find your mind disengaged and free? Can you say, '*Deleo dehinc
omnes ex animo mulieres*'?[275] If so, stand fast in the liberty wherewith
Christ hath made you free. Be not entangled again in that yoke of
bondage.[276] Beware of the very first approach, and watch and pray   10
that you enter not into temptation.

I hope Mr. Drake[277] is determined to contract no acquaintance
with any man that knows not God. Let him have sense and learning
and every other recommendation, still it will not quit cost;[278] it is
necessary to be courteous to all. But that does not imply intimacy.   15
He knows, and we know, the value of time. See that you improve
every part of

> The least of these a serious care demands;
> For though they're little, they are golden sands.[279]   20

I am,
        Your affectionate brother,

[John Wesley]

25

Source: published transcription; Telford, *Letters*, 3:206.

---

[275] Terence, *Eunuch*, Act 2, Scene 3 (l. 96); 'Henceforth I blot out all women from my
mind'.

[276] See Gal. 5:1.

[277] Samuel Drake; see 26:596, n. 9 in this edn.

[278] To 'quit cost' is to 'cover the expense' or 'prove adequate'.

[279] From a manuscript poem by John Gambold, 'On Listening to the Vibrations of a
Clock,' as published by JW in *MSP* (1744), 3:195.

To Samuel Furly

LONDON
NOVEMBER 26, 1756

My Dear Brother,

You would do well to meet earlier in the evening—at seven, if not
5   sooner—and to begin your meeting with close examination of each
other's progress for the day past. I am afraid an hour and half is too
little. At Oxford we always met at six. You should likewise have your
eyes all round, to see if you can't add another to your number. Probably some parts of the *Serious Call* or *Christian Perfection* might be
10 a means of awakening her again.[280] But whether it would or not is
very uncertain. For when a person has once quenched the Spirit,
we cannot be assured God will restore it again. However, one would
spare no pains in a case of such importance, and there are such instances of God's longsuffering that we cannot despair of any.
15   I have lately been reading Mr. Hutchinson's *Works*.[281] And the
more I read, the less I like them. I am fully convinced of one thing
in particular, which I least of all expected: he did not understand
Hebrew; not critically—no, not tolerably. I verily believe Thomas
Walsh understands it far better at this day than he did to the day
20 of his death. Let us understand the love of God, and it is enough.
    I am,
                    Your affectionate brother,

[John Wesley]

Source: published transcription; Telford, *Letters*, 3:206–7.

---

[280] Wesley is commending William Law's *A Serious Call to a Devout and Holy Life* (1729)
and Law's *Practical Treatise upon Christian Perfection* (1726); surely in the abridged versions
that JW published in 1744 & 1743 respectively.

[281] John Hutchinson (1674–1737), was an eccentric Hebraist who argued that the Old
Testament revealed all scientific truth when read properly (without the vowel points). He was
a sharp critic of Newtonian science and advocate of high-church views, who became influential
in the Bristol area and at Oxford, particularly among those of non-juror leanings. Hutchinson's
twelve-volume *Philosophical and Theological Works* were published in 1748–49; but JW was
reading the more recent *Abstract from the Works of John Hutchinson* (1753), as evident when he
read an excerpt to his lay preachers a few days earlier (see JW, *Journal*, Nov. 22, 1756, 21:81 in
this edn.).

To [Edward Perronet][282]

[LONDON]
DECEMBER 1756

I do not see that *diocesan* episcopacy is *necessary*, but I do, that it is highly expedient. But whether it were or no, the spirit shown in those verses is wrong from end to end.

Neither John Edwards[283] nor any other separatist can ever be expected to own prejudice, pride, or interest to be his motive. Nevertheless, I do and must blame every one of them for the act of separating. Afterwards, I leave them to God.

The apostles had not the 'Lordships' or the *revenues*, but they had the *office* of *diocesan* bishops. But let that point sleep. We have things to think of which are *magis ad nos*.[284] Keep from proselyting others, and keep your opinion till doomsday—stupid, self-inconsistent, unprimitive, and unscriptural as it is.

I have spoken my judgment concerning lay administering at large, both to Charles Perronet and Nicholas Norton.[285] I went as far as I could with a safe conscience. I must follow my conscience, and they their own. They who dissuade people from attending the Church and sacrament do certainly 'draw them from the church'.

Source: published transcription; Whitehead, *Life*, 2:289.

To Samuel Furly

SNOWSFIELDS, London
DECEMBER 4, 1756

Dear Sammy,

I did not mention any particular book because I did not recollect any that was particularly proper. But either Mr. Allen's *Alarm* in the

---

[282] Whitehead names the recipient only as 'a friend', but opening reference to verse disparaging the episcopacy makes clear that JW is writing Edward Perronet (son of Vincent Perronet; see 26:428 in this edn.). Perronet had just published *The Mitre*, a ferocious attack in verse on the Church of England that insisted the Lord's Supper was not a priestly rite, but could be celebrated in any small gathering of Christians. This soon ended his connection to the Wesley brothers. Cf. CW's letter to JW, Nov. 16, 1756.

[283] Orig., 'J. E.'; but the reference is clear: John Edwards (b. 1717), one of the preachers who had been associated with JW from 1749, but formed an Independent congregation in Leeds in 1754; see Atmore, *Memorial*, 117–18.

[284] 'More [important] for us.'

[285] See JW to Nicholas Norton, Sept. 3, 1756.

Christian Library or *Vindiciae Pietatis* may do well.[286] I saw nothing amiss in your meeting with Mr. Drake but that the time was too short. You should read the closest and most searching books you can and apply them honestly to each other's heart.

5   As to yourself, *principiis obsta*[287]—the *first* look or thought! Play not with the fire, no, not a moment. Then it cannot hurt you.

Mr. Drake must determine for himself as to conversing with those gentlemen. If he *feels* any hurt from it, he must abstain. If not, he may converse with them sparingly, that is, if there be but a 10 faint, distant prospect of doing them any good.

I have no receipts or proposals, so they may be sent in my next. I have answered about an hundred and forty pages of John Taylor,[288] but it has cost me above an hundred and twenty. Sammy, never trifle more! I am,

15   Yours affectionately,

J. Wesley

Address: 'To / Mr Samuel Furly / In Queen's College / Cambridge'.
Postmark: '7/DE'. *Charge*: '3'.
Source: holograph; MARC, DDWes 5/29.

To Dorothy Furly[289]

LONDON,
DECEMBER 22, 1756

20   It is a happy thing if we can learn obedience by the things which we suffer. Weakness of body and heaviness of mind will, I trust, have this good effect upon you. The particular lesson which you have now to learn is to be faithful in (comparatively) little things,

---

[286] Joseph Alleine (1634–68), *An Alarm to Unconverted Sinners* (1672; *Christian Library*, 24:161–25:26); and Richard Alleine, *Vindiciae Pietatis: Or, A Vindication of Godlinesse* (1660; *Christian Library*, 30:145–31:107). Richard Alleine's *Vindiciae Pietatis* would serve as the basis of Wesley's covenant prayers.

[287] Latin, 'Resist the beginnings'.

[288] Cf. JW to his wife, June 18, 1756.

[289] Dorothy Furly was the sister of JW's friend and correspondent Samuel Furly. She would later marry John Downes (see JW to Furly, July 16, 1763).

particularly in conversation. God hath given you a tongue. Why? That you may praise him therewith, that all your conversation may be, for the time to come, 'meet to minister grace to the hearers'.[290] Such conversation and private prayer exceedingly assist each other. By resolutely persisting (according to your little strength) in all works of piety and mercy, you are waiting on God in the old scriptural way. And therein he will come and save you. Do not think he is afar off. He is nigh that justifieth,[291] that sanctifieth. Beware you do not thrust him away from you. Rather say,

> My heart would *now* receive thee, Lord:
> Come in, my Lord, come in![292]

Write as often, and as freely and fully as you please to
Your affectionate brother and servant,

J. Wesley

Source: published transcription; Benson, *Works*, 16:314–15.

To Samuel Furly

[1756–57?[293]]

My Dear Sammy,

I shall expect to hear you are confined in Bedlam soon. You say you cannot understand this and that. Understand! We can understand nothing. But however little we can understand, we can understand this: God is wise and I am foolish, and that he wills all men to be saved.

I am,
Yours affectionately,

J. Wesley

---

[290] Cf. Eph. 4:29.

[291] See Isa. 50:8.

[292] CW, 'Hymn on Tit. 2:14', st. 14, *HSP* (1742), 247 (emphasis added by JW).

[293] The letter is undated. This date range is suggested by similarities in letters of April 16, 1756 and Feb. 11, 1757.

Source: published transcription; A Wesleyan Minister [possibly Thomas L. Withington], *Temporal Prosperity and Spiritual Decline; or, Free Thoughts on Some Aspects of Modern Methodism* (London: Hamilton, Adams, and Co., 1866), 268. There is also a manuscript transcription in an 1889 letter by Thomas Withington to George Stampe, which suggests that Withington either owned or saw the original. The 1889 letter is held at Duke, Rubenstein, Frank Baker Collection of Wesleyana, Box WF.

1757

To Matthew Errington[1]

LONDON
JANUARY 8, 1757

My Dear Brother,

You have done well in sending me a particular account. The bill came safe, and is accepted. But Michael's[2] senseless delay has distressed me much. He ought to have been here the 28th of November, and to have then brought with him all the money he could procure. For the time to come, if he should take another journey, I must punctually fix beforehand how many days he is to stay in every place.

I hope you all continue a family of love, and that the stewards and you are in harmony with each other. I should be glad to see poor Becky, especially if I find her all alive to God. We have a sickly family here: my wife, Jenny,[3] Sally Clay,[4] ill of paralytic; Thomas Walsh and Jemmy Morgan[5] of consumptive disorders. But all is best. I am,
Your affectionate brother,

J. Wesley

Source: holograph; MARC, MAM JW 2/87 (address portion missing).

---

[1] This letter initiates JW's correspondence with Matthew Errington (1711–88), a tailor converted in 1741 in London, where he helped care for a while for the Foundery; he moved to Newcastle in 1749 and served as JW's book steward at the Orphan House in Newcastle until his death; see Vickers, *Dictionary*, 111.

[2] Michael Fenwick.

[3] Jeanne Vazeille.

[4] On Sarah Clay, see 26:466 in this edn.

[5] James Morgan (1736–74) became one of JW's traveling lay preachers in 1755. By 1766 ill health led him to settle in Dublin. See Atmore, *Memorial*, 281–86.

73

To Samuel Furly

[LONDON]
FEBRUARY 11, 1757

The times and seasons of bestowing comfort and all other spiritual blessings the Father hath reserved in his own power. And there
5   may be many wise reasons unknown to us (who are of yesterday and know nothing) why he does not answer every prayer as soon as we offer it. Indeed, one very common reason is, sin lieth at the door—perhaps sin of omission, the not following the light, not using the power we have. I know not that this is your case. Possibly God may
10   see good to take this way to break the stubbornness of your will and destroy your pride of understanding. Certainly you are in the hands of him that loves you, and that will speedily deliver, if you persevere in waiting for him and in rejecting all comfort but that which flows from the Spirit of adoption crying in your heart, 'Abba Father!'[6]
15

Address: 'To / Rev. S. Furly, / Kippax' (given by Telford).
Source: holograph; privately held (current owner unknown, Wesley Works Editorial Project Archive includes a photocopy that is possibly incomplete, with no salutation or signature shown).

To Samuel Furly

LONDON
MARCH 8, 1757

Dear Sammy,
I have preached on that subject again and again, and shall do
20   when it comes my way. Pray look into Mr. Taylor's note on that verse of 2 Tim.: 'taken captive at his will'.[7] See the verse he cites from Homer.[8] Consult the book and tell me whether his assertion be true or false.

---

[6] Rom. 8:15.
[7] 2 Tim. 2:26. JW refers here to John Taylor's *The Scripture-Doctrine of Original Sin Proposed to Free and Candid Examination* (3rd edn.; London, 1750), 152. Wesley was at work on a response to Taylor, which he published later this year; on this point, see 12:269 in this edn.
[8] In a note on p. 154, Taylor referred to Homer's *Iliad*, Book V, line 698, in his attempt to explain the Greek expression translated 'to revive'.

Hutcheson's *Moral Philosophy* is a solemn trifle.[9] His Latin is not easy and natural. It is abundantly too laboured and thence less easy to be understood. This is an essential defect in his language.

Have not time? Why have not you time? When I was at the university, I had always time to do whatever I would. And so I should now, but that

> ... *aliena negotia centum*
> *per caput et circa saliunt latus.*[10]

Last week you was in great danger. Thomas Walsh and I were within twelve miles of Cambridge. But the Norwich coach could not go out of its way. So you are escaped.

Above all knowledge, know Christ. I am,

> Your affectionate brother,

> > J. Wesley

Source: holograph; Gateshead, Co. Durham, England, Public Library (framed, so no access to *address*, *postmark*, or indications of postal *charge*).

To Samuel Furly

LEWISHAM
MARCH 24, 1757

Dear Sammy,

I am glad you are so fully employed. I think you need not speak to each of the women every day; at least, not for an hour altogether. You may say all you have to say in less time. But whatever you do, or leave undone, you must, absolutely must, find time for exercise. Otherwise, you are penny wise and pound foolish, for one fit of sickness will cost you more time than you have saved in several years. Nay, you already lose much time by your past want of exercise,

---

[9] Francis Hutcheson, *Philosophiae Moralis Institutio Compendiaria, Ethices et Jurisprudentiae Naturalis Elementa Continens* (Glasgow, 1742); English translation: *System of Moral Philosophy* (3 vols.; London, 1755).

[10] Horace, *Satires*, II.vi.33–34; 'A hundred matters from other people encompass me about my head and on every side'.

namely in sleep. Why do I need less sleep than you? Because I constantly use more exercise.

All Passion Week I purpose spending in London. On Easter Sunday I hope to be at Bedford, in my way to the north. I thank
5 Mr. Drake and you for the trouble you have taken.[11] κακοπάθητε ὡς καλοὶ στρατιῶται.[12] I am,
    Your affectionate brother,

J. Wesley

Address: 'To / Mr Furly / At Queen's College / Cambridge'.
Postmark: '25/MR'. *Charge*: '3'.
Source: holograph; MARC, MAM JW 3/16.

To Thomas Olivers

10   LEWISHAM
MARCH 24, 1757

Dear Tommy,

We should neither be forward nor backward in believing those who think they have attained the second blessing.[13] Of those in
15 Courtmatrix and Ballingarrane I can form no judgment yet. Barely to feel no sin, or to feel constant peace, joy, and love, will not prove the point. We have known some who remained in that state for several years, and yet have afterwards lost almost all they had received.

In the two sermons on this subject, the Minutes of the Con-
20 ference, the preface to the second and third volumes of Hymns, and some of our controversial writings, you have a full account of Christian perfection.[14] 1) It undoubtedly implies salvation from all sin, inward and outward, into all holiness. 2) Without it none can be admitted into heaven, nor be completely happy upon earth. But

[11] The reference is apparently to Samuel Drake; see 26:596, n. 9 in this edn.

[12] Cf. 2 Tim. 2:3 (Greek), 'Endure as good soldiers'; Wesley has altered the expression by making it plural and using a simpler form of the verb.

[13] There was currently a flurry of Methodists claiming the 'second blessing', a term that JW used on occasion for entire sanctification or Christian perfection. This letter reflects Wesley's high interest in such claims, yet desire to test their validity.

[14] Wesley refers specifically to Sermon 17, 'The Circumcision of the Heart' (1:398–414 in this edn.); Sermon 40, *Christian Perfection* (2:97–121 in this edn.); the Doctrinal Minutes of 1749 (10:778–85 in this edn.); and the prefaces to *HSP* 1740 and *HSP* 1742 (13:42–53 in this edn.).

we must speak very tenderly on this head, for it is far better to *lead* men than to *drive*. Study to recommend it rather as amiable and desirable than as necessary. 3) A *gradual* growth in grace precedes, but the gift itself is always given *instantaneously*. I never knew or heard of any exception; and I believe there never was one. 4) One fruit given at the same instant (at least usually) is a direct, positive testimony of the Spirit that the work is done, that they cannot fall away, that they cannot sin. In consequence of this they have no slavish fear, but uninterrupted light, love, and joy, with continual growth in wisdom, holiness, and happiness, till they are filled with all the fullness of God.

Beware of pride and stubbornness. Consult brother Hopper in all things.[15] Be obstinate only in pressing on to perfection.

My love to Fanny and Sally Moore. They forget me as soon as I cross the water. Peace be with your spirit. I am,
Your affectionate brother,

J. Wesley

Address: 'To / Mr Tho. Olivers'.
Source: holograph; Drew, Methodist Archives.

To Potential Subscribers[16]

[LONDON]
[MARCH 25, 1757]

Proposals for Printing by Subscription,

The Doctrine of Original Sin

By John Wesley

Occasioned by the Writings of Mr.[17] John Taylor

---

[15] I.e., Christopher Hopper, who was apparently the senior itinerant supervising Olivers during this stationing in Ireland.

[16] There were at least two published versions of this appeal for subscriptions to JW's *The Doctrine of Original Sin*. The version printed in Felix Farley's *Bristol Journal* is followed here, with substantive variants in other printings noted. JW's volume was published later that year (see 12:155–481 in this edn.).

[17] June 25, Newcastle, has 'Dr.' in this and the other four instances.

Conditions:

I. The work will contain about five hundred pages, octavo, on good paper and new leather.[18]

5   II. The price to subscribers of a book in quires is five shillings, half to be paid at the time of subscribing.

III. Subscribers for six will have a seventh *gratis*.

IV. The work is ready to be put into the press.

10   Subscriptions are taken in by T. Trye, near Gray's Inn Gate, Holbourn; Robinson, in Ludgate Street; J. Hodges, at London Bridge; and at the Found[e]ry, in Upper Moorfields, London; J. Fox, Westminster Hall; and J. Jolliffe, St. James's Street, Westminster. By J. Palmer, in Wine Street; J. Wilson, in Peter
15   Street, and J. Long, in Tower Lane, Bristol. By W. Shent, in Leeds; and R. Akenhead,[19] in Newcastle upon Tyne.[20]

London, March 25, 1757

It has been constantly affirmed by Mr. John Taylor's admirers 'that his book upon *Original Sin* has never been answered'. And it is
20   in some sense true. Indeed presently after the publication of it Dr. [David] Jenning[s] published a tract which contained strong and pertinent remarks on many parts of it. Not long after, Mr. [Samuel] Hebden of Suffolk wrote several excellent treatises on the same subject, in which the most considerable arguments used by Mr.
25   Taylor are calmly and solidly refuted. Dr. [Isaac] Watts then wrote his ingenious book entitled *The Ruin and Recovery of Human Nature*, some parts of which strike at the very foundation of Mr. Taylor's hypothesis. Lastly, Mr. [James] Hervey has, in his *Dialogues*, many beautiful strokes, whereby he rescues the Scripture from Mr.
30   Taylor's misrepresentations.[21] Nevertheless, as none of these have followed him step by step, from the beginning of his book to the end, it is still confidently affirmed, 'That he is *unanswered*, and therefore, *unanswerable*'.

---

[18] June 25, Newcastle, omits 'octavo' and 'and new leather'.

[19] April 23, 30 alter to 'R. Fleming'.

[20] June 25, 'Subscriptions are taken by James Fleming, Michael Calendar, and at the Orphan House.'

[21] For details on each of these earlier responses to Taylor see the editorial introduction to JW, *The Doctrine of Original Sin*, 12:132–36 in this edn.

Is there not then a loud call for some person to treat him in a different manner? To examine this *unanswered, unanswerable* work from the very beginning to the end? To weigh every argument there advanced both 'in the balance of the sanctuary'[22] and (wherever the nature of the thing admits) in the scale of impartial reason? 5

This is what I have attempted to do, although with this great disadvantage (besides many others) that I have not time to weigh every point so throughly and answer it so fully as the importance of it requires. Nevertheless I flatter myself the impartial reader will find a clear and rational answer (if not very correctly or elegantly 10 expressed) to every argument Mr. Taylor has advanced. And I trust this is done 'in the spirit of meekness';[23] without anger, without bitterness, and without contempt. I think I speak the truth only. And I know I 'speak' that 'truth in love'.[24] Though not with coolness or indifference, as being most thoroughly[25] convinced the whole cause 15 of *revealed religion* is at stake, and that it stands or falls with the doctrine of *original sin*. Could I once be persuaded to give up this, I must give up the Christian system with it. Nor could I ever after concern myself with any other religion than that of Seneca or Marcus Antoninus.[26] 20

I would only add that, as I have here *one* point of view, I meddle with no other[27] controversy. I touch not in any degree on things disputed between Remonstrants and Counter-Remonstrants, or any other Christians. No serious Christian of any denomination will find here any positions that '[en]gender strife',[28] or any that will not 25 be allowed by all who agree to the plain sense of that weighty declaration, 'As in Adam all died, so in Christ shall all be made alive.'[29]

Source: *Felix Farley's Bristol Journal*, April 16, 23, and 30, 1757; *Newcastle Journal*, June 25, 1757.

---

[22] Cf. John Gill, *Exposition of the Old Testament* (1763–65), commenting on Prov. 11:1, 'A false balance is an abomination to the Lord': 'This may be understood of balances and weights in religious affairs; the balance of the sanctuary is the word of God, with which all doctrines are to be weighed, and, if found wanting, they are to be rejected.'

[23] 1 Cor. 4:21.

[24] Cf. Eph. 4:15.

[25] June 25, 'throughly'.

[26] Apr. 16 & June 25, 'Antonius'.

[27] June 25 omits 'other'.

[28] 2 Tim. 2:23.

[29] 1 Cor. 15:22.

To Mary (Goldhawk/Vazeille) Wesley

LIVERPOOL
APRIL 22, 1757

Now, my dear Molly, you do just as you should. I was really uneasy for want of hearing from you. Thus far God has brought me safe
5 and well, but I have left my companions behind me. John Haime[30] could reach no farther than Leicester (but he hopes to meet me at Manchester). Joseph Jones[31] held out to Poole, near Nantwich. But having forgot his bags at Bilbrook, he was obliged to go back for them. Brother Lucas[32] came with me from Chester today, but he also
10 must leave me on Monday, and go into the round. I shall then want simple Michael,[33] for without a companion in travel, I am like a bird without a wing, especially in this place which is at present the seat of war, for poor James Schol[e]field sets me at open defiance.[34] But I am not afraid of that, I fear only fair words, and that weapon he is not at
15 present inclined to use. I suppose he has carried off about half the society by telling them how cruelly I have treated him.

I expect brother [William] Atkinson will give you every week an account of the books sold. I am sorry I forgot to mention it to him. Your labour in the printing-house was well bestowed, as also in get-
20 ting the books collated. Now, my love, go on to overcome evil with good. By the grace of God, you are able.

I am afraid Jemmy Rouquet's head is not quite right.[35] I have written him a long, mild, loving answer. Pray let the *Notes*[36] (in quires) be sent down to Leeds directly, and with them two hundred
25 of each sort of proposals.

The post constrains me to break off. Grace and peace, my dear life, be with you and Jenny and Noah forever![37]

---

[30] On John Haime, see 26:98 in this edn.

[31] Joseph Jones was one of the first Methodist itinerants, but settled in Somerset in 1760; see Atmore, *Memorial*, 225–26.

[32] Richard Lucas (d. 1766), an itinerant at least as early as 1755; see 10:273 in this edn.; and Atmore, *Memorial*, 246.

[33] Presumably Michael Fenwick.

[34] Cf. JW, *Journal*, April 21, 1757 (21:93–94 and n. 63 in this edn.).

[35] James Rouquet (1730–76) was a descendant of Huguenot refugees to England who became one of JW's close colleagues. He was educated at St. John's College, Oxford, and converted under George Whitefield's influence while in school. JW appointed Rouquet as Master of Kingswood School between 1751 and 1754. He then became an itinerant preacher. In 1765 Rouquet was ordained as a priest and served the remainder of his life in parishes around Bristol. Cf. A. Barrett Sackett, *James Rouquet and His Part in Early Methodism* (Broxton, Cheshire, 1972).

[36] A second edition of the *NT Notes* was published this year.

[37] This is Wesley's first reference to his stepson Noah Vazeille (1747–1809), along with Jeanne.

Adieu!

Pray tell Mr. Blackwell I stay here ten days, then six days at Mr. Philips in Manchester, and seven more in or near Leeds.

Pray put the enclosed into the post directly.

Address: 'To / Mrs Wesley'.

No *postmark* or indications of postal *charge*; apparently delivered by hand.

Source: holograph; WHS Library, Heaton bequest.

To Joseph Cownley

Liverpool
April 23, 1757

Dear Joseph,

Your letter came to me here. Ted Perronet says Dr. Turner[38] expects no fee at all, but will do you all the service he can. I sent to the Dr. before I left London. He said he had wrote his thoughts on your case at large, but had not yet had time to transcribe them. But he does not think it is a desperate case. When I talked with him concerning it, he said: 1) no physician hitherto seems to have understood it; 2) a proper course of medicines will probably remove the whole disorder; and if not, 3) an entire milk diet will hardly fail to restore your health.

I will write to London, that he may send his thoughts directly. Meantime I advise you to apply, not a murdering blister, but a large treacle-plaster to your head, renewing it in twelve hours if you find any benefit.

If after all Dr. Turner does not cure you, I am *almost certain* electrifying will.[39] Courage, Joseph! I trust your deliverance draws nigh! If it does, be not less, but tenfold more serious.

With love to Suky,[40] I am,

Your affectionate friend and brother,

J. Wesley

---

[38] See JW's letter to his wife, July 10, 1756, where he urges her to see Dr. Turner.

[39] JW's *Primitive Physick* (1747 with numerous republications thereafter) suggests electrification as a treatment for a number of ailments.

[40] I.e., Cownley's wife.

Ten days hence I go to Manchester, and then to Leeds. At Manchester we have an electrifying machine.

I am obliged by the state of things there, to go into Yorkshire, before I go to Scotland. Therefore I shall not be at Berwick till June
5   9, at Alnwick till Sat. June 11th, nor at Morpeth, Placey, and Newcastle till June 13th.

Address: 'To Mr Joseph Cownley / At the Orphan-house / Newcastle
    upon Tyne / North Post Manchester'.
Postmark: 'LIVER / POOL'. *Charge*: '3'.
Source: holograph; Wesley's Chapel (London), LDWMM 1994/1995.

To Mary (Goldhawk/Vazeille) Wesley

LIVERPOOL
APRIL 24, 1757

10   I see plainly, my dear Molly, you are resolved to make me love you better and better. Be as careful as ever you will (only not so as to make yourself sick) and as diligent as ever you can. This is one of the talents which God has given you. O use it to the uttermost! Put forth all your strength in things temporal as well as
15   in things spiritual. Whatsoever your hand findeth to do, do it with your might. What a blessed rule is that of Kempis. 'Do what is in thee, and God will supply what is lacking'![41] Only, my love, watch over your own spirit! Take heed that it be not sharpened. Fret not thyself because of the ungodly, but in quietness and patience pos-
20   sess your own soul.[42]

I believe my letter to the stewards will stir them up. What if you gave it to Thomas Butts and desired him and John Matthews[43] to second it? If they speak to William Atkinson in good earnest, it will certainly do good, one way or the other.

---

[41] Thomas à Kempis, *Imitation of Christ*, IV.xii.2.

[42] See Luke 21:19.

[43] John Matthews was a London supporter of JW, who married his stepdaughter Jeanne Vazeille on July 24, 1757; JW records in his *Journal* that he was at Matthews's side when he died on Dec. 28, 1764 (21:497 in this edn.).

Now I have burnt your letter. My health continues to a miracle. Ten days hence I shall probably see John Haime and Joseph Jones if he finds his way back from Bilbrook.

It grows late, but I could not persuade myself to lose one post, though I cannot tell you how much I am, dear Molly, 5
Your affectionate husband, lover, and friend,

John Wesley

My dear sister Hacket was to have a cag of the elder wine.[44] Has she had it? 10

Address: 'To / Mrs Wesley'.
No *postmark* or indications of postal *charge*; apparently delivered by hand.
Source: holograph; MARC, MAM JW 5/57.

To Dorothy Furly

Birstall
May 18, 1757

The great point is to pick out in Bristol, as in all places, such acquaintance as have a deep fear of God, a continual consciousness of 15
his presence, and a strong thirst after his whole image. Such I take most of the leaders of bands to be; and such are many of the poor in the society. But extremely few of the rich or honourable Methodists are of that number. My dear sister, I have been in pain for you on their account. When I talked with you last, you could relish the sim- 20
plicity of the gospel. You were athirst for all the mind that was in Christ, and wanted to walk just as he walked. O let none persuade you, either by example or advice, to make any, the least, deviation from that good way. Make no abatement; do not soften the plain, rough gospel; do not 25

Measure back your steps to earth again.[45]

---

[44] A 'cag' was a barrel or wooden vessel containing four or five gallons. Elderberries (genus *sambucus*) were used to produce a fruit wine.
[45] Cf. Thomas Parnell, 'The Hermit', l. 227; retained in JW's abridged form in *MSP* (1744), 1:275.

Be not, either inwardly or outwardly, conformed to this world; but
be a Christian altogether.

    Health you shall have if health be best. And he that gives it will
give a blessing with it, an increase of spiritual as well as of bod-
5   ily strength—but it is strength to labour, not to sit still. And this
strength will either increase or decrease in the same proportion
with your sense of his love. You may lose this sense either 1) by
committing sin; or 2) by omitting duty; or 3) by giving way to pride,
anger, or any other inward sin; or 4) by not watching unto prayer, by
10 yielding to indolence or spiritual sloth. But it is no more necessary
that we should ever lose it than it is necessary we should omit duty
or commit sin. Mr. [William] Law, therefore, speaking on this head,
betrays deep ignorance both of the Scripture and the inward work
of God. You are more liable to receive hurt from his late writings
15 than from any others which I know.[46] I shall write to Sammy[47] in the
morning. It would not have been amiss if you had spoken freely to
me concerning him. Why should not you, now you have in some
measure broke that natural shyness, speak all that is in your heart
to, dear Miss Furly,
20   Your truly affectionate friend and brother,

                                 J. Wesley

Source: published transcription; Benson, *Works*, 16:315–16.

To Ebenezer Blackwell

WHITEHAVEN
MAY 28, 1757

25 Dear Sir,

    Does the rule still hold, 'Out of sight out of mind'? I am afraid it
does with poor Miss Freeman,[48] as she does not give me one line in

---

[46] To help protect his followers from this danger, in 1768 Wesley published *An Extract from the Rev. Mr. Law's Later Works*, highlighting views he found problematic; see *Bibliography*, No. 312.

[47] Samuel Furly, her brother.

[48] Mary Freeman (1731–1815), was a cousin of Ebenezer Blackwell, born in England but descended on her maternal side from Italian aristocratic roots. She was educated at a convent

answer to the long letter I wrote from Liverpool.[49] I was in hopes we might have interchanged several letters in less than six weeks' time. As for you, I presume you are full of business, and yet not so full of temporal business as to exclude the thoughts of higher concerns, business that will endure when earth and the works of it are burned 5 up. Were anything temporal even to damp or lessen (though not destroy) our care and zeal for things eternal, what could countervail the loss? What could make us amends for the damage thereby sustained? Sometimes, indeed, we may go through abundance of business, and yet have God in all our thought. But is this the case 10 always? Are not even lawful, nay necessary, things at other times a grievous hindrance, especially when we undertake them without any suspicion of danger, and consequently without any prayer against that danger?

In this respect, as in many others, I have lately had peculiar rea- 15 son to be thankful. In every place people flock about me for direction in secular as well as spiritual affairs; and I dare not throw even this burden off my shoulders, though I have employment enough without it. But it is a burden, and no burden. It is no encumbrance, no weight upon my mind. If we see God in all things and do all for 20 him, then all things are easy.

I think it is fourteen or fifteen days since my wife wrote to me. I am afraid she is not well, or is angry at my brother, and consequently, with me. If any letters for me come enclosed to Mr. Belchier,[50] I will be obliged to you if you will (not send them to her, but) direct them 25 to me at Newcastle, where I hope to be in a few days.[51] Wishing all grace and peace to you and yours, I am, dear sir,
> Your most affectionate servant,

> > John Wesley

I breakfasted at Keswick last Tuesday. 30

---

in Rome, and a devoted Roman Catholic her whole life. But she also became close friends with Charles and Sarah Wesley and their children (perhaps influencing their son Samuel in his decision to convert to the Church of Rome). Freeman never married, but about 1784 she formally changed her name to Mary Freeman Shepherd, in honor of her uncle Nathaniel Shepherd, who was her godfather and benefactor.

[49] JW had been in Liverpool Apr. 21–30.

[50] William Belchier, of Epsom, a Member of Parliament; see JW's letter to Blackwell dated Mar. 15, 1755 (26:283 and fn. 14 in this edn.).

[51] He arrived in Newcastle on June 19.

Address: 'To / Mr Blackwell / In Exchange Alley / London'.
Postmarks: '3 / IV' (June 3) 'COCKER / MOUTH'. *Charge*: '4'.
Endorsement: 'Rev'd Mr John Wesley / Whitehaven 28. May 1757'.
Source: holograph; Bridwell Library (SMU).

To Sarah Crosby[52]

NEWCASTLE-UPON-TYNE
JUNE 14, 1757

My Dear Sister,

I was concerned at not hearing from you for so long a time,
5   whereas I would not willingly pass a fortnight without it. Whenever
you have leisure write, whether any one else does or not. I shall be
here near three weeks, and then at York. It comforts me to hear that
your love does not decrease. I want it to increase daily. Is there not
height and depth in him with whom you have to do, for your love to
10   rise infinitely higher and to sink infinitely deeper into him than ever
it has done yet? Are you fully employed for him, and yet so as to
have some time daily for reading and other private exercises? If you
should grow cold, it would afflict me much. Rather let me always
rejoice over you. As for me, I seem only to be just beginning to aim
15   feebly at God, though I have found more liberty in the respects you
mention lately than of a long season.

    Dear Sally, never forget to pray for,
      Your affectionate brother,

John Wesley

20

Source: published transcription; Benson, *Works*, 16:331.

---

[52] This is the first surviving letter from JW to Mrs. Sarah Crosby (1729–1804; maiden
name unknown), although it alludes to earlier correspondence. Crosby became one of JW's
most prolific correspondents, with at least twenty letters from JW to her surviving, beginning
with this one and ending with a letter in June 1789. Crosby was drawn into the Wesleyan revival
under JW's preaching and joined the Foundery society in London in 1750 (see her autobiographical letter to JW, Aug. 7, 1757). In early 1757 Crosby met Mary Bosanquet, the beginning
of a long friendship and shared ministry. Both women became prominent female preachers
among Wesley's followers, with Crosby pioneering the way.

To Dorothy Furly

Newcastle-Upon-Tyne
June 14, 1757

You have reason to praise God for what he has done and to expect all that he has promised. Indeed, if it were required that you should work this in yourself, your impotence might be a bar to your expectations. And so might your unworthiness, if God required any merit of yours in order to his working in you. But what impotence in you can be a bar to the almighty power of God? And what unworthiness can hinder the free love of God? His love in and through Christ Jesus? So that all the promises lie fair before you. The land flowing with milk and honey, the Canaan of his perfect love, is open. Believe, and enter in![53]

It is an observation of one of the ancients that it is far easier not to desire praise than not to be pleased with it. A bare conviction that it is, generally speaking, deadly poison may prevent our desiring it, but nothing less than humble love filling the heart will prevent our being pleased with it, for the sense of honour is as natural to man as the sense of tasting or feeling. But when that which is spiritual is fully come, this which is corruptly natural shall be done away.

Whatever enemies you have, it is enough that you have a friend who is mightier than them all. O let him reign in your heart alone! Do not spare to speak with all freedom to, dear Miss Furly,
    Your affectionate brother and servant,

J. Wesley

Source: published transcription; Benson, *Works*, 16:216–17.

To Dorothy Furly

[Sunderland]
June 18, 1757

I am the more jealous over you because I know you are liable to be much influenced by fair words, especially when they are spoken by

---

[53] An example of JW's use of Exodus imagery, specifically the land of promise, to describe the goal of entire sanctification.

persons of sense and in an agreeable manner. And flesh and blood are powerful advocates for conformity to the world, particularly in little things. But, blessed be God, we have an unction from the Holy One ready to teach us of all things. O let us attend to this
5   inward teaching, which indeed is always consonant with the word. Then the word, applied by the Spirit, shall be a light in all our ways and a lamp in all our paths.[54]

Fight on and conquer! Change of place, as you observe, is but a little thing. But God has, in some measure, changed your heart,
10   wherein you have great reason to rejoice. And, having received the first fruits of the Spirit, righteousness, peace, and joy in the Holy Ghost, patiently and earnestly wait for the great change, whereby every root of bitterness may be torn up.

You may profitably converse with even those honourable Chris-
15   tians if you watch and pray that they do not infect you 1) with *mystical* notions, which stand in full opposition to plain old Bible divinity, or 2) with their odd, senseless jargon of a 'catholic spirit', whereby they have themselves suffered great loss. The spirit of the world, I think, you are aware of already, and indeed there is danger
20   in every approach to it.

I have heard from both Mrs. Gaussen[55] and Miss Bosanquet.[56] There is a poor, queer old woman in Bristol (if she is not gone to paradise) with whom it might do you good to talk. John Jones knows her. Her name is Elizabeth Edgecomb. Peace be with your
25   spirit.

I am, dear Miss Furly,
Your affectionate brother and servant,

John Wesley

Source: published transcription; Benson, *Works*, 16:317–18.

---

[54] See Ps. 119:105.

[55] Mrs. Gaussen was a friend of Charles and Sarah Wesley in Bristol. JW commends her to Furly again in his letter of Sept. 25, 1757.

[56] This is the first mention of Mary Bosanquet (1739–1815) in JW's correspondence. For details on Bosanquet see the note on JW's letter to her of July 25, 1761.

To Sarah Crosby

[NEWCASTLE-UPON-TYNE]
JULY 1, 1757

My Dear Sister,

Certainly you judge right. Do not entangle yourself with the things of this world. Neither give occasion to any to speak re- 5
proachfully. Therefore accept of no deed or writing whatsoever which should tie her down to do anything for you one day longer than she would do without it. What she will do day by day without hurting herself or any one else is liable to no exception. O stand fast in glorious liberty, and be subject to no creature, only so far as love 10
constrains. By this sweetest and strongest tie, you are now subject to, dear Sally,

Your affectionate friend and brother,

J. Wesley

15

I shall look for a letter at York.

Address: 'To / Mrs Crosby / At Mr Kent's Bricklayers / In the Tenter
Ground / Near Upper Moorfields / London'.
Postmarks: '4/JY' 'NEW / CASTLE'.
Source: holograph; WMC Museum.

To Dorothy Furly

YORK
JULY [11,[57]] 1757

Dear Miss Furly,

20

I cannot write to you now so fully as I would, but I must send a few lines. Mere temptation certainly does not weaken without yielding to temptation. Yet a heaviness and soreness may remain upon the spirit till there is a fresh discovery of the love of God.

[57] Although the printed version of the letter has 'July 1', JW's *Journal* shows that he was not in York until July 11 (21:114 in this edn.).

A jealous fear of offending God is good. But what have you to do with any other fear? Let love cast it all out, and at the same time make you tenfold more afraid of doing anything, small or great, which you cannot offer up as an holy sacrifice, acceptable to God
5   through Jesus Christ.

All who are without this fear (and much more all who call it 'legal', who revile the precious gift of God, and think it an hindrance to 'the growing up in Christ'[58]) are antinomians in the inmost soul. Come not into their secret, my dear Miss Furly, but pray for more
10   and more of that 'legal spirit', and you will more and more rejoice
          Your affectionate servant,

                                        John Wesley

Source: published transcription; Benson, *Works*, 16:318.

                        To Samuel Furly

                                        YORK
15   JULY 12, 1757

Dear Sammy,

In all my experience I never knew one so much altered for the worse as Charles Perronet[59] in so short a time. I am afraid that enemy is in real, actual possession of his understanding; though God,
20   I hope, has still hold of his heart. Certainly, the conversing with him at present would not be profitable to you.

Nothing could be more seasonable than the notes you give me concerning Mary Bosanquet.[60] I was just going to answer a letter from one who can say anything to her without offence.[61] So that
25   proper advice may be now[62] conveyed to her with great probability of success.

     [58] Cf. Eph. 4:15.
     [59] Orig., 'C. P.'; see the concerns that JW expresses about him in letters to Nicholas Norton (Sept. 3, 1756), and Sarah Ryan (Dec. 14, 1757).
     [60] Orig., 'M. B.'.
     [61] Likely Sarah Crosby.
     [62] Orig., 'may be now be'.

I hope you will write to Mr. Drake[63] without delay. He is in danger, for every possible snare is laid for him. His aunt here, Mrs. Dickens,[64] has been of great service to him. He was hurried hence by his mother (a woman bitter of spirit) to keep him out of my way.

You may direct your next to me at Mr. Hutton's[65] in Epworth,   5
Lincolnshire, by Thorne bag.

Dear Sammy, fight on!

Adieu.

Miss Tancred, a gay, giddy girl, a mere coquet, is put in the way   10
of Mr. Drake. Warn him earnestly, to keep clear of her.

Address: 'To / Mr Furly / At Mr Greenwoods, Upholsterer / In Rood Lane / London'.

Postmark: smudged and undecipherable. *Charge*: '4'.

Endorsement: '1757 July'.

Source: holograph; Emory, MARBL, Wesley Family Papers, 1/26.

To Dorothy Furly

TREMENEARE
SEPTEMBER 6, 1757

Why you should be afraid on account of anything you said to   15
me, I do not know. Certainly, if you had said whatever was in your heart, it might have been a means of lessening your burden and not of increasing it. I believe you have often a desire, and almost a resolution, of saying a great deal to me; but when you come to write or speak, your heart fails. Why should it? Why should you repress   20
yourself? I should not despise but love you for your openness. It is the fruit and the proof of an honest heart. I know you are weak. I know a little of your particular weaknesses. But so much the more am I concerned for you as a tender, sickly flower. Away then with this reserve. It answers no end but to trouble and embarrass you.   25

[63] Samuel Drake; see 26:596, n. 9 in this edn.

[64] Telford (*Letters*, 3:220) corrects this to 'Mrs. Dickson', without giving a rationale.

[65] George Stevenson described William Hutton as a 'mercer and grocer, a man in good repute in the town', with whom Wesley stayed when at Epworth; *Memorials of the Wesley Family* (London, 1876), 348.

Tell me freely and plainly any difficulty you meet with, any enemy against whom you want help. Use me as a friend, as I hope you will use sister Crosby, and you will find it a blessing to your soul. It will again bring the promise of holiness near, which indeed always

5 seems to be far off when we give way to any known sin, when we any way grieve the Spirit of God. There may be some rare cases wherein God has determined not to bestow his perfect love till a little before death, but this I believe is uncommon. He does not usually put off the fulfilling of his promises. Seek, and you shall

10 find;[66] seek earnestly, and you shall find speedily. Lift up the hands that hang down.[67] Deny yourself, take up your cross,[68] whether that of meeting your class, or any other. Fight on, and victory is at hand!

I am, dear Miss Furly,
    Your affectionate servant,

15
                        J. Wesley

Source: published transcription; Benson, *Works*, 16:318–19.

To Mary (Goldhawk/Vazeille) Wesley

HELSTON
SEPTEMBER 15, 1757

It is a blessed thing to overcome evil with good.[69] You are at pres-
20 ent the mistress of Kingswood house and the women there are to follow your direction. If they do not know it, I desire brother Parkinson to tell them so, only in a mild and loving manner. I desire him also to tell them I will allow no one in that house to drink tea twice a day.

25
Source: published excerpt, *Wesley's Chapel Magazine* 8, no. 30 (June 1938): 11.

---

[66] See Matt. 7:7.
[67] See Heb. 12:12.
[68] See Matt. 16:24, Luke 9:23.
[69] See Rom. 12:21.

To Samuel Walker[70]

PENRYN
SEPTEMBER 19, 1757

Reverend and Dear Sir,

Nothing can be more kind than the mentioning to me whatever you think is amiss in my conduct. And the more freedom you use in doing this, the more I am indebted to you. I am thoroughly convinced that you 'wish me well', and that it is this, together with a 'concern for the common interests of religion', which obliges you to speak with more plainness than otherwise you would. The same motives induce me to lay aside all reserve and tell you the naked sentiments of my heart.

Two years since, eleven or twelve persons of Falmouth were members of our society. Last year I was informed that a young man there had begun to teach them new opinions, and that soon after offence and prejudice crept in and increased till they were all torn asunder. What they have done since I know not, for they have no connection with us. I do 'exert myself' so far as to separate from us those that separate from the Church. But in a thousand other instances I feel the want of more resolution and firmness of spirit. Yet sometimes that may appear irresolution which is not so. I exercise as little authority as possible, because I am afraid of people's depending upon me *too much* and paying me more reverence than they ought.

But I proceed to the substance of your letter. You say, 1. 'If you still hold the essence of justifying faith to be in assurance, why did you encourage John Hingeston to believe his state good?'

Assurance is a word I do not use because it is not scriptural. But I hold a divine evidence or conviction that Christ loved *me* and gave himself for *me* is essential to, if not the very essence of, justifying faith. John Hingeston told me he had more than this, even a clear conviction that his sins were forgiven, although he said that conviction was not so clear now as it had been in times past.

---

[70] Replying to a letter of Walker that it quotes repeatedly. JW would be in Truro, where Walker was vicar, the next day, and likely hand delivered this letter dealing with issues between them. Walker was one of a group of Evangelical clergy (that within a year or so would include CW) who insisted on canonical conformity to the Church of England and believed that itinerant preaching violated the canons of the Church and perhaps the laws of the realm, specifically the Toleration Act of 1689. In addition to addressing specific issues that Walker raised, JW pleads for Walker to allow people in his parish to identify themselves voluntarily with the Wesleyan societies and to hear Wesley and other preachers sent by the Wesleyan Conference. JW sent a similar appeal to Henry Venn on June 22, 1763.

2. 'If you believed Mr. Vowler[71] to be a gracious person and a gospel minister, why did you not in justice to your people leave them to him?'

John Hingeston assured me that Mr. Vowler also had a clear conviction of his being reconciled to God. If so, I could not deny his being a gracious person; and I heard him preach the *true* though not the *whole* gospel. But had it been the whole, there are several reasons still why I did not give up the people to him. 1) No one mentioned or intimated any such thing, nor did it once enter into my thought. But if it had, 2) I do not know that everyone who preaches the truth has wisdom and experience to guide and govern a flock. I do not know that Mr. Vowler in particular has. He may or he may not. 3) I do not know whether he could or would give that flock all the advantages for holiness which they now enjoy, and to leave them to him before I was assured of this would be neither justice nor mercy. 4) Unless they were also assured of this, they could not in conscience give up themselves to him, and I have neither right nor power to dispose of them contrary to their conscience.

'But they are his already by legal establishment.' If they receive the sacrament from him thrice a year and attend his ministrations on the Lord's Day, I see no more which the law requires. But to go a little deeper into this matter of 'legal establishment', does Mr. Conon[72] or you think that the King and Parliament have a right to prescribe to me what pastor I shall use? If they prescribe one which I know God never sent, am I obliged to receive him? If he be sent of God, can I receive him with a clear conscience till I *know* he is? And even when I do, if I believe my former pastor is more profitable to my soul, can I leave him without sin? Or has any man living a right to require this of me?

I 'extend this to every gospel minister in England'. Before I could with a clear conscience leave the Methodist society even to such an one, all these considerations must come in.

And with regard to the people, far from thinking that 'the withdrawing our preachers' from such a society without their consent would prevent a separation from the Church, I think it would be the direct way to cause it.[73] While we are with them, our advice has

---

[71] James Vowler (d. 1758), whose 'thundering sermons' Wesley had heard at St. Agnes a fortnight before, on Sept. 4, 1757; see JW, *Journal* (21:122 in this edn.). See also a biographical notice about James Vowler in the *Christian Observer* (1877): 232–33.

[72] George Conon was the master of Truro Grammar School and had been influential in Samuel Walker's conversion; see *WHS* 28 (1952): 106, n. 1; and 21:25, n. 95 in this edn.

[73] JW is pleading with Walker not to reject Wesleyan itinerant preachers who visit his area.

weight and keeps them to the Church. But were we totally to withdraw, it would be of little or no weight. Nay, perhaps resentment of our unkindness (as it would probably appear to them) would prompt them to act in flat opposition to it. 'And will it not be the same at your death?' I believe not. For there will be no resentment 5
in this case, and the last advice of a dying friend is not likely to be so soon forgotten.

3. But 'was there no inconsistency in your visiting Mr. Vowler as a gospel minister when you do not give up your people to him?' No. My receiving him as a gospel minister did not imply any obligation 10
so to do.

4. 'If that was not the design of your visit, you should not have visited him at all.' Does that follow? I visited him because he desired it, as a brother and fellow labourer.

5. 'Does not this conduct on the whole savour of a party spirit 15
and show a desire to please the Methodists as Methodists?' I am not conscious of any such spirit, or of any desire but that of pleasing all men for their good to edification. I have as great a desire thus to please you as any Methodist under heaven.

You add one thing more, which is of deep importance and de- 20
serves a particular consideration. 'You spoke to Mr. Vowler of your being as one man. Nothing is so desirable. But really before it can be effected, something must be done on your part more than paying us visits; which, as far as I can see, can serve no other purpose in the present circumstances than to bring us under needless 25
difficulties.'

I did indeed speak to Mr. Vowler of our being as one man. And not to him only, but to several others, for it lay much upon my heart. Accordingly I proposed that question to all who met at our late Conference, 'What can be done in order to a close union with 30
the clergy who preach the truth?'[74] We all agreed that nothing could be more desirable. I in particular have long desired it, not from any view to my own ease or honour or temporal convenience in any kind, but because I was deeply convinced it might be a blessing to my own soul and a means of increasing the general work of God. 35

But you say, 'Really, before it can be effected, something must be done on your part.' Tell me what, and I will do it without delay, however contrary it may be to my ease or natural inclination, provided only that it consists with my keeping a conscience void of offence

---

[74] The Conference had met in London beginning on August 4, but no detailed minutes have survived; cf. 10:279 in this edn.

toward God and toward man. It would not consist with this to give up the flock under my care to any other minister, till I and they were convinced they would have the same advantages for holiness under him which they now enjoy.

5 But 'paying us visits can serve no other purpose than to bring us under needless difficulties.' I will speak very freely on this head. Can our conversing together serve 'no other purpose'? You seem then not to have the least conception of *your own* wanting any such thing! But whether you do or not, I feel I do. I am not in *memet totus teres atque* 10 *rotundus.*[75] I want more light, more strength, for my personal walking with God; and I know not but he may give it me through you. And (whether you do or no) I want more light and strength for guiding the flock committed to my charge. May not the Lord send this also by whom he will send? And by you as probably as by any other? 15 It is not improbable that he may by you give me clearer light, either as to doctrine or discipline. And even hereby how much comfort and profit might redound to thousands of those for whom Christ hath died? Which, I apprehend would fully compensate any 'difficulties' that might arise from such conversation.

20 But what difficulties are those? All that are the necessary consequence of your sharing our reproach. And what reproach is it which we bear? Is it the reproach of Christ or not? It arose first while my brother and I were at Oxford, from our endeavouring to be real Christians. It was increased abundantly when we began to preach 25 repentance and remission of sins and insist that we are justified by faith. For this cause were we excluded from preaching in the churches. (I say for *this*—as yet there was no field-preaching.) And this exclusion occasioned our preaching elsewhere, with the other irregularities that followed. Therefore all the reproach consequent 30 thereon is no other than the reproach of Christ.

And what are we the worse for this? It is not pleasing to flesh and blood. But is it any hindrance to the work of God? Did he work more by us when we were honourable men? By no means. God never used us to any purpose till we were a proverb of reproach. Nor have 35 we now a jot more of dishonour, of evil report, than we know is necessary, both for us and for the people to balance that honour and good report which otherwise could not be borne.

You need not, therefore, be so much afraid of or so careful to avoid this. It is a precious balm. It will not break your head, neither 40 lessen your usefulness. And, indeed, you cannot avoid it any other-

---

[75] Cf. Horace, *Satires* II.vii.86; 'complete in himself, a smooth, rounded sphere'.

wise than by departing from the work. You do not avoid it by standing aloof from us; which you call *christian*, I *worldly*, prudence.
I speak as a fool. Bear with me.[76] I am clearly satisfied that you have
far more faith, more love, and more of the mind which was in Christ
than I have. But have you more gifts for the work of God or more   5
fruit of your labour? Has God owned you more? I would he had a
thousand-fold! I pray God that he may! Have you at present more experience of the wisdom of the world and the devices of Satan? Or of
the manner and method wherein it pleases God to counterwork them
in this period of his providence? Are you sure God would add noth-   10
ing to you by me beside what he might add to me by you? Perhaps
when the time is slipped out of your hands, when I am no more seen,
you may wish you had not rejected the assistance of even
    Your affectionate brother,

                                        J. W.   15

Address: 'To/ the Revd Mr Walker / In Truro'.
No *postmark* or indications of postal *charge*; apparently delivered by hand.
Endorsement: 'JW to SW Sep. 19th 1757'.
Source: holograph; MARC, MAM JW 5/38. Wesley published a transcrip-
    tion with only minor variants in *Arminian Magazine* 3 (1780): 48–54.

To an Unidentified Man[77]

                                   TRURO
                       SEPTEMBER 20, 1757

Dear Sir,
    The longer I am absent from London, and the more I attend the
service of the Church in other places, the more I am convinced   20
of the unspeakable advantage which the people called Methodists
enjoy. I mean even with regard to public worship, particularly on
the Lord's Day.[78] The church where they assemble is not gay or

---

[76] See 2 Cor. 11:1.

[77] This letter stands in striking contrast to the letter of the previous day to Rev. Samuel
Walker, where JW stressed his encouragement of Methodists to attend Church of England
worship. While the recipient is not named, Ebenezer Blackwell is a likely candidate.

[78] This description of formal Methodist worship focuses on the West Street Chapel (that
JW and his brother CW leased in 1743), which had an altar consecrated in its medieval past that
allowed them to celebrate the Lord's Supper within the canonical boundaries of the Church
of England.

splendid, which might be an hindrance on the one hand; nor sordid
or dirty, which might give distaste on the other; but plain as well as
clean. The persons who assemble there are not a gay, giddy crowd,
who come chiefly to see and be seen; nor a company of goodly, for-
5   mal, outside Christians, whose religion lies in a dull round of duties; but a people most of whom know, and the rest earnestly seek, to
worship God in spirit and in truth. Accordingly they do not spend
their time there in bowing and courtesying, or in staring about
them, but in looking upward and looking inward, in hearkening to
10   the voice of God, and pouring out their hearts before him.

It is also no small advantage that the person who reads prayers
(though not always the same) yet is always one who may be supposed to speak from his heart,[79] one whose life is no reproach to his
profession, and one who performs that solemn part of divine ser-
15   vice, not in a careless, hurrying, slovenly manner, but seriously and
slowly, as becomes him who is transacting so high an affair between
God and man.

Nor is their solemn addresses to God interrupted either by the
formal drawl of a parish clerk, the screaming of boys who bawl out
20   what they neither feel nor understand, or the unseasonable and unmeaning impertinence of a voluntary on the organ.[80] When it is seasonable to sing praise to God, they do it with the spirit and with the
understanding also; not in the miserable, scandalous doggerel of
Hopkins and Sternhold,[81] but in psalms and hymns which are both
25   sense and poetry,[82] such as would sooner provoke a critic to turn
Christian than a Christian to turn critic.[83] What they sing is there-

[79] JW is not here contrasting extemporary prayer (in Puritan fashion) with reading from
the Book of Common Prayer. He is instead stressing the manner in which prayers are read from
the BCP at West Street Chapel.

[80] JW occasionally affirmed the use of organs in church services, but generally disap-
proved of voluntaries. His *Journal* for Easter Sunday, April 7, 1751, noted, 'After preaching I
went to the new church and found an uncommon blessing at a time when I least of all expected
it, namely, whilst the organist was playing a voluntary!' (20:382 in this edn.). Cf. Samuel J. Ro-
gal, 'John Wesley and the Organ: The Superfluous Pipes,' in *Church Music* 74:2 (1974): 27–31.

[81] Thomas Sternhold, John Hopkins, and others, *The Whole Book of Psalms Collected into
English Metre* (London,1562); a collection of Psalms in 'common metre' that was used broadly
in Church of England worship at the time.

[82] I.e., using JW's *Collection of Psalms and Hymns* (that had grown through several editions to an enduring form in 1744), which was designed for formal worship, in comparison to
the various volumes he also published of *Hymns and Sacred Poems* for broader Methodist use.

[83] In 1738 John Byrom had written a similar line to CW, 'I do not at all desire to discourage your publication. But when you tell me that you write not for the critic but for the Christian, it occurs to my mind that you might as well write for both, or in such a manner that the
critic may by your writing be moved to turn Christian, rather than the Christian turn critic'
(letter of Mar. 3, 1738; in Richard Parkinson, ed., *The Private Journal and Literary Remains of
John Byrom* [Manchester, 1856], 2:196).

fore a proper continuation of the spiritual and reasonable service; being selected for that end (not by a poor humdrum wretch who can scarce read what he drones out with such an air of importance) but by one who knows what he is about and how to connect the preceding with the following part of the service. Nor does he take just 'two staves',[84] but more or less, as may best raise the soul to God; especially when sung in well-composed and well-adapted tones not by a handful of wild, unawakened striplings, but by a whole serious congregation; and then not lolling at ease, or in the indecent posture of sitting drawling out one word after another, but all standing before God, and praising him lustily and with a good courage.

Nor is it a little advantage as to the next part of the service to hear a preacher whom you know to live as he speaks, speaking the genuine gospel of present salvation through faith, wrought in the heart by the Holy Ghost, declaring present, free, full justification, and enforcing every branch of inward and outward holiness. And this you hear done in the most clear, plain, simple, unaffected language, yet with an earnestness becoming the importance of the subject and with the demonstration of the Spirit.

With regard to the last and most awful[85] part of divine service, the celebration of the Lord's Supper, although we cannot say that either the unworthiness of the minister or the unholiness of some of the communicants deprives the rest of a blessing from God, yet do they greatly lessen the comfort of receiving.[86] But these discouragements are removed from you. You have proof that he who administers fears God, and you have no reason to believe that any of your fellow communicants walk unworthy of their profession. Add to that the whole service is performed in a decent and solemn

---

[84] Although 'two staves' might appear to refer to musical harmony (i.e., music with a melody and figured bass written out), it is more likely that JW is using 'stave' in the archaic sense of a 'line of verse'. It was customary for a parish clerk to 'line out' the words of a metrical psalm for parishioners to sing. JW's point would be, then, that the careful leader does not simply give out two lines at a time, but whatever length of lines is appropriate to convey the sense of the lines to the congregants before they sing them. I am indebted to Dr. Nicholas Temperley for this insight into the meaning of 'staves'.

[85] I.e., most solemn, or 'full of awe'.

[86] In the fourth century Donatist controversy, St. Augustine decisively rejected the suggestion that the validity of the sacraments was dependent upon the worthiness of ministers or celebrants, by stressing the faithfulness of Christ as their ultimate source. Augustine's stance was formally endorsed in the Twenty-sixth Article of Religion of the Church of England. Thus JW treads carefully here, arguing that while a minister's unworthiness may not invalidate the efficacy of the sacrament, it is nevertheless of comfort to recipients to believe that the ministers of the sacrament and other recipients reflect appropriate Christian holiness.

manner, is enlivened by hymns suitable to the occasion, and concluded with prayer that comes not out of feigned lips.

Surely then, of all the people in Great Britain, the Methodists would be the most inexcusable should they let any opportunity slip
5   of attending that worship which has so many advantages, should they prefer any before it, or not continually improve by the advantages they enjoy! What can be pleaded for them if they do not worship God in spirit and in truth,[87] if they are still outward worshippers only, approaching God with their lips while their hearts are far
10   from him?[88] Yea, if, having known him, they do not daily grow in grace and in the knowledge of our Lord Jesus Christ?[89]

J. W.

Source: published transcription; *Arminian Magazine* 3 (1780): 101–3.

To Dorothy Furly

St. Austell, Cornwall
15   September 25, 1757

My Dear Sister,
It is a rule with me to take nothing ill that is well meant. Therefore you have no need ever to be afraid of my putting an ill construction on anything you say, for I know you mean only to save your soul. In
20   most genteel, religious people there is so strange a mixture that I have seldom much confidence in them. I love the poor; in many of them I find pure, genuine grace, unmixed with paint, folly, and affectation. But I think Mrs. Gaussen is upright of heart, and perhaps you may find one or two gentlewomen like her.[90]
25   It is plain God sees it best for you frequently to walk in a thorny path. By this means he aims at destroying your pride of heart, and breaking your stubborn will. You have had large experience that there is no substantial or lasting happiness but in him. O be true to yourself and to your own experience. Do not seek it where it cannot

---

[87] See John 4:24.
[88] See Isa. 29:13; Matt. 15:8.
[89] See 2 Pet. 3:18.
[90] On Mrs. Gaussen, see JW's letter to Dorothy Furly, June 18, 1757.

be found. Hew out to yourself no more broken cisterns,[91] but let all the springs of your happiness be in him.

You cannot be too careful to keep out of the way of anything that has been the occasion of sin. And it is very possible to show civility and moderate respect to any person without coming in the way of danger. All private conversation may be avoided, and ought to be, at all hazards. Do not run yourself into temptation, and God will deliver you from evil.

Nature and the devil will always oppose private prayer, but it is worthwhile to break through. That it is a cross will not hinder its being a blessing; nay, often the more reluctance, the greater blessing.

I think it was not you who advised poor Sam to be a *mere regular* clergyman,[92] unconnected with the Methodists. Certainly this is the best way to preferment; but it is not the best way to heaven, or to do good upon each. When it is too late, the awakened clergy will probably see this.

I am,
>   Your affectionate brother,

>>>>   J. Wesley

Source: published transcription; Benson, *Works*, 16:319–20.

To Samuel Furly

K<small>INGSWOOD</small>
O<small>CTOBER</small> 14, 1757

Dear Sammy,

In the sermon on 'Justification by Faith' (in the first volume of *Sermons*[93]) my sentiments are expressed at large. There is certainly no such assertion in Scripture as 'The righteousness of Christ is imputed to us'. Yet we will not deny it if men only mean thereby that 'we are accepted through his merits' or 'for the sake of what

---

[91] See Jer. 2:13.

[92] Her brother Samuel Furly; cf. JW's letter of Apr. 8, 1758 to Samuel Furly in which he offers to recommend Furly for ordination.

[93] I.e., Sermon 5, 'Justification by Faith', 1:182–99 in this edn.

he has done and suffered for us'. If they mean anything more, we cannot but deny it.

Mr. Hervey[94] is a deeply-rooted antinomian, that is, a Calvinist consistent with himself (which Mr. Whitefield is not, nor Robert
5 Bolton,[95] nor any Calvinist who is not an antinomian). But in truth *ornatus est pro suis instratibus*,[96] by the Scotch writer of the *Letters to the Author of 'Theron and Aspasio'*,[97] a man of admirable sense and learning, but a Calvinist and antinomian to the bone, as you may judge from his vehement anger at Messrs. Erskine,[98] Cudworth,[99]
10 and Hervey for their *legality*! I am,
     Your affectionate brother,

          J. Wesley

Source: holograph; MARC, MA 1995/020 (address portion missing).

To Dorothy Furly

BRISTOL
OCTOBER 21, 1757
15

My Dear Sister,

God will do his own work in his own manner, and exceeding variously in different persons. It matters not whether it be wrought in a more pleasing or painful manner, so it is wrought; so nature is
20 subdued, pride and self-will dethroned, and the will of God done in us and by us. Therefore trouble not yourself about the experience of others. God knows *you*, and let him do with you as he sees best.

---

[94] Rev. James Hervey; on whom, see 25:581 in this edn.

[95] Robert Bolton (1572–1631); JW included a number of Bolton's writings in *Christian Library*, 7:160–9:193.

[96] 'He is adorned by his own trappings.'

[97] In June 1757 Robert Sandeman published (under a pseudonym 'Palaemon') a set of *Letters on 'Theron and Aspasio'*. JW had just read this volume and was busy preparing a *Sufficient Answer*; see 13:345–56 in this edn.

[98] John Erskine (1721–1803), an evangelical clergyman of the Church of Scotland, staunchly Calvinist in theology; see JW's letter to Erskine of Apr. 24, 1765. See *ODNB*.

[99] William Cudworth (1717–63), a preacher associated with George Whitefield and the Calvinist Methodists for a time, before turning Independent.

I judge your late distress to be partly the effect of disease, but chiefly preternatural. In the third *Journal* there is a case nearly parallel, only the symptoms were more severe. For in a moment, Lucretia Smith felt such a cloud spread over her that she could not believe there was a God or an after-state.[100] You did right to pray, as you could pray, and this is the best method which can be taken in heaviness or darkness of any kind. Then, if sin be the cause, it will be discovered. But take care that you do not refuse any help. Even rough speakers may be of service. Only spread what they say before the Lord, and he will turn it to good.

I am,

    Your affectionate brother,

J. Wesley

Source: published transcription; Benson, *Works*, 16:320–21.

To Sarah Ryan[101]

NEWBURY
NOVEMBER 8, 1757

My Dear Sister,

In the hurry of business I had not time to write down what you desired—the rules of our family.[102] So I snatch a few minutes to do

---

[100] Cf. JW, *Journal*, Dec. 24, 1740, 19:175 in this edn.

[101] Sarah Ryan (1724–68), maiden name unknown, was spiritually awakened under Whitefield's preaching at age seventeen. She married about age twenty, but was soon deserted by her husband. About eighteen months later she married a sailor named Ryan, who may have been abusive during his times home from the sea. Through the influence of the wife of the sailor's captain, who was a Methodist, Ryan began attending JW's Foundery in London. She participated in a class meeting and established a friendship with Sarah Crosby. In 1754 she experienced a strong spiritual renewal. Over the next year, partly in conversation with JW, she decided not to follow her husband to New England, where he had moved (see *AM* 2 [1779]: 296–310).

In 1757 JW appointed Ryan housekeeper at the Kingswood School in Bristol. Ryan's letter of Aug. 10 accepting this position is the second surviving item in their correspondence. Ryan was one of JW's most spiritually intimate correspondents, provoking the jealousy of his wife Mary when she intercepted a letter of JW to Ryan (see the letters of Jan. 20 and 27, 1758). By 1762 Ryan had left Bristol, and spent her final years working closely with Mary Bosanquet in ministering to orphans.

[102] That is, the students and staff living together at Kingswood School.

it now, and the more cheerfully because I know you will observe them.

1. The family rises, part at four, part at half an hour after.

2. They breakfast at seven, dine at twelve, and sup at six.

3. They spend the hour from five to six in the evening (after a little joint prayer) in private.

4. They pray together at nine, and then retire to their chambers, so that all are in bed before ten.

5. They observe all Fridays in the year as days of fasting or abstinence.

You in particular I advise, suffer no impertinent visitant, no unprofitable conversation, in the house. It is a city set upon an hill, and all that is in it should be 'holiness to the Lord'.[103]

On what a pinnacle do you stand! You are placed in the eye of all the world, friends and enemies. You have no experience of these things, no knowledge of the people, no advantages of education, not large natural abilities, and are but a novice, as it were, in the ways of God! It requires all the omnipotent love of God to preserve you in your present station. Stand fast in the Lord, and in the power of his might![104] Show that nothing is too hard for him. Take to thee the whole armour of God,[105] and do and suffer all things through Christ strengthening thee.[106] If you continue teachable and advisable, I know nothing that shall be able to hurt you.

Your affectionate brother,

[John Wesley]

Source: published transcription; Jackson, *Works* (3rd), 12:201–2.

---

[103] Zech. 14:20.
[104] See Eph. 6:10.
[105] See Eph. 6:11.
[106] See Phil. 4:13.

To Sarah Ryan[107]

NORWICH
NOVEMBER 22, 1757

My Dear Sister,

May the peace and love of God spring up in your heart as in time past, and more abundantly! You have refreshed my bowels in the Lord. I feel your words, and praise God on your behalf. I not only excuse but love your simplicity; and whatever freedom you use, it will be welcome.

Surely God will never suffer me to be ashamed of my confidence in you. I have been censured for it by some of your nearest friends, but I cannot repent of it.[108] Will not you put forth all your strength (which indeed is not yours, it is the Spirit of the Father which now worketh in you): 1) in managing all things pertaining to the house, so as to adorn the gospel of God our Saviour? 2) in feeding the sheep he has committed to your immediate care, and carrying the weak and sickly in your bosom? 3) in assisting, quickening, and directing the family at Kingswood, whom I trust you will always bear upon your heart? 4) in reproving, stirring up, or confirming all whom the providence of God shall put into your hands? And lastly, [5)] in watching over and helping forward in the ways of God one who has more need of help than all the rest, and who is always willing to receive it from *you*, because you always speak the truth in love?

Do you find no interruption or abatement at any time of your joy in the Lord?[109] Do you continually see God, and that without any cloud or darkness or mist between? Do you pray without ceasing,[110] without ever being diverted from it by anything inward or outward? Are you never hindered by any person or thing? By the power or subtlety of Satan, or by the weakness or disorders of the body pressing down the soul? Can you be thankful for everything

---

[107] Replying to Ryan's letter of Nov. 13.

[108] Mary Wesley and others had questioned the propriety of appointing a woman with such a reputation as that of Sarah Ryan to the important role at Kingswood. See the introductory note on the previous letter.

[109] These are typical questions that JW addressed to those who had claimed Christian perfection, or being saved from all sin (see his letter to Ryan of Nov. 30). He was not trying to call their claim into question, but seeking to understand this experience of God's gracious work.

[110] See 1 Thess. 5:17.

without exception?[111] And do you feel all working together for good?[112] Do you do nothing, great or small, merely to please yourself? Do you feel no touch of any desire or affection, but what springs from the pure love of God? Do you speak no words but
5   from a principle of love and under the guidance of his Spirit? O how I long to find you unblameable in all things, and holy as he that hath called you is holy![113]

I am,

Yours, etc.,

J. W.
10

Source: published transcription; *Arminian Magazine* 5 (1782): 46–47.

To Sarah Ryan[114]

LONDON
NOVEMBER 30, 1757

My Dear Sister,

Your letter came in a seasonable time, as rain in a time of drought.
15   How fain would we excuse those we love! I would gladly acquit those who severely condemn each other. The wrong to myself is not worth a thought; it gives me not a moment's uneasiness. But I am pained for others, who, if they do not sin against God, yet give great occasion to the enemy to blaspheme.[115]
20   You may learn an excellent lesson herefrom. Suppose you are saved from sin, it is certain that you are not saved from a possibility of mistake. On this side, therefore, Satan may assault you. You may be deceived either as to persons or things. You may think better or (which is far more strange) you may think worse of them than they

---

[111] See 1 Thess. 5:18.
[112] See Rom. 8:28.
[113] See 1 Pet. 1:15.
[114] Replying to Ryan's letter of Nov. 29.
[115] JW was currently mediating a disturbance in the London society over 'some imprudent words spoken by one who seemed to be strong in the faith', which had become a case where 'one side flatly affirmed, the other flatly denied'; see JW, *Journal*, Nov. 26–30, 1757, 21:132 in this edn.

deserve. And hence words or actions may spring which, if not sinful in *you*, are certainly wrong in themselves, and which will and must appear sinful to those who cannot read your heart. What grievous inconvenience would ensue! How would the good that is in you be evil spoken of! How would the great gift of God be doubted of, if 5 not disbelieved and denied for your cause! Therefore in the name of God I exhort you, keep close every moment to the unction of the Holy One! Attend to the still, small voice![116] Beware of hearkening to the voice of a stranger! My eyes ache, my head aches, my heart aches. And yet I know not when to have done. O speak nothing, act 10 nothing, think nothing, but as you are taught of God!

> Still may he with your weakness stay,
>   Nor for a moment's space depart;
> Evil and danger turn away, 15
>   And keep your hand, your tongue, your heart.[117]

So shall you always comfort, not grieve,
  Your affectionate brother,

20
          J. W.

Source: published transcription; *Arminian Magazine* 5 (1782): 101–2.

To Walter Sellon[118]

LONDON
DECEMBER 1, 1757

My Dear Brother,
    If only one stone were removed out of the way, the thing might be 25 immediately effected. Only prevail upon John Brandon[119] to spend a month or two in London or any other part of England, and I will immediately send another preacher to Leicester, Ashby, and the

---

[116] See 1 Kgs. 19:12.

[117] CW, Hymn on 2 Tim. 4:5, st. 3, *HSP* (1742), 217.

[118] On Walter Sellon, see 26:121 in this edn.

[119] John Brandon of Leicester, who had apparently just begun to itinerate, though official lists are spotty until 1765, where he appears (see 10:304 in this edn.).

adjacent places. But during the present scarcity of labourers we cannot spare a second for that small circuit, till you spare us the first.

5 It is surprising that, from one end of the land to the other, so little good is done in a regular way. What have you to do but to follow that way which the providence of God points out? And when they drive you from Smisby, you know where to have both employment and the things needful for the body. I think also it will be highly profit-able for your soul to be near those who have more experience in the 10 ways of God. I am,
Your affectionate brother,

J. Wesley

Source: nineteenth-century transcription; MARC, MA 1977/487; appar-ent source for Jackson, *Works* (3rd), 14:200–201.

To Sarah Ryan[120]

LEWISHAM
15   DECEMBER 14, 1757

My Dear Sister,
I find by Mr. P—n's[121] last letter that he is deeply offended, that his former affection (so he speaks) 'is degenerated into a cold es-teem, and that he no longer regards me as a dear friend, but as an 20 austere master'. Has he not a little affected *you*? He does not speak with passion, but his words distil as the dew. The God whom you serve send forth his light and his truth, and direct you in every thought!
Do you never find any *wandering thoughts* in prayer?[122] Or useless 25 thoughts at other seasons? Does the corruptible body never press

---

[120] Replying to Ryan's letter of Dec. 13.

[121] Thus the reading in *AM*. Telford (*Letters*, 3:243) substitutes 'Perronet' with no expla-nation, but the degree of alienation between JW and both Charles and Edward Perronet at this point was such that one doubts they would even speak of 'cold esteem' for Wesley.

[122] This was one of the more debated issues among those claiming Christian perfection. JW eventually devoted an entire sermon to it: Sermon 41, *Wandering Thoughts*, 2:125–37 in this edn.

down the soul, and make it muse about useless things? Have you so great a command over your imagination as to keep out all unprofitable images? At least to banish them the moment they appear, so that they neither trouble nor sully your soul? Do you find every *reasoning* brought into captivity to the obedience of Christ? Is there no vanity or folly in your *dreams?* No temptation that almost overcomes you? And are you then as sensible of the presence of God, and as full of prayer, as when you are waking?

I can hardly avoid trembling for you still. Upon what a pinnacle do you stand! Perhaps few persons in England have been in so dangerous a situation as you are now.[123] I know not whether any other was ever so regarded both by my brother and me at the same time. What can I do to help you? The Father of mercies help you, and with his favourable kindness surround you on every side! May the eternal Spirit help you in every thought, word, and work to serve the living God! I am,

  Your affectionate brother,

J. W.

Source: published transcription; *Arminian Magazine* 5 (1782): 155–56.

---

[123] JW may be referring to Ryan's informing him that she had received a letter from a woman (Mary Wesley?) who had seen the last letter that he had sent Ryan.

1758

To Thomas Foulkes[1]

[c. 1758][2]

My Dear Brother,

The glory of the Wesleyan Methodists is not to dispute with anybody concerning their opinion. We know that the kingdom of
5　heaven is not meat and drink, nor opinions of any sort. What we need is that mind which was in Christ, to teach us to walk as Christ walked. But one cannot lay hold on this except by a life of constant and complete self-denial. There is a great danger of your being inconstant in this, unless you have vigilant Christians about you.
10　In Chester you would certainly enjoy such; how it is at Bala I know not.

The best books I know for one in your situation are *Serious Call* and *Christian Perfection* by Mr. Law; I mean the abbreviated edition of them which I published years ago. I am grateful to you for the
15　note you sent in your letter. David is poor enough, but he is increasing in grace. Let us safeguard that matter, and all will be well. I am,
　　　Your affectionate friend,

　　　　　　　　　　　　　　　　　　J. Wesley

Source: published transcription; an English translation by Griffith T. Roberts (*WHS* 31 [1957]: 197) of a Welsh translation (in *Yr Eurgrawn Wesleyaidd* [1829]: 366) of an originally English letter that has not survived.

---

[1] Thomas Foulkes (1731–1802), a native of Llandrillo, Merionethshire (Meirionnydd), had a conversion experience and became a member of a Wesleyan society at Neston in Cheshire, c. 1756. On his return to Wales in 1757 or 1758 he joined a Calvinistic Methodist society at Bala, but remained a member of the Wesleyan society at Chester. See Robert Thomas Jenkins, "Foulk(e)s, Thomas," in *Welsh Biography Online*.

[2] Griffith T. Roberts suggested that JW's letter to Foulkes was written soon after Foulkes's return to Wales, hence its placement at the beginning of 1758 in this edn.

To George Merryweather[3]

LONDON
JANUARY 16, 1758

My Dear Brother,

If the work of God does so increase at Yarm, we must not let the opportunity slip. Therefore let the travelling preacher be there either every Sunday evening, or at least every other Sunday. 5

No person must be allowed to preach or exhort among our people whose life is not holy and unblameable, nor any who asserts anything contrary to the gospel which we have received.[4] And if he does not own his fault and amend it, he cannot be a leader any longer. 10

Peace be with you all. I am,
Your affectionate brother,

J. Wesley

Address: 'To / Mr George Merryweather / In Yarm / Yorkshire'.
Postmark: '17/IA'. *Charge*: '4'.
Endorsement: 'Jany 1758'.
Source: holograph; Wesley's Chapel (London), LDWMM 1992/410/1.

To Sarah Ryan[5]

[LONDON]
JANUARY 20, 1758 15

My Dear Sister,

How did you feel yourself under your late trial? Did you find no stirring of resentment, no remains of your own will, no desire or wish that things should be otherwise? In one sense you *do* desire it, because you desire that God should be glorified in all things. But 20 did not the falling short of that desire lessen your happiness? Had

---

[3] This letter initiates John Wesley's correspondence with George Merryweather, a merchant of Yarm whom Wesley had known since at least 1748 when Merryweather invited Wesley to preach there; see Vickers, *Dictionary*, 229–30.

[4] See Gal. 1:8–9.

[5] This is not a direct response to Ryan's letter of Dec. 20, 1757, because JW was in Bristol from Dec. 25, 1757 through Jan. 12, 1758. Their correspondence resumes now that he has departed.

you still the same degree of communion with God, the same joy in
the Holy Ghost? I never saw you so much moved as you appeared
to be that evening. Your soul was then greatly troubled, and a variety of conflicting passions—love, sorrow, desire, with a kind of de-
5   spair—were easy to be read in your countenance. And was not your
heart unhinged at all? Was it not ruffled or discomposed? Was your
soul all the time calmly stayed on God, waiting upon him without
distraction? Perhaps one end of this close trial was to give you a
deeper knowledge of yourself and of God, of his power to save, and
10   of the salvation he hath wrought in you.

Most of the trials you have lately met with have been of another
kind, but it is expedient for you to go through both evil and good
report. The conversing with you, either by speaking or writing, is
an unspeakable blessing to me. I cannot think of you without think-
15   ing of God. Others often lead me to him, but it is, as it were, going
round about; you bring me straight into his presence.[6] Therefore,
whoever warns me against trusting you, I cannot refrain, as I am
clearly convinced he calls me to it.

I am,
20   Your affectionate brother,

J. W.

Source: published transcription; *Arminian Magazine* 5 (1782): 214–15.

To Sarah Ryan[7]

[LONDON]
JANUARY 27, 1758

My Dear Sister,
25   Last Friday,[8] after many severe words, my ———[9] left me, vowing
she would see me no more. As I had wrote to you the same morn-

---

[6] The depth of spiritual intimacy expressed in this letter stands in contrast with the
business-like tone JW struck in letters to his wife Mary in this period. Mary Wesley intercepted
this very letter, and her reading it was a key event leading to the separation between Mary and
JW (see JW to Ryan, Jan. 27).

[7] JW had clearly not received Ryan's response to his letter dated Jan. 20; she wrote her
response the same day as the current letter.

[8] I.e., Jan. 20.

[9] JW discreetly omits the identification of his wife, Mary Wesley, in this published version.

ing, I began to reason with myself till I almost doubted whether I had done well in writing or whether I ought to write to you at all. After prayer that doubt was taken away, yet I was almost sorry that I had written that morning. In the evening, while I was preaching at the chapel, she came into the chamber where I had left my clothes, searched my pockets, and found the letter there which I had finished but had not sealed. While she read it, God broke her heart, and I afterwards found her in such a temper as I have not seen her in for several years. She has continued in the same ever since. So I think God has given a sufficient answer with regard to our writing to each other.

I still feel some fear concerning you. How have you found yourself since we parted? Have you suffered no loss by anything? Has nothing damped the vigour of your spirit? Is honour a blessing, and dishonour too? The frowns and smiles of men? Are you one and the same in ease or pain, always attentive to the voice of God? What kind of humility do you feel? What have you to humble you, if you have no sin?[10] Are you wise in the manner of spending your time? Do you employ it all, not only well, but as well as it is possible? What time have you for reading? I want you to live like an angel here below, or rather like the Son of God. Woman, walk thou as Christ walked; then you cannot but love and pray for,

Your affectionate brother,

J. W.

Source: published transcription; *Arminian Magazine* 5 (1782): 268–69.

To Dorothy Furly

Lewisham,
February 9, 1758

Undoubtedly you may arise now and receive power from on high. You are hindered chiefly by not understanding the *freeness* of the

---

[10] Once again JW probes Ryan's experience in light of her claim to entire sanctification (see the letters of Nov. 22 & Dec. 14, 1757; and several that follow), which JW understood to include no longer committing sin in the specific sense of 'a voluntary transgression of a known law of God'; cf. JW, 'Thoughts on Christian Perfection' (1760), Q. 6, 13:61–62 in this edn.

gift of God. You are perpetually seeking for something in yourself to move him to love and bless you. But it is not to be found there. It is in himself and in the Son of his love. He did *then* give you a proof of this in that fresh evidence of pardon, and he is ready to give it you again today, for he is not weary of well doing. But even after this you may or you may not use the power which attends that peace. And if you ask for more power, it shall be given you; for you have an Advocate with the Father.[11] O cast yourself upon him. Learn more of that lesson,

> Thy salvation to obtain,
> Out of myself I go;
> Freely thou must heal my pain,
> Thy unbought mercy show.[12]

How much of it may you find in this hour! Look up and see redemption near!
    I am,
        Your affectionate brother and servant,

                            J. Wesley

Source: published transcription; Benson, *Works*, 16:321–22.

To Sarah Ryan[13]

London
February 10, 1758

My Dear Sister,
    Your last letter was seasonable indeed. I was growing faint in my mind. The being continually watched over for evil; the having every word I spoke, every action I did (small and great) watched over with no friendly eye; the hearing a thousand little, tart, unkind reflections in return for the kindest words I could devise,

---

[11] See 1 John 2:1.
[12] CW, Hymn on John 1:29, st. 5, *HSP* (1742), 28.
[13] Replying to her letter of Feb. 1.

Like drops of eating water on the marble,
At length have worn my sinking spirits down.[14]

Yet I could not say, 'Take thy plague away from me.'[15] But only,
'Let me be purified, not consumed.'[16]   5
What kind of humility do you feel? Is it a sense of sinfulness? Is it
not a sense of helplessness, of dependence, of emptiness, and, as it
were, nothingness? How do you look back on your past sins, either
of heart or life? What tempers or passions do you feel while you
are employed in these reflections? Do you feel nothing like pride   10
while you are comparing your present with your past state, or while
persons are showing their approbation of or esteem for you? How
is it that you are so frequently charged with pride? Are you careful
to abstain from the appearance of it? O how important are all your
steps! The Lord God guide and support you every moment!   15
    I am,
        Yours, etc.,

                                                        J. W.

Source: published transcription; *Arminian Magazine* 5 (1782): 381–82.

To Sarah Ryan[17]

MALDON
FEBRUARY 20, 1758   20

My Dear Sister,
    Is your eye altogether single? Is your heart entirely pure? I know
you gave up the whole to God once, but do you stand to the gift?
Once your will was swallowed up in God's, but is it now, and will
it be so always? The whole Spirit and power of God be upon you,   25

---

[14] Cf. Nicolas Rowe, *Tamerlane: A Tragedy* (1701), Act IV, Scene I; JW has substituted 'sinking spirits' for Rowe's 'boasted courage'.

[15] Ps. 39:11 (BCP).

[16] Cf. Mal. 3:2, 6.

[17] JW is apparently responding to Ryan's comment in her letter of Feb. 8: 'What shall I do that I may work the works of God? O my dear sir, help me by your prayers.'

establish, strengthen, settle you, and preserve your spirit, soul, and body, spotless and unblameable unto the coming of Jesus Christ!
    I am,
5   Yours, etc.,

J. W.

Source: published transcription; *Arminian Magazine* 5 (1782): 438.

To Samuel Furly[18]

[SUNDON]
MARCH 7, 1758

10   Dear Sammy,
    You have done well in writing to me the first week of this month. I should be glad if you would continue that regularly. And you have done exceeding well in giving me the full, particular account of that (shall I say unlucky?) accident. For really *non satis mihi constiterat,*
15   *cum aliquane animi mei molestia an potirer libenter [...] accepi.*[19] I am grieved. I am troubled for the consequences that may ensue. But I am pleased. I rejoice that the Lord has carried on such a work of conviction in that poor Pharisee. Yea, I cannot but be exceeding glad *me non laborem inanem cepisse.*[20]
20   Neither am I sorry but rather well satisfied that you lent her that little 'awakening tract'. Upon the first hearing of this, indeed, my spirit was troubled. Confusion of mind seized me, struck partly with fear, partly with sorrow, and partly with astonishment. But what need we fear? Or wherefore are we cast down? The Lord God
25   Omnipotent reigneth.[21] And cannot he make all things turn to his glory? How long shall the boasting enemy triumph? Not longer (at least) than the breath is in his nostrils; and then shall all his vain thoughts perish. But they have not yet won the day. Who knoweth

---

[18] Furly had completed his B.A. at Cambridge in January and was in London, where he would be ordained Deacon in May.
[19] Cf. Cicero, *Epistolae*, xiii.1.1–2 (*Letters*, 63.1–2): 'I was not quite sure whether to accept it with distress or pleasure' (Loeb).
[20] Cf. Terence, *Hecyra* ('The Mother-in-Law'), Act 3, Scene 2 (l. 344), '[That I not] labour in a useless task' (Loeb).
[21] See Rev. 19:6.

but the Lord may give peace and love and power and the spirit of a sound mind to her who for a season is sorely vexed with the cruel overwhelming power of Satan? At a moment when the ungodly think not of it, the Lord may arise and maintain his own cause and put to silence the vauntings of the proud. So that all that are around may see it and fear, and acknowledge, 'This is the Lord's doing'.[22]

What he does now we know not yet. It is our part to wait patiently to see what he will do. *Quietus esto*.[23] Be calm in the midst of this storm. I pity you, indeed, who are in the very midst of it. For my own part I leave the matter without concern in his hands who will not, cannot do wrong. But not without taking much shame unto myself. I did not order my conversation aright all the time I was in the place. I was afraid of giving offence, therefore I assumed too much the appearance of one of them. I did not dare to be altogether singular, to be constantly, steadily serious before them. Now by this circumstance the Lord has rebuked me and taught me wisdom. Here he has permitted no small offence to arise from a quarter I could neither foresee nor prevent. Where now is all my worldly prudence? What is become of my fearful caution? The Lord hath blasted it. Not indeed with the breath of his mouth, but with the rushing torrent of his sudden providence. Mark this, and settle it in thine heart that the Lord will be feared, honoured, and obeyed even in the midst of lions; or will make us feel the weight of his uplifted hand. I feel this moment my just punishment for my base cowardice. This sin sets heavier upon my conscience at this time than almost all my crimes and all the transgressions of my youth. And one sin lying upon the conscience is a load of misery.[24]

There is not now time to give you any particular relation of myself, that affair having spun out my letter too long. In study at present I make but a slow progress. I am not at all content with myself in this point. I have just entered upon Lord Clarendon's *History*,[25] which is such an account of the ways, vices, and passions of men as one who did not know the corruption of human nature could scarce be induced to believe of his fellow creatures.

I shall conclude this letter with affirming that I would to God such a deep work of conviction was wrought in your heart and mine as God has begun in that poor distressed woman. I wish we also felt the arrows of the Lord fastened in our conscience even as she has

---

[22] Mark 12:11.
[23] 'Be at rest.'
[24] The preceding three paragraphs are a single paragraph in the original.
[25] Edward Hyde, Earl of Clarendon, *The History of the Rebellion and Civil Wars in England*, 6 vols. (2nd edn.; Oxford, 1705–6).

done. O when shall we with that piercing sense repent of all our
sins and all our backslidings? Is not the time now come? We are
spared today. God knoweth whether we shall be tomorrow. But this
we know, that whatever knowledge, whatever gifts we have, purity
5   of heart alone will be of true worth in the end. To the earnest pur-
suit of which I commend your being,
> Yours, etc.,

> [John Wesley]

Endorsement: '(1) It is the *love* of God. It hath in it heights, depths, *strength*
    stronger than death. / (2) — of God in Christ. Sweetness of it. Better
    than all. Subject to no change.'
Source: manuscript copy (in the hand of John Jones[26]); Huntington Li-
    brary, Manuscripts, HM 57036.

To Jonathan Pritchard

LIVERPOOL
10   MARCH 25, 1758

Dear Jonathan
    I am persuaded what you say is true. John Nelson[27] may be useful
at Chester, and at other places in this circuit.[28] So I have appointed
him to come without delay. If there be a supply for other places, he
15   may spend a week with you; but no place must be neglected.
    O Jonathan, make the best of life! With love to your wife and all
the brethren, I am,
> Your affectionate brother,

20   J. Wesley

Address: 'To / Mr Jonathan Pritchard / In Broughton, near / Chester'.
Postmark: 'LIVER/POOL'. *Charge*: '3'.
Source: holograph; WHS Library.

---

[26] This identification is owed to Richard Heitzenrater.
[27] On John Nelson, see 26:106 in this edn.
[28] See an earlier letter from JW to Pritchard concerning the administration of the Chester
circuit, Jan. 16, 1753, 26:499–500 in this edn.

To Sarah Ryan[29]

DUBLIN
APRIL 4, 1758

My Dear Sister,
  Oh that I could be of some use to you! I long to help you forward
in your way. I want to have your understanding a mere lamp of light,   5
always shining with light from above! I want you to be full of divine
knowledge and wisdom, as Jordan in the time of harvest.[30] I want
your words to be full of grace, poured out as precious ointment.[31]
I want your every work to bear the stamp of God, to be a sacrifice
of a sweet-smelling savour,[32] without any part weak, earthly or hu-   10
man, all holy, all divine! The great God, your Father and your love,
bring you to this self-same thing! Begin, soldier of Christ, child of
God! Walk worthy of the vocation wherewith thou art called![33] Remember the faith! Remember the Captain of thy salvation![34] Fight!
Conquer! Die—and live for ever!   15
  I am,
       Yours, etc.,

                                                          J. W.

Source: published transcription; *Arminian Magazine* 5 (1782): 494.

To Elizabeth Hardy[35]

DUBLIN
APRIL 5, 1758   20

  It is with great reluctance that I at length begin to write: first,
because I abhor disputing, and never enter upon it but when I am,

---

[29] Possibly replying to Ryan's letter of Mar. 20.
[30] See Josh. 3:15.
[31] See Matt. 26:7.
[32] See Eph. 5:2; Phil. 4:18.
[33] Eph. 4:1.
[34] Heb. 2:10.
[35] *AM* labels this simply 'To Miss H—'. But related letters of May 1758 and Dec. 26,
1761 are specified as being to Elizabeth Hardy. Little is known of Hardy beyond these letters.
Telford says she lived in Bristol.

as it were, dragged into it by the hair of the head; and next, because I have so little hope that any good will arise from the present dispute. I fear your passions are too deeply interested in the question to admit the force of the strongest reason. So that, were it not for the tender regard I have for you, which makes your desire a motive I cannot resist, I should not spend half an hour in so thankless a labour, and one wherein I have so little prospect of success.

'The doctrine of perfection', you say, 'has perplexed you much since some of our preachers have placed it in so dreadful a light, one of them affirming a believer, till perfect, is under the curse of God and in a state of damnation; another, if you die before you have attained it, you will surely perish.'

By 'perfection' I mean 'perfect love', or the loving God with all our heart, so as to rejoice evermore, to pray without ceasing, and in everything to give thanks.[36] I am convinced every believer may attain this, yet I do not say he is in a state of damnation or under the curse of God till he does attain. No, he is in a state of grace and in favour with God as long as he believes. Neither would I say, 'If you die without it, you will perish'; but rather, 'Till you are saved from unholy tempers, you are not ripe for glory. There will, therefore, more promises be fulfilled in your soul before God takes you to himself.'

'But none can attain perfection unless they first believe it attainable.' Neither do I affirm this. I know a Calvinist in London who never believed it attainable till the moment she did attain it, and then lay declaring it aloud for many days till her spirit returned to God.

'But you yourself believed twenty years ago that we should not put off the infection of nature but with our bodies.' I did so. But I believe otherwise now, for many reasons, some of which you afterwards mention. How far Mr. [James] Rouquet or Mr. [Thomas] Walsh may have mistaken these I know not. I can only answer for myself.

'The nature and fitness of things' is so ambiguous an expression that I never make use of it. Yet if you ask me, 'Is it fit or necessary in the nature of things that a soul should be saved from all sin before it enters into glory?' I answer, it is. And so it is written, 'No unclean thing shall enter into it.'[37] Therefore, whatever degrees of holiness

---

[36] See 1 Thess. 5:16–18.
[37] Rev. 21:27.

they did or did not attain in the preceding parts of life, neither Jews nor heathens any more than Christians ever did or ever will enter into the New Jerusalem unless they are cleansed from all sin before they enter into eternity.

I do by no means exclude the Old Testament from bearing witness to any truths of God. Nothing less! But I say the experience of the *Jews* is not the standard of *Christian* experience and that therefore, were it true 'The Jews did not love God with all their heart and soul', it would not follow 'Therefore no Christian can', because we may attain what they did not.

'But', you say, 'either their words do not contain a promise of *such perfection*, or God did not fulfil this promise to them to whom he made it.' I answer, he surely will fulfil it to *them to whom he made it*—namely, to the Jews *after their dispersion into all lands*. And to these is the promise made, as will be clear to any who impartially considers the 30th chapter of Deuteronomy, wherein it stands.

I doubt whether this perfection can be proved by Luke 6:40. From 1 John 3:9 (which belongs to all the children of God) I never attempted to prove it. But I still think it is clearly described in those words, 'As he is, so are we in this world.'[38] And yet it doth not now appear 'what we shall be' when this vile body is 'fashioned like unto his glorious body',[39] when we shall see him, not in a glass, but face to face, and be transformed into his likeness.

Those expressions (John 13:10), 'Ye are clean, clean every whit,' are allowed to refer to justification only. But that expression, 'If we walk in the light as he is in the light',[40] cannot refer to justification only. It does not relate to justification at all, whatever the other clause may do. Therefore those texts are by no means parallel, neither can the latter be limited by the former, although it is sure the privileges described in both belong to every adult believer.

Not[41] only abundance of particular texts, but the whole tenor of Scripture declares, Christ came to 'destroy the works of the devil',[42] to 'save us from our sins';[43] all the works of the devil, all our sins, without any exception or limitation. Indeed, should 'we say we have no sin'[44] to be saved or cleansed from, we should make him come in

---

[38] 1 John 4:17.
[39] Phil. 3:21.
[40] 1 John 1:7.
[41] Orig., 'But not'.
[42] 1 John 3:8.
[43] Cf. Matt. 1:21.
[44] 1 John 1:8.

vain. But it is at least as much for his glory to cleanse us from them all before our death as after it.

'But St James says, "In many things we offend all";[45] and whatever "we" might mean if alone, the expression "we all" was never 5 before understood to exclude the person speaking.'[46] Indeed it was. It is unquestionably to be understood so as to exclude Isaiah, the person speaking, 'We are all as an unclean thing. We all do fade as a leaf; and our iniquities, like the wind, have taken us away' (44:6). For this was not the case with Isaiah himself. Of himself he says, 10 'My soul shall be joyful in my God; for he hath clothed me with the garments of salvation. He hath covered me with the robe of righteousness' (41:10). Here the prophet, like the apostle, uses the word 'we' instead of 'you' to soften the harshness of an unpleasing truth.

In this chapter the apostle is not cautioning them against censur- 15 ing others, but entering upon a new argument wherein the second verse has an immediate reference to the first, but none at all to the thirteenth of the preceding chapter.[47]

I added, "'We offend all" cannot be spoken of all [...] Christians, for immediately there follows the mention of one who "offends 20 not," as the "we" before-mentioned did.'[48] You answer, 'His not offending *in word* will not prove that he does not offend *in many things*.' I think St James himself proves it in saying, 'He is able to bridle also the whole body',[49] to direct all his actions as well as words according to the holy, perfect will of God, which those, and those 25 only, are able to do who love God with all their hearts. And yet these very persons can sincerely say, 'Forgive us our trespasses.' For as long as they are in the body, they are liable to mistake and to speak or act according to that mistaken judgement.[50] Therefore they cannot abide the rigour of justice, but still need mercy and forgiveness.

30 Were *you* to ask, 'What if I should die this moment?' I should answer, I believe you would be saved, because I am persuaded none that has faith can die before he is made ripe for glory. This is the doctrine which I continually teach which has nothing to do with

---

[45] James 3:2.

[46] Hardy is specifically rejecting Wesley's treatment of this verse in Sermon 40, *Christian Perfection*, II.17 (2:114–15 in this edn.).

[47] James 2:13, 'For he shall have judgment without mercy that hath showed no mercy, and mercy rejoiceth against judgment.'

[48] Sermon 40, *Christian Perfection*, II.17 (2:115 in this edn.).

[49] James 3:2.

[50] Another instance of JW's distinction between such trespasses and 'sin properly so called', or 'a voluntary transgression of a known law of God'; cf. JW, 'Thoughts on Christian Perfection' (1760), Q. 6, 13:61–62 in this edn.

justification by works. Nor can it discourage any who have faith, neither weaken their peace, nor damp their joy in the Lord. True believers are not distressed hereby, either in life or in death; unless in some rare instance wherein the temptation of the devil is joined with a melancholy temper.

Upon the whole, I observe your great argument turns all along on a mistake of the doctrine. Whatever warm expressions may drop from young men, we do not teach that any believer is under condemnation. So that all the inferences drawn from this supposition fall to the ground at once.

Your other letter I hope to consider hereafter. Though I have great reason to apprehend your prejudice will still be too strong for my arguments. However, whether you expect it or not, I must wish for *your perfection*. You of all people have most need of perfect love, because this alone casts out fear.

I am, with great sincerity,
    Your affectionate brother and servant,

John Wesley

Source: published transcription; *Arminian Magazine* 3 (1780): 223–27.

To Samuel Furly

DUBLIN
APRIL 8, 1758

Dear Sammy,
    Very probably I may procure your admission into orders with a title or without.[51]

[51] Anglican polity, spelled out in Edmund Gibson's *Codex Juris Ecclesiastici Anglicani* (1713, 1:168–78), mandated that a candidate for ordination either as a deacon or a priest had to hold a 'title' to a specific position. For example, a person ordained as a deacon might be given the title of curate in a parish where there was a priest willing to work with him. JW may have been hoping to find ordination for Furly that permitted him to itinerate. If so, he was not successful (see JW's letter to Furly, May 3, 1758). Furly was ordained deacon on May 21, 1758 by the Bishop of London and served briefly at Bow Church, Cheapside, moving in Nov. 1758 to be curate in Lakenheath, Suffolk.

It is not strange that any one should stifle the first convictions; neither ought that to discourage you at all. Speak again. Be instant εὐκαίρως, ἀκαίρως,[52] and by-and-by you will see the effect.

Ten, perhaps twenty people, being dissatisfied they know not why, cry out, 'Everybody is dissatisfied.' Far from it. There wanted a little evil report to balance the good report.

O Sammy, be all in earnest! Press through things temporal! Expect not happiness from any creature! Here we are, whether for life or for death we know not. But God knows, and that is enough! I am,

> Your affectionate brother,

> J. Wesley

Address: 'To / Mr Furly'.
No *postmark* or indications of postal *charge*; apparently delivered by hand.
Endorsement: '1758'.
Source: holograph; MARC, MAM JW 3/17.

To Dorothy Furly

DUBLIN
APRIL 13, 1758

But if you find such a surprising alteration at Bonner's Hall,[53] what need have you of removing to Bristol? Perhaps a lodging there might answer the purpose of health full as well as one at Clifton, and the purpose of religion considerably better.[54] There are few in that neighbourhood from whom I should hope you would receive much profit, except Sarah Ryan. If she abides in her integrity, she is a jewel indeed; one whose equal I have not yet found in England.

You ought not to drink much tea, and none without pretty much cream (not milk) and sugar. But I believe, were you to drink nettle-tea for a few mornings, it would do you more good than any other. It

---

[52] 2 Tim. 4:2: 'in season, out of season'.
[53] Bonner's Hall, in the parish of Hackney in Middlesex, was a manor house that had been a palace of the Bishops of London.
[54] Clifton was adjacent to Hot Wells, a mineral springs many visited to seek its health benefits. It was also the location of one of Lady Huntingdon's homes; JW may be trying to protect Furly from Calvinist influences that she would meet with there.

seems best for you to have frequent returns of weakness. It may be needful to fix seriousness upon your spirit by a lasting impression that there is but a step between you and eternity. But sickness alone will not do this—no, nor even the near approach of death. Unless the Spirit of God sanctify both, a man may laugh and trifle with his last breath.

You will overcome trifling conversation and the fear of man not by yielding, but by fighting. This is a cross which you cannot be excused from taking up. Bear *it*, and it will bear *you*. By prayer you will receive power so to do, to be a good soldier of Jesus Christ. But it is more difficult to resist hurtful desire; I am most afraid you should give way to this. Herein you have need of all the power of God. O stand fast! Look up and receive strength! I shall be glad to hear that you are more than conqueror,[55] and that you daily grow in the vital knowledge of Christ. Peace be with your spirit.

I am,

Your affectionate servant,

J. Wesley

Source: published transcription; Benson, *Works*, 16:322–23.

To Elizabeth Hardy[56]

[MAY 1758 ?]

Without doubt it seems to you that yours is a peculiar case. You think there is none like you in the world. Indeed there are. It may be ten thousand persons are now in the same state of mind as you. I myself was so a few years ago. I felt the wrath of God abiding on me. I was afraid every hour of dropping into hell. I knew myself to be the chief of sinners.[57] Though I had been very innocent in the account of others, I saw my heart to be all sin and corruption. I

---

[55] See Rom. 8:37.

[56] This may be JW's response to the 'second letter' mentioned in his earlier reply (Apr. 5) to Hardy. The manuscript is undated, but placed here because of the close connection in theme to the earlier letter.

[57] See 1 Tim. 1:15.

was without the knowledge and the love of God, and therefore an abomination in his sight.

But I had an advocate with the Father, Jesus Christ the righteous.[58] And so have you. He died for your sins, and he is now pleading for
5   you at the right hand of God. O look unto him and be saved! He loves you freely, without any merit of yours. He has atoned for all your sins.

See all your sins on Jesus laid![59]

10   His blood has paid for all. Fear nothing; only believe. His mercy embraces you; it holds you in on every side. Surely you shall not depart hence till your eyes have seen his salvation.

I am, madam,[60]

Address: The manuscript is pasted on a board that has been cut to expose: 'For M. Hardy'.

Source: holograph; Wesley's Chapel (London), LDWMM 1997/6731.

To Samuel Furly

TULLAMORE
15   MAY 1, 1758

Dear Sammy,

Two conversations I have had with the Bishop of Londonderry,[61] and *processimus pulchre*.[62] I intend to write to him in a few days, and then I shall be able to form a better judgement. He loves the Method-
20   ists from his heart. But he is not free from the fear of man. Yet I have much hope that love will conquer fear. Will it not conquer all sin?

Why do you not go every afternoon to visit the sick? Can you find a more profitable employment? I am,

Your affectionate brother,
25

J. Wesley

---

[58] See 1 John 2:1.

[59] CW, 'For the Anniversary Day of One's Conversion', st. 14, *HSP* (1740), 122.

[60] The manuscript page ends at this point.

[61] The Bishop of Derry since 1747 had been William Barnard (1697–1768). JW was consulting Barnard about the possibility of Furly being ordained without requirement of a title (see the letter of Apr. 8 above).

[62] 'We are proceeding well.'

To Ebenezer Blackwell[63]

CASTLEBAR
JUNE 5, 1758

Dear Sir,

I suppose my wife is now in London, as the letters I received thence in the last frank[64] were open; for she still insists on her right of reading all the letters which are sent to me. And I have no friend or servant where she is who has honesty and courage to prevent it. I find since I left England all my domestics have changed their sentiments, and are convinced she is a poor, quiet creature that is barbarously used. I should not at all wonder if my brother and you were brought over to the same opinion.

Since I came into this kingdom I have wrote several times. But I have not received one line in answer. So I sit still.[65] I have learned by the grace of God in every state to be content. I have in this respect done what *I* ought and what *I* could. Now let God do what seemeth him good. What a peace do we find in all circumstances when we can say, 'Not as I will, but as thou wilt!'[66]

I have now gone through the greatest part of this kingdom—Leinster, Ulster, and the greater half of Connaught. Time only is wanting. If my brother could take care of England and give me but one year for Ireland, I think every corner of this nation would receive the truth as it is in Jesus. They want only to hear it; and they

[63] JW's letter to Sarah Ryan of Jan. 27, 1758 indicates that his wife Mary had vowed to leave him after reading a letter from JW to Ryan. This letter shows Wesley's growing concern over his wife's reading letters addressed to him.

[64] The word 'frank' denoted a parcel of letters marked for free delivery.

[65] The version of the letter given in Tyerman begins at this point, omitting all the previous material. It also omits the following sentences: 'I have in this respect done what *I* ought and what *I* could. Now let God do what seemeth him good.'

[66] The fragmentary copy at Emory University ends at this point. In addition, everything in this paragraph after 'So I sit still' is struck through, as if for omission. This material is not shown as struck through in the copy at MARC, but it too lacks the remaining material in the letter up to 'My best wishes attend you'.

will hear me, high and low, rich and poor. What a mystery of providence is this! In England they may hear, but will not. In Ireland they fain would hear, but cannot. So in both, thousands perish for lack of knowledge. So much the more blessed are your ears, for they
5 hear; if you not only hear the word of God, but keep it.

I hope you find public affairs changing for the better. In this corner of the world we know little about them; only we are told that the great little king in Moravia is not swallowed up yet.[67]

Till near the middle of next month I expect to be at Mr. Beau-
10 champ's in Limerick. I hope you have a fruitful season in every respect. My best wishes attend you all.[68] I am, dear sir,

Your affectionate servant,

J. Wesley

Source: This letter is reconstructed from three sources: 1) a ms. fragment at Emory, MARBL, John Wesley Collection, 1/28; 2) a nineteenth-century ms. transcription at MARC, MA 1977/609; and 3) a published transcription in Tyerman, *John Wesley*, 2:304–5.

To Ebenezer Blackwell

BANDON
15 JULY 12, 1758

Really, sir, you had made me almost angry at an innocent person—I mean, innocent of the fault supposed. I wrote to Mr. Downing[69] nearly at the time I wrote to you; and seeing no name, I read part of your letter as from him, and thought 'My wife did very wrong
20 to trouble him with matters of this kind, which might do him more

---

[67] During the Seven Years War, Prussian King Frederick the Great invaded Moravia, then part of the Hapsburg monarchy, in May 1758. At the end of June, the Austrian army aligned with the Hapsburg empire won an unexpected victory over the Prussian army in the battle of Domstadtl.

[68] The copy at MARC lacks the word 'all' and summarises the concluding 'your affectionate servant' to 'yr affect.'

[69] George Downing (c. 1729–1809) was a priest in the Church of England sympathetic with the Evangelical revival, at least with its 'regular' wing who stressed conformity to church law. He was rector of Ovington, Essex, and also served as chaplain to William Legge, the second Earl of Dartmouth.

harm than good'. Time and patience will remove many other troubles, and show them to have no more foundation than this.

While you have so eloquent a person[70] at your elbow, and I am two or three hundred miles off, I have little to say. It may be time enough when I return to London. At present I would only make   5
two or three cursory remarks.

1) That letter was not *left on a chair*, but *taken out of my* pocket.[71]

2) It was not *letters*, but *a letter* of mine (and one which did not signify a straw) which Sarah Crosby some time since showed to three or four persons, and of which she will hear these ten years.[72] I   10
write to her when I judge it my duty so to do; but I have not wrote these ten or twelve weeks.

3) If you softened or salved over anything I wrote in the letter from Bedford,[73] you did her an irreparable damage. What *I* am is not the question there, but what *she* is, of which I must needs be a   15
better judge than you, for I wear the shoe—as you must needs be a better judge of Mrs. [Elizabeth] Blackwell's temper than I.

4) 'She is now full of anger.' High day! Anger! For what? Why because when Captain Dansey called upon me in Dublin (on the 7th of April) and asked, 'Sir, have you any commands? I am just sailing for   20
Bristol', I said, 'Yes. Here is a letter. Will you deliver it with your own hands?'[74] He promised he would, and that was our whole conversation.

5) But suppose he delivered this about the 12th of April, why did she not write for a month before? What excuse or pretence for this?

6) I certainly will, as long as I can hold a pen, assert my right of   25
conversing with whom I please. Reconciliation or none, let *her* look to that. If the unbeliever will depart, let her depart. That right I will exert just when I judge proper, giving an account only to God and my own conscience. Though (as it happens) the last letter I wrote to Sarah Ryan was in the beginning of May.[75]   30

7) My conscience bears me witness before God that I have been as 'cautious as I ought to have been'; for I have rigorously kept my rule, 'To *do* everything and *omit* everything which I could with a safe conscience for peace sake'.

But there is no fence against a flail, against one that could tell   35
Thomas Walsh calmly and deliberately (he begs this may not be

---

[70] Apparently referring to Mary Wesley.

[71] See JW's letter to Sarah Ryan, Jan. 27, 1756.

[72] 'years' is clear in the manuscript, but JW perhaps meant to write 'weeks'.

[73] JW was in Bedford Mar. 9–10; no letter to his wife of this date has survived.

[74] No letter from JW to his wife has survived from this period either.

[75] This letter has not survived.

mentioned again, nor his name brought into the question), 'His parting words to me were, "I hope I shall see your wicked face no more."' Can you ever be safe against being deceived by such an one but by not believing a word you hear?

5   In a week or two I shall be looking out for a ship. You people in England are bad correspondents. Both Mr. Downing, Mr. Venn,[76] and Mr. Madan[77] are a letter in my debt; and yet I think they have not more business than I have. How unequally are things distributed here! Some want time, and some want work! But all will be set

10   right hereafter. There is no disorder on that shore.

    Wishing all happiness to you and all that are with you, I remain, dear sir,

            Yours most affectionately,

                               J. W.

Address: 'To / Mr Blackwell / In Change Alley / London'.
Postmarks: 'DUBLIN' and '28 / IY'. *Charge*: '4'.
Endorsement: 'Rev'd Mr. John Westly / Bandon 12 July 1758'.
Source: holograph; Emory, MARBL, Wesley Family Papers, OBV1, p. 4.

To [Elizabeth (Hastings) Rawdon, Countess of Moira ?][78]

15   Cork
                                  July 21, 1758

Madam,
    If faith implied no more than a system of right opinions, one could not reasonably doubt of the faith, of so eminent a defender of sev-

20 eral Christian doctrines as Mr. H. was. But if it implies a divine evidence of things not seen;[79] in particular, of God's love to *me*; then

[76] On Henry Venn (1725–97), see 26:535 in this edn.
[77] Martin Madan (1725–90) was a 'spiritual son' of JW, awakened under his preaching. But Madan soon aligned with more Calvinist-leaning evangelicals like Lady Huntingdon, David Jones, William Romaine, and George Whitefield.
[78] While the address portion of the letter is missing, it is directed to the wife of a peer. When a transcription was published in *WHS* 19 (1934): 144–45, it was identified as to Elizabeth (Hastings) Rawdon. This would fit the fact that Elizabeth and her husband John Rawdon, 1ˢᵗ Earl of Moira, were supporters of JW in Ireland. Likewise, the owner of the letter in 1934 was in Ireland. See also JW's letter to Elizabeth Rawdon of Mar. 18, 1760.
[79] See Heb. 11:1; Wesley's consistent definition of 'faith'; cf. Sermon 43, *The Scripture Way of Salvation*, II:1–2, 2:160–61 in this edn.

I cannot but doubt of the faith of every man on earth who does not possess (in some good degree) all the Christian tempers, in the front of which lowliness and meekness stand. But from many eye- and ear-witnesses I have learned that Mr. H. did not possess these tempers. And if he did not, he had not Christian faith, how well so ever he defended the Christian doctrine. Of his death indeed I never received any account, but if the hope he therein expressed was the fruit of deep repentance for his uncommon pride, ungovernable passion, and high contempt of all his opponents, it was true Christian hope; and I should not then doubt but he is lodged in Abraham's bosom.[80]

It is an easy thing to make allowances to any who (so far as we can judge) have the mind that was in Christ.[81] I love and reverence all the externals of religion, but what are all these to the Kingdom of God within us? Let us spend the most, and the choicest of our time on confirming and enlarging this! I want holy tempers and can scarce waste a thought on any thing which does not conduce to these. O that his Lordship and you may abound in them more and more! I am, madam,
Your affectionate servant for Christ's sake,

John Wesley

Endorsement: 'Mr. John Wesley July 1758'.
Source: holograph; MARC, MAM JW 4/50 (address portion missing).

To the Rev. Samuel Furly

CORK
JULY 28, 1758

Dear Sammy,
Your conjecture is right. I never received the letter you speak of, nor heard before that you was in Holy Orders.[82] I hope you are also in great earnest to save your own soul as well as those that hear you.

---

[80] See Luke 16:23. JW understood the expressions 'paradise' and 'the bosom of Abraham' to denote the intermediate state of a believer between death and the final judgment; see Sermon 73, 'Of Hell', I:4, 3:35 in this edn.

[81] See Phil. 2:5.

[82] Cf. the previous letters from JW to Furly of Apr. 8 and May 3, 1758. Furly was ordained deacon on May 21, 1758.

You have need to pray much for steadiness of spirit and seriousness in conversation. If there be added to this the ornament of a
meek and quiet spirit, your words will not fall to the ground.

There will be danger, if you write so much, of writing in a dry
5 and formal manner. We may suffer loss either by writing too little
or too much. Observe every step you take. Walk circumspectly, and
God will be with you. I am,
Your affectionate brother,

J. Wesley

10 We expect to sail in three or four days.

Address: 'To / The Revd Mr Furly'.
No *postmark* or indications of postal *charge*; apparently delivered by hand.
Source: holograph; Melbourne, Queen's College, JW2.

To the Rev. Samuel Furly

BRISTOL
SEPTEMBER 2, 1758

Dear Sammy,
I know no way to cure men of curiosity but to fill them with the
15 love of God. If a great majority of those who attended the Thursday
sermon were Methodists, I know not but it was right to put Mr.
Charles in your place. Otherwise it would be wrong, for 'him that
escapes the sword of Jehu shall Elisha slay'.[83] Every preacher whom
God has sent will have a message to some souls who have not been
20 reached by any other. And the more persons attend his preaching
the better, the more room there is for God to work.

Mr. Jones's book I have found and will send by Jemmy Morgan.
Mr. Holloway's probably I shall find by and by.

I wish you would carefully read over the *Directions for Married
25 Persons*.[84] It is an excellent tract. You need to have your heart full of
grace, or you will have your hands full of work. Universal watchful-

---

[83] 1 Kgs. 19:17.
[84] JW published in 1753 an abridged edition of William Whateley's *Directions for Married
Persons: Describing the Duties Common to Both, and Peculiar to Each of Them* (orig., 1619); see
Bibliography, No. 165.i.

ness is absolutely necessary in order to our victory over any evil.
Whatever you do, do with your might.

I am,

Your affectionate brother,

J. Wesley 5

Address: 'The Revd Mr Furly'.

No *postmark* or indications of postal *charge*; apparently delivered by hand.

Source: holograph; MARC, MAM JW 2/98.

To [William Allwood][85]

BRISTOL
SEPTEMBER 13, 1758

My Dear Brother,

Enquire *why* brother Gibbs[86] was not liked at those places and tell
him frankly what has been amiss. Write again and hasten brother 10
Tobias.[87] Lincolnshire is now fully supplied without him.

Thomas Mitchell[88] is fast in Sussex as yet; I have letter upon letter to desire he may not leave it, and I suppose he will not stir from
thence till I ⟨go[89]⟩ myself and fetch him.

I ⟨know⟩ no reason at all why you should not feel always what 15
you felt then. The gifts of God are all without repentance on *his*
part. He is willing to give always what he gives once, and what more
than you feel, Ruth Hall[90] experiences—it is all for *you*. Only be not

---

[85] While the address is not visible, William Allwood had been assigned to serve the York circuit the previous month with Thomas Mitchell and Thomas Tobias (see 10:287 in this edn.), one of Wesley's itinerant preachers on the York 'Round' or circuit (see 21:206, n. 9 in this edn.) JW often spelled his last name 'Alwood', but his own signature included the second 'l'.

[86] This is apparently John Gibbs, who was accepted as an itinerant at the August 1758 Conference (see 10:282 in this edn.); perhaps he had been preaching in York previously, or maybe he stayed in York even though he was assigned by Conference to Cornwall (see 10:286 in this edn. and JW's letter to Allwood on Oct. 15, 1758).

[87] Thomas Tobias (d. 1767) was a native of Wales who appears in the Minutes as a travel-ing preacher in 1755 (10:272 in this edn.) and served until his death in early 1767. See Atmore, *Memorial*, 428–30.

[88] On Thomas Mitchell, see 26:474 in this edn.

[89] A small portion of the manuscript is torn away, but can be reconstructed in the two lines affected.

[90] This is JW's first mention of Mrs. Ruth Hall (maiden name unknown). She was born in Woolley, Yorkshire in 1732, converted in York in 1752, married in 1753, and claimed entire

afraid of knowing yourself, of seeing the inbred monster's face. I
am, with love to her and all our friends,
        Your affectionate brother,

                                                            J. Wesley

Postmark: '19/SE'.[91]
Source: holograph; privately held (current owner unknown, Wesley Works
    Editorial Project Archive includes a copy).

To the Printer of the *Leedes Intelligencer*[92]

BRISTOL
SEPTEMBER 13, 1758

Sir,
    I was a little surprised at one of your papers which was sent me
lately, wherein was inserted a letter supposed to be wrote by me and

---

sanctification in 1757. JW carried on extensive correspondence with her between 1759 and
1762, though only his published transcriptions of her letters survive. See 'A Short Account of
Ruth Hall', *AM* 4 (1781): 477–80.
    [91] Nothing more of the address can be seen, but Ruth Hall lived in York.
    [92] The *Leedes Intelligencer* printed in its Aug. 29, 1758 issue a letter (included in the online
'in-letters' file), falsely purporting to be by JW, addressing criticisms of his *Address to the Clergy*.
    Now printing JW's disavowal, the editor added the following comment:
    'We think ourselves obliged to declare that the *Expostulatory Letter* was not printed, as
Mr. Wesley imagines, at Leedes. Mr. Wesley best knows the motives that have induced him to
publish a number of volumes, and if he candidly judges of others by himself, he may possibly
have abundance of reason to be convinced, even without reading a page of it, that the *Expostulatory Letter* was merely a device to get a little money. Whether the author of that letter be a
follower of Mr. Wesley or not, he may, for ought that appears in the letter, be as sincerely desirous of promoting the interest of true religion as Mr. Wesley himself. There are some doubts
proposed which it seems no way unbecoming [for] the younger disciples, at least, of Mr. Wesley
to entertain. And if he would fairly remove those doubts, this would tend, one would presume,
more to their satisfaction and be more suitable to the character he assumes than to treat the
performance with contempt. The like treatment (in the least degree) of any thing that he has
published, his followers have been taught to call not answering but railing. And if they can be
satisfied with the like practice in him which they so warmly condemn in others, this proves
nothing but Mr. Wesley's great ability to impose upon the understanding of his admirers.
    'The letter signed J. W. printed in our paper of the 29th of August we really believed to be
Mr. Wesley's own writing. And since he does not plainly deny it to be his, it may, at least till he
think proper to explain himself further, be looked upon as a necessary paternal admonition to
some of his over-zealous disciples, though he may not be unwilling to have the world amused by
Mr. [John] Hampson's daring disavowal of that *miserable* letter. However this be, if Mr. Wesley
thinks it expedient to clear the point with more precision, we shall readily give what he shall
send for that purpose a place in our paper.'

containing a kind of answer to an *Expostulatory Letter* printed (as I imagine) at Leedes some time since.[93] I was not likely to answer that harmless thing, for in truth I never read a page of it—being convinced by reading a few lines that it was merely a device to get a little money. Nevertheless, if the author will subscribe his real name, perhaps some farther notice may be taken of him, by, sir,

    Your humble servant,

John Wesley

Source: published transcription; *Leedes Intelligencer* (Sept. 28, 1758), p. 4.

To Francis Okeley[94]

SALISBURY
OCTOBER 4, 1758

Dear Sir,

The plain reason why I did not answer you before is I had no heart to write, for I had no expectation of doing any good. And why should I trouble myself or you to no purpose? However, I will once more cast my bread upon the waters,[95] and leave the event to God.

1. You say, 'I cannot preach because I have not faith.'[96] That is not the thing; you do not speak simply. The direct reason why you did not preach at Bristol was because you would not displease the Brethren. They have still hold of your heart. The chain enters into your soul, therefore you could not even seem to *act against them*.

[93] [Richard Fawcett], *An Expostulatory Letter to the Rev. Mr. Wesley, occasioned by his 'Address to the Clergy'* (London: J. Wilkie, 1757). A note to this letter says that Griffith Wright, the printer of the *Leedes Intelligencer*, also sells this *Expostulatory Letter*.

[94] Francis Okeley (1719–94), a fellow member with JW of the Fetter Lane society in 1738, had cast his lot with the Moravians as this group split. He ministered most of his life among the Moravians, though frequently became dissatisfied and moved around. For a short time in 1758 he had joined JW in his tour of Ireland, but as this letter shows he quickly made clear that he would not align with Wesley if it meant disavowing his Moravian 'Brethren'. For more on Okeley, see 21:136, n. 45 in this edn.

[95] Cf. Eccl. 11:1.

[96] As JW states later, he is quoting from and replying to a letter that Okeley wrote to CW, which does not appear to have survived.

2. 'I am not convinced, and cannot be so, that what *now passes* for faith …' Hold! Do you mean that what *now passes* for faith among the Methodists is not true Christian faith, that we have not a right conception of faith? I know the teachers among *the Brethren* have
5   not. But the conception which we now have of faith is the same which the apostles had, for we conceive faith to be 'a divine ἔλεγχος of things not seen',[97] particularly of this, that Christ loved *me* and gave himself for *me*. Did St. Paul conceive it to be either less or more? *You* know he did not.

10   'But I am not convinced, and cannot be so, that this is experienced by most that profess it'—suppose in the united society at Bristol. I know you are not convinced of this and that you cannot be so. But the hindrance lies in your heart, not your understanding. You *cannot* because you *will not*; so much of the old prejudice
15   still remains, and says, *non persuadebis etiamsi persuaseris.*[98] But you *ought* to be convinced that *most of them* who there profess it truly experience what they profess. For (unless they are an whole heap of wilful liars, which you *ought* not to think without proof) they have those fruits which cannot possibly subsist without true
20   Christian faith. They have a peace that passes all understanding[99] and banishes the fear of death. They have the love of God shed abroad in their heart,[100] overcoming the love of the world. And they have abiding power over all sin, even that which did easily beset them.[101] Now, what excuse have you for not being convinced
25   that *they* have faith, who have fruits which nothing but faith can produce?

3. 'But they seem at best to have the *letter of the new covenant* and the *spirit of the old*.' How so? What is the spirit of the new covenant? Is it not love, the love of God and man? *This spirit* they have; it is
30   the great moving spring both of their desires, designs, words, and actions. This also cannot be denied, unless they are the vilest liars upon earth. I speak now more confidently, having last week (together with my brother) examined all one by one.

4. 'But still you have not found what you expected among the
35   Methodists, nor can you see your way clear to join them.' I think this was the sum of what you wrote to my brother. But what did

---

[97] Heb. 11:1; ἔλεγχος is the term translated 'conviction' in this verse.
[98] Aristophanes, *Plutus*, 1. 60; which JW translated, 'Thou shalt not persuade me, though thou dost persuade me' in Sermon 83, 'On Patience', §11, 3:177 in this edn.
[99] See Phil. 4:7.
[100] See Rom. 5:5.
[101] See Heb. 12:1.

you expect to have found among them? Faith and love and holiness (whether in your own soul or not) you did find among them—at least, you *ought to* have found them, for there they are, which neither men nor devils can deny. What else did you expect to find? Or why cannot you see your way clear to join them? I will tell you why. You have at least five strong reasons to the contrary: 1) a wife, 2) a mother, 3) children, 4) cowardice, 5) love of ease. But are these reasons good in the sight of God? I will not affirm that.

5. 'However, *the Brethren* are good men, and I dare not oppose them.' If they are not *the only people* of God[102] (which they cannot be if the Scriptures are true), they are not good men; they are very wicked men. They are as a body deceiving and being deceived. They are liars, proud, boasters, despisers of those that are good, slaves to an ungodly man, and continually labouring to enslave others to him. O take warning at last! Have no commerce with them! Come not near the tents of these wicked men,[103] whose words are smoother than oil, and yet they are very swords![104] I dare not but oppose them, for in many places they have wellnigh destroyed the work of God. Many souls, once full of faith and love, they have caused to draw back to perdition. Many they have driven into the deep and then triumphed over them. Beware it be not so with *you*. You have greatly resisted the Spirit in this matter! Remember Richard Viney[105]—a pillar of salt, not because he came out of Sodom, but because he *looked back*![106]

    I am, dear sir,

        Your affectionate brother and servant,

                J. Wesley

Endorsement: in JW's hand, 'Oct. 8 [*sic*], 1758 / to Mr O'.
Source: manuscript copy by secondary hand for JW; MARC, MA 1977/609.

---

[102] JW assumes that the Brethren are making this claim.

[103] Num. 16:26.

[104] Ps. 55:21.

[105] Richard Viney was one of the earliest English adherents of the Moravians in London. He was later ejected from the Moravian community and sought fellowship with Wesley, but ended up creating a disturbance in the Wesleyan society in Birstall; see 19:159, n. 26 & 25:583, n. 7 in this edn.

[106] See Gen. 19:26.

To William Allwood

RYE, IN SUSSEX
OCTOBER 15, 1758

My Dear Brother,

It is very difficult to determine suddenly whether a person is or is
5 not renewed. If sister Hatton is, it will appear more and more clearly.
If she is not, let her earnestly and patiently wait for it. I wrote to
sister Ruth Hall and hope she will find time to send me an answer.

The books you will, I suppose, receive shortly, if you have not
already. Thomas Tobias is a serious man and will not do the work
10 of the Lord deceitfully. If you see good, let brother Gibbs go at
any time into Lincolnshire, and John Hacking[107] come to you in his
place.

I believe another preacher will come from London, but Thomas
Mitchell cannot yet be spared from these parts. There has never
15 been any preaching in this county before, and now the kingdom of
God is come upon them unawares.

O Billy, be much in prayer! I am,
Your affectionate friend and brother,

J. Wesley

Address: 'To / Mr Allwood / At Mr John Hall's / In Newgate Street /
York'.
Postmark: '17/OC'.
Source: holograph; MARC, MAM JW 6/42; part of a double letter (now
separate) to John Johnson, with address information on back of that
sheet, MAM JW 3/73.

---

[107] John Hacking, an itinerant since at least 1755, had been appointed to Lincolnshire at
the 1758 Conference; see 10:287 in this edn.

To John Johnson[108]

My Dear Brother,

Would it not be best for Nicholas Manners[109] to come up to me in London immediately? Would it not be the most likely means to   5
settle his sentiments?

I am exceedingly glad you go abroad when you can. O let us work while the day is! In great haste, I am,

Your ever affectionate brother,

J. Wesley   10

Source: holograph; MARC, MAM JW 3/73 (part of double letter with previous).

To Mary (Goldhawk/Vazeille) Wesley

My Dear Love,

I had a pleasant ride to Ingatestone[110] in the coach. I then took horse and came to Maldon by dinnertime. Between ten and eleven   15
this morning we set out from Maldon, and in three hours found honest brother Arvin here. If I find no particular reason to alter my design, I purpose going on toward Norwich on Monday.

You obliged me on Tuesday afternoon by inviting my sister Hall[111] to drink tea with you; and likewise by leaving Betty Duchesne with   20
me till she had said what she had to say. My dear, this is the way (as I have often told you) to secure a person's affections:

---

[108] John Johnson (1725–1803) was a native of Somerset who became a Methodist itinerant in 1753 (see 10:260 in this edn.) and spent most of his career preaching in Ireland. He was for a while General Assistant for the Irish work, but became about this time the center of some dissent. See Vickers, *Dictionary*, 182.

[109] Nicholas Manners was a prospective itinerant, whose brother John was appointed to Ireland along with John Johnson in 1758 (10:287 in this edn.).

[110] Orig., 'Ingotstone'; Ingatestone and Maldon are both in Essex.

[111] I.e., Martha (Wesley) Hall.

> Let all his ways be unconfined,
> And clap your padlock on his mind.[112]

Believe me, there is no other way; leave every one to his own
5   conscience. For why am I judged, says St. Paul, of another's
conscience?[113] Every one must give an account of himself to God.
And even if a man acts contrary to good conscience, can you re-
claim him by violent methods? Vain thought!

10   By force beasts act, and are by force restrained;
> The human mind by gentle means is gained.[114]

Either by gentle means or by none at all. Or if there be an exception, if a rod be for a fool's back,[115] the wife is not the person who is
15   to use it towards her husband.

If it please God to bring me safe to Norwich, I hope to have a letter from you there. Peace be with your spirit. I am,
> Your affectionate husband,

John Wesley

Address: 'To / Mrs Wesley / At the Foundery / London'.
Postmark: '28 / OC'. *Charge*: '3'.
Source: holograph; MARC, MAM JW 5/58.

To Thomas [Brisco?[116]]

20

Dear Tommy,
I hope you will set out for Wednesbury on Monday. But from
thence I would not have [left unfinished].

Source: holograph; MARC, MAM JW 4/63, [p. 11].

---

[112] The concluding couplet of Matthew Prior, 'An English Padlock', changing 'her' to 'his'.
[113] See 1 Cor. 10:29.
[114] Matthew Prior, 'Solomon', Book II, ll. 257–58.
[115] See Prov. 14:3.
[116] JW started this letter on a half sheet, probably to Thomas Brisco, who was assisting him this year. But it was not completed and the sheet was bound into a notebook for JW's copy letters, where a copy of the letter of Sarah Ryan to JW on Nov. 12, 1758 is transcribed over it.

To Sarah Ryan

…[117] Yesterday I transcribed C. P.'s[118] questions, with a little alteration. A few of them I will put to *you*, which I know you will answer with all plainness. (The four first questions.[119])

As to myself, I am still cold and faint, though (as I told you) a little revived since I wrote freely. Pray that God may at length lift up the hands that hang down and the feeble knees![120]

Source: manuscript copy by JW for records; MARC, MAM JW 4/63, p. 9.

To Sarah Moore[121]

My Dear Sister,

Praise God for what he hath already done. Let those give thanks whom the Lord hath redeemed and delivered from the hand of the enemy,[122] but you know a greater deliverance is at hand. What have you to do but to fight your way through the world, the flesh, and the devil? It is a good though a painful fight. Unless you yield, you cannot but conquer. It is true you will first conquer by little and little. For

> More of this life and more we have
> As the old Adam dies.[123]

---

[117] Wesley's transcription begins with a dash, indicating an elision (i.e., this is an extract).

[118] Possibly Charles Perronet.

[119] The questions are given in his transcription of Ryan's response on Nov. 12 (online).

[120] See Heb. 12:12.

[121] Sarah Moore was born at King's Lynn, Norfolk in 1738, and moved with her parents to Sheffield four years later. She began to teach at a school in Sheffield in her seventeenth year; and at eighteen was appointed the first class-leader at Hallam, walking there from Sheffield every week for two years. The first Quarterly Meeting was held in her house at Fargate between 1756 and 1760, and the society held its meetings there. She married Samuel Knutton, a popular local preacher at Sheffield, in 1772. See Everett, *Sheffield*, 80.

[122] Moore had apparently written Wesley about the sudden death of a young man who had been disrupting Methodist services; cf. Everett, *Sheffield*, 126.

[123] Cf. CW, 'Christ Our Sanctification', st. 3, *HSP* (1740), 97.

But there is also an instantaneous conquest: in a moment sin shall be no more. You are gradually dying for a long time. But you will die in a moment. O hasten to that happy time! Pray, strive, hope for it!
  I am,
5   Your affectionate brother,

                                              J. Wesley

Source: published transcription; Everett, *Sheffield*, 1:126.

To the Rev. James Hervey[124]

LONDON,
NOVEMBER 29, 1758

Dear Sir,
10   A week or two ago, in my return from Norwich, I met with Mr. Pierce of Bury, who informed me of a conversation which he had had a few days before. Mr. Cudworth, he said, then told him 'that he had prevailed on Mr. Hervey to write against me,[125] who likewise, in what he had written, referred to the book which he (Mr. Cud-
15   worth) had lately published'.[126]
    Every one is welcome to write what he pleases concerning me. But would it not be well for you to remember that before I published anything concerning you I sent it to you in a private letter; that I waited for an answer for several months, but was not favoured
20   with one line; that when at length I published part of what I had sent you, I did it in the most inoffensive manner possible—in the latter end of a larger work, purely designed to *preserve* those in connexion with me from being tossed to and fro by various doctrines?[127]

---

[124] On James Hervey, see 13:321–22 & 25:581 in this edn.

[125] James Hervey was drafting a set of letters in reply to Wesley. But his health was declining fast (he died on Dec. 25), and perhaps persuaded by this letter, he decided not to make them public (entrusting them to the care of his brother William). The letters were known, however, among some of Hervey's associates and in 1764 one of these associates published them surreptitiously. Thus in Nov. 1764 Wesley wrote one more (posthumous) response to Hervey; see 13:377–90 in this edn.

[126] William Cudworth, a staunch Calvinist, had recently published *A Preservative in Perilous Times* (London, 1758), which included extended critiques of two publications by JW.

[127] Wesley's letter was sent privately to Hervey in Oct. 1756, and not published until June 1758 in *A Preservative against Unsettled Notions in Religion*; see 13:323–44 in this edn.

What, therefore, I may fairly expect from my friend is to mete to me with the same measure, to send to me first in a private manner any complaint he has against me, to wait as many months as I did, and if I give you none or no satisfactory answer, then to lay the matter before the world, if you judge it will be to the glory of God.   5

But, whatever you do in this respect, one thing I request of you. Give no countenance to that insolent, scurrilous, virulent libel which bears the name of William Cudworth. Indeed, how you can converse with a man of his spirit I cannot comprehend. O leave not your old, well-tried friends! The new is not comparable to them.   10 I speak not this because I am *afraid* of what any one can say or do to *me*. But I am really concerned for you. An evil man has gained the ascendant over you, and has persuaded a dying man, who had shunned it all his life, to enter into controversy as he is stepping into eternity! Put off your armour, my brother! You and I have no   15 moments to spare. Let us employ them all in promoting peace and goodwill among men. And may the peace of God keep your heart and mind in Christ Jesus![128] So prays,

Your affectionate brother and servant,

J. Wesley

Source: published transcription; *Arminian Magazine* 1 (1778): 136–37.

To Augustus Montague Toplady[129]

LONDON   20
DECEMBER 9, 1758

Dear Sir,

I verily believe no single person since Mahomet has given such a wound to Christianity as Dr. Taylor.[130] They are his books, chiefly

---

[128] See Phil. 4:7.

[129] Augustus Montague Toplady (1740–88) had been converted after hearing a sermon in 1755 preached at Coolamain by James Morris, one of JW's preachers. Sometime there after he and JW began to correspond, with this being the first surviving letter of JW to the 18 year-old Toplady (a prior letter is referred to in Toplady to JW, Sept. 13, 1758). Toplady would shortly align with the Calvinist Methodists and become a strong critic of JW's Arminianism; see, for example, JW, *The Consequence Proved* (1771), 13:422–28 in this edn. See *ODNB*.

[130] JW had published his response to John Taylor's *The Scripture-Doctrine of Original Sin* in 1757; see 12:117ff in this edn.

that upon *Original Sin,* which have poisoned so many of the clergy and indeed the fountains themselves—the universities in England, Scotland, Holland, and Germany.

5   If you do not immediately see the fruit of your labour in conversing with this or that person, still there is no reason to think it lost. The wind bloweth when as well as where it listeth.[131] We know the help that is done, God doth it himself. And it is fit he should do it in his own time as well as manner.

   If you continue to walk humbly and simply with God,[132] there is 10 no need the darkness should ever return. God is willing to give the love, the joy, the peace always which he gives once. Only, hear his voice, and follow it with all diligence. Do whatever he calls you to, be it ever so grievous to flesh and blood, and shun whatever you find lessens your communion with him.

15   Nothing but almighty grace can amend that child. She had a taste of it once; and she may again. It would be well to put her in the way of it as frequently as may be.

   I have not had my health so well for many years. How many are the mercies of God! We want only thankful hearts.

20   Have you had yet any thoughts as to your future life, in what way you might most glorify God? I am, dear sir,
      Your affectionate servant,

                     John Wesley

Address: 'To / Mr Toplady / in Trinity College / Dublin'.
Source: holograph; MARC, MA 2008/016.

To an Unidentified Man[133]

My Dear Brother,

   From time to time I have had more trouble with the society at Leeds than with all the other societies in Yorkshire. And now I hear

---

[131] See John 3:8.
[132] See Micah 6:8.
[133] The letter was likely directed to John Hampson or one of JW's other preachers stationed in Leeds.

that *the leaders* insist that such and such persons be put out of the society! I desire the leaders may know their place and not stretch themselves beyond their line. Pray let me judge who should be put out of a Methodist society and who not. I desire Faith and Ann Hardwick may not be put out of the society, unless some fresh mat-   5
ter appear against them; and if any new matter does appear, let it be laid before *me.*

He shall have judgement without mercy who hath shown no mercy![134] I am,

Your affectionate brother,   10

J. Wesley

Source: holograph; Huntington Library, HM 57037 (address portion missing).

To Mary (Goldhawk/Vazeille) Wesley

NORWICH
DECEMBER 23, 1758

Dear Molly,

I was much concerned the night before I left London at your   15
unkind and unjust accusation.[135] You accused *me* of unkindness, cruelty, and what not. And why so? Because I insist on choosing my own company, because I insist upon conversing, by speaking or writing, with those whom I (not you) judge proper! For more than seven years this has been a bone of contention between you   20
and me, and it is so still. For I will not, I cannot, I dare not give it up. 'But then *you* will rage and fret and call me names.' I am sorry for it. But I cannot help it. I still do and must insist that I have a right to choose my own company. Then you will 'denounce against me all the curses from Genesis to the Revelation'. You may so. But   25
you gain no ground hereby, for still I cannot give up my right. Nay, but 'you will say all manner of evil of me'. Be it so, but still I stand just where I was. Then 'you will show my private letters to all the

---

[134] See James 2:13.
[135] JW left London on Dec. 18 according to his *Journal* (21:173 in this edn.).

world'. If you do, I must assert my right still. All this will not extort
it from me, *nor anything else which you can do*. You may therefore as
well *allow* it now as after we have squabbled about it (if we live so
long) seven years longer, for it is my right by all the laws of God and
5 man, and a right which I never can part with. O do not continue
to trouble yourself and me and to disturb the children of God by
still grasping at a power which must be denied you by him who is
nevertheless,
         Your truly affectionate husband,

10   John Wesley

Address: 'To Mrs Wesley / At the Foundery / London'.
Postmarks: (top of date stamp illegible) '/DE' and 'NOR / WICH'.
   Charge: '4'.
Source: holograph; MARC, MAM JW 5/59.

To Dorothy Furly

[COLCHESTER]
DECEMBER 28, 1758

My Dear Sister,
      I thought it long since I heard from you, but I imputed it to your
15 illness. And I did not desire you should do anything which would
put you to pain or increase your bodily weakness.
      When you seemed confident of receiving the promise in a few
days, I did not judge it needful to say anything to the contrary, both
because I was persuaded that expectation would be a quickening to
20 your soul, and because I knew you had one near you who was able
to advise you in any emergency. See that your desires do not cool,
and you shall not be ashamed of this confident expectation. So long
as it is tempered with resignation, it can do you no disservice. And
what else is there worthy of a desire? Health you shall have if health
25 be best, even bodily health. But what is that in comparison of an
healthful mind? And this you are sure to have.
      I scruple Sarah Ryan's drinking tar-water because it is so ex-
tremely nauseous. Neither will it profit if it occasion costiveness,[136]

---

[136] Constipation.

unless stewed prunes be taken every second or third night instead of it. I rather wish she would resume the medicine I formerly prescribed, only taking care not to catch cold with it. Perhaps in a few days you may see,

    Your affectionate brother, 5

                                   J. Wesley

Source: published transcription; Benson, *Works*, 16:323.

1759

To the Rev. Samuel Furly

London
February 17, 1759

Dear Sammy,

James Kershaw[1] is an independent minister. Probably, if we live
till another Conference, he may be in connexion with us. Hitherto
he acts as an independent. We have no society at Kenninghall.[2]

I take John Pearse to be an honest man. As soon as he sees the
truth he will preach it. Dolly Furly was considerably better in
health before I came from Bristol. And she was all athirst for God.
I think her soul prospers more and more.

I will desire Mr. Gilbert[3] to see whether the four volumes of the
Library which you mention can be spared. And if they can, if they
are not necessary for the making up of sets, they will be sent with
the last *Journal* and the *Pilgrim's Progress*.[4]

It is very possible the day of grace may be at end before the day
of life is. But I believe this is very rarely the case. I have narrowly
observed, and have found but one indisputable instance in thirty
years.

Nancy[5] must give me credit for her letter a little longer, for I am
at present much straitened for time. March 1 I hope to be at Mr.
Berridge's,[6] whence I must strike off for Colchester, so that you

---

[1] James Kershaw (1730–97), one of JW's first itinerants, who had withdrawn from riding
the circuit; see Atmore, *Memorial*, 237 or Vickers, *Dictionary*, 190.

[2] Orig., 'Renninghall'; this is surely a misprint for Kenninghall, Norfolk, which was near
Lakenheath, Suffolk, where Furly was placed as curate in late Nov. 1758.

[3] Nicholas Gilbert, an itinerant preacher since 1744, was currently stationed in London,
and helping care for JW's publications (see 10:260 in this edn.).

[4] The books in question are volumes from JW's *Christian Library*, installment 9 of his
Journal (which had just been released), and his abridged republication of Bunyan's *Pilgrim's
Progress* (*Bibliography*, No. 79).

[5] Ann (Bloodworth) Furly, Samuel's wife, whom he married in June 1758.

[6] John Berridge (1716–93), vicar of Everton, Bedfordshire, had met JW in 1758, and was
drawn into the evangelical revival. At this point his parish was a center for the work of JW's
preachers in the East Midlands (see the account of the revival in late May 1759 in JW's *Journal*,
21:195–200 in this edn.). Berridge later embraced Calvinist views and attacked JW's theology.
See Vickers, *Dictionary*, 28; and *ODNB*.

will not see me this spring unless you come to Everton. I am, dear Sammy,

> Yours affectionately,

> [J. Wesley]

Source: published transcription; Telford, *Letters*, 4:50–51.

To an Unidentified Woman

London   5
February 21, 1759

Probably, Miss —,[7] this may be the last trouble of the kind which you will receive from me. Therefore you may forgive me this, and the rather when you consider my motives to it. You know I can have no temporal view. I can have none but a faint, distant hope (be-   10 cause with God all things are possible) of doing some service to one whom I love. And this may answer the question which you might naturally ask, 'What would you have! What do you want with *me*!' I want you, not to be a convert to my opinions, but to be a member of Christ, a child of God, and an heir of his kingdom. Be anything   15 as to outward profession, so you are lowly in heart, so you resist and conquer every motion of pride, and have that mind in you which was also in Christ Jesus. Be what you please besides; only be meek and gentle, and in patience possess your soul, so that one may truly say to you,   20

> Calm thou ever art within,
> All unruffled, all serene.[8]

Hear what preacher you will, but hear the voice of God, and be-   25 ware of prejudice and every unkind temper. Beware of foolish and hurtful desires or they will pierce you through with many sorrows.

---

[7] This and a subsequent letter of Mar. 20 were published in *AM* together as directed to the same unidentified recipient. Telford suggests 'Miss Johnson', with no indication of why he makes that association.

[8] CW, 'The Beatitudes', ll. 79–80, *HSP* (1749), 1:37.

In one word, be anything but a trifler, a trifler with God and your own soul. It was not for this that God gave you

> A mind superior to the vulgar herd.[9]

5

No, Miss —, no! But that you might employ all your talents to the glory of him that gave them. O do not grieve the Holy Spirit of God! Is he not still striving with you! Striving to make you not almost but altogether a Christian! Indeed, you must be all or noth-
10   ing—a saint or a devil, eminent in sin or holiness! The good Lord deliver you from every snare, and guide your feet in the way of peace! How great a pleasure would this give to all your real friends, and in particular to,
      Your affectionate servant for Christ's sake,

15

John Wesley

Source: published transcription; *Arminian Magazine* 2 (1780): 161–62.

To the Rev. Samuel Furly

[EVERTON]
MARCH 2, 1759

I hope to be at Leeds on Easter Monday. So Mr. Venn[10] has
20   opened your eyes! Poor Sammy!

Source: holograph; MARC, MA 1977/477 (JW's postscript on a letter of Charles Perronet to Furly).

---

[9] Cf. Matthew Prior, 'Solomon', Book I, l. 681, 'And turn superior to the vulgar herd'.
[10] Henry Venn, an evangelical clergyman who became vicar of Huddersfield in 1759, and was supportive of Methodist activity in his parish.

To Ebenezer Blackwell

EVERTON
MARCH 2, 1759

Dear Sir,

When it is probable I may alter my judgement or practice, I am very willing to speak upon any head. But when I am clearly and 5 fully fixed, then I do not speak, for it would be lost labour. For this reason I did not speak the other night, because I was fully fixed.

My wife picks my lock and steals my papers. Afterwards she says, 'You cannot trust me.' I answer, 'I cannot, till you restore what you stole and promise to steal no more.' She replies, 'I will burn them, 10 or lodge them with another, on such terms.' I answer nothing. Do you ask why so? I answer to *you*: 1) I will not *consent* my goods shall be *burnt*, much less accept it as a favour. I require her to *restore* them. 2) I will not thank her for lodging them with another. I require that they be restored to *me*. 3) I will not so much as consider *the terms*; 15 I require the restitution of my own goods without *any terms*. And I know you would do so were it your case. And so would any man of common sense. 'But she will not restore them.' Then she must keep them. But let her not blame *me* because I cannot trust her.

Permit me to add one word to *you*. You think yourself a match for 20 her, but you are not. By her exquisite art she has already made you think ill of two very deserving women.[11] And you have been more than once much puzzled what to think of me! Nor could you help thinking me *a little* in the wrong. I am almost afraid she likewise entertains you with the faults of many in the society, the knowing 25 of which (be they real or feigned) does you no good at all. O sir, let us look inward, let us *live at home*! The more we know of our own faults and the less of other people's, the more will the work of God prosper in our hearts.

Wishing all happiness to you and yours, I am, dear sir, 30
Your affectionate servant,

John Wesley

Address: 'To / Mr Blackwell / In Change Alley / London'.
No *postmark* or indications of postal *charge*; apparently delivered by hand.
Endorsement: 'Revd Mr John Wesley / Everton 2nd March 1759'.
Source: holograph; MARC, MAM JW 1/63.

[11] Sarah Ryan and Sarah Crosby.

To William Allwood

NORWICH
MARCH 6, 1759

Dear Billy,
    You spoil my plan. I had appointed, with God's leave, to be at
5 Wakefield on Wednesday, April 18. But you tell me I must be at York.
If I must, who can help it? Then I must set out from Epworth that
morning, dine at Selby about noon, and so go on in the afternoon
for York.[12] But I hope you will begin the building directly. I suppose
Dr. Cockburn has my plan.[13] Lose no time. I have some money in
10 my hands for you.[14] The King's business requireth haste.[15] You may
still direct your letters to London. I am,
        Your affectionate friend and brother,

                                        [J. Wesley]

Address: 'To Mr. Will. Alwood, At Mr. John Hall's, / In Newgate Street,
    York'.
Source: published transcription; Telford, *Letters*, 4:55.

To Dorothy Furly

NORWICH
15   MARCH 6, 1759

My Dear Sister,
    I shall always be glad to hear from you when you can write with-
out hurting yourself. But I am almost afraid to write, for fear of
tempting you to answer whether you can or not.

---

[12] JW's *Journal* for Apr. 18, 1759 (21:187 in this edn.) indicates that he did just this.
[13] Dr. Thomas Cockburn of York, a younger classmate of CW at Westminster, who had
become a supporter of the Methodist movement in York. He later moved to Jamaica, where he
died in 1768.
[14] Probably funds raised for a new preaching house at York.
[15] 1 Sam. 21:8.

Since you left Kingswood, I hope you use the water at the Hot Wells as often as possible.[16] If anything medicinal profit you, probably it will be this. But perhaps God will not suffer you to be healed by outward medicines. It may be he is determined to have all the glory of his own work. Meantime he designs by this weakness of body to keep your soul low as a weaned child. There is a wonderful mystery in the manner and circumstances of that mighty working whereby he subdues all things to himself and leaves nothing in the heart but his pure love alone.

I have no doubt but God will give you the answer to that prayer,

> Let me thy witness live,
> When sin is all destroyed!
> And then my spotless soul receive,
> And take me home to God![17]

I am, my dear sister,
    Your affectionate brother,

J. Wesley

Source: published transcription; Benson, *Works*, 16:323–24.

To Matthew Lowes[18]

My Dear Brother,

Lawrence Coughlan,[19] who was at first appointed for Whitehaven, is to set out from Colchester on Monday and to stay at

---

[16] Furly has apparently now gone to Clifton, just south of Bristol and adjacent to Hot Wells (see the letter of Apr. 13, 1758).

[17] CW, Hymn for Believers #15, st. 7, *HSP* (1749), 1:219.

[18] Matthew Lowes (1721–94) served as an exhorter for several years, before becoming an itinerant preacher in 1755; see Atmore, *Memorial*, 244–46.

[19] Lawrence Coughlan, of Irish ancestry, first shows up in the list of itinerants in 1758 (see 10:281 in this edn.). He would have a colorful ministry, reaching to North America and including being ordained twice. See 21:175, n. 91 in this edn.; and Atmore, *Memorial*, 80–83.

Whitehaven till the Conference in the beginning of August. Till
he comes, I desire you diligently to inquire whether the bulk of
the society are for or against W. Wilson's preaching. If they are
against it, he had better not preach at Whitehaven (but he may
5   preach anywhere else) till I come. If the bulk of them are for it, let
him preach at some times; at others brother Browning may read a
sermon.[20] But if he does speak, let him take care to conclude the
whole service within the hour.

Certainly, rather than any flame should have arisen concerning it,
10 brother Hodgson and the rest ought to have dropped their opposition. What would not one do (except sin) that brotherly love may
continue! I am,
                Your affectionate brother,

                                    [J. Wesley]

Address: 'To Mr. Matthew Lowes, At the Methodist / Preaching-house,
    In Whitehaven'.
Source: published transcription; Telford, *Letters*, 4:56–57.

To Selina (Shirley) Hastings, Countess of Huntingdon[21]

15   NORWICH
                                    MARCH 10, 1759

The agreeable hour which I spent with your Ladyship the last
week recalled to my mind the former times, and gave me much matter of thankfulness to the giver of every good gift. I have found
20 great satisfaction in conversing with those instruments whom God
has lately raised up. But still there is I know not what in them whom
we have known from the beginning, and who have borne the burden
and heat of the day, which we do not find in those who have risen
up since, though they are upright of heart. Perhaps, too, those who
25 have but lately come into the harvest are led to think and speak

---

[20] Neither Wilson nor Browning are listed among itinerants at this point. Wilson may
have been an exhorter.

[21] This is the first surviving personal letter from JW to Selena (Shirley) Hastings, Countess of Huntingdon (as compared to his preface to *MSP*, 26:114–16 in this edn.). JW consistently addressed her as 'Lady Huntingdon'.

more largely of justification and the other first principles of the doctrine of Christ. And it may be proper for *them* so to do. Yet *we* find a thirst after something farther. We want to sink deeper and rise higher in the knowledge of God our Saviour. We want all helps for walking closely with him whom we have received, that we may 5 the more speedily come to the measure of the stature of the fullness of Christ.[22]

Mr. Berridge[23] appears to be one of the most simple as well as most sensible men of all whom it has pleased God to employ in reviving primitive Christianity. I designed to have spent but one night 10 with him, but Mr. Gilbert's[24] mistake (who sent him word I would be at Everton on Friday) obliged me to stay there another day, or multitudes of people would have been disappointed. They come now twelve or fourteen miles to hear him, and very few come in vain. His word is with power. He speaks as plain and home as John 15 Nelson, but with all the propriety of Mr. Romaine and tenderness of Mr. Hervey.[25]

At Colchester likewise the word of God has free course—only no house will contain the congregation. On Sunday I was obliged to preach on St. John's Green. The people stood on a smooth sloping 20 ground, sheltered by the walls of an old castle, and behaved as men who felt that God was there.

I am persuaded your Ladyship still remembers in your prayers,
Your willing servant for Christ's sake,

John Wesley 25

Source: published transcription; Seymour, *Huntingdon*, 1:398–99, compared with *Wesleyan Methodist Magazine* 80 (1857): 691–92.

[22] See Eph. 4:13.
[23] JW had stayed at Everton with John Berridge on Mar. 1 and 2 (see *Journal*, 21:178–79 in this edn.).
[24] Nicholas Gilbert, who was assisting JW in London this year.
[25] JW compares one of his itinerant preachers known to Lady Huntingdon with two evangelical clergy with whom she worked closely, William Romaine and James Hervey (now deceased).

To Ebenezer Blackwell

NORWICH
MARCH 12, 1759

Dear Sir,
   You have entirely satisfied me as to what I was afraid of.[26] We are
5   at present upon pretty good terms. And I am not without hope that
this good understanding will continue for some time longer. I am
sure it will, if he who has the hearts of all men in his hand sees it to
be expedient for me.
   You have never yet spoken to me with more freedom than was
10 agreeable to me. Your freedom is the best proof of your friendship.
There are not many that will deal freely with me. Nor indeed are
there many from whom I would desire it, lest it should hurt themselves without profiting me. But I do desire it of *you*; and do not
doubt but it will profit me, as it has done in time past.
15   I know not if in all my life I have had so critical a work on my
hands as that wherein I am now engaged. I am endeavouring to
gather up those who were once gathered together and afterwards
scattered by James Wheatley.[27] I have reunited about seventy of
them, and hope this evening to make up an hundred. But many
20 of them have wonderful spirits, having been always accustomed to
teach their teachers. So that how they will bear any kind of discipline I cannot well tell.
   At Colchester the case is far otherwise. About an hundred and
sixty simple, upright people are there united together, who are as
25 little children, minding nothing but the salvation of their souls.
Only they are greatly distressed for a larger house. What we could
have done last Sunday I know not, but that, the day being mild,
I took the field and preached on St. John's Green. I see but one
way—to build a commodious house; and I desired them to look out
30 for a piece of ground. It is true they are poor enough. But if it be
God's work, he will provide the means.

---

[26] Referring to tensions with his wife Mary, see the letter of Mar. 2.
   [27] Wheatley had been expelled from Methodist itinerancy in 1751 for sexual immoral-
ity (see 26:464–65 in this edn.). He became an independent preacher, and built a chapel in
Norwich called the Tabernacle, which grew for a while, until further indiscretions by Wheatley
came to light. In the aftermath, in Nov. 1758 Wheatley offered to lease the Tabernacle to JW
(see *Journal*, Nov. 3, 1758, 21:170 in this edn.), who was exploring how he could minister to
this bruised and scattered society.

Wishing an increase in all grace both to Mrs. [Elizabeth] Black-well, Mrs. Dewal,[28] and you, I remain, dear sir,
    Your very affectionate servant,

John Wesley

Address: 'To / Mr Blackwell / In Change Alley / London'.
Postmarks: 'NOR / WICH' and '14 / MR'. *Charge*: '4'.
Endorsement: 'Revd Mr John Westley / Norwich 12 March 1759'.
Source: holograph; MARC, MAM JW 1/64.

To an Unidentified Woman

COLCHESTER   5
MARCH 20, 1759

My wife, Miss —,[29] surprised me last night by informing me you
are left mistress of a large fortune. Shall I say, agreeably surprised
me! I cannot tell. Because I believe there is another world, and I do
not know what influence this change may have on your condition.   10
Therefore I am in fear and in hope. You may be hereby far more
happy or far more miserable in eternity! O make a stand! Consider
the situation you are in. Perhaps never before were you in so great
danger. You know a little of your natural tempers. Now you have
means of indulging and thereby inflaming them to the uttermost.   15
And how many will incite you so to do! How few will dare to warn
you against it! Now what food will you have for *pride*! What infinite
temptations to think more highly than you ought to think! You do
so already. But O where will you stop! The good Lord arrest the
storm in mid career! How impetuously now, unless God interpose,   20
must *self-will* whirl you along! How deeply, unless he help, will you
shortly be immersed in practical atheism, as ten thousand things
will concur to drive God out of your thoughts, as much as if he
were not in the world! But, above all, how will you escape from being swallowed up in *idolatry*, love of the world, such as you never   25
knew before!

---

[28] Hannah Dewal (d. 1762), who lived with the Blackwell family at Lewisham.

[29] The publication of this and the prior letter of Feb. 21 together in *AM* implies that they
are to the same recipient, whom Telford suggested was 'Miss Johnson'.

Hitherto you have been greatly superior to every delicacy in *food*. But even this may assault you now, and perhaps raise in you other *desires* which you are now a stranger to. At present you are above the follies of *dress*; but will you be so a twelvemonth hence? May

5   you not easily slide into the 'pride of life',[30] in this as well as other instances, especially considering how your *vanity* will be gratified thereby! For who will not *admire* and *applaud* your admirable taste! It will only remain for you to *marry* some agreeable person that has much wit and sense with little or no religion; then it is finished!

10 Either you will be thoroughly miserable in this world or miserable to eternity.

'But what business is this of yours! Cannot you let me alone! What have I to do with you!' Believe me, I could very easily let you alone, if I had not a real and tender goodwill toward you, and if I

15 did not know (what perhaps you do not) that you have need even of me. You want friends who understand you well, and who dare tell you the whole, plain truth; and yet not in a surly, imperious manner, for then you could not receive it. I have endeavoured to do this once more. Will not you forgive me! I cannot but think, if you do

20 not thank, you will at least excuse,
    Your affectionate servant,

                                                      John Wesley

Source: published transcription; *Arminian Magazine* 2 (1780): 162–64.

To William Allwood

Norwich
March 29, 1759

25 Dear Billy,
    I believe each window may stand eight foot (the bottom of it) from the ground, and be four foot broad and six or seven high, arched at the top.[31]

---

[30] 1 John 2:16.
[31] At the new preaching house in York; see the previous letter of Mar. 6.

If you think it would do good, I should have no objection to preaching at Selby about eleven o'clock, as I come from Epworth on Wednesday, April 18.

Oblige Dr. Cockburn as far as possibly you can. We can *bear* with little tempers, though we do not *approve* of them.

I can say little now to what Thomas Tobias writes of. I should think a patient, mild man might quiet two scolding women.

Billy, pray and labour with your might! You may direct your next to me at Epworth. I am,

Your affectionate friend and brother,

J. Wesley

I doubt sister Hall[32] forgets me.

Source: holograph; privately held (current owner unknown, Wesley Works Editorial Project Archive includes a copy of front side only).

To Mary (Goldhawk/Vazeille) Wesley

My Dear Molly,

I must write once more. Then, if I hear nothing from you, I have done.

Above a year ago, while I suspected nothing less, you opened my bureau and took out many of my letters and papers. Mr. Blackwell advised me, before you, if you refused to restore them, to send that instant for a smith and break open your bureau and take my own, to prevent which you restored them. But it was not long before you robbed me again, and showed my private letters to more than twenty different persons on purpose to make them have an ill opinion of me. For the same end you spoke much evil of me while I was several hundred miles off.[33]

---

[32] Ruth Hall.

[33] JW defines 'evil-speaking' as 'speaking evil of an absent person' in Sermon 49, 'The Cure of Evil-speaking', §1, 2:252 in this edn.

Your pretence was that I conversed with sisters Ryan and Crosby.[34] I know it was only a pretence, and told your friends the humouring you herein would leave matters just where they were. I knew giving a person drink would not cure a dropsy.[35] How-
5   ever, at their instance I made the experiment. I broke off all correspondence with them, whether by speaking or writing.[36] For a while, having gained your point, you was in a good humour. Afterwards it was just as I said. You robbed me again. And your sin (as before) carried its own punishment, for the papers you had
10   stole harrowed up your soul and tore your poor fretful spirit in pieces.

Notwithstanding this, you wrote me two loving letters.[37] (I hope, not with a design of reading them to other people; which I shall not suspect if you assure me you have not read or shown
15   them in part or in whole to any one.) So that I was a little surprised when at our meeting in Colchester I found you thoroughly out of humour.[38] It really seemed as if you was heartily vexed by the papers you had taken, and so were resolved to have it out with me. Accordingly you could not refrain from throwing squibs[39] at
20   me even in company, and from speaking with such keenness when we were alone as I think no wife ought to speak to an husband— such as I apprehend you could not have used decently to any but Noah Vazeille.[40]

Perhaps you may now take the greater liberty, because, having
25   stripped me of all my papers, you imagine it is now absolutely impossible for me to justify myself. But you are under a mistake. To all that know me, my word is a sufficient justification. And if anything more is needful, I know One that is able to say to the grave, 'Give back!' Yea, and if he say it to jealousy, cruel as the grave, it shall hear
30   and obey his voice.

---

[34] I.e, his correspondence with Sarah Ryan and Sarah Crosby.

[35] 'Dropsy' was the term for swelling of bodily tissue due to accumulating liquid (i.e., an edema); thus, JW is saying that you do not cure a problem by giving in to it.

[36] Indeed, there is no evidence of correspondence between JW and Crosby or Ryan after Dec. 1758, until the mid 1760s.

[37] These letters have not survived, because Mary requested JW to destroy her letters after he received them.

[38] JW was in Colchester on Mar. 19, 1759, though his *Journal* makes no mention of Mary's presence there; see 21:179 in this edn.

[39] 'Squibs': broken firecrackers, a term used to describe caustic conversational insults.

[40] Mary's son by her first husband, who would be 12 years old at the time.

Wishing you the blessing which you now want above any other, namely, unfeigned and deep repentance, I remain,
Your much injured yet still affectionate husband,

John Wesley

Address: 'To / Mrs Wesley / At the Foundery / London'.
Postmarks: '13/AP' and 'LIN/COLN'. *Charge*: '4'.
Source: holograph; MARC, MAM JW 5/60.

To [James Lowther][41]

[WHITEHAVEN]   5
MAY 16, 1759

Dear Sir,

Since I received your favour I have had many thoughts on worldly and Christian prudence. What is the nature of each? How do they differ? How may we distinguish one from the other?   10

It seems *worldly prudence* either pursues *worldly ends*—riches, honour, ease, or pleasure—or pursues Christian ends on *worldly maxims* or by *worldly means*. The grand maxims which obtain in the world are: The more power, the more money, the more learning, and the more reputation a man has, the more good he will do. And   15 whenever a Christian, pursuing the noblest ends, forms his behaviour by these maxims, he will infallibly (though perhaps by insensible degrees) decline into worldly prudence. He will use more or less of conformity to the world, if not in sin, yet in doing some things that are good in themselves yet (all things considered) are not good   20 to him, and perhaps at length using guile or disguise, simulation or dissimulation, either seeming to be what he is not, or not seeming to be what he is. By any of these marks may worldly prudence be discerned from the wisdom which is from above.

---

[41] *AM* does not give the name of the recipient of either this or a follow-up letter on July 1. Telford identifies it as James Lowther (1736–1802), eventually Earl of Lonsdale. Lowther had inherited a family estate in Whitehaven (where JW was currently preaching) on the death of Sir William Lowther, his uncle (see JW's comment in *Journal*, May 19, 1759, 21:192 in this edn.). Being just 23 years of age, and recently elected a Member of Parliament for Cumberland, James Lowther had sent JW an inquiry about prudence. See *ODNB*.

This, *Christian prudence*, pursues *Christian maxims* and by *Christian means*. The ends it pursues are holiness in every kind and in the highest degree, and usefulness in every kind and degree. And herein it proceeds on the following maxims: The help that is done
5　upon earth, God doeth it himself. It is he that worketh all in all,[42] and that, not by human power. Generally he uses weak things to confound the strong,[43] not by men of wealth (most of his choicest instruments may say, 'Silver and gold have I none'[44]), not by learned or wise men after the flesh (no, the foolish things hath God
10　chosen[45]), not by men of reputation, but by the men that were as the filth and offscouring of the world.[46] All which is for this plain reason, 'that no flesh may glory in his sight.'[47]

Christian prudence pursues these ends upon these principles, by only Christian means. A truly prudent Christian, while in things
15　purely indifferent he becomes all things to all men,[48] yet wherever duty is concerned, matters the example of all mankind no more than a grain of sand. His word is then,

　　　… *Non me, qui caetera, vincit*
20　　*impetus; et rapido contrarius evehor orbi.*[49]

He will not, to gain the favour or shun the hate of all, omit the least point of duty. He cannot prevail upon himself on any account or pretence to use either simulation or dissimulation. There is no guile in
25　his mouth,[50] no evasion or ambiguity. Having one desire, one design, to glorify God with his body and with his spirit; having only one fear,

　　Lest a motion, or a word,
　　Or thought arise to grieve his Lord;[51]
30

Having one rule, the Word of God; one guide, even his Spirit; he goes on in childlike simplicity. Continually seeing him that is invisible, he

---

[42] See 1 Cor. 12:6.
[43] See 1 Cor. 1:27.
[44] Acts 3:6.
[45] See 1 Cor. 1:27.
[46] See 1 Cor. 4:13.
[47] 1 Cor. 1:29.
[48] See 1 Cor. 9:22.
[49] Cf. Ovid, *Metamorphoses*, ii.1.72–73; 'nor does the swift motion which overcomes all else overcome me, but I drive clear contrary to the swift circuit of the universe' (Loeb).
[50] See 1 Pet. 2:22.
[51] Cf. Isaac Watts, 'Song of Solomon, 2:14ff', st. 2, *Hymns and Spiritual Songs* (London, 1709), 53; included by JW in *Collection of Psalms and Hymns* (1737), 31.

walks in open day. Looking unto Jesus,[52] and deriving strength from him, he goes on in his steps, in the work of faith, the labour of love, the patience of hope, till he is called up to be ever with the Lord.

Oh that this were in all points your own character! Surely you desire it above all things. But how shall you attain? Difficulties and hindrances surround you on every side! Can you bear with my plainness? I believe you can? Therefore I will speak without any reserve. I fear you have scarce one friend who has not more or less of the prudence which is not from above. And I doubt you have (in or near your own rank) hardly one example of true Christian prudence! Yet I am persuaded your own heart advises you right, or rather God in your heart. Oh that you may hearken to his voice alone, and let all creatures keep silence before him![53] Why should they encumber you with Saul's armour![54] If you essay to go forth thus, it will be in vain. You have no need of this, neither of his sword or spear, for you trust in the Lord of hosts.[55] O go forth in his strength! and with the stones of the brook you shall overthrow all your enemies. I am, dear sir, Your obedient servant for Christ's sake,

John Wesley

Source: published transcription; *Arminian Magazine* 3 (1780): 445–47.

To Clayton Carthy[56]

Newcastle-Upon-Tyne 20
June 12, 1759

Dear Clayton,

I hope you have received the sermon upon the New Birth.[57] I can easily send you one a week. I have finished eight, and am now transcribing the fourth. You should supply any word that is wanting.

---

[52] See Heb. 12:2.

[53] See Hab. 2:20.

[54] See 1 Sam. 17:38–40, for this extended comparison to David.

[55] See Ps. 84:12 and similar verses.

[56] Clayton Carthy does not appear in any list of itinerants. He was apparently serving as JW's book steward in Bristol, assisting with compiling the fourth volume of *Sermons on Several Occasions*, which JW finished in early Oct. 1759 (see *Journal*, 21:231 in this edn.).

[57] Sermon 45, 'The New Birth' (2:187–201 in this edn.).

Go east, west, north, or south, to Norton[58] or elsewhere, and speak sense or nonsense for a quarter of an hour. I believe it will avail both for your soul and body more than you imagine.

I do 'think what is doing'.[59] By this post (to leave that poor sinner
5   without excuse) I have wrote once more in the following words:

> I make you one more offer. Only leave off
> speaking against me behind my back (whereby you
> do not hurt me, but the cause of God) and restore my
10   papers to me, and you will find me,
>   Your still affectionate husband,

My part is to go on my way and to finish my work. I am, dear Clayton,
15   Yours affectionately,

                       J. Wesley

Address: 'To / Mr Carthy / At the New Room in / Bristol'.
Source: holograph; Wesley's Chapel (London), LDWMM 1997/6773 (bottom half of address section is missing).

To [James Lowther][60]

[NEWCASTLE-UPON-TYNE]
JULY 1, 1759

Dear Sir,
20   Considering the variety of business which must lie upon you, I am not willing to trouble you too often, yet cannot any longer delay to return thanks for your favour of May 21st. How happy is it that there is an higher wisdom than our own to guide us through the mazes of life, that we have an unction from the Holy One to teach us of all
25   things where human teaching fails! And it certainly must fail in a thousand instances. General rules cannot reach all particular cases, in some of which there is such a complication of circumstances that

---

[58] Norton St Philip between Bath and Frome.

[59] Carthy had apparently asked if JW was aware of the turmoil being caused by his estrangement with his wife Mary.

[60] On recipient, see the prior letter of May 16, 1759.

God alone can show what steps we should take. There is one circumstance in your case which claims your peculiar attention, and makes it necessary often to check that boldness and simplicity which otherwise would be both your duty and pleasure. But oh how easily may you comply too far, and hurt yourself in hopes of gaining another; nay, perhaps hurt the other too, by that very compliance which was designed to help! And who is able to lay the line, to determine how far you should comply, and where fix your foot! May the God of wisdom direct you in all your steps! And I conceive he will rather do this by giving you light directly from himself in meditation and private prayer than by the advice of others, who can hardly be impartial in so tender a point. Is it not, then, advisable that you should much commune with God and your own heart? You may then lay aside all the trappings that naturally tend to hide you from yourself, and appear naked, as a poor sinful worm, before the great God, the creator of heaven and of earth, the great God, who is your father and your friend, who hath prepared for you a kingdom, who calls you to forget the little things of earth, and to sit down with him on his throne. O may you dwell on these things till they possess your whole soul and cause you to *love* the honour which cometh of God only!

 I am, dear sir,
   Your obedient servant,

            John Wesley

Source: published transcription; *Arminian Magazine* 3 (1780): 276–77.

To the Rev. Dr. John Taylor[61]

HARTLEPOOL
JULY 3, 1759

Rev. Sir,
 I esteem you as a person of uncommon sense and learning. But your doctrine I cannot esteem, and some time since I believed it my

---

[61] John Taylor (1694–1761), long-time pastor of a Presbyterian congregation in Norwich, had assumed the role of tutor at Warrington Academy in late 1757. He was a prominent voice among the 'rational dissenters', and JW's most extended apologetic treatise was a response to Taylor's *Scripture-Doctrine of Original Sin* (1740). For more details on Taylor and this work, see the editorial introduction to JW's *Doctrine of Original Sin*, 12:117–54 in this edn., and *ODNB*.

duty to speak my sentiments at large concerning your doctrine of *Original Sin.*[62] When Mr. Newton[63] of Liverpool mentioned this, and asked whether you designed to answer, you said you thought not, 'for it would only be a *personal controversy* between John Wes-
5   ley and John Taylor.' How gladly, if I durst, would I accept of this discharge from so unequal contest! For I am thoroughly sensible, humanly speaking, it is *'formica contra leonem'.*[64] How gladly, were it indeed no other than a *personal* controversy! But certainly it is not. It is a controversy *de re*[65] if ever there was one in this world.
10 Indeed, concerning a thing of the highest importance—nay, all the things that concern our eternal peace. It is *Christianity* or *heathenism*? For take away the scriptural doctrine of redemption or justification, and that of the new birth, the beginning of sanctification, or which amounts to the same, explain them as you do, suitably to
15 your doctrine of original sin, and what is Christianity better than heathenism? Wherein (save in rectifying some of our *notions*) has the religion of St. Paul any preeminence over that of Socrates or Epictetus?

This is, therefore, to my apprehension, the least a *personal contro-*
20 *versy* of any in the world. Your person and mine are out of the question. *The point* is, Are *those things* that have been believed for many ages throughout the Christian world real, solid *truths*, or *monkish dreams* and vain imaginations?

But farther, it is certain between you and me there need be no
25 *personal* controversy at all. For we may agree to leave each other's person and character absolutely untouched, while we sum up and answer the several arguments advanced as plainly and closely as we can.[66]

Either I or you mistake the whole of Christianity from the begin-
30 ning to the end! Either my scheme or yours is as contrary to the

---

[62] See JW, *Doctrine of Original Sin*, 12:155–481 in this edn.

[63] John Newton (1725–1807), a native of London and a former slave-trader, had a conversion experience on board his ship in March 1748. He continued to practice the slave trade through about 1756, when he abandoned it and became active in the Evangelical revival. He was currently supporting himself as a tax collector in the port of Liverpool, while seeking to be ordained. He would finally be ordained in 1764 and become vicar at Olney. He is best known for his hymns and his writings against the slave trade. He and JW had been in correspondence since at least early 1758 (see Newton to JW, Apr. 3). See *ODNB*.

[64] 'An ant against a lion'.

[65] 'On the very thing' or 'on a serious matter'.

[66] This challenge seems to have encouraged Taylor to collect a few observations on Wesley's volume. Taylor died before publishing these observations, but they were issued posthumously as *A Reply to the Reverend John Wesley's Remarks on 'The Scripture-Doctrine of Original Sin'* (London, 1767). There is no evidence that JW ever saw Taylor's response.

scriptural as the Koran[67] is. Is it mine, or yours? Yours has gone through all England and made numerous converts. I attack it from end to end. Let all England judge whether it can be defended or not!

Earnestly praying that God may give you and me a right understanding in all things, I am, rev. sir,

> Your servant for Christ's sake,

> J. W.

Source: published transcription; JW, *Journal*, July 3, 1759 (21:205–6 in this edn.).

To the Rev. Thomas Goodday[68]

YARM
JULY 6, 1759

Rev. and Dear Sir,

The few minutes I had the pleasure of spending with Mrs. Goodday and you made me desirous of your farther acquaintance.[69] I believe you will have no great taste for your former acquaintance, any farther than you find profitable for their souls. Indeed if you did not help *them*, they would hurt *you*, and the more if they were civil and good natured. 'Harmless men', so called, are the most mischievous of all. God deliver you and me out of their hands!

I have been often afraid lest you should light on another kind of mischievous creatures, called pre-deist[70] men. These are continually palming upon us the wisdom of the world, under the notion of Christian wisdom, hereby damping our zeal for God and destroying the childlike simplicity of faith. These, if we hearken to them,

---

[67] I.e., Quran.

[68] Thomas Goodday (1705–68) matriculated at Queen's College, Oxford, but never graduated. He was perpetual curate of Monkwearmouth from 1744 to his death. He became a close friend of JW, allowing him to preach in his church and hold services in a building next to his home; see JW, *Journal*, May 31, 1761, 21:326 in this edn. The transcriber of this letter mistakenly identifies it as to 'John' Goodday.

[69] Wesley would have passed through Monkwearmouth as he rode north from Sunderland to South Shields on June 23–24, 1759 (*Journal*, 21:203 in this edn.). This appears to be his first contact with Goodday.

[70] The transcriber marks this as a questionable reading.

will soon bring us again into bondage to worldly shame and the fear of man. And I know few clergymen in England, except Mr. Grimshaw,[71] who are not touched with it more or less. O sir, regard not man but God! Let his Spirit be your constant guide! When he convinces you that this or that would be to his glory, confer not with flesh and blood.[72] It is enough that God is on your side.

To him I commend you and yours. I am, dear sir,
    Your affectionate brother,

John Wesley

Source: privately held (current owner unknown; MARC, MA 1977/609 includes a transcription made in 1971).

To the Rev. Samuel Furly

YARM
JULY 7, 1759

Dear Sammy,

Our Conference at Leeds is to begin on Wednesday, August 1. I hope to see you at it.[73] If you are in Yorkshire some days sooner, we shall have more time together. Your present call to Kippax is clear.[74] When you are called farther, that will be clear also.

What avails all knowledge but that which ministers to the knowledge of Christ, and which qualifies us for saving our own souls and the souls of them that hear us? What knowledge you have of other things retain, but secure this in all and above all. I am, with love to Nancy, dear Sammy,
    Yours affectionately,

J. Wesley

---

[71] I.e., William Grimshaw of Haworth; see his letter to JW, May 30, 1747, 26:243 in this edn.

[72] Gal. 1:16.

[73] There is no record that Furly attended this or any of the Conferences. While repeatedly courted by JW, he did not become active in the Methodist connexion.

[74] Furly was preparing to move from Lakenheath to Kippax, Yorkshire, still as curate. He would come to know Lady Huntingdon while at Kippax.

Address: 'To / The Revd Mr Furly / At Lakenheath, Near Brandon / Suffolk / Turn at Caxton'.

Charge: '4'.

Source: holograph; Oklahoma City, Oklahoma, The Green Collection, GC.PPR.007734.1.

To Miss C—

YORK
JULY 15, 1759

Dear Miss C—,

Your letter gave me much satisfaction, though it was long before I received it. Now I find you can speak freely to me, and as you have   5
found the way, I hope to hear from you a little oftener. In a few days I hope to be at Leeds. Why should you not give me the pleasure of hearing from you there?

At present you are a captive of unbelief, though an unwilling captive. But I trust you shall ere long know One that bringeth the pris-   10
oners out of captivity. You can say from your heart,

> I would not to the foe submit,
>   I hate the tyrant's chain;
> Bring, Lord, the prisoner from the pit,   15
>   Nor let me cry in vain.[75]

And you will not cry in vain; only cry on, though it be weariness and pain to slothful flesh and blood. If instability and ingratitude were sufficient to prevent either present or future salvation, then   20
would no child of Adam ever have been saved from the foundation of the world. But these and all manner of sin are washed away by the blood of the covenant. You want only to be acquainted with this to have it sprinkled upon your heart. And how soon may it be? Why not now? If you have nothing to pay, leave all your harmlessness,   25
your good desires or works, all you have and are behind! Are you to be saved *freely*? Then be it as thou wilt!

[75] Cf. CW, Hymn 27, st. 4, *Redemption Hymns* (1747), 39.

Freely the gift of God receive,
Pardon and peace in Jesus find.[76]

5 Away with your preparation! The Lord himself prepare your heart
and then hearken thereto! Away with your reasoning! Be a little
child! Sink down before the Saviour of sinners, the lover of *your*
soul! Let him have the glory over you. What hinders?
Dear Miss C—, be not reserved or fearful when you speak to,
Your affectionate brother and servant,

10

J. Wesley

Source: published transcription; *Wesleyan Methodist Magazine* 70 (1847):
766–67.

To an Unidentified Man

EVERTON
AUGUST 6, 1759

Dear Sir,
In the *Minutes* of the Conference we observe ⟨that 'poring⟩
15 too much upon our inbred sin' may bring ⟨us 'under a⟩ kind of
bondage',[77] that is, when we fix, as it were, *both* eyes of the mind
upon it, whereas one only should be fixed upon this, and the other
constantly upon Christ. One with whom I was speaking a day or
two ago, who seems to be entered into rest, by looking at *sin alone*
20 had lost all her joy and peace, and almost her faith, and was like
a condemned unbeliever; while her friend (whom I j⟨udge to⟩ be
higher in grace than her) only felt an ine⟨xpress⟩ible want and emptiness (yet consistent with peace as well as with love) till she was
filled with the fullness of God. O tread in her steps! Be simple,
25 little, nothing; yet be loved of God, yet a member of Christ, a child
of God, an heir of all his promises! Be still, ⟨and know that⟩ he

---

[76] CW, 'The Fifty-Fifth Chapter of Isaiah', st. 4, *HSP* (1740), 2; the original has 'Frankly'
in place of 'Freely'.
[77] See Disciplinary Minutes, June 17, 1747, Q. 22, 10:805–6 in this edn.

is God![78] *Obmutesce, pulvis et cinis.*[79] ‹…› Καὶ γενήσεται γαλήνη ἡ μεγάλη[80] ‹…›

Source: holograph; MARC, MA 1995/020 (the ms. is severely damaged, with address portion entirely missing and only a large fragment of text).

To Dorothy Furly

LONDON
AUGUST 19, 1759

My Dear Sister,   5
The observing that rule might prevent abundance of mischief. I wish others would observe it as well as you. Thomas Walsh was a good and a wise man, yet there were some circumstances, not commonly known, which easily account for the darkness he went through before he went to paradise.[81]   10
I hope you have *talked* with Cornelius Bastable as well as heard him preach. He is an uncommon monument of the power of grace, strengthening the understanding as well as renewing the heart. For so weak a head and so bad a temper as he once had I do not know among all our preachers.[82]   15
Probably the difference between you and others lies in words chiefly. All who expect to be sanctified at all expect to be sanctified *by faith*. But meantime they know that faith will not be given but to them that *obey*. *Remotely*, therefore, the blessing depends on our works, although *immediately* on simple faith.   20
Enjoy while you may the advantage which I had once, and shall have again when God sees best. I am,
        Your affectionate brother,

J. Wesley

---

[78] See Ps. 46:10.

[79] 'Be silent, dust and ashes.'

[80] Cf. Matt. 8:26, 'καὶ ἐγένετο γαλήνη μεγάλη'; but JW has made it future tense: 'and there shall be a great calm'.

[81] Thomas Walsh's death in Apr. 1759 in Bristol (while Furly was in nearby Clifton) was accompanied with significant suffering and spiritual struggle; see *EMP*, 3:258–68.

[82] Cornelius Bastable (c. 1725–75), apparently a native of Middlezoy, Somerset, began 'exhorting' in 1747 and came to JW's attention as a promising prospective preacher in Sept. 1748. He appears in the Minutes as a 'probationary helper' in 1750, but did not advance to the regular itinerancy, likely because he married Catherine Stockdale (1726–86) in Cork in 1752 (see 10:205, 237 in this edn.). The couple was currently living in the Bristol area.

Certainly *you* may say to *me* whatever you have a mind, either by writing or speaking.

Source: published transcription; Benson, *Works*, 16:324–25.

To [the Rev. Thomas Jones][83]

LONDON
AUGUST 22, 1759

5   Sir,

Nothing is more certain than that the kingdom of God is not divided against itself;[84] that peace and joy in the Holy Ghost are no ways obstructive of righteousness, even in the highest degree of it. Hold fast, therefore, that whereunto you have attained,[85] and in

10   peace and joy wait for perfect love. We know 'this is not of works, lest any man should boast',[86] and it is no more of *sufferings* than it is of works. Nothing is absolutely pre-required but a sense of our want; and this may be a calm, peaceful, yea, a joyful sense of it. When I was lately in Rotherham, I talked with eleven persons who

15   seem to be perfected in love.[87] Of these Jane Green (the wife of one of our preachers[88]) was *facile princeps*[89]—higher and deeper in experience than them all—and she never was in darkness or heaviness one hour during the second conviction. Only she felt in a manner not to be expressed her own foolishness, emptiness, and nothing-

20   ness. And in this state she quietly continued till God said, 'Be thou clean'.[90]

While I was riding (since Christmas) three- or four-and-twenty hundred miles I found no want of strength. But when my work was at an end, so was my strength. When I want it, I shall have it again. I

[83] The transcription does not identify the recipient; Telford titles 'To Mr. Jones'. Rev. Thomas Jones had recently initiated contact with JW (see his letter of Mar. 21, 1759), and would be a fitting person for JW to ask for input on revising *NT Notes*.

[84] See Mark 3:25.

[85] See Phil. 3:16.

[86] Eph. 2:9.

[87] See JW, *Journal*, Aug. 2, 1759, 21:221 in this edn.

[88] Apparently a local preacher, as there were no itinerants of that name at the time.

[89] 'Easily the leader'.

[90] See Matt. 8:3 and parallels.

thought you was to have been here in October, but God's time is the best! He doth all things well. Why should we not trust him in all! I am, dear sir,

Ever yours,

[John Wesley] 5

Will you take the time and pains to read the *Notes* critically over, and give me your alterations and additions before I print another edition![91]

Source: secondary manuscript transcription; MARC, MA 1983/027 (Mather scrapbook).

To Richard Tompson

LONDON 10
AUGUST 22, 1759

I am afraid you would hardly save yourself harmless, by the publication of those letters.[92] However, if you are inclined to run the hazard, I do not object. Only it would be needful to advertise the readers, that what I wrote was in haste, just as I could snatch a little 15
time now and then, to answer the private letter of a private friend, without any thought of its going any farther.

I am,

Your affectionate brother,

J. Wesley 20

Source: published transcription; Tompson, *Original Letters*, 6.

[91] JW and CW spent December revising *NT Notes*, resulting in its definitive 3rd edn.; see JW, *Journal*, Dec. 12, 1759, 21:236 in this edn.

[92] Tompson included this letter in the preface to his publication of the interchange of letters between him and JW in 1755–56.

To the Editor of *Felix Farley's Bristol Journal*

BRISTOL,
OCTOBER 20, [1759]

Sir,

Since I came to Bristol I heard many terrible accounts concern-
5 ing the French prisoners at Knowle. As that 'they were so wedged
together that they had no room to breathe, that the stench of the
rooms where they lodged was intolerable, that their food was only
fit for dogs, that their meat was carrion, their bread rotten and un-
wholesome, and that in consequence of this inhuman treatment,
10 they died in whole shoals.'[93]

Desiring to know the truth, I went to Knowle on Monday, and
was showed all the apartments there.[94] But how was I disappointed!
1) I found they had large and convenient space to walk in, if they
chose it, all the day. 2) There was no stench in any apartment which
15 I was in, either below or above. They were all sweeter and cleaner
than any prison I have seen either in England or elsewhere. 3) Being
permitted to go into the larder, I observed the meat hanging up, two
large quarters of beef. It was fresh and fat, and I verily think as good
as I ever desire to eat. 4) A large quantity of bread lay on one side.
20 A gentleman took up and cut one of the loaves. It was made of good
flour, was well-baked, and perfectly well-tasted. 5) Going thence
to the hospital, I found that even in this sickly season there are not
thirty persons dangerously ill out of twelve or thirteen hundred. 6)
The hospital was sweeter and cleaner throughout than any hospital
25 I ever saw in London. I think it my duty to declare these things, for
clearing the innocence and the honour of the English nation.[95]

Yet one thing I observed with concern. A great part of these men
are almost naked, and winter is now coming upon them in a cold
prison and a colder climate than most of them have been accus-
30 tomed to. But will not the humanity and generosity of the gentlemen of Bristol prevent or relieve this distress? Did they not make
a notable precedent during the late war? And surely they are not
weary of well-doing.[96] Tuesday night we did a little according to our
power, but I shall rejoice if this be forgotten through the abundance

---

[93] The prison at Knowle, now a Bristol suburb but then a distinct village, was utilised in the Seven Years War and beyond.

[94] See JW, *Journal*, Oct. 15, 1759; 21:231 in this edn.

[95] When the *London Chronicle* republished this letter, it explained, 'The following letter will give pleasure as the honour of the nation is vindicated by it'.

[96] See Gal. 6:9.

administered by their liberality in a manner which they judge most proper. Will it not be both for the honour of their city and country, for the credit of our religion, and for the glory of God, who knows how to return it sevenfold into their bosom?

I am,   5

Your humble servant,

John Wesley

Source: published transcription; *Felix Farley's Bristol Journal* (Oct. 20, 1759). Reprinted in *London Chronicle* (Oct. 25–27, 1759), p. 408; and *Universal Chronicle or Weekly Gazette* (Oct. 27–Nov. 3, 1759), p. 347.

To Mary (Goldhawk/Vazeille) Wesley

COLEFORD
OCTOBER 23, 1759

Dear Molly,   10

I will tell you simply and plainly the things which I dislike. If you remove them, well. If not, I am but where I was.

I dislike 1) your showing any one my letters[97] and private papers without my leave. This never did any good yet, either to you or me or any one. It only sharpens and embitters your own spirit. And the   15
same effect it naturally has upon others. The same it would have upon me, but that (by the grace of God) I do not think of it.[98] It can do no good. It can never bring me nearer, though it may drive me farther off.[99] And should you do as you often threaten, then the matter is over. ⟨I[100]⟩ know what I have to do.[101]   20

In all this you are fighting against yourself. You are frustrating your own purpose, if you want me to love you. You take just the wrong way. No one ever was *forced* to love another. It cannot be. Love can only be won by *softness*; foul means avail nothing. But you say, 'I have tried fair means, and they did not succeed.' If they   25

---

[97] The ms. has a series of comments in this paragraph that are not in JW's hand (likely by Mary). Here is the first: 'Not being fit to be seen.'
[98] The comment is added: 'NO.'
[99] The comment is added: 'Imposable.'
[100] A small repair covers where this word would surely appear.
[101] The comment is added: 'Belye me as you have been?'

do not, none will. Then you have only to say, 'This evil is of the Lord.[102] I am clay in his hand.'[103]

I dislike 2) not having the command of my own house, not being at liberty to invite even my nearest relations so much as to drink a
5   dish of tea without disobliging *you*.

I dislike 3) the being myself a prisoner in my own house; the having my chamber door watched continually so that no person can go in or out but such as have your good leave.

I dislike 4) the being but a prisoner at large, even when I go abroad,
10   inasmuch as you are highly disgusted if I do not give you an account of every place I go to and every person with whom I converse.

I dislike 5) the not being safe in my own house. My house is *not* my castle. I cannot call even my study, even my bureau, my own. They are liable to be plundered every day. You say, 'I plunder you
15   of nothing but papers.' I am not sure of that. How is it possible I should? I miss money too, and he that will steal a pin will steal a pound. But were it so, a scholar's papers are his treasure—my journal in particular. 'But I took only such papers as relate to Sarah Ryan and Sarah Crosby.' That is not true. What are Mr. Landey's
20   letters to them? Besides, you have taken parts of my journal which relate neither to one nor the other.

I dislike 6) your treatment of my servants (though, indeed, they are not properly mine). You do all that in you lies to make their lives a burden to them. You browbeat, harass, rate them like dogs, make
25   them afraid to speak to me. You treat them with such haughtiness, sternness, sourness, surliness, ill-nature, as never were known in any house of mine for near a dozen years. You forget even good breeding, and use such coarse language as befits none but a fishwife.[104]

I dislike 7) your talking against me behind my back, and that ev-
30   ery day and almost every hour of the day; making my faults (real or supposed) the standing topic of your conversation.

I dislike 8) your slandering me, laying to my charge things which you know are false. Such are (to go but a few days back): that I beat you, which you told James Burges;[105] that I rode to Kingswood with
35   Sarah Ryan, which you told Sarah Rigby; and that I required you, when we were first married, never to sit in my presence without my leave, which you told Mrs. Lee, Mrs. Fry, and several others, and stood to it before my face.

---

[102] See 2 Kgs. 6:33.
[103] See Isa. 64:8.
[104] A woman that sells fish; connoting a vulgar woman.
[105] Burges lived in Bristol and had been an early supporter of the Kingswood School; see JW, *Journal*, Oct. 25, 1757, 21:129–30 in this edn.

I dislike 9) your common custom of saying things not true. To instance only in two or three particulars. You told Mr. Ireland,[106] 'Mr. Vazeille learnt Spanish in a fortnight.' You told Mr. Fry, 'Mrs. Ellison[107] was the author as to my intrigue in Georgia.' You told Mrs. Ellison 'you never said any such thing; you never charged her with it.' You also told her 'that I had laid a plot to serve you as Susannah was served by the two elders.'[108]

I dislike 10) Your extreme, immeasurable bitterness to all who endeavour to defend my character (as my brother, Joseph Jones, Clayton Carthy), breaking out even into foul, unmannerly language, such as ought not to defile a gentlewoman's lips if she did not believe one word of the Bible.

And now, Molly, what would any one advise you to that has a real concern for your happiness? Certainly 1) to show, read, touch those letters no more, if you did not restore them to their proper owner; 2) to allow *me* the command of my own house, with free leave to invite thither whom I please; 3) to allow me my liberty there that any who will may come to me without let or hindrance; 4) to let me go where I please and to whom I please without giving an account to any; 5) to assure me you will take no more of my papers nor anything of mine without my consent; 6) to treat all the servants where you are, whether you like them or no, with courtesy and humanity, and to speak (if you speak at all) to them, as well as others, with good nature and good manners; 7) to speak no evil of me behind my back; 8) never to accuse me falsely; 9) to be extremely cautious of saying anything that is not strictly true, both as to the matter and manner; and 10) to avoid all bitterness of expression till you can avoid all bitterness of spirit.

These are the advices which I now give you in the fear of God and in tender love to your soul. Nor can I give you a stronger proof that I am,

Your affectionate husband,

John Wesley

Address: 'To / Mrs Wesley'.
No *postmark* or indications of postal *charge*; apparently delivered by hand.
Source: holograph; Harvard University, Houghton Library, MS Eng 870 (44).

[106] James Ireland of Bristol (see the letter of Nov. 4, 1759).
[107] I.e., Susanna (Wesley) Ellison, JW's sister. At this point Susanna (or 'Suky') was living in London.
[108] Referring to the story in the apocryphal book of Susanna, included by the Catholic Church in the book of Daniel.

To the Editor of the *London Chronicle*

THE FOUNDERY [LONDON]
SUNDAY EVENING, NOVEMBER 4, 1759

Sir,

5   An hour or two ago I was informed that a letter is inserted in your yesterday's paper,[109] relating to one which I wrote at Bristol and which was since reprinted in London (p. 408).[110] I therefore think it my duty, being thus publicly required, to give a farther account of the steps I have taken.

10   On Tuesday, October 16 last, I made a collection at the New Room in Bristol for the French prisoners confined at Knowle. The money contributed then, and the next day, was about three and twenty pounds. I judged it best to lay this out in shirts and waistcoats, and accordingly bought, of Mr. Zephaniah Fry, in the Castle, check shirts and woollen cloth to the amount of eight pounds, ten shillings and

15   sixpence, and of Mrs. Sarah Coole in Wine Street, check linen to the amount of five pounds, seventeen shillings. The linen was immediately delivered out, partly to two or three poor women, who were to make them at the common price, partly to others, who were willing to make them for nothing; the woollen to John Heath in Castle

20   Ditch, who agreed to make the waistcoats at twenty-one pence each, and to whom (being poor) I advanced five shillings. The money remaining I lodged in the hands of Mr. James Ireland of Horse Street, as he speaks French readily, and Mr. John Salter, of Badminster, who had been with me both at the prison and the hospital. I directed

25   these 1) to give a waistcoat and two shirts to every one who was remanded from the hospital to the prison, and to keep about half the clothes which our money would procure, to be thus bestowed from time to time; 2) to dispose of the other half in the prison to those whom they should judge most needy and most deserving.

30   I am, sir,
Your very humble servant,

John Wesley

Source: published transcription; *London Chronicle* (Nov. 3–6, 1759), p. 440.[111]

[109] This unsigned letter to the editor (*London Chronicle*, Nov. 1–3, 1759, p. 431), while focused on appealing to upper class British for aid for the French prisoners, had described the apparent Methodist contribution as 'some little succour' and suggested the amount given was unclear.
[110] I.e., JW's letter to *Felix Farley's Bristol Journal*, Oct. 20, 1759, which was reprinted in the *London Chronicle*.
[111] An extract of this letter was reprinted in 1791, when questions were raised immediately after JW's death about his propriety in dealing with funds raised among his people; see *Lloyd's Evening Post* (1791), p. 244; and *Morning Chronicle* (Mar. 11, 1791), p. 4.

To the Rev. Samuel Furly

LONDON
NOVEMBER 21, 1759

Dear Sammy,

At present you are just *where* you ought to be and *as* you ought to be. It is of great use to be in suspense.[112] Nothing more effectually breaks our will. While you stay, you do well to give all the assistance you can to the society. They must be weak and undisciplined as yet. Probably they want you more than once a month.

I doubt not of Abraham's being perfected in love. But he was rather under the evangelical than the legal dispensation.[113] And none can doubt but all the Jewish believers were perfected before they died. But that many of them were perfected *long before* they died, I see no reason to think. The Holy Ghost was not *fully* given before Jesus was glorified. Therefore 'the law' (unless in a very few exempt cases) 'made nothing perfect'.[114]

It is certain the word 'perfect' in the Old Testament bears several senses. But we lay no stress upon the word at all. The thing is *pure love*. The promise of this was given by Moses, but not designed to be fulfilled till long after. See Deuteronomy 30:1–6. By the whole tenor of the words it appears it was *then*, when he had 'gathered' the Jews 'from all nations', that God was so to 'circumcise their hearts'.[115] However, this may be fulfilled in you and me. Let us hasten toward it!

With love to Nancy, I am,
    Your affectionate friend and brother,

J. Wesley

Address: 'To / The Revd Mr Furly / At Kippax, Near Ferry-bridge / Yorkshire'.
Postmarks: '22/10'; place stamp illegible. *Charge*: '4'.
Source: holograph; Melbourne, Queen's College, JW3.

---

[112] Furly's current role as curate at Kippax was not permanent; he was assisting Henry Crook, vicar of Kippax (see JW's letter to Furly, June 19, 1760).

[113] See this distinction in Sermon 40, *Christian Perfection*, II.8, 2:108 in this edn.

[114] Heb. 7:19.

[115] JW consistently took this concluding phrase as referring to entire sanctification; see Sermon 17, 'The Circumcision of the Heart', 1:398–414 in this edn.

To Mary (Goldhawk/Vazeille) Wesley

BEDFORD
NOVEMBER 24, 1759

My Dear Molly,

You have been much upon my thoughts this morning. Shall I tell
5   you what I thought? Then take it[116] in good part. Take it kindly, as
it is kindly meant.

What do you gain by keeping my papers, or at least think you
gain? Why, this: you gain the satisfaction of showing them, or parts
of them, to others; you gain the power of justifying *yourself*, and of
10   hurting (at least by vexing) *me*; you gain occasion to make people
think ill of *me*, and to make them think well of *you*. And hereby you
make yourself more friends and me more enemies.

Very well. But are you quite sure of this? Is it *pure satisfaction*
which you gain by showing them? Is there not often a doubt whether
15   you do right, a secret misgiving which spoils the satisfaction? Will
the *showing* them justify you for *taking* them? Is it not rather adding
sin to sin? And will not even men of the world say, 'What a wretch
is this, first to *rob*, then to *expose* her own husband'? If, therefore,
you make them think ill of me, you do not make them think well of
20   *yourself*. If you make me more enemies, you do not make yourself
one more friend. Nay, all these after a time are less your friends
than ever they were before.

But what if you did gain by it all that you suppose, would it
make amends for what you lose thereby? You totally lose my es-
25   teem, you violently shock my love, you quite destroy my confidence. You oblige me to lock up everything as from a thief; to
stand continually upon my guard, to watch all the time you are
near me, as never knowing what you may steal next and expose
to all the world. You cut yourself off from joint prayer. For how
30   can I pray with one that is daily watching to do me hurt? You cut
yourself off from all friendly intercourse with many who would
otherwise rejoice to converse with and serve you. You rob yourself
of many precious opportunities of public prayer and attending the
Lord's Table.

35   Now, how dearly must you love *justifying* yourself and *blackening*
me, if you will do it at this expense?

---

116 Orig., the word 'it' is doubled at the end of one line and at the beginning of the next.

O Molly, throw the fire out of your bosom! Shun as you would a serpent those that stir it up. And see in a true light,
Your affectionate husband,

John Wesley

Address: 'To / Mrs Wesley / At the Foundery / London'.
Postmark: '26/NO' (twice stamped). *Charge*: '3'.
Source: holograph; MARC, MAM JW 5/61.

To Mr. I'Ans.[117]

LONDON 5
DECEMBER 11, 1759

Sir,

I return you thanks for transmitting that letter to me. I am glad our little service was so well accepted.[118] If I should see Bristol again before those poor men return home, I would use what interest I 10 have in order to assist them a little farther. I am, sir,
Your most humble servant,

John Wesley

Address: 'To Mr I'Ans. in Bristol'.
Endorsement: 'London 11th December. 1759. Parson John Wesley's thanks for sending him the French Prisoners Letter of thanks for Collection on their behalfe. / Recd Mr. Wiggington 18th Do. And inserted a paragraph of thanks in Mr. Felix Farley's News-Paper'.
Source: holograph; National Library of Scotland, MS. 588, no. 1292.

---

[117] The manuscript is possibly abbreviating the name I'Anson. Thomas and Bryan I'Anson, brothers who shared a legal practice in Westminster and often assisted the Wesley brothers (see 21:308, n. 73 in this edn.), are possible recipients, though it is not clear they would be in Bristol.

[118] I.e., assistance in providing winter clothing for French prisoners held in Knowle, described in the letters of Oct. 20 and Nov. 4 above.

1760

To George Merryweather[1]

My Dear Brother,

I received yours with the bill a day or two ago. I wish you would
5 everywhere recommend two books in particular—*The Christian
Pattern* and the *Primitive Physick*.[2] 'Tis a great pity that any Methodist should be without them.

I wonder brother Mather[3] does not write to me. He should not
forget his friends. I hope the gentleman with whom I breakfasted at
10 Yarm[4] has not forsaken you. Even the rich *may* enter into the kingdom, for with God all things are possible.

See that you stir up the gift of God that is in you.[5] What is our
Lord's word to *you*? 'Let the dead bury their dead; but follow thou
me!'[6] I am,
15   Your affectionate brother,

J. Wesley

Address: 'To / Mr George Merryweather / In Yarm / Yorkshire'.
Postmarks: '26/IA' (double stamped) and a triangular mark that is illegible.
    Charge: '4'.
Endorsement: 'Jany 1760'.
Source: holograph; Wesley's Chapel (London), LDWMM 1992/410/2.

---

[1] George Merryweather was a merchant in Yarm on Tees, who became in the late 1740s an active promoter and generous patron of Methodism, especially within the extensive Yarm circuit; see *WHS* 44 (1983): 47, 80–81.

[2] I.e., JW's abridged version of Thomas à Kempis's *The Imitation of Christ* (*Bibliography*, No. 45) and his collection of medical advice (*Bibliography*, No. 138 and Vol. 32 in this edn.).

[3] Alexander Mather (1733–1800) was converted under JW's preaching in London in 1754 and became an itinerant in 1757. For more detail, see *EMP*, 2:158–239; Atmore, *Memorial*, 256–66; and 21:309, n. 78 in this edn.

[4] Perhaps Mr. Waldy, a landed proprietor in Yarm to whom JW referred in a letter to Merryweather of Dec. 28, 1767.

[5] See 2 Tim. 1:6.

[6] Matt. 8:22.

To the Editor of *Lloyd's Evening Post*

WINDMILL HILL[7] [LONDON]
FEBRUARY 18, 1760

Sir,

On Sunday, December 16 last, I received a £20 bank bill from an
anonymous correspondent, who desired me to lay it out in the manner   5
I judged best for the use of poor prisoners.[8] I immediately employed
some in whom I could confide to inquire into the circumstances of
those confined in Whitechapel and New Prison.[9] I knew the former
to have very little allowance even of bread, and the latter none at all.
Upon inquiry they found one poor woman in Whitechapel Prison   10
very big with child and destitute of all things. At the same time I
casually heard of a poor man who had been confined for nine months
in the Poultry Counter,[10] while his wife and three children (whom
he before maintained by his labour) were almost perishing through
want. Not long after, another poor woman, who had been diligent   15
in helping others, was herself thrown into Whitechapel Prison. The
expense of discharging these three and giving them a few necessar-
ies amounted to £10 10s. One pound fourteen shillings I expended
in stockings and other clothing, which was given to those prisoners
who were in the most pressing want. The remainder, seven pounds   20
sixteen shillings, was laid out in bread, which was warily distributed
thrice a week. I am therefore assured that the whole of this sum was
laid out in real charity. And how much more noble a satisfaction must
result from this to the generous benefactor (even supposing there
were no other world, supposing man to die as a beast dieth[11]) than he   25
could receive from an embroidered suit of clothes or a piece of plate
made in the newest fashion? Men of reason, judge!

I am, sir,

Your humble servant,

30

John Wesley

Feb. 23, 1760

I began this letter some days since, but had not leisure to finish it.

---

[7] The location of the Foundery.

[8] Probably due to publicity about JW's help offered the French prisoners held in Knowle
prison in Bristol, described in earlier letters of Oct. 20 and Nov. 4, 1759.

[9] Whitechapel was a debtor's prison serving Stepney and Hackney; New Prison was located in Clerkenwell and held persons accused of petty or serious crimes.

[10] More commonly known as 'Poultry Compter', this was a sheriff's prison in London
City.

[11] See Eccles. 3:19.

Source: published transcription; *Lloyd's Evening Post and British Chronicle*
(Feb. 22–24, 1760), p. 190; reprinted in *Universal Chronicle and Westminster Journal* (Feb. 23–Mar. 1, 1760), p. 67.

To the Rev. Samuel Furly

LONDON
FEBRUARY 25, 1760

Dear Sammy,
    At present I have but just time to tell you I hope to be at Leeds
5   on Tuesday, March 11.
    Your manner of proposing your objection puts me in mind of
your friend Mr. Dodd. You speak *ex cathedra*.[12] But the matter is
not so clear as it appears to you. It is, however, a point, though considered long ago, worth considering again and again. But you must
10   stay your stomach till you either see or hear again from,
        Your affectionate brother,

J. Wesley

Source: holograph; Toronto, United Church of Canada Archives, 97.002C,
3-3 (address portion missing).

To Jane Catherine March[13]

WEDNESBURY
MARCH 4, 1760

15   Certainly the more freedom you use, the more advantage you will
find. But at the same time it will be needful continually to remem-

---

[12] Latin 'from the teaching office'; i.e., as if delivering a papal pronouncement.
[13] This is the first of a sequence of letters in the *Methodist Magazine* for 1791 attributed to
John Wesley and addressed 'To a Member of the Society', running from 1760 to 1777. Telford
gathered a convincing array of evidence pointing to "Miss March" as the recipient of these
letters (*Letters*, 4:85). Jane Catherine March (c. 1744–1820) was the daughter of prosperous
merchant Thomas March (d.1754) and his wife Jane (née Lisle) of St. Peter Le Poer parish
in London. The teen-age March had recently become connected to some London Methodist,
likely through friendship with Mary Bosanquet. Miss March inherited a significant family
estate, and never married. She eventually settled in Bristol, where she was buried Feb. 26, 1820.

ber from whom every good and perfect gift cometh.[14] If he blesses our intercourse with each other, then we shall never repent of the labour.

It is a blessing indeed when God uncovers our hearts and clearly shows us what spirit we are of. But there is no manner of necessity that this self-knowledge should make us *miserable*. Certainly the highest degree of it is well consistent both with peace and joy in the Holy Ghost. Therefore how deeply soever you may be convinced of pride, self-will, peevishness, or any other inbred sin, see that you do not let go that confidence whereby you may still rejoice in God your Saviour. Some, indeed, have been quite unhappy though they retained their faith, through desire on the one hand and conviction on the other. But that is nothing to you; you need never give up anything which you have already received. You will not, if you keep close to that:

> For this my *vehement* soul *stands still*;
> Restless, *resigned*, for this I wait.[15]

We have a fuller, clearer knowledge of our own members than of those belonging to other societies, and may therefore, without any culpable partiality, have a better opinion of them.

It is a great thing to spend all our time to the glory of God. But you need not be scrupulous as to the precise time of reading and praying; I mean, as to the dividing it between one and the other. A few minutes one way or the other are of no great importance.

May he who loves you fill you with his pure love! I am,
    Your affectionate brother,

John Wesley

Source: published transcription; *Methodist Magazine* 22 (1799): 47–48.

---

[14] See Jas. 1:17.
[15] CW, 'The Just Shall Live By Faith', st. 19, *HSP* (1740), 164; emphasis added by JW.

To an Unidentified Man[16]

MANCHESTER
MARCH 17, 1760

Sir,

5   The humanity which you showed during the short time I had
the pleasure of conversing with you at Lewisham emboldens me to
trouble you with a line in behalf of a worthy man.

I apprehend the collector at Northwich in Cheshire has informed
the Honourable Board that 'Mr. James Vine is a preacher at Northwich and makes disturbances in the town'. That he attends the
10   preaching of the Methodists is true. But it is not true that he is
a preacher. It is likewise true that the rabble of Northwich have
sometimes disturbed our congregations.[17] But herein Mr. Vine was
only concerned as a sufferer, not an actor. I know him to be a careful, diligent officer, and a zealous lover of King George.

15   Wishing you all temporal and spiritual blessings, I remain, sir,
Your obedient servant,

John Wesley

Endorsement: 'Revd Mr John Wesley / Manchester 18 March 1760'.
Source: holograph; Bridwell Library (SMU), address portion missing.

To Elizabeth (Hastings) Rawdon, Countess of Moira[18]

LIVERPOOL
MARCH 18, 1760

20   My Lady,

It was impossible to see the distress into which your Ladyship
was thrown by the late unhappy affair without bearing a part of it,

---

[16] Although Thomas Jackson listed the recipient of this letter as Ebenezer Blackwell in
his editions of JW's *Works* (probably because it refers to Lewisham where Blackwell lived),
Telford pointed out that it is not in the more familial style in which JW typically wrote to
Blackwell. Telford suggested that the letter was probably addressed to someone in authority in
the Excise Office whom JW met at Mr. Blackwell's at Lewisham (*Letters*, 4:86).

[17] JW reports being attacked later in Northwich in his *Journal*, Aug. 3, 1762, 21:382 in
this edn.

[18] Elizabeth (Hastings) Rawdon (1731–1808) was the oldest daughter of Selina, Countess
of Huntingdon, and the third wife of John Rawdon, having married him in 1752. The Rawdons
hosted JW at Moira (13 miles southwest of Belfast), and he preached in front of their home on
May 1 and 12, 1760 (see *Journal*, 21:252, 260 in this edn.). JW refers to his host in the *Journal*
account as the Earl of Moira, a title not awarded until 1761 but true by the time that this installment of the *Journal* was published.

without sympathising with you.[19] But may we not see God therein? May we not both hear and understand his voice? We must allow it is generally 'small and still',[20] yet he speaks sometimes in the whirlwind. Permit me to speak to your Ladyship with all freedom, not as to a person of quality, but as to a creature whom   5
the Almighty made for himself and one that is in a few days to appear before him.

You *were* not only a nominal but a real Christian. You *tasted* of the powers of the world to come.[21] You knew God the Father had accepted you through his eternal Son, and God the Spirit bore wit-   10
ness with your spirit that you were a child of God.[22]

But you fell among thieves,[23] and such as were peculiarly qualified to rob you of your God. Two of these in particular were sensible, learned, well-bred, well-natured, moral men. These did not assault you in a rough, abrupt, offensive manner. No, you would then have   15
armed yourself against them, and have repelled all their attacks. But by soft, delicate, unobserved touches, by pleasing strokes of raillery, by insinuations rather than surly arguments, they by little and little sapped the foundation of your faith, perhaps not only of your *living* faith, your 'evidence of things not seen',[24] but even of   20
your *notional*. It is well if they left you so much as an assent to the Bible or a belief that Christ is God over all![25] And what was the consequence of this? Did not your love of God grow cold? Did not you 'measure back your steps to earth again'?[26] Did not your love of the world revive, even of those poor, low trifles, which in your very   25
childhood you utterly despised?

Where are you now? Full of faith? Looking into the holiest, and seeing him that is invisible? Does your heart now glow with love to

---

[19] A cousin of Lady Rawdon, Lawrence Shirley, Fourth Earl Ferrers, had shot and killed the steward of his family estate on Jan. 18, 1760. The case was now heading towards trial in the House of Lords, at which Earl Ferrers would be convicted, despite his plea of insanity. He was executed on May 5, 1760.

[20] 1 Kgs. 19:12.

[21] See Heb. 6:5.

[22] See Rom. 8:16.

[23] See Luke 10:30.

[24] Heb. 11:1.

[25] One of the men JW may be referring to is Elizabeth's brother, Francis Hastings (1729–89), who become Earl of Huntingdon in 1749. Francis spent the early 1750s in Europe—particularly in France, where he was influenced by deistic thinkers. Cf. JW's comments on Francis in his letter to Mary Bishop, Feb. 7, 1778.

[26] Cf. Thomas Parnell, 'The Hermit', l. 227; retained in JW's abridged form in *MSP* (1744), 1:275.

him who is daily pouring his benefits upon you? Do you now even desire it? Do you now say (as you did almost twenty years ago),

> Keep me dead to all below,
> 5   Only Christ resolved to know;
> Firm, and disengaged, and free,
> Seeking all my bliss in thee?[27]

Is your taste now for heavenly things? Are not you a lover of
10   pleasure more than a lover of God?[28] And oh what pleasure! What is the pleasure of visiting, of modern conversation? Is there any more reason than religion in it? I wonder what rational appetite does it gratify? Setting religion quite out of the question, I cannot conceive how a woman of sense can—*relish*, should I say? No, but—*suffer* so
15   insipid an entertainment.
   Oh that the time past may suffice! Is it now not high time that you should awake out of sleep? Now God calls aloud! My dear Lady, now hear the voice of the Son of God and live![29] The trouble in which your tender parent is now involved may restore all that
20   reverence for her which could not but be a little impaired while you supposed she was 'righteous over-much'.[30] Oh how admirably does God lay hold of and 'strengthen the things that remain'[31] in you—your gratitude, your humane temper, your generosity, your filial tenderness! And why is this but to improve every right temper,
25   to free you from all that is irrational or unholy; to make you all that you *were*, yea, all that you *should* be; to restore you to the whole image of God? I am, my Lady,
   Yours, etc.,

J. Wesley

Source: published transcription; *Arminian Magazine* 6 (1783): 102–4.

---

[27] CW, 'Hymn on John 16:24', st. 4, *HSP* (1739), 220.
[28] See 2 Tim. 3:4.
[29] See John 5:25.
[30] Eccl. 7:16.
[31] Rev. 3:2.

To Mary (Goldhawk/Vazeille) Wesley

LIVERPOOL
MARCH 23, 1760

Poor Molly! Could you not hold out a little longer; not one month, not twenty days? Have you found out a pretence already for talking in the old strain? A thin one indeed. But, such as it is, 5
it may serve the turn for want of a better. 'You have taken a bed to pieces. And you want to put it in my study. And I do not tell you whether you may or no'! Truly I cannot look upon this whole affair as any other than a pretence. For what need had you to take the bed in pieces at all? And what need was there (if it was taken in pieces) 10
that it should lie just in the one little room which I have, when you have four rooms to yourself?

Alas! That to this hour you should neither know your duty nor be willing to learn it! Indeed, if you were a wise [woman], whether a good woman or not, you would long since have given me a *carte* 15
blanche.[32] You would have said, 'Tell me what to do, and I will do it. Tell me what to avoid, and I will avoid it. I promised to *obey* you, and I will keep my word. Bid me do *anything*, *everything*. In whatever is not sinful, I *obey*. You *direct*, I will follow the direction.'

This it had been your wisdom to have done long ago, instead of 20
squabbling for almost these ten years.[33] This it is both your wisdom and your duty to do now, and certainly better late than never. This must be your indispensable duty, till 1) I am an adulterer, 2) you can prove it. Till then I have the same right to claim obedience from *you* as you have to claim it from Noah Vazeille.[34] Consequently every act 25
of disobedience is an act of rebellion against God and the King, as well as against,

Your ((affectionate[35])) husband,

John Wesley

Address: 'To / Mrs Wesley / At the Foundery / London'.
Postmarks: '29/MR' and 'WARR / INGTON'. *Charge*: '4'.
Source: holograph; MARC, MAM JW 5/61A.

[32] Orig. 'Chart Blanche'; indicating full freedom or approval.
[33] They were married in February 1751. This comment implies that they had been at odds from the beginning in their marriage, though their early correspondence does not reveal this.
[34] Her son by her first marriage, now 13 years old.
[35] The word 'affectionate' has been very deliberately scored through in the ms.

To Jane Catherine March

LIVERPOOL
MARCH 29, 1760

Having a little longer reprieve, I snatch the opportunity of writing a few lines before we embark.[36] Prayer is certainly the grand
5   means of drawing near to God, and all others are helpful to us only
so far as they are mixed with or prepare us for this. The comfort of
it may be taken away by wandering thoughts, but not the benefit.
Violently to fight against these is not the best and speediest way to
conquer them, but rather humbly and calmly to ask and wait for his
10   help, who will bruise Satan under your feet.[37] You may undoubtedly
remain in peace and joy until you are perfected in love. You need
neither enter into a dispute when persons speak wrong, nor yet betray the truth; there is a middle way. You may simply say, 'I believe
otherwise, but I think and let think. I am not fond of contending on
15   this or any other head lest I receive more hurt than I can do good.'
Remember your calling. Be

> A simple follower of the Lamb,
> And harmless as a little child.[38]

20

Source: published transcription; *Methodist Magazine* 22 (1799): 48.

To Jane Catherine March

DUBLIN,
APRIL 16, 1760

Eltham is a barren soil indeed. I fear scarce any are to be found
there who know anything of the power of religion, and not many
25   that have so much as the form. But God is there, and he can supply
every want. Nothing contributes to seriousness more than humility,
because it is a preparation for every fruit of the Holy Spirit; and the
knowledge of our desperate state by sin has a particular tendency

---

[36] Wesley's *Journal* for this period indicates that the ship on which he had planned to sail to Dublin on Mar. 29 had been delayed by fog, so they postponed their departure until the next day; see 21:249 in this edn.

[37] See Gen. 3:15; Rom. 16:20.

[38] CW, 'Psalm 32', st. 2, *CPH* (1743), 70.

to keep us earnest after deliverance; and that earnestness can hardly consist with levity, either of temper or behaviour.

Those who have tasted of the goodness of God are frequently wanting in declaring it. They do not, as they ought, stir up the gift of God which is in every believer by exciting one another to contin- 5
ual thankfulness and provoking each other to love and good works. We should never be content to make a drawn battle, to part neither better nor worse than we met. Christian conversation is too precious a talent to be thus squandered away.

It does not require a large share of natural wisdom to see God 10
in all things, in all his works of creation as well as of providence. This is rather a branch of spiritual wisdom, and is given to believers more and more as they advance in purity of heart.

Probably it would be of use to you to be as regular as you can; I mean, to allot such hours to such employments. Only not to be 15
troubled when providence calls you from them. For the best rule of all is *to follow the will of God.*

Source: published transcription; *Methodist Magazine* 22 (1799): 49.

To the Rev. John Berridge

Dublin
April 18, 1760

Dear Sir, 20

Disce, docendus adhuc quae censet amiculus;[39] and take in good part my mentioning some particulars which have been long on my mind, and yet I knew not how to speak them. I was afraid it might look like taking too much upon me or assuming some superiority over you. But love casts out, or at least overrules, that fear.[40] So I will speak 25
simply, and leave you to judge.

It seems to me that, of all the persons I ever knew save one, you are the *hardest to be convinced.* I have occasionally spoken to you on many heads; some of a speculative, others of a practical nature. But I do not know that you was ever convinced of one, whether of 30

---

[39] Horace, *Epistles*, I.xvii.3; 'learn the views of your humble friend, who still needs some teaching' (Loeb).
[40] See 1 John 4:18.

great importance or small. I believe you retained your[41] own opinion in every one, and did not vary an hair's breadth. I have likewise
doubted whether you were not full as *hard to be persuaded* as to be
convinced, whether your will does[42] not adhere to its first bias, right
5   or wrong, as strongly as your understanding; I mean with regard
to any impression which another may make upon them. For perhaps you readily, too readily, change of your own mere motion, as
I have frequently observed great *fickleness* and great stubbornness
meet in the same mind. So that it is not easy to please you long, but
10 exceeding *easy* to offend you. Does not this imply the 'thinking'
very 'highly of yourself',[43] particularly of your own understanding?
Does it not imply, what is always connected therewith, something
of *self sufficiency*? 'You can stand alone. You care for no man. You
need no help from man.'[44] It was not so with my brother and me
15 when we were first employed in this great work. We were deeply
conscious of our own insufficiency, and though in one sense we
trusted in God alone, yet we sought his help from all his children,
and were glad to be taught by any man. And this, although we were
really alone in the work. For there were none that had gone before
20 us therein, there were none then in England who had trod that path
wherein God was leading us. Whereas *you* have the advantage which
we had not, you tread in a beaten path. Others have gone before you
and are going now in the same way, to the same point. Yet it seems
you *choose* to stand alone. What was necessity with *us* is choice with
25 *you*. You like to be unconnected with any, thereby tacitly condemning all.

But possibly you go farther yet. Do not you explicitly condemn
all your fellow labourers, blaming one in one instance, one in another, so as to be thoroughly pleased with the conduct of none?
30 Does not this argue a vehement proneness to condemn, a very high
degree of *censoriousness*? Do you not censure even *peritos in sua
arte*?[45] Permit me to relate a little circumstance to illustrate this.
After we had been once singing an hymn at Everton, I was just
going to say, 'I wish Mr. Whitefield would not try to mend my
35 brother's hymns. He cannot do it. How vilely he has murdered that
hymn, *weakening* the sense as well as *marring* the poetry!' But how
was I afterwards surprised to hear it was not Mr. Whitefield, but

---

[41] Orig. 'you'.
[42] Orig. 'do'.
[43] Rom. 12:3.
[44] JW appears to be quoting Berridge.
[45] 'Those skilled in their particular art.'

Mr. B[erridge]![46] In very deed it is not easy to *mend* his hymns any more than to imitate them. Has not this aptness to find fault frequently shown itself in abundance of other instances, sometimes with regard to Mr. Parker or Mr. Hicks,[47] sometimes with regard to me? And this may be one reason why you take one step which was   5
scarce ever before taken in Christendom—I mean, the discouraging the new converts from reading, at least, from reading anything but the Bible. Nay, but get off the consequence who can. If they ought to *read* nothing but the Bible, they ought to *hear* nothing but the Bible, so away with sermons, whether spoken or written!   10
I can hardly imagine that you discourage reading even our little tracts, out of jealousy, lest we should undermine you or steal away the affections of the people. I think you cannot easily suspect this. I myself did not desire to come among them, but you desired me to come. I should not have obtruded myself either upon them or   15
you, for I have really work enough, full as much as either my body or mind is able to go through. And I have, blessed be God, friends enough—I mean, as many as I have time to converse with. Nevertheless, I never repented of that I spent at Everton, and I trust it was not spent in vain.   20

I have not time to throw these thoughts into a smoother form, so I give you them just as they occur. May the God whom you serve give you to form a right judgement concerning them, and give a blessing to the rough sincerity of, dear sir,

Your affectionate servant,   25

John Wesley

Source: published transcription; *Arminian Magazine* 3 (1780): 499–501.

[46] Berridge would later publish his own collection of *Sion's Songs or Hymns* (London, 1785).

[47] William Parker, a Methodist sympathiser in Bedford; and William Hicks, rector of nearby Wrestlingworth, whom Berridge had converted to the Evangelical camp; see JW, *Journal*, Oct. 8, 1759, 21:171, n. 79 in this edn.

To Ebenezer Blackwell

Newry
April 26, 1760

Dear Sir,

I hope your lameness is now at an end, but not the benefit you have
reaped from it. May we not in every trial, great or small, observe the
hand of God? And does he send any sooner than we want it or longer
than we want it? I found the inflammation which I had in my eyes
last month came just in the right time.[48] The danger is that anything
of this kind should pass over before the design of it is answered.

Whether Miss [Mary] Freeman should make use of Lough
Neagh, or Lough Leighs (forty miles nearer Dublin), I suppose she
is not yet able to determine till I can send her some farther information, and that I cannot do to my own satisfaction till I am upon the
spot. For though Lough Neagh is scarce fifteen miles from hence,
yet I can hardly find any one here who knows any more of the circumstances of it than if it lay in the East Indies.

Hitherto I have had an extremely prosperous journey, and all the
fields are white to the harvest.[49] But that the labourers are few is not
the only hindrance to the gathering it in effectually. Of those few,
some are careless, some heavy and dull, scarce one of the spirit of
Thomas Walsh. The nearest to it is Mr. [James] Morgan, but his
body too sinks under him, and probably will not last long.

In a few days I expect to be at Carrickfergus, and to have from
those on whose word I can depend a full account of that celebrated
campaign.[50] I believe it will be of use to the whole kingdom. Probably the government will at last awake and be a little better prepared
against the next encounter.

When you have half an hour to spare, I hope you will give it me
under your own hand that Mrs. [Elizabeth] Blackwell and you are
not only in good health, but labouring more than ever after an
healthful mind, and trampling the world and the devil under your
feet. I am, dear sir,

Your ever affectionate servant,

John Wesley

The week after next I shall spend mostly at Sligo.

---

[48] Cf. JW, *Journal*, Mar. 24, 1760, 21:248 in this edn.
[49] See John 4:35.
[50] See his next letter to Blackwell on May 7.

Endorsement: 'Revd Mr John Wesley / Newry 26 April 1760'.
Source: holograph; Bridwell Library (SMU), address portion missing.

To Ebenezer Blackwell

CARRICKFERGUS
MAY 7, 1760

Dear Sir,

I can now give you a clear and full account of the late proceedings of the French here, as I now lodge at Mr. Cobham's, under the same 5 roof with Mons. Cavenac, the French Lieutenant-General.[51] When the people here saw three large ships about ten in the morning anchor near the town, they took it for granted they were English, till about eleven the French began landing their men. The first party came to the north gate between twelve and one. Twelve 10 soldiers planted on the wall (there were an hundred and sixty in the town) fired on them as they advanced, wounded the General, and killed several. But when they had fired four rounds, having no more ammunition, they were obliged to retire. The French then entered the town (at the same time that another party entered at 15 the east end of it), keeping a steady fire up the street, till they came near the Castle. The English then fired hotly from the gate and walls, killed their second General (who had burst open the gate and gone in sword in hand), with upwards of fourscore men. But, having no more cartridges nor any man that knew how to make them, 20 they thought it best to capitulate. They agreed to furnish such a quantity of provisions in six hours, on condition the French should not plunder. But they began immediately to serve themselves with meat and drink, having been in such pressing want that, before they landed, the men were glad to eat raw oats to sustain nature. And 25 some hours after, no provisions being brought, they took all they could find, with a good deal of linen and wearing apparel, chiefly from the houses whose inhabitants were run away. But they neither hurt nor affronted man, woman, or child, nor did any mischief for mischief's sake, though many of the inhabitants affronted them, 30

---

[51] French naval forces occupied Carrickfergus on Feb. 21, 1760, surprising town leaders. After five days, British troops from Belfast recaptured the town. This incident in the Seven Years War is referred to as the Battle of Carrickfergus.

cursed them to their face, and even took up pokers or other things to strike them.

I have had much conversation with Mons. Cavenac, who speaks Latin pretty readily. He is a Lieutenant-Colonel in the King's Guards and a Knight of the Order of St. Louis. (Indeed, all the soldiers were picked men drafted out of the Guards, and more like officers than common men.) I found him not only a very sensible man but thoroughly instructed even in heart religion. I asked him 'if it was true that they had a design to burn Carrick and Belfast'. (After one General was wounded and the other killed, the command had devolved upon him.) He cried out, 'Jesu, Maria! We never had such a thought! To burn, to destroy, cannot enter into the head or the heart of a good man.' One would think the French king sent these men on purpose to show what officers he has in his army. I hope there are some such in the English army. But I never found them yet. I am, dear sir,
　　　　Your affectionate servant,

　　　　　　　　　　　　　　　　　　John Wesley

Endorsement: 'Revd Mr John Wesley / Carrickfergus 7 May 1760'.
Source: holograph; Bridwell Library (SMU), address portion missing.

To John Rawdon, Earl of Moira[52]

SLIGO
MAY 18, 1760

My Lord,

I have taken the liberty to speak to Lady Rawdon all that was in my heart,[53] and doubt not but your Lordship will second it on every proper occasion. The late awful providence[54] I trust will not pass

---

[52] John Rawdon (1720–93), was at this point Baron of Moira; in 1761 he was elevated to Earl of Moira.

[53] JW was in Moira at the Rawdons' estate on May 1, 1760 (see *Journal*, 21:251–52 in this edn.), so he is probably referring to a conversation he had with Lady Rawdon, not just his letter to her of Mar. 18, 1760.

[54] Elizabeth Rawdon's cousin, the Earl of Ferrers, had been executed on May 5, 1760.

over without a suitable improvement. God has spoken aloud, and happy are they that hear and understand his voice.

In one respect I have been under some apprehension on your Lordship's account also. I have been afraid lest you should exchange the simplicity of the gospel for a philosophical religion. O my Lord, why should we go one step farther than this, 'We love him because he first loved us'?[55] I am,

> Your Lordship's most obedient servant,

> John Wesley

We go to Castlebar tomorrow, thence to Loughrea.

Source: holograph; Duke, Rubenstein, Frank Baker Collection of Wesleyana, Box WF 1 (address portion missing).

To Dorothy Furly

ATHLONE
JUNE 1, 1760

My Dear Sister,

I am persuaded it is not a little thing which will make me angry at *you*. I hope your thinking evil of me would not, for you may have many reasons so to do.

Try, perhaps by prayer and a little resolution you may avoid hearing those disputes about holiness. It implies no more than this. If John Jones or any other begins a discourse concerning the errors or sins of absent persons, tell him, 'I beg you would say no more on this head. I dare not, and I will not, hear, unless those persons were present.' If one begins any caution of that kind, stop him, only with mildness and good humour; say, 'I believe you speak out of kindness, but I must not hear. It both distresses and hurts my soul. Therefore, if you really wish my welfare, be silent, or let us call another cause.' Where you see good, you may add, 'I consulted Mr. Wesley on this head, and this was the advice he gave me.'

[55] 1 John 4:19.

No one ever 'walked in the light as God is in the light' (I mean in the full sense of the expression) till 'the blood of Jesus Christ had cleansed him from all sin.'[56] 'If we are perfectly saved, it is through his blood.' This is the plain meaning of the text, and it may be ful-
5   filled in you before you sleep. God is sovereign in sanctifying as well as justifying. He will act *when* as well as *how* he pleases, and none can say unto him, 'What dost thou?'

When the lungs are ulcerated, cold bathing not only does no hurt but is the most probable cure. Sammy is a letter in my debt. I do
10   not know but he is providentially called to this kingdom. I have now finished more than half my progress, having gone through two of the four provinces. Who knows whether I shall live to go through the other two? It matters not how long we live, but how well. I am, my dear sister,
15   Your affectionate brother,

John Wesley

Source: published transcription; Benson, *Works*, 16:325–26.

To the Rev. Samuel Furly

Dear Sammy,
20   Certainly you cannot remove without giving Mr. Crook a quar-ter's warning.[57] If you do remove, you need be under no concern about repaying, nor about those you leave behind. Our preachers, when it is needful, must allow them a little more time.

How easy it is to puzzle a cause, and to make a thousand plausible
25   objections to any proposition that can be advanced? This makes me quite out of conceit with *human understanding* and *human language*. So confused is the clearest apprehension! So ambiguous the most determinate expressions!

---

[56] 1 John 1:7.
[57] Henry Crook was vicar of Kippax, where Furly was a curate in training. In Apr. 1761 Furly moved to become a 'permanent curate' at Slaithwaite, Yorkshire.

Lay aside the terms 'Adamic law', gospel law, or any law. The thing is beyond dispute, and you may as well demand a scriptural proof that two and two make four.

Adam in Paradise *was able* to apprehend *all* things distinctly and to *judge truly* concerning them; therefore it was his duty so to do. But no man living *is* now *able* to do this; therefore neither is it the duty of any man now living. Neither is there any man now in the body who does or can walk in this instance by that rule which was bound upon Adam. Can anything be more plain than this: that Adam *could*, that I *cannot*, avoid mistaking? Can anything be plainer than this: if he *could* avoid it, he *ought*? Or than this: if I *cannot*, I *ought not*? I mean it is not my duty, for the clear reason that no one can do the impossible. Nothing in the sermon on the law contradicts this.[58] If anything does, it is wrong.

Oh what a work might be done in this kingdom if we had six zealous, active, punctual men in it! Be *you* one. I am, dear Sammy,
   Your affectionate brother,

J. Wesley

Address: 'To / The Revd Mr Furly / At Kippax, near Ferrybridge / Yorkshire'.
Postmark: '12/IY'. *Charge*: '4'.
Endorsement: '1760'.
Source: holograph; Melbourne, Queen's College, JW4.

To the Rev. Charles Wesley

COOLALOUGH[59]
JUNE 23, 1760

[[Dear Brother,]]
   Where you are I know not, and how you are I know not, but I hope the best.[60] Neither you nor John Jones has ever sent me your

---

[58] I.e., JW, Sermon 34, 'The Original, Nature, Properties, and Use of the Law', 2:4–19 in this edn.

[59] Orig., 'Coolylough'.

[60] There is no surviving evidence of correspondence between JW and CW between December 1756 and early 1760. This is the first surviving letter of JW to CW after that hiatus.

remarks upon that tract in the late volume of Sermons.[61] You are
not kind. Why will you not do all you can to make me wiser than I
am? Samuel Furly told me his objections at once, so we canvassed
them without loss of time. Do you know what is done, anything or
5   nothing, with regard to the small edition of the Notes?[62]

Mr. I'Anson writes me a long account of the Sussex affair.[63] It
is of more consequence than our people seem to apprehend. If we
do not exert ourselves, it may drive us to that bad dilemma, leave
preaching or leave the Church. We have reason to thank God it is
10   not come to this yet. Perhaps it never may.

In this kingdom nothing is wanting but a few more zealous and
active labourers. James Morgan, John Johnson, and two or three
more do their best; the rest spare themselves. I hope Sally and your
little ones are well. Where and how is my wife? I wrote to her on
15   Saturday last.

Adieu!

Where must the Conference be, at Leeds or Bristol? If we could but
chain or gag[64] the blatant beast, there would be no difficulty.

Address: 'To / The Revd Mr C. Wesley'.
No *postmark* or indications of postal *charge*; apparently delivered by hand.
Endorsement: in CW's hand, 'Wants to be found fault with, doubts whether
to leave the Church. Dreads the Blatant Beast.' and 'B. June 23. 1760'.
Source: holograph; MARC, DDWes 3/12.

[61] There were four tracts included in vol. 4 of JW's *Sermons on Several Occasions*, which
had been published in early 1760, but JW is referring to 'Thoughts on Christian Perfection'
(pp. 241–68 in that volume; 13:54–80 in this edn.), which he had included to address growing
debate within Methodist societies over the doctrine.

[62] The first two editions of *NT Notes* were issued in the large quarto format. JW was
inquiring about progress on the new edition, which he had decided to print in his favoured
duodecimo size. This smaller size resulted in the third edition being spread over three volumes, the first of which was published in late summer 1760 and the other two a year apart (see
Bibliography, No. 209).

[63] A Methodist preacher had preached at the home of Thomas Osborne at Rolvenden in
Kent, three miles from Sussex, on Mar. 13, 1760. The preacher and Osborne were each fined
£20 by a local magistrate. The Quarter Sessions confirmed their convictions, but the Court of
King's Bench overturned them; see Tyerman, *John Wesley*, 2:359.

[64] Orig., 'gagg'.

To Jane Catherine March

Sligo
June 27, 1760

A day or two ago I was quite surprised to find among my papers a
letter of yours, which I apprehend I have not answered.

Every one, though born of God in an instant, yea and sanctified in   5
an instant, yet undoubtedly grows by slow degrees both after the former and the latter change. But it does not follow from thence that there
must be a considerable tract of time between the one and the other. A
year or a month is the same with God as a thousand. If he wills, to do
is present with him. Much less is there any necessity for much suffer-   10
ing. God can do his work by pleasure as well as by pain. It is therefore
undoubtedly our duty to pray and look for full salvation every day,
every hour, every moment, without waiting till we have either done
or suffered more. Why should not this be the accepted time?

Certainly your friend will suffer loss if he does not allow himself   15
time every day for private prayer. Nothing will supply the want of this;
praying with others is quite another thing. Besides, it may expose us
to great danger. It may turn prayer into an abomination to God, for

> Guilty we speak, if subtle from within   20
> Blows on our words the self-admiring sin![65]

O make the best of every hour!

Source: published transcription; *Methodist Magazine* 22 (1799): 147.

To Mary (Goldhawk/Vazeille) Wesley

Ennis, Near Limerick
July 12, 1760   25

My Dear,

Though you have not answered my two last, I will not stand upon
ceremony. I am now looking toward England again, having wellnigh gone through this kingdom. In a few days I purpose moving
toward Cork, where I shall probably take ship for Bristol. There the   30
Conference is to begin, if it please God to give me a prosperous

---

[65] John Gambold, 'Religious Discourse', st. [3], *HSP* (1739), 59.

voyage, on Wednesday, August 27. If there be no ship ready to sail from Cork on or about August 20th, I design, God willing, to return straight to Dublin, and embark there.[66]

My desire is to live peaceably with all men, with *you* in particular.
5 And (as I have told you again and again) everything which is in my power I do and will do to oblige you—everything you desire, unless I judge it would hurt my own soul, or yours, or the cause of God. And there is nothing which I should rejoice ⟨in[67]⟩ more than the having
10 you always with me, provided only that I could keep you in a good humour, and that you would not speak against me behind my back.

I still love you for your indefatigable industry, for your exact frugality, and for your uncommon neatness and cleanliness, both in your person, your clothes, and all things round you. I value you for
15 your patience, skill, and tenderness in assisting the sick. And if you could submit to follow my advice, I could make you an hundred times more useful both to the sick and healthy in every place where God has been pleased to work by my ministry. O Molly, why should these opportunities be lost? Why should you not
20

Catch the golden moments as they fly,
And by few fleeting hours ensure eternity?[68]

If you really are of the same mind with me, if you want to make the
25 best of a few days, to improve the evening of life, let us begin today! And what we do, let us do with our might! Yesterday is past, and not to be recalled; tomorrow is not ours. Now, Molly, let us set out.

Let us walk hand in hand,
30 To Immanuel's land![69]

If it please God we meet again, let us meet for good. Had you rather we should lodge at the room or at Mr. Stonehouse's?[70] Peace be with your spirit! I am, dear Molly,
35   Your affectionate husband,

John Wesley

---

[66] He embarked on August 24th from Dublin according to his *Journal* (21:272 in this edn.).

[67] There is a small hole in the ms., but the missing text is clear.

[68] Adapted from Samuel Wesley Jr.'s poem on the death of JW's Oxford friend William Morgan, which JW appended to the preface of the first installment of his *Journal*, 18:134 in this edn.

[69] An adaptation of CW, 'On a Journey', st. 6, *HSP* (1749), 2:244.

[70] Rev. George Stonehouse (see 25:570 in this edn.) retired after the death of his wife in 1751 to East Brent in Somerset, about twenty miles from Bristol.

Address: 'To / Mrs Wesley / At the Foundery / Near Moorfields / London'.
Postmarks: '23/IY' and 'LIMERICK'. *Charge*: illegible.
Source: holograph; MARC, MAM JW 5/62.

To John Trembath[71]

CORK
AUGUST 17, 1760

My Dear Brother,
The conversation I had with you yesterday in the afternoon gave me a good deal of satisfaction. As to some things which I had heard 5 (with regard to your wasting your substance, drinking intemperately, and wronging the poor people of Siberton), I am persuaded they were mistakes; as I suppose it was that you *converse much* with careless, un-awakened people. And I trust you will be more and more cautious in all these respects, abstaining from the very appearance of evil. 10

That you had not always attended the preaching when you might have done it you allowed, but seemed determined to remove that objection, as well as the other of using such exercises or diversions as give offence to your brethren. I believe you will likewise endeavour to avoid light and trifling conversation, and to talk and behave 15 in all company with that seriousness and usefulness which become a preacher of the gospel.

Certainly some years ago you was alive to God. You experienced the life and power of religion. And does not God intend that the trials you meet with should bring you back to this? You cannot 20 stand still. You know this is impossible. You must go forward or backward. Either you must recover that power and be a Christian altogether, or in a while you will have neither power nor form, inside nor outside.

Extremely opposite both to one and the other is that aptness to 25 ridicule others, to make them contemptible, by exposing their real or supposed foibles. This I would earnestly advise you to avoid. It hurts yourself, it hurts the hearers, and it greatly hurts those who are so exposed and tends to make them your irreconcilable enemies. It has also

---

[71] John Trembath of St. Gennys, Cornwall, one of JW's itinerant preachers since 1743. See JW's similar letter of reproof to Trembath on Sept. 21, 1755, 26:589–90 in this edn.

sometimes betrayed you into speaking what was not strictly true. O beware of this above all things! Never amplify, never exaggerate anything. Be rigorous in adhering to truth. Be exemplary therein. Whatever has been in time past, let all men now know that John Trembath
5　abhors lying, that he never promises anything which he does not perform, that his word is equal to his bond. I pray be exact in this; be a pattern of truth, sincerity, and godly simplicity.

What has exceedingly hurt you in time past, nay and I fear to this day, is want of reading. I scarce ever knew a preacher read so little.
10　And perhaps by neglecting it, you have lost the taste for it. Hence your talent in preaching does not increase. It is just the same as it was seven years ago. It is lively, but not deep. There is little variety, there is no compass of thought. Reading only can supply this, with meditation and daily prayer. You wrong yourself greatly by omitting this. You
15　can never be a deep preacher without it any more than a thorough Christian. Oh begin! Fix some part of every day for private exercises. You may acquire the taste which you have not. What is tedious at first will afterwards be pleasant. Whether you like it or no, read and pray daily. It is for your life. There is no other way, else you will be a trifler
20　all your days and a pretty, superficial preacher. Do justice to your own soul, give it time and means to grow. Do not starve yourself any longer. Take up your cross, and be a Christian altogether. Then will all the children of God rejoice (not grieve) over you, and in particular,

　　　　Yours, etc.,
25
　　　　　　　　　　　　　　　　　　　　　　J. Wesley

Source: published transcription; *Arminian Magazine* 3 (1780): 448–49.

To John Oliver[72]

[c. August 1760]

30　You have set your hand to the gospel-plough, therefore, never look back. I would have you come up to London this winter. Here is everything to make the man of God perfect.

---

[72] John Oliver (b. 1732) was converted and joined the Methodist society in Stockport in 1748. He was accepted on trial as a traveling preacher about 1760, and is listed in the Minutes as an itinerant through at least 1782 (10:521 in this edn.). See his autobiographical reflections in *AM* 2 (1779): 417–32.

Source: published extract; *Arminian Magazine* 2 (1779): 425, in 'An Account of Mr. John Oliver, Written by Himself'.

To the Rev. Samuel Furly

LAUNCESTON
SEPTEMBER 4, 1760

Dear Sammy,

People in England, and in Ireland much more, are apt to veer from north to south. In May last Mr. Archdeacon[73] wanted to see 5
me, of all people in the world, and was ready (as he sent me word), not only to receive me into his church and house, but to go with me wherever I went. In July he is quite of another mind, having found I take too much upon me.[74] Either this is owing (as I much fear) to a false brother, who, after eating of my bread, privately lifts up his 10
heel against me, or he was struck to the heart on reading the *Appeals* and some of our other writings, and has now by the assistance of the neighbouring clergy, worn off the impression. That he was provided with a curate before he received yours,[75] I do not believe. However, all is well. 15

Most of our preachers had very near left off preaching on practical religion. This was, therefore, earnestly recommended to them in the Conference at London. I am glad they followed the advice which was then given, which may be done without neglecting to speak on justification. This I choose to do on Sundays chiefly, and 20
wherever there is the greatest number of unawakened hearers.

I thought I had sent to *you* the answer to those queries which I sent a copy of to the printer in Bristol. But whether you have it or no, do *you* preach according to *your* light, as I do according to mine.

I am now entering into Cornwall, which I have not visited these 25
three years, and consequently all things in it are out of order.[76]

---

[73] Apparently the current Archdeacon of York, Edmund Pyle (1726–77).

[74] Wesley was in York in April and then again in July 1759, according to his *Journal*.

[75] Furly had apparently sent an application to the Archdeacon in his continued quest for a new position; see JW to Furly, June 19, 1760.

[76] See JW's *Journal* entry for the previous day (Sept. 3), where he found at Launceston 'the small remains of a dead, scattered society. And no wonder, as they have had scarce any discipline, and only one sermon in a fortnight' (21:273–74 in this edn.).

Several persons *talk* of sharing my burden, but none *does* it. So I must wear out one first. I am, dear Sammy,
        Your affectionate brother,

J. Wesley

Address: 'To / The Revd Mr Furly / At Kippax near Ferry-bridge ‹/ Yorkshire[77]›'.
No *postmark* or indications of postal *charge*; possibly delivered by hand.
Source: holograph; Melbourne, Queen's College, JW5.

To the Editor of the *London Chronicle*

5   [St. Just]
                                            September 17, 1760

Sir,
    As you sometimes insert things of a religious nature in your paper, I shall count it a favour if you will insert this.
10   Some years ago I published *A Letter to Mr. Law*,[78] and about the same time *An Address to the Clergy*.[79] Of the former Mr. Law gives the following account in his *Collection of Letters* lately published:[80]

        To answer Mr. Wesley's letter seems to be quite
15   needless, because there is nothing substantial or
        properly argumentative in it. I was once a kind of
        oracle to Mr. W[esley]. I judged him to be much
        under the power of his *own spirit*. To this was owing
        the false censure which he published against the
20   mystics as enemies to good works (pages 128, 130).
        His letter is such a juvenile composition of emptiness
        and pertness as is below the character of any man
        who had been serious in religion for half a month.

[77] An image of the ms. letter is cut off after 'Ferry-bridge', but Wesley consistently placed 'Yorkshire' on a separate line in the addresses of his letters to Furly at Kippax.
[78] JW, *A Letter to the Rev. Mr. Law, Occasioned by Some of His Late Writings* (1756); *Bibliography*, No. 215.
[79] JW, *An Address to the Clergy* (1756); *Bibliography*, No. 216.
[80] William Law, *A Collection of Letters on the Most Interesting and Important Subjects* (London: printed for J. Richardson, 1760).

It was not ability but necessity that put his pen into his hand. He had preached much against my books, and forbid his people the use of them; and for a cover of all this he promised from time to time to write against them; therefore an answer was to be made at all adventures. He and the Pope conceive the same reasons for condemning the mystery revealed by Jacob Boehme (page 190).

Of the latter he gives this account:

> The pamphlet you sent is worse than no advice at all; but infinitely beyond Mr. Wesley's Babylonish *Address to the Clergy*, almost all of which is empty babble, fitter for an old *grammarian* that was grown *blear-eyed* in mending dictionaries than for one who had tasted of the powers of the world to come (page 198).

I leave others to judge whether an answer to that letter be quite needless or no, and whether there be anything *substantial* in it. But certainly there is something *argumentative*. The very queries relating to Jacob [Boehme]'s philosophy are arguments, though not in form; and perhaps most of them will be thought conclusive arguments by impartial readers. Let these likewise judge if there are not arguments in it (whether conclusive or no) relating to that entirely new system of divinity which he has *revealed* to the world.

It is true that Mr. Law, whom I love and reverence *now*, was *once* 'a kind of oracle to me'. He thinks I am still 'under the power of' my 'own spirit', as opposed to the Spirit of God. If I am, yet my censure of the mystics is not at all owing to this, but to my reverence for the oracles of God—which, while I was fond of them, I regarded less and less; till at length, finding I could not follow both, I exchanged the mystic writers for the scriptural.

It is sure, in exposing the philosophy of Boehme, I use ridicule as well as argument. And yet I trust I have by the grace of God been in some measure 'serious in religion', not 'half a month' only, but ever since I was six years old,[81] which is now about half a century. I do not know that the pope has condemned him at all,

---

[81] Telford indicates that this was the age when JW's father admitted him to the Lord's Supper (*Letters*, 4:106, n. 1).

or that he has any reason so to do. My reason is this, and no other: I think he contradicts Scripture, reason, and himself, and that he has seduced many unwary souls from the Bible way of salvation. A strong conviction of this, and a desire to guard others against that
5 dangerous seduction, laid me under 'a necessity' of writing that letter. I was under no other necessity, though I doubt not but Mr. Law *heard* I was, and very seriously *believed* it. I very rarely mention his books in public. Nor are they in the way of one in an hundred of those whom he terms 'my people', meaning, I suppose,
10 the people called 'Methodists'. I had therefore no temptation, any more than power, to 'forbid the use' of them to the Methodists in general. Whosoever informed Mr. Law of this wanted either ability or integrity.

He is so deeply displeased with the *Address to the Clergy* because
15 it speaks strongly in favour of learning. But still, if *this part* of it is only 'fit for an old *grammarian* grown *blear-eyed* in mending dictionaries', it will not follow that '*almost all* of it is mere empty babble'; for a large part of it much more strongly insists on a single eye and a clean heart. Heathen philosophers may term this 'empty
20 babble', but let not Christians either account or call it so!
    I am, sir,
        Your humble servant,

                      John Wesley

Source: published transcription; *London Chronicle* (Sept. 25–27, 1760), p. 309. JW also published in his *Journal*, Sept. 17, 1760 (21:277–80 in this edn.).

To the Rev. Charles Wesley

REDRUTH
25   SEPTEMBER 21, 1760

[[Dear Brother,]]
    I do not apprehend that letter to be any proof of L. A.'s understanding. I believe you had not time to consider it. Do you really think *she* was the indicter? That she was the transcriber of it I al-

low, but is not the hand of Joab in this?[82] Did you not take knowledge not only of the sentiments but the very language of honest James R.?[83]

Your message by John Jones seems to supersede the necessity of my writing, yet I think of sending a few civil lines without entering into the merits of the cause. Is it not an excellent copy of our friend's[84] countenance to 'beg leave to live apart'? *Quis enim negat?*[85] If the unbeliever will depart, let her depart. But she will as soon leap into the sea.

I speak everywhere of bribery and run goods.[86] I suppose John Jones has sent you the Minutes of the Conference.[87] On Friday se'nnight I hope to preach at Shepton Mallet at noon and at Bristol in the evening. *Vive hodie!*[88]

[[Adieu.]]

I should think if you was *solus cum solo*,[89] the point to be insisted on with John Gambold would be, 'You went to the Moravians to find happiness. Have you found it? What have you gained by the exchange?' It is time enough, I suppose, for me to write; for you cannot go to London soon.

Address: in JW's hand 'To / The Revd Mr C. Wesley / in'. Then, in a different hand, 'In Charles Street / Stokescroft / Bristol'.
No *postmark*. *Charge*: '4'.
Endorsement: in CW's hand, 'B. Sept 21. 1760 / She asks to part'.
Source: holograph; MARC, DDWes 3/13.

---

[82] See 2 Sam. 14:19.

[83] Apparently James Relly (1722–78), in which case JW is speaking ironically, for he viewed Relly as an antinomian; see JW, *Journal*, July 5, 1756, 21:3 in this edn.

[84] I.e., Mary (Goldhawk/Vazeille) Wesley.

[85] 'For who denies [this]?'

[86] The expression 'run goods' referred to items smuggled into coastal areas. The Cornish coast where Redruth is located was notorious for smuggling activities. The Conference of 1763 adopted a minute exhorting preachers to 'Extirpate smuggling, buying or selling uncustomed goods, out of every society, particularly in Cornwall, and in all seaport towns' (10:851 in this edn.).

[87] The Conference had been held at Bristol on August 29–30, 1760.

[88] 'Live today', the motto on his seal.

[89] 'One on one.'

To the Rev. Charles Wesley

PLYMOUTH DOCK
SEPTEMBER 28, 1760

[[Dear Brother,]]
I have no objection to the bestowing another reading upon Mr.
5   Law's *Letters*. But I think I have answered them *quantum sufficit*[90]
by the letter in *Lloyd's Evening Post*;[91] only, if need be, it may be inserted in some of the monthly magazines. Since I wrote that letter I
have procured (which I could not before) the *Address to the Clergy*.
It is amazing! Nothing is more plain than that he never read it. I
10   doubt whether he ever *saw* it.
I care not a rush for ordinary means, only that it is our duty to
try them. All our lives and all God's dealings with us have been extraordinary from the beginning.[92] We have all reason, therefore, to
expect that what has been will be again. I have been preternaturally
15   restored more than ten times. I suppose you will be thus restored
for the journey, and that by the journey as a natural means your
health will be re-established, provided you determine to spend all
the strength which God shall give you in his work.
Cornwall has suffered miserably by my long absence and the un-
20   faithfulness of the preachers. I left seventeen hundred in the societies, and I find twelve hundred.
If possible, you should see Mr. Walker.[93] He has been near a
month at the Hot Wells. He is absolutely a Scot in his opinions, but
of an excellent spirit.
25   Mr. Stonehouse's horse performs to a miracle. He is considerably
better than when I had him.
On Friday evening (if nothing extraordinary occur) I hope to be
at Bristol between five and six. Probably I shall leave Shepton Mallet at two. My love to Sally.
30   [[Adieu.]]

---

[90] 'As much as is needed'.
[91] JW's memory has failed him; his letter responding to Law, on Sept. 17, 1760, was published in the *London Chronicle*, not *Lloyd's Evening Post* (see above).
[92] On the distinction between ordinary and extraordinary means, see Sermon 121, 'Prophets and Priests', 4:75–84 in this edn.
[93] Samuel Walker, vicar of Truro. A subsequent letter to Ebenezer Blackwell (July 16, 1761), noted that Walker was near death.

If John Fisher[94] is at Bristol, pray desire him to send what Thomas Seccomb left (with an account) to his poor mother.[95]

Address: 'To / The Revd Mr C. Wesley / in / Bristol'.
Postmark: 'PLYMOUTH', no date stamp. *Charge*: '4'.
Endorsement: in CW's hand, 'B. Sept. 28. 1760 on Law / my health'.
Source: holograph; MARC, DDWes 3/14.

To Jane Catherine March

LONDON
NOVEMBER 11, 1760

Conviction is not condemnation. You may be convinced, yet not 5
condemned; convinced of useless thoughts or words, and yet not
condemned for them. You are condemned for nothing if you love
God and continue to give him your whole heart.

Certainly spiritual temptations will pass through your spirit, else
you could not feel them. I believe I understand your state better 10
than you do yourself. Do not perplex yourself at all about what you
shall call it. You are a child of God, a member of Christ, an heir of
the kingdom. What you have hold fast[96] (whatever name is given to
it), and you *shall have* all that God has prepared for them that love
him. Certainly you do need more faith, for you are a tender, sickly 15
plant. But see,

> Faith while yet you ask is given;
> God comes down, the God and Lord
> That made both earth and heaven![97]   20

---

[94] John Fisher, an Irish Methodist, had been a travelling preacher between 1751–60. He now appears to be assisting JW with administrative matters; see the letter to Abigail Brown on Nov. 21.

[95] Thomas Seccomb, one of JW's preachers from Cornwall, had died recently while serving in Ireland, at the home of Lord Rawdon. See Atmore, *Memorial*, 379–80; and Crookshank, *Ireland*, 1:139.

[96] See Phil. 3:16.

[97] Cf. CW, 'Psalm 121', st. 1, *CPH* (1743), 86; original begins 'Help, while yet I ask …'.

You cannot live on what he did yesterday. Therefore he comes today! He comes to destroy that tendency to levity, to severe judging, to anything that is not of God.

Peace be with your spirit!

Source: published transcription; *Methodist Magazine* 22 (1799): 147–48.

To the Editor of *Lloyd's Evening Post*[98]

Spirat tragicum satis et feliciter audet. Hor.[99]

5   [LONDON]
                                                              NOVEMBER 17, 1760

Sir,

In your last paper we had a letter from a very angry gentleman (though he says he had 'put himself into *as good humour* as pos-
10   sible'), who *personates* a clergyman, but is, I presume, in reality a retainer to the theatre. He is very warm against the people vulgarly called Methodists, 'ridiculous impostors', 'religious buffoons', as he styles them; 'saint-errants' (a pretty and quaint phrase), full of 'inconsiderateness, madness, melancholy, enthusiasm'; teaching a
15   'knotty and unintelligible *system*' of religion—yea, a 'contradictory or self-contradicting'; nay, a 'mere illusion', a 'destructive scheme, and of pernicious consequence'; since 'an *hypothesis* is a very slippery foundation to hazard our *all* upon'.

Methinks the gentleman has a little mistaken his character. He
20   seems to have exchanged the sock for the buskin.[100] But, be this as it may, general charges prove nothing. Let us come to particulars. Here they are: 'The basis of Methodism is the *grace of assurance*' (excuse a little impropriety of expression), '*regeneration* being only a preparative to it.' Truly this is somewhat 'knotty and unintelligible'.

---

[98] Replying to a letter to the editor by 'Philodemus' in *Lloyd's Evening Post and British Chronicle* (Nov. 12–14), pp. 467–68.

[99] Horace, *Epistles*, II.i.166; 'he has some tragic inspiration, and is happy in his ventures' (Loeb).

[100] The 'sock' and 'buskin' refer to comedic and tragic characters, respectively. A buskin was an elevated shoe that placed tragic actors higher than comedic actors, who wore only a sock.

I will endeavour to help him out. The fundamental doctrine of the people called Methodists is, 'Whosoever will be saved, before all things it is necessary that he hold the true faith';[101] the faith which works by love;[102] which, by means of the love of God and our neighbour, produces both inward and outward holiness. This faith is an evidence of things not seen.[103] And he that thus believes is regenerate, or born of God, and he has the witness in himself[104] (call it assurance or what you please). The Spirit itself witnesses with his spirit that he is a child of God.[105] 'From what scripture' every one of these propositions 'is collected' any common concordance will show. 'This is the true portraiture of Methodism', so called. 'A religion superior to this' (the love of God and man) none can 'enjoy', either in time or in eternity.

But the Methodists do not hold 'good works meritorious'. No; neither does ours, or any other Protestant church. But meantime they hold it is their bounden duty, as they have time, to do good unto all men.[106] And they know the day is coming wherein God will reward every man according to his works.[107]

But they 'act with sullenness and sourness, and account innocent gaiety and cheerfulness a crime almost as heinous as sacrilege'. Who does? Name the men. I know them not, and therefore doubt the fact. Though it is very possible you account that kind of gaiety innocent which I account both foolish and sinful.

I know none who denies that true religion, that is, love, the love of God and our neighbour, 'elevates our spirits, and renders our minds cheerful and serene'. It must, if it be accompanied, as we believe it always is, with peace and joy in the Holy Ghost,[108] and if it produces a conscience void of offence toward God and toward man.[109]

But they 'preach up religion only to accomplish a *lucrative* design, to *fleece* their hearers, to accumulate *wealth*, to *rob* and *plunder*,

---

[101] The first line of the Athanasian Creed, one of the three creeds authorised by Anglican Article of Religion 8 and included in the Book of Common Prayer. JW changed the word 'catholic' in this sentence from the Athanasian Creed to 'true', which later led to an accusation that he had altered the creed (see the letter of Dec. 20 below).

[102] See Gal. 5:6.
[103] See Heb. 11:1.
[104] See 1 John 5:10.
[105] See Rom. 8:16.
[106] See Gal. 6:10.
[107] See Rev. 22:12.
[108] See Rom. 14:17.
[109] See Acts 24:16.

which they esteem meritorious'. We deny the fact. Who is able to prove it? Let the affirmer produce his witnesses, or retract.

This is the sum of your correspondent's charge, not one article of which can be proved. But whether it can or no, 'we have made them', says he, 'a theatrical scoff and the common jest and scorn of every chorister in the street'. It may be so. But whether you have done well herein may still admit of a question. However, you cannot but wish 'we had some formal Court of Judicature erected' (happy Portugal and Spain![110]) 'to take cognizance of such matters'. Nay, *cur optas quod habes?*[111] Why do you wish for what you have already? The court is erected. The holy, devout playhouse is become the House of Mercy,[112] and does take cognizance hereof 'of all pretenders to sanctity, and happily furnishes us with a discerning spirit to distinguish betwixt right and wrong'. But I do not stand to their sentence. I appeal to Scripture and reason, and by these alone consent to be judged.

> I am, sir,
> Your humble servant,

> John Wesley

Source: published transcription; *Lloyd's Evening Post* (Nov. 17–19, 1760), p. 482; JW also published in his *Journal*, Nov. 17, 1760 (21:286–87 in this edn.).

Voters in Durham[113]

[LONDON]
NOVEMBER 20, 1760

I desire earnestly all who love me to assist him, to use the utmost of their power. What they do let them do it with all their might.[114]

---

[110] An allusion to the Courts of Inquisition in Spain and Portugal.

[111] Horace, *Satires*, I.iii.126; translated by JW immediately after.

[112] The name of the prison in which those condemned by the Spanish Courts of Inquisition were held.

[113] According to Thwaites, JW wrote these lines in support of the Whig candidate Sir Thomas Clavering (1719–94), later Baronet of Axwell (from 1768), who was running for Parliament in Durham in 1760. Clavering lost, but ran again in 1761 and 1768, succeeding in being elected in the latter year.

[114] See Col. 3:23.

Let not sloth nor indolence hurt a good cause. Let them not rail at the other candidates; they may act earnestly and yet civilly. Let all you do be done in charity, and at the peril of your souls receive no bribe. Do your duty without being tired, and God will pay you in this world, and in the world to come.   5

Source: published transcription; William Thwaites, *Methodism in Durham City* (Durham: G. H. Procter, 1909), 10–11.

To Abigail Brown

LONDON
NOVEMBER 21, 1760

Dear Abby,

I cannot advise. You must follow your own conscience. Act as you are fully persuaded in your own mind. Consider first what is best   10
with regard to eternity, and then take your measures accordingly. Mr. Fisher[115] will assist you in whatever you would have done, and if you want money, I have desired him to help you to it. Speak freely to me, if you love me, and believe me to be, dear Abby,
Your sincere friend and affectionate brother,   15

[John Wesley]

Source: published transcription; Telford, *Letters*, 4:111–12.

To the Editor of *Lloyd's Evening Post*

LONDON
NOVEMBER 22, 1760

Sir,

Just as I had finished the letter published in your last Friday's paper, four tracts came to my hands: one wrote, or procured to be wrote, by   20

---

[115] John Fisher; see JW to CW, Sept. 28, 1760.

Mrs. Downes;[116] one by a clergyman in the county of Durham;[117] the third by a gentleman of Cambridge;[118] and the fourth by a member (I suppose, dignitary) of the Church of Rome.[119] How gladly would I leave all these to themselves, and let them say just what they please, as my day is far spent and my taste for controversy is utterly lost and gone. But this would not be doing justice to the world, who might take silence for a proof of guilt. I shall therefore say a word concerning each. I may, perhaps, some time say more to one or two of them. The letter which goes under Mrs. Downes's name scarce deserves any notice at all, as there is nothing extraordinary in it but an extraordinary degree of virulence and scurrility. Two things only I remark concerning it, which I suppose the writer of it knew as well as me: 1) that my letter to Mr. Downes was both wrote and printed *before Mr. Downes died;*[120] 2) that when I said, *Tibi parvula res est* ('Your ability is small'),[121] I had no view to his fortune, which I knew nothing of, but, as I there expressly say, to his wit, sense, and talents as a writer.

The tract wrote by the gentleman in the north is far more bulky than this. But it is more considerable for its bulk than for its matter, being little more than a dull repetition of what was published some years ago in *The Enthusiasm of the Methodists and Papists Compared.*[122] I do not find the author adds anything new, unless we may bestow that epithet on a sermon annexed to his *Address*, which I presume will do neither good nor harm. So I leave the Durham gentleman, with Mrs. Downes, to himself and his admirers.

The author of the letter to Mr. Berridge is a more considerable writer. In many things I wholly agree with him, though not in ad-

---

[116] *The Widow Downes's Answer to the Rev. Mr. John Wesley's Letter which was addressed to her late husband the Rev. Mr. Downes, just at the time of his decease* (London: Stanley Crowder, 1760); the letter is dated Apr. 1, 1760, and included among the online transcriptions. Anne (née Balguy) Downes was the wife of Rev. John Downes (c. 1691–1759), rector of St. Michael, Wood Street, who had published *Methodism Examined and Exposed* (London, 1759), to which JW had replied in Nov. 1759 with *A Letter to the Rev. Mr. Downes* (9:350–66 in this edn.).

[117] Alexander Jephson, *A Friendly and Compassionate Address to All Serious and Well-Disposed Methodists* (London, 1760). On Jephson, see 21:288, n. 28 in this edn.

[118] 'Academicus' [John Green, D.D.], *The Principles and Practices of the Methodists Considered* (London, 1760). On Green, see JW's letter of Apr. 2, 1761.

[119] [Richard Challoner], *A Caveat against the Methodists* (London, 1760). Challoner (1691–1781) was Vicar Apostolic of the London District of the Catholic Church, and titular Bishop of Doberus.

[120] JW's *Letter* to Rev. Downes was dated Nov. 17, 1759; Downes died eight days later.

[121] Horace, *Epistles*, I.xviii.29; 'your means are but trifling' (Loeb).

[122] George Lavington, *The Enthusiasm of Methodists and Papists Compared* (London, 1749–51); answered by JW, *Letter to the Author of the Enthusiasm of Methodists and Papists Compared* (1750), 11:361–76 in this edn.

miring Dr. Taylor. But there is a bitterness even in him which I should not have expected in a gentleman and a scholar. So in the very first page I read, 'The Church, which most of *your graceless fraternity* have deserted.' Were the fact true (which it is not), yet is the expression to be commended? Surely Dr. G[reen] himself thinks it is not. I am sorry too for the unfairness of his quotations. For instance: he cites me (p. 53) as speaking of 'faith shed abroad in men's hearts like lightning'. *Faith shed abroad* in men's hearts! I never used such an expression in my life. I do not talk after this rate. Again he quotes, as from me (p. 57), so I presume Mr. Wesley means 'a behaviour does not pretend to add the least to what Christ has done'. But be these words whose they may, they are none of mine. I never spoke, wrote, no nor read them before. Once more, is it well judged for any writer to show such an utter contempt of his opponents as you affect to do with regard to the whole body of people vulgarly termed Methodists? 'You may keep up', say you, 'a little bush-fighting in controversy; you may skirmish awhile with your feeble body of irregulars, but you must never trust to your skill in reasoning' (p. 77). Upon this I would ask: 1) If these are such poor, silly creatures, why does so wise a man set his wit to them? 'Shall the King of Israel go out against a flea?'[123] 2) If it should happen that any one of these silly bush-fighters steps out into the plain, engages hand to hand, and foils this champion by mere dint of reason, will not his defeat be so much the more shameful as it was more unexpected? But I say the less at present, not only because Mr. Berridge is able to answer for himself, but because the title page bids me expect a letter more immediately addressed to myself.

The last tract, entitled *A Caveat against the Methodists*, is in reality a caveat against the Church of England, or rather against all the churches in Europe who dissent from the Church of Rome. Nor do I apprehend the writer to be any more disgusted at the Methodists than at Protestants of every denomination, as he cannot but judge it equally unsafe to join to any society but that of Rome. Accordingly all his arguments are levelled at the Reformed churches in general, and conclude just as well if you put the word 'Protestant' throughout in the place of the word 'Methodist'. Although, therefore, the author borrows my name to wound those who suspect nothing less, yet I am no more concerned to refute him than any other Protestant in England; and still the less, as those arguments are refuted over and over in books which are still common among us.

[123] 1 Sam. 24:14, 26:20.

But is it possible any Protestants, nay Protestant clergymen, should buy these tracts to give away? Is then the introducing popery the only way to overthrow Methodism? If they know this, and choose popery as the smaller evil of the two, they are consistent 5 with themselves. But if they do not intend this, I wish them more seriously to consider what they do.

I am, sir,
    Your humble servant,

John Wesley

Source: published transcription; *Lloyd's Evening Post* (Nov. 24–26, 1760), pp. 505–6; JW also published in his *Journal*, Nov. 22, 1760 (21:287–90 in this edn.).

To Charles Gray[124]

[DECEMBER 1760?[125]]

10

Sir,
    Since I had the pleasure of waiting upon you, I have been often reflecting on the account given us of the Indians in Paraguay.[126] It is

---

[124] The holograph has no address page and the salutation is simply 'Sir'. We are following the transcription published in *WMM* in identifying the recipient as Charles Gray (1696–1782), who served as MP (five times) from Colchester. This transcription was made by a descendent of Gray who had access to the holograph, which was owned by another family member. By contrast, Telford (apparently unaware of the *WMM* transcription) identifies the recipient as Dr. Jemmett Browne (1703–82), a prelate of the Church of Ireland. This reflects an endorsement in pencil on the holograph: 'During an hundred and fifty years there has not been a crime committed amongst the Indians of Paraguay which has been thought worthy of capital punishment.' This same sentence is copied in ink, with a further sentence added, 'Doctor Brown said the above was an answer to the letter within wrote with a pencil by himself.' The endorsement is clearly secondary, perhaps by Telford himself. We judge the account of the letter's provenance in *WMM* more reliable.

[125] The holograph is undated and there is no way to date it definitively. We have chosen 1760 as a likely date because Muratori's *Relation of the Missions in Paraguay* (1759) was receiving broad notice in settings like the *Critical Review* (Sept. 1760, p. 210). This date also fits with JW's comment about his 'first' reading on the topic (and, contrary to a claim in *WMM*, is consistent with JW's hand at the time). Telford placed it c. 1768, assuming it was in response to news of the Jesuits being expelled from the Rio de la Plata region (including Paraguay and most of what is now Argentina) in 1767–68.

[126] Likely referring to Ludovico Antonio Muratori, *A Relation of the Missions in Paraguay* (London: Marmaduke, 1759; Italian orig., 1743).

about four and twenty years since I read the first account of them, translated from a French author.[127] It then made much the same impression on my mind which I believe it has now made on yours. Permit me, sir, to speak my free thoughts concerning it, which I shall be glad to alter upon better information. 5

I am thoroughly persuaded that true, genuine religion is capable of working all those happy effects which are said to be wrought there, and that in the most ignorant and savage of humankind. I have seen instances of this. No Indians are more savage than were the colliers of Kingswood, many of whom are now an humane, hospitable peo- 10 ple, full of love to God and man, quiet, diligent in business, in every state content, every way adorning the gospel of God their Saviour.

But the difficulty with me lies here. I am not persuaded that the Romish missionaries (very few excepted) either know or teach true, genuine religion. And of all their missionaries, generally speaking, 15 the Jesuits are the worst. They teach nothing less than the true, genuine religion of Jesus Christ.[128] They spend their main strength in teaching their converts, so-called, the opinions and usages of their church. Perhaps the most religious that ever was among them was their 'East Indian apostle', Francis Xavier. And from his own letters 20 (four volumes of which I had[129]) it plainly appears, that, whether he knew it himself or no, he never taught one tittle of the religion of the heart, but barely opinions and externals.

Now what virtue, what happiness, can possibly spring from such a root as this? Allowing, then, that the Paraguay converts have peace 25 and plenty, allowing they have moral honesty, allowing they have an outward form of religion (and thus far I know not but their guides may bring them), I cannot believe they have gone one step farther or that they know what true religion is. Do their instructors experience the inward kingdom of God—righteousness, and peace, and 30 joy in the Holy Ghost?[130] And, if not, are they likely to lead others any farther than they have gone themselves? Can they point out

Th' eternal sunshine of the spotless mind,
Each prayer accepted, and each wish resigned? [...] 35

---

[127] This is almost certainly Armédée François Frézier, *A Voyage to the South-Sea, and along the Coasts of Chili and Peru, in the years 1712, 1713, and 1714; particularly describing the genius and constitution of the inhabitants, as well Indians as Spaniards ... and an account of the settlement, commerce, and riches of the Jesuits in Paraguay* (London: J. Bowyer, 1717; French orig., 1716). JW would have read it in preparation for his ministry in Georgia.

[128] I.e., 'There *is* nothing they teach *less* than ...'.

[129] Francis Xavier (1506–52). *Epistolarum libri quatuor* (Orig., 1596).

[130] See Rom. 14:17.

> Desires composed, affections ever even;
> Tears that delight, and sighs that waft to heaven?[131]

5   And, without this, who can be happy? Who can avoid feeling many
dull, heavy hours? Let the Indians eat, drink, dance, play; all this
will not fill up the blanks of life. Their highest enjoyments will carry
them no farther than 'sauntering Jack and idle Joan' in Prior.[132]
What can carry them any farther but heart-religion, 'fellowship
with the Father and with the Son'?[133] O, may you and yours always
10   experience this better part, which alone takes away the weariness of
life, which alone gives that heartfelt, that unceasing joy, the pledge
and earnest of life eternal!
     I am, sir,
          Your very humble servant,
15
                                                John Wesley

Source: holograph; MARC, MAM JW 2/18. Published transcription;
Wesleyan Methodist Magazine 82 (1859): 799–800.

To Mr. Somebody, alias Philodemus, alias T. H.[134]

LONDON
DECEMBER 1, 1760

Sir,
     I am very happy in having given you 'infinite pleasure by my
20   animadversions upon your letter', and therefore cannot but add a
few more, hoping they may give you still farther satisfaction. It is,
indeed, great condescension in you to bestow a thought upon me,
since 'it is only losing time' (as you observe in your last), as you
'judge arguing with Methodists is like pounding fools in a mortar'.
25   However, do not despair; perhaps, when you have pounded me a
little more, my *foolishness* may *depart from me.*

---

[131] Alexander Pope, *Eloisa to Abelard*, ll. 209–10, 213–14.
[132] Matthew Prior, 'An Epitaph', *Poems on Several Occasions* (London, 1721), 1:250.
[133] Cf. 1 John 1:3.
[134] Replying to 'Somebody' [a.k.a. 'Philodemus'], Nov. 20, 1760; and 'T. H.', Nov. 20, 1760.

I really was so foolish as to think that by saying 'We *Churchmen*' you assumed the character of a 'clergyman'. Whether you 'retain' to the 'theatre' or no is easily shown: tell your name, and the doubt is cleared up.[135] But who or what you are affects not me. I am only concerned with what you say.

But you complain, I have 'passed over the most interesting and material circumstances' in your letter. I apprehend just the contrary. I think nothing in it is passed over which is at all material. Nor will I knowingly pass over anything material in this, though I am not a dealer in many words.

You say: 1) 'You have impiously apostatised from those principles of religion which you undertook to defend.' I hope not. I still (as I am able) defend the Bible, with the Liturgy, Articles, and Homilies of our Church. And I do not defend or espouse any other principles, to the best of my knowledge, than those which are plainly contained in the Bible as well as in the Homilies and Book of Common Prayer.

You blame me 2) for teaching heterodox doctrine concerning faith and good works (I am obliged to put the meaning of many of your straggling sentences together as well as I can). As to the former, which you still awkwardly and unscripturally style 'the grace of assurance' (a phrase I never use), you say: 'You have given it a true Methodistical gloss. But where are the proofs from Scripture? Not one single text.' Sir, that is your ignorance. I perceive the Bible is a book you are not acquainted with. Every sentence in my account is a text of Scripture. I purposely refrained from quoting chapter and verse, because I expected you would betray your ignorance, and show that you was got quite out of your depth. As your old friend Mr. Vellum says, 'You will pardon me for being jocular.'[136]

To one who seriously desired information on this point I would explain it a little farther. *Faith* is an evidence or conviction of things not seen,[137] of God, and the things of God. This is faith in general. More particularly it is a divine evidence or conviction that Christ loved *me* and gave himself for *me*.[138] This directly leads us to 'work out our salvation with fear and trembling';[139] not with slavish, painful fear, but with the utmost diligence, which is the proper import

---

[135] In his letter to the editor on Nov. 17, 1760, Wesley suggested that 'Philodemus' '*personates* a clergyman, but is, I presume, in reality a retainer to the theatre'.

[136] Joseph Addison, *The Drummer*, Act. 4, scene 2.

[137] See Heb. 11:1.

[138] See Gal. 2:20.

[139] Phil. 2:12.

of that expression. When this evidence is so heightened as to exclude all doubt, it is the *plerophory* or *full assurance* of faith.[140] But any degree of true faith prompts the believer to be zealous of good works.

5   On this head you say: 'Your definition of good works' (truly I gave none at all) 'is still more extraordinary. You shall have it in your own words, where you quarrel with me for esteeming them meritorious, "No, neither does ours or any other Protestant church. But meantime they hold it is their bounden duty as they have time to do good

10   unto all men. And they know the day is coming wherein God will render to every man according to his works." Admirable contradiction! Was you intoxicated, or *jure divino*[141] mad? Is man to be judged for his deeds done in this life, when it is immaterial whether he does any or not? These are your own words, sir.' What? That 'it is

15   immaterial whether he does any good works or not'? Hey-day! How is this? O, I cry your mercy, sir. Now I find where the shoe pinches. You have stumbled on an hard word which you do not understand. But give me leave, sir, to assure you (you may take my word for once) that 'meritorious' and 'material' are not all one. Accordingly

20   not only the Church of England but all other Protestant churches allow good works to be material, and yet (without any contradiction) deny them to be meritorious.

They all likewise allow that the genuine fruit of faith is righteousness, peace, and joy in the Holy Ghost;[142] and consequently that

25   cheerfulness or serenity of spirit (a mixture of that peace and joy) is so far from being a crime that it is the undoubted privilege of every real Christian. I know no Methodist (so called) who is of another mind. If you do, tell me the man. I believe 'it is not your intention to do this'. But you must either do it or bear the blame.

30   You blame me 3) for allowing of lay preachers. This is too knotty a point to be settled at present. I can only desire those who want farther information therein to read calmly *A Letter to a Clergyman*[143] or the latter part of the third *Appeal to Men of Reason and Religion.*[144]

35   You blame me 4) for acting from 'a lucrative principle', though you 'deny you used the word "robbing"'. (True, for you only said,

---

[140] See Heb. 10:22.
[141] 'By divine law'.
[142] See Rom. 14:17.
[143] JW, *A Letter to a Clergyman* (1748), 9:247–51 in this edn.
[144] JW, *A Farther Appeal to Men of Reason and Religion, Part III*, III, 11:289–331 in this edn.

'To rob and plunder'.) In proof of this you refer to the houses I have built (in Bristol, Kingswood, and Newcastle-upon-Tyne). But don't you know, sir, those houses are none of mine? I made them over to trustees long ago. I have food to eat and raiment to put on; and I *will have no more* till I turn Turk or pagan.

I am, sir, in very good humour,
Your well-wisher,

John Wesley

P. S. It is not very material whether 'T. H.', 'Somebody', and 'Philodemus' are the same individual or not. I have subjoined his questions with my answers, though they have all been answered fifty times before.

Q. 1. Whether a very considerable body of the Methodists do not declare that there can be no good hopes of salvation without *assurance*?

A. Yes, if you mean by that term a divine evidence or conviction that Christ loved *me* and gave himself for *me*.[145]

Q. 2. Whether they do not put a greater confidence in what they call regeneration than in the moral or social duties of life?

A. No. They hold the due discharge of all these duties to be absolutely necessary to salvation. The latter part of this query, 'on the mercy of the Divine Being', seems to have lost its way.

Q. 3. Whether the stage in later years has ever ridiculed anything really serious?

A. Yes, a thousand times. Who that reads Dryden's, Wycherley's, or Congreve's plays can doubt it?

Q. 4. Whether anything can be religious that has not right reason to countenance it?

A. No. True religion is the highest reason. It is indeed wisdom, virtue, and happiness in one.

Source: published transcription; *Lloyd's Evening Post* (Dec. 1–3, 1760), p. 530.

[145] See Gal. 2:20.

To the Rev. Samuel Furly

London
December 9, 1760

Dear Sammy,

I am determined to publish nothing against Mr. Hervey unless
5 his answer to my letter is published. Indeed, it is not his; it is Mr.
Cudworth's, both as to matter and manner.[146] So let it pass for the
present.

Richard Tompson (who lives in Prince's Square, Ratcliff High-
way) told me honestly, 'Sir, I want a little money, and I can have
10 it by printing the letters which passed between you and me.' I answered, 'You know I never designed my letters for public view, but
you may print them if you please. I am quite indifferent about it.'[147]

When I say 'I have no time to write largely in controversy', I
mean this. Every hour I have is employed more to the glory of God.
15 Therefore, if short answers to opponents will not suffice, I cannot
help it. I will not, I cannot, I dare not spend any more time in that
kind of writing than I do. 'Well, but many think you ought.' Undoubtedly they do, but I am to be guided by my own conscience.

I am laying another plot for *you*. Mr. Fletcher is rector of Made-
20 ley, in Shropshire.[148] If he takes you to be his curate, probably you
may be ordained priest. I will write to him about it.

I am, with love to Nancy,
    Your affectionate friend and brother,

25 J. Wesley

Address: 'To / The Rev Mr Furly / At Kippax, near Ferry bridge / York-
    shire'.
Postmark: '9/DE' but no indication of the place, nor of postal *charge*.
Source: holograph; Melbourne, Queen's College, JW6.

---

[146] Cf. JW to James Hervey, Nov. 29, 1758. Hervey's manuscript letters to JW had not
yet been published.

[147] Cf. JW to Richard Tompson, Aug. 22, 1759.

[148] On John Fletcher, see 26:613 in this edn. He had been installed as vicar of Madeley in
Shropshire in Oct. 1760.

To Mr. 'T. H.', alias 'Philodemus', alias 'Somebody', alias 'Stephen Church', alias 'R. W.'[149]

LONDON
DECEMBER 12, 1760

Patience, dear sir, patience! Or I am afraid your choler will hurt your constitution as well as your argument. Be composed, and I will 5 answer your queries, 'speedily, clearly, and categorically'. Only you will give me leave to shorten them a little, and to lay those together which have some relation to each other.

Permit me likewise, before I enter upon particulars, to lay a few circumstances before you which may add some light to the subject 10 and give you a clearer knowledge of the people with whom you are so angry.

About thirty years since, I met with a book written in King William's time, called *The Country Parson's Advice to his Parishioners*.[150] There I read these words: 'If good men of the Church will unite 15 together in the several parts of the kingdom, disposing themselves into friendly societies, and engaging each other in their respective combinations to be helpful to each other in all good, Christian ways, it will be the most effectual means for restoring our decaying Christianity to its primitive life and vigour and the supporting of our 20 tottering and sinking Church.'[151] A few young gentlemen then at Oxford approved of and followed the advice. They were all zealous Churchmen, and both orthodox and regular to the highest degree. For their exact regularity they were soon nicknamed Methodists. But they were not then, or for some years after, charged with any 25 other crime, real or pretended, than that of being 'righteous overmuch'.[152] Nine or ten years after, many others 'united together in the several parts of the kingdom, engaging in like manner to be helpful to each other in all good, Christian ways'. At first all these were of the Church, but several pious Dissenters soon desired to 30

---

[149] Despite this longer title in the *London Magazine*, the letter is mainly JW's reply to that of 'Stephen Church' [i.e., John Cook], Nov. 3. 1780, as the title indicates in *London Chronicle*; though he appends a response to 'R. W.'

[150] [Anonymous], *A Country Parson's Advice to his Parishioners* (London: Benj. Tooke, 1680). The work thus antedated the accession of William and Mary by eight years, but it was reprinted many times and Wesley may have seen a later printing. His diary indicates that he had read the book since at least his time in Georgia; see 18:339, 342–44, 346–48, 422, and 431 in this edn.

[151] Ibid., p. 81.

[152] Eccl. 7:16.

unite with them. Their one design was to forward each other in true, scriptural Christianity.

Presently the flood-gates were opened, and a deluge of reproach poured upon them from all quarters. All manner of evil was spo-
5 ken of them, and they were used without either justice or mercy, and this chiefly (I am sorry to say it) by the members of our own Church. Some of them were startled at this, and proposed a question, when they were met together at Leeds, 'whether they ought not to separate from the Church'. But after it had been fairly and
10 largely considered, they were one and all satisfied 'that they ought not'.[153] The reasons of that determination were afterwards printed and lately reprinted and strongly enforced by my brother.[154] *Hinc illae lacrymae!*[155] This, I presume, has occasioned your present queries. For though you talk of 'our episcopal communion', I doubt not
15 but you are either a papist or a dissenter. If I mistake, you may easily set me right by telling your *real* name and place of abode.

But, in spite of all we could say or do, the cry still continued, 'You have left the Church, you are no ministers or members of it.' I answer (as I did fourteen years ago to one who warmly affirmed
20 this): 'Use ever so many exaggerations, still the whole of the matter is, 1) I often use extemporary prayer; 2) wherever I can, I preach the gospel; 3) those who desire to *live the gospel*, I advise how to watch over each other and to put from them such as walk disorderly.'[156] Now, whether these things are right or wrong, this single point I
25 must still insist upon. All this does not prove either that I am no *member* or that I am no minister of the Church of England. Nay, nothing can prove that I am no *member* of the Church, till I either am *excommunicated* or *renounce* her communion, and no longer join in her 'doctrine and in the breaking of bread and in prayer'.[157] Nor
30 can anything prove I am no *minister* of the Church, till I either am deposed from my ministry or *voluntarily renounce her* and wholly cease to teach her doctrines, use her offices, and obey her rubrics.[158]

---

[153] See the Minutes of the Leeds Conference, May 6, 1755; 10:271–72 in this edn.

[154] JW published 'Reasons against a Separation from the Church of England' in *Preservative against Unsettled Notions in Religion* (1758); in 1760 CW reissued it as a separate pamphlet, adding his own exhortation and seven hymns; see 9:334–49 in this edn.

[155] Horace, *Epistles*, I.xix.41; 'Hence these tears', or more loosely, 'So that's the explanation' (Loeb).

[156] JW, *Principles of a Methodist Farther Explained* (1746), III:9; 9:195 in this edn.

[157] Acts 2:42.

[158] Cf. JW's definition of the Church of England in a paper read at the 1755 Leeds Conference: 'that body of people, nominally united, which profess to uphold the doctrine contained

Upon the same principle that I still preach and endeavour to assist those who desire to *live the gospel*, about twelve years ago I published proposals for printing *A Christian Library: Consisting of Extracts from and Abridgements of the Choicest Pieces of Practical Divinity which have been published in the English Tongue.*[159] And I have done what I proposed. Most of the tracts therein contained were wrote by members of our own Church, but some by writers of other denominations, for I mind not who speaks but what is spoken.

On the same principle, that of 'doing good to all men, of the ability that God giveth',[160] I published *Primitive Physick; or an Easy and Natural Method of Curing Most Diseases;*[161] and, some years after, a little tract entitled *Electricity made Plain and Useful.*[162] On the same, I printed an English, a Latin, a French, and a short Hebrew Grammar,[163] as well as some of the Classics, and a few other tracts, *in usum juventutis Christianae.*[164]

This premised, I now proceed to the queries.

Q. 1. 'Why have you not cleared yourself of those reflections that you stand charged with by a learned author?' *A.* I have thoroughly cleared myself in three letters to that learned author which were published immediately after his tracts.[165]

Q. 2. 'Can you consistently charge your people to attend the worship of our Church and not Dissenters' meetings?' I can. This is consistent with all I have written and all I have done for many years. 'But do not you call *our Church* a "mere rope of sand"?' No: look again into the *Plain Account*, and you will see (if you care to see) that those words are not spoken of *our Church.*[166]

in the Articles and Homilies, and to use Baptism, the Lord's supper and Public Prayer, according to the Common Prayer Book' (see 9:568 in this edn.).

[159] *Bibliography*, No. 165.

[160] 1 Pet. 4:11.

[161] *Bibliography*, No. 138; Vol. 32 in this edn.

[162] *The Desideratum; or, Electricity Made Plain and Useful* (1760), *Bibliography*, No. 239; Vol. 32 in this edn.

[163] *A Short English Grammar* (1748), *Bibliography*, No. 149; *A Short Latin Grammar* (1748), *Bibliography*, No. 150; *A Short French Grammar* (1750), *Bibliography*, No. 189; *A Short Hebrew Grammar* (1751), *Bibliography*, No. 190. Wesley would later complete the set with *A Short Greek Grammar* (1765), *Bibliography*, No. 262.

[164] 'For the use of Christian young people.' See *Bibliography*, Nos. 152, 172, 173, 174, 179, 180.

[165] JW assumes Cook is referring to George Lavington's *The Enthusiasm of Methodists and Papists Compared* (1749–51), and points to his three replies to Lavington (11:353–436 in this edn.).

[166] In *Plain Account of the People Called Methodists*, I:11 (9:259 in this edn.), JW used this phrase to describe the condition of 'parishioners' and not as a general reference to the Church of England. Cf. a parallel use in the *Farther Appeal, Part III*, III:[16], 11:301 in this edn.

Q. 6. 'But do not you hold doctrine contrary to hers?' No. 'Do not you make a dust about words?' No. 'Do not you bewilder the brains of weak people?' No.

Q. 11. 'Do not you in print own episcopacy to be *jure divino?*'[167]
5   Not that I remember. Can you tell me where? But this I own—I have no objection to it; nay, I approve it highly.

Q. 16. 'But are you not guilty of *canonical disobedience* to your bishop?' I think not. Show me wherein.

Q. 17. 'Did not you suffer your lay preachers at Leeds to debate
10   whether they should separate from the Church?' Yes, and encouraged them to say all that was in their hearts. 'Why did you do this?' To confirm their adherence to it; and they were so confirmed that only two out of the whole number have since separated from it.

Q. 18. 'If most votes had carried the day, what had followed?' *If*
15   the sky should fall!'[168]

Q. 12. 'What did you propose by preaching up to the people a solemn covenant?'[169] To conform them in fearing God and working righteousness. I shall probably do the same again shortly. And if you desire any farther information, you are welcome to hear every
20   sermon which I preach concerning it.

Q. 13. 'Was not this intended to cut them off from ever communicating with any company of Christians but yourselves?' No; nothing less. It was not intended to cut them off from anything but the devil and his works.

25   *Q.* 14. 'Do not you commend the Quakers?' Yes, in some things. 'And the French prophets?'[170] No.

Q. 15. 'Do not you stint your lay preachers to *three or four* minutes only in their public prayers?' I advise them 'not *usually* to exceed *four or five* minutes either *before or after sermon*'. *Preservative*, p.
30   244.[171] At other times I do not object to a longer prayer.

Q. 3. 'Is not your Christian Library an odd collection of mutilated writings of Dissenters of all sorts?' No. In the first ten volumes there is not a line from any Dissenter of any sort; and the great-

---

[167] 'By divine law'.

[168] I.e., Wesley is charging Cook with committing the fallacy of a 'question contrary to fact'.

[169] JW introduced a covenant renewal service (drawing again on *A Country Parson's Advice*) among Methodists at least as early as Christmas Day, 1747 (see *Journal*, 20:203 in this edn.); the practice took on more prominence in the mid 1750s; see JW, *Journal*, Aug. 6, 1755, 21:23 in this edn.

[170] JW was critical from his first encounter with the French prophets; see *Journal*, Jan. 28, 1739, 19:32–34 in this edn.

[171] I.e., 'Reasons Against Separation', III.3, 9:340 in this edn.

est part of the other forty is extracted from Archbishop Leighton, Bishops Taylor, Patrick, Kenn, Reynolds, Sanderson, and other ornaments of the Church of England.

Q. 4. 'Is not this declaring that you have a superior privilege beyond all men to print, correct, and direct as you please?' I think not. I suppose every man in England has just the same privilege.

Q. 5. 'Is it not performed according to the first proposals and the expectation of the subscribers?' It is performed according to the first proposals; nor could any subscriber reasonably expect more.

Q. 7. 'Why did you not in your New Testament distinguish those places with italics where you altered the old translation?'[172] Because it was quite needless, as any who choose it may easily compare the two translations together. 'But should you not have given the learned a good reason for every alteration?' Yes, if I had wrote for the learned. But I did not, as I expressly mention in the preface.

Q. 8. 'Do not you assume too much in philosophy and physic as well as in theology?' I hope not.

Q. 9. 'Why did you meddle with electricity?'[173] For the same reason as I published the *Primitive Physick*, to do as much good as I can.[174]

Q. 10. 'Why did you marry a person you could have no issue by?'[175] Did you or I know that?

Q. 19. 'Are you a clergyman at all?' Yes. 'Are you not a Quaker in disguise?' No. 'Do not you betray the Church, as Judas his Master, with a kiss?' No. 'If you be in the wrong, God confound your devices.' I say the same thing. 'If in the right, may he display it to all people!' Amen! In his own time.

I take this opportunity to answer the queries also which occur in the 614th page:[176]

1. 'If the operations of the Spirit overpower the natural faculties, must they not destroy free agency?' I neither teach nor believe that the ordinary operations of the Spirit do overpower the natural faculties.

---

[172] I.e., *NT Notes*, where JW provided his own translation of the Greek text, frequently varying from the Authorised Version.

[173] In addition to publishing the *Desideratum*, JW had procured a machine that generated electrical shocks and was experimenting on the health benefits of being electrified; see JW, *Journal*, Nov. 9, 1756, 21:81 in this edn.

[174] This is altered in the reprint in the *London Chronicle*: 'to do what good I can'.

[175] The implication may be that JW married Mary Vazeille for her money.

[176] I.e., the letter from 'R. W.' in the November issue.

2. 'If every man be furnished with an inward light as a private guide and director, must it not supersede the use and necessity of revelation?' This affects the Quakers, not the Methodists, who allow no inward light but what is subservient to the written Word, and to be judged thereby. They are therefore no 'enthusiasts'. Neither is it yet proved that they are 'deluded' at all. They follow no *ignis fatuus*,[177] but 'search the Scriptures'[178] freely and impartially. And hence their doctrines are not 'the dogmas of particular men', but are all warranted by Scripture and reason.

I am, sir,

Your sincere well-wisher,

John Wesley

Source: published transcription; *London Magazine* 29 (Dec. 1760), pp. 651–53; reprinted in *London Chronicle* (Dec. 27–30, 1760), p. 628.[179]

To Jane Catherine March

[LONDON]
DECEMBER 12, 1760

You may blame yourself, but I will not blame you for seeking to have your every temper, and thought, and word, and work suitable to the will of God. But I doubt not you seek this *by* faith, not *without* it; and you seek it *in* and *through* Christ, not *without* him. Go on. You shall have all you seek, because God is love. He is showing you the littleness of your understanding and the foolishness of all natural wisdom. Certainly peace and joy in believing are the grand means of holiness, therefore love and value them as such.

'Why is the law of works superseded by the law of love?' Because Christ died. 'Why are we not condemned for coming short even of this?' Because he lives and intercedes for us. I believe it is impos-

---

[177] 'Foolish light'; referring to a pale light sometimes reported to be seen in swamps.
[178] John 5:39.
[179] The reprinted letter is dated Dec. 26, and introduced with the line, 'You will oblige me by inserting in your paper the following answer to a letter published last month in the *London Magazine*'. This reprinted version provides several corrections of punctuation and one variant that is noted.

sible not to come short of it, through the unavoidable littleness of our understanding. Yet the blood of the covenant is upon us, and *therefore* there is no condemnation.[180]

I think the extent of the law of love is exactly marked out in the 13th of the Corinthians.[181] Let faith fill your heart with love to him 5 and all mankind, then follow this loving faith to the best of your understanding, meantime crying out continually, 'Jesus is all in all to me.'

Source: published transcription; *Methodist Magazine* 22 (1799): 148.

To Mr. 'T. H.', alias 'E. L.', etc. etc.[182]

[LONDON]
[DECEMBER 20, 1760] 10

What, my good friend again! Only a little disguised with a new name and a few scraps of Latin! I hoped, indeed, you had been pretty well satisfied before; but since you desire to hear a little farther from me, I will add a few words, and endeavour to set our little controversy in a still clearer light. 15

Last month you publicly attacked the people called Methodists without either fear or wit. You charged them with 'madness, enthusiasm, self-contradiction, imposture', and what not! I considered each charge and, I conceive, refuted it to the satisfaction of all indifferent persons. You renewed the attack, not by *proving* anything 20 but *affirming* the same things over and over. I replied, and without taking notice of the dull, low scurrility, either of the first or second letter, confined myself to the merits of the cause, and cleared away the dirt you had thrown.

You now heap together ten paragraphs more, most of which re- 25 quire very little answer. In the first you say: 'Your *foolishness* becomes the wonder and admiration of the public.' In the second: 'The *public* blushes for you, till you give a better solution to the articles demanded of you.' In the third you cite my words, I still

---

[180] See Rom. 8:1.

[181] I.e., 1 Cor. 13.

[182] Replying to 'E. L.', Dec. 10, 1760; whom JW clearly assumes is the same person as 'Philodemus', 'T. H.', etc.

maintain 'the Bible, with the Liturgy, and Homilies of our Church; and do not espouse any other principles but what are consonant to the Book of Common Prayer.' You keenly answer: 'Granted, Mr. Methodist. But whether or no you *would not* espouse other princi-
5   ples, if you durst, is evident from some *innovations* you have already introduced, which I shall attempt to *prove* in the subsequent part of my answer.' Indeed, you won't. You neither *prove*, nor *attempt* to prove, that I *would* espouse other principles if I durst. However, you give me a deadly thrust: 'You falsify the first Article of the Athana-
10   sian Creed.' But how so? Why, I said: 'The fundamental doctrine of the people called Methodists is, whosoever will be saved, before all things it is necessary that he hold the true faith.' Sir, shall I tell you a secret? It was for the readers of *your* class that I changed the hard word 'catholic' into an easier.[183]
15   In the fourth paragraph you say: 'Did you never use that phrase "the grace of assurance"?' Never, that I remember, either in preaching or writing. Both your ears and eyes have been very *unhappy* if they informed you I did. And how many soever look either sorrowful or joyful, that will not prove the contrary. 'But produce
20   your texts.' What, for a phrase I never use? I pray you, have me excused.[184] But (as I said before) 'from what scripture every one of my propositions is collected any common concordance will show.' To save you trouble, I will for once point out those scriptures: 'Whosoever will be saved must believe' (Mark 16:16; Acts 16:31); 'This
25   faith works by love' (Gal. 5:6); it is 'an evidence of things not seen' (Heb. 11:1); 'He that believes is born of God' (1 John 5:1); 'He has the witness in himself' (verse 10); 'The Spirit itself witnesses with his spirit that he is a child of God' (Rom. 8:16[185]).
In the fifth you say: 'You embrace any shift to twist words to your
30   own meaning.' This is saying just nothing. Any one may *say* this of any one. To *prove* it is another point.
In the sixth you say: 'No Protestant divine ever taught your doctrine of assurance.' I hope you know no better, but it is strange you should not. Did you never see Bishop Hall's *Works*? Was not he a
35   Protestant divine? Was not Mr. Perkins,[186] Bolton, Dr. Sibbs, Dr. Preston, Archbishop Leighton? Inquire a little farther; and don't run thus hand over head, asserting you know not what. By 'assurance' (if we *must* use the expression) I mean 'a confidence which a

---

[183] I.e., JW changed 'catholic faith' to 'true faith'.
[184] See Luke 14:19.
[185] Orig., '8:15'.
[186] Orig., 'Parkins'.

man hath in God that by the merits of Christ his sins are forgiven and he reconciled to the favour of God.'[187] Stop! Do not run your head into a noose again. These are the words of the Homily.

In the seventh you grant 'that works are not *meritorious* unless accompanied with faith'. No, nor then neither. But pray don't talk of this any more till you know the difference between 'meritorious' and 'rewardable', otherwise your ignorance will cause you to blunder on without shame and without end.

In your eighth you throw out an hard word, which somebody has helped you to (*Thaumaturg*, what is it?[188]) about *lay preachers*. When you have answered the arguments in the *Farther Appeal to Men of Reason and Religion*, I will say something more upon that head.[189]

In the ninth you say something, no way material, about the houses at Bristol, Kingswood, and Newcastle; and in the last you give me a fair challenge to a 'personal dispute'. Not so. You have fallen upon me in public, and to the public I appeal. Let all men, not any single umpire, judge whether I have not fully refuted your charge, and cleared the people called Methodists from the foul aspersions which, without why or wherefore, you had thrown upon them. Let all my countrymen judge which of us have spoken the words of truth and soberness, which has *reason* on his side, and which has treated the other with a *temper* suitable to the gospel.

If the general voice of mankind gives it against you, I hope you will be henceforth less flippant with your pen. I assure you, as little as you think of it, the Methodists are not such fools as you suppose. But their desire is to live peaceably with all men;[190] and none desires this more than,

John Wesley

Source: published transcription; *Lloyd's Evening Post* (Dec. 24–26, 1760), p. 610.

---

[187] From *Homilies* (1683), 'Of Salvation', Pt. III; included in JW's published abridgement, *The Doctrine of Salvation, Faith, and Good Works*, I.15, 12:37 in this edn.

[188] From θαυματουργός; 'wonder worker'.

[189] That is, the defense of lay preachers in JW, *A Farther Appeal to Men of Reason and Religion, Part III*, III, 11:289–331 in this edn.

[190] See Rom. 12:18, Heb. 12:14.

1761

To the Editor of the *London Chronicle*

[LONDON]
JANUARY 1, 1761

Sir,

Of all the seats of woe on this side hell, few I suppose exceed or
even equal Newgate.[1] If any region of horror could exceed it a few
years ago, Newgate in Bristol did, so great was the filth, the stench,
the misery, and wickedness which shocked all who had a spark of
humanity left. How was I surprised, then, when I was there a few
weeks ago! 1) Every part of it, above stairs and below, even 'the pit'
wherein the felons are confined at night, is as clean and sweet as a
gentleman's house, it being now a rule that every prisoner wash and
clean his apartment thoroughly twice a week. 2) Here is no fighting
or brawling. If any thinks himself ill-used, the cause is immediately
referred to the keeper,[2] who hears the contending parties face to
face and decides the affair at once. 3) The usual grounds of quarrel-
ling are removed, for it is very rarely that any one cheats or wrongs
another, as being sure, if anything of this kind is discovered, to be
committed to a closer confinement. 4) Here is no drunkenness suffered, however advantageous it might be to the keeper as well as
the tapster. 5) Nor any whoredom, the women prisoners being narrowly observed and kept separate from the men, nor is any woman
of the town *now* admitted; no, not at any price. 6) All possible care
is taken to prevent idleness. Those who are willing to work at their
callings are provided with tools and materials, partly by the keeper,
who gives them credit at a very moderate profit, partly by the alms
occasionally given, which are divided with the utmost prudence
and impartiality. Accordingly at this time, among others, a shoemaker, a tailor, a brazier, and a coachmaker are working at their
several trades. 7) Only on the Lord's Day they neither work nor
play, but dress themselves as clean as they can, to attend the public

[1] Newgate prison in London.
[2] Abel Dagge, the keeper of Newgate Prison, had been converted under the influence of
George Whitefield's preaching in 1737 and opened the pulpit there to Methodist preachers;
see JW to James Hutton, May 7, 1739, 25:641–42 in this edn. Dagge established a reputation
for civil treatment of the prisoners, being described as 'the tender gaoler' in Samuel Johnson,
Lives of the English Poets (Dublin, 1779), 3:71.

service in the chapel, at which every person under the roof is present. None is excused unless sick, in which case he is provided gratis both with advice and medicines. 8) And, in order to assist them in things of the greatest concern (besides a sermon every Sunday and Thursday), they have a large Bible chained on one side of the   5
chapel, which any of the prisoners may read. By the blessing of God on these regulations the prison now has a new face. Nothing offends either the eye or ear, and the whole has the appearance of a quiet, serious family. And does not 'The Keeper of Newgate' deserve to be remembered full as well as 'The Man of Ross'?[3] May   10
the Lord remember him in that day! Meantime will not one follow his example?

    I am, sir,
        Your humble servant,

                                 John Wesley   15

Source: published transcription; *London Chronicle* (Jan. 6–8, 1761), p. 32; republished by JW in *Journal*, Jan. 2, 1761 (21:295–96 in this edn.).

To the Author of the *Westminster Journal*[4]

L<small>ONDON</small>
J<small>ANUARY</small> 7, 1761

Sir,
    I hope you are a person of impartiality. If so, you will not insert what is urged on one side of a question only, but likewise what is   20
offered on the other.

---

[3] John Kyrle (1637–1724), was a man of wealth who lived simply in Ross-on-Wye and dedicated his resources to the service of the poor. He was celebrated under the title 'The Man of Ross' by Alexander Pope in *Moral Essays* (1754), Epistle iii, line 250.
    [4] JW gives this identification when reprinting the letter in his *Journal*. Unfortunately no copies of the *Westminster Journal* for the relevant time period appear to survive. Thus the text here follows JW's *Journal*. There are surviving copies of the *London Chronicle*, where JW republished the letter with a revised introduction (as noted below).

Your correspondent[5] is doubtless a man of sense, and he seems to write in a good humour, but he is extremely little acquainted with the persons of whom he undertakes to give an account.[6]

5 There is 'gone abroad', says he, 'an ungoverned spirit of enthusiasm, propagated by knaves and embraced by fools.' Suffer me now to address the gentleman himself.[7] Sir, you may *call* me both a knave and a fool. But *prove* me either the one or the other if you can. 'Why, you are an enthusiast.' What do you mean by the term? A believer in Jesus Christ? An asserter of his equality with the Father 10 and of the entire Christian revelation? Do you mean one who maintains the antiquated doctrines of the new birth and justification by faith? Then I am an enthusiast. But if you mean anything else, either prove or retract the charge.

The enthusiasm which has lately gone abroad is faith which 15 worketh by love.[8] Does this 'endanger government itself'? Just the reverse. Fearing God, it honours the king.[9] It teaches all men to be subject to the higher powers, not for wrath, but for conscience' sake.[10]

But 'no power in England ought to be independent of the su- 20 preme power.' Most true; yet 'the Romanists own the authority of a pope, independent of civil government.' They do, and thereby show their ignorance of the English constitution. 'In Great Britain we have many popes, for so I must call all who have the *souls and bodies* of their followers devoted to them.' Call them so, and wel- 25 come. But this does not touch *me*; nor Mr. Whitefield, Jones, or Romaine,[11] nor any whom I am acquainted with. None of us have our followers thus 'devoted to us'. Those who follow the advice we constantly give are devoted to God, not man. But 'the Methodist proclaims he can bring into the field twenty-five thousand men.'

---

[5] JW is responding to a letter published in the *Westminster Journal* and the *Gazetteer*. Copies of these two publications for the relevant period have not been located, but the general argument can be reconstructed from JW's extracts.

[6] The *London Chronicle* replaces these opening paragraphs with: 'Sir, / Be pleased to insert in your paper what follows. It is an answer to a letter published in the *Westminster Journal* and the *Gazetteer*. / Sir, …'.

[7] The *London Chronicle* text addresses the interlocutor directly from the beginning: 'Sir, "There is gone abroad" (you say) "an ungoverned spirit of enthusiasm, propagated by knaves, and embraced by fools."' It then omits 'Suffer me now to address the gentleman himself', and proceeds from that point as the text in JW, *Journal*.

[8] See Gal. 5:6.

[9] See 1 Pet. 2:17.

[10] See Rom. 13:1, 5.

[11] George Whitefield; Thomas Jones (1729–62), vicar of St. Saviour's, Southwark; and William Romaine—three leading Evangelical/Calvinist clergymen in the Church of England.

What Methodist? Where and when? Prove this fact, and I will allow you I am a Turk.

'But it is said they are all good subjects. Perhaps they are, because under a Protestant government they have all the indulgence they can wish for.' And do you seriously wish for a popish government to abridge them of that indulgence? 'But has not a bad use been made of this? [1)] Has not the decency of religion been perverted?' Not in the least. The decency of religion is never so well advanced as by advancing inward and outward religion together. 2) 'Have not the minds of the vulgar been darkened to a total neglect of their civil and social duties?' Quite the contrary. Thousands in London as well as elsewhere have been enlightened to understand and prevailed on to practice those duties as they never did before. 3) 'Has not the peace of many families been ruined?' The lost peace of many families has been restored. In others a furious opposition to true religion has occasioned division, as our Lord foretold it would. 4) 'Have not the circumstances of many industrious tradesmen been hurt?' I believe not. I know no instance. But I know an hundred tradesmen in London who began to be industrious since they began to fear God, and their circumstances, low enough till then, are now easy and affluent.

I am almost ashamed to spend time upon these threadbare objections, which have been answered over and over. But if they are advanced again, they must be answered again, lest silence should pass for guilt.

'But how can the Government distinguish between tenderness of conscience and schemes of interest?' Nothing more easy. 'They may withdraw the licenses of such.' Sir, you have forgot the question. Before they *withdraw them* they are to *distinguish* whether they are such or no. And how are they to do this? 'Oh, it is very easy'! So you leave them as wise as they were before.

But 'the Methodist who pretends to be of the Church of England in forms of worship *and differs from her in point of doctrine* is not, let his presences be what they will, a member of that Church.' Alas, sir! your friends will not thank you for this. You have broke their heads sadly. Is no man of the Church, let him pretend what he will, who *differs from her in point of doctrine? Au! obsecro; cave dixeris!*[12]

---

[12] JW pieces together two phrases from Terence: *Eunuch*, Act 4, Scene 3 (l. 657) and *Adelphi* (*The Brothers*), Act 3, Scene 4 (l. 458); 'O, I beg you,' 'be careful about what you have said' (Loeb).

I know not but you may stumble upon *scandalum magnatum*.[13] But stay, you will bring them off quickly. 'A truly good man may *scruple signing and swearing* to Articles that his mind and reason cannot approve of.' But is he a truly good man who *does not scruple* signing
5   and swearing to Articles which he cannot approve of? However, this does not affect *us*, for we do not differ from our Church *in point of doctrine*. But all do who deny justification by faith; therefore, according to you, they are no members of the Church of England.

'Methodists preachers', you allow, 'practice, sign, and swear
10   whatever is required by law', a very large concession, 'but the reserves they have are incommunicable and unintelligible.' Favour us, sir, with a little proof of this. Till then, I must plead not guilty. In whatever I sign or swear to I have no *reserve* at all. And I have again and again communicated my thoughts on most heads to all
15   mankind, I believe intelligibly, particularly in the *Appeals to Men of Reason and Religion*.

But 'if Methodism, as its professors pretend, be a *new* discovery in *religion* [...]'. This is a grievous mistake. We pretend no such thing. We aver it is the one *old religion*; as old as the Reformation, as
20   old as Christianity, as old as Moses, as old as Adam.

'[...] They ought to discover the whole ingredients of which their nostrum is composed, and have it enrolled in the public register, to be perused by all the world.' It is done. The whole ingredients of Methodism (so called) have been discovered in print over and over;
25   and they are enrolled in that public register, the Bible, from which we extracted them at first. 'Else they *ought not to be tolerated*.' We allow it, and desire toleration on no other terms. 'Nor should they be suffered to add or alter one grain different from what is so registered.' Most certainly. We ought neither to add or diminish, nor
30   alter whatever is written in that Book.

I wish, sir, before you write concerning the Methodists again, you would candidly read some of their writings. Common report is not a sure rule of judging. I should be unwilling to judge of you thereby.

To sum up the matter. The whole ingredients of our religion
35   are love, joy, peace, longsuffering, gentleness, goodness, fidelity, meekness, temperance. Against these, I think, there is no law,[14] and

---

[13] English law in this period distinguished between common libel or slander, defamation of a commoner, and *scandalum magnatum*, defamation of a peer or a high state official; see George Wingrove Cooke, *A Treatise on the Law of Defamation: With Forms of Pleadings* (London, 1844), 25–26.

[14] See Gal. 5:22–23.

therefore I still apprehend they may be *tolerated*, at least in a Christian country.

I am, sir,

Your sincere well-wisher,

John Wesley 5

Source: published transcription; JW, *Journal*, Jan. 5, 1761 (21:297–99 in this edn.); revised reprint in *London Chronicle* (Jan. 15–17, 1761), p. 61.

To Dorothy Furly

NORWICH
JANUARY 18, 1761

My Dear Sister,

I have sometimes wondered that not one of all the clergymen we 10
have known should ever cleave to me for God's sake, nor one man
of learning, which would ease me exceedingly. Tommy Walsh designed it,

But death had quicker wings than love.[15] 15

Perhaps it was not best, because I am so immeasurably apt to pour
out all my soul into any that loves me.

It is well for sister Clarke that she is landed safe.[16] And it is well
for us, who are still amidst the waves, that he is with us whom the 20
winds and the seas obey.[17] He is steering you to the haven where
you would be. You may well trust your soul with him and let him do
with you as seemeth him good.

---

[15] Samuel Wesley Jr., 'Epigram from the Greek', *Poems on Several Occasions* (Cambridge, 1743), 66; included by JW in *MSP* (1744), 3:58. On Thomas Walsh, who died in Apr. 1759, see 26:430 in this edn.

[16] Mary Clarke owned a house in Christopher Alley, Moorfields, where 'a few of the most lively souls in the London society gathered' in the mid 1750s; both Sarah Ryan (before going to Bristol) and Sarah Crosby boarded with Clarke, and it was in her home that Mary Bosanquet first met them. See Henry Moore, *The Life of Mrs. Mary Fletcher* (1818), 34–35.

[17] See Matt. 8:27 and parallels.

Certainly nothing can be of greater importance than the behaviour both of those who are renewed and of those who are known to be pressing after it. You have need to weigh every step you take. When and where do you meet now? And who are they that meet? Pray send
5 the enclosed to your neighbour; and let all of you love and pray for,
Your affectionate brother,

J. Wesley

Source: published transcription; Benson, *Works*, 16:326.

To the Rev. Samuel Furly

LAKENHEATH
FEBRUARY 2, 1761

10 Dear Sammy,
Your friends here,[18] particularly brothers Evans and Kitchener, desire to be remembered to you and yours. But they are sorry you have so soon forgot them, otherwise you should have given them one letter in six months. Did you receive your books? If so, you
15 should have sent them word and put them out of their pain.
God is very merciful to the people of Lakenheath. Mr. Goudicheau,[19] who has served the cure since you left it, is an honest, serious man, and preaches the truth to the uttermost of his power. He has done much good, especially by defending the doc-
20 trines and preachers of the gospel in his conversation. Mr. Pearse has not been here for many months, so that the people now are wholly under our care.
I wish you would read over what I have published, regularly, and minute[20] down in order what you object to or stand in doubt. I am
25 doing the same myself. From your papers and mine we might then draw up an *index expurgatorius*.[21] And as the tracts are continually

---

[18] Furly had served as curate in Lakenheath from Nov. 1758 to June 1759.

[19] JW met a Mr. Goudicheau, a former Catholic priest, in London in Dec. 1758, whom he described as 'now ready to perish for want of bread, though of an unblemished character' (*Journal*, Dec. 8, 1758, 21:172–73 in this edn.). It is possible that Wesley helped him obtain the curacy of Lakenheath as a point of entry into the Anglican priesthood.

[20] I.e., record.

[21] 'List of things to remove'; the term is sometimes used for a list of prohibited books, but JW uses it here to refer to a list of errata and corrigenda for his works.

reprinting, most things that need it may be corrected before I die. This would be doing a substantial piece of service to the whole body of Methodists.

If there be any inconsistency in the Thoughts upon Perfection,[22] it is not for want of consideration. I have reviewed them again and again, I suppose six times at least, since they were printed. And I can discern none. Nay the oftener I read them, the more I am persuaded that whether there be truth in them or no, there is perfect consistency. I find that tract is 'generally received', even by the clergy, as any I have wrote for many years.

Mr. Fletcher says, 'He cannot do it.'[23] So when the other clergymen here follow his example, I must send for *you*, just as you are. For I can do nothing at the chapels without help.

With love to Nancy, I am, dear Sammy,
    Your affectionate friend and brother,

                  J. Wesley

Address: 'To / The Revd Mr Furly / At Kippax, near Ferrybridge / By Caxton bag / Yorkshire'. *Seal*: black, dove with twig, and over 'NUNTIA PACIS', in an octagonal frame.
Postmark: 'NEWMARKET'.
Endorsement: 'to support ye fall[in]g Prop of a darl[in]g Hypothesis'.
Source: holograph; MARC, MAM JW 3/18.

To Sarah Crosby

LONDON
FEBRUARY 14, 1761

My Dear Sister,

Miss _____[24] gave me yours on Wednesday night. Hitherto, I think you have not gone too far. You could not well do less.[25] I

---

[22] JW, 'Thoughts on Christian Perfection' (1760), 13:57–80 in this edn.

[23] JW had tried to persuade Fletcher to take on Furly as a curate, so that he could be ordained a priest (and apparently then assist JW in broadening sacramental access for Methodists); see JW to Furly, Dec. 9, 1760.

[24] This was likely Mary Bosanquet, a close friend of Crosby and a supporter of women exhorting or preaching.

[25] An extract of Sarah Crosby's diary published in the *Methodist Magazine* (1806, p. 518) indicated that Crosby had gone from London to Derby in early 1761 and had found great crowds in Methodist meetings there. On February 8, in particular, she estimated the group at

apprehend all you can do more is, when you meet again, to tell them simply, 'You lay me under a great difficulty. The Methodists do not allow of women preachers. Neither do I take upon me any such character. But I will just nakedly tell you what is in my heart.' This will

5 in a great measure obviate the grand objection and prepare for John Hampson's coming.²⁶ I do not see that you have broken any law. Go on calmly and steadily. If you have time, you may read to them the Notes²⁷ on any chapter before you speak a few words, or one of the most awakening sermons, as other women have done long ago.

10 The work of God goes on mightily here both in conviction and conversion. This morning I have spoken with four or five who seem to have been set at liberty within this month. I believe within five weeks six in one class have received remission of sins and five in one band received a second blessing. Peace be with you all! I am,

15 Your affectionate brother,

J. Wesley

Source: published transcription; Benson, *Works*, 16:332.

To Mr. 'G. R.', alias 'R. A.', alias 'M. H.', alias 'R. W.'²⁸

LONDON
FEBRUARY 17, 1761

Dear Sir,

20 As you are stout, be merciful; or I shall never be able to stand it. Four attacks in one month! And pushed so home! Well, I must defend myself as I can.

---

about 200, and noted there was no preacher available. Her diary states, 'I was not sure whether it was right for me to exhort in so public a manner, and yet I saw it impracticable to meet all these people by way of speaking particularly to each individual. I therefore gave out an hymn, and prayed, and told them part of what the Lord had done for myself, persuading them to flee from all sin.'

²⁶ John Hampson (c.1732–95), became a Methodist itinerant in 1752, took a hiatus 1765–76, and withdrew entirely in 1784 in a dispute over how leadership would be structured on JW's death; see Atmore, *Memorial*, 176–78; and Vickers, *Dictionary*, 148.

²⁷ I.e., *NT Notes*.

²⁸ JW is responding to four letters published in the Dec. 1760 and Jan. 1761 issues of *London Magazine*. The title of his response has a misprint 'M. K.' in the original.

Indeed, your first attack under the character of G. R. is not very desperate. You first give a short history of Montanism, [then] innocently say, 'It would fill a volume to draw a parallel between Montanism and Methodism.' According as it was drawn. But if it contained nothing but truth, it would not fill a nutshell.[29] You add: 'Such a crude composition is this Methodism that there is scarce any one pestilent heresy that has infested the Church but what is an actual part of their doctrine.' This is easily said, but till you can *prove* it, it will pass for nothing.

In your second letter you say: 'The present troublers of our Israel are that heterogeneous mass, the Methodists.' Heterogeneous! An hard word, a very hard word! Pray, sir, what is the meaning of it? 'They are avowed enemies to the doctrine and discipline of the Church.' Surely not *avowed* enemies (if they are secret ones, which no man can prove). They flatly disavow any such thing. 'Have faithfully copied the worst of men in the worst of times.' This means nothing, it is mere garniture of the dish. 'If such men's enthusiastical notions be the true doctrine of Jesus Christ, better would it be to be a Jew, a Turk, an infidel, than a Christian.' This proves nothing but what was pretty plain before, namely, that you are very angry. 'Notions repugnant to common sense and to the first principles of truth and equity.' My fundamental notions are that true religion is love, the love of God and our neighbour, the doing all things to the glory of God, and doing to all men as we would be done to. Are these notions repugnant to common sense or to the first principles of truth and equity? 'What punishment do they deserve?' they who walk by this rule? By nature they deserve hell; but by the grace of God, if they endure to the end, they will receive eternal life.

In your third letter you say: 'None of the principles of the Methodists have a more fatal tendency than the doctrine of *assurance*.' I allow it; and it is past your skill to prove that *this* has any fatal tendency at all, unless as you wonderfully explain it in the following words: 'They insist that themselves are sure of salvation, but that all others are in a damnable state!' Who do? Not I, nor any that I know but papists. Therefore all that you add to disprove this, which no one affirms, is but beating the air, 'But St. Paul commands us to

---

[29] Despite the distance Wesley places between himself and Montanism in this letter, he had written in 1750, '1) that the Montanists, in the second and third centuries, were real, scriptural Christians; and 2) that the grand reason why the miraculous gifts were so soon withdrawn, was not only that faith and holiness were wellnigh lost, but that dry, formal, orthodox men began even then to ridicule whatever gifts they had not themselves, and to decry them all as either madness or imposture' (*Journal*, Aug. 15, 1750, 20:356–57 in this edn.).

pass the time of our sojourning here in fear.' Indeed, he does not; your memory fails. But St. Peter does, and that is as well.[30]

Your fourth (for want of a better) is to serve for a reply to my answer. In this you stoutly say: 'Sir, your performance is frivolous and fallacious.' Very well, but others must judge of that. 'Shocks, sir, or violent operations of the Spirit are too fully evidenced by your trances, ecstasies, and I know not what.' I assure you, neither do I. But if you please to tell me, when you *do* know a little of the matter, I will give you what satisfaction I can. 'These appear in the practices of your followers, and as such must destroy free agency.' Nay, sir, you[31] are now too severe, especially in that keen 'as such'! 'As you then assert such practices, you are (excuse the harshness of the expression) an enemy to religion and a deceiver of the people.' Sir, I do excuse you. I am pretty well used to such expressions. If they hurt not you, they hurt not me. 'Until you publish in plain, intelligible words your scheme of principles, it is impossible to say what you are.' I have done it ten times over, particularly in *The Principles of a Methodist*, the *Appeals to Men of Reason and Religion*, and (what I am not without hope might be intelligible even to you) *Instructions for Children*.[32] 'I must be plain with you. You seem, sir, to have as much knowledge of the Scriptures as a Mahometan.' Sir, I thank you, and I presume you do not expect any other answer to this. 'That you are an enthusiast, a very great enthusiast, not I, let your own Journals demonstrably prove.' Nay, why not *you*? I fear my Journals will not give such proof as will satisfy any impartial person. 'As to dogmas, I do not know that it is good English. I know it is false dog-Latin.' Now, I really thought it was neither Latin nor English. I took it to be mere heathen Greek.

Whenever you please to favour the public with your name and place of abode, you may perhaps (if I have leisure) hear farther from,

Your humble servant and well-wisher,

John Wesley

Source: published transcription; *London Magazine* (Feb. 1761), pp. 91–92.

---

[30] 1 Pet. 1:17.

[31] Orig., 'your'.

[32] A basic catechism that JW published in 1745; *Bibliography*, No. 101, and Vol. 16 in this edn.

To Sarah Moore

My Dear Sister,

I hope to spend a night or two with you at Sheffield in my return
from Newcastle. Probably I may see Hallam too. I am glad to hear   5
you are athirst for God. Look for him. Is he not nigh at hand?[33]
Beware of unbelief. Receive a blessing now! I am,
    Your affectionate brother,

John Wesley   10

Source: published transcription; Everett, *Sheffield*, 1:156.

To Christopher Hopper[34]

My Dear Brother,

I stepped over from Manchester hither yesterday, and am to return thither tomorrow. I cannot fix my route through Scotland till   15
I hear from Mr. Gillies,[35] but I expect to be at Aberdeen in four or
five weeks and at Newcastle about the middle of May.

My best friend (such she undoubtedly is in a sense) remains still
in London.[36] I do not expect any change till the approach of death,
and I am content. With regard to *me* all is well.   20

John Nelson and John Manners[37] both write to me from York that
they wish Thomas Olivers would spend some time longer in the
Newcastle circuit. I wish so too. I think it would be better for himself

---

[33] See Jas. 4:8.

[34] On Christopher Hopper, see 26:406 in this edn.

[35] John Gillies; see 26:504 in this edn.

[36] I.e., his wife Mary.

[37] John Manners (1731–64) was converted by Methodist preaching about 1755, and is
listed as a travelling preacher by 1758 (see 10:282 in this edn.). He helped spark a revival in
Dublin in 1762. See Atmore, *Memorial*, 247–50.

and for many others. O let us follow after the things which make for peace! I am,

Yours affectionately,

J. Wesley

5

Alas! Alas! So poor Jacob Rowell[38] says: 'Mr. Wesley has nothing to do with his round, and all the societies in it but Barnard Castle are willing to separate.' In God's name, let one of you go into that round without delay!

10

Address: 'To / Mr Christopher Hopper / in / Newcastle upon Tyne'.
Seal: black, dove with twig, the words 'NUNTIA PACIS'.
Postmark: 'LEEDS'.
Source: holograph; MARC, MAM JW 3/52.

To the Rev. James Rouquet

MANCHESTER
MARCH 30, 1761

Dear Jemmy,

The thing you mention has been much in my thoughts, and in-
15   deed for some years last past. The dreadful consequences which have arisen from the disunion of Christian ministers, especially those whom God has lately employed, are too glaring to be hid from any who do not wilfully shut their eyes. How often has this put a sword into the hand of the common enemy! How often has it
20   made the children of God go heavily! And how many of them has it turned out of the way! On the other hand, how many and how great are the advantages which would flow from a general *union*, of those at least who acknowledge each other to be messengers of God! I know nothing[39] which I would not do or leave undone to promote
25   it, and this has been my settled determination for at least ten years

---

[38] Jacob Rowell (1722–84) became a Methodist exhorter in 1749 and appears in the Minutes as an itinerant by 1752 (10:251 in this edn.). He laboured mainly in the northeast, and JW valued his preaching, though had to restrain (as here) his inclination to separation from the Church of England. See Atmore, *Memorial*, 378.

[39] Telford at this inserted editorially: '[except sin]'.

last past. But all my overtures have been constantly rejected; almost all of them stand aloof, and at length they have carried their point. I let them alone.

> I'll give the fruitless contest o'er.[40]   5

However, if you can think of any expedient which is likely to avail, I will make a fresh trial. God has lately done great things. Mr. Berridge and Whitefield were much knit to us. The grand breach is now between the irregular and regular clergy.[41] The latter say: 10 'Stand by yourselves; we are better than you!' And a good man is continually exhorting them so to do, whose steady advice is so very civil to the Methodists. But we have nothing to do with them. And this man of war is a dying man—it is poor, honest Mr. Walker.[42]

Finding all other means ineffectual, on Monday the 2nd instant 15 I opened my wife's bureau and took what I found of my own. (No notes, bills, or papers of hers—in saying this, she only does as she uses to do.) Some hours after, she talked like an Empress Queen; on which I told her plainly, '*While you are in this mind* I will neither bed nor board with you.' On ... following I found her of a better 20 mind, so on Saturday and Sunday we were together as usual. But if we should live to meet again, and she behaves as she did on that day, I should think it my bounden duty to do as I did then. I judge her case to be proper lunacy. But it is a preternatural, a diabolical lunacy, and therefore *at those times* (I know what I say) I do not think 25 my life is safe with her. And yet I feel just as much resentment toward her as I do to Sally Rouquet.[43]

Peace be with you and yours,

[John Wesley]

Source: published transcription; Telford, *Letters*, 4:142–44.

---

[40] Cf. JW's rendering of 'The Dialogue', st. 2, by George Herbert, in *HSP* (1739), 121; 'Give the needless contest o'er'.

[41] JW identifies himself on this occasion with the 'irregular clergy', that is, those who support itinerancy.

[42] Samuel Walker of Truro died on July 19, 1761.

[43] James Rouquet's wife; in other words, JW is claiming he feels no resentment toward Mary.

To the Rev. John Green[44]

[CHESTER]
APRIL 2, 1761

Rev. Sir,

 I have no desire to dispute, least of all with one whom I believe
5 to fear God and work righteousness.[45] And I have no time to spare.
Yet I think it my duty to write a few lines with regard to those you
sent to Mr. Bennet.[46]

 You therein say: 'If you sent me the books to inform me of an error
which I had publicly advanced, pardon me if I say I know numbers
10 who call themselves Methodists assert their assurance of salvation at
the very time they wallow in sins of the deepest dye.' Permit me, sir, to
speak freely. I do not doubt the fact. But 1) those who are connected
with *me* do not *call themselves* Methodists. Others call them by that
nickname, and they cannot help it, but I continually warn them not to
15 pin it upon themselves. 2) We rarely use that ambiguous expression
of 'Christ's righteousness imputed to us'. 3) We believe a man may be
a real Christian without being 'assured of his salvation'. 4) We know
no man can be assured of salvation while he lives in any sin whatever.
5) The wretches who talk in that manner are neither Methodists nor
20 Moravians, but followers of William Cudworth, James Relly, and
their associates, who abhor us as much as they do the pope, and ten
times more than they do the devil. If *you* oppose these, so do *I*, and
have done privately and publicly for these twenty years.

 But you say: 'Such as do not profess this doctrine will not be af-
25 fected by my sermon.' Indeed they will, for the world (as you yourself did) lump all that are called Methodists together. Consequently
whatever you then said of Methodists in general falls on *us* as well as
them, and so *we* are condemned for those very principles which we
totally detest and abhor. A small part of the *Preservative*[47] (had you
30 taken the pains to read it) would have convinced you of this. 'Did
you send them to convince me of some important truth? I have the
New Testament.' So have I, and I have read it for above these fifty

---

[44] John Green was Dean of Lincoln, and became Bishop of Lincoln in Dec. 1761. He
published pseudonymously *The Principles and Practices of the Methodists Considered* (London,
1760), to which JW responded briefly in his letter to *Lloyd's Evening Post* dated Nov. 22, 1760.
See *ODNB*.

[45] See Acts 10:35.

[46] The identity of 'Mr. Bennet' is unclear (his former colleague, John Bennet, having died
in 1759). Perhaps this is a confused reference to John Berridge, the veiled addressee of Green's
earlier tract.

[47] *Preservative against Unsettled Notions in Religion* (1758).

years, and for near forty with some attention. Yet I will not say that
Mr. Green may not convince me of some truth which I never yet
learned from it. I want every help, especially from those who strive
both to preach and to live the gospel. Yet certainly I must dissent
from you or you from me wherever either conceives the other to 5
vary from it. Some of my writings you 'have read'. But allow me to
ask, Did not you read them with much prejudice or little attention?
Otherwise surely you would not have termed them 'perplexing'.
Very few lay obscurity or intricacy to my charge. Those who do
not allow them to be *true* do not deny them to be *plain*. And if they 10
believe me to have done any good at all by writing, they suppose
it is by this very thing, by speaking on practical and experimental
religion more plainly than others have done.

I quite agree we 'neither can be better men nor better Christians
than by continuing members of the Church of England'. And not 15
only her doctrines but many parts of her discipline I have adhered
to at the hazard of my life. If in any point I have since varied therefrom, it was not by choice but necessity. Judge, therefore, if they
do well who throw me into the ditch, and then beat me because my
clothes are dirty! 20

Wishing you much of the love of God in your heart and much of
his presence in your labours, I remain, reverend sir,
      Your affectionate brother,

John Wesley

Source: published transcription; *Arminian Magazine* 3 (1780): 670–71.

To the Rev. George Downing

LIVERPOOL 25
APRIL 6, 1761

Dear Sir,

Let who will speak, if what is spoken be true, I am ready to subscribe it. If it be not, I accept no man's person. *Magis amica veritas.*[48]

---

[48] 'Truth is a better friend.' A common expression of which this is a phrase was *Amicus
Plato, sed magis amica veritas*, 'Plato is a friend, but truth is a better friend.'

I had an agreeable conversation with Mr. Venn,[49] who I suppose is now near you. I think he is exactly as regular as he ought to be.[50] I would observe every punctilio of order, except where the salvation of souls is at stake. There I prefer the end before the means.

5   I think it great pity that the few clergymen in England who preach the three grand scriptural doctrines, original sin, justification by faith, and holiness consequent thereon,[51] should have any jealousies or misunderstandings between them. What advantage must this give to the common enemy! What an hindrance is it to

10   the great work wherein they are all engaged! How desirable is it that there should be the most open, avowed intercourse between them! So far, indeed, as they judge it would be for the glory of God, they may openly declare wherein they disagree.

But surely, if they are ashamed to own one another in the faces of

15   all mankind, they are ashamed of Christ; they are ashamed of him that sends if they dare not avow whom he has sent. Excuses, indeed, will never be wanting. But will these avail before God? For many years I have been labouring after this—labouring to unite, not scatter, the messengers of God. Not that I want anything from them. As

20   God has enabled me to stand almost alone for these twenty years, I doubt not but he will enable me to stand either with them or without them. But I want all to be helpful to each other, and all the world to know we are so. Let them know who is on the Lord's side.[52] You, I trust, will always be of that number. O let us preach and live

25   the whole gospel! The grace of our Lord be with your spirit![53]

I am, dear sir,

Your ever affectionate brother and servant,

John Wesley

Source: published transcription; *Arminian Magazine* 3 (1780): 672–73.

[49] Henry Venn had become vicar of Huddersfield in the West Riding of Yorkshire in 1759, where JW had breakfast with him on Mar. 25, 1761 (*Journal*, 21:313 in this edn.).

[50] Downing was sympathetic and met regularly with clergy from both the Wesleyan and Calvinist wings of the Evangelical revival (see the occasion CW describes in a letter to his wife Sarah, Feb. 27, 1759). But he was uncomfortable with any type of irregularity in church law, such as lay preaching; see the following letter to William Legge, whom he served as chaplain.

[51] An epitome of the distinctive notes of Evangelical preaching: original sin leading to repentance and 'awakening', justification typically involving 'assurance of pardon', and the quest for holiness (sanctification).

[52] See Exod. 32:26.

[53] See Gal. 6:18.

To William Legge, 2nd Earl of Dartmouth[54]

LIVERPOOL
APRIL 10, 1761

Dear Sir,

1. In order to answer the question more clearly which Mr. [Downing[55]] has proposed to you, it may be well to look a little backward. Some years since, two or three clergymen of the Church of England, who were above measure zealous for all her rules and orders, were convinced that religion is not an external thing, but 'righteousness and peace and joy in the Holy Ghost',[56] and that this righteousness and peace and joy are given only to those who are justified by faith. As soon as they were convinced of these great truths they preached them, and multitudes flocked to hear. For these reasons, and no others, real or pretended (for as yet they were strictly *regular*), because they *preached such doctrine*, and because *such multitudes followed* them, they were forbid to preach in the churches. Not daring to be silent, they preached elsewhere, in a school, by a riverside, or upon a mountain, and more and more sinners forsook their sins and were filled with peace and joy in believing.

2. But at the same time huge offence was taken at their 'gathering congregations' in so *irregular* a manner; and it was asked,

a) 'Do you judge that the Church with the authority of the State has power to enact laws for her own government?'

I answer: If a dispensation of the gospel is committed to me, no Church has power to enjoin me silence. Neither has the State, though it may *abuse* its power and enact laws whereby I suffer for preaching the gospel.

b) 'Do you judge it your duty to submit to the laws of the Church and State as far as they are consistent with a good conscience?'

I do. But 'woe is me if I *preach not* the gospel'.[57] This is not consistent with a good conscience.

c) 'Is it a law of the Church and State that none of her ministers shall *gather congregations* but by the appointment of the bishop? If

---

[54] William Legge, the second Earl of Dartmouth (1731–1801) was one of the leading Evangelical noblemen of the eighteenth century. Educated at Trinity College, Oxford, he succeeded his grandfather as Earl of Dartmouth in 1750, and would also play a leading role in events related to the American revolution. See *ODNB*.

[55] The person is not identified in *AM*, but George Downing held the position of chaplain to Dartmouth—the parallel to the priest of the German nobleman speaking against Luther posited near the end of the letter.

[56] Rom. 14:17.

[57] 1 Cor. 9:16.

any do, does not she forbid her people to attend them? Are they not subversive of the good order of the Church? Do you judge there is anything sinful in such a law?'

5   I answer: 1) If there is a law that a minister of Christ who is not suffered to preach the gospel in the church should not preach it elsewhere, I do judge that law to be absolutely sinful. 2) If that law forbids Christian people to hear the gospel of Christ out of their parish church when they cannot hear it therein, I judge it would be sinful for them to obey it. 3) This preaching is not subversive of any
10 'good order' whatever. It is only subversive of that vile *abuse of the good order* of our Church whereby men who neither preach nor live the gospel are suffered publicly to overturn it from the foundation, and in the room of it to palm upon their congregations a wretched mixture of dead form and maimed morality.

15   d) 'If these premises be allowed.'

They cannot be allowed. So, from nothing, nothing follows.

3. It was objected farther,

a) 'In every nation there must be some settled order of government, ecclesiastical and civil.'
20   There must, but put *civil* out of the question. It only tends to puzzle the cause.

b) 'The Scriptures likewise enjoin this.'

They do, that 'all things' in the church be 'done in order'.[58]

c) 'There is an ecclesiastical order established in England, and it
25 is a lawful one.'

I believe it is in general not only lawful but highly commendable.

d) But Mr. [Downing] tells you: 'You are born under this establishment. Your ancestors supported it, and were ennobled on that account.' These points, I think, are not very material. But that
30 which follows is. 'You have by deliberate and repeated acts of your own engaged yourself to defend it. Your very rank and station constitute you a formal and eminent guardian of it.'

A guardian of what? What is it that you have 'deliberately engaged yourself to defend'? The constitution of the Church of Eng-
35 land. And is not her *doctrine* a main part of this constitution, a far more essential part thereof than any rule of external *order*? Of this, then, you are a formal guardian, and you have deliberately engaged yourself to defend it. But have you deliberately engaged to defend her *orders* to the destruction of her *doctrine*? Are you a guardian of
40 this *external circumstance* when it tends to destroy the *substance* of

---

[58] Cf. 1 Cor. 14:40.

her constitution? And if you are engaged, at all events, to defend her *order*, are you also to defend the *abuse* of it? Surely no. Your rank, your station, your honour, your conscience, all engage you to oppose this.

e) 'But how can it consist with the duty arising from all these to give *encouragement, countenance*, and *support* to principles and practices that are a direct renunciation of the established constitution, and that in their genuine issue' (or natural tendency) 'are totally subversive of it?'

Are the principles of those clergymen a 'direct renunciation' of the established constitution? Are their practices so? Are either the one or the other 'totally subversive of it'? Not so. Their fundamental principles are the very principles of the Established Church. So is their practice too, save in a very few points wherein they are constrained to deviate. Therefore it is no ways inconsistent with your duty to *encourage, countenance*, and *support* them; especially seeing they have no alternative. They must either be *thus far* irregular or destroy their own souls, and let thousands of their brethren perish for lack of knowledge.

f) Nay, but their 'principles and practices are of this character. For, 1) they gather congregations and exercise their ministerial office therein in every part of this kingdom, directly contrary to the restraint laid on them at their ordination and to the design of that parochial distribution of duty settled throughout this nation. 2) They maintain it lawful for men to preach who are not episcopally ordained, and thereby contradict the Twenty-third Article. 3) They disclaim all right in the bishops to control them in any of these matters, and say that, rather than be so controlled, they would renounce all communion with this Church. 4) These principles they industriously propagate among their followers.'

I answer: 1) They do gather congregations everywhere and exercise their ministerial office therein. But this is not contrary to any restraint which was laid upon them at their ordination, for they were not ordained to serve any particular parish. And it is remarkable that Lincoln College was founded *ad propagandam Christianam fidem et extirpandas haereses.*[59] But were it otherwise, suppose

---

[59] 'For propagating the Christian faith and extirpating heresies.' JW had cited the statutes of Lincoln College in this manner in the *Farther Appeal, Part I*, VI:9 (11:183 in this edn.) and in the *Principles of a Methodist Farther Explained*, III:5 (9:190 in this edn.). A text of the statutes governing Lincoln College does not show this language, though it is clear that the intent of Richard Fleming and Thomas Rotherham, the founders of the College, was to train clergy to preach in opposition to the errors of heretics, *haereticorum sectas plus solito invalescere*, 'to

a parish minister to be either ignorant or negligent of his duty, and
one of his flock adjures me for Christ's sake to tell him what he
must do to be saved, was it ever the design of our Church that I
should refuse to do it because he is not of my parish? 2) 'They
5   maintain it lawful for men to preach who are not episcopally ordained.' In some circumstances they do, particularly where thousands are rushing into destruction, and those who are *ordained* and
appointed to watch over them neither care for nor know how to
help them. 'But hereby they contradict the Twenty-third Article,
10 to which they have subscribed.' They subscribed it in the simplicity of their hearts, when they firmly believed none but episcopal
ordination valid. But Bishop Stillingfleet has since fully convinced
them this was an entire mistake.[60] 3) 'They disclaim all right in the
bishops to control them in any of these matters.' In every point of
15 an indifferent nature they obey the bishops for conscience' sake,
but they think *episcopal* authority cannot reverse what is fixed by
divine authority. Yet they are determined never 'to renounce communion with the Church' unless they are cast out headlong. If it be
said, 'Nay, but if I varied from the Church at all, I would throw off
20 my gown and be a professed Dissenter', what! Would you *profess* to
dissent when you did not? If *you* would, they dare not do it. They
love the Church, and therefore keep to all her doctrine and rules
as far as possibly they can, and if they vary *at all*, it shall not be an
hair's breadth farther than they cannot help. 4) 'These principles
25 they industriously propagate among their followers.' Indeed they
do not. The bulk of their followers know just nothing of the matter.
They industriously propagate among them nothing but inward and
outward holiness.

g) 'Now these are oppositions to *the most fundamental principles*
30 and *essentially constituent* parts of our establishment, and not of
ours only, but of every ecclesiastical establishment that is or ever
has been in the Christian world.'

---

invalidate the sects of heretics more than [has been] customary'; *Statutes of the Colleges of Oxford* (1853), vol. 1, p. 8 of the section on Lincoln College.

[60] Edward Stillingfleet's *Irenicum* (1659) had convinced JW in the 1740s that episcopacy
was an extension of the office of presbyters or elders and thus that presbyters had the same
inherent right to ordain as bishops; see his letter to CW, July 16, 1755. JW would cite this
principle in his letter 'To Dr. Coke, Mr. Asbury, and Our Brethren in North America', of September 1784, justifying his actions in undertaking to ordain elders and to consecrate Thomas
Coke as a 'superintendent', though in that letter he attributed his changing views to Peter King
rather than Stillingfleet. The 23rd Article of Religion became the main source of controversy
between 'regular' and 'irregular' (i.e., itinerant) clergy. It ruled out preaching or administration
of the sacraments unless a minister had been 'lawfully called, and sent to execute' these offices.

'The most fundamental principles'! No more than the tiles are the most fundamental principles of an house. Useful doubtless they are, yet you must take them off if you would repair the rotten timber beneath. 'Essentially constituent parts of our establishment'! Well, we will not quarrel for a word. Perhaps the doors may be essentially 5 constituent parts of the building we call a church. Yet, if it were on fire, we might innocently break them open or even throw them for a time off the hinges. Now this is really the case. The timber is rotten, yea, the main beams of the house, and they want to place that firm beam, salvation by faith, in the room of salvation by works. 10 A fire is kindled in the Church, the house of the living God—the fire of love of the world, ambition, covetousness, envy, anger, malice, bitter zeal; in one word, of ungodliness and unrighteousness. O who will come and help to quench it? Under disadvantages and discouragements of every kind, a little handful of men have made 15 a beginning, and I trust they will not leave off till the building is saved or they sink in the ruins of it.

4. To sum up the whole. A few irregular men openly witness those truths of God which the regular clergy (a few excepted) either suppress or wholly deny. 20

Their word is accompanied with the power of God, convincing and converting sinners. The word of those is not accompanied with power; it neither wounds nor heals.

The former witness the truth and the power of God by their own life and conversation; therefore the world, men who know not God, 25 hate them and speak all manner of evil against them falsely. The latter are of the world; therefore the world loves its own and speaks honourably of them.

Which of these ought you to hear, those who declare or those who deny the truth of God? That word which is the power of God unto 30 salvation,[61] or that which lulls men on to destruction? The men who live as well as preach the gospel, or those whose lives are no better than their doctrine?

'But they are irregular.'

I answer: 1) That is not their choice. They must either preach 35 irregularly or not at all. 2) Is such a circumstance of weight to turn the scale against the substance of the gospel? If it is, if none ought to speak or hear the truth of God unless in a *regular* manner, then (to mention but one consequence) there never could have been any reformation from popery. For here the entire argument for 'Church 40

[61] See Rom. 1:16.

order' would have stood in its full force. Suppose one had asked a German nobleman to hear Martin Luther preach; might not his priest have said (without debating whether he preached the truth or not): 'My lord, in every nation there must be *some settled order*
5 of government, ecclesiastical and civil. There is an *ecclesiastical order* established in Germany. You are born under this establishment. Your ancestors supported it, and your very rank and station constitute you a formal and eminent guardian of it. How, then, can it consist with the duty arising from all these to give *encouragement*,
10 *countenance*, and *support* to principles and practices that are a direct renunciation of the *established constitution*?' Had the force of this reasoning been allowed, what had become of the Reformation?

Yet it was right, though it really was a subversion of the whole *ecclesiastical constitution* with regard to doctrine as well as disci-
15 pline. Whereas this is no such thing. The *doctrine* of the *Established* Church, which is far the most essential part of her *constitution*, these preachers manifestly confirm, in opposition to those who *subvert* it. And it is the opposition made to them by those subverters which constrains them in *some* respects to deviate from her discipline, to
20 which in *all others* they conform for conscience. Oh what pity that any who preach the same doctrine, and whom those subverters have not yet been able to thrust out, should join with them against their brethren in the common faith and fellow witnesses of the common salvation!
25 I am, dear sir,
Your willing servant for Christ's sake,

John Wesley

Source: published transcription; *Arminian Magazine* 4 (1781): 219–26.

To Mary (Goldhawk/Vazeille) Wesley

WHITEHAVEN
APRIL 24, 1761

My Dear Molly,
30 Although I have not had any answer to my former letters, yet I must trouble you once more, and repeat the advice I gave you be-

fore, 'Beware of tale-bearers.' God has given you plenty of temporal blessings, and if you only avoid this snare (to which your natural temper lays you open), you may have plenty of spiritual too. Indeed he mingles afflictions with your cup. But may not these be blessings also? May they not be admirable means to break the impetuosity and soften the harshness of your spirit? Certainly they may. Certainly they have this effect on many. And why not on *you* likewise? Is not everything contrary to your will intended to conquer it? And to bring it into a full subordination to the will of God? And when once this is done, what can hurt you? Then you are invulnerable. You are defended from head to foot by armour which neither the world nor the devil can pierce. Then you will go on unmoved, through honour and dishonour, through evil report and good report. You will happily experience in your own soul the truth of that fine observation, 'In the greatest afflictions which can befall the just, either from heaven or earth, they remain immovable in virtue, and perfectly submissive to God, by an inward, loving regard to him uniting all the powers of their soul.'[62]

I am with much sincerity, dear Molly,
Your affectionate husband,

John Wesley

What is become of the Chancery suit?[63] Of Noah? Of John and Jenny Matthews and poor Anthony?[64]

Address: 'To / Mrs Wesley / At the Foundery / London'.
Seal: red, almost complete, dove with twig, 'NUNTIA PACIS' in octagonal frame.
Postmarks: '27/AP' and 'WHITE/HAVEN'. *Charge*: '4'.
Source: holograph; MARC, MAM JW 5/63.

---

[62] A translation from a letter of the Jansenist leader Jean Duvergier de Hauranne, Abbé de Saint-Cyran (1581–1643), that John Wesley had included in his *Farther Thoughts Upon Christian Perfection*, II.3, 13:125 in this edn.

[63] JW records in his *Journal* that he consulted with attorneys 'in order to prevent another chancery suit' on Feb. 21, 1761 (21:308 in this edn.). He does not detail the substance of the suit, but notes that (by the time this extract of the *Journal* was published) the suit 'did not go on'.

[64] Noah, her son; her daughter Jeanne (Vazeille) Matthews and husband; and her son John Anthony Vazeille (b. 1738) who was still alive (in India) in 1765.

To Thomas Olivers

WHITEHAVEN
APRIL 25, 1761

My Dear Brother,

I have a desire to ask you some questions on two or three heads,
5   which you may answer as particularly as you please.

    1. Have you read over *The Doctrine of Original Sin*? I mean the
book wrote in answer to Dr. Taylor?[65] Have you read it with attention and prayer? Do you understand it? Have you seriously considered it? Is there anything in it which you think wrong? Or does it
10   express your own judgement?

    2. Have you read over the sermons in the first and fourth volumes
on justification and the new birth?[66] Do you think you thoroughly
understand them? Is there anything in them which you cannot
agree to?

15   3. Have you read over the Thoughts upon Perfection in the fourth
volume?[67] Did you read them with humility and prayer? With calmness and deliberation? Have you considered them again and again,
crying to God for help? Is there anything in them which you do not
understand, or which you think is not right?

20   On all these heads you may speak freely to, dear Tommy,
    Your affectionate friend and brother,

J. Wesley

Address: 'To / Mr Tho. Olivers / at Mr John Hall's / In Newgate Street /
Cross Post / York / Direct to Newcastle'. Then, in a different hand,
'To / Mr Tho. Olivers / at the Orphin House / Newcastle upon
Tine'.

Seal: black, almost entirely intact, dove with twig, 'NUNTIA PACIS' in
octagonal frame.

Postmarks: date stamp is illegible; 'YORK'. *Charge*: '4' over the original
address; '4' over the second address.

Source: holograph; MARC, MAM JW 4/30.

[65] JW, *The Doctrine of Original Sin* (1757), 12:117–481 in this edn.

[66] JW, Sermon 5, 'Justification by Faith', 1:181–99 in this edn.; and Sermon 45, 'The
New Birth', 2:186–201 in this edn.

[67] JW, 'Thoughts on Christian Perfection', 13:57–80 in this edn.

To Elizabeth Booth[68]

SUNDERLAND
MAY 29, 1761

My Dear Sister,

It is a long time to the first of August. Before that time many of us may be in Abraham's bosom. If I am at Sheffield that morning, very probably I may be at Woodseats[69] the same day at noon. I do not know but George Tizzard may be in that round some time longer.[70] O what cause have we to praise God for all the wonders he has wrought? I am, with love to brother Booth,

Your affectionate brother,

J. Wesley

I return to Newcastle in a day or two.

Source: holograph; MARC, MAM JW 1/100 (address portion missing).

To John Hosmer[71]

NEWCASTLE-UPON-TYNE
JUNE 7, 1761

My Dear Brother,

I apprehend, if you will give another careful reading to those four pages, 244–47,[72] you will find all your objections anticipated

---

[68] Elizabeth Booth (fl. 1740–65) was one of the earliest members of the Methodist society at Woodseats, about three miles south of Sheffield. She was instrumental in the conversion of her husband Jonathan Booth, whom Wesley greets at the conclusion of the letter. JW described the bizarre illness of their daughter, also Elizabeth (born c. 1743) in his *Journal*, June 5, 1753, 20:461–63 in this edn.

[69] Orig., 'Woodsets'.

[70] George Tizzard (fl. 1755–70) served as a Methodist itinerant between 1759–61, never appearing in the spotty Minutes from that period. He left to become first a Baptist preacher and then to obtain ordination as a priest in the Church of England on Apr. 1, 1767; cf. Atmore, *Memorial*, 426–28; and Everett, *Sheffield*, 1:159–60.

[71] John Hosmer (d. 1780), of Darlington, Staffordshire, was one of the earliest Methodists in that area and became an itinerant preacher in 1758. He subsequently settled in Sunderland and practiced as a surgeon. See Atmore, *Memorial*, 200–201.

[72] These page numbers refer to the fourth volume of JW, *Sermons* (1760), which cover Questions 4–6 of 'Thoughts on Christian Perfection'; see 13:59–62 in this edn.

or answered. However, I do not think much of answering them over again. Your words are: 'You say, "A mistake is not a sin, if love is the sole principle of action; yet it is a transgression of the *perfect* law"; therefore *perfect love* is not the *perfect law*'! Most sure, for by the 'perfect law' I mean that given to Adam at his creation. But 'the loving God with all his heart' was not *the whole of that law*. It implied abundantly more, even *thinking*, *speaking*, and *acting right* in *every* instance, which he was then *able*, and therefore *obliged*, to do. But none of his descendants are able to do this. Therefore love is the fulfilling of *their* law.

Perhaps you had not adverted to this. The law of love, which is the *whole law* given to us, is only *one* branch of *that perfect law* which was given to Adam in the beginning. His law was far wider than ours, as his faculties were more extensive. Consequently many things might be transgressions of the latter which were not of the former.

'... But if ignorance be a transgression of the perfect law.' Whoever said or thought so? Ignorance is not, but *mistake* is. And this Adam was able to avoid; that kind of ignorance which was in him not constraining him to mistake, as ours frequently does.

'But is "a voluntary transgression of a known law" a proper definition of "sin"?' I think it is of all such sin as is imputed to *our* condemnation. And it is a definition which has passed uncensured in the Church for at least fifteen hundred years.[73]

To propose any objections that naturally arise is right, but beware you do not *seek* objections. If you once begin this, you will never have done. Indeed, this whole affair is a 'strife of words'.[74] The thing is plain. All in the body are liable to mistakes, practical as well as speculative. Shall we *call* them 'sins' or no? I answer again and again, *call* them just what you please.

John Wesley

Source: published transcription; *Arminian Magazine* 6 (1783): 104–5.

---

[73] 1 John 3:4 had defined sin as 'the transgression of the law.' A long strain of Christian theology had referred to both voluntary as well as involuntary sins. For example, the *Apostolic Constitutions* (8:8), an ancient text with which Wesley was familiar, asked forgiveness for 'all their offenses, both voluntary and involuntary'.

[74] 1 Tim. 6:4.

To George Merryweather

NEWCASTLE-UPON-TYNE
JUNE 7, 1761

My Dear Brother,

I had allotted two nights for Yarm, but by the advice of our brethren here I have made a little alteration in my plan. On Wednesday and Thursday the 18th instant I am to be at Stockton. On Friday evening and Saturday noon I purpose (with God's leave) to preach at Yarm. On Saturday evening I am to be at Hutton Rudby,[75] which is nearer the centre of our societies. I am,

> Your affectionate brother,

> J. Wesley

Address: 'To / Mr George Merryweather / in / Yarm'.
Postmark: 'NEW/CASTLE'. *Charge*: '9'.
Endorsement: 'June 1761'.
Source: holograph; Wesley's Chapel (London), LDWMM 1998/6887 (address half is detached).

To Martha (Wesley) Hall

NEAR NEWCASTLE-UPON-TYNE
JUNE 14, 1761

Dear Patty,

Why should any of us live in the world without doing a little good in it? I am glad you have made a beginning. See that you are not weary of well doing,[76] for it will often be a cross. But bear the cross, and it will bear *you*. The best fruit grows under the cross.

I have often thought it strange that so few of my relations should be of any use to me in the work of God. My sister Wright was, of whom I should least have expected it; but it was only for a short season.[77] My sister Emily and you, of whom one might have expected

---

[75] Hutton Rudby in N. Yorkshire; orig. 'Hutton Rugby'.
[76] See Gal. 6:9.
[77] Mehetabel (Wesley) Wright died Mar. 21, 1750.

more, have, I know not how, kept at a distance, and sometimes cav-
illed a little, at other times, as it were approved, but never heartily joined in the work. Where did it stick? Did you not thoroughly
understand what my brother and I were doing? Did you not *see* the
5   truth? Or did the cause lie in your heart? You had no *will* to join hand
in hand. You wanted resolution, spirit, patience. Well, the day is far
spent. What you do, do quickly. 'Life for delay no time will give!'[78]

‹My[79]› work in the country cannot be finished before ‹the› latter
end of August, as the circuit is now larger by ‹some› hundred miles
10   than when I was in the North two ‹years› ago. O let the one thing[80]
be ever uppermost in ‹our› thoughts!

To promote either your temporal or eternal good will always be a
pleasure to, dear Patty,

‹Your affectionate brother,[81]›

15

‹John Wesley›

Endorsement: 'I am obliged to my dear B[rother] for t[his]'.
Source: holograph; MARC, DDWes 5/2 (address portion is largely missing).

To Jane Catherine March

STOCKTON,
JUNE 17, 1761

I apprehend your great danger now is this: to think you *never shall*
receive *that blessing* because you have not received it yet. Nay, per-
20   haps you may be tempted to believe that there is no such thing, and
that those who *thought* they had received it were mistaken as well
as you. This danger will be increased if some who professed to be
sanctified long ago, and yet have not received this blessing, affirm
there is no such thing, and begin to warn others against falling into
25   *this delusion*. But keep close to your rule, the Word of God, and to

---

[78] Cf. Abraham Cowley's translation of an epigram of Martial (Book II, Epigram 90): 'life
for delays and doubts no time does give'.

[79] The left-hand side of this page is torn off; the missing text is reconstructed.

[80] See Luke 10:42.

[81] The bottom of the page is torn off after 'Dear Patty'; JW's typical closing is reconstructed.

your guide, the Spirit of God, and never be afraid of expecting *too much*. As yet you are but a babe. Oh what heights of holiness are to come! I hope you do not forget to pray for me. Adieu!

Source: published transcription; *Methodist Magazine* 22 (1799): 148.

To the Editor of the *London Gazette*[82]

YARM, Yorkshire,   5
JUNE 19, 1761

This moment I was shown the *London Gazette* published the 13th instant. I read therein that, 'It has been represented to the King that a letter, afterwards inserted, was lately found near Haverhill in the County of Suffolk, signed five hundred of the Gospel Legion.'[83]   10
I am amazed. So bold an insult on the royal authority I never heard or read before. Who are they that dare to represent that letter as any other than a vile, shameless forgery, invented purely to throw scandal on a handful of quiet people who are no more likely to raise a mob than to conquer a kingdom? I never was at Haverhill in my   15
life,[84] but I well know both Mr. Berridge and his principles.[85] He *suffers* wrong from many, but *does* it to none. He promotes peace, but never violates it. He loves and reverences his Majesty King

---

[82] JW composed this letter and sent it to London on June 19, but it was not then printed; thus he resent it to the *Leedes Intelligencer*, where it was published on Sept. 1, 1761 (see below).

[83] The text of the supposed letter, which appeared in *London Gazette* (June 6–9, 1761), p. 3, and was reprinted (June 9–13, 1761), p. 2, reads (retaining original spelling):

Mr. Carter   Bumstead

On the receipt of this goo and tell Hemsted Pickett and Milleway and all the resst of your Heaverill gang of the bandity that so vilinously oppoose the gorspel being preeched that if we meet with any more affronts or abuse when we come again as we intend to doo on the 17th instant we are resolved to reveng itt on your parssons or houses for as we have lifted up under the banner of Christ we are on and all determin'd to stand by on another[;] our number is larg and our caus good therefor we sett all your mallis att defians[.] Don't say you had no notis or worning for wee are so prepar'd that we fear you not therefor tak care what you doo[.] I am order'd by my brethren in the Lord to sighne for the rest

                your friendly Moneter Five Hundred   or the Gospel Legion.

[84] JW rode through Haverhill the following year and reports 'we were saluted with one huzza, the mob of that town having no kindness for Methodists'; *Journal*, Jan. 5, 1762, 21:347 in this edn.

[85] Apparently John Berridge was associated with a group called the Gospel Legion.

George, and spends his whole time, strength and fortune in advancing true scriptural Christianity, that is, the love of God and man.
I am, sir,
Your humble servant,

5   John Wesley

Source: published transcription; *Leedes Intelligencer* (Sept. 1, 1761), p. 4.

To the Rev. Samuel Furly

YORK
MONDAY, JUNE 29, 1761

Dear Sammy,
Since you could not meet me at York, meet me at Tadcaster, on
10   this day sevennight. I hope to be there between eleven and twelve.
The same evening I am to be at Otley.
Adieu!

Address: 'To the Revd Mr Furly'.
Seal: red with complete example of dove, twig, and 'NUNTIA PACIS' in octagonal frame.
No *postmark* or indications of postal *charge*; apparently delivered by hand.
Source: holograph; MARC, MAM JW 3/19.

To Alexander Coats[86]

OTLEY
JULY 7, 1761

15   My Dear Brother,
The perfection I teach is perfect love—loving God with all the
heart, receiving Christ as prophet, priest, and king, to reign alone

---

[86] Alexander Coats (d. 1765) was a native of Scotland who became an itinerant preacher in 1741. He had a gift for languages, having studied Gaelic, Danish, and Dutch in addition to Greek, Hebrew, and Latin. At the time of his death in 1765, John Wesley referred to him as the 'oldest preacher in our connexion'; see Atmore, *Memorial*, and JW, *Journal*, Oct. 6, 1765, 22:23 in this edn. On the spelling of his last name, see 10:281, n. 981 in this edn.

over all our thoughts, words, and actions. The papists neither teach nor believe this; give even the devil his due. They *teach* there is no perfection here which is not consistent with 'venial sins', and among venial sins they commonly reckon simple fornication. Now, I think this is so far from the perfection I teach that it does not come 5 up to any but Mr. Relly's perfection.[87]

To say Christ will not reign alone in our hearts in this life, will not enable us to give him *all* our hearts, this in my judgement is making him *a half-saviour*. He can be no more, if he does not *quite save* us from our sins. I pray, then, be not quite so peremptory. Who exalts 10 Christ most? Those who call on him to be the *sole monarch* of the heart, or those who allow him only to *share* the power and to govern *most* of the thoughts and tempers? Who honour him most? Those who believe he heals all our sickness, takes away *all* our ungodliness, or those who say he heals only the *greater part* of it, till death does 15 what he cannot do? I know no creature (of us) who says, 'Part of our salvation belongs to Christ and part to us.' No; we all say, Christ alone saves us from *all* sin, and your question is not about the *author* but the measure of salvation. Both agree it is *all Christ*, but is it *all salvation* or only *half salvation* he will give? 20

Who was Pelagius? By all I can pick up from ancient authors, I guess he was both a wise and a holy man. But we know nothing but his name, for his writings are all destroyed, not one line of them left.

But brother Coats, *this way* of talking is highly offensive. I ad- 25 vise you 1) if you are willing to labour with us, preach no doctrine contrary to ours. I have preached twenty years in some of Mr. Whitefield's societies, yet to this day I never contradicted him among his own people. I did not think it honest, neither necessary at all. I could preach salvation by faith, and leave all controversy 30 untouched. I advise you, 2) avoid all those strong, rhetorical exclamations 'Oh horrid!' 'Oh dreadful!' and the like, unless when you are strongly exhorting sinners to renounce the devil and all his works. 3) Acquaint yourself better with the doctrine we preach, and you will find it not dreadful but altogether lovely. 4) Observe that 35 if forty persons think and speak wrong, either about justification or sanctification (and perhaps fancy they have attained both), this is no objection to the doctrines themselves. They must bear their

---

[87] James Relly (c. 1722–78), was a native of Wales converted under George Whitefield's preaching. He became a Calvinistic Methodist minister and published a hymn-book and a treatise on *The Union of Christ and His Church* (1759), which JW took to teach antinomianism.

own burden. But this does not at all affect the point in question.
5) Remember, as sure as you are that 'believers cannot fall from
grace', others (wise and holy men too) are equally sure they can,
and you are as much obliged to bear with them as they are to bear
5   with you. 6) Abstain from all controversy in public. Indeed, you
have not a talent for it. You have an honest heart, but not a clear
head. Practical religion is your point. Therefore, 7) keep to this:
repentance toward God, faith in Christ, holiness of heart and life,
a growing in grace and in the knowledge of Christ,[88] the continual
10   need of his atoning blood, a constant confidence in him, and all
these every moment to our life's end. In none of these will any of
our preachers contradict you or you them.

When you leave this plain path and get into controversy, then
they think you 'invade the glories of our adorable King and the
15   unspeakable rights and privileges and comforts of his children', and
can *they* then 'tamely hold their peace'?

O Sander, know the value of peace and love! I am,
	Your affectionate brother,

20	J. Wesley

Source: published transcription; *Arminian Magazine* 6 (1783): 105–7.

To the Printer of the *Leedes Intelligencer*

25	BRADFORD
	JULY 15, 1761

Sir,

I cannot conceive how it is that no notice is taken in our public
papers of the late earthquakes at Shaftesbury in Dorsetshire.[89]
30	The account which I received from one upon the spot, whose
word I can depend upon, is as follows:

---

[88] See 2 Pet. 3:18.
[89] A series of earthquakes shook the Shaftesbury area of Dorset beginning on June 9,
1761, at 11:45 am; Charles Davison, *A History of British Earthquakes* (Cambridge, 1924), 323.

June 9, 1761. This morning it was very rough and
windy till near eleven. Then it began to be very warm
and so calm, there was scarce wind enough to move
the leaves on the trees. Soon after there was heard a
great rumbling noise much resembling thunder. This
was not over before the earth began to reel to and
fro like a drunken man. The houses were so shaken
hereby that the people ran out as fast as possible.
Some were obliged to catch hold of the things that
were near to avoid falling, and saw the bedsteads in
the room move up and down several times. Several
chimneys were shaken down.

An house two miles from Shaftesbury was much
damaged. It is a large old building sixty foot long.
Part of the chimney is thrown into the garden, part
of the end wall is moved in a surprising manner, as if
the house has been running an end. The side walls are
greatly shattered, the timbers shaken asunder, and the
tenons[90] drawn out of the mortises. Indeed the whole
building is so shattered that it must be rebuilt.

The shocks were repeated almost daily, and
usually several times a day, until June 21. I do not
know whether they are over yet.

A few days before the first earthquake, a piece of
meadow ground sixty yards long and ten foot broad
sunk three foot. It is torn all over, with openings in
some parts two yards long and a half a yard broad.
In two or three places also the ground is heaved up,
exactly in the shape of graves.

I am, sir,
    Your humble servant,

                John Wesley

Source: published transcription; *Leedes Intelligencer* (July 21, 1761), p. 3.

[90] Orig., 'tenners'.

To Ebenezer Blackwell

BRADFORD
JULY 16, 1761

Dear Sir,
Methinks it is a long time since I saw or heard anything of you.
5 I hope, however, that Mrs. [Elizabeth] Blackwell and you are not
only alive, but more alive than ever, seeking and enjoying something
more than King George is likely to find either at his wedding or his
coronation.[91] And can you likewise give me a comfortable account
of Miss [Mary] Freeman, both as to her health and her spirit? I
10 often think of her, and sometimes have a mind to send her another
letter, though she is one in my debt already.
Mr. [Henry] Venn was so kind as to come over hither yesterday
and spend the evening with us. I am a little embarrassed on his account, and hardly know how to act. Several years before he came
15 to Huddersfield some of our preachers went thither, carrying their
lives in their hands, and with great difficulty established a little,
earnest society. These eagerly desire them to preach there still, not
in opposition to Mr. Venn (whom they love, esteem, and constantly
attend), but to supply what they do not find in his preaching. It is
20 a tender point. Where there is a gospel ministry *already*, we do not
desire preach. But whether we can leave off preaching because
such an one comes *after* is another question, especially when those
who were awakened and convinced by us beg and require the continuance of our assistance. I love peace, and follow it, but whether I
25 am at liberty to purchase it at such price I really cannot tell.
I hear poor Mr. Walker is near death.[92] It seems strange that, when
there is so great a want of faithful labourers, such as him should be
removed. But the will of God is always best, and what he does we
shall know hereafter! I have been for some days with Mr. [William]
30 Grimshaw, an Israelite indeed.[93] A few such as him would make a
nation tremble. He carries fire wherever he goes. Mr. Venn informs
me that Mr. Whitefield continues very weak.[94] I was in hope, when
he wrote to me lately, that he was swiftly recovering strength. Per-

[91] George III had acceded to the throne in October of the previous year when his father died, and his marriage and coronation were anticipated at this time. He married Princess Charlotte of Mecklenburg-Strelitz on Sept. 8 and their coronation followed on Sept. 22.

[92] Samuel Walker of Truro died three days later, on July 19.

[93] See John 1:47.

[94] Whitefield underwent a lengthy illness in 1761 that left him 'semi-invalid' and forced him to leave off preaching for many months; see Stuart C. Henry, *George Whitefield: Wayfaring Witness* (New York, 1957), 209.

haps, sir, you can send me better news concerning him. What need have we, while we do live, to live in earnest! I am, dear sir,
    Your affectionate servant,

John Wesley

If you have not a mind for me to write again, you must not write yourself. For about a fortnight I shall be at or near Leeds.

Endorsement: 'Revd Mr John Wesley, / Bradford, 16 July 1761'.
Source: holograph; Philadelphia, Historical Society of Pennsylvania Library, Dreer Collection, English Clergy (address portion missing).

To Mary Bosanquet[95]

[LEEDS]
[JULY 25, 1761?[96]]

If Sally Ryan takes bark at all, I beg she will take it (let her be obstinate) only in one of these two ways:
    Infuse an ounce of bark, finely powdered, in a quart of good, soft mountain wine.[97] After it has stood 24 hours, it is fit for use. Let her take a small wine glass full (pouring it off clear) when she feels anything like the gout in her stomach. Or,
    Divide an ounce of bark powdered into sixteen parts. Mix an equal quantity of dried Seville[98] orange peel. Pour a large dish of

[95] Mary Bosanquet was the daughter of a wealthy London merchant and mistress of a manor in Leytonstone, Essex. Starting in 1762 Bosanquet gathered a group of women, including Sarah Crosby and Sarah Ryan, into a community that converted her house in Leytonstone into an orphanage and school. In 1768 the group moved to Yorkshire to continue their work in the north. While she had long planned to remain single, in 1781 Bosanquet married John Fletcher. See Henry Moore, *The Life of Mrs. Mary Fletcher* (1817). JW had been in correspondence with Mary Bosanquet since at least Jan. 1761 (see her reply of Feb. 1761). This is JW's first surviving letter to Bosanquet.

[96] JW gives no date or indication of the place from which the letter was sent, but a stamp indicates it was mailed from Leeds. It is addressed to Hoxton Square, where Mary Bosanquet lived from 1761 to early 1763. The date stamp is in the 20s, and seems to be '27'. In July 1762 JW was in Ireland, but his *Journal* indicates that he was just leaving the Leeds area July 27, 1761 (21:338 in this edn.). Thus the letter was most probably written a day or two earlier.

[97] A sweet, fortified wine from Málaga in Andalusia, now referred to as Málaga wine.

[98] Orig., 'Sevil'.

green tea on one of these, and cover it with a saucer two or three minutes. Then let her drink it, sweetened or unsweetened, leaving the bark and peel behind. I think to take it fasting is best, for eight or sixteen mornings.

Address: 'To / Miss Bosanquet / [Hoxto]n Square, near / London'.
Seal: Red wax seal with dove and olive branch.
Stamps: 'LEEDS'. Postmark: '2[7] / IU'.
Endorsement: 'Palsingham in ye Kent charg / 743'.
Source: holograph; MARC, MA 1983/027 (Mather scrapbook).

To the Rev. Henry Cantrell[99]

MATLOCK BATH
JULY 29, 1761

Reverend Sir,
I doubt whether your hearing will be restored. But probably it may be helped by small shocks of the electric machine given from ear to ear, which we have frequently found to restore the tone of relaxed nerves or fibres. At first I believed cold bathing would have been of use. Now I fear it would not. Wishing you all health of soul and body, I am, reverend sir,
Your affectionate brother and servant,

John Wesley

Address: 'To / the Revd Mr Cantrell / in / Derby'.
No *postmark* or indications of postal *charge*; apparently delivered by hand.
Endorsement: 'Mr. J. Wesley's letter of / Hardship of Hearing. / July ye 29th. 1761.'
Source: holograph; University of Sydney (Australia), Rare Books and Special Collections Library, Wesley College Collection.

---

[99] Henry Cantrell (baptised 1684, d. 1762) was educated at Emmanuel College, Cambridge, ordained deacon in 1705 and priest in 1709. He served as vicar of St Alkmund's church in Derby from 1712 to the time of his death in 1762. See *ODNB*.

To Ebenezer Blackwell

NORWICH
AUGUST 15, 1761

Dear Sir,

As you are encompassed with a thousand temptations, and some of them of the most dangerous kind, it is an unspeakable blessing that you still continue with your face heavenward. And if you have resolution to break through a thousand hindrances and allow some time every day for private prayer, I doubt not but you will receive every gospel blessing in this world and in the world to come.

Mr. Venn and I have had some hours' conversation together and have explained upon every article.[100] I believe there is no bone of contention remaining, no matter of offence, great or small. Indeed fresh matter will arise *if* it be sought, but it shall not be sought by *me*. We have amicably compromised the affair of preaching. He is well pleased that our preacher should come once a month.

That story was one of those which we cleared up. But Mr. Oddie,[101] the person of whom it was told, will be in town next week and can himself give you full satisfaction concerning it. On this day sennight I hope to be in town, and tomorrow sennight at West Street Chapel.

With sincere love to Mrs. [Elizabeth] Blackwell and Mrs. [Hannah] Dewal, I am, dear sir,

Your very affectionate servant,

John Wesley

I thank you for sending me the letters.

Endorsement: 'Revd. Mr John Wesley / Norwich 15 August. 1761'.
Source: holograph; Emory, MARBL, Wesley Family Papers, 1/38 (address portion missing).

---

[100] See JW's previous letter to Blackwell, July 16, 1761, where Wesley notes negotiations with Venn concerning the issue of Methodist itinerants preaching in Venn's parish.

[101] James Oddie (c. 1730–90) served as an itinerant between 1752 and 1771, mainly in the north; see Armore, *Memorial*, 298–300; and Vickers, *Dictionary*, 259.

To the Editor of the *Leedes Intelligencer*

[LONDON]
[C. AUGUST 28, 1761]

Sir,

As an answer to your late correspondent A. B., be pleased to in-
5   sert in their paper the following letter, which I sent to London,
according to the date, and expected to have seen in the next week's
Chronicle.

YARM, YORKSHIRE
JUNE 19, 1761

10

This moment I was shown the *London Gazette* published the 13th
instant. I read therein that, 'It has been represented to the King
that a letter, afterwards inserted, was lately found near Haverhill in the County of Suffolk, signed five hundred of the Gospel
15   Legion.' I am amazed. So bold an insult on the royal authority I
never heard or read before. Who are they that dare to represent that
letter as any other than a vile, shameless forgery, invented purely to
throw scandal on a handful of quiet people who are no more likely
to raise a mob than to conquer a kingdom? I never was at Haverhill
20   in my life, but I well know both Mr. Berridge and his principles. He
suffers wrong from many, but *does* it to none. He promotes peace, but
never violates it. He loves and reverences his Majesty King George,
and spends his whole time, strength and fortune in advancing true
scriptural Christianity, that is, the love of God and man.

25   I am, sir,
            Your humble servant,

John Wesley

Source: published transcription; *Leedes Intelligencer* (Sept. 1, 1761), p. 4.

To the Rev. Samuel Furly

LONDON
SEPTEMBER 8, 1761

Dear Sammy,

I hope we have effectually provided against that evil disease, the *scribendi cacoethes*,[102] in our preachers, as we have agreed that none shall publish anything for the time to come till he has first submitted it to the judgement of his brethren met in Conference.

That is really a fine passage which you cite from Mr. Ridley.[103] He is an excellent writer. I have often seen that text cleared up before, but never in so convincing a manner.

What all our brethren think concerning that circumstance of entire sanctification, that it is instantaneous (although a gradual growth in grace both precede and follow it) you may see in the minutes of the Conference, wherein it was freely debated.[104] Any of the good, old Puritans would have been no less amazed, had they come into one of our congregations and heard us declare that God willeth every man without exception to be saved.[105]

O Sammy, shake off the *disputandi cacoethes*[106] and be a quiet, simple, loving Christian! I am, with love to Nancy,

Your affectionate friend and brother,

J. Wesley

You scorn to fear receiving any hurt from Mr. [Henry] Venn. Therefore I fear he does hurt you.

Address: 'To / The Revd Mr Furly / At Kippax, near Ferrybridge / Yorkshire'.
Postmark: '8/SE'.

---

[102] Juvenal, *Satires* vi.51–52; 'itch for writing' (Loeb).

[103] Furly had likely quoted from Glocester Ridley, *The Difference and Respective Use of the Moral, Civil, and Ceremonial Law* (London, 1753), since he and JW had been discussing this topic earlier; see JW to Furly, June 19, 1760.

[104] The Conference that met Sept. 1–5, 1761 focused on the doctrine of entire sanctification, but the minutes do not survive; see 10:191–92 in this edn. Peter Jaco conveyed to CW a somewhat different emphasis, reporting, 'It is determined that there are no texts of Scripture which will absolutely support instantaneous perfection; that there is no state in this world which will absolutely exempt the person in it from sin, and that therefore they have need of caution, etc.'; cited in 10:292 in this edn.

[105] See 1 Tim. 2:4.

[106] An 'itch for disputing', parallel to the phrase quoted from Juvenal above.

Endorsement: 'Mr. Wesley Septr. 8th, 1761.'
Source: holograph; Middletown, Connecticut, Wesleyan University, Literary and Historical Manuscripts Collection.

To Matthew Lowes

LONDON
SEPTEMBER 8, 1761

My Dear Brother,

　　If local preachers who differ from us will keep their opinions to
5　themselves, then they may preach in our societies; otherwise they
must not. And upon this condition we are all willing to receive William Darney[107] into connexion with us.

　　The sooner you set out for Whitehaven the better. The society
there need not be frightened at a married preacher, considering we
10　have paid forty pounds of their debt out of the collection. And if the
expense for wives be too heavy, I will help them out.

　　Do all you can to propagate the books in that circuit and to fulfil
the office of an Assistant.[108] I am, with love to sister Lowes,

　　　　Your affectionate friend and brother,

15

J. Wesley

Address: 'To / Mr Lowes / At the Orphan House / Newcastle upon Tyne'.
Postmark: '8/SE'. *Charge*: '4'.
Source: holograph; WHS Library.

---

[107] On William Darney, see 26:537, n. 20 in this edn.

[108] When JW first began recruiting and assigning travelling lay preachers, they were referred to variously as 'helpers' or 'assistants', even in the Minutes (see June 29, 1744, 10:139 in this edn.). But in 1749 a distinction was standardised where 'assistant' referred to the senior supervising itinerant in a circuit, and 'helper' was retained as the title for other itinerant preachers (see Minutes, Nov. 16, 1749, QQ. 2–4, 10:232 in this edn.).

To [Grace Walton?][109]

LONDON
SEPTEMBER 8, 1761

‹My Dear Sis›ter,[110]

If a few more persons come in when you are meeting, ‹you may› either enlarge four or five minutes on a question you had, ‹or give› a short exhortation (perhaps for five or six minutes), ‹and then› sing and pray. This is going as far as I think any woman ‹should do.› For the words of the apostle are clear.[111] I think as always ‹that the› meaning is this: 'I suffer not a woman to teach in a ‹congr›egation, nor thereby to assert authority over the man' ‹whom› God has invested with this prerogative; whereas teaching …[112]

[I] ask you some more questions, which you may answer as soon as you have opportunity.

Had you then, or have you had since, a witness that you would never finally perish? Have you a witness that sin shall *never enter* more? Have you a witness that you shall no more offend God? If so, what need have you to watch against sin? Do you ever use self-examination? At what times, or in what manner? Do you always see God? Does no cloud ever interpose? Are you as sure you see him as that you are alive? Does nothing ever dim your sight of God? Have you an experimental proof of the ever blessed Trinity? Is your mind always stayed on God? Do your thoughts never wander from him in prayer, in business, or in travelling?

What are you looking for now?[113]

I am,
Your affectionate brother,

J. Wesley

[109] Bryant's transcription does not identify a recipient. Telford (*Letters*, 164) assigned the first portion of the letter to Grace Walton, because of JW's comment of writing on this topic to Grace Walton in his later letter to Sarah Crosby, Mar. 18, 1769. Lacking clear alternatives, we leave this as a possible, though questionable identification.

[110] Bryant notes that a left-hand portion of this page of the holograph was torn off; the missing text is reconstructed, often as suggested by Bryant or the initial recipient of his transcription, F. F. Bretherton.

[111] 1 Tim. 2:11–12.

[112] The ms. is broken off at this point. We might surmise that JW went on to endorse women speaking in a more restricted context or venue than a 'congregation', as in his letter to Sarah Crosby, Feb. 14, 1761.

[113] Bryant indicates that the last three paragraphs and the closing were distinct from the first in the original manuscript. It is unclear whether he means they are written perpendicular to the other text on the same page or are on a separate page. Telford (*Letters*, 165) treats these paragraphs as a separate letter directed to Sarah Ryan. While the letter is similar to ones JW wrote to Ryan in 1757–58, there is no evidence they had resumed correspondence at this point. On balance, it seemed best to treat this as a single letter.

Address: 'Mr. John Smith's / Writer in Galley Gate / Aberdeen, Scotland'.
Source: holograph; privately held (current owner unknown, transcription
by E. G. H. Bryant in 1940 held at Duke, Rubenstein, Frank Baker
Collection of Wesleyana, Box WF 1[114]).

To the Rev. Charles Wesley

LONDON
SEPTEMBER 8, 1761

[[Dear Brother,]]
Our Conference ended, as it began, in peace and love.[115] All found
5   it a blessed time:

Excepto, quod non simul esses, caetera laeti.[116]

The minutes John Jones can help you to, who sets out hence in two
10   or three days. The right hand of the Lord bringeth mighty things
to pass.[117] Not the least of them is that [[my wife]] cordially loves
Thomas Maxfield.[118]
Why should not Bath be supplied from Bristol? Order it so. I
have no objection. They will by that means often have a more able
15   preacher than they would otherwise have.
If he does not linger by the way, a preacher may be at Bristol on
Thursday night.
I do not at all think (to tell you a secret) that the work will ever be
destroyed, Church or no Church. What has been done to prevent
20   the Methodists leaving the Church you will see in the minutes of
the Conference.[119]
I told you before, with regard to Norwich, *dixi*.[120] I have done at
the last Conference all I *can* or *dare* do. Allow me liberty of conscience, as I allow you.

[114] Bryant's transcription was judged by Frank Baker to be more accurate than the text
given in Telford, *Letters*; a conclusion seconded in Paul Chilcote, *John Wesley and the Women
Preachers of Early Methodism* (Lanham, MD, 1991), 296.

[115] The Conference had met Sept. 1–5 in London; cf. 10:291–92 in this edn.

[116] Horace, *Epistles*, I.x.50; 'Happy on all counts, save you are not with me' (Loeb).

[117] Ps. 188:16 (BCP).

[118] Thomas Maxfield had been converted in May 1739, and became one of JW's earliest
itinerant ministers about two years later. See Atmore, *Memorial*, 266–69; Vickers, *Dictionary*,
225; and 25:653 in this edn.

[119] Unfortunately, these minutes do not survive.

[120] 'I have spoken.' CW was likely still complaining about how JW had handled an instance of Methodist lay preachers officiating over the Lord's Supper at Norwich.

On Monday sennight I hope to set out for Bristol.
My love to Sally.
   [[Adieu!]]

I know not what you will do with an exceeding honest mad woman,   5
Mrs. Greer, of Newry, in Ireland, who, I hear, is embarking for
Bristol. She comes without her husband's consent.

Peter Jaco desires to take a journey to Canterbury before he returns to Bristol.[121]

I doubt not the Moravians will be courteous. And I fear that is   10
all. Pray tell brother Sheen I am satisfied with his letter.[122] He may
stay at Bristol till I come. And be so kind as to tell Isaac I approve of
his reasons, and think he ought to go home; but have the stewards
found one fit to succeed him?[123]

Address: 'To / The Revd Mr C. Wesley / in / Bristol'.
No *postmark* or indications of postal *charge*; apparently delivered by hand.
Endorsement: in CW's hand, 'Sept 8. 1761 / B. *dixi!*'
Source: holograph; MARC, DDWes 3/15.

To Thomas Rankin[124]

[c. October 14, 1761]   15

... You will never get free of all those evil reasonings till you give
yourself wholly up to the work of God! ...[125]

Source: published extract; *Methodist Magazine* 34 (1811): 726.

---

[121] Jaco wrote to CW explaining the actions of the Conference in regard to Christian
perfection, and explaining that he was given leave to stay in Canterbury and the south through
the end of the year because of his poor health; see 10:292, n. 1020 in this edn.

[122] Sheen (his Christian name is not known) appears repeatedly in letters of CW to his
wife in the early 1760s. He was a book steward in Bristol and likely keeping records for Kingswood School; see JW to CW, Dec. 26, 1761.

[123] Isaac is apparently another book steward, or a master at Kingswood.

[124] Thomas Rankin (1738–1810) was a native of Scotland who had lived for a brief period
in South Carolina, then returned to the UK where he was converted under the influence of
George Whitefield and other Evangelical preachers. He had travelled preaching independently
from 1759, but by 1762 was serving under direction of JW and Conference (see 10:294 in this
edn.). He would later return to North America as Wesley's General Superintendent (1773–78).
See *EMP*, 5:135–217; and Vickers, *Dictionary*, 288.

[125] This brief line, from a memoir published in the *Methodist Magazine* for 1811 (the year
after Rankin's death), is the first known correspondence between Rankin and JW.

To Matthew Lowes

LONDON
OCTOBER 30, 1761

My Dear Brother,
 The thing is settled. Thomas Newall[126] is to labour with you in
5 the Whitehaven Circuit. And see that you break up fresh ground.
In the meantime William Darney is to divide the Allendale circuit
with Thomas Hanby.[127]
 As to maintenance, first let the society do what they can. And
they have good encouragement. Secondly, at Christmas I will make
10 up what is wanting to you and sister Lowes. 'Dwell in the land, and
be doing good, and verily thou shalt be fed.'[128] I am,
 Your affectionate friend and brother,

J. Wesley

15

See that you perform the *whole* office of an Assistant.[129]

Endorsement: 'Writen octr 30, 1761'.
Source: holograph; MARC, MAM JW 3/98 (address portion missing).

To an Unidentified Helper/Assistant

LONDON
DECEMBER 14, 1761

20 My Dear Brother,
 You do well to write. You should not write seldomer than once in
two or three months.

---

[126] Thomas Newall (fl. 1760–85) served as an itinerant from this year, so this is likely his
first circuit appointment. He served as an itinerant preacher through 1780, and was preaching
in circuits as late as 1786. See John Lenton, *John Wesley's Preachers* (Milton Keynes: Paternoster, 2009), 301–2.

[127] Thomas Hanby (b. 1733) became an itinerant in 1754 and served in Staffordshire,
Northumberland, and other northern circuits. In 1785 John Wesley ordained him as an elder
for Methodist work in Scotland, and he presided at the 1794 Annual Conference. See Atmore,
Memorial, 179–81; *EMP*, 2:131–57; Vickers, *Dictionary*, 148.

[128] Ps. 37:3.

[129] Defined in Minutes, Nov. 16, 1749, QQ. 7–10, 10:233–34 in this edn. (= Disciplinary
Minutes, §71, 10:828).

I am glad to hear, there is an increase of the work of God, in the northern societies. Be exact in every point of discipline. Keep the Rules,[130] and God will keep *you*.

I wish you yourself would talk with Mr. Greer. Go to him on purpose. And ask him expressly, whether he is willing to receive Mrs.   5
Greer again, and upon what terms?[131] Perhaps, if she would never hear the preaching more. Would he allow her liberty of conscience?
I am,

> Your affectionate brother,

> J. Wesley   10

Source: holograph; Melbourne, Queen's College, JW7 (mounted so no access to address side).

To Elizabeth Hardy

> LONDON
> DECEMBER 26, 1761

Dear Sister,

The path of controversy is a rough path. But it seems smoother while I am walking with *you*; so that I could follow *you* through all   15
its windings, only my time will not permit.

The plain fact is this. I know many who love God with all their heart, mind, soul, and strength.[132] He is their one desire, their one delight, and they are continually happy in him. They love their neighbour as themselves.[133] They feel as sincere, fervent, constant   20
a desire for the happiness of every man, good or bad, friend or enemy, as for their own. They rejoice evermore, pray without ceasing, and in everything give thanks.[134] Their souls are continually streaming up to God in holy joy, prayer, and praise. This is plain, sound, scriptural experience, and of this we have more and more living   25
witnesses.

---

[130] I.e., the General Rules; see 9:69–75 in this edn.
[131] See JW to CW, Sept. 8, 1761 on Mr. and Mrs. Greer.
[132] See Deut. 6:5; Matt. 22:37 and parallels.
[133] See Matt. 22:39 and parallels.
[134] See 1 Thess. 5:16–18.

But these souls dwell in a shattered, corruptible body, and are so pressed down thereby that they cannot *exert* their love as they would by always thinking, speaking, and acting *precisely right*. For want of better bodily organs, they sometimes inevitably think, speak, or act
5 wrong. Yet I think they need the advocacy of Christ, even for these involuntary defects, although they do not imply a defect of *love*, but of *understanding*. However that be, I cannot doubt the fact. They are *all love*, yet they cannot *walk* as they desire. 'But are they *all love* while they grieve the Holy Spirit?' No surely; they are then fallen
10 from their steadfastness, and this they may do even after they are sealed. So that, even to such, strong cautions are needful. After the heart is cleansed from pride, anger, and desire, it may suffer them to re-enter. Therefore I have long thought some expressions in the hymns are abundantly too strong,[135] as I cannot perceive any state
15 mentioned in Scripture from which we may not, in a measure at least, fall.

Persons who talked of being 'emptied before they were filled' were for some time a great stumbling-block to me too. But I have since considered it thus: The great point in question is, 'Can we be
20 saved from all sin or not?' Now, it may please God to act in that uncommon manner, purposely to clear this point, to satisfy those persons that they are saved from all sin before he goes on in his work.

Forgive me, dear Miss Hardy, that I do but just touch upon the heads of your letter. Indeed, this defect does not spring from the
25 want of love, but only from want of time. I should not wonder if *your* soul was one of the next that was filled with pure love. Receive it freely, thou poor bruised reed! It is able to make *thee* stand.
    I am,
        Your affectionate friend and brother,

30   John Wesley

Source: published transcription; *Arminian Magazine* 5 (1782): 271–72.

[135] JW is referring specifically to hymns of CW, some of which JW had included in *HSP* (1739), *HSP* (1740), and *HSP* (1742), but particularly some in later volumes that CW published without submitting to JW's editorial review. For example, JW's personal copy of *HSP* (1749) survives, with his reactions to CW's text often written in the margins (see the annotated copy available on the website of The Center for Studies in the Wesleyan Tradition, Duke Divinity School).

To the Rev. Charles Wesley

LONDON
DECEMBER 26, 1761

[[Dear Brother,]]

Spend as many hours in the congregation as you will or can. But exercise alone will strengthen *your lungs*. Or electrifying, which I wonder you did not try long ago. Never start at its being a quack medicine. I desire no other; particularly since I was so nearly murdered by being cured of my ague *secundum artem*.[136] You should always (and I hope you do) write standing and sloping.

We are always in danger of enthusiasm, but *I think no more now than any time these twenty years*. The word of God runs indeed, and loving faith spreads on every side. Don't take my word or any one's else, but *come and see*. Tis good to be in London now.

It is impossible for me to correct my own books. I sometimes think it strange that I have not one *preacher that* will and can. I think every one of them owes me so much service.

Is it right that my sister Patty should suffer Mr. Hall to live with her?[137] I almost scruple giving her the sacrament, seeing he does not even pretend to renounce Betty Rogers.[138] Was it right for William Baynes[139] to carry on his affair with Sammy Whittaker without consulting either you or me?

Pray tell brother Sheen I am hugely displeased at his reprinting the *Nativity Hymns* and omitting the very best hymn in the collection,

All glory to God in the sky, etc.[140]

---

[136] 'According to the art'; that is, by standard medical practices.

[137] Westley Hall, the unfaithful husband of JW and CW's sister Martha ('Patty'), having run off with one of his mistresses to the West Indies in 1755, had now returned and was seeking reconciliation with Martha.

[138] Elizabeth Rogers was one of Westley Hall's mistresses, with whom he had a child.

[139] William Baynes (d. 1778) served as a master at Kingswood School for several years (see JW, *Journal*, Oct. 25, 1757, 21:129 in this edn.; and Hastling et al., *Kingswood*, Register, 186). He obtained ordination in 1760 and moved to assist JW as a curate at the chapels in London (see *Journal*, Dec. 27, 1777, 23:73 in this edn.).

[140] Hymn 18, the concluding hymn of *Hymns for the Nativity of Our Lord* (London, 1745), 23–24. The hymn had actually been omitted in one strand of republications, beginning with the 2nd edition, published in Bristol in 1745. JW may have just became aware of this strand on seeing the 6th edition, just issued in Bristol. Or JW may be the one who restored this hymn in 4th edition, published in Bristol in 1750, and was chagrined to find that Sheen had used an earlier edition as the model in preparing the 1761 reprint. In any case, Hymn 18 was restored in printings from 1762 onwards.

I beg they may never more be printed without it. Omit one or two, and I will thank you. They are *namby-pambical.*

I wish you would give us *two or three invitatory* hymns. We want such exceedingly. My love to Sally. *My wife gains ground.*

5   Adieu!

Endorsement: in CW's hand, 'B. Dec. 26. 1761 No danger / of enthusiasm'.
Source: holograph; MARC, DDWes 3/16 (address portion missing).

To an Unidentified Man

LONDON
DECEMBER 31, 1761

My Dear Brother,

None can blame you for desiring to build when your present
10   house will not contain the congregation. And considering your
number, there is an handsome subscription so that you have no reason to delay on that account. But you must be assured of a good title
to the land wherever you build, else you are doing nothing. Peace be
with your spirits! I am,

15   Your affectionate brother,

J. Wesley

Source: holograph; WMC Museum.

1762

To Christopher Hopper

NORWICH
JANUARY 18, 1762

My Dear Brother,

Public affairs do look exceeding dark, and the clouds gather more and more.[1] Yet the Lord sitteth above the water-floods, and remaineth a King for ever. And he (whatever be the lot of his enemies) shall give his people the blessing of peace.[2]

If you do not establish good order in the Orphan House,[3] it is pity you should go there. This is the very design of your master. For this end are you sent. Do just as I would do in every instance if I were in your place. Act just the thing that is right, whoever is pleased or displeased. I hereby give it under my hand I will stand by you with all my might.

I am glad you have had a free conversation with Thomas Olivers. There is good in him, though he is a rough stick of wood. But love can bow down the stubborn neck. By faith and love we shall overcome all things.

Peace be with you and yours. I am,

> Your ever affectionate brother,

[John Wesley]

I set out for London tomorrow.

Source: published transcription; Jackson, *Works* (3rd), 12:289–90.

---

[1] In the midst of the Seven Years War against France, Britain had declared war on Spain on Jan. 4, 1762. Spain returned the favour on the very day this letter was written.

[2] See Ps. 29:10–11 (BCP).

[3] In Newcastle-upon-Tyne.

To the Rev. Samuel Furly

LONDON
JANUARY 25, 1762

Dear Sammy,

But that I have pretty near attained to the happiness *nil admirari*,[4]
5   I should have a little wondered at your long silence. But it is not
strange, if 'Time changes thought,'[5] and it would not surprise me
much, if in a year or two more, you should

<blockquote>

Wonder at the strange man's face
10   As one you ne'er had known.[6]
</blockquote>

If you entangled yourself with no kind of promise to the archbishop, I doubt not but your ordination will prove a blessing.[7] The
care of a parish is indeed a weighty thing, which calls for much and
15   earnest prayer. In managing it you must needs follow *your own* conscience, whoever is pleased or displeased. Then, whether your *success be less or more*, you will by-and-by give up your account with joy.

I myself hear frequently unscriptural as well as irrational expressions from those at whose feet I shall be joyous to be found in the
20   day of the Lord Jesus. But blasphemy I never heard from one of
them, either teacher or hearer. What is wide of Scripture or reason
I mildly reprove, and they usually receive it in love. Generally they
are convinced. When I cannot convince, I can bear them, yea, and
rejoice at the grace of God which is in them.

25   Sammy, beware of the impetuosity of your temper! It may easily
lead you awry. It may make you evil affected to the excellent ones
‹of the› earth.[8] Don't expect propriety of speech from uneducated
persons. The longer I live, the larger allowances I make for human
infirmities. I exact more from myself and less from others. Go thou
30   and do likewise! I am, with love to Nancy,

Your ever affectionate friend and brother,

J. Wesley

Take nothing, absolutely nothing, at second hand.

---

[4] 'To be surprised by nothing'.

[5] Cf. Matthew Prior, 'Henry and Emma', l. 166: 'Time changes thought; and flattery conquers truth'.

[6] Adapted from William Congreve, 'Doris', ll. 55–56. JW also quotes these lines in *Journal*, May 1, 1762 (21:364 in this edn.); and May 13, 1765 (21:508).

[7] Furly had been ordained a priest on Nov. 29, 1761, by Robert Hay, Archbishop of York.

[8] The words 'of the' are supplied as there is a tape over the page at this point. Cf. Acts 14:2 and Ps. 16:3 (BCP).

Address: 'To / The Revd Mr Furly / At Kippax near Ferrybridge'.
Postmark: barely legible, '2 [illegible letter] / [illegible letter] A'.
Source: holograph; MARC, MAM JW 3/20.

To Matthew Lowes

LONDON
JANUARY 25, 1762

Dear Matthew,
I ordered Mr. Franks[9] to pay the eight pounds bill today, which is four pounds more than I had in my hands. What we shall do for money till the next Conference I do not know. But the earth is the Lord's and the fullness thereof.[10]   5

You do well to be exact in discipline. Disorderly walkers will give us neither credit nor strength. Let us have just as many members as walk by one rule. I will beg or borrow for William Newall, anything but steal.[11]

My wife joins in love to you and yours. I am,   10
    Your affectionate friend and brother,

                                        J. Wesley

Source: holograph; MARC, MA 2014/20.

To Jane Catherine March

LONDON
JANUARY 30, 1762

When you was justified, you had a direct witness that your sins   15
were forgiven. Afterward this witness was frequently intermitted, and yet you did not doubt of it. In like manner, you have had a direct witness that you are saved from sin, and this witness is frequently

---

[9] Samuel Franks was JW's general steward in London, covering both books and the Foundery in London from 1759 through at least 1773; see 10:307, 873 in this edn.

[10] See Ps. 24:1.

[11] The identity of this William Newall is unknown. The spelling of the first name is clear, but it may be JW's mistaken reference to the itinerant preacher Thomas Newall.

intermitted, and yet even then you do not doubt of it. But I much doubt if God withdraws either the one witness or the other without some occasion given on our part. I never knew any one receive the abiding witness[12] gradually. Therefore I incline to think this also is
5   given in a moment. But there will be still, after this, abundant room for a gradual growth in grace.

Source: published transcription; Jackson, *Works* (3rd), 13:48.

To Matthew Lowes

LONDON
FEBRUARY 13, 1762

My Dear Brother,
10   Order concerning brother Newall as you see good.[13] If he is not wanted in the Manchester round, I believe he would be welcome in James Oddie's.

You must not be surprised if there is a deadness in many places during the winter season. But the spring will return. Fear nothing.
15   Hope belongs to us. Fight on, and conquer. I am,
    Your affectionate friend and brother,

[John Wesley]

Source: published transcription; Telford, *Letters*, 4:170.

To Thomas Rankin

LONDON
FEBRUARY 20, 1762

20 My Dear Brother,
    By all means go into Sussex again. And you may continue in that circuit till another preacher comes. I trust God has sent you thither

[12] See John 14:16.
[13] Thomas Newall, who was specified to labour with Matthew Lowes in the Whitehaven circuit in JW to Lowes, Oct. 30, 1761.

for the good of others and of your own soul. Be exact in observing and in enforcing all the rules of our society. Then you will see more and more fruit of your labour. I am,
    Your affectionate brother,

[John Wesley]   5

Source: published transcription; Jackson, *Works* (3rd), 12:304.

To the Rev. Samuel Furly

Dear Sammy,

Facile credimus quae fieri volumus.[14] So I am easily persuaded of the continuance of your friendship. But your long silence had a sus- 10 picious aspect, especially when it fell out just at the time of your preferment.[15]

The danger of most of those in London who believe they are saved from sin is quite opposite to what you suppose, so diametrically opposite that I can sometimes scarce clear them of antinomi- 15 anism. They speak *so much* of the blood of Christ, they lay *so great* stress upon his atonement, influence, and intercession in all their prayers, thanksgivings, and conversations, that I have been more than once in fear lest *Moravianism* should steal back upon us. Never yet did I hear any men, except Moravians, so aggrandise Christ. I 20 am at present only afraid of their honouring the Son *more* than they honour the Father.

But suppose I heard one of these to say, 'I do not now pray for pardon'. Although I know this is wrong, yet I should impute it *wholly* to the littleness of his understanding, not to the badness of 25 the heart. This is not a crime of the deepest dye—if it be indeed any *crime* at all.

---

[14] 'We easily believe the things we desire to be'; a variation of a commonly quoted Latin phrase, *quod volumus, facile credimus*, 'We easily believe that which we want.'

[15] I.e., Furly's ordination as priest, in preparation for becoming perpetual curate of Slaithwaite in the West Riding of Yorkshire.

The whole religion which I prize lies in the thirteenth chapter to the Corinthians. Now this religion has never in my memory so increased as it does at this day. Herein I rejoice. And I take no thought for the morrow. God will see to that.

5   Bishop Green has published to Mr. Berridge and Mr. Whitefield, and promised a letter to me also.[16] It will be time enough, when this appears, to take a little notice of all three at once.

In autumn we shall probably have our Conference at Leeds.[17] I expect to go from Bristol to Cork next month. I am, with love to
10   Nancy, dear Sammy,
        Yours affectionately,

J. Wesley

Address: 'To / The Revd Mr Furly / At Kippax, near Ferry Bridge / Yorkshire'.
Postmarks: '23/[illegible]'. *Charge*: '4'.
Source: holograph; Huntington Library, Manuscripts, HM 57038.

To Unidentified Correspondent[18]

LONDON
MARCH 1, 1762

15   My Dear Brother,
        I rejoice to hear that you continue in the good way.
        Never leave off a duty because you are tempted in it. You may be more tempted than usual on fasting days, and yet you may receive a blessing thereby.
20   I expect to be either in Dublin or Cork about the end of this month.

---

[16] Bishop John Green (1706–79) published *The Principles and Practices of the Methodists Considered, in Some Letters ... the first to the Reverend Mr. B[erridg]e* (London: W. Bristow, 1760); and *The Principles and Practices of the Methodists Farther Considered, in a letter to the Reverend Mr. George Whitefield* (Cambridge: J. Bentham, 1761). JW commented on the first work shortly after it was published, in his letter to the editor of *Lloyd's Evening Post*, Nov. 22, 1760. The letter Wesley anticipated addressed to himself from Green was never published; hence, neither was Wesley's fuller response.

[17] The Conference convened on Aug. 10, 1762, in Leeds; see 10:293–94 in this edn.

[18] Telford (*Letters*, 4:171) identifies the recipient as Henry Brooke (1738–1806), even though the manuscript has no addressee information. Brooke is not a possibility, because his earliest contact with Methodism was in 1764–65; see his letter to JW in Apr. 1765.

I have not, since I have been in London, heard anything of Tommy Bethell.[19] I believe the letters are safely delivered. I am,
Your affectionate brother,

J. Wesley

Source: holograph; Toronto, Canada, United Church of Canada Archives, 97.002C, 3-4 (address portion missing).

To Christopher Hopper

LONDON
MARCH 1, 1762

My Dear Brother,

Public commotions fill the minds and hands of those who might otherwise employ themselves in hindering the course of the gospel. And probably they are of great use to give more seriousness and thoughtfulness to a young and inexperienced Prince.[20]

I am glad you are in the Orphan House, were it only that you may drop a word in season to Thomas Olivers. This day fortnight I am to set out for Ireland. When will you set out for Scotland? They want you sadly at Aberdeen. Shall I send you two or three guineas for your journey? James Kershaw may spend a month or two in Newcastle circuit to supply your pl‹ace›.[21] I think it is of importance. Much good may ‹be› done, by you in particular. We join in love to y‹ou› all. I am,
Ever yours,

J. Wesley

Address: In Wesley's hand, at the top of the page, 'To Mr Hopper'.
Source: holograph; MARC, MAM JW 3/53 (address portion missing).

[19] Orig., 'Bethel'. Thomas Bethell (fl. 1755–85) was a member of the Methodist society in Dublin who may have served as a local exhorter and later ran a prayer meeting; cf. JW to Thomas Rutherford, July 29, 1782.

[20] George III, who had acceded to the throne in October 1760, was facing the public concern in light of the recent mutual declarations of war between Britain and Spain.

[21] A small tear on the left side of the ms. obscures some letters in this and following cases. This is one of the first evidences that Kershaw, who had withdrawn for about five years, was returning to itinerancy.

To Matthew Lowes

LONDON
MARCH 11, 1762

Dear Matthew,

I have enclosed that part of the Minutes of the Conference which
5　relates to discipline.[22] In the other paper (which you may read in
every society just before you visit the classes) you see the design of
the general yearly collection, to which *every* Methodist in England
is to contribute something.[23] If there is any who cannot give an halfpenny in a year, another will give it for him.

10　I believe no money was put to any other use than that for which it
was allotted at the Conference. Something was allotted for Whitehaven; I can't now remember how much.

The society here has subscribed near three hundred pounds. I am,
Your affectionate friend and brother,

15

J. Wesley

Endorsement: 'written March 11th / 1762 / From the Revd Mr Wesley'.
Source: holograph; MARC, MAM JW 3/99 (address portion missing).

To the Rev. Samuel Furly

BRISTOL
MARCH 20, 1762

Dear Sammy,

You who have conversed with him are the best judge of Mr. Hol-
20　lin's present state. So I refer the matter to the Assistant and you.
Satisfy yourselves, and you satisfy me.

Still, Sammy, I take knowledge you are a young man, and as such,
extremely peremptory. So was I, till I was more than thirty years
old. So I may well make allowance for *you*. I was likewise as much
25　*bigoted* to my own opinions as you can be for your life. That is, I
thought them deeply *important*, and that all contrary opinions were

---

[22] See 10:806–35 in this edn.

[23] This would be the yearly collection for Kingswood School, which was instituted by the
1756 Conference; see Minutes, Aug. 28, 1756, 10:277–78 in this edn.

damnable errors. Have patience and you will see farther. In a few years you will find out that neither these are half so *necessary* to salvation, nor those half so destructive as you now imagine.

I know none that denies that every true saint will *die at the feet of mercy*, and will stand, even at the day of Judgement, as a *redeemed sinner*. But I deny that any *justified* believer has any *real guilt*. Guilt cannot consist with justification; they are directly opposite to each other. And yet I believe that a truly sanctified person does involuntarily fall short in divers instances of the rule marked out in the 13th chapter to the Corinthians. And that on *this* account, they continually need their Advocate with the Father. And I never talked with one person who denied it. I do not believe there is one such in the London society. But there are many who abound in bowels of mercy and tenderness towards all men. I know many thousands of awakened and believing souls, but I know *none like them*. Sometimes I have disliked some of their opinions, and frequently some of their expressions. But I admire their tempers, and their holy, unblamable, useful lives adorn the doctrine of God our Saviour. On him alone they depend. He is their God and their all. They live in him and walk in him. They are filled and clothed with humility. They spread the knowledge and love of Christ wherever they converse. And to these chiefly it is owing, that within this year, near four hundred members are added to that society.

General charges prove nothing. When my brother has told me ten times, 'You are credulous', I have asked, 'Show me the instances'. He could not do it. No, nor any man else. Indeed, jealousy and suspiciousness I defy and abhor, as I do hell-fire. But I believe nothing, great or small, without such kind of proof as the nature of the thing allows.

How does Mr. [Henry] Venn go on, in his soul and in his labours? And how are you employing yourself? O seek, enjoy Christ alone. I am, with love to Nancy, dear Sammy,
>   Your affectionate brother,

>   J. Wesley

I expect to be at Mr. Bennet's in Boughton, near Chester, on the 31st instant, in my way to Ireland.

Address: 'Cross Post / To / The Revd Mr Furly / At Kippax near Ferrybridge / Yorkshire'.
Postmarks: 'B / RIS / TOL' and (twice stamped) '23 / MR'. *Charge*: '3'.
Endorsement: 'On the Contr. of Perfcn'.
Source: holograph; MARC, MAM JW 3/21.

To Thomas Rankin

BRISTOL
MARCH 20, 1762

My Dear Brother,

 You should act as an Assistant in Sussex. Therefore see that our
5 Rules be everywhere observed; and spread our books wherever
you go, particularly Kempis, *Primitive Physick*, and *Instructions for
Children.*[24]

 Before eight weeks are ended the societies will be able to secure
you an horse. O be simple! Be a little child before God! I am,
10   Your affectionate brother,

            J. Wesley

Read and pray much.

Address: 'To / Mr Tho. Rankin / At Mr Barker's / In Sevenoaks / Kent'.
Postmarks: '22 / MR' and 'BRIS / TOL'. *Charges*: '4' marked over with
 '6'.
Source: holograph; privately held (current owner unknown, Wesley Works
 Editorial Project Archive includes a copy).

To Jane Catherine March

[ATHLONE]
15   MAY 13, 1762

 You did well to write. 'It is good to hide the secrets of a king,
but to declare the loving-kindness of the Lord.'[25] Have you never
found any wandering since? Is your mind *always* stayed on God?
Do you find *every* thought brought into captivity to the obedience
20 of Christ? Do no *vain* thoughts (useless, trifling, unedifying) lodge
within you? Does not the corruptible body at *some times* more or
less press down the soul? Has God made your very *dreams* devout?

---

[24] I.e., JW's abridged version of Thomas à Kempis's *The Imitation of Christ* (*Bibliography*,
No. 45); his collection of medical advice (*Bibliography*, No. 138 and Vol. 32 in this edn.); and
the basic catechism that JW published in 1745 (*Bibliography*, No. 101, and Vol. 16 in this edn.).
[25] Tobit 12:7.

I have known Satan assault in their sleep (endeavouring to terrify or affright) those whom he could not touch when they were awake.

As to your band, there are two sorts of persons with whom you may have to do—the earnest and the slack. The way you are to take with the one is quite different from that one would take with the other. The latter you must *search*, and find out why they are slack; exhort them to repent, be zealous, do the first works. The former you have only to encourage, to exhort to push forward to the mark, to bid them grasp the prize so nigh! And do so yourself. Receive a thousand more blessings. Believe more. Love more. You cannot love enough. Beware of sins of omission. So shall you fulfil the joy of,
> Your affectionate brother,

> J. Wesley

Source: published transcription; *Methodist Magazine* 22 (1799): 149.

To the Rev. Samuel Furly

[CASTLEBAR]
MAY 21, 1762

Dear Sammy,

This morning I came hither, and received yours. The post-boys in Ireland do not ride Pegasus.

A sermon of Archbishop Sharp's fully convinced me about thirty years ago that it is inconsistent with charity to charge any man with those *consequences* of his doctrine which he disavows.[26] I always did so before, but not since. Otherwise what work should I make with poor George Whitefield.

Another thing I was not so soon nor so easily convinced of; namely, that in spite of all my logic *I cannot so prove* any one point in the whole compass of philosophy or divinity as not to leave room for strong objections, and probably such as I could not answer. But

---

[26] John Sharp (1645–1714) was Archbishop of York from July 1691. JW read his *Fifteen Sermons Preached on Several Occasions* (London, 1700) at Oxford and while in Savannah (see Diary, June 30, 1736, 18:398 in this edn.). In the first sermon of the collection, on Rom. 14:19, Sharp stated, 'Another thing that would make for peace is this, never to charge upon men the consequences of their opinions when they expressly disown them'.

if I could, my answer, however guarded, will give room to equally strong objections. And in this manner, if the person is a man of sense, answers and objections may go on *in infinitum*.

I am therefore weary of altercation. Once or twice I give my rea-
5 sons. If they do not convince, I have done. My day is far spent, so that I have no hours to spare for what I verily believe will profit nothing.

As to that particular expression, 'Dying at the feet of mercy', I have only farther to add, I do not care, as it is not a scriptural
10 phrase, whether any one takes or leaves it. It is enough for me if he says from the heart

> Every moment, Lord, I need
> The merit of thy death.
15 Never shall I want it less
> When thou the grace hast given,
> Fill'd me with thy holiness,
> And seal'd the heir of heaven;
> I shall hang upon my God,
20 Till I thy perfect glory see,
> Till the sprinkling of thy blood
> Shall speak me up to thee.[27]

I wish Mr. Venn may have more and more success. Has he pub-
25 lished his book concerning gospel ministers?[28] I still think it is not prudence, but high imprudence, for any of those who preach the essential gospel truths to stand aloof from each other. I cannot but judge there ought to be the most cordial and avowed union between them. But I rejoice that the shyness is not, and never was, on my
30 side. I have done all I could, and with a single eye. For as long as God is pleased to continue with me, I want no man living. I have all things and abound. How happy is the man that trusts in him![29]

I expect our Conference will begin at Leeds on Tuesday the 10th of August. Peace be with you and yours! I am, dear Sammy,
35   Your affectionate friend and brother,

J. Wesley

---

[27] Cf. CW, 'Isaiah 32:2', sts. 5–6, *HSP* (1742), 146.

[28] JW may mean Henry Venn's *The Duty of a Parish Priest* (1760). But he had met with Venn since it appeared; cf. *Journal*, Mar. 25, 1761, 21:313 in this edn.

[29] See Ps. 34:8.

Address: 'To / The Revd Mr Furly / At Slaithwaite, Near Huddersfield / Yorkshire / Turn at Chester'.
Postmarks: '31 / MA' and an illegible place stamp. *Postage*: '4'.
Source: holograph; MARC, MAM JW 3/22.

To Jane Lee[30]

LIMERICK
JUNE 7, 1762

My Dear Sister,

You did well to write freely. The more largely you write, the more welcome your letters will be; and your soul is now so feeble and　　5 tender that it needs every help.

It is certain that God has made bare his arm and wrought a great deliverance for you.[31] He has more fully revealed his Son in you. He has purified your heart. He has saved you from pride, anger, desire. Yea, the Son has made you free, and you are free indeed.[32]　　10 Stand fast, then, my dear friend, in this glorious liberty.[33] Stand fast by simple faith! Look unto Jesus![34] Trust him, praise him forever. Lean upon him alone! And be not careful about this or that name for the blessing you have received. Do not reason one moment what to call it, whether perfection or anything else. You have faith, hold　　15 it fast. You have love, let it not go. Above all, you have Christ! Christ is yours! He is your Lord, your love, your all! Let him be your portion in time and in eternity! Send word just how you are in every particular to,

Your affectionate brother,　　　　　　　　　　　　　　20

J. Wesley

---

[30] Jane ('Jenny') Esther Lee was a native of Larne, County Antrim, in Northern Ireland. She met John Wesley at some point on a trip to visit her grandmother in Limerick and became a frequent correspondent. In October 1763 she married James Freeman, a local preacher from Dublin. See *WHS* 8 (1912): 98; citing Robert Redman Belshaw, *John Lee and Charles Wesley's Hymns* (Dublin: Ponsonby & Givvs, 1902), 11, 14. This is apparently JW's first letter to her.

[31] See Isa. 52:10.

[32] See John 8:36.

[33] See Gal. 5:1.

[34] See Heb. 12:2.

Address: 'To / Miss Jenny Lee'.

No *postmark* or indications of postal *charge*; apparently delivered by hand.

Source: holograph; Baltimore, Maryland, Lovely Lane Museum Library, United Methodist Historical Society of the Baltimore-Washington Conference.

To Christopher Hopper

CORK
JUNE 18, 1762

My Dear Brother,

So your labour has not been in vain. I shall expect an account of
5   the remaining part of your journey too. And you will be able to inform me of the real character and behaviour of Robert Miller also.[35]
I do not rightly understand him. But I see James Kershaw and he
do not admire one another.

Pray let me know as particularly as you can how William Fugill[36]
10 has behaved in Scotland, and what has hindered the increase of the
work at Edinburgh. I thought the society would have been doubled
before now.

I expect to be in Dublin on Saturday, July 24. Then providence
will determine how I shall go forward, and whether I am to embark
15 for Parkgate, Liverpool, or Holyhead in my way to Leeds, where I
hope to meet you all on August 10.[37] I am,

Yours affectionately,

J. Wesley

20 I hope you will all exert yourselves in the midsummer collection for
Kingswood.[38]

---

[35] It is unclear whether this is the Robert Miller, perhaps serving now as a local preacher, who became an itinerant about 1789 (see 10:678 in this edn.).

[36] William Fugill (d. 1800) was a native of Rothwell, near Leeds. He had been itinerating for about 10 years, but this letter reveals JW's growing concern about him. He was expelled in 1764. See Atmore, *Memorial*, 147–48.

[37] The Conference met at Leeds on Aug. 10; see 10:293–94.

[38] See JW to Hopper, Mar. 11, 1762.

Address: 'To / Mr Hopper'.

No *postmark* or indications of postal *charge*; apparently delivered by hand.

Source: holograph; Duke, Rubenstein, Frank Baker Collection of Wesleyana, Box WF 1.

To Jane Lee

CORK
JUNE 18, 1762

My Dear Sister,

It is observed in Mr. [Gaston] De Renty's *Life* that God himself does often give desires that he will not suffer to take effect.[39]   5
Such probably may be your desire of death. God may make it a
blessing to you, though he does not intend to fulfil it soon. But he
will withhold no manner of thing that is good. Do you now find a
witness in yourself that you are saved from sin? Do you see God
always? And always feel his love? And in everything give thanks?[40]   10
My dear Jenny, you shall see greater things than these! The Lord is
your shepherd. Therefore can you lack nothing.[41] O cleave close to
him! Christ is yours! All is yours! Trust him, praise him evermore.
Pray for,

Your affectionate brother,   15

J. Wesley

Source: published transcription; *WHS* 17 (1929): 69–70.

---

[39] JW published *An Extract of the Life of Monsieur De Renty, a Late Nobleman of France*
(1741, *Bibliography*, No. 43).

[40] See 1 Thess. 5:18.

[41] See Ps. 23:1.

To Howell Powell[42]

CORK
JUNE 28, 1762

My Dear Brother,

This is nothing strange, but have patience and all will be well. I do
5 not enquire after men's opinions, but their spirit. It lies upon you not
only not to begin, but not to be led into a dispute. If a man say, 'A believer may fall from grace and may be saved from all sin', it would be
your wisdom either to be quite silent, as I generally am in such cases,
or to say mildly, 'You and I may love alike, if we do not think alike'.
10

So skilful fencers suffer heat to tire.[43]

I desired the leaders might take their turn in reading, only that
you would read on Sunday. Steadfastness and gentleness will carry
15 you through. Bear all and conquer all. S— B— will think better.
Give him time. He has many trials. But I dare not therefore put him
in an office he is not qualified for. I am,

Your affectionate brother,

John Wesley

Source: published transcription; Matthew Simpson (ed.), *Cyclopedia of
Methodism* (5th edn.; Philadelphia: Louis H. Everts, 1883), 2:730–31.

To Ebenezer Blackwell

20 DUBLIN
JULY 28, 1762

Dear Sir,

It was seven or eight weeks before I could prevail upon any of our
brethren in England to let me know whether 'Mr. Blackwell, an em-

---

[42] Howell Powell (1730–1820) was born in Derbyshire and came to reside in County
Cork, Ireland, where he was converted under the influence of Evangelical preachers. He had
become the tutor to the family of the Earl of Bandon at Bandon, County Cork, and met John
Wesley in 1758 in that town.

[43] Cf. George Herbert, 'The Church Porch', l. 36, 'As cunning fencers suffer heat to tire';
included by JW in *MSP* (1744), 1:29.

inent banker, died at his house in Lewisham' or not. John Maddern was the first who occasionally told me he was alive.[44] Now, a messenger of good news should be rewarded. But what can be done for this poor man, in truth I cannot tell. He hinted at a distance as if he would be much obliged if I would be bound for his behaviour. But how could I be bound for a thousand pounds who am not worth a groat? I could not, therefore, but advise him to give up the thought of being in a banker's shop, as I see no manner of probability of his procuring such sureties as are requisite.

Indeed, I heartily wish he was in any way of business, as he is capable of almost anything.

The people in this kingdom have been frightened sufficiently by the sickness and by the Levellers, whose design undoubtedly was deep laid and extended to the whole kingdom.[45] But they broke out too soon. Nothing should have *appeared* till a French or Spanish squadron came.[46] The nation is not now in the same state as it was in 1641.[47] Then there were not four thousand soldiers in the kingdom; now there are near twenty thousand.

I hope you and yours have escaped the general disorder or have found it a blessing. It little matters whether we escape pain or suffer it, so it be but sanctified. Without some suffering we should scarce remember that we are not proprietors here, but only tenants at will, liable to lose all we have at a moment's warning. Happy it were if we continually retained a lively impression of this on our minds. Then should we more earnestly seek that portion which shall never be taken from us.

In two or three days I am likely to embark in order to meet our brethren at Leeds. There I hope to have it under your own hand that both you, Mrs. [Elizabeth] Blackwell, Mrs. [Hannah] Dewal, and Miss [Mary] Freeman are alive in the best sense. I am, dear sir,
Your affectionate servant,

J. Wesley

---

[44] John Maddern (fl. 1740–65) was a native of Cornwall who served as an itinerant, 1747–56, as English master at Kingswood School 1756–57, and then as a local preacher in London. See Hastling et al., *Kingswood*, Register, 193; and Vickers, *Dictionary*, 220.

[45] An agrarian uprising originated in Limerick in November 1761, and spread to a number of Irish counties, including Cork where JW was traveling at this time. Historians refer to the propagators as 'Whiteboys', but in the eighteenth century they were more commonly called 'Levellers', recalling the Levellers of the English Revolution (1640s through 1650s).

[46] At this point in the Seven Years War, Britain was at war with both Spain and France.

[47] JW refers to the Irish Rebellion of 1641 against British rule.

Address: 'To / Mr Blackwell / In Change Alley / London'.
Postmarks: 'DUBLIN' and '4 / AV'. *Postage*: '4' [?].
Endorsement: 'Rev'd Mr John Wesley / Dublin 28 July 1762'.
Source: holograph; Emory, MARBL, Wesley Family Papers, OBV1, p. 5.

To the Rev. Samuel Furly

DUBLIN
JULY 30, 1762

Dear Sammy,

'If I am unanswered, then I am unanswerable.' Who can deny the
5   consequence? By such an argument you carry all before you and
gain a complete victory. You put me in mind of the honest man who
cried out while I was preaching, '*Quid est tibi nomen?*'[48] and, upon
my giving no answer, called out vehemently, 'I told you he did not
understand Latin!'
10   I do sometimes understand, though I do not answer. This is often
the case between you and me. You love dispute, and I hate it. You
have much time, and I have much work. *Non sumus ergo pares.*[49]
But if you will dispute the point with Nicholas Norton, he is your
match. He has both leisure and love for the work.[50]
15   For me, I shall only once more state the case. Here are forty or
fifty people who declare (and I can take their word, for I know them
well), each for himself, 'God has enabled me to rejoice evermore,
and to pray and give thanks without ceasing.[51] He has enabled me to
give him all my heart, which I believe he has cleansed from all sin. I
20   feel no pride, no anger, no desire, no unbelief, but pure love alone.' I
ask, 'Do you, then, believe you have no farther need of Christ or His
atoning blood?' Every one answers, 'I never felt my want of Christ so
deeply and strongly as I do now. I feel the want of Christ my priest
as well as king, and receive all I have in and through him. Every
25   moment I want the merit of his death, and I have it every moment.'
    But you think, 'They cannot want the merit of his death if they
are saved from sin.' They think otherwise. They know and feel the

---

[48] 'What is your name?'
[49] 'We are therefore not equals.'
[50] See JW to Nicholas Norton, Sept. 3, 1756.
[51] See 1 Thess. 5:16–18.

contrary, whether they can *explain* it or no. There is not one, either in this city or in this kingdom, who does not agree in this.

Here is a plain fact. You may dispute, reason, cavil about it, just as long as you please. Meantime I know by all manner of proof that these are the happiest and the holiest people in the kingdom. Their 5 light shines before men.[52] They are zealous of good works, and labour to abstain from all appearance of evil.[53] They have the mind that was in Christ, and walk as Christ also walked.[54]

And shall I cease to rejoice over these holy, happy men because they mistake in their judgement? If they do, I would to God you 10 and I and all mankind were under the same mistake, provided we had the same faith, the same love, and the same inward and outward holiness! I am, dear Sammy,
> Yours affectionately,

> J. Wesley 15

Will not you meet us at Leeds on the 10th of August?[55]

Address: 'To / The Revd Mr ⟨Furb⟩y / Near Huddersfield / Yorkshire'.
Postmark: '7/AV'.
Endorsement: 'From Chester' 'JW'.
Source: holograph; New Room (Bristol).

To Dorothy Furly

St. Ives
September 15, 1762

My Dear Sister, 20

Whereunto you have attained hold fast.[56] But expect that greater things are *at hand*, although our friend[57] talks as if you were not to expect them till the article of death.

---

[52] See Matt. 5:16.
[53] See Titus 2:14; 1 Thess. 5:22.
[54] See 1 Cor. 2:16; 1 John 2:6.
[55] I.e., at JW's annual Conference with his preachers.
[56] See Phil. 3:16.
[57] I.e., her brother Samuel.

Certainly sanctification (in the proper sense) is 'an instantaneous deliverance from all sin', and includes 'an instantaneous power then given always to cleave to God'. Yet this sanctification (at least, in the lower degrees) does not include a power never to think an *useless* thought nor ever speak an *useless* word. I myself believe that *such* a perfection is inconsistent with living in a corruptible body, for this makes it impossible 'always to think right'. While we breathe we shall more or less *mistake*. If, therefore, Christian perfection implies this, we must not expect it till after death.

I want you to be *all love*. This is the perfection I believe and teach. And this perfection is consistent with a thousand nervous disorders, which that high-strained perfection is not. Indeed, my judgement is that (in this case particularly) to overdo is to undo, and that to set perfection too high (so high as no man that we ever heard or read of attained) is the most effectual (because unsuspected) way of driving it out of the world.

Take care you are not hurt by anything in the *Short Hymns* contrary to the doctrines you have long received.[58] Peace be with your spirit! I am,

Your affectionate brother,

J. Wesley

Source: published transcription; Benson, *Works*, 16:327.

To the Rev. Samuel Furly

ST. IVES
SEPTEMBER 15, 1762

Spectatum satis, ac donatum iam rude, quaeris,
Maecenas, iterum antiquo me includere ludo?
Non eadem est aetas, non mens.[59]

[58] CW's *Short Hymns on Select Passages of the Holy Scriptures* (1762) specifically emphasise a gradual process of sanctification in contrast to the teachings of Thomas Maxfield, George Bell, and others. See JW to Thomas Maxfield, Nov. 2, 1762; and the brief survey of the "London Blessing" controversy in 12:22–23 in this edn.

[59] Horace, *Epistles*, I.i.2–4; '... you, Maecenas, seek to shut me up again in my old school, though well tested in the fray, and already presented with the foil. My years, my mind are not the same' (Loeb).

I have entirely lost my taste for controversy. I have lost my readiness in disputing. And I take this to be a providential discharge from it. All I can now do with a clear conscience is (not to enter into a formal controversy about the new birth, or justification by faith, any more than Christian perfection, but) simply to *declare* my judgement on any point, and the grounds of that judgement, and to *explain* myself as clearly as I can, upon any difficulty that may arise concerning it.

So far, Sammy, I can go with *you*, but no farther. I still say (and without any self-contradiction) I know no persons living, who are so deeply conscious of their needing Christ both as prophet, priest, and king as those who believe themselves, and whom I believe, to be cleansed from all sin—I mean from all pride, anger, evil desire, idolatry, and unbelief. These very persons more feel their own ignorance, littleness of grace, coming short of the full mind that was in Christ,[60] and walking less ἀκριβῶς[61] than they might have done after their divine pattern, are more convinced of the insufficiency of all they are, have, or do to ⟨bear the[62]⟩ eye of God without a mediator, are more pe⟨netrated⟩ with the sense of the want of him than ever they were before. If Mr. Madan or you say 'that "coming short" is sin,' be it so; I contend not.[63] But still I say: 'There are they whom I believe to be scripturally "perfect". And yet these never felt their want of Christ so deeply and strongly as they do now.'

If in saying this I have 'fully given up the point', what would you have more? Is it not enough that I leave you to 'boast your superior power against the little, weak shifts of baffled error'? 'Canst thou not be content,' as the Quaker said, 'to lay John Wesley on his back, but thou must tread his guts out?'[64]

Here are persons exceeding holy and happy, rejoicing evermore, praying always, and in everything giving thanks,[65] feeling the love of God and man every moment, feeling no pride or other evil temper. If these are not 'perfect', that scriptural word has no meaning.

[60] See Phil. 2:5; 1 Cor. 2:16.

[61] Greek, 'accurately' or 'circumspectly'; cf. Eph. 5:15 (AV), 'walk circumspectly'.

[62] The ms. is torn at the right-hand bottom of this page; the missing words are reconstructed in this and the following instance.

[63] Like most Calvinist Methodists, Martin Madan was critical of any claim to Christian perfection. Within a couple of months of this letter he published *Some Quaeries Humbly Offered to Those who Profess Sinless Perfection*; see both his queries and JW's responses in 13:591–96 in this edn.

[64] JW identifies this Quaker as living in Cornwall in *Letter to Mr. Potter* (1758), §5 (vol. 14 in this edn.).

[65] See 1 Thess. 5:16–18.

Stop. You must not cavil at *that* word, you are not wiser than the Holy Ghost. But if you are not, see that you teach 'perfection' too. 'But are they not "sinners"?' Explain the term one way, and I say, 'Yes', another, and I say, 'No'. 'Are they cleansed from *all sin*?' I
5 believe they are, meaning from all sinful tempers. 'But have they then need of Christ?' I believe they have, in the sense and for the reasons above mentioned.

Now, be this true or false, it is no contradiction. ⟨It is co⁶⁶⟩nsistent with itself, and I think consistent with ⟨right r⟩eason and the whole
10 oracles of God.

O Sammy, let you and I go on to perfection. God grant we may so run as to attain!⁶⁷ I am,

Your affectionate friend and brother,

J. Wesley

Address: 'The Revd Mr Furly / At Slaithwaite, near Huddersfield / Yorkshire'.
Postmark: '20/SE'. *Charge*: '4' and possibly '8'.
Endorsement: 'Mr J. Wesley to Mr Furly Sept. 15, 1762'.
Source: holograph; Drew, Methodist Archives.

To Jane Catherine March⁶⁸

15 BRISTOL
OCTOBER 9, 1762

Though I have very little time, I must write a few lines. I thank you for your comfortable letter. Some have more of heat and some of light. The danger is that one should say to the other, 'I have no
20 need of thee';⁶⁹ or that any should mistake his place and imagine himself to be what he is not. Be not backward to speak to any whom you think are mistaken either in this or other things. A loving word

---

⁶⁶ The same tear of the page also affected the left bottom of this second page of the letter.
⁶⁷ See 1 Cor. 9:24.
⁶⁸ JW is replying to her letter of Oct. 7, 1762.
⁶⁹ 1 Cor. 12:21.

spoken in faith shall not fall to the ground.[70] And the more freely
you speak to *me* at any time or on any head, the more you will oblige,
    Your ever affectionate brother,

J. Wesley

Source: published transcription; *Methodist Magazine* 22 (1799): 149.

To the Rev. Samuel Furly

BRISTOL
OCTOBER 13, 1762

My Dear Brother,

In general, when I apprehend, 'Certainly this is a contradiction',
if I find other persons of equal sagacity with myself, of equal natural and acquired abilities, apprehend it is not, I immediately suspect
my own judgement. And the more so because I remember I have
been many times *full as sure* as I am now, and yet afterwards I found
myself mistaken.

As to this particular question, I believe I am able to answer every
objection which can be made. But I am not able to do it without
expending much time which may be better employed. For this reason I am persuaded it is so far from being my duty to enter into a
formal controversy about it that it would be a wilful sin, it would
be employing my short residue of life in a less profitable way than
it may be employed.

The proposition which I will hold is this: 'A person may be
cleansed from all *sinful tempers*, and yet need the atoning blood.' For
what? For 'negligences and ignorances'; for both words and actions
(as well as omissions) which are, in a sense, transgressions of the
perfect law. And I believe no one is clear of these till he lays down
this corruptible body.

Now, Sammy, dropping the point of contradiction, tell me simply
what you would have more? Do you believe evil tempers remain till
death? All, or some? If some only, which?

[70] See Matt. 10:29.

I love truth wherever I find it; so if you can help me to a little more of it, you will oblige, dear Sammy,

Yours, etc.,

J. Wesley

Source: published transcription; *Arminian Magazine* 6 (1783): 107–8.

To the Rev. Thomas Maxfield[71]

CANTERBURY
NOVEMBER 2, 1762

5

Without any preface or ceremony, which is needless between you and me, I will simply and plainly tell what I dislike in your doctrine, spirit, or outward behaviour. When I say *yours*, I include brother
10 Bell and Owen,[72] and those who are most closely connected with them.

1) I like your doctrine of *perfection*, or pure love—love excluding sin. Your insisting that it is merely by *faith*; that consequently it is *instantaneous* (though preceded and followed by a gradual work),
15 and that it may be *now*, at this instant.

But I dislike your supposing man may be as perfect 'as an angel'; that he can be *absolutely* perfect; that he can be *infallible*, or above being *tempted*; or that the moment he is pure in heart he *cannot fall* from it.

[71] A controversy had been brewing for months over claims about Christian perfection among Methodists, particularly in the London society, as many of the previous letters reflect. CW was particularly frustrated with JW's reluctance to discipline Thomas Maxfield and George Bell, who were leaders of the contingent championing 'angelic' perfection. In his *Journal* JW records that on Nov. 1, 1762, 'I went down to Canterbury. Here I seriously reflected on some late occurrences, and, after weighing the matter thoroughly, wrote as follows' (21:394 in this edn.). He then gave the text of this letter.

As the letter reminds Maxfield, in May 1762 (or thereabouts) JW had told him not to preach at Snowsfield, on pain of being removed from the connexion. Maxfield did so, but the final breach did not come until April 1763. This letter is JW's attempt to lay out specific grounds of disagreement with Maxfield's teachings and practices, providing Maxfield the possibility of clearing himself of these charges, following the biblical mandate to tell a member of the community of their faults privately before making a public break with them (Matt. 18:15–17).

[72] Daniel Owen was a member of the London Society active in the perfectionist party, who withdrew with Bell in 1763.

I dislike the saying, This was not known or taught among us till within two or three years. I grant, You did not know it. You have over and over denied instantaneous sanctification to *me*. But I have known and taught it (and so has my brother, as our writings show) above these twenty years.[73]

I dislike your directly or indirectly depreciating justification: saying a justified person is not 'in Christ',[74] is not 'born of God',[75] is not 'a new creature',[76] has not a 'new heart',[77] is not 'sanctified',[78] not a 'temple of the Holy Ghost';[79] or that he 'cannot please God',[80] or cannot 'grow in grace'.[81]

I dislike your saying that one saved from sin needs nothing more than 'looking to Jesus',[82] needs not to hear or think of anything else— 'Believe, believe' is enough—that he needs no *self-examination*, no times of *private prayer*; needs not mind *little*, or *outward* things; and that he *cannot be taught* by any person who is not in the same state.

I dislike your affirming that justified persons in general persecute them that are saved from sin, that *they* have persecuted *you* on *this* account, and that for *two years* past *you* have been more persecuted by 'the two brothers'[83] than ever you was by the world in all your life.

2) As to your spirit, I like your confidence in God and your zeal for the salvation of souls.[84]

But I dislike something which has the appearance of *pride*, of overvaluing yourselves and undervaluing others, particularly the preachers, thinking not only that they are *blind* and that they are not sent of God, but even that they are *dead*, dead to God, and walking in the way to hell; that 'they are going *one* way', you *another*; that 'they have *no life* in' them! Your speaking of *yourselves* as though *you* were the *only men* who knew and taught the gospel; and as if

---

[73] At this point, John Wesley was playing down his brother's move in this period towards a doctrine of sanctification that emphasised its gradual and progressive nature; cf. John Tyson, *Charles Wesley on Sanctification* (Grand Rapids: Zondervan, 1986), 227–301.

[74] Rom. 16:7, etc.

[75] 1 John 3:9, etc.

[76] Gal. 5:15.

[77] Ezek. 18:31, etc.

[78] John 17:19, etc.

[79] 1 Cor. 6:19.

[80] Rom. 8:8.

[81] 2 Pet. 3:18.

[82] Heb. 12:2 (*NT Notes*).

[83] I.e., John and Charles Wesley.

[84] See 1 Pet. 1:9.

not only *all the clergy* but *all the Methodists* besides, were in utter darkness.

I dislike something that has the appearance of *enthusiasm*: over-valuing *feelings* and *inward impressions*; mistaking the mere work of *imagination* for the voice of the Spirit; expecting the end without the means; and undervaluing *reason, knowledge*, and *wisdom*, in general.

I dislike something that has the appearance of *antinomianism*: not magnifying the law and making it honourable; not enough valuing *tenderness of conscience*, and exact *watchfulness* in order thereto; using *faith* rather as contradistinguished from *holiness* than as productive of it.

But what I most of all dislike is your *littleness of love* to your brethren, to your own society: your want of *union of heart* with them and 'bowels of mercies'[85] toward them; your want of *meekness, gentleness, long-suffering*, your 'impatience of contradiction';[86] your counting every man your enemy that reproves or admonishes you in love; your *bigotry* and *narrowness* of spirit, loving in a manner only those that love *you*; your *censoriousness*, proneness to *think hardly* of all who do not exactly agree with you: in one word, your *divisive spirit*. Indeed, I do not believe that any of you either design or desire a separation. But you do not enough *fear, abhor*, and *detest* it, shuddering at the very thought. And all the preceding tempers tend to it and gradually prepare you for it. Observe, I tell you before! God grant you may immediately and affectionately take the warning!

3) As to your outward behaviour, I like the general tenor of your life, devoted to God and spent in doing good.

But I dislike your slighting any, the very least, rules of the bands or society and your doing anything that tends to hinder others from exactly observing them. Therefore,

I dislike your appointing such meetings as hinder others from attending either the public preaching or their class or band, or any other meeting which the rules of the society or their office requires them to attend.

I dislike your spending so *much time* in several meetings, as many that attend can ill spare from the other duties of their calling, unless they omit either the preaching or their class or band. This naturally tends to dissolve our society by cutting the sinews of it.

---

[85] Col. 3:12.
[86] Cf. Heb. 12:3.

As to your more public meetings, I like the praying fervently and largely for all the blessings of God. And I know much good has been done hereby, and hope much more will be done.

But I dislike several things therein: (i) the singing or speaking or praying of several at once; (ii) the praying to the Son of God only, 5 or more than to the Father; (iii) the using improper expressions in prayer: sometimes too bold, if not irreverent, sometimes too pomp- ous and magnificent, extolling yourselves rather than God and tell- ing him what you *are*, not what you *want*; (iv) using poor, flat, bald hymns; (v) the never kneeling at prayer; (vi) your using postures or 10 gestures highly indecent; (vii) your screaming, even so as to make the words unintelligible; (viii) your affirming people *will* be justi- fied or sanctified just now; (ix) the affirming *they are*, when they are not; (x) the bidding them say, I believe; (xi) the bitterly condemning any that oppose, calling them wolves, etc., and pronouncing them 15 hypocrites or not justified.

Read this calmly and impartially before the Lord in prayer. So shall the evil cease and the good remain. And you will then be more than ever united to,

Your affectionate brother, 20

J. Wesley

Source: published transcription; JW, *Journal*, Nov. 1, 1762 (21:394–97 in this edn.).

To Emma Moon[87]

CANTERBURY
NOVEMBER 5, 1762

My Dear Sister,

Ten times I believe I have been going to answer your last, and 25 have been as often hindered. Surely Satan does not approve of our

---

[87] Emma Moon (fl. 1755–88) was a native of Potto, near Yarm in the North Riding of Yorkshire. The wife of a sheep-raiser, she was converted under the influence of an older Meth- odist woman from Birstall. See Tyerman, *John Wesley*, 2:409. Moon's first surviving letter to JW was dated Mar. 11, 1762. This is JW's first letter to Moon, reply to one that has not survived.

corresponding together. And no wonder, seeing he does not like what tends to the furtherance of the kingdom of God. And this your letters always do. I find an animating, strengthening power in them. And this is what I particularly want. For I often feel a
5 feebleness of soul, a languor of spirit, so that I cannot as I would press forward toward the mark.[88] This I am particularly sensible of when I am in company with serious, good-natured people, who are not alive to God, and yet say nothing that one can well reprove. I am then apt to sit silent, and make as it were a drawn battle. I want
10 vigour of spirit to break through, whether they will hear or whether they will forbear. Help me forward, my friend, by your prayers.

If that fever continues in the country still, you may cure all that are taken ill near you.[89] But it must be helped at the beginning. First, no bleeding, no blistering; these are extremely hurtful. Sec-
15 ondly, give the patient a pint of spring water sweetened with a large spoonful of treacle, lying down in bed. If this is taken at the beginning of the fever, I never once knew it fail.

How does the work of God now go on round about you? Is brother Cotty[90] able to preach? And can John Manners do anything? I want
20 much to know the particulars of Miss Romaine's[91] experience. I wish she would write to me. Do you find a growth in grace? In lowliness, meekness, patience? May our Lord make all grace to abound in you!

I am, my dear sister,
25 Your affectionate friend and brother,

J. Wesley

Address: 'To Mrs. Emma Moon'.
Source: published transcription; *WHS* 11 (1918): 174–75.

---

[88] See Phil. 3:14.

[89] The *Annual Register* for 1762 described an outbreak of disease that sounds like influenza: 'Numbers of people have been lately affected by colds, which attacked them with violent pains in the stomach, head, and bones; it is the opinion of the faculty that it is in the air, the distemper being so common' (London: Dodsley, 1763), 82.

[90] James Cotty was apparently already an itinerant preacher, though the first surviving Minutes that list him are in 1765 (10:304 in this edn.). He served up to the time of his death in 1780 (see 10:486).

[91] Miss Romaine was apparently a member of a Methodist society near Yarm.

To the Rev. Charles Wesley

LONDON
DECEMBER 11, 1762

[[Dear Brother,]]

For eighteen or twenty days I heard with both ears, but rarely opened my mouth. I think I now understand the affair, *at least* as well as any person in England.[92]
The sum is this: 1. The meeting in Beech Lane, before I came to town, was like a bear-garden, full of noise, brawling, cursing, swearing, blasphemy, and confusion. 2. Those who prayed were partly the occasion of this, by their horrid screaming, and unscriptural, enthusiastic expressions. 3. Being determined either 'to *mend* them or *end* them', I removed the meeting to the Foundery. 4. Immediately the noise, brawling, cursing, swearing, blasphemy, and confusion ceased. 5. There was less and less screaming and less of unscriptural and enthusiastic language. 6. Examining the society, I found about threescore persons who had been convinced of sin and near fourscore who were justified at these meetings. So that on the whole they have done some hurt and much good. I trust they will now do more good, and no hurt at all. Seven persons had left the society on this account; but four of them are come back already.

I bought the ground before Kingswood School of Margaret Ward, and paid for it with my own money. Certainly, therefore, I have a right to employ it as I please. What can any reasonable man say to the contrary?

I have answered the Bishop, and had advice upon my answer.[93] If the devil owes him a shame, he will reply. He is a man of sense, but I verily think he does not understand Greek!

I should be glad to see Mr. Nitschmann.[94] What is all beside loving faith! We join in love to Sally and you.

Adieu!

Address: 'To / The Revd Mr C. Wesley / in / Bristol'.
Postmark: '11/DE'. *Charge*: '4'.

---

[92] 'The affair' is the controversy over claims to instantaneous absolute perfection in the London society; see JW, *Journal*, Nov. 24–Dec. 8, 1762, 21:398–400 in this edn.

[93] JW had completed the manuscript of his *Letter to the Right Reverend the Lord Bishop of Gloucester* (William Warburton) in late November and sent it to CW to review; see 11:459–538 in this edn.

[94] Orig., 'Nitchman'. David Nitschmann (1695–1772), a Moravian bishop whom Wesley had met in Georgia; cf. 18:137, n. 9 in this edn.

Endorsement: in CW's hand, 'Dec. 11, 1763 [*sic*] B. slight-healer'.
Source: holograph; MARC, DDWes 3/18.

To the Rev. Samuel Furly

LONDON
DECEMBER 20, 1762

Dear Sammy,

Charles Perronet, the author of that remark on 2 Peter 3:13, does
5   not believe Christ will reign at all upon earth, nor any millennium
till we come to heaven. The argument by which he endeavours to
prove that St. Peter there speaks only to what will precede the day
of judgement is this: 'If those expressions, a "new heavens" and a
"new earth" refer only to this world where they occur in Isaiah,
10   then they refer to nothing more where they are used by St. Peter.'[95]
I should never have suspected Dr. Sherlock of writing anything
in a burlesque way. He never aimed at it in his controversy with Dr.
South, and seemed exceeding angry at his opponent for doing so.
Probably he knew himself to be overmatched by the Doctor, and
15   therefore did not care to engage him on his own ground. 'But why
should you be angry', says Dr. South, 'at wit? It *might* have pleased
God to make you a wit too.'[96]
I think the danger in writing to Bishop Warburton is rather that
of saying too much than too little. The least said is the soonest
20   amended, and leaves an ill-natured critic the least to take hold of.
I have therefore endeavoured to say as little upon each head as
possible. If he replies, I shall say more.[97] But I rather think he will
not, unless it be by a side stroke when he writes on some other
subject.

---

[95] Furly (and JW) were apparently referring to a manuscript by Perronet. In *AM* (1781)
JW published several items left in manuscript by Perronet at his death. This specific quotation
appears in none of these, nor in Perronet's tract *A Search into the Prophecies* (London, 1770).

[96] William Sherlock (1641–1707) published *A Vindication of the Doctrine of the Holy and
Ever-Blessed Trinity* in 1690. Robert South (1634–1716) responded with *Animadversions upon
Dr. Sherlock's book …* (1693). Sherlock replied in *A Defense of Dr. Sherlock's Notion of a Trinity
in Unity* (1694). South countered with *Tritheism Charged upon Dr. Sherlock's New Notion of
the Trinity* (1695). And Sherlock rebutted in *A Letter out of the Country to a Friend in the City*
(1695).

[97] Warburton did not reply, so JW did not elaborate.

How does the work of God prosper at Huddersfield and Slaithwaite? Do you begin to see the fruit of your labours? And does your
own soul prosper? What signifies all but this, to save our own souls
and them that hear us? I am, dear Sammy,
    Your affectionate friend and brother,   5

                                                        J. Wesley

Address: 'To / The Revd Mr Furly / At Slaithwait, near Huddersfield /
Yorkshire'.
Postmark: '21 / DE'. *Charge*: '4'.
Source: holograph; MARC, MAM JW 3/23.

To the Rev. Charles Wesley

[[Dear Brother,]]
    But how to come to the speech of the colliers is the question, as   10
there are an hundred miles between us, as this is too critical a time
for me to be out of London.
    I am satisfied with the learning of John Jones (as there is no point
of learning in debate between us) and the judgement of John Matthews, Charles Perronet, and James Morgan. Yet 'tis certain his ad-   15
mirers will still think him unanswerable.
    I believe several in London have imagined themselves saved from
sin 'upon the word of others', and these are easily known. For that
work does not stand. Such imaginations soon vanish away. Some
of these and two or three others are still wild, though I think Mrs.   20
[[Garbrand]] exceeds them all.[98]
    But the matter does not stick here. I could play with all these if
[[I could but set Thomas Maxfield]] right. He is *mali caput et fons*;[99]
so inimitably wrong-headed, and so absolutely unconvincible! And
yet (what is exceeding strange) God continues to bless his labours.   25

---

[98] Edward Perronet identifies this as the 'later famous Mrs. Garbrand of the Strand near
Brentford—whose *chief* accomplishments were her intemperate love ...', and describes her as
'a visionary enthusiast' (in a manuscript cited in 21:489, n. 35, and 21:428, n. 52 in this edn.).
[99] 'The head and fount of evil'.

My kind love to Sally!
[[Adieu.]]

I shall soon try your patience with a long letter.

Address: 'To / The Revd Mr Charles Wesley / at the New Room / Bristol'.
Postmark: '23/DE'. *Charge*: '4'.
Endorsement: in CW's hand, 'Dec. 23. 1762 / B. palliating'.
Source: holograph; MARC, DDWes 3/19.

1763
To the Rev. Charles Wesley

LONDON
JANUARY 5, 1763[1]

[[Dear Brother,]]

You take me right. I am far from pronouncing my remarks *ex cathedra*.[2] I only desire they may be fairly considered.

I was a little surprised to find Bishop Warburton so entirely unacquainted with the New Testament, and, notwithstanding all his parade of learning, I believe he is no critic in Greek.

If [[Thomas Maxfield]] continues as he is, it is impossible he should long continue with us. But I live in hope of better things. Meantime *festina lente!*[3]

I baptised two Turks two or three weeks ago. They *seem* to be strong in faith and their story is very probable, but I am not *sure* it is true. I wait for farther evidence.[4]

This week I have begun to speak my mind concerning five or six honest enthusiasts.[5] But I move only an hair's breadth at a time, and by this means we come nearer and nearer to each other. No sharpness will profit. There is need of a lady's hand as well as a lion's heart.

Mr. Whitefield has fallen upon *me* in public open-mouthed, and only not named my name. So has Mr. Madan.[6] But let them look to it. I go on my way. I have a sufficient answer as to George Bell but I will not give it before the time.[7]

We join in love to you both. My wife gains ground. She is quite peaceable and loving *to all*.

[[Adieu!]]

---

[1] Orig., '1762'; but both CW's endorsement and the content of the letter show that it was 1763.

[2] 'From the cathedral'; or with the authority of a papal edict. CW was reviewing JW's manuscript of the forthcoming *Letter to the ... Bishop of Gloucester* (William Warburton).

[3] 'Hasten slowly,' i.e., aim for an appropriate balance of speed and diligence.

[4] The 'Turks' turned out to have been impostors. See JW, *Journal*, Dec. 4, 1762 (21:399 in this edn.), and Jan. 5, 1763 (21:401–2); and JW to CW, Feb. 8 and Feb. 26, 1763.

[5] Referring to Thomas Maxfield, George Bell, and others; cf. JW to Maxfield, Nov. 2, 1762.

[6] Martin Madan had published *Some Quaeries Humbly Offered to Those who Profess Sinless Perfection*; see both his queries and JW's responses in 13:591–96 in this edn.

[7] See JW to the *London Chronicle*, Jan. 7, 1763.

Address: 'To / The Revd Mr Chas. Wesley / in Bristol'.

Postmark: '6 / IA' but with no place stamp. *Charge*: '4'.

Endorsement: in CW's hand, 'B. festina lente! / Jan. 5. 1763 / quot [illegible] tot errores!'.[8]

Source: holograph; MARC, DDWes 3/17.

To the Editor of the *London Chronicle*

WINDMILL HILL[9] [LONDON]
JANUARY 7, 1763

When I returned to London two or three months ago, I received various accounts of some meetings for prayer which had lately been
5 held by Mr. Bell[10] and a few others. But these accounts were contradictory to each other. Some highly applauded them, others utterly condemned; some affirmed they had done much good, others that they had done much hurt. This convinced me that it was requisite to proceed with caution and to do nothing rashly. The first point
10 was to form my own judgement, and that upon the fullest evidence. To this end I first talked with Mr. Bell himself, whom I knew to be an honest, well-meaning man. Next I told him they were at liberty, for a few times, to meet under my roof. They did so, both in the society room at the Foundery and in the chapel at West Street. By this
15 means I had an opportunity of hearing them myself, which I did at both places. I was present the next meeting after that which is mentioned by Mr. Dodd and Mr. Thompson in the *Public Ledger*.[11] The same things which they blame I blame also, and so I told him the same evening. And I was in hopes they would be done away, which
20 occasioned my waiting till this time. But having now lost that hope, I have given orders that they shall meet under my roof no more.

---

[8] 'As many [illegible] as errors'.

[9] The location of the Foundery.

[10] George Bell (fl. 1760s) was a corporal in the Life Guards, converted in London about 1758. In late 1761 through 1762 he presided over an enthusiastic prayer meeting in Beech Lane, London, which drew increasing attention (see JW to CW, Dec. 11, 1762). Bell eventually claimed unique spiritual privileges, the power to heal miraculously, and predicted that the world would end on Feb. 28, 1763. When Wesley resisted these claims, Bell withdrew from Methodism, never to return.

[11] No copy of the *Public Ledger* containing the account by Dodd and Thompson appears to survive.

What farther steps it will be necessary for me to take is a point I
have not yet determined.[12] I am, sir,
>   Your humble servant,

>   John Wesley

Source: published transcription; *London Chronicle* (Jan. 15–18, 1763),
p. 63; abridged reprint in *Scots Magazine* (Jan. 1763), p. 57.

To Jane Lee

>   LONDON   5
>   JANUARY 13, 1763

My Dear Sister,
>   Fasting does not always imply the totally abstaining from all food,
but the using a smaller quantity, or less pleasing food at one time
than at another.[13] I do not advise *you* to fast in the former sense. I   10
believe you ought not to do it. But if you fasted in the latter sense
on a Friday, you would find a blessing.
>   Certainly you do want more faith, more love, more of the image
of God. And is it not at hand? Look up and receive! O what have
you received already? And is there more yet? Only believe, and all   15
the promises are yea and amen![14] Today you may drink deeper into
his love than ever you have done yet! Let me hear from time to time,
how your soul prospers. I am, my dear sister,
>   Your affectionate brother,

>   J. Wesley   20

Address: 'To / Miss Jenny Lee'.
No *postmark* or indications of postal *charge*; apparently delivered by hand.
Source: holograph; Drew, Methodist Archives.

[12] See the follow-up letter of Feb. 29, where JW announces that Bell is no longer a Methodist.
[13] See JW, Sermon 27, 'Upon Our Lord's Sermon on the Mount, VII', I.2–5 (1:595–96 in this edn.), which distinguishes different degrees of fasting and abstinence.
[14] See 2 Cor. 1:20.

To the Rev. Thomas Maxfield

LONDON
JANUARY 26, 1763

My Dear Brother,

5 For many years I and all the preachers in connexion with me have taught that every believer may and ought to grow in grace. Lately you have taught or seemed to teach the contrary. The effect of this is, when I speak as I have done from the beginning those who believe what *you* say will not bear it. Nay, they will renounce con-10 nexion with us—as Mr. and Mrs. Coventry did last night.[15] This breach lies wholly upon *you*. You have contradicted what I taught from the beginning. Hence it is that many cannot bear it, but when I speak as I always have done, they separate from the society. Is this for *your* honour, or to the glory of God?

O Tommy, seek counsel, not from man, but God; not from brother 15 Bell, but Jesus Christ! I am,

Your affectionate brother,

J. W.

Source: published transcription; JW, *Journal*, Feb. 5, 1763 (21:405 in this edn.).

To the Rev. Charles Wesley

LONDON
FEBRUARY 8, 1763

20 [[Dear Brother,]]

I think now the sooner you could be here the better, for the mask is thrown off. George Bell, John Dixon, Joseph Calvert, Benjamin Biggs, etc., etc., have quitted the society and renounced all fellowship with us.[16] I wrote to Thomas [Maxfield], but was not favoured 25 with an answer. This morning I wrote a second time, and received

---

[15] This is recounted in JW, *Journal*, Jan. 25, 1763, 21:403 in this edn.

[16] JW details several members of the London society withdrawing in *Journal*, Jan. 28–Feb. 5, 21:403–6 in this edn.

an answer indeed! The substance is, 'You take too much upon you. We *will not* come up.'

I know all the history of the Turk.[17] I must leave London on Friday to bury Mrs. Perronet. She died on Saturday morning.[18]

The answer to the Bishop (who has broke his leg) is forthcoming.[19] Mr. Madan wrote the *Queries*.[20] I let him have the last word. I should not wonder if a *dying* saint were to prophesy. Listen to Sally Colston's last words![21]

Molly Westall died last week in huge triumph.[22]

John Jones does good. I have seen the Colonel.[23] James Morgan has lately been in a violent storm, and is scarce alive.[24] I advise him to retire to Kingswood for a season. We need all your prayers. God is preparing thoroughly to purge his floor.[25] O let us be instant εὐκαίρως ἀκαίρως![26]

We join in love to Sally.

[[Adieu!]]

Address: 'To / The Revd Mr C. Wesley / in / Bristol'.

Postmark: '8/FE'. *Charge*: '4'.

Endorsement: in CW's hand: 'B. Feb. 8. 1763 himself / confirming my prophecy of the Ranters'.

Source: holograph; MARC, DDWes 3/20.

[17] Cf. JW to CW, Jan. 5, 1763.

[18] JW administered the Lord's Supper to Charity (Goodhew) Perronet, the wife of Vincent Perronet, on Jan. 10 (21:402, n. 44 in this edn.) and performed her funeral on Feb. 11 (21:406).

[19] JW's lengthy *Letter to the Right Rev. the Lord Bishop of Gloucester* was published in March 1763 in London and Dublin.

[20] *Some Quaeries Humbly Offered to Those who Profess Sinless Perfection*; see both Madan's queries and JW's (unpublished) responses in 13:591–96 in this edn.

[21] Sarah Colston (or Coulston) was a member of the Bristol society; see her letter to JW, June 6, 1745, published in JW, *Journal*, Aug. 12, 1745, 20:82–83 in this edn.

[22] Molly was likely the wife of the itinerant Thomas Westell (whose last name JW often spelled Westall); on Thomas, see 26:222 in this edn.

[23] Bartholomew Gallatin (d. 1779), a Swiss army officer who become a British citizen in 1737 and rose to the rank of Lieutenant Colonel in the British Army by 1759; cf. 26:432 in this edn.

[24] Morgan had sided with John Wesley in his differences with Thomas Maxfield, as revealed in the letter from Maxfield to JW, Dec. 28, 1761.

[25] See Matt. 3:12; Luke 3:17.

[26] 'In season, out of season' (2 Tim. 4:2).

To the Printer of the *London Chronicle*

LONDON
FEBRUARY 9, 1763

Sir,

I take this opportunity of informing all whom it may concern
5 1. that Mr. Bell is not a member of our society;[27] 2. that I do not believe either the end of the world or any signal calamity will be on the
28th instant;[28] and 3. that not one in fifty (perhaps not one in five
hundred) of the people called Methodists believe any more than I
do either this or any other of his prophecies. I am, sir,
10   Your humble servant,

John Wesley

Source: published transcription; *London Chronicle* (Feb. 8–10, 1763),
p. 143.

To the Rev. Charles Wesley

LONDON
FEBRUARY 26, 1763

[[Dear Brother,]]
15 I perceive *verba fiunt mortuo*;[29] so I say no more about your coming to London. Here stand I; and I *shall* stand, with or without human help, if God is with me.[30]

Yesterday Mr. Madan and I, with a few more, gave the full hearing
to the famous Turk and his associate.[31] He is an exquisite wretch—
20 was originally a Spanish Jew, afterwards a Turk, then a papist, then
a Jew again, then a Protestant, and now at last (under Mr. Lom-

---

[27] George Bell withdrew from the London society on Feb. 4; see JW, *Journal*, 21:403 in
this edn.

[28] JW's *Journal* for Feb. 28 states that he spoke at Spitalfields and 'largely showed the
absurdity of the supposition that the world was to end that night' and then 'went to bed at my
usual time and was fast asleep by ten o'clock' (21:407 in this edn.).

[29] Cf. Plautus, *Poenulus* ('The Little Carthaginian'), Act 4, Scene 2 (l. 840) '*verba faciet
mortuo*'; 'They would be words for a dead man'.

[30] Echoing the words of Martin Luther at the Diet (Council) of Worms.

[31] See JW to CW, Feb. 8, 1763, referring to JW's baptism of two Muslims.

bardi's wing) a zealous papist! Concerning his companion we are still in doubt. We *fear* he is little better, though we cannot prove it.

Mr. Gaussen tells us the stroke will come tomorrow evening; the rest say not till Monday.[32] Let us live today!

I labour for peace; but they still make themselves ready for battle. 5
Peace be with you and yours!

Adieu!

Address: 'To / The Revd Mr Wesley / in / Bristol'.
Postmark: '28 / FE' or '26 / FE' (unclear). *Charge*: '4'.
Endorsement: in CW's hand, 'Febr. [[Fb]] 26, 1763; B[rother]'s [[of prophets]] / Turks & Prophets'.
Source: holograph; MARC, DDWes 3/21.

To the Rev. Charles Wesley

LONDON
MARCH 6, 1763

[[Dear Brother,]] 10

Tomorrow I set out for Norwich, which I have delayed as long as possible. I am likely to have rough work there, but the turbulent spirits must bend or break.[33]

That story of Thomas Maxfield is not true. But I doubt more is true than is good. He is a most incomprehensible creature. I can- 15 not convince him that separation is any evil, or that speaking in the name of God, when God has not spoken, is any more than an *innocent mistake*. I know not what to say to him or do with him. He is really *mali caput et fons*.[34]

Mr. Neal has grievously peached his associates. But I shall not 20 hastily saddle myself with him and his seven children.

The week after Easter week I hope to visit the classes in Bristol, or the week following. James Morgan is love-sick, John Jones

---

[32] Referring to George Bell's prophecy of the end of the world.

[33] Despite his apprehensions, JW's *Journal* for Mar. 8ff (21:408 in this edn.) indicates that he spent 'a few quiet, comfortable days in Norwich, Yarmouth, and Colchester, without any jar or contention'.

[34] 'The head and source of [the] evil'; perhaps a version of the more common expression, *fons et origo mali*, 'the source and origin of [the] evil.'

physic-sick; so that I have scarce one hearty helper but Lawrence Coughlan![35] We join in love to you both.

    Adieu!

Address: 'To / The Revd Mr Wesley in / Bristol'.
Postmark: '8/MR'. *Charge*: '4'.
Endorsement: in CW's hand, 'B. of Prophet Md / March 6. 1763'.
Source: holograph; MARC, DDWes 3/22.

To the Rev. Samuel Furly

Norwich
March 10, 1763

Dear Sammy,

    When we revised the notes on St. Peter, our brethren were all of the same opinion with you. So we set Charles's criticism aside, and let the note stand as it was.[36]

    I have not read Dr. Newton on the *Prophecies*.[37] But the bare text of the Revelation from the time I first read it satisfied me as to the general doctrine of the millennium. But of the particulars I am willingly ignorant since they are not revealed.[38]

    I scarce ever yet repented of saying too little, but frequently of saying too much. To the Bishop I have said more than I usually do, and I believe as much as the occasion requires. But I spare him. If he replies, I shall probably speak more plainly, if[39] not more largely.[40]

---

[35] Lawrence Coughlan (d. 1784), an Irish Catholic convert to Methodism, was an itinerant preacher by 1758. He was one of the preachers ordained by Gerasimos Avlonites in 1764, then by Anglican Bishop Richard Terrick in 1765. He was sent as a SPCK missionary to Conception Bay, Newfoundland, 1767–73. See Atmore, *Memorial*, 80–83; and Vickers, *Dictionary*, 80.

[36] It is unclear if the note in question related specifically to 2 Pet. 3:13, which Furly had made a focus of an earlier inquiry; see JW to Furly, Dec. 20, 1762.

[37] Isaac Newton's *Observations upon the Prophecies of Daniel, and the Apocalypse of St. John*, 2 vols. (Dublin: S. Powell, 1733).

[38] While disavowing any claim to certainty, JW retained in *NT Notes*, in the comments on Rev. 20:4–5, the suggestion by Johann Albrecht Bengel that there will be two distinct millennia, with Christ's second advent occurring after the first millennial age, but prior to the second.

[39] Orig., in Telford, 'it'.

[40] Another reference to William Warburton, Bishop of Gloucester.

A notion has lately started up in London, originally borrowed from the Moravians, which quite outshoots my notions of perfection as belonging only to fathers in Christ—namely, that every man is saved from all (inward) *sin* when he is justified, and that there is *no sin*, neither anger, pride, nor any other, in *his heart* from that moment unless he loses justifying faith.[41]

How will you disprove this position? In particular, by what New Testament authority can you overthrow it? These questions have puzzled many poor plain people. I should be glad of your answer to them at large.

It is a doubt whether I shall be able to leave London this summer, unless now and then for a week or two. Next week I am to return thither.—I am, dear Sammy,

> yours affectionately,
>
> [John Wesley]

Source: published transcription; Telford, *Letters*, 4:204–5.

To the Editor of *Lloyd's Evening Post*[42]

[LONDON]
MARCH 18, 1763

Sir,

A pert, empty, self-sufficient man who calls himself 'Philodemas' (I hope not akin to Samuel Johnson in the *Public Ledger*[43]) made use of your paper a few days ago to throw abundance of dirt at the people called Methodists. He takes occasion from the idle prophecy of Mr. Bell, with whom the Methodists, so called, have nothing to do, as he is not, nor has been for some time, a member of their society.[44] Had he advanced anything new or any particular charge, it would have deserved a particular answer. But as his letter contains nothing

---

[41] JW wrote Sermon 13, 'On Sin in Believers' (1:317–34 in this edn.) eighteen days later, in response to this set of issues; see JW, *Journal*, Mar. 28, 1763, 21:408 in this edn.

[42] Replying to the letter of 'Philodemas' in *Lloyd's Evening Post* (Mar. 2–4, 1763).

[43] Samuel Johnson contributed a 'Weekly Correspondent' column in the *Public Ledger* in the early 1760s.

[44] See JW to the editor of the *London Chronicle*, Feb. 9, 1763, stating formally that Bell was no longer a member of the Wesleyan society.

but dull, stale, general slanders, which have been confuted ten times over, it would be abusing the patience of your readers to say any more concerning it. To Bishop Warburton, bringing particular charges, I have given particular answers, I hope to the satisfaction
5 of every reasonable and impartial man.[45]

    I am, sir,
        Your humble servant,

                               John Wesley

Source: published transcription; *Lloyd's Evening Post* (Mar. 21–23, 1763), p. 275.[46]

To Selina (Shirley) Hastings, Countess of Huntingdon

LONDON
10 [MARCH 20, 1763[47]]

My Lady,
    For a considerable time I have had it much upon my mind to write a few lines to your Ladyship; although I cannot learn that your Ladyship has ever inquired whether I was living or dead. By
15 the mercy of God I am still alive, and following the work to which He has called me; although without any help, even in the most trying times, from those I might have expected it from. Their voice seemed to be rather, 'Down with him—down with him, even to the ground.' I mean (for I use no ceremony or circumlocution) Mr.
20 Madan, Mr. Haweis,[48] Mr. Berridge, and (I am sorry to say it) Mr. Whitefield. Only Mr. Romaine has shown a truly sympathising

---

[45] Referring to JW, *Letter to the Right Rev. the Lord Bishop of Gloucester* (11:467–538 in this edn.).

[46] The editor added the following comments after the letter: 'It cannot be interesting to the public to have a controversy on points of a religious nature carried on in a newspaper. We have inserted a letter signed Philodemas, and now give our readers one from Mr. Wesley in answer to it. We have received another letter from Philodemas, which for the reason above-mentioned, is left at the publisher's.'

[47] The letter as given in Seymour is undated, but he also gives the Countess's endorsement that it was received on Mar. 21.

[48] Thomas Haweis (1734–1820), a native of Cornwall, had studied at Oxford but did not take a degree there. He had been ordained as deacon and priest by Thomas Secker, then serving as Dean of St. Paul's, London, in 1757. He served as Martin Madan's curate at the Lock Chapel, London, and subsequently as rector of All Saints', Northampton. In later life he was chaplain to Lady Huntingdon and kept her personal papers.

spirit and acted the part of a brother. I am the more surprised at this because he owed me nothing, only the love which we all owe one another. He was not my son in the gospel, neither do I know that he ever received any help through me. So much the more welcome was his kindness now. The Lord repay it sevenfold into his bosom![49]

As to the prophecies of those poor, wild men, George Bell and half a dozen more, I am not a jot more accountable for them than Mr. Whitefield is; having never countenanced them in any degree, but opposed them from the moment I heard them. Neither have these extravagances any foundation in any doctrine which I teach. The loving God with all our heart, soul, and strength, and the loving all men as Christ loved us, is and ever was, for these thirty years, the sum of what I deliver, as pure religion and undefiled.

However, if I am bereaved of my children, I am bereaved! The will of the Lord be done!

> Poor and helpless as I am,
> Thou dost for my vileness care:
> Thou hast called me by my name!
> Thou dost all my burdens bear.[50]

Wishing your Ladyship a continual increase of all blessings, I am, my Lady,

Your Ladyship's servant for Christ's sake,

John Wesley

Endorsement: 'Received at Brightstone,[51] March 21, 1763'.
Source: published transcription; Seymour, *Huntingdon*, 1:329–30.

[49] Apparently Lady Huntingdon gave William Romaine this letter and asked for his comment on it. A part of his letter to her, dated Mar. 26, was as follows: 'Enclosed is poor Mr. John's letter. The contents of it, as far as I am concerned, surprised me, for no one has spoken more freely of what is now passing among the people than myself. Indeed, I have not preached so much as others whose names he mentions, nor could I. My subject is one and I dare not vary from it. The more I read and preach upon the all-sufficiency of the adorable Jesus, the more I am determined to know nothing but him and him crucified. But whatever stands in my way of exalting him I would tread upon it as the merest dross and dung. A perfection out of Christ, call it grace, and say it is grace from him, yet with me it is all rank pride and damnable sin. Oh! Madam, we should be careful of his glory and not give it to another, least of all to ourselves .... I pity Mr. John from my heart. His societies are in great confusion, and the point which brought them into the wilderness of rant and madness is still insisted on as much as ever. I fear the end of this delusion. As the late alarming providence has not had its proper effect, and "perfection" is still the cry, God will certainly give them up to some more dreadful thing. May their eyes be opened before it be too late!' (in Seymour, *Huntingdon*, 1:330).

[50] Cf. CW, Hymn VI, st. 5, *Hymns for Times of Trouble and Persecution* (1744), 13.

[51] I.e., 'Brighthelmstone'; now known as Brighton.

To an Unidentified Woman

LONDON
MARCH 21, 1763

My Dear Sister,

5 My coming into the country is quite uncertain till I see what turn
things here will take. I am glad to hear the work of God prospers
among you.

[Yours affectionately,

John Wesley]

Source: published transcription; Telford, *Letters*, 4:207.

To the Editor of the *London Chronicle*

LONDON
APRIL 5, 1763

10

Sir,

Some time since, I heard a man in the street bawling, 'The Scripture Doctrine of Imputed Righteousness asserted and maintained
by the Rev. John Wesley!'[52] I was a little surprised, not having pub-
15 lished anything on the head; and more so when, upon reading it
over, I found not one line of it was mine, though I remembered
to have *read* something like it. Soon after (to show what I really
do maintain) I published *Thoughts on the Imputed Righteousness of
Christ*,[53] mentioning therein that 'pious fraud' which constrained
20 me so to do.

The *modest* author of the former publication now prints a second edition of it, and faces me down before all the world—yea, and
proves that it is *mine*!

Would you not wonder by what argument? Oh, the plainest in
25 the world. 'There is not', says he, 'the least fraud in the publication nor imposition on Mr. Wesley, for the words are transcribed

---

[52] I.e., selling the first edition of a booklet of this title published anonymously by William
Mason around 1760–61; see 13:367–69 in this edn.

[53] Published in 1762; see 13:370–74 in this edn.

from the ninth and tenth volumes of his *Christian Library*.' But the
Christian Library is not Mr. Wesley's writing. It is 'Extracts from
and Abridgements of' other writers; the subject of which I highly
approve, but I will not be accountable for every expression. Much
less will I *father* eight pages of I know not what which a shameless   5
man has picked out of that work, tacked together in the manner he
thought good, and then published in my name.

He puts me in mind of what occurred some years since. A man
was stretching his throat near Moorfields and screaming out, 'A
full and true account of the death of the Rev. George Whitefield!'   10
One took hold of him, and said, 'Sirrah! what do you mean? Mr.
Whitefield is yonder before you.' He shrugged up his shoulders,
and said, 'Why, sir, an honest man must do something to *turn a
penny*.' I am, sir,

     Your humble servant,   15

                   John Wesley

Source: published transcription; *London Chronicle* (Apr. 5–7, 1763),
pp. 335–36.

To Jane Catherine March

[LONDON]
APRIL 7, 1763

The true gospel touches the very edge both of Calvinism and   20
Antinomianism, so that nothing but the mighty power of God can
prevent our sliding either into the one or the other.

The nicest point of all which relates to Christian perfection is
that which you inquire of. Thus much is certain: they that love
God with all their heart and all men as themselves are scriptur-   25
ally perfect. And surely such there are, otherwise the promise of
God would be a mere mockery of human weakness. Hold fast this.
But then remember on the other hand, you have this treasure in an
earthen vessel; you dwell in a poor, shattered house of clay, which
presses down the immortal spirit. Hence all your thoughts, words,   30
and actions are so imperfect, so far from coming up to the standard

(that law of love which, but for the corruptible body, your soul
would answer in all instances), that you may well say till you go to
him you love,

5   Every moment, Lord, I need
           The merit of thy death.[54]

John Wesley

Source: published transcription; *Methodist Magazine* 22 (1799): 149–50.

To an Unidentified Friend

[c. May 1763]

10   At your instance I undertake the irksome task of looking back
upon things which I wish to forget for ever. I have had innumerable
proofs (though such as it would now be an endless task to collect
together) of all the facts which I recite. And I recite them as briefly
as possible, because I do not desire to aggravate anything, but barely
15   to place it in a true light.
    1. Mr. Maxfield was justified while I was praying with him in
Baldwin Street, Bristol.[55]
    2. Not long after, he was employed by me as a preacher in London.
    3. Hereby he had access to Mrs. Maxfield,[56] whom otherwise he
20   was never likely to see, much less to marry; from whence all his
outward prosperity had its rise.
    4. He was by *me* (by those who did it at *my* instance) recom-
mended to the Bishop of Derry to be ordained priest, who told him

---

[54] CW, 'Isaiah 32:2', st. 5, *HSP* (1742), 146.
    [55] JW described Maxfield's dramatic conversion experience in a letter of May 28, 1739 to
John Hutton (25:653 in this edn.), and then in his *Journal* for May 21, 1739 (19:61 in this edn.).
However, a note in a ms. by Edward Perronet stated that Maxfield himself claimed to have been
converted under the influence of George Whitefield (see 21:408, n. 67).
    [56] Elizabeth, née Branford, one of George Whitefield's early followers, who was indepen-
dently wealthy.

then (I had it from his own mouth), 'Mr. Maxfield, I ordain *you* to assist that good man, that he may not work himself to death.'[57]

5. When a few years ago many censured him much, I continually and strenuously defended him, though to the disgusting several of the preachers and a great number of the people.

6. I disgusted them, not barely by defending him but by commending him in strong terms from time to time, both in public and private, with regard to his uprightness as well as usefulness.

7. All this time Mr. Maxfield was complaining (of which I was frequently informed by those to whom he spoke) that he was 'never so ill represented by the rabble in Cornwall' as by *me* and my brother.

8. Four or five years since, a few persons were appointed to meet weekly at the Foundery. When I left London, I left these under Mr. Maxfield's care, desiring them to regard *him* just as they did *me*.

9. Not long after I was gone, some of these had dreams, visions, or impressions, as they thought from God. Mr. Maxfield did not put a stop to these. Rather he encouraged them.

10. When I returned, I opposed them with my might, and in a short time heard no more of them. Meanwhile, I defended and commended Mr. Maxfield as before and, when I left the town again, left them under his care.

11. Presently visions and revelations returned. Mr. Maxfield did not discourage them. Herewith was now joined a contempt of such as had them not, with a belief that they were proofs of the highest grace.

12. Some of our preachers opposed them roughly. At this, they took fire and refused to hear them preach but crowded after Mr. Maxfield. He took no pains to quench the fire, but rather availed himself of it to disunite them from other preachers and attach them to himself. He likewise continually told them they were 'not to be *taught by man*', especially by those who had *less grace than themselves*. I was told of this likewise from time to time. But he denied it. And I would not believe evil of *my friend*.

13. When I returned October 1762, I found the society in an uproar and several of Mr. Maxfield's most intimate friends formed into a detached body. Enthusiasm, pride, and great uncharitableness appeared in many who once had much grace. I very tenderly reproved them. They would not bear it. One of them, Mrs. Coventry, cried out, 'We will not be browbeaten any longer; we will *throw*

---

[57] Maxfield was ordained by William Barnard, who was Bishop of Derry from 1747 to the time of his death in 1768.

off the mask.' Accordingly a few days after, she came and, before an hundred persons, brought me hers and her husband's tickets and said, 'Sir, we will have no more to do with *you*; Mr. Maxfield is our teacher.' Soon after, several more left the society (one of whom was George Bell), saying, '*Blind* John is not capable of teaching *us*; we will keep to Mr. Maxfield.'

14. From the time that I heard of George Bell's prophecy I explicitly declared against it, both in private in the society, in preaching, over and over, and at length in the public papers. Mr. Maxfield made no such declaration.[58] I have reason to think he believed it. I know many of his friends did, and several of them sat up the last of February, at the house of his most intimate friend, Mr. [Benjamin] Biggs, in full expectation of the accomplishment.

15. About this time one of our stewards,[59] who at *my desire* took the chapel in Snowsfields *for my use*, sent me word, 'The chapel was *his*, and Mr. Bell should exhort there whether I would or no.' Upon this, I desired the next preacher there to inform the congregation that while things stood thus, neither I nor our preachers could in conscience preach there any more.

16. Nevertheless, Mr. Maxfield did preach there. On this, I sent him a note, desiring him not to do it and adding, 'If you do, you thereby renounce connexion with *me*.'

17. Receiving this, he said, 'I *will* preach at Snowsfields.' He did so and *thereby* renounced connexion. On *this* point and no other we divided. By *this* act the knot was cut. Resolving to do this, he told Mr. Clementson, 'I am to preach at the Foundery no more.'

18. From this time, he has spoke all manner of evil of *me*, his father, his friend, his greatest earthly benefactor. I cite Mr. [John] Fletcher for one witness of this and Mr. [Martin] Madan for another. Did he speak evil of me to Mr. Fletcher one day only? Nay, but every day, for six weeks together. To Mr. Madan he said (among a thousand other things, which he had been twenty years raking together), 'Mr. Wesley *believed and countenanced all* which Mr. Bell said. And the *reason* of our parting was *this*. He said to me one day, "Tommy, I will tell the people, you are the greatest gospel preacher in England. And you shall tell them, I am the greatest." For *refusing to do this* Mr. Wesley put me away!'

---

[58] In *A Vindication of the Rev. Mr. Maxfield's Conduct* (London, 1767), Maxfield states that he consistently tried to keep Bell and the others 'within bounds', and when he heard Bell's prophecy he immediately 'stood up and set aside all that he had said about it' (p. 16).

[59] Maxfield identifies the steward as 'Mr. Arvin' (ibid., pp. 9–10).

Now, with perfect calmness, and I verily think without the least touch of prejudice, I refer to your own judgement, what connexion I ought to have with Mr. Maxfield, either till I am satisfied these things are not so, or till he is thoroughly sensible of his fault.

Source: published transcription; JW, *Journal*, April 28, 1763 (21:408–11 in this edn.).

To an Unidentified Man

[c. May 1763] 5

⟨…[60]⟩ not so ⟨…⟩
⟨…⟩ receive the sense they ⟨…⟩
which I have been insisting on ⟨…⟩
And I do not know that ⟨…⟩ Guilford[61] ⟨had any other⟩ objection to
them than I ⟨…⟩ more or less, than 'By grace ⟨ye are⟩ saved through 10
faith'?[62] And whenever we give up this fundamental truth, the work of God, by us, will come to an end.

It is true, saving faith is both the gift and the work of God; yea, and a work of omnipotence. But still this does not exclude any man, because God is ready to work it in every man, there being nothing 15
more sure, taking the words in a sound sense, than that 'every man may believe, if he will'.

The matters in question between Mr. Maxfield and me may sleep till I have the pleasure of seeing you. Wishing you all light and love, I remain, dear sir, 20
Your affectionate brother and servant,

J. Wesley

Source: holograph; MARC, MAM JW 6/43 (fragmentary and mounted, no address or postmark visible).

[60] At least the top third of the page is missing or tattered, resulting in several holes where reconstruction is essentially impossible.
[61] Joseph Guilford (d. 1777) had been a soldier, was converted under the influence of Thomas Olivers, and became an itinerant in 1761; see Atmore, *Memorial*, 169–71.
[62] Eph. 2:8.

Letter Endorsing John Johnson

I desire that none of our preachers would oppose John Johnson, but rather assist him all they can. I have no objection to his preach-
5   ing in any of our societies.

John Wesley

Source: holograph; privately held (current owner unknown, Wesley Works Editorial Project Archive includes a transcription by Frank Baker).

To Sir Archibald Grant, 2nd Baronet[63]

Sir,
10   Mr. Naish returns you his sincere[64] thanks for your seasonable relief.
On Saturday the 21st instant, I expect to be at Edinburgh, and on the Tuesday evening following at Aberdeen. I apprehend you will hardly be in the country so soon, otherwise I should gladly have
15   waited upon you there.
I am, sir,
Your most obedient servant,

John Wesley

Address: 'To / Sir Archibald Grant, Bart / At Duncan Grant's Esq / in Redlion Square / Holborn'.

[63] JW made the acquaintance of Sir Archibald Grant, 2nd Baronet (1696–1778), in May 4–7, 1761 (*Journal*, 21:318–19 in this edn.), and visited his estate at Monymusk in Aberdeenshire again on June 7, 1764 (21:469) and June 10, 1766 (22:43). From 1729 through his expulsion from Parliament in 1731, Grant had been a member of the Parliamentary Gaols Committee, which visited Fleet and Marshalsea prisons, which may have given him a special sensitivity to the needs of Mr. Naish now in Fleet prison. See *ODNB*.

[64] Orig., 'you his sincere you his sincere'; duplicating words from one line to the next.

Endorsement: 'Mr John Westley / Abt charity to Mr Naish / In Fleet prison / Recd 9th May 1763'.
Source: holograph; Edinburgh, National Records of Scotland, Grant Family of Monymusk Papers, GD345/1169/1/24.

To Penelope (Madan) Maitland[65]

[LONDON]
MAY 12, 1763

Dear Madam,

Both in the former and in the farther Thoughts on Perfection[66] I have said all I have to say on that head. Nevertheless, as you seem to desire it, I will add a few words more. 5

As to *the word*, it is scriptural. Therefore neither you nor I can in conscience object against it, unless we would send the Holy Ghost to school and teach him to speak who made the tongue.

By that word I *mean* (as I have said again and again) 'so loving 10 God and our neighbour as to rejoice evermore, pray without ceasing, and in everything give thanks'.[67] He that experiences this is scripturally perfect. And if you do not yet, you may experience it. You surely will, if you follow hard after it, for the Scripture cannot be broken. 15

What, then, does their arguing prove who object against 'perfection'? Absolute and infallible perfection? I never contended for it. Sinless perfection? Neither do I contend *for this*, seeing the term is not scriptural. A perfection that fulfils the whole law, and so needs not the merits of Christ? I acknowledge none such—I do now, and 20 always did, protest against it.

'But is there no sin in those that are "perfect"?' I believe not, but be that as it may, they feel none, no temper but pure love while they rejoice, pray and give thanks continually. And whether sin is *suspended* or *extinguished*, I will not dispute; it is enough that they 25

---

[65] Penelope Maitland (1730–1805), was one of nine children of Martin Madan (Sr.) and Judith Cowper Madan, and a sister of the Rev. Martin Madan. She married General Sir Alexander Maitland in 1754. JW is replying to her letter of May 2, 1763.

[66] I.e., both in 'Thoughts on Christian Perfection' (1760; 13:54–80 in this edn.) and *Farther Thoughts upon Christian Perfection* (1762; 13:92–131).

[67] See 1 Thess. 5:16–18.

feel nothing but love. This you allow we should daily press after. And this is all I contend for. O may God give you to taste of it today! I am, dear madam,
        Your very affectionate servant,

5
                                              J. Wesley

Source: published transcription; *WHS* 5 (1906): 145–46, which is taken from a commonplace book in the Madan family and more complete than *AM* 20 (1797): 351–52.

To Jane Lee

ABERDEEN
MAY 26, 1763

My Dear Sister,
    If you are likely to fall into a consumption, I believe nothing will
10 save your life, but the living two or three months upon buttermilk churned daily in a bottle.[68] Change of air may do something, if you add riding every day. Else it will avail but little.
    Your conscience will not be clear unless you find fault wherever occasion requires. Thou shalt in any wise rebuke thy brother, and
15 not suffer sin upon him.[69] Regard none who speak otherwise; you have but one rule, the oracles of God. His Spirit will always guide you according to his Word. Keep close to him, and pray for, dear Jenny,
        Your affectionate brother,
20
                                              J. Wesley

Address: 'To / Miss Jenny Lee'.
Seal: red, broken, '*Nuntia Pacis*'.
No *postmark* or indications of postal *charge*; apparently delivered by hand.
Source: holograph; Upper Room Museum, L-183.

[68] 'Consumption' was the common term denoting the latter stages of tuberculosis up to the 1750s. Jane Lee's sister Elizabeth had died of the disease in March 1762. Wesley prescribed buttermilk for consumption in his *Primitive Physick*, s.v. 'Consumption'.
[69] See Lev. 19:17.

To Ann Foard[70]

NEWCASTLE-UPON-TYNE
JUNE 3, 1763

My Dear Sister,

I take your writing exceeding kindly, particularly at this time. You
do refresh my bowels in the Lord. Sometimes I thought there was   5
a kind of strangeness in your behaviour. But I am now persuaded
it sprung only from caution, not from want of love. When you believed you had the pure love of God, you were not deceived. You
really had a degree of it, and s‹ee[71]› that you let it not go. Hold th‹e›
beginning of your confidence steadfast unto the end. Christ and all   10
he has is yours! Never quit your hold! Woman, remember the faith!
The Lord increase it in you sevenfold! How wonderfully does he
often bring to our remembrance what we have read or heard long
ago? And all is good which he sanctifies. My dear sister, continue to
love and pray for,   15
        Your affectionate brother,

J. Wesley

Address: 'Miss Foard'.
No *postmark* or indications of postal *charge*; apparently delivered by hand.
Source: holograph; MARC, MAM JW 3/1.

To the Rev. Henry Venn

BIRMINGHAM
JUNE 22, 1763[72]

Reverend and Dear Sir,   20

Having at length a few hours to spare, I sit down to answer your
last, which was particularly acceptable to me, because it was wrote

---

[70] Ann Foard (1741–99) was a native of Southwark, London. She had joined a Methodist
society in 1761, and in 1772 married John Thornton, an undertaker. Wesley carried on correspondence with her from this date through the time of her marriage.

[71] The manuscript has a missing fragment at this point and in the next line.

[72] Orig., in *AM* '1765'; a clear misprint as JW was in Ireland at this time in 1765. He was
in Birmingham on June 22, 1763, according to his *Journal*.

with so great openness. I shall write with the same. And herein you and I are just fit to converse together, because we both like to speak blunt and plain, without going a great way round about. I shall likewise take this opportunity of explaining myself on some other
5   heads. I want you to understand me inside and out. Then I say, *Sic sum: si placeo, utere.*[73]

Were I allowed to boast myself a little, I would say I want[74] no man living; I mean, none but those who are now connected with me, and who bless God for that connexion. With these I am able
10   to go through every part of the work to which I am called. Yet I have laboured after union with all whom I believe to be united with Christ. I have sought it again and again, but in vain. They were resolved to stand aloof. And when one and another sincere minister of Christ has been inclined to come nearer to me, others have dili-
15   gently kept them off, as though thereby they did God service.

To this poor end the doctrine of perfection has been brought in head and shoulders. And when such concessions were made as would abundantly satisfy any fair and candid man, they were no nearer; rather farther off, for they had no desire to be satisfied.
20   To make this *dear* breach wider and wider, stories were carefully gleaned up, improved, yea invented and retailed, both concerning me and 'the perfect ones'. And when anything very bad has come to hand, some have rejoiced as though they had found great spoils.

By this means, chiefly, the distance between you and me has in-
25   creased ever since you came to Huddersfield. And perhaps it has not been lessened by that honest, well-meaning man Mr. Burnett[75] and by others, who have talked largely of my dogmaticalness, love of power, errors, and irregularities. My dogmaticalness is neither more nor less than a 'custom of coming to the point at once',[76] and
30   telling my mind flat and plain without any preface or ceremony. I could, indeed, premise something of my own imbecility, littleness of judgement, and the like: but 1) I have no time to lose, I must dispatch the matter as soon as possible; 2) I do not think it frank or ingenuous. I think these prefaces are mere artifice.

---

[73] Terence, *Phormio*, Act 3, Scene 2 (l. 527), 'That's how I am. If you like me, do business with me' (Loeb).

[74] I.e., lack or need.

[75] Orig., 'Burnet'. Rev. George Burnett had been curate of Huddersfield from 1759, curate of Elland (four miles away from Huddersfield) from 1761, and perpetual curate there from 1762 until the time of his death in 1793.

[76] JW is apparently echoing Venn's self-description back to him, as he does later in the letter.

The *power* I *have* I never *sought*. It was the undesired, unexpected result of the work God was pleased to work by me. I have a thousand times sought to devolve it on others, but as yet I cannot. I therefore suffer it till I can find any to ease me of my burden.

If any one will convince me of my *errors*, I will heartily thank him. I believe all the Bible as far as I understand it, and am ready to be convinced. If I am a heretic, I became such by reading the Bible. All my notions I drew from thence, and with little help from men, unless in the single point of justification by faith. But I impose my notions upon none; I will be bold to say there is no man living farther from it. I make no opinion the term of union with any man. I think, and let think. What I want is holiness of heart and life. They who have this are my brother, sister, and mother.[77]

'But you hold perfection.' True; that is, loving God with *all* our heart, and serving him with *all* our strength.[78] I teach nothing more, nothing less than this. And whatever infirmity, defect, ἀνομία,[79] is consistent with this, any man may teach and I shall not contradict him.

As to *irregularity*, I hope none of those who cause it do then complain of it. Will they throw a man into the dirt and beat him because he is dirty? Of all men living, those clergymen ought not to complain who believe I preach the gospel (as to the substance of it). If they do not ask me to preach in their churches, *they* are accountable for my preaching in the fields.

I come now directly to your letter, in hopes of establishing a good understanding between us. I agreed to suspend for a twelvemonth our stated preaching at Huddersfield, which had been there these many years.[80] If this answered your end, I am glad; my end it did not answer at all. Instead of coming nearer to me, you got farther off. I heard of it from every quarter, though few knew that I did, for I saw no cause to speak against *you* because you did against *me*. I wanted you to do more, not less good, and therefore durst not do or say anything to hinder it. And, lest I should hinder it, I will make a farther trial and suspend the preaching at Huddersfield for another year.

1. To clear the case between us a little farther. I must now adopt your words: 'I, no less than you, preach justification by faith only, the absolute necessity of holiness, the increasing mortification of

---

[77] See Matt. 12:50 and parallels.

[78] See Deut. 6:5, Luke 10:27, and parallels.

[79] 'Matters not legal in nature'.

[80] JW's earlier discussion with Venn is described in JW's letters to Ebenezer Blackwell on July 16, 1761 and Aug. 15, 1761.

sin, and rejection of all past experiences and attainments. I abhor, as you do, all antinomian abuse of the doctrine of Christ, and desire to see my people walking even as he walked. Is it, then, worth while, in order to gratify a few bigoted persons or for the sake of
5   the minute differences between us', to encourage 'all the train of evils which follow *contention for opinions* in little matters as much as in great?'

   2. If I was as strenuous with regard to perfection on one side as you have been on the other, I should deny you to be *a sufficient*
10   preacher. But this I never did. And yet I assure you I can advance such reasons for all I teach as would puzzle you and all that condemn me to answer, but I am sick of disputing. Let them beat the air and triumph without an opponent.

   3. 'None', you say, 'preach in your houses who do not hold the
15   very same doctrine with you.' This is not exactly the case. You are welcome to preach in any of those houses, as I know we agree in the main points, and whereinsoever we differ you would not preach there contrary to me. 'But would it not give you pain to have any other teacher come among those committed to your charge, so as
20   to have your plan disconcerted, your labours depreciated, and the affections of your flock alienated?' It has given me pain when I had reason to fear this was done, both at Leeds, Birstall, and elsewhere. And I was 'under a temptation of speaking against you', but I refrained even among my intimate friends. So far was I from publicly
25   warning my people against one I firmly believed to be much better than myself.

   4. Indeed, I trust 'the bad blood is now taken away'. Let it return no more. Let us begin such a correspondence as has never been yet, and let us avow it before all mankind. Not content with not weaken-
30   ing each other's hands, or speaking against each other directly or indirectly (which may be effectually done under the notion of exposing this and that error), let us defend each other's characters to the uttermost against either ill- or well-meaning evil-speakers. I am not satisfied with 'be very civil to the Methodists, but have nothing to
35   do with them'. No, I desire to have a league offensive and defensive with every soldier of Christ. We have not only one faith, one hope, one Lord,[81] but are directly engaged in one warfare. We are carrying the war into the devil's own quarters, who therefore summons all his hosts to war. Come, then, ye that love him, to the help of the
40   Lord, to the help of the Lord against the mighty! I am now wellnigh

----

[81] See Eph. 4:5.

miles emeritus senex, sexagenarius;[82] yet I trust to fight a little longer.
Come and strengthen the hands till you supply the place of,
   Your weak but affectionate brother,

John Wesley

Source: published transcription; *Arminian Magazine* 5 (1782): 495–99.

To the Rev. Richard Hart[83]

LONDON   5
JULY 11, 1763

Dear Sir,

Abundance of business has prevented my writing so soon as I
desired and intended, nor have I time now to write so largely as I
could wish, and as your openness and frankness would otherwise   10
constrain me to do. But I cannot delay any longer to write a little,
lest I should seem to slight your correspondence.

What you before observed is of great importance, viz., 'If it be the
professed aim of the gospel to convince us that *Jesus* is the *Christ*; if
I, a sinner, am convinced of the reality of this fact, am not I, who be-   15
lieve, authorised to expect life, not through any condition, or any act,
inward or outward, performed by me, but singly through the name
which Jesus assumed, which stands for his whole character or merit?'

Here is the hinge on which Mr. Sandeman's whole system turns.[84]
This is the strength of his cause, and you have proposed it with all   20
the strength and clearness which he himself could devise.

Yet suffer me to offer to your consideration a few queries concerning it.

---

[82] 'An old, retired soldier, sixty years of age.' *Miles emeritus* was a common Latin phrase
designating a retired Roman soldier who was eligible to receive land in payment for his services.
JW typically celebrated his birthday on the 28th of June (recalculated relative to the Gregorian
calendar), so when he wrote this letter he was within a week of his sixtieth birthday.

[83] Richard Hart (c. 1727–1808) studied at Oxford (Christ Church) and was ordained
priest in 1752 by Edward Willes, Bishop of Bath and Wells. He was curate at Freshford, Somerset, then vicar of St. George's, Bristol, in the vicinity of Kingswood, from 1759. JW noted in
1759 that he had delayed Methodist preaching so as not to coincide with a stated time at which
Hart was to preach; *Journal*, Sept. 27, 1759, 21:230–31 in this edn.

[84] See JW, *Sufficient Answer to 'Letter to the Author of "Theron and Aspasio'* " (1757;
13:345–56 in this edn.), a book published by Robert Sandeman.

Is every one who is convinced of the reality of this fact, 'Jesus is the Christ', a gospel believer? Is not the devil convinced of the reality of this fact? Is, then, the devil a gospel believer?[85]

5   I was convinced of the reality of this fact when I was twelve years old,[86] when I was without God in the world.[87] Was I then a gospel believer? Was I then a child of God? Was I then in a state of salvation?

Again, you say, 'I who believe am authorised to expect life, not through any condition or act, inward or outward, performed by me.'

'I who believe.' But cannot you as well expect it without believing? If not, what is believing but a condition? For it is something *sine qua non*.[88] And what else do you, or I, or any one living mean by a condition? And is not believing an inward act? What is it else? But you say, 'not performed by me'. By whom, then? God gives me the power to believe. But does he believe for me? He works faith in me.

15   But still is it not I that believe? And if so, is not believing an inward act performed by me?

Is not, then, this hypothesis (to waive all other difficulties) contradictory to itself?

I have just set down a few hints as they occurred. Wishing you an

20   increase of every blessing, I am, dear sir,

Your very affectionate brother,

John Wesley

Source: published transcription; *Arminian Magazine* 20 (1797): 360–61.

To Dorothy Furly

LONDON
JULY 16, 1763

25   My Dear Sister,

1. So far as I know what will make me most holy and most useful, I know what is the will of God.

---

[85] A point made in JW, Sermon 1, 'Salvation by Faith', I.2, 1:119–20 in this edn.

[86] See JW, *A Second Letter to the Author of 'The Enthusiasm of Methodists and Papists Compared'*, § 14, 11:394 in this edn.

[87] See Eph. 2:12.

[88] 'Without which, not,' i.e., a necessary condition without which the claim could not be true.

2. Certainly it is possible for persons to be as devoted to God in a married as in a single state.

3. I believe John Downes is thoroughly desirous of being wholly devoted to God, and that if you alter your condition at all, you cannot choose a more proper person.[89]

I am, my dear sister,
        Your affectionate brother,

John Wesley

Source: published transcription; Benson, *Works*, 16:327–28.

To Eliza Bennis[90]

My Dear Sister,

You did well to write. This is one of the means which God generally uses to convey either light or comfort. Even while you are writing you will often find relief; frequently while we propose a doubt it is removed.

There is no doubt but what you at first experienced was a real foretaste of the blessing, although you were not properly possessed of it till the Whitsunday following.[91] But it is very possible to cast away the gift of God, or to lose it by little and little, though I trust this is not the case with you. And yet you may frequently be in heaviness, and may find your love to God not near so warm at some times as it is at others. Many wanderings likewise, and many deficiencies, are consistent with pure love, but the thing you want is the abiding witness of the Spirit touching this very thing. And this you

---

[89] Dorothy Furly married John Downes in June 1764.

[90] This is JW's first letter to Eliza Bennis (1725–1802), replying to her letter of Aug. 2. JW would write at least 26 more letters to Bennis by Dec. 1776. A native of Limerick, Bennis had been married in 1744 (maiden name unknown), and was converted in 1749 under the influence of Methodist preachers in her area. She and her husband later moved to Waterford and then to Philadelphia in the 1790s, where she died in 1802.

[91] Bennis's Aug. 2 letter to JW described an experience of entire sanctification that occurred at the Lord's Supper on Pentecost Sunday 1763.

may boldly claim on the warrant of *that* word, 'We have received the Spirit that is of God, that we may *know the things which are freely given to us of God.*'[92]

    I am, my dear sister,
5   Your affectionate brother,

John Wesley

Source: published transcription; Bennis, *Correspondence*, 11–12.

To Christopher Hopper

BRISTOL
SEPTEMBER 3, 1763

My Dear Brother,
10   I am much inclined to think you will be more useful this year than ever you have been in your life. From the first hour abate nothing of our Rules, whether of society or bands. Be a Methodist all over. Be exact in everything. Be zealous. Be active. Press on to the one thing,[93] and carry all before you. How much may be done before
15 summer is at an end! Their little misunderstandings at Edinburgh you will soon remove by hearing the parties face to face.[94] I hope a preacher is gone northward, and brother Roberts come southward.[95] I hate delay. The King's business requires haste![96]

    I am, with love to sister Hopper,
20   Yours most affectionately,

J. Wesley

[92] 1 Cor. 2:12.

[93] See Luke 10:42.

[94] Hopper's 'Autobiography' indicates that he was in London for the Conference in July (19–23), and then was assigned to Edinburgh. He and his wife lived in 'a little dark room at Edinburgh, encompassed round with old black walls, disagreeable enough, but we had a good season; many poor sinners were converted to God. We saw the fruit of our labours, and rejoiced' (*EMP* 1:212).

[95] Robert Roberts (1731–99) was a native of Upton near Chester who became an itinerant preacher in 1759; cf. letter of Nov. 2, 1763 (below), in which Wesley complains of his lack of punctuality. Roberts was named in the Deed of Declaration of 1784. See Atmore, *Memorial*, 367–73; and *EMP*, 2:262–76.

[96] See 1 Sam. 21:8.

Take the field everywhere as often as possible. Who goes to the Highlands, now, quickly?

Address: 'To / Mr Hopper'.
Source: holograph; Bridwell Library (SMU).

To George Merryweather

LONDON
OCTOBER 5, 1763

My Dear Brother   5
Your letter was sent from hence to Bristol. But I had left Bristol before it came.[97]
I have no objection to Mr. [Peter] Jaco's coming to Yarm to open the house. But I suppose he cannot stay long. He will soon be wanted again in his own circuit.   10
It is strange that the number of hearers should decrease if you have regular preaching. I hope the morning preaching is never omitted. If it be, everything will droop.
What relates to the account I will give Mr. Franks. Probably he will find where the mistake lies.[98]   15
O be in earnest! I am,
      Your affectionate brother,

J. Wesley

Address: 'To / Mr George Merryweather / in Yarm / Yorkshire'.
Postmark: '4/OC'. *Charge*: '4'.
Endorsement: 'Octr 1763 / On Mr Jaco's opening / the Chapel'.
Source: holograph; Wesley's Chapel (London), LDWMM/1998/ 6888/1-2.

---

[97] JW left Bristol on Sept. 27.

[98] Samuel Franks continued as JW's book steward and accountant at the Foundery. The reverse of the address side of the letter sheet has detailed accounting figures in Franks's hand referring to the accounts of Peter Jaco.

To Lady Frances (Erskine) Gardiner[99]

WELLING
NOVEMBER 2, 1763

My Dear Lady,

You are again a messenger of glad tidings. Many were formerly of
5 opinion that our preaching would not be received in north Britain,
and that we could be of no use there. But they had forgotten that the
Lord sendeth by whom he *will* send and that he hath the hearts of
all men in his hand. I have never seen the fields more white for the
harvest than they were from Edinburgh to Aberdeen last summer.[100]
10 And if I live to take another journey into the north, especially if I
should have a little more time to spare, I doubt not I should find an
open door as far as Caithness[101] and perhaps the Isles of Orkney.

The harvest surely has not been more plenteous for many hundred years. But there is the same complaint still, the labourers are
15 few.[102] We found this particularly at our last Conference. We had
none to spare, and very hardly enough to supply our stated circuits.
Mr. [Robert] Roberts was allotted for Newcastle circuit, whence I
have had complaint upon complaint. He ought to have been there
long ago. Several congregations have suffered loss for want of him.
20 All our preachers should be as punctual as the sun, never standing
still or moving out of their course.

I trust your Ladyship is still pressing on to the mark, expecting and receiving blessing upon blessing. O how can we sufficiently
praise him who deals so bountifully with us! I am, my dear Lady
25   Your affectionate servant,

John Wesley

Address: 'To / The Right Honourable / The Lady Frances Gardiner / in /
Edinburgh'.
Postmark: '3/NO'. *Charge*: '6'.
Source: holograph; MARC, MAM JW 3/26.

[99] This is the only surviving letter from JW to Lady Frances Gardiner (d. 1766), the
widow of Col. James Gardiner and the daughter of David Erskine, fourth Lord of Candross
and ninth Earl of Buchan. Her husband, Col. Gardiner, had been killed at the Battle of
Prestonpans in the 1745 Highland uprising. JW had read Philip Doddridge's *Some Remarkable
Passages in the Life of the Honourable Colonel James Gardiner* in 1747 (*Journal*, Oct. 20, 1747,
21:195 in this edn.), and in 1751 he rode by Preston Field and saw the place of battle (*Journal*,
Apr. 24, 1751, 20:385). Lady Gardiner wrote to JW on July 25, 1763, that she had heard him
preach at the High School yard in Edinburgh on May 29 of that year. See *ODNB*.
[100] See John 4:35.
[101] Orig., 'Cathness'.
[102] See Matt. 9:37 and parallels.

To Christopher Hopper

WELLING
NOVEMBER 2, 1763

My Dear brother,

'Dundee', you say, 'would be thankful for a preacher.' But who would give him things needful for the body? He cannot live upon air, 5 and we now expect that Scotland should bear its own burden. John Hampson you must think of no more. But I doubt our Newcastle friends are out of all patience for want of Robert Roberts. In spring you will need a fourth preacher. But what would he have to do?

Why, then, I think you must get the plat without Canongate.[103] 10 'The earth is the Lord's and the fullness thereof.'[104] Sevenpence halfpenny! Pshaw! Let it be eightpence, even money. By-and-by we may give Mr. Trail more work.[105] O let us work in this fruitful season! We join in love to sister Hopper and you. I am,

Yours affectionately, 15

[John Wesley]

Source: published transcription; Jackson, *Works* (3rd), 12:291.

To Dorothy Furly

LEWISHAM
DECEMBER 15, 1763

My Dear Sister,

It has seemed to me for some time that God will not suffer Cor- 20 nelius Bastable to *live* at Cork.[106] He may starve there, but he cannot live. The people are not worthy of him.

---

[103] This would be the land in Low Calton, on which construction began on an octagonal chapel the following year; cf. JW, *Journal*, Apr. 24, 1765, 21:504 in this edn.

[104] Ps. 24:1.

[105] This may be the same Mr. Trail in Bristol later, about whose preaching JW had some concerns; see JW to CW, Jan. 11, 1765.

[106] Remember that Bastable had married Catherine Stockdale of Cork in 1752. The couple would return to Bristol after JW's judgment about the prospects of staying in Cork proved correct.

Salvation from sin is a deeper and higher work than either you or Sarah Ryan can conceive. But do not imagine (as we are continually prone to do) that it lies in an indivisible point. You experienced a taste of it when you were justified, you since experienced the thing itself, only in a low degree, and God gave you his Spirit that you might know the things which he had freely given you. Hold fast the beginning of your confidence steadfast unto the end. You are continually apt to throw away what you have for what you want. However, you are right in looking for a farther instantaneous change as well as a constant gradual one. But it is not good for you to be quite alone. You should converse frequently as well as freely with Miss Johnson,[107] and any other that is much alive. You have great need of this.

    I am, my dear sister,
        Your affectionate brother,

                         J. Wesley

Source: published transcription; Benson, *Works*, 16:328.

---

[107] Elizabeth ('Betsy') Johnson (1720–98), whom JW frequently commended as a spiritual example and counsellor, especially to women; see 23:281, n. 13 in this edn.

1764

To Selina (Shirley) Hastings, Countess of Huntingdon

LONDON
JANUARY 8, 1764

My Lady,

Shall I tell your Ladyship just what is in my mind, without any disguise or reserve? I believe it will be best so to do. And I think 5
your Ladyship can bear it.

'When Lady Huntingdon' (says my brother) 'invites me to Brighthempston,[1] will you bear me company?' I answered, 'Yes', being under no apprehension of his claiming my promise suddenly. And indeed I was perfectly indifferent about it, being in no 10
want of employment. It was therefore little concern to me, that Mr. Whitefield, Madan, Romaine, Berridge, Haweis were sent for over and over, and as much notice taken of my brother and me, as of a couple of postillions. It only confirmed me in the judgment I had formed for many years, I am too rough a preacher for tender ears. 15
'No, that is not it; but you preach perfection.' What! Without why or wherefore? Among the unawakened? Among babes in Christ? No. To these I say not a word about it. I have two or three grains of common sense. If I do not know how to suit my discourse to my audience at these years, I ought never to preach more. 20

But I am grieved for your Ladyship. This is no mark of catholic spirit, but of great narrowness of spirit. I do not say this because I have any desire to preach at Brighthelmstone.[2] I could not now if your Ladyship desired it, for I am engaged every week till I go to Bristol in my way either to Ireland or Scotland. 25

But this I wish even your perfection, the establishment of your soul in love! I am, my Lady,

Your Ladyship's affectionate and obedient servant,

John Wesley

Address: 'To / The Right Honourable / The Countess of Huntingdon / At Brighthempston / Sussex'.

[1] One of a number of variations on the name of the city that is now Brighton.
[2] Another variant for Brighton.

347

Seal: red, very complete, two birds and 'L'Amitie'.
Postmark: '9/IA'.
Source: holograph; Cambridge, The Cheshunt Foundation, Westminster
College, Archives, E4/3/1.

To the Rev. Samuel Furly

LONDON
JANUARY 14, 1764

Dear Sammy,
    I shall never think much of paying postage for a letter from *you*.
5 We are all here now in great peace, and God is both widening and
deepening his work.
    In that text I generally consider, 1) what is implied in 'gaining the
whole world', 2) what in losing one's own soul, and then 3) what an
ill bargain it would be to gain the whole world at that price.[3]
10   I hope you are still pressing on to the mark[4] and counting all
things loss for the excellency of the knowledge of Christ.[5] I am
(with love to Nancy), dear Sammy,
        Your affectionate brother,

John Wesley

Address: 'To / Miss Gideon'.[6]
No *postmark* or indications of postal *charge*; apparently delivered by hand.
Source: holograph; Harvard University, Houghton Library, MS Hyde 77
(5.372).

---

[3] Mark 8:36. See Wesley's later sermon, 'The Important Question' (3:180–98 in this edn.), which follows this three-point outline.
[4] See Phil. 3:14.
[5] See Phil. 3:8.
[6] This address may indicate that a Miss Gideon was to deliver the letter to Furly by hand; CW mentions a Miss Gideon assisting him in London, in a letter to his wife on July 3, 1764.

To John Valton[7]

LONDON
JANUARY 31, 1764

It is certainly right, with all possible care to abstain from all outward evil, but this profits only a little. The inward change is the one thing needful for you.[8] You must be born again, or you will never   5
gain an uniform and lasting liberty. Your whole soul is diseased, or rather dead, dead to God, dead in sin. Awake, then, and arise from the dead, and Christ shall give you light.[9] To seek for a particular deliverance from one sin only is mere lost labour. If it could be attained, it would be little worth, for another would arise in its place;   10
but indeed, it cannot before there is a general deliverance from the guilt and power of all sin. This is the thing which you want, and which you should be continually seeking for. You want to be justified freely from all things, through the redemption which is in Jesus Christ. It might be of use if you should read over the first volume   15
of *Sermons* seriously and with prayer.[10] Indeed, nothing will avail without prayer. Pray, whether you can or not. When you are cheerful, and when you are heavy, still pray. Pray with many or with few words, or with none at all. You will surely find an answer of peace. And why not now?   20
    I am, etc.

J. W.

Source: published transcription; *Arminian Magazine* 6 (1783): 406–7.

---

[7] This is the first letter from JW to John Francis Valton (1740–94), a native of London who became an itinerant preacher in 1775. He had been assigned in December 1763 to the royal gunpowder magazine (depot) at Purfleet on the Thames in Essex, east of London, and had a conversion experience early in 1764 following his receiving this letter. See Atmore, *Memorial*, 431–36; and *EMP*, 6:1–136.

[8] See Luke 10:42.

[9] See Eph. 5:14; and CW's sermon on this text, 'Awake, Thou That Sleepest', 1:142–58 in this edn.

[10] The first volume of JW's *Sermons on Several Occasions* focused on the need for awakening, repentance, and the new birth.

To Thomas Hanson[11]

LONDON
FEBRUARY 15, 1764

Dear Tommy,
    Brother [Samuel] Franks received the bill you mention.
5   I wish Ev. Wall[12] may be able to procure business. It is not an easy thing.
    The old proverb says, 'half is more than the whole'. Certainly half the people who called themselves a society, well united together, are better than twice as many, who are only as a rope of sand.
10   If the country societies are thoroughly regulated, they are well able to maintain one preacher. Indeed they *must* for I will no longer burden others for *them*.
    If the elderly man and woman (you should have told me their names) are real Christians, let them come into the house directly.
15   If you are not yet cleansed from all sin, believe, and you shall be.
I am, dear Tommy,
            Your affectionate friend and brother,

J. Wesley

Address: 'To / Mr Hanson / At the Tabernacle, in / Norwich'.
Postmark: '16/FE'.
Source: holograph; WMC Museum.

To Thomas Hanson[13]

LONDON
FEBRUARY 25, 1764

20   Dear Tommy,
    Thomas Mott[14] is inclined to teach school at Norwich. I am in-

---

[11] Thomas Hanson (d. 1804) was a native of Yorkshire who became an itinerant preacher c. 1760. He appears in the Minutes of Conference from 1765 (10:304 in this edn.) through at least 1791 (10:763). See *EMP*, 6:201–10.

[12] The first name appears over a fold in the letter and is illegible. It could be 'Ew', and a third letter of the name may be in the fold. This Mr. Wall has not been identified.

[13] The last name is not given, but Thomas Hanson was serving as an itinerant in Norwich at the time, as seen from the letter of Feb. 15 above.

[14] Thomas Mott (also sp. 'Motte') was admitted as a preacher in 1769, according to the early Methodist historian William Myles, *Chronological History of the People Called Methodists*

clined to think it might do well. And when you judge it proper, I hope he may likewise be of use in preaching.

I thank sister Flight[15] for her letter. Go on, in the name of God, and prosper. I am,

Your affectionate brother,   5

J. Wesley

No *address* or *postage* marks appear on back side.

Source: holograph; Naperville, Illinois, North Central College, Oesterle Library Special Collections, Philip and Elsie Sang Autograph Collection.

To the Rev. Charles Wesley

London
March 1, 1764

[[Dear Brother,]]   10

If the parties require it, I will re-hear the cause of William Warren and Abraham Ore.[16] But I do not apprehend there is anything to be said, more than what you have heard already.

I read Rollin's *Belles-Lettres* several years ago. Some things I liked, some I did not. Mark in him what you admire, and I will give   15 it a second reading and a farther consideration.[17]

You 'have no thoughts of venturing to London before May'! Then I must indeed 'do the best I can'. So I will comply with the advice

---

of the Connexion of the Late Rev. John Wesley (London, third edition, 1803), 302. He served in Ireland on the Tandragee circuit in 1770 (see 10:383 in this edn.) and died at Kilwarlin in that circuit in the summer of 1771 (see JW, *Journal*, July 1, 1771, 22:283 in this edn.).

[15] A society member named Mary Flight appeared in the earliest class lists from Norwich, in 1785, and was listed as a class leader in 1788: Norfolk Record Office document FC16/1, 'A list of the Societys [*sic*] in the Norwich Circuit 1785'.

[16] Nothing is known of this matter beyond this reference, apparently a matter of discipline in the Bristol society.

[17] Charles Rollin, *De la Manière d'Enseigner et d'Étudier les Belles Lettres* (4 vols.; Paris, 1726–28); published in English as *The Method of Teaching and Studying the Belles Lettres* (4 vols.; London, 1734).

of the stewards, as well as my own judgement, and insist upon John
Jones's assisting me on Sunday.[18] I have delayed all this time purely
out of tenderness to *you*.

    [[Adieu.]]

5

Address: 'To / The Revd Mr C. Wesley in / Bristol'.
Postmark: 'BATH'. *Charge*: '4'.
Endorsement: in CW's hand, 'B. Mar. 1. 1764 / ordaining J. J. in pure ten-
    der / ness to me!'
Source: holograph; MARC, DDWes 3/23.

To Jane (Lee) Freeman[19]

LONDON
MARCH 2, 1764

My Dear Sister,

Such love as yours is need not be ashamed. You must make me
amends for anything past that looks unkind by altering it for the
time to come.

10

You have no reason to doubt of the work of God. It partly shines
by its own light. And when that is not sufficient (as in times of
temptation), a clear witness shall be superadded. And see that you
strengthen your brethren, particularly those who are tempted to
give up their confidence. O lift up the hands that hang down![20] Help
those especially who did once taste of pure love.

15

---

[18] To enable John Jones to assist him fully, JW arranged for him to be ordained a priest
by a man who claimed to be the (Greek) Orthodox Bishop Erasmus (Gerasimos Avlonites) of
Arcadia in Crete; cf. A. B. Sackett, 'John Wesley and the Greek Orthodox Bishop' in *WHS* 38
(1971–72): 81–88, 97–102. This explains CW's comment in his endorsement about 'ordaining
J. J.'. Jones continued to serve as JW's assistant until 1769, when he left the post for health
reasons. Jones was subsequently (re-)ordained by Richard Terrick, Bishop of London in 1770
and took a parish. He remained friendly with the Wesley brothers, but was no longer active in
Methodist circles.

[19] This is JW's first letter to the former Jane Esther Lee, after her marriage in Oct. 1763
to James Freeman, a local preacher from Dublin; cf. *WHS* 8 (1912): 98.

[20] See Heb. 12:12.

My will has nothing to do in my coming over this spring. If a ship be ready, I shall embark.[21] O Jenny, look up and receive more! I am,
        Your affectionate brother,

                                                                    J. Wesley

Address: 'To / Mrs Jane Freeman'.
No *postmark* or indications of postal *charge*; apparently delivered by hand.
Endorsement: 'Revd J. Wesley to / Jane Freeman / 2 March 64'.
Source: holograph; MARC, MAM JW 3/7.

To the Rev. Samuel Furly

                                                        LEWISHAM
                                                    MARCH 6, 1764

Dear Sammy,
    After showing what is implied in 'gaining the whole world,' and what in 'losing our own soul,'[22] I ask how is it possible that any man should consent to gain the whole world at the price of losing his own soul? How amazing is it that any man living should do this? But in order to abate this amazement, consider the suppositions on which he proceeds: 1) that a life of sin is a life of happiness, 2) that a life of religion is a life of misery, and 3) that he shall certainly live twenty, forty, or sixty years. Under the second of these articles you have a fair occasion of describing both false and true religion.
    For eight or ten weeks Mr. [Thomas] Maxfield has been laid up by a lingering illness. This has contributed not a little to the peace of our society, who in general mind one thing, to save their own souls, and seldom strike first, though they sometimes strike again, especially when they are attacked without fear or wit, which has generally been the case.
    You have encouragement to go on at Slaithwaite, seeing already your labour is not in vain. I hope you add private to public application, visiting the poor people from house to house, and distributing

---

[21] JW did not return to Ireland until May 1765.
[22] Mark 8:36; this biblical passage and its application had been the subject of JW's previous letter to Furly on Jan. 14.

little books. By this means only that deplorable ignorance will be removed.

I doubt you had a dunce for a tutor at Cambridge, and so *set out*
wrong. Did he never tell you that, of all men living, a clergyman
should '*talk* with the vulgar'? Yea, and *write*, imitating the language
of the *common people* throughout, so far as consists with *purity* and
propriety of speech? *Easiness*, therefore, is the first, second, and
third point; and *stiffness*, *apparent* exactness, *artificialness* of style,
the main defect to be avoided, next to solecism and impropriety.[23]

You *point* wrong, Sammy; you aim at a wrong mark. If he was a
standard for any one (which I cannot possibly allow), yet Dr. Middleton[24] is no standard for a preacher; no, not for a preacher before
the University. His diction is stiff, formal, affected, unnatural. The
art glares, and therefore shocks a man of true taste. Always to talk or
write like him would be as absurd as always to walk in minuet step.
O tread natural, tread easy, only not careless. Do not blunder or
shamble into impropriety. If you *will* imitate, imitate Mr. Addison
or Dr. Swift.[25] You will then both save trouble and do more good.

I am, with love to Nancy, dear Sammy,

          Your ever affectionate brother,

                                                J. Wesley

Address: 'To / The Revd Mr Furly / At Slaithwaite / Near Huddersfield
/ Yorkshire'.
Postmark: '6/MR'. *Charge*: '4'.
Source: holograph; Buckhannon, West Virginia, West Virginia Wesleyan
    College, Annie Merner Pfeiffer Library, West Virginia Annual Con-
    ference (United Methodist Church) Archives.

---

[23] Wesley consistently claimed to write and speak in a natural and 'familiar' style. The
preface to JW, *Sermons on Several Occasions*, vol. 1, claimed that 'Nothing here appears in an
elaborate, elegant, or oratorical dress' (par. 2), and 'I design plain truth for plain people' (par.
3); see 1:103–4 in this edn. Similarly, in 'Directions concerning Pronunciation and Gesture',
JW exhorts, 'Endeavour to speak in public just as you do in common conversation. Attend to
your subject, and deliver it in the same manner as if you were talking of it to a friend' (vol. 16
in this edn.).

[24] Dr. Conyers Middleton (1683–1750), to whom Wesley had addressed a lengthy letter
on Jan. 4, 1749, refuting Middleton's claim that miraculous gifts ceased in the Christian church
after the period of the apostles, was taken by some eighteenth-century writers as an exemplar
of prose. See vol. 14 in this edn.

[25] Joseph Addison (1672–1719) was known not only for his prose writings but also for
sacred poetry. Jonathan Swift (1667–1745), who had been Dean of St. Patrick's Cathedral,
Dublin, was among Wesley's most favoured authors.

To an Unidentified Woman[26]

WEDNESBURY
MARCH 25, 1764

My Dear Sister,

I am glad you wrote, and that you write so freely. There needs no reserve between you and me. It is very easy for you to judge 5 concerning what you have heard. Who are they that 'always praise me' (that is, to my face)? I really know none such. *You* are said to do so. But I think you are clear of the accusation. Certain it is, then, I cleave to none *upon this account*. For I know not the men.

But you 'do not take those to be your real friends who tell you 10 what they think wrong'. Do I not take Sally Ryan and Mary Bosanquet to be my real friends? And certainly they have told me more of this kind than all the world besides.

Do you now find an uninterrupted communion with God? Is he in *all* your thoughts? In what sense do you pray always and in ev- 15 erything give thanks? Are you always happy? Is your will wholly subject to the will of God? Do you feel no repugnance to any of his dispensations? Continue to pray for, my dear sister,

  Your affectionate brother,

              J. W. 20

Source: JW's transcribed copy; MARC, MA 1977/157, JW III.7, item numbered '111'.

---

[26] During his preaching tour in 1764 JW transcribed into a notebook a set of exchanges with an unidentified woman. Telford supposed that the woman was Sarah Ryan, and titled JW's letters of Mar. 25 and Apr. 23 accordingly (*Letters*, 4:233, 240). But JW's reference to Ryan in this letter is as a third party, not the letter recipient. Moreover, the tone of this set of exchanges does not fit the 'reprimand' letter that JW sends Sarah Ryan in June 28, 1766. Perhaps the most that can be said with confidence is that the recipient of this letter was currently associated with Sarah Ryan and Mary Bosanquet. One possibility would be Sarah Crosby.

To the Rev. Thomas Hartley[27]

DERBY
MARCH 27, 1764

Dear Sir,

5   Your book on the millennium and the mystic writers was lately
put into my hands.[28] I cannot but thank you for your strong and
seasonable confirmation of that comfortable doctrine, of which I
cannot entertain the least doubt as long as I believe the Bible. I
thank you likewise for your remarks on that bad performance of
the Bishop of Gloucester, which undoubtedly tears up by the roots
10 all real, internal religion.[29] Yet at the same time I cannot but bewail
your vehement attachment to the mystic writers, with whom I conversed much for several years, and whom I then admired perhaps
more than you do now. But I found at length an absolute necessity
of giving up either them or the Bible. So after some time I fixed
15 my choice, to which I hope to adhere to my life's end. It is only the
extreme attachment to these which can account for the following
words: 'Mr. Wesley does in several parts of his Journals lay down
some marks of the new birth, not only doubtful but exceptionable,
as particularly where persons appeared agitated or convulsed under
20 the ministry, which might be owing to other causes rather than any
regenerating work of God's Spirit' (p. 385).

Is this *true*? In what *one* part of my Journals do I lay down any
doubtful, much less exceptionable, marks of the new birth? In no
part do I lay down those agitations or convulsions as any marks of
25 it at all. Nay, I *expressly declare* the contrary in those very words
which the Bishop himself cites from my Journal. I declare, 'These
are of a disputable nature: they may be from God, they may be from
nature, they may be from the devil.'[30] How is it, then, that you tell

[27] Thomas Hartley (1708/9–84), a native of London, had been educated at St. John's
College, Cambridge. Ordained priest in 1732, he was rector of Winwick, Northamptonshire,
from 1744. See *ODNB*.
[28] Thomas Hartley, *Paradise Restored: Or, a Testimony to the Doctrine of the Blessed Millennium, or Christ's Glorious Reign with His Saints on Earth: To which is added A Short Defence
of the Mystical Writers, written against The Doctrine of Grace, issued by Bishop Warburton in 1763*
(London, 1764). Wesley began reading this work on Feb. 5, and commented on the work in his
Journal for that date (21:442–43 in this edn.).
[29] William Warburton, *The Doctrine of Grace*. The first edition is dated 1763, but released
in Nov. 1762; when JW began his response, *Letter to ... Bishop of Gloucester*, 11:459–538 in
this edn.
[30] Cf. JW, *Journal*, June 22, 1739, 19:73 in this edn.

all the world Mr. Wesley lays them down in his Journals as marks of the new birth?

Is it *kind*? Would it not have been far more kind, suppose I had spoken wrong, to tell me of it in a *private* manner? How much more unkind was it to accuse me to all the world of a fault which I never 5 committed!

Is it *wise* thus to put a sword into the hands of our common enemy? Are we not both fighting the battle of our Lord against the world as well as the flesh and the devil?[31] And shall I furnish them with weapons against *you*, or you against *me*? Fine diversion for the 10 children of the devil! And how much more would they be diverted if *I* would furnish my quota of the entertainment by falling upon *you* in return! But I bewail the change in your spirit. You have not gained *more* lowliness or meekness since I knew you. O beware! You did not use to *despise* any one. This you have *gained* from the authors 15 you admire. They do not express *anger* toward their opponents, but *contempt* in the highest degree. And this, I am afraid, is far more antichristian, more diabolical, than the other. The God of love deliver you and me from this spirit and fill us with the mind that was in Christ. So prays, dear sir, 20

Your still affectionate brother,

J. Wesley

Source: published transcription; *Arminian Magazine* 6 (1783): 498–500.

To an Unidentified Assistant or Helper

SHEFFIELD
MARCH 29, 1764

My Dear Brother, 25

Is it true that you have baptised several children since the conference? If it is, I cannot but interpret it as a clear renunciation of connexion with us. And if this be the case, it will not be proper for

---

[31] Cf. the BCP Litany, 'from all the deceits of the world, the flesh, and the devil, *Good Lord, deliver us*'.

you to preach any longer in our societies. But the land is wide. You have room enough to turn to the right hand or to the left.[32] I am,
    Your affectionate brother,

J. Wesley

No *address, postmarks*, or indications of *postage* paid.
Endorsement: 'Baptism by / L. Preacher'.
Source: holograph; Huntington Library, Manuscripts, HM 57039.

To William Legge, 2nd Earl of Dartmouth[33]

5

SCARBOROUGH
APRIL 19, 1764

Dear Sir,
    It has pleased God to give your Lordship both the will and the power to do many things for his glory (although you are often
10 ashamed you have done so little, and wish you could do a thousand times more). This induces me to mention to your Lordship what has been upon my mind for many years, and what I am persuaded would be much for the glory of God, if it could once be effected. And I am in great hopes it will be, if your Lordship heartily under-
15 take it, trusting in him alone.
    Some years since, God began a great work in England. But the labourers were few. At first those few were of one heart. But it was not so long. First one fell off, then another, and another, till no two of us were left together in the work besides my brother and me.
20 This prevented much good and occasioned much evil. It grieved our spirits and weakened our hands. It gave our common enemies huge occasion to blaspheme. It perplexed and puzzled many sincere Christians. It caused many to draw back to perdition.[34] It grieved the Holy Spirit of God.[35]

---

[32] See Gen. 24:49.
[33] JW specifies Lord Dartmouth as the recipient of this letter in his letter to Lady Huntingdon the next day.
[34] See Heb. 10:39.
[35] See Eph. 4:30.

As labourers increased, disunion increased. Offences were multiplied. And instead of coming nearer to, they stood farther and farther off from each other. Till at length those who were not only brethren in Christ, but fellow-labourers in his gospel, had no more connection or fellowship with each other than Protestants have 5 with papists. But ought this to be? Ought not those who are united to one common head and employed by him in one common work, to be united to each other? I speak now of those labourers who are ministers of the Church of England. These are chiefly Messrs. Per- 10 ronet, Romaine, Shirley, Madan, Haweis, Hartley, Downing, Jesse, Adam, Talbot, Stillingfleet, Riland, Fletcher, Johnson, Boddiley,[36] Andrews, Jane, Hart, Sims, Brown, Sellon, Boddiley (of Hayfield), Venn, Burnet, Richardson, Furly, Crook, Eastwood, Conyers, Bentley, King, Berridge, Hicks, Whitefield, [John and Charles] Wesley.[37] 15

---

[36] The listing of 'Boddiley' twice was intentional, since the location is added the second time. The best candidate for this first listing is George Baddelley (born c. 1726), who took his BA from Oxford, Pembroke in 1747, was ordained priest in 1749, and was appointed rector of Markfield, Leicestershire in 1750. While JW never names the rector in his *Journal*, he comments frequently on being welcomed to preach in the Markfield church through this period; see June 10, 1753 (20:464 in this edn.), July 31, 1757 (21:119), and July 31, 1770 (22:243).

[37] Biographical details for most of these clergymen are given in 21:454–55, n. 69 in this edn. We have added notes only for those missing there and not already identified in this volume. We list them here by full names (correcting JW's spelling on occasion) and their current ecclesiastical assignment; partly to show that JW was grouping them by region:

Vincent Perronet (1693–1785), vicar of Shoreham, Kent
William Romaine (1714–95), lecturer at St. Dunstan and curate at St. Olave's, London
Walter Shirley (1725–86), rector of Loughrea, County Galway, Ireland
Martin Madan (1726–90), chaplain of Lock Hospital, London
Thomas Haweis (1734–1820), rector of Aldwinkle, Northamptonshire [see 21:309, n. 77]
Thomas Hartley (1708/9–84), rector of Winwick, Northamptonshire
George Downing (c. 1729–1803?), rector of Ovington, Essex
William Jesse (c. 1739–1815), curate of Chigwell, Essex
Thomas Adam (1701–84), rector of Winteringham, Lincolnshire
William Talbot (c. 1719–74), vicar of Kineton, Warwickshire
Edward Stillingfleet (c. 1732–95), vicar of West Bromwich, Staffordshire
John Riland (1736–1822), curate of Sutton Coldfield, Warwickshire
John William Fletcher (1729–85), vicar of Madeley, Shropshire
Samuel [not John, as in vol. 21] Johnson (c. 1727–84), curate of Cirencester Gloucestershire
George Baddelley, rector of Markfield, Leicestershire
John Andrews (born c. 1730), vicar of Stinchcombe, Gloucestershire
Joseph Jane (1716–95), rector of Iron Acton, Gloucestershire
Richard Hart (c. 1727–1808), vicar of St. George's, Bristol, Gloucestershire
Richard Symes (c. 1722–c. 1794), rector of St. Werburgh's, Bristol, Gloucestershire
James Brown (c. 1730–91), rector of Portishead, Somerset
Walter Sellon (1715–92), curate of Smisby and Breedon, Leicestershire

Not excluding any other clergymen who agree in these essentials—I. Original sin, II. Justification by faith, III. Holiness of heart and life—provided their life be answerable to their doctrine.

'But *what union* would you desire among these?' Not an union in *opinions*. They might agree or disagree touching absolute decrees on the one hand and perfection on the other. Not an union in *expressions*. These may still speak of the 'imputed righteousness', and those of the 'merits of Christ'. Not an union with regard to *outward order*. Some may still remain *quite regular*, some *quite irregular*, and some *partly regular* and *partly irregular*.[38] But these things being as they are, as each is persuaded in his own mind, is it not a most desirable thing, that we should

1. Remove hindrances out of the way? Not *judge* one another, not *despise* one another, not *envy* one another? Not be *displeased* at one another's *gifts* or *success*, even though greater than our own? Not *wait* for one another's halting, much less *wish* for it, or *rejoice* therein?

Never *speak* disrespectfully, slightly, coldly, or unkindly of each other. Never *repeat* each other's faults, mistakes, or infirmities, much less *listen* for and *gather* them up. Never say or do anything to hinder each other's usefulness, either directly or indirectly.

Is it not a most desirable thing that we should

2. *Love our brethren? Think well* of and *honour* one another? *Wish* all good, all grace, all gifts, all success, yea greater than our own, to each other? *Expect* God will answer our wish. *Rejoice* in every appearance thereof, and *praise* him for it? *Readily believe* good of each other, as readily as we once believed evil?

Speak respectfully, honourably, kindly of each other. *Defend* each other's character. Speak all the good we can of each other. Recom-

---

John Baddeley (1706–64), rector of Hayfield, Derbyshire [see 21:5, n. 18]
Henry Venn (1725–97), rector of Huddersfield, Yorkshire
George Burnett (1734–93), vicar of Elland, Yorkshire
John Richardson (c. 1735–91), perpetual curate of Haworth, Yorkshire
Samuel Furly (1732–95), perpetual curate of Slathwaite, Yorkshire
Henry Crooke (1708–70), vicar of Kippax, Yorkshire
Jonas Eastwood (d. 1772), curate of Cleckheaton, Yorkshire
Richard Conyers (1725–86), vicar of Helmsley, Yorkshire [see 21:452, n. 62]
Roger Bentley (1734–95) possibly assistant to Crooke at Kippax, Yorkshire
John King (c. 1724–1812), rector of Partonhall, Bedfordshire
John Berridge (1716–93), vicar of Everton, Bedfordshire
William Hicks, rector of Wrestlingsworth, Bedfordshire [see 21:171 in this edn.]
George Whitefield (1714–70), itinerant
John and Charles Wesley, itinerants

[38] In this as in his previous letter to Legge, 'irregular' denotes those who advocated itinerant preaching and lay preaching.

mend one another where we have influence. Each *help* the other on in his work and *enlarge* his influence by all the honest means we can?

This is the *union* which I have long sought after. And is it not the duty of every one of us so to do? Would it not be far better for ourselves? A means of promoting both our holiness and happiness? Would it not remove much *guilt* from those who have been faulty in any of these instances? And much *pain* from those who have kept themselves pure? Would it not be far better for the *people*? Who suffer severely from the clashings and contentions of their leaders. Would it not be better even for the poor, blind *world*, robbing them of their sport, 'Oh', say they, 'how can *we* believe them? They cannot agree among themselves, one confutes the other.' Would it not be better for the *whole work* of God, which would then deepen and widen on every side?

'But it will never be; it is utterly impossible.' Certainly it is *with men*. Who imagines *we* can do this? That it can be effected by any *human power*? All *nature* is against it, every infirmity, every *wrong temper* and *passion*; love of honour and praise, of power, of pre-eminence; anger, resentment, pride; long-contracted habit, and prejudice lurking in a thousand forms. The *devil* and all his angels are against it. For if this takes place, how shall his kingdom stand? All *the world*, all that know not God, are against it, though they may be overruled for a season. Let us settle this in our hearts, that we may be cut off from all dependence on our own strength or wisdom.

But surely 'with God all things are possible'.[39] Therefore 'all things are possible to him that believeth'.[40] And this union is proposed only to them that believe, and therefore speak.

I am, my Lord,

Your Lordship's affectionate and obedient servant,

J. W.

Source: published transcriptions; *The Evangelical Register* 1 (1824): 38–40; and JW, printed circular letter, Oct. 15, 1766.[41]

[39] Matt. 19:26.
[40] Mark 9:23.
[41] The holograph of this letter does not appear to survive. JW published a transcription in the circular letter that he sent to various Evangelical clergy in Oct. 1766 (*Bibliography*, no. 298); but this version was revised, as indicated by the inclusion of John Newton and James Rouquet in the list of clergy, neither of whom were ordained in Apr. 1764. JW revised the letter further when publishing in 1768 the extract of his *Journal* covering April 19, 1764 (21:455–58 in this

To Selina (Shirley) Hastings, Countess of Huntingdon

WHITBY
APRIL 20, 1764

My Lady,

5   Since I had the pleasure of seeing your Ladyship, I have had many thoughts upon the subject of our conversation.[42] The result I here send to your Ladyship, which I have as yet communicated to none but my Lord Dartmouth.

[THE text of the previous letter, minus the opening paragraph and personal closing, appears here.]

10   Who knows but it may please God to make your Ladyship an instrument in this glorious work? In effecting an union among the labourers in his vineyard? That he may direct and bless you in all your steps is the prayer of, my Lady,

Your Ladyship's affectionate and obedient servant,

15

John Wesley

Source: published transcription; *The Evangelical Register* 1 (1824): 38–40, reprinted in *WHS* 12 (1919): 29–34.

---

edn.). The most reliable source for the bulk of this letter is JW's letter to Lady Huntingdon the next day, in which he transcribes what he had just sent to Lord Dartmouth (a transcription that does *not* include Newton or Rouquet!). The only items missing in this transcription are the opening paragraph and closing remarks addressed directly to Lord Dartmouth, which are based on the 1766 circular letter (since this material is made less personal in the 1768 extract of the *Journal*). The differences between this original letter to Dartmouth and its form in the 1766 circular letter will be noted when that letter appears in vol. 28.

    [42] JW's conversation with Lady Huntingdon was likely in mid-March when he was in Bristol (near her home in Clifton) and met with several 'serious clergymen' to discuss the possibility of a closer union in their work; see JW, *Journal*, Mar. 16, 1764, 21:444 in this edn. JW had similar conversation with clergy as he rode north into Yorkshire (see Apr. 17–18, 1764; 21:452–53).

To an Unidentified Person[43]

[HUTTON RUDBY]
APRIL 23, [1764]

Do you always find a *direct witness* that you are saved from sin?
How long have you had this? Have you as clear and *strong* an evidence of eternal as of temporal things? Do you never find what they   5
call 'lowness of spirits'? How far do you find *wandering thoughts*?

Source: JW's transcribed copy; MARC, MA 1977/157, JW III.7, item
numbered '113'.

To Elizabeth (Harvey) Woodhouse[44]

[HUTTON RUDBY]
APRIL 23, 1764

My Dear Sister,
    I have often thought of you since I saw you.[45] Your openness gave   10
me much pleasure, and I found I could speak as freely to you as if
we had been acquainted for many years. You seem to me to have suffered loss for want of Christian conversation. Your mind was open
to instruction or advice. You did not shun it; rather you panted after
it. But alas, how few had you to advise with! How few to lead you on   15
in the royal way! I believe I do not wrong you when I say your heart
is panting after Christ. You desire all that he has purchased for you:

A pardon written in his blood,
The favour and the peace of God; [...]   20

---

[43] The correspondent is not named, although it is likely to be the same person to whom
Wesley wrote on Mar. 25 (see above), since it appears in the same notebook of transcriptions.

[44] This letter initiates John Wesley's correspondence with Elizabeth (neé Harvey) Woodhouse. She was apparently the daughter of John Harvey of Finningley Park, Yorkshire, and
Lord of the manor at Wroot, Lincolnshire; the eldest son of James (d. 1786) and Elizabeth
Harvey of Old Warden, Bedfordshire (who also held the manor in Yorkshire). John's younger
brother Edmund Harvey (1740–1823) graduated St. John's, Oxford in 1764, and was installed
by John as rector of Finningley. Their sister Elizabeth Harvey (1741–1807) never married,
living in Hinxworth, Hertfordshire, where she became a generous supporter of the Methodist cause. The younger Elizabeth Harvey married Gervase Woodhouse, and they resided at
Owston Ferry, Lincolnshire.

[45] JW had been in Epworth on Mar. 31–Apr. 3, 1764.

> The speechless awe that dares not move,
> And all the silent heaven of love.[46]

And all things are ready![47] Behold the Lamb of God![48] Is he not at
5   your right hand? Look unto Jesus! Take the blessing! Do not delay!
Now is the accepted time![49] Believe, and all is yours! I am, my dear
sister,
>   Your affectionate brother,

>   [John Wesley][50]

10

I shall stay two or three weeks at Newcastle-upon-Tyne.

Address: 'To / Mrs Woodhouse: / At Mr Hutton's / In Epworth, near
     Thorne / Yorkshire'.
Postmark: None visible. *Charge*: '3'.
Endorsement: 'April 64'.
Source: holograph; Emory, MARBL, Wesley Family Papers, 1/42.

To George Merryweather

>   NEWCASTLE-UPON-TYNE
>   MAY 7, 1764

My Dear Brother,
15   I thank you for the receipts.
     There is nothing more sure than that God is able and willing to
give always what he gives once. And it is most certainly his design
that whatever he has given you should abide with you forever. But
this can only be by simple faith. In this, reasoning is good for noth-
20 ing. See that both of you be as little children![51] Your help is all laid

---

[46] CW, Hymn on Luke 14:17, sts. 7–10, *HSP* (1749), 1:260; JW has combined the first
two lines of st. 7 with the last two lines of st. 10.
[47] See Matt. 22:4 and parallels.
[48] See John 1:29.
[49] See 2 Cor. 6:2.
[50] The signature appears to have been cut out.
[51] See Matt. 18:3.

up above in the hand of him that loves you. Look unto him,[52] and receive what you want! Believe yourselves to heaven! I am,
Your affectionate brother,

J. Wesley

Address: 'To / Mr George Merryweather / In Yarm / Yorkshire'.
Postmark: 'NEWCASTLE'. Charge: '9'.
Endorsement: 'May 1764'.
Source: holograph; Wesley's Chapel (London), LDWMM/1998/6889.

To Thomas Newall

NEWCASTLE-UPON-TYNE
MAY 7, 1764

My Dear Brother,
Pray tell brother Johnson,[53] 1) I am satisfied about the horse, 2) I don't know what rules they are which he speaks of.

I suppose the Conference will begin at Bristol the second week in August.[54]

I have often complained that most of our preachers were unfaithful to each other, not [saying] freely to each other what they thought amiss. I doubt that has been the case between you and John Atlay.[55] 'Tis well if you have spoke freely to him. You don't know what good you might do thereby. A hint or two will do nothing. Take the opportunity when you give him my letter, and your labour will not be in vain.

Press all our believers strongly and explicitly to go on to perfection. I am,
Your affectionate brother,

J. Wesley

For the present *you* must act as an Assistant.

---

[52] See Heb. 12:2.
[53] Possibly the itinerant Thomas Johnson.
[54] It began on Aug. 6 according to the *Journal* (21:485 in this edn.).
[55] Orig., 'Atley'. John Atlay (1736–c. 1805) was a native of Yorkshire who had become a Methodist in the 1750s and an itinerant preacher in 1763. In 1773 he began serving as JW's book steward in London. See Tyerman, *John Wesley*, 552–60; Vickers, *Dictionary*, 14.

Address: 'To Mr Newall / At Mr John Hall's / In Newgate Street / York'.
Postmark: None visible. *Charge*: indicated but illegible.
Source: holograph; MARC, MAM JW 4/22.

To Cradock Glascott[56]

NEWCASTLE-UPON-TYNE
MAY 13, 1764

Dear Sir,

It is an unspeakable blessing that God has given you to taste of
5   the powers of the world to come.[57] And he is willing to give always
what he gives once. You need lose nothing of what you have received; rather expect to receive more every moment, grace upon
grace. And be not content till you are a Christian altogether, till
your soul is all love, till you can rejoice evermore, and pray without
10   ceasing, and in everything give thanks.[58]

If you are not already, it might be of use to you to be acquainted
with Mr. Crosse, of Edmund Hall.[59] He has a sound judgement and
an excellent temper, and you have need of every help, that you may
not lose what God hath wrought, but may have a full reward.

15   A little tract wrote by Bishop Bull, entitled *A Companion for Candidates for Holy Orders*, was of much service to me.[60]

In order to be well acquainted with the doctrines of Christianity
you need but one book (beside the New Testament), Bishop Pearson
On the Creed.[61] This I advise you to read and master thoroughly—it

---

[56] Cradock Glascott (1742–1839) took his BA at Jesus College, Oxford, in 1766 and was ordained priest on Dec. 21 of that year by John Green, Bishop of Lincoln. He served as a chaplain of Lady Huntingdon until 1781, when he became vicar of Hatherleigh, Devonshire. JW had travelled with Glascott's father on his first trip to Wales; cf. JW to Thomas Price, Dec. 6, 1739, 21:703 in this edn.

[57] See Heb. 6:5.

[58] See 1 Thess. 5:16–18.

[59] John Crosse (1739–1816) was a native of London influenced by Methodism in his early life. He matriculated in St. Edmund Hall, Oxford, in 1762 and took his BA in 1768. He was subsequently ordained and served a number of Anglican parishes. See *ODNB*.

[60] George Bull, *A Companion for the Candidates of Holy Orders; Or, The Great Importance and Principal Duties of the Priestly Office* (London: George James, 1714). JW records reading this volume in his Oxford diary, shortly before being ordained deacon.

[61] One of Wesley's most frequently recommended readings: John Pearson, *An Exposition of the Creed* (London: Roger Daniel for John Williams, 1659).

is a library in one volume. But above all be much in prayer, and God will withhold no manner of thing that is good! I am,
> Your affectionate servant,

J. Wesley

Address: 'To Mr Charles Glascott / In Jesus College / Oxon'.
Postmarks: '14/MA' and 'NEWCASTLE'. *Charge*: numerous marks over the address.
Source: holograph; MARC, MA 1998/015.

To Selina (Shirley) Hastings, Countess of Huntingdon

NEWCASTLE[-UPON-TYNE]   5
MAY 16, 1764

My Dear Lady,

I am much obliged to your Ladyship for your encouraging answer,[62] which plainly speaks an heart devoted to God and longing for the furtherance of his kingdom. I have likewise received an exceeding friendly letter from Mr. [Richard] Hart, testifying a great desire of union between the preachers of the gospel. Only he carries the point considerably farther than I do, proposing a free debate concerning our several opinions. Now this, I fear, we are not yet able to bear. I fear it might occasion some sharpness of expression, if not of spirit too, which might tear open the wounds before they are fully closed. I am far from being assured that I could bear it myself, and perhaps others might be as weak as me. To me, therefore, it still seems most expedient to avoid disputings of every kind—at least, for a season, till we have tasted each other's spirits and confirmed our love to each other. I own freely I am sick of disputing; I am weary to bear it. My whole soul cries out 'Peace! Peace!'[63] at least with the children of God, that we may all unite our strength to carry on the war against the 'rulers of the darkness of this world'.[64] Still, I ask but one thing—I can require no more: 'Is thy *heart* right,

---

[62] Lady Huntingdon was replying to JW's letter of Apr. 20; unfortunately, the reply does not survive.
[63] Jer. 8:11.
[64] Eph. 6:12.

as my heart is with thine? If it be, give me thy hand.'[65] 'Let us take sweet counsel together and strengthen each other in the Lord.'[66]

And the advantage in the proposal I make is this: If it should be (which God forbid!) that I should find none to join with me therein, I will (by God's help) comply with it myself—none can hinder this. And I think my brother will be likeminded; yea, and all who act in connexion with us.

Probably it might contribute much to this end, if those of our brethren who have opportunity would be at Bristol on Thursday the ninth of August.[67] We might then spend a few hours in free conversation, either apart from or in conjunction with the other preachers. I apprehend, if your Ladyship could then be near, it might be of excellent service in confirming any kind and friendly disposition which our Lord might plant in the hearts of his servants. Surely, if this can be effectually done, we shall again see Satan as lightning fall from heaven.[68]

Then,

> The children of thy faith and prayer
> Thy joyful eyes shall see,
> Shall see the prosperous Church, and share
> In her prosperity![69]

I am, my dear Lady,
Your Ladyship's most affectionate and obedient servant,

John Wesley

Source: manuscript transcriptions; MARC, MA 1977/502 (leaf 42), and MARC, MA 1977/609. Both are apparently nineteenth-century copies, the first in the hand of Eliza Tooth. There are no major differences between the two transcriptions.

---

[65] 2 Kings 10:15.
[66] Ps. 55:15 (BCP).
[67] JW's Conference with his preachers was set for Bristol on Aug. 6, so he envisioned a conversation with Lady Huntingdon and preachers in connexion with her following it.
[68] See Luke 10:18.
[69] CW, 'Psalm 128', st. 7, *CPH* (1743), 94.

To an Unidentified Correspondent

MAY 22, 1764

Do you never find any tendency to *pride*? Do you find nothing like *anger*? Is your mind never *ruffled*, put *out of tune*? Do you never feel any useless *desire*? Any desire of pleasure? Of ease? Of approbation? Of increase of fortune? Do you find no *stubbornness*, *sloth* or 5 *self-will*? No *unbelief*?

Source: published transcription; *Arminian Magazine* 5 (1782): 434.

To the Rev. Charles Wesley

HADDINGTON
MAY 25, 1764

[[Dear Brother,]]

Is there any reason why you and I should have no farther inter- 10 course with each other? I know none; although possibly there are persons in the world who would not be sorry for it.

I hope you find peace and unity in the south, as we do in the north. Only the Seceders and Mr. Sandeman's friends are ready to eat us up.[70] And no wonder, for these, as well as deists and Socinians, I op- 15 pose *ex professo*.[71] But how do Thomas Maxfield and his friends go on? Quietly, or *gladiatorio animo*?[72] And how are John Jones, [John] Downes, and [John] Richardson?[73] And my best friend, and yours?[74]

The frightful stories wrote from London had made all our preachers in the north afraid even to mutter about perfection, and 20 of course the people on all sides were grown good Calvinists in that point. Tis what I foresaw from the beginning, that the devil would

---

[70] There had been two notable secessions from the Church of Scotland that led to separate presbyteries, in 1733 and in 1761. A smaller secession by the followers of John Glas and Robert Sandeman had occurred around 1730.

[71] 'expressly'.

[72] Terence, *Phormio*, Act 5, Scene 8 (l. 964), 'like gladiators' (Loeb).

[73] This would be John Richardson (1734–92), who had taken the BA at St. John's College, Cambridge in 1756, been ordained priest in 1757, and served curacies in Leek, Battle Abbey, and Ewhurst near Rye. At the latter he came into contact with a Methodist society and deepened his religious experience. Removed from his curacy, he offered his service to JW in 1762. See Atmore, *Memorial*, 356–65.

[74] I.e., Mary Wesley and Sarah Wesley.

strive by Thomas Maxfield and company to drive perfection out of the kingdom.

O let you and I hold fast whereunto we have attained,[75] and let our yea be yea, and our nay, nay![76] I feel the want of some about me that are all faith and love. No man was more profitable to me than George Bell, while he was simple of heart. O for heat and light united!

My love to Sally.

Adieu!

No *address*, *postmarks*, indications of postal *charges*, or evidence of a *seal*.
Endorsement: in CW's hand, 'B. / Maxfd driving out Pn'.
Source: holograph; MARC, DDWes 3/24.

To Dorothy Furly

EDINBURGH
MAY 28, 1764

My Dear Sister,

Certainly it would be right to spend some time in setting down both the outward providences of God and the inward leadings and workings of his Spirit as far as you can remember them. But observe withal you are called to be a good steward of the mammon of unrighteousness.[77] You must therefore think of this too in its place, only without anxiety. Otherwise that neglect of your calling will hinder the work of God in your heart. You are not serving mammon by this, but serving Christ; it is part of the task which *he* has assigned you. Yet it is true your heart is to be free all the time, and see that you stand fast in the liberty wherewith Christ hath made you free.[78]

I thought your name had been altered before now.[79] In a new station you will have need of new watchfulness. Still redeem the time. Be steadily serious and follow your own conscience in all things.

---

[75] See Phil. 3:16.
[76] See Matt. 5:37 and Jas. 5:12.
[77] See Luke 16:9.
[78] See Gal. 5:1.
[79] Furly married John Downes in the next month, June 1764.

I am, my dear sister,
    Your affectionate brother,

                                          J. Wesley

In my return from the Highlands, I expect to spend a day at   5
Newcastle-upon-Tyne, the 18th or 19th of June.

Source: published transcription; Benson, *Works*, 16:328–29.

To Matthew Errington

EDINBURGH
MAY 30, 1764

O Matthew, how is this? There is not one Milton here, nor one
set of the Philosophy.[80] Pray send immediately twelve sets of the   10
Philosophy and twenty Miltons (if you have more than twenty at
Newcastle, for you must not be left without some); and see that they
be here before I return, which I expect will be on Saturday fortnight. So on Tuesday fortnight, June 19th, you will (if God permit)
see me at Newcastle.   15
    The word of God has free course in north Britain, even among
honourable and right honourable sinners. I am, with love to all,
dear Matthew,
        Your affectionate brother,

                                          J. Wesley   20

I hope to spend two days with you, and to preach at the Fell at three
on Thursday, 21st.[81]

---

[80] JW is chiding Errington, as book steward in Newcastle, responsible for the north of
Britain, that two of Wesley's recent publications have not made it to Edinburgh: *An Extract
from Milton's Paradise Lost* (1763, *Bibliography*, No. 253); and *Survey of the Wisdom of God in
the Creation, or A Compendium of Natural Philosophy* (1763, *Bibliography*, No. 259).

[81] JW preached at Gateshead Fell, Co. Durham, on June 20; cf. *Journal*, 21:473 in this
edn.

Send also[82]

24 Plain Accounts		[none]
50 Character of a Methodist		
100 Rules of Society		[60]
30 Primitive Physick, if you have them.		
12 Earnest Appeals		[none]
30 Answer to Bp. Warburton		[20]
20 Kempis. Lose not a day.		
40 Short Hymns.		

Address: 'To / Mr Matthew Errington / At the Orphan House / Newcastle upon Tyne'.

Postmark: 'MY/31'. *Charge*: '5'.

Endorsement: 'answer'd'; and see also Errington's notes on his inventory shown in square brackets above in the transcription.

Source: holograph; MARC MAM JW 2/88.

To Darcy (Brisbane) Maxwell, Lady Maxwell of Pollok[83]

NEWCASTLE-UPON-TYNE
JUNE 20, 1764

Will it be agreeable to my dear Lady Maxwell that I trouble her with a letter so soon? And that I write with so little ceremony? That I use no compliment, but all plainness of speech? If it be not, you must tell me so, and I shall know better how to speak for the time to come. Indeed, it would be unpleasing to me to use reserve. The regard I feel for you strongly inclines me to 'think aloud', to tell you every thought which rises in my heart.

I think God has taken unusual pains, so to speak, to make you a Christian, a Christian indeed, not in name, worshipping God in

---

[82] This postscript appears overleaf in John Wesley's hand but with Errington's notes on his inventory indicated in square brackets.

[83] Scottish native Darcy Brisbane (1742–1810) married Sir Walter Maxwell, Fourth Baronet Pollock, in 1759. He and an infant son died two years later. She became involved with Methodist societies and would become one of Wesley's most prominent benefactors. Wesley probably met her when he visited Edinburgh in May 1764. See *MM* 39 (1816): 721ff; Vickers, *Dictionary*, 225; and *ODNB*.

spirit and in truth,[84] having in you the mind that was in Christ,[85] and walking as Christ also walked.[86] He has given you affliction upon affliction. He has used every possible means to unhinge your soul from things of earth, that it might fix on him alone. How far the design of his love has succeeded I could not well judge from a   5
short conversation. Your Ladyship will therefore give me leave to inquire, is the heaviness you frequently feel merely owing to weakness of body and the loss of near relations? I will hope it is not. It might, indeed, at first spring from these outward pressures. But did not the gracious Spirit of God strike in, and take occasion from   10
these to convince you of sin, of unbelief, of the want of Christ? And is not the sense of this one great cause, if not the greatest, of your present distress? If so, the greatest danger is, either that you should stifle that conviction, not suffering yourself to be convinced that you are *all sin*, the chief of sinners, or that you should heal   15
the wound slightly, that you should rest before you *know* Christ is yours, before his Spirit witnesses with your spirit that you are a child of God.[87] My dear Lady, be not afraid to know yourself, yea, to know yourself as you are known. How soon, then, will you know your advocate with the Father, Jesus Christ the righteous?[88]   20
And why not this day? Why not this hour? If you feel your want, I beseech the God and Father of our Lord Jesus Christ to look upon you now! O give thy servant power to believe, to see and feel how thou hast loved her! Now let her sink down into the arms of thy love, and say unto her soul, 'I am thy salvation'.[89]   25

With regard to particular advices, I know not how far your Ladyship would have me to proceed. I would not be backward to do anything in my power, and yet I would not obtrude. But in any respect you may command, my dear Lady,

Your Ladyship's affectionate servant,   30

John Wesley

Source: published transcription; *Methodist Magazine* 35 (1812): 311–12.

[84] See John 4:24.
[85] See Phil. 2:5.
[86] See 1 John 2:6.
[87] See Rom. 8:16.
[88] See 1 John 2:1.
[89] Ps. 35:3.

To Jane Catherine March

WHITEHAVEN
JUNE 24, 1764

You give me an agreeable account of the state of things in London, and such as calls for much thankfulness. From different letters
5 I find that there is at length a calm season, God having rebuked the wind and the seas. But I am concerned for you. I cannot doubt a moment but you were saved from sin. Your every act, word, thought was love, whatever it be now. You were in a measure a living witness of the perfection I believe and preach, the only perfection of which
10 we are capable while we remain in the body. To carry perfection higher is to sap the foundation of it and destroy it from the face of the earth. I am jealous over you. I am afraid lest, by grasping at a shadow, you should have let go the substance; lest, by aiming at a perfection which we cannot have till hereafter, you should cast away
15 that which now belongs to the children of God. This is love filling the heart. Surely it did fill yours, and it may do now, by simple faith. O cast not away your confidence, which hath great recompense of reward![90] Converse much with those who are all alive, who strive not to pull you down but to build you up. Accursed be that humility
20 by which shipwreck is made of the faith. Look up and receive power from on high.[91] Receive all you had once, and more than all. Give no place to evil reasoning. You have need to be guarded by a steady and yet tender hand. Be as a little child. The Lord is at hand.[92] He is yours, therefore shall you lack nothing.
25 I am, etc.,

[John Wesley]

Source: published transcription; Jackson, *Works* (3rd), 14:206.

---

[90] See Heb. 10:35.
[91] See Luke 24:49.
[92] See Phil. 4:5.

To Sarah Moore

LEEDS
JULY 5, 1764

My Dear Sister,

I am fully convinced that Thomas Bryant's staying another year in the Sheffield Circuit would neither be good for him nor for the people.[93] I know his strength, and I know his weakness. But he shall go no farther than the Leeds Circuit, from whence he may now and then step over to Sheffield, and the Sheffield preacher to Leeds.

Sally, see that you walk circumspectly. The eyes of many are upon you, and, above all, the eye of God! I am,
        Your affectionate brother,

J. Wesley

Source: holograph; Emory, MARBL, Wesley Family Papers, 1/43 (address portion missing).

To Darcy (Brisbane) Maxwell, Lady Maxwell of Pollok

MANCHESTER
JULY 10, 1764

My Dear Lady,

Till I had the pleasure of receiving yours, I was almost in doubt whether you would think it worth your while to write or not. So much the more I rejoiced when that doubt was removed, and removed in so agreeable a manner. I cannot but think of you often;[94] I seem to see you just by me, panting after God, under the heavy pressure of bodily weakness and faintness, bereaved of your dearest

---

[93] Thomas Bryant (d. 1797) appeared as an itinerant in the Minutes of the 1758 Bristol Conference, where he was appointed to Cornwall (10:281 and 286 in this edn.). He was one of the Methodist preachers who would be ordained by the Greek church leader Gerasimos Avlonites (Erasmus Aulonita) later this year, and dismissed from the Methodist connection on Jan. 7, 1765. In May 1765, Bryant led a secession of members of the Sheffield society who built a Chapel on Scotland Street. Their society would become one of the founding constituencies of the Methodist New Connexion in 1797. See Vickers, *Dictionary*, 46.

[94] See Phil. 1:3.

relatives, convinced that you are a sinner, a debtor that has nothing to pay, and just ready to cry out,

> Jesu, now I have lost my all,
> 5   Let me upon thy bosom fall.[95]

Amen, Lord Jesus![96] Speak, for thy servant heareth![97] Speak thyself into her heart! Lift up the hands that hang down and the feeble knees.[98] Let her see thee full of grace and truth,[99] and make her glad 10 with the light of thy countenance.[100]

Do not stop, my dear Lady, one moment 'because you have not felt sorrow enough'. Your friend above has felt enough of it for you.

> O Lamb of God, was ever pain,
> 15   Was ever love like thine![101]

Look, look unto him, and be thou saved! He is not a God afar off;[102] he is now hovering over you with eyes of tenderness and love! Only believe! Then he turns your heaviness into joy.[103] Do not think you 20 are not humble enough, not contrite enough, not earnest enough. You are nothing, but Christ is all, and he is yours! The Lord God write it upon your heart,[104] and take you for an habitation of God through the Spirit.[105]

O that you may be ever as dead to the world as you are now![106] I 25 apprehend the greatest danger from that quarter. If you should be induced to seek happiness out of Christ, how soon would your good desires vanish! Especially if you should give way to the temptation to which your person, your youth, and your fortune will not fail to expose you. If you escape this snare, I trust you will be a real Chris-30 tian, having the power as well as the form of religion.[107] I expect you will then have likewise better health and spirits, perhaps tomorrow. But O, take Christ today! I long to have you happy in him! Surely

---

[95] Cf. CW, 'Come, Lord Jesus!', st. 9, *HSP* (1742), 205.
[96] See Rev. 22:20.
[97] See 1 Sam. 3:10.
[98] See Heb. 12:12.
[99] See John 1:14.
[100] See Ps. 4:6.
[101] Samuel Wesley Sr., 'On the Crucifiction', st. 4, *CPH* (1737), 47 and *HSP* (1739), 132.
[102] See Jer. 23:23.
[103] Cf. Jas. 4:9 (inverted).
[104] See Jer. 31:33.
[105] See Eph. 2:22.
[106] See Col. 3:2–3.
[107] See 2 Tim. 3:5.

few have a more earnest desire of your happiness than, my very dear Lady,

Your Ladyship's most affectionate servant,

John Wesley

Source: published transcription; *Methodist Magazine* 35 (1812): 312.

To an Unidentified Man[108]

WIGAN

JULY 13, 1764

Dear Sir,

There was one thing when I was with you that gave me pain. You are not in the society. But why not? Are there not sufficient arguments for it to move any reasonable man? Do you not hereby make an open confession of Christ, of what you really believe to be *his* work, and of those whom you judge to be in a proper sense *his* people and his messengers? By this means do not you encourage his people and strengthen the hands of his messengers? And is not this the way to enter into the spirit, and share the blessing, of a Christian community? Hereby likewise you may have the benefit of the advices and exhortations at the meeting of the society, and also of provoking one another, at the private meetings, to love and to good works.[109]

The ordinary objections to such an union are of little weight with *you*. You are not afraid of the *expense*. You already give unto the Lord as much as you need do then. And you are not *ashamed* of the gospel of Christ,[110] even in the midst of a crooked and perverse generation.[111] Perhaps you will say, 'I am joined in *affection*'. True, but not to so good effect. This *joining half-way*, this being a friend to, but not a member of, the society, is by no means so open a confession of the work and servants of God. Many go thus far who dare not go farther, who are ashamed to bear the reproach of an entire union. Either *you* are ashamed or you are not. If you are, break

---

[108] JW presents this in the *Journal* as a letter for all 'those to whom it belongs'.
[109] See Heb. 10:24.
[110] See Rom. 1:16.
[111] See Phil. 2:15.

through at once; if you are not, come into the light and do what those well-meaning cowards dare not do. This imperfect union is not so *encouraging* to the people, not so *strengthening* to the preachers. Rather it is weakening their hands, hindering their work, and laying a stumbling-block in the way of others. For what can any man think who knows you are so well acquainted with them and yet do not join in their society? What can he think, but that you know them *too well* to come any nearer to them; that you know that kind of union to be *useless*, if not *hurtful*. And yet by this very union is the whole (external) work of God upheld throughout the nation, besides all the spiritual good which accrues to each member. O delay no longer, for the sake of the work, for the sake of the world, for the sake of your brethren. Join them inwardly and outwardly, heart and hand, for the sake of your own soul. There is something not easily explained in the 'fellowship of the Spirit',[112] which we enjoy with a society of living Christians. You have no need to give up your share therein and in the various blessings that result from it. You have no need to exclude yourself from the benefit of the advice and exhortations given from time to time. These are by no means to be despised, even supposing you have yourself more understanding than him that gives them. You need not lose the benefit of those prayers which experience shows are attended with a peculiar blessing. 'But I do not care to meet a class; I find no good in it.' Suppose you find even a dislike, a loathing, of it; may not this be natural or even diabolical? In spite of this, break through, make a fair trial. It is but a 'lion in the way'.[113] Meet only six times (with previous prayer) and see if it do not vanish away. But if it be a cross, still bear it for the sake of your brethren. 'But I want to gain my friends and relations.' If so, stand firm. If you give way, you hurt them, and they will press upon you the more. If you do not, you will probably gain them. Otherwise you confirm both their wrong notions and wrong tempers. Because I love you I have spoken fully and freely. To know that I have not spoken in vain will be a great satisfaction to,

Your affectionate brother,

J. W.

Source: published transcription; JW, *Journal*, July 13, 1764 (21:478–79 in this edn.).

---

[112] Phil. 2:1.
[113] I.e., a poor excuse for not participating; see Prov. 26:13.

To Ebenezer Blackwell

LIVERPOOL
JULY 14, 1764

Dear Sir,

My brother informs me that you have been so extremely ill that
your life was hardly expected.[114] I really am under apprehensions 5
lest that chariot should cost you your life. If, after having been accustomed to ride on horseback for many years, you should now exchange a horse for a carriage, it cannot be that you should have good
health. It is a vain thing to expect it. I judge of your case by my own.
I must be on horseback for life, if I would be healthy. Now and then, 10
indeed, if I could afford it, I should rest myself for fifty miles in a
chaise. But without riding near as much as I do now, I must never
look for health.[115]

In the meantime I trust both Mrs. Blackwell and you are looking
for health of a nobler kind. You look to be filled with the spirit of 15
love and of a healthful mind. What avails everything else? Everything that passes away as an arrow through the air?

> The arrow is flown!
> The moment is gone! 20
> The millennial year
> Rushes on to the view, and eternity's here![116]

You want nothing more of this world. You have enough, and, by the
peculiar blessing of God, know you have. But you want a thousand 25
times more faith. You want love. You want holiness. The Lord God
supply all your wants from the riches of his mercy in Christ Jesus![117]

I am, dear sir,
Your very affectionate servant,

[John Wesley] 30

Next week I shall set my face toward Bristol.

Source: published transcription; Jackson, *Works* (3rd), 12:176.

---

[114] Blackwell recovered and lived to the spring of 1782.

[115] In Feb. 1772 some of Wesley's friends attempted to raise money 'to prevent my riding
on horseback', but there is no evidence that they succeeded at that time; see *Journal* for Feb.
21, 1772, 22:308 in this edn.

[116] CW, 'Hymn V', st. 2, *Hymns for New-Year's-Day* (1750), 9.

[117] See Phil. 4:19.

To the Rev. Samuel Furly

LIVERPOOL
JULY 15, 1764

Dear Sammy,

I have had many thoughts since we parted on the subject of our
5   late conversation. I send you them just as they occur. 'What is it
that constitutes a good style?' Perspicuity and purity, propriety,
strength, and easiness, joined together. Where any one of these is
wanting, it is not a good style. Dr. Middleton's style wants easiness.
It is stiff to an high degree.[118] And stiffness in writing is full as great
10   a fault as stiffness in behaviour. It is a blemish hardly to be excused,
much less to be imitated. He is pedantic. 'It is pedantry', says the
great Lord Boyle, 'to use an hard word where an easier will serve.'[119]
Now, this the Doctor continually does, and that of set purpose. It is
abundantly too artificial. *Artis est celare artem*,[120] but his art glares
15   in every sentence. He continually says, 'Observe how fine I speak!'
Whereas a good speaker seems to forget he speaks at all. His full
round curls naturally put one in mind of Sir Cloudesley Shovell's[121]
peruke, that

20   Eternal buckle takes in Parian stone.[122]

Yet this very fault may appear a beauty to you, because you are apt
to halt on the same foot. There is a stiffness both in your carriage
and speech and something of it in your very familiarity. But for
25   this very reason you should be jealous of yourself and guard against
your natural infirmity. If you imitate any writer, let it be South,
Atterbury, or Swift,[123] in whom all the properties of a good writer
meet. I was myself once much fonder of Prior than Pope,[124] as I

---

[118] JW returns to the critique of Middleton's writing style that he began in JW to Furly, Mar. 6, 1764.

[119] Charles Boyle, Earl of Orrery, *Dr. Bentley's Dissertation on the Epistles of Phalaris, and the fables of Aesop, Examined* (London: Thomas Bennet, 1698), 93.

[120] 'It is [characteristic] of art to conceal art.'

[121] Orig., 'Shovel's'.

[122] Alexander Pope, *Moral Essays*, Epistle 3, l. 296; see in JW, *MSP* (1744), 2:13. A 'peruke' was a style of wig. The reference is to tasteless excess in ornamentation. A monument to Sir Cloudesley Shovell (1650–1701) in Westminster Abbey was frequently cited as an example of over-ornamentation.

[123] To Jonathan Swift, invoked in his letter of Mar. 6, JW adds now Robert South (1634–1716) and Francis Atterbury (1663–1732) as writers/preachers to emulate.

[124] Comparing Matthew Prior (1664–1721) to Alexander Pope (1688–1744). See JW, 'Thoughts on the Character and Writings of Mr. Prior', *AM* 5 (1782): 600–3, 660–66.

did not then know that stiffness was a fault. But what in all Prior can equal for beauty of style some of the first lines that Pope ever published?

> Poets themselves must die[125], like those they sung,   5
> Deaf the praised ear, and mute the tuneful tongue;
> E'en he whose heart now melts in tender[126] lays,
> Shall shortly want the generous tear he pays.
> Then from his eyes thy much-loved form[127] shall part;
> And the last pang shall tear thee from his heart: 10
> Life's idle business at one gasp be o'er,
> The Muse forgot, and thou beloved no more.[128]

Here is style! How clear, how pure, proper, strong! And yet how amazingly easy! This crowns all: no stiffness, no hard words,   15 no apparent art, no affectation. All is natural, and therefore consummately beautiful. Go thou and write likewise.[129]

As for me, I never think of my style at all, but just set down the words that come first. Only when I transcribe anything for the press, then I think it my duty to see every phrase be clear, pure, and   20 proper. Conciseness (which is now, as it were, natural to me) brings *quantum sufficit* of strength. If, after all, I observe any stiff expression, I throw it out, neck and shoulders.

Clearness in particular is necessary for you and me, because we are to instruct people of the lowest understanding. Therefore we,   25 above all, if we think with the wise, yet must speak with the vulgar. We should constantly use the most common, little, easy words (so they are pure and proper) which our language affords. When I had been a member of the university about ten years, I wrote and talked much as you do now. But when I talked to plain people in the Castle   30 or the town, I observed they gaped and stared. This quickly obliged me to alter my style and adopt the language of those I spoke to. And yet there is a dignity in this simplicity, which is not disagreeable to those of the highest rank.

I advise *you*, Sammy, sacredly to abstain from reading any stiff   35 writer. A bystander sees more than those that play the game. Your

---

[125] Pope: 'fall'.

[126] Pope: 'mournful'.

[127] Pope: 'closing eyes thy form'.

[128] From Alexander Pope, 'Elegy to the Memory of an Unfortunate Lady', the concluding lines, *Miscellany Poems* (London: Bernard Lintot, 1726), 1:162.

[129] Cf. Luke 10:37.

style is much hurt already. Indeed, something might be said if you was a learned infidel writing for money or reputation. But that is not the case. You are a Christian minister, speaking and writing to save souls. Have this end always in your eye, and you will never designedly use an hard word. Use all the sense, learning, and fire you have; forgetting yourself, and remembering only these are the souls for whom Christ died, heirs of an happy or miserable eternity!

I am, with love to Nancy,

Your affectionate friend and brother,

J. Wesley

Address: 'To / The Revd Mr Furly / At the Revd Mr Venn's / in Huddersfield / Yorkshire' and also 'Cross Post'.

No *postmarks* or indications of postal *charges*.

Source: holograph; MARC, WCB, D5/16.

To William Legge, 2nd Earl of Dartmouth[130]

LAMPETER
JULY 26, 1764

My Lord,

Upon an attentive consideration, it will appear to every impartial person that the uniting of the serious clergy in the manner I proposed in a former letter is not a matter of indifferency, but what none can reject unless at the peril of his own soul. For every article therein mentioned is undeniably contained in the royal law, the law of love, and consequently the observance thereof is bound upon every man as indispensably necessary to salvation. It will appear, farther, that every single person may observe it, whether the other will or no. For many years I, for instance, have observed this rule in every article. I labour to do so now; and will by God's help, whatever others do, observe it to the end.

I rejoice that your Lordship so heartily concurs in doing what is in your power to promote a general observance of it. Certainly this

---

[130] JW is replying to Lord Dartmouth's response to the proposal in his letter of Apr. 19, 1764.

is not possible to be effected by merely human means, but it seems
your Lordship has taken one good step towards it by communicating it to several. I am persuaded, at the same time, your Lordship's
wish is that it might take place everywhere. The same step I purpose to take, by sending to each of those gentlemen the substance of   5
what I wrote to your Lordship, and desiring them to tell me freely
whatever objections they have against such an union.[131] As many
of those as are grounded on reason, I doubt not will be easily answered. Those only which spring from some wrong temper must
remain till that temper is subdued. For instance: First, 'We cannot   10
unite', says one, 'because we cannot trust one another.' I answer to
your *reason* or *understanding*, no matter whether we can or no, thus
far we must unite—trust or not—otherwise we sin against God.
Secondly, I can trust *you*; why cannot you trust me? I can have no
private end herein. I have neither personal hopes nor fears from   15
you. I want nothing which you can give me, and I am not afraid
of your doing me any hurt, though you may hurt yourself and the
cause of God. But I cannot answer your *envy, jealousy, pride,* or
credulity, as long as those remain. Objections, however cut off, will
spring up again like Hydra's heads.[132]   20
    If your Lordship has heard any objections, I should be glad to
know them. May I be permitted to ask, have not the objections you
have heard made some impression upon your Lordship? Have they
not occasioned (if I may speak freely) your Lordship's standing
aloof from me? Have they not set your Lordship farther and farther   25
off, ever since I waited upon you at [Blackheath[133]]? Why do I ask?
Indeed, not upon my own account. *Quid mea? Ego in portu navigo.*[134]
I can truly say, I neither fear nor desire anything from your Lordship. To speak a rough truth, I do not desire any intercourse with
any persons of quality in England. I mean for my own sake; they   30
do me no good, and I fear I can do none to them. If it be desired,
I will readily leave all those to the care of my fellow labourers.[135] I

---

[131] See the formal circular letter that JW sent out Oct. 15, 1766 (vol. 28 in this edn.).

[132] Alluding to Hydra of Greek mythology.

[133] The location is left blank in *AM*; the most likely location was Lord Dartmouth's
manor in Blackheath, just southeast of London. In this case, though JW does not record it in
his *Journal*, it likely took place in early March 1764, just before Wesley left for Bristol to discuss
the matter with several clergy; see JW, *Journal*, Mar. 16, 1764, 21:444 in this edn. JW had not
been back to London since that time and the writing of this letter.

[134] *Quid mea?* can be translated, 'What [of this] is mine?' The remainder is from Terence,
Andria ('The Woman of Andros'), Act 3, Scene 1 (l. 480), 'my ship's in harbour' (Loeb).

[135] William Romaine, Charles Wesley, and George Whitefield, in particular, were much
more comfortable ministering among the upper classes than was JW.

will article with them so to do rather than this shall be any bone of contention.

Were I not afraid of giving your Lordship pain, I would speak yet still farther. Methinks you desire I should, that is, to tell you once for all every thought that rises in my heart. I will then. At present I do not want *you*, but I really think you want *me*.[136] For have you a person in all England who speaks to your Lordship so plain and downright as I do? Who considers not the *Peer*, but the *man*? Not the *Earl*, but the *immortal spirit*? Who rarely commends, but often blames, and perhaps would do it oftener if you desired it? Who is jealous over you with a godly jealousy, lest you should be less a Christian by being a nobleman? Lest, after having made a fair advance towards heaven, you should

> Measure back your steps to earth again?[137]

O my Lord, is not such a person as this needful for you in the highest degree? If you have any such, I have no more to say, but that I pray God to bless him to your soul. If you have not, despise not even the assistance which it may please God to give you by, my Lord,
Your Lordship's ready servant,

J. Wesley

Source: published transcription; *Arminian Magazine* 6 (1783): 162–64.

To Darcy (Brisbane) Maxwell, Lady Maxwell of Pollok

LONDON
AUGUST 17, 1764

My Dear Lady,

Since I had the pleasure of yours, I have hardly had an hour that I could call my own. Otherwise I should not have delayed writing so long, as I have a very tender regard for you and an earnest desire

---

[136] JW used 'want', as he does typically, in the sense of 'need'.
[137] Cf. Thomas Parnell, 'The Hermit', l. 227; retained in JW's abridged form in *MSP* (1744), 1:275.

that you should be altogether a Christian. I cannot be content with your being ever so harmless or regular in your behaviour, or even exemplary in all externals; nay, more than all this you have received already, for you have the fear of God. But shall you stop here? God forbid! This is only the beginning of wisdom.[138] You are not to end here. Fear shall ripen into love. You shall know (perhaps very soon) that love of God which passeth knowledge.[139] You shall witness the kingdom of God within you,[140] even righteousness, peace, and joy in the Holy Ghost.[141]

It is no small instance of the goodness of God towards you that you are conscious of your want, your 'want of living faith divine'.[142] And his goodness herein is more remarkable, because almost all your neighbours would set you down for a right good believer. O beware of those flatterers! Hold fast the conviction which God hath given you! Faith, living, conquering, loving faith, is undoubtedly the thing you want. And of this you have frequently a taste to encourage you in pressing forward. Such is the tender mercy of him that loves you! Such his desire that you should receive all his precious promises! Do not think they are afar off. Do not imagine you must stay long years or months before you receive them. Do not put them off a day, an hour! Why not now? Why should you not look up this instant, and see, as it were, Jesus Christ set forth, evidently set forth, crucified before your eyes?[143] O hear his voice! 'Daughter! Be of good cheer! Thy sins are forgiven thee!'[144] Say not in thy heart, who shall go up into heaven, or who shall go down into the deep? No. The word is nigh thee, even in thy mouth and in thy heart.[145] 'Lord, I believe; help my unbelief.'[146]

Joy in the Holy Ghost is a precious gift of God, but yet tenderness of conscience is a still greater gift, and all this is for *you*. Just ready,

> The speechless awe which dares not move,
> And all the silent heaven of love.[147]

[138] See Ps. 111:10; Prov. 9:10.
[139] See Eph. 3:19.
[140] See Luke 17:21.
[141] See Rom. 14:17.
[142] CW, 'Hymn 42', st. 1, *Redemption Hymns* (1747), 52.
[143] See Gal. 3:1.
[144] Cf. Matt. 9:2, 22.
[145] See Rom. 10:6–8.
[146] Mark 9:24.
[147] CW, 'Hymn on Luke 14:7', st. 10, *HSP* (1749), 1:260.

I am no great friend to solitary Christianity.[148] Nevertheless, in so peculiar a case as yours, I think an exception may be admitted. It does seem most expedient for *you* to retire from Edinburgh, at least for a season, till God has increased your strength. For the company of those who know not God, who are strangers to the religion of the heart, especially if they are sensible, agreeable persons, might quite damp the grace of God in your soul.

You cannot oblige me more than by telling me all that is in your heart; there is no danger of your tiring me. I do not often write so long letters myself. But when I write to *you*, I am full of matter. I seem to see you just before me, a poor, feeble, helpless creature, but just upon the point of salvation, upright of heart (in a measure), full of real desires for God, and emerging into light. The Lord take you whole! So prays, my dear Lady,

Your affectionate servant,

John Wesley

Address: 'To / The Lady Maxwell'.
Source: manuscript transcription, not JW's hand except for possible annotation; MARC, MA 1977/609.

To Thomas Rankin

Bristol
September 21, 1764

Dear Tommy,

I sometimes wonder that all our preachers are not convinced of this, that it is of unspeakable use to spread our practical tracts in every society. Billy Penington in one year sold more of these in Cornwall than had been sold for seven years before.[149] So may you,

---

[148] JW stressed his opposition to anchoritic ('solitary') forms of mysticism in the preface to *HSP* (1739), p. viii: 'Directly opposite to this is the gospel of Christ. Solitary religion is not to be found there. "Holy solitaries" is a phrase no more consistent with the gospel than holy adulterers. The gospel of Christ knows of no religion, but social; no holiness but social holiness.'

[149] William Penington (c. 1734–67) of Yorkshire entered the itinerant ministry around 1760 (records are spotty for this period). He is well documented from 1765 to his death in 1767. See Atmore, *Memorial*, 314–17 (who spells the last name 'Pennington').

if you take the same method. Carry one sort of books with you the first time you go the round, another sort the second time, and so on. Preach on the subject at each place, and after preaching, encourage the congregation to buy and read the tract.

Neither James Michel nor William Thomas was without blame.[150] We must make allowance when they tell their own story, but if they now behave well, it is all we desire.

Some years since, there was something done in the way you mention concerning brother Triggs. I remember two or three of our brethren from the west coming to London, recommended by Billy Roberts.[151] The particulars he can best inform you of, as well as what success they had. Peace be with your spirit! I am,
>   Your affectionate friend and brother,

>   J. Wesley

Address: 'To / Mr Tho. Ranken / In St Ives / Cornwall'.
Postmark: stylised 'B/RIS/TOL'. *Charge*: '4'.
Source: holograph; Garrett-Evangelical, William Colbert Collection.

To Darcy (Brisbane) Maxwell, Lady Maxwell of Pollok

>   [BRISTOL]
>   SEPTEMBER 22, 1764

My Dear Lady,

You need be under no manner of apprehension of writing too often to me. The more frequent your letters are, the more welcome they will be. When I have not heard from you for some time, I begin to be full of fears. I am afraid either that your bodily weakness increases or that your desires after God grow cold. I consider you are at present but a tender, sickly plant, easily hurt by any rough blast. But I trust this will not be so long, for you have a strong helper. And the Lord, whom you serve, though feebly and imperfectly, will

---

[150] Telford changed 'Michel' to 'Mitchell'. Neither of these two men can be identified with any confidence.

[151] William Roberts (1728–97) was a native of Cornwall who became an itinerant in 1750 but left the itinerancy after a few years, settling into a career in business in Tiverton. He continued to support the Methodist work in this capacity. See Atmore, *Memorial*, 346–56.

suddenly come to his temple.[152] When, Lord? Are all things ready now?[153] Here is the sinner; one whose mouth is stopped, who has nothing to pay, who pleads neither her own harmlessness, nor works, nor good desires, nor sincerity, but can adopt that strange word,

5

> I give up every plea beside,
> Lord, I am damned; but thou hast died.[154]

He *has* died; therefore you shall live. O do not *reason* against him!
10 Let him take you now! Let him take you just as you are and make you what is acceptable in his sight.[155]

It gives me pleasure indeed to hear that God has given you resolution to join the society. Undoubtedly you will suffer reproach on the account, but it is the reproach of Christ. And you will have large
15 amends when the Spirit of glory and of God shall rest upon you.[156] Yet I foresee a danger. At first you will be inclined to think that *all* the members of the society are in earnest. And when you find that *some* are otherwise (which will always be the case in so large a body of people), then prejudice may easily steal in and exceedingly
20 weaken your soul. O beware of this rock of offence![157] When you *see* anything amiss (upon hearsay you will not readily receive it), remember our Lord's word, 'What is that to thee? Follow thou me.'[158] And I entreat you do not regard the half-Methodists (if we must use the name). Do not mind them who endeavour to hold Christ in one
25 hand and the world in the other. I want *you* to be all a Christian, such a Christian as the Marquis De Renty or Gregory Lopez was,[159] such an one as that saint of God, Jane Cooper,[160] all sweetness, all

---

[152] See Mal. 3:1.
[153] See Luke 14:17.
[154] CW, 'Gal. 3:22', st. 12, *HSP* (1739), 94.
[155] See Ps. 19:14.
[156] See 1 Pet. 4:14.
[157] See 1 Pet. 2:8.
[158] John 21:22.
   [159] JW frequently highlights these two as models of serious Christian piety. Indeed, he published *An Extract of the Life of Monsieur De Renty* in 1741 (*Bibliography*, No. 43); and included an abridgement of *The Holy Life of Gregory Lopez* (1675) in the *Christian Library*, 50:337–406.
   [160] Jane Cooper, born in 1738 at Higham in Norfolk, moved to London about 1756, was converted, and became a devout Methodist domestic servant. In failing health for some time, she died of smallpox and was buried by JW on Nov. 25, 1762 (see *Journal*, 21:399 in this edn.). In 1764 JW published *Letters wrote by Jane Cooper* (*Bibliography*, No. 260). His preface offered strong praise: 'Here are no extravagant flights, no mystic reveries, no unscriptural enthusiasm. The sentiments are all just and noble, the result of a fine natural understanding, cultivated

gentleness, all love. Methinks you *are* just what she *was* when I saw her first. I shrink at the thought of seeing you what she was when I saw her last. But why should I?[161] What is all the pain of one that is glorifying God in the fires with 'Father, into thy hands I commend my spirit'?[162]

May I not take upon me to give you one advice more? Be very wary how you contract new acquaintance. All, even sincere people, will not profit you. I should be pained at your conversing frequently with any but those who are of a deeply serious spirit and who speak closely to the point. You need not condemn *them*, and yet you may say, 'This will not do for *me*.'

May he that loves you richly supply all your wants[163] and answer your enlarged desires! So prays, my very dear Lady,

Your affectionate servant,

J. Wesley 15

Source: published transcription; Benson, *Works*, 16:187–89.

To Ann Foard

BRISTOL
SEPTEMBER 29, 1764

My Dear Sister,

I am glad you wrote. You should do it oftener, and the more freely the better. None shall see your letters, so that you need be under no apprehension of any inconvenience following.

In the Thoughts upon Perfection and in the Farther Thoughts,[164] you have a *clear, consistent* account of it. Did you never hear any one

---

by conversation, thinking, reading, and true Christian experience' (pp. 5–6). The collection includes twenty-one of her letters, written between Aug. 29, 1757 and Sept. 29, 1762, at the height of the perfection controversies, and many of them touching upon the subject.

[161] Two years after this letter, JW published an extended account of Jane Cooper's death as 'a living and a dying witness of Christian perfection' in §24 of *A Plain Account of Christian Perfection*, see 13:182–86.

[162] Luke 23:46.

[163] See Phil. 4:19.

[164] 'Thoughts on Christian Perfection' (1760; 13:54–80 in this edn.) and *Farther Thoughts upon Christian Perfection* (1762; 13:92–131).

speak of it in the *manner* I do there? Or does ‹___¹⁶⁵› speak of it in a *different* manner? Does not ‹___› speak in the same manner with ‹___›? Wherein do they differ? And does not ‹___¹⁶⁶›. Nancy, do not start but speak freely. It may be of more service than you are aware
5   of. And be assured, you will bring no inconvenience upon *yourself*.
    I was likewise grieved at the danger you was in of stopping short. Certainly you may attain that blessing *soon*. And I am thoroughly persuaded you *did* taste of it, though how you lost it I know not. It will be eternally true, 'If thou canst believe, all things are possible
10 to him that believeth.'¹⁶⁷ Meanwhile, faith is the voice of God in the heart, proclaiming himself. Have this faith and you have salvation. And this is the very thing you want. When this is joined with a strong understanding, it is well; but it may exist with a very weak understanding. This is the case with Mrs. W.¹⁶⁸ whose understand-
15 ing is extremely weak, and yet she has strong faith, and such as exceedingly profits *me*, though I take knowledge, the treasure is in an earthen vessel. I see *all* that is of nature, and this does not hinder my rejoicing in *all* that is of God. This is one branch of *simplicity*. While *reason* assisted from above enables me to discern the precious
20 from the vile, I make my full use of the former without losing one moment in thinking upon the latter. Perhaps *reason* (enlightened) makes me *simple*. If I *knew less* of human nature (forgive me for talking so much of myself) I should be more apt to stumble at the weakness of it. And if I had not (by nature or by grace) some *clearness* of
25 apprehension. It is owing to this (under God) that I never staggered at all at the reveries of George Bell. I saw instantly, at the beginning and from the beginning, what was right and what was wrong. But I *saw* withal, 'I have many things to speak, but you cannot bear them now.'¹⁶⁹ Hence many imagined I was *imposed* upon and applauded
30 themselves in their greater perspicacity, as they do at this day. 'But if you knew it', says his friend to Gregory Lopez, 'why did not you

---

¹⁶⁵ Someone has cutout several places in the manuscript where JW named persons. See the similar cutouts in the letter of Oct. 12; as explained there, the names cut out here likely include Sarah Ryan and Sarah Crosby.

¹⁶⁶ This cutout is longer, running half a line.

¹⁶⁷ Mark 9:23.

¹⁶⁸ See JW's more extended description of Mrs. W. in *Journal*, Sept. 14, 1763, 21:428 in this edn. See also the letters from her that he published in *AM*, starting with one dated Apr. 18, 1761.

¹⁶⁹ John 16:12.

tell me?' I answer with him, 'I do not speak all I know, but what I judge needful.'[170]

Still, I am persuaded there is no state under heaven from which it is not possible to fall. But I wish *you* was *all love*, and then you would not need to take any thought for the morrow. 5

The usual preaching may be at Combe of Saturday evening, and at the Grove on Sunday morning.[171] I *bear* the rich, and love the poor. Therefore I spend *almost all* my time with them.

My dear sister,
Adieu! 10

Write to me at London, and write freely.

Address: 'To / Miss Foard'.
No *postmark* or indications of postal *charge*; apparently delivered by hand.
Endorsement: 'Thinkst thou to treat Almighty Pow'r / Is but the Bus'ness of an Hour? / O who that gets So dear a Guest / But once enshrin'd within his Breast, / Would, for this worlds Impertinence, / Neglect him there, or drive him thence?'[172]
Source: holograph; WHS Ireland Archives.

To Christopher Hopper

BRISTOL
SEPTEMBER 29, 1764 15

My Dear Brother,

My judgement is this, that it is best for you to be at Edinburgh (but in a more airy lodging, if it can be had for love or money) before the end of next month, James Kershaw at Dundee, and Tommy Hanby at Aberdeen. If you have either love or pity for him, let 20 him not stay too long at Dundee. His mind is by no means strong enough to bear that weight of applause. At any rate, take him out of

---

[170] Francisco de Losa, *The Holy Life of Gregory Lopez*, Abraham Woodhead, tr. (London, 1675), 124; summarised in JW's abridgement, *Christian Library*, 50:381.

[171] Monkton Combe (often called simply 'Combe') was about 5 km south of Bath. Combe Grove at that time was simply a house built in a grove nearby, where JW preached on Sept. 17 (see *Journal*, 21:488 in this edn.). Foard may have been present, and appears to have asked about the times of regular Methodist preaching at these sites.

[172] From a poem 'On Retirement' (author unidentified), in David Lewis, ed., *Miscellaneous Poems by Several Hands* (London: J. Watts, 1730), 183–85.

the furnace, or he will be consumed. And you well know a change
is best for the people as well as best for him. Is it not easiest for him
and you to change at a day appointed, and then for you to stay at
Dundee till you are relieved by James Kershaw?

5   Peace be with your spirits! I am,
           Your affectionate friend and brother,

                                                        J. Wesley

I hope you have been at Sir Archibald [Grant]'s.

Address: 'To / Mr Christopher Hopper / in / Aberdeen'.
Postmarks: stylised 'B/RIS/TOL' and '1/OC'. *Charge*: '4'.
Source: holograph; Bridwell Library (SMU).

To the Rev. Samuel Furly

10   YARMOUTH
                                               OCTOBER 11, 1764

Dear Sammy,
     I have delayed writing thus long, because I was not inclined to
draw the saw of controversy, particularly on a subject not very im-
15   portant and with a person not very easy to be convinced. I simply
told you my thoughts concerning style and concerning yourself.[173]
If you can profit by them, well; if not, there is no harm done. I
wanted to have you write in the most excellent way. If you prefer
any other, you may. I have no prejudice for or against any writer. But
20   I may say, without much vanity, I know a good style from a bad one,
and it would be a shame if I did not, after having spent five-and-
forty years (with some natural understanding, much attention, and
a free acquaintance with many eminent men) in reading the most
celebrated writers in the English tongue.
25   Observing *you* to want one of the things essential to a good style,
namely, *easiness*, I warned you of it, and (to make the reason of my
caution more clear) enlarged a little upon the head. You reply, '*Harmony* is essential to a good style.' It may be so. I have nothing to
say to the contrary. In the very lines I quoted there is admirable

---

[173] See JW to Furly, July 15, 1764.

harmony, *nihil supra*.[174] The soul of music breathes in them, but there is no stiffness. The lines are as easy as harmonious. This is the perfection of writing.

Whether *long* periods or *short* are to be chosen is quite another question. Some of those you transcribe from Swift are long, but they are *easy* too, entirely easy, void of all stiffness, and therefore just such as I advise you to copy after. The paragraphs cited from Hawkesworth[175] are far inferior to them; not more harmonious, but more stiff and artificial. That from Wharton is worst of all, stiff as a stake, all art and no nature.[176] I know not what taste they can have who admire his style; certainly they must prefer Statius to Virgil.

That 'poor people understand long sentences better than short' is an entire mistake. I have carefully tried the experiment for thirty years, and I find the very reverse to be true. Long sentences utterly confound their intellects; they know not where they are. If you would be understood by them, you should seldom use a word of many syllables or a sentence of many words. Short sentences are likewise infinitely best for the careless and indolent. They strike them through and through. I have seen instances of it an hundred times. Neither are the dull and stupid enlightened nor the careless affected by long and laboured periods half so much as by such short ones as these, 'The work is great. The day is short. And long is the night wherein no man can work.'[177]

But the main thing is, let us be all alive to God.[178] Let Christ reign alone in our hearts.[179] Let all that mind be in us which was in Christ Jesus.[180] And let us walk as Christ also walked.[181]

Peace be with you and yours! I am,

Your affectionate friend and brother,

J. Wesley

Source: published transcription; *United Methodist Free Churches Magazine* 9 (1866): 250–51.

[174] 'Nothing better'.

[175] Orig., 'Hawksworth'. John Hawkesworth (c. 1715–73), an English writer and editor who followed Samuel Johnson as a reporter on parliamentary debates for the *Gentleman's Magazine*. JW revealed his distaste for Hawkesworth again in a comment on his book about the voyages of Captain Cook; JW, *Journal*, Nov. 17, 1773, 22:394–95 in this edn.

[176] Perhaps the author Henry Wharton (1664–95), who had written *Anglia Sacra* (1691), a collection of biographies of English bishops and Archbishops.

[177] John 9:4.

[178] See Rom. 6:11.

[179] See Col. 3:15. The KJV read 'Let the peace of God rule in your hearts', but JW was aware that the text in Greek and Latin had 'peace of Christ'.

[180] See Phil. 2:5.

[181] See 1 John 2:6.

To Ann Foard

[NORWICH]
OCTOBER 12,[182] 1764

My Dear Sister,

That great truth, 'that we are saved by faith',[183] will never be
5   worn out; and that sanctifying as well as justifying faith is the free
gift of God.[184] Now, with God one day is as a thousand years.[185] It
plainly follows that the quantity of time is nothing to him. Centuries, years, months, days, hours, and moments are exactly the same.
Consequently he can as well sanctify in a day after we are justified
10   as an hundred years. There is no difference at all unless we suppose
him to be such an one as ourselves. Accordingly we see, in fact, that
some of the most unquestionable instances of sanctifying grace were
sanctified within a *few days* after they were justified. I have seldom
known so devoted a soul as Sally Hooley, at Macclesfield, who was
15   sanctified within nine days after she was *convinced of sin*.[186] She was
then twelve years old, and I believe was never afterwards heard to
speak an improper word or seen to do an *improper thing*. Her look
struck an awe into all that saw her. She is now in Abraham's bosom.

Although, therefore, it *usually* pleases God to interpose *some time*
20   between justification and sanctification, yet, as it is expressly observed in the *Farther Thoughts*, we must not fancy this to be an
invariable rule. All who think this must think 'we are sanctified
by works', or (which comes to the same) by sufferings, for otherwise what is *time* necessary for? It must be either to do or to suffer.
25   Whereas, if nothing be required but simple faith, a moment is as
good as an age.

The truth is, we are continually forming *general* rules from our
own *particular* experience. Thus ⟨Sarah Ryan[187]⟩ having gone about
and about herself, which took up a considerable time, might very
30   naturally suppose *all* who are sanctified must stay for it near as long
a time as she did. Again, if God has so rooted and grounded *her* in
love (which I neither affirm nor deny) that she *cannot* now fall from

---

[182] This is the date given in *AM*, but the postmark suggests that it may have been Oct. 17.
[183] Eph. 2:8.
[184] See Rom. 5:15.
[185] See 2 Pet. 3:8.
[186] JW recounts the story of Ann Hooly (who apparently went by 'Sally') in his *Journal*, Aug. 6, 1762, 21:385 in this edn.
[187] As in the letter of Sept. 29, the names of persons mentioned are cut out of the manu-
script. JW's transcription in *AM* has 'S— R—' in this and three following instances; for which
Sarah Ryan is the almost certain referent. Cf. JW's letter to Ryan, June 28, 1766.

him, she very naturally thinks this is the case with *all* that are sanctified. Formerly ⟨Sarah Crosby[188]⟩ drew the same inference from *her own* experience, and was as positive that she *could not fall* from that state or sin as ⟨Sarah Ryan⟩ can be now.

But 'none can be sanctified without a deep knowledge of themselves and of the devices of Satan.' They may without the latter, which God will give them in due time. And the former he can give in a moment, and frequently does, of which we have fresh instances almost every day.

In the Thoughts on Perfection it is observed that, before any can be assured they are saved from sin, they must not only feel no sin but 'have a direct witness' of that salvation.[189] And this several have had as clear as ⟨Sarah Ryan⟩ has, who afterwards fell from that salvation, although ⟨Sarah Ryan⟩, to be consistent with her scheme, must deny they ever had it, yea, and must affirm that witness was either from nature or the devil. If it was really from God, is he well pleased with this?

I know not how to reconcile speaking *sharply* or *roughly*, or even a seeming *want of meekness*, with perfection. And yet I am fearful of condemning whom God has not condemned. What I cannot understand I leave to him.

How is it that you make me write longer letters to *you* than I do almost to any one else? I know not how. I find a greater concern for your welfare. I want you to be exactly right. This occasions my not thinking much of any pains that may give *you* help or satisfaction. The Lord touch your heart *now*, that all your tempers, thoughts, words, and works may be holiness unto our God.[190]

Address: 'To Miss Ford at Mr Alcocks / Milliner, In Green dragon Cort / Southwark / London'.[191]
Postmarks: 'NORWICH' and '17/OC'.
Endorsement: 'Revd John Wesley / to Ann Thornton'.[192]
Source: holograph; MARC, MAM JW 3/2; compared to JW's published transcription in *Arminian Magazine* 5 (1782): 608–9.

---

[188] This name is also cut out in the manuscript; with *AM* reading 'S— C—'. What remains visible on the edges of the cut-out portion corresponds to 'S Crosby', making Sarah Crosby the certain referent; cf. JW to Sarah Crosby, Oct. 5, 1765.

[189] See 'Thoughts on Christian Perfection', Q. 26, 13:73 in this edn.

[190] Cf. Jer. 2:3. JW ends here, without his typical closing line and signature.

[191] While the body of the letter is in JW's hand, the address is not.

[192] Ann Foard married John Thornton in 1772, so the endorsement is evidently after that year.

To Jane Catherine March

[NORWICH]
OCTOBER 13, 1764

I do not see that you can speak otherwise than you do in your band. If you sought their approbation, that would be wrong, but you may suffer it without blame. Indeed, in these circumstances you must, since it is undeniably plain that the doing otherwise would hurt rather than help their souls. I believe Miss F___[193] thought she felt evil before she did, and by that very thought gave occasion to its re-entrance. You ought not to speak explicitly to many, very few would understand or know how to advise you. For some time I thought M___[194] did, and was therefore glad of your acquaintance with him, hoping he would lead you by the hand in a more profitable manner than I was able to do. But I afterwards doubted. The Lord send you help by whom he will send!

From what not only you but many others likewise have experienced, we find there is very frequently a kind of wilderness state, not only after justification, but even after deliverance from sin; and I doubt whether the sermon upon that state might not give you light in this case also.[195] But the most frequent cause of this second darkness or distress, I believe, is evil reasoning. By this, three in four of those who cast away their confidence are gradually induced so to do. And if this be the cause, is there any way to regain that deliverance but by resuming your confidence? And can you receive it unless you receive it freely, not of works, but by mere grace? This is the way; walk thou in it.[196] Dare to believe! Look up and see thy Saviour near! When? Tomorrow or today? Nay, today hear his voice! At this time, at this place! Lord, speak. Thy servant heareth![197]

Source: published transcription; *Methodist Magazine* 22 (1799): 200.

---

[193] Likely Ann Foard.
[194] Almost certainly Thomas Maxfield.
[195] Sermon 46, 'The Wilderness State', 2:202–21 in this edn.
[196] See Isa. 30:21.
[197] See 1 Sam. 3:9–10.

To the Printer of the *St. James's Chronicle*

[LONDON]
OCTOBER 27, 1764

Sir,

Your last paper contained a letter to me.[198] If you
please to insert a few lines in answer, you will oblige,   5
Your humble servant,

John Wesley

One may know Hercules by his foot.[199] In the letter of Oct. 13,
I easily take knowledge of my old friend,[200] though dating from   10
Gravesend, who is no Presbyterian, but *a kind of* Churchman.

The doctor has much time, and I have much work; therefore I
shall take no farther notice of his innocent performance than to
touch upon one or two little mistakes, which may easily be removed.

He says, 'you apply Στοργὴ to religious opinions'. Indeed I do   15
not, nor ever did, and I cite the Doctor himself to prove the contrary, whose words in the very same paragraph are, 'what you mean
by *storge* here is something like that fondness which papists express
for all the members of their Church'.

The other mistake is of greater importance. He says, you are 'fully   20
*persuaded that the Dissenters in general are in a more damnable state than
those who live without God in the world.*' And this he puts in *italics*, to
persuade the reader not only that these are my words, but that this
is a sentiment which I lay a peculiar stress upon. I charge this upon
his conscience before God, as a deliberate, wilful falsehood. He well   25
knows nothing under heaven can be more contrary to my firm, settled persuasion, declared an hundred times, all manner of ways, both
in public and private. Two sermons I printed many years ago, one

---

[198] *St. James's Chronicle* for Oct. 23–25, 1764, on the second page, contained a two-
column letter dated from Gravesend and signed 'A Presbyterian,' severely questioning JW's
professions of loyalty to the Church of England given his more recent statements that the
Church stood in need of reformation and might not tolerate the reformation it needed.

[199] A Latin proverb, *Ex pede Herculem*: '[You can tell it is] Hercules from his foot'.

[200] JW assumes this letter is by John Cook, M.D., who had published a letter to Wesley
under the pseudonym 'Stephen Church' on Nov. 3, 1760. For John Cook's disavowal, see his
letter to *St. James's Chronicle*, dated Nov. 12, 1764. 'A Presbyterian' was likely Mr. Eglesham,
schoolmaster in Gravesend (see his follow-up letter dated Nov. 5, 1764).

on 'Bigotry', the other on 'Catholic Spirit', which express the very opposite sentiment to this, in the strongest terms, from beginning to end.[201] I believe 'the kingdom of God is not meats and drinks', not externals of any kind, not opinions, or modes of worship, but 'righteousness, and peace, and joy in the Holy Ghost'.[202] And whoever 'in these serveth God, the same is my brother, and sister, and mother'.[203]

5

Source: published transcription; *St. James's Chronicle* (November 1–3, 1764), p. 1.

To the Printer of the *St. James's Chronicle*

LONDON
OCTOBER 29, 1764

10 Sir,

The words inserted as mine in your last paper I absolutely disclaim.[204] I never said, 'If any of you have any money in the public funds, it would be less sin, to take it out and cast it into the depth of the sea, than to let it continue there.' I believe a man may let money

15 continue there without any sin at all.

Whoever desires to see my full deliberate thoughts on this subject, may read the sermon on 'the mammon of unrighteousness'.[205] And this I am ready to defend against any that will set his name. But I do not love fighting in the dark. I am,

20   Your humble servant,

John Wesley

PS. The further remarks of the 'Presbyterian' Doctor of physic, I may, perhaps, have leisure to read by and by.

---

[201] Sermon 38, 'A Caution Against Bigotry', 2:61–80; and Sermon 39, 'Catholic Spirit', 2:81–95 in this edn.

[202] Rom. 14:17.

[203] Matt. 12:50; Mark 3:35.

[204] JW is replying to a letter from 'Solicitus', dated Oct. 24, and published in *St. James's Chronicle* (Oct. 25–27, 1764), p. 3.

[205] JW refers to Sermon 50, 'The Use of Money', 2:263–80 in this edn. It is based on Luke 16:9, 'Make unto yourselves friends of the mammon of unrighteousness ...'.

Source: published transcription; *The St. James's Chronicle* (November 8–10, 1764), p. 1. Reprinted in *Ipswich Journal* (Nov. 17, 1764), p. 1.

To Thomas Rankin

LONDON
NOVEMBER 2, 1764

My Dear Brother,

At the request of several of our preachers I have at length abridged Dr. Goodwin's Treatise on Justification.[206] I trust it will stop the   5
mouths of gainsayers concerning imputed righteousness, and teach them (at least the most candid) to speak as the oracles of God.

I desire *you* to read the proposal and preface in every society within your circuit, then enforce it, as you see best, both in public and private conversation. Spare no pains. Exert yourself. See   10
what you can do. Give this proof of your love for the truth, for the people, and for

Your affectionate friend and brother,

J. Wesley

15

N.B. Be careful to keep an exact list of all the subscribers' names in each society, and also to leave a copy thereof with the person who takes care of the books.

Address: 'To Mr T. Rankin / St Ives'.
Source: manuscript transcription, with JW's signature;[207] Emory, MAR-BL, Wesley Family Papers, 1/44.

---

[206] The Puritan author John Goodwin (1593–1665) published a *Treatise on Justification* in 1642. In response to Calvinistic claims about the doctrine of imputed righteousness, Wesley published an extract of Goodwin's *Treatise* in 1765 (*Bibliography*, No. 266).

[207] The text appears to be in the hand of Joseph Cownley. This was surely one of numerous copies of this letter, sent to JW's scattered Assistants, to raise subscriptions for the volume.

To Thomas Rankin

LONDON
NOVEMBER 6, 1764

Dear Tommy,

If the Crowan or [St.] Buryan²⁰⁸ society are able to bear the ex-
5   pense of building themselves, we have no objection. But we must
not increase our debt this year. This is what we determined. If you
do build, build large enough.

In general, we do not pay rent out of the public stock, but get help
from friends in the circuit. For once we may allow forty shillings.

10   I shall write to Plymouth Dock this post. I hope John Catermole
(a sound man) will come and help you.²⁰⁹ I shall either mend William Darney or end him. He must not go on in this manner.

Spread the little tracts wherever you go. You know the solid good
which results therefrom.

15   Go on; spend and be spent for a good master. I am, dear Tommy,
Your affectionate friend and brother,

J. Wesley

Address: 'To / Mr Tho Rankin / At Mr Joseph Andrew's / In Redruth /
Cornwall'.
Postmark: '6/NO'. *Charge*: '4'.
Source: holograph; Emory, MARBL, Wesley Family Papers, 1/45.

---

²⁰⁸ Orig., 'Burian'. Both societies were in Cornwall.

²⁰⁹ John Catermole (d. c. 1799) traveled briefly as a helper about 1763, then went to study
and assist at Kingswood, while preaching occasionally. He returned to the itinerant ranks in
1765, but by 1771 it was clear that his temperament did not suit this calling and he settled again.
See Atmore, *Memorial*, 73.

To the Rev. Charles Wesley

LONDON,
DECEMBER 7, 1764

[[Dear Brother,]]

Be so kind as to show this to Thomas Lewis[210] and Mark Davis[211] so I may answer theirs and yours together.

What need of a formal petition? Would it not be just as effectual for me to write a letter to the Corporation, in the name of all the Bristol Methodists—urging first, Mr. Witherspoon's argument against the English theatre;[212] secondly, the matter of fact, the actual mischief done thereby; and then gently and respectfully making the application? What think you? *Ecquid novisti rectius?*[213] Send me word without delay.

Sister Suky was in huge agonies for five days, and then died in the full assurance of faith. Some of her last words (after she had been speechless for some time) were, 'Jesus is come! Heaven is here!'[214]

I am like Simonides. The more I think, the less able I am to answer the king's question: to prove the necessity, expediency, or propriety of an atonement to an unconvinced sinner.[215]

Indeed, you ought to have said something to Thomas Maxfield's letter, had it been only what you say now. He is Thomas Maxfield still. *Cerebrum non habet.*[216] Mr. [John] Richardson is better and better.

James Wheatley (the jewel!) has given me warning to quit the

---

[210] Thomas Lewis was a General Steward in Bristol at this time (see 10:873 in this edn.), and a friend of CW.

[211] Mark Davis (1734–1803) was accepted as an itinerant at the Dublin Conference in 1756, shortly after joining the Dublin society (Crookshank, *Ireland*, 1:131). He was currently serving in Wiltshire as an Assistant. Davis left the itinerant ranks in 1768 to set up a school in London (see 10:353 in this edn.).

[212] John Witherspoon (1723–94) had published *A Serious Inquiry into the Nature and Effects of the Stage* in 1757.

[213] 'Do you know anything better?'

[214] Susanna (née Wesley) Ellison, the elder sister of John and Charles, died the very day of this letter.

[215] Telford explains that 'Simonides of Ceos spent his last days at the Court of Hiero, tyrant of Syracuse, who begged him to explain the being and nature of the Deity. Simonides asked for a day to reflect, and when the question was repeated on the morrow he asked for two days, then four, and so on. Hiero grew weary of waiting, and wanted to know the reason for his strange behaviour. Simonides replied, "The longer I deliberate, the greater obscurity I find"' (Telford, *Letters*, 4:276).

[216] 'He has no brain.'

Tabernacle in spring; so I am preparing to build at Norwich, for no place already built can be procured for love or money.[217]

I think verily there is no need that you and I should be such strangers to each other. Surely we are old enough to be wiser.

5   Come, I will give you a little work. Translate for me into good English the Latin verses that occur in the *Earnest Appeal*; and why not those three Greek ones?[218]

Ἦ, καὶ κυανέῃσιν ἐπ' ὀφρύσι νεῦσε Κρονίων,....[219]

I have answered poor Mr. Hervey's last tract so far as it is per-
10 sonal.[220] My love to Sally. *Vivamus!*[221]

Adieu!

I will see to the 6 lb.

15 You *should* send C. Perronet's book immediately.[222]
The Tax of the Apostolic Chamber.

Address: 'To / The Revd Mr Charles Wesley / in / Bristol'.
Postmark: '8/DE'. *Charge*: '4'.
Endorsement: in CW's hand, 'Dec. 7. 1764 / B. / poor S Suky saved / at last! Why shd — / despair?'
Source: holograph; Emory, MARBL, Wesley Family Papers, 1/46.

[217] JW had been renting the Tabernacle in Norwich from Wheatley since 1758 (see *Journal*, Nov. 3, 1758, 21:170 in this edn.).

[218] While he refers specifically to the *Earnest Appeal to Men of Reason and Religion*, JW is lumping with this the three-part sequel, *Farther Appeal* .... There are only two Latin quotations in *Earnest Appeal*, and no Greek. JW was at work on a new edition of the *Appeals*, but ended up publishing only the *Earnest Appeal* (6th edn.) the following year. He published the full set next in his collected *Works*, vol. 14 (1772). Vol. 32 of *Works* (1774) included an appendix giving English translations for various Latin and Greek items, including those in the *Appeals*. It is unclear who did the translations. The relevant Latin and Greek passages (with suggested English translation in footnotes) can be found on 11:51, 217, 274, and 303 in this edn.

[219] Homer, *Iliad*, i.528ff. The translation that JW supplied in *Works* (1774) was 'Jove spake, and nodded with his sable brow, / And huge Olympus to his centre shook'.

[220] James Hervey's manuscript letters addressed to JW, which he left unpublished at his death in 1758, in the care of his brother, had been surreptitiously published by one of their associates in mid 1764 as *Aspasio Vindicated, and the Scripture-Doctrine of Imputed Righteousness Defended against the Objections and Animadversions of the Rev. John Wesley, in Eleven Letters* ([Leeds: Griffith Wright,] 1764). JW became aware of this volume and crafted an answer in late Nov. He published this 'answer' as the Preface to his abridgement of John Goodwin's *Treatise on Justification*; see 13:377–90 in this edn.

[221] 'Let us live!'

[222] Possibly a reference to C[harles] P[erronet], *A Letter to Mr. P——e : Occasioned by the late frequent disturbances made during the time of prayer and exhortation, in an independent meeting in Beach-Lane* (London, 1762).

To Sarah Moore

LONDON
DECEMBER 8, 1764

My Dear Sister,

Your business is by every possible means to calm the intemperate
spirits on both sides.[223] There has been much ill blood, and many un- 5
kind sayings, which had been better let alone. Now, at least, let there
be by general agreement an entire cessation of arms. Our God is a
God of peace; and all his children should with all their might labour
after it. I have heard something of the kind you mention, but not in the
same manner you relate it. However, let it die and be forgotten. I am, 10
    Your affectionate brother,

J. Wesley

Source: published transcription; Everett, *Sheffield*, 1:188–89.

To Thomas Rankin

LONDON
DECEMBER 15, 1764 15

Dear Tommy,

I will send a man down to William Darney that is as rough as himself, namely, Thomas Bryant.[224] But he is much changed for the better,
and I think will not now jar with you. You need not, indeed, be very
near one another; Cornwall is wide enough. Otherwise let Thomas 20
Bryant stay in Devonshire and Peter Price move westward.[225] John
Catermole sticks fast at Kingswood, and can get no farther.

I wish you could conquer John Paynter too.[226] And who knows?
Love may do the deed.

[223] See JW to Sarah Moore, July 5, 1764, on the controversy over Thomas Bryant.

[224] JW referred to problems with William Darney in his letter to CW, Dec. 7, 1764. He
mentioned problems with Thomas Bryant in his letters to Sarah Moore of July 5 and Dec. 8,
1764.

[225] Peter Price was admitted as a preacher in 1765 (10:303 in this edn.), after one year on
trial. He served as a master at Kingswood School from 1765–68; cf. Hastling et al., *Kingswood*,
Register, 195.

[226] John Paynter was a native of Crowan, Cornwall, mentioned in JW, *Journal*, Apr. 12,
1744, 20:24 in this edn.

Want of sleep will occasion hoarseness. You should sleep at least
six hours in twenty-four, either at once or at twice.

For hoarseness look into the *Primitive Physick*, and try, one after another if need be, the garlic, the apple, the conserve, and the
5   balsam. I know not how you will procure subscribers to Goodwin
while you are pressing the general subscription.[227]

I am, dear Tommy,
              Your affectionate friend.

[John Wesley]

10

Source: published transcription; Jackson, *Works* (3rd), 12:306.

To the Mayor and Corporation of Bristol

LONDON
DECEMBER 20, 1764

Gentlemen,

Both my brother and I and all who have any connexion with us are
15   extremely sensible of our obligations to you for the civility which
you have shown us on all occasions, and we cannot but feel ourselves deeply interested in whatever we apprehend in any degree to
concern your honour or the general good and prosperity of the City
of Bristol. This occasions my giving you the present trouble, which
20   (whether it has any farther effect or no) you will please to receive as
a testimony of the high regard we shall ever retain for you.

The endeavours lately used to procure subscriptions for building
a new playhouse in Bristol have given us not a little concern, and
that on various accounts: not barely as most of the present stage
25   entertainments sap the foundation of all religion, as they naturally
tend to efface all traces of piety and seriousness out of the minds
of men; but as they are peculiarly hurtful to a trading city, giving
a wrong turn to youth especially gay, trifling, and directly opposite to the spirit of industry and close application to business; and,
30   as drinking and debauchery of every kind are constant attendants

---

[227] I.e., how to fulfill the exhortation in JW's letter of Nov. 2, while gathering the yearly
collection for Kingswood School; see Minutes, Aug. 28, 1756, 10:277–78 in this edn.

on these entertainments, with indolence, effeminacy, and idleness, which affect trade in an high degree.[228]

It was on these very considerations that the Corporation at Nottingham lately withstood all solicitations, and absolutely forbade the building a new theatre there, being determined to encourage nothing of the kind. And I doubt not but thousands will reap the benefit of their wise and generous resolution.

It does not become me, gentlemen, to press anything upon you, but I could not avoid saying this much, both in behalf of myself and all my friends.

Wishing you the continuance and increase of every blessing, I remain, gentlemen,

> Your obliged and obedient servant,

> > John Wesley

[[Dear brother,]]

I suppose it is of little consequence in whose hand this is transmitted. Let it be accompanied by prayer and good must follow, one way or the other. Let us work while the day is.[229]

> Adieu.[230]

Address: 'To / The Revd Mr C. Wesley / in / Bristol'.
Postmark: '19/DE' [*sic*]. *Charge*: '4'.
Source: holograph; MARC, DDWes 3/25.

To the Rev. Charles Wesley

LONDON
DECEMBER 31, 1764

[[Dear Brother,]]

Pray tell Thomas Lewis I believe one I spoke to yesterday will make us a good housekeeper. She is selling off her things, and can come in two or three weeks.

---

[228] Despite these concerns of the Wesley brothers, the Theatre Royal was built on King Street, opening in 1766.

[229] Cf. John 9:4.

[230] The note to CW appears on the back of the address half and is thus detachable, so that the letter to the Mayor and Corporation of Bristol could be delivered without the affixed note.

John Matthews sent for me between 2 and 3 on Friday morning.[231]
One had a little before asked him how he found himself, and he answered, 'The Lord protects, for ever near.' When I came, he was
perfectly sensible. I began to pray at three, and before I had spoken
5 many words his soul was set at liberty, without a groan. Here is a
subject for y‹our pen.[232›] He has had 'the witness', in *my* sense, for
several months—that is, he *knew* he was in the favour of God, and
had *no doubt* of going to heaven.[233]

I hope Goodwin is above three-quarters printed.[234]
10 You know doctors differ. I could trust Dr. Turner as well as any.[235]
I shall say a word to the preachers in Ireland. I really thought
Mark Davis had had more wit and more modesty.

I do not yet find anything on the atonement fit for a deist. Pray
inquire of your learned friends.
15 My love to Sally.
[[Adieu.]]

I have sent you by Miss Billo the Preface to Goodwin and the
Appeals. You will English the Latin verses, and produce the nearest
20 and correctest edition of them which has ever appeared.[236]

No *address*, *postmark*, or indications of postal *charge*; apparently delivered
by hand.
Endorsement: in CW's hand, 'B. Dec. 31, 1764 / J. Mathews death'.
Source: holograph; MARC, DDWes 3/26.

---

[231] John Matthews, husband of JW's step-daughter Jeanne (Vazeille), had been dying of
consumption since at least August; see JW, *Journal*, Aug. 27, 1764, 21:487 in this edn.

[232] There is a hole in the paper and the words in brackets are supplied.

[233] Charles Wesley did in fact write a manuscript poem 'On the Death of Mr. John Mat-
thews, Dec. 28, 1764', surviving in MARC, MA 1977/583/20. A transcription is available in
S T Kimbrough, Jr., and Oliver Beckerlegge, eds., *The Unpublished Poetry of Charles Wesley*
(Nashville, 1992), 3:335–37 (or on the CSWT website; see p. xv above).

[234] I.e., JW's extract of John Goodwin's *Treatise on Justification*.

[235] JW had recommended Dr. Turner to his wife in a letter of July 10, 1756.

[236] Cf. JW to CW, Dec. 7, 1764. There is no evidence that CW prepared the English
translations requested at this time. Only the *Earnest Appeal* was issued in a new edition in 1765,
and there was no English translation provided for the Latin verse.

1765

To *London Magazine* / 'Philosophaster'[1]

[LONDON]
JANUARY 4, 1765

Sir,

If you please to insert in your magazine my
answer to a letter directed to me in November last,   5
you will oblige,
      Your humble servant,

John Wesley

Sir,   10
    I am obliged to you for your queries and remarks, and so I shall be
to any who will point out anything wherein they think I have been
mistaken. It would not be strange if there should be many mistakes
in the *Compendium of Natural Philosophy*, as philosophy is what for
many years I have only looked into at leisure hours. Accordingly in   15
the preface of that treatise I said, 'I am thoroughly sensible there are
many who have more ability as well as leisure for such a work than
me, but as none of them undertakes it, I have myself made some
little attempt in the following volumes.'[2]
    Q. 1. 'You say the sun revolves upon his axis once in twenty-seven   20
hours. Should it not be once in twenty-seven days nearly?' Yes, it
should. This was an error of the press.

---

[1] JW published *Survey of the Wisdom of God in the Works of Nature: Or, A Compendium of Natural Philosophy* in 1763. The main source of this work was Johann Franz Buddeus, *Elementa Philosophiae Theoreticae* (Halle: Glauche-Hallensis, 1706), which JW translated and abridged. But he also interspersed material from other writers, resulting in some contradictory claims. A writer taking the pseudonym 'Philosophaster' ('the little philosopher'), in the Nov. issue of *London Magazine* (pp. 570–73), pointed out a few of these problems and challenged the caution Wesley exhibited concerning recent scientific advances, particularly in astronomy. This is JW's reply.

[2] JW, *Survey*, Preface, §3, p. 4.

Q. 2. 'You say he is *supposed* to be abundantly larger than the earth. Is it not *demonstrable* that he is so?' I do not know whether it is or no.

Q. 3. 'You tell us the moon turns always the same side to the earth. Should it not be *nearly* the same?' Yes.

Q. 4. 'You say it does not appear that she moves round her own axis. How, then, do you account for her turning always the same side to the earth?' I think, full as well without the supposition as with it. But I do not undertake to *account* for anything.

Q. 5. 'Why do you say the moon is *supposed* to be forty-five times smaller than the earth when the moon's bulk is nicely known?' It is not *known* by me; nor, I doubt, by any man else.

Q. 6. 'You say Jupiter is supposed to be twenty-five times larger than the earth, and in the next page that his diameter is supposed to be 130,655 miles. If so, is he not 4,096 times larger than the earth?' Undoubtedly. But I do not undertake to defend either one supposition or the other.

Q. 7. 'You inform us that even a good eye seldom sees more than an hundred stars at a time. Do you mean at one look?' Yes.

Remark 1. 'You say (p. 148), "Even with respect to the distance of the sun, it is wisest to confess our ignorance, and to acknowledge we have nothing to rest upon here but mere uncertain conjecture."' I did not say this of the distance of the sun in particular. My words (p. 146[3]) are: 'With regard to *their* distance from the earth (the distance of all the bodies in the solar system), there is such an immense difference in the calculations of astronomers, even with respect to the distance of the sun, that it is wisest to confess our ignorance,' namely, with regard to *their* distance.

To prove that we are not ignorant hereof you say: 'The knowledge of the sun's distance depends on finding its parallax, or the angle that the semi-diameter of the earth appears under at the sun; which angle is so very minute that an error of a single second will give the distance very considerably greater or less than the true distance.' It will, and therefore I doubt whether the distance of any heavenly body can ever be known by this means.[4]

---

[3] JW has the page correct; 'Philosophaster' had given the wrong citation (p. 148). This may be Wesley's subtle reminder of human fallibility to his opponent.

[4] 'Philosophaster' responded to this and subsequent places where Wesley doubted calculations based on parallax, asserting that accurate parallax measurements could be made by calculating the relative size of the shadow that the moon casts on earth during a lunar eclipse and the size of the moon's image in respect to the sun during a solar eclipse (*London Magazine*, March 1765, 129–30).

'But Mr. Keill[5] says: "We are assured, by various methods made use of to obtain the sun's parallax, that his distance from us is more than twenty-eight millions of miles.'" He may be assured, but I am not. 'He says farther: "Two eminent astronomers have since determined the sun's distance to be about seventy-six millions of miles." Now, if the least distance possible is *absolutely determined*, how can it be wisest to confess our ignorance?' If it be. But I doubt it cannot be determined at all, at least, not by the sun's parallax, 'seeing this is so very minute that an error of a single second will give the distance very considerably greater or less than the true.'

Remark 2. 'In page 143 you tell us' — the whole paragraph runs thus, 'It is now almost universally supposed that the moon is just like the earth, having mountains and valleys, seas with islands, peninsulas and promontories, with a changeable atmosphere, wherein vapours and exhalations rise and fall, and hence it is generally inferred that she is inhabited like the earth, and, by parity of reason, that all the other planets, as well as the earth and moon, have their respective inhabitants.' (I take this to be the very strength of the cause. It was this consideration chiefly which induced me to think for many years that all the planets were inhabited.) 'But after all comes the celebrated Mr. [Christian] Huygens, and brings strong reasons why the moon is not, and cannot be, inhabited at all, nor any secondary planet whatever. Then' (if the first supposition sinks, on which all the rest are built) 'I doubt that we shall never prove that the primary are. And so the whole hypothesis of innumerable suns and worlds moving round them vanishes into air.'

In order to prove that there are innumerable suns you say,

1) 'It is found by observations on the parallax of the earth's orbit that a fixed star is ten thousand times farther from the sun than we are.' I can build nothing on these observations, till parallaxes can be taken with greater certainty than they are at present. Therefore I shall want proof that any one fixed star is one thousand times farther from the sun than we are.

2) 'They are fiery bodies.' I suppose they are, but this cannot be proved from their distance till that distance itself is proved.

3) 'It is demonstrable that Sirius is as big as the sun.' Demonstrate it who can.

---

[5] Orig., 'Keil'. The reference is to the Scottish mathematician and astronomer John Keill (1671–1721), a student of Isaac Newton who in 1725 had published a work entitled *Introductio ad Veram Astronomiam (Introduction to True Astronomy*, published at Leiden).

4) 'Seeing the fixed stars are not much less than the sun, they are to be esteemed so many suns.' Not much less! How is this proved? To argue from the distance is to prove *ignotum per aeque ignotum.*[6]

'You see, sir, the hypothesis of innumerable suns is so far from vanishing into air that it is almost altogether founded on demonstration.' Indeed, I do not see one tittle of demonstration yet from the beginning to the end.

In order to prove that the planets are inhabited you say,

1) 'The earth is spherical, opaque, enlightened by the sun, casting a shadow opposite thereto, and revolving round it in a time exactly proportioned to its distance. The other planets resemble the earth in all these particulars. Therefore they likewise are inhabited.' I cannot allow the consequence.

2) 'The earth has a regular succession of day and night, summer and winter. So probably have all the planets. Therefore they are inhabited.' I am not sure of the antecedent. But, however that be, I deny the consequence.

3) 'Jupiter and Saturn are much bigger than the earth.' Does this prove that they are inhabited?

4) 'The earth has a moon, Jupiter has four, Saturn five, each of these larger than ours. They eclipse their respective planets, and are eclipsed by them.' All this does not prove that they are inhabited.

5) 'Saturn's ring reflects the light of the sun upon him.' I am not sure of that. And, till the fact is ascertained, no certain inference can be drawn from it.

6) 'But is it probable God should have created planets like our own and furnished them with such amazing apparatus, and yet have placed no inhabitants therein?' Of their apparatus I know nothing. However, if all you assert be the *probability* of their being inhabited, I contend not.

7) 'They who affirm that God created those bodies, the fixed stars, only to give us a small, dim light, must have a very mean opinion of the divine wisdom.' I do not affirm this. Neither can I tell for what other end he created them. He that created them knows. But I have so high an opinion of the divine wisdom that I believe no child of man can fathom it. It is our wisdom to be very wary how we pronounce concerning things which we have not seen.

Remark 3. 'Suppose some intelligent beings in one of the planets, who were

---

[6] 'An unknown by an equally unknown.'

Slaves to no sect, who sought no private road,
But looked through nature up to nature's God,[7]

viewed the Earth from thence; they would argue it must be
inhabited, as we argue the other planets are. But the superstitious   5
would oppose this doctrine, and call it mere uncertain conjecture.'
I see no argument in this. But perhaps I do not understand it.
Are you applauding the supposed inhabitants of Venus for not being *slaves* to the *Christian sect*? Otherwise what has *superstition* to do
in the case? Why is this dragged in by head and shoulders? If there   10
be superstition here, it is on *your* side, who believe because you will
believe, who assent to what you have no evidence for, and maintain
what you cannot prove. At present you are the *volunteer* in faith, you
swallow what chokes my belief.
Remark 4. 'You quote Dr. Rogers.'[8] But I do not undertake to   15
defend his hypothesis or any other. 'Our best observators could
never find the parallax of the sun to be above eleven seconds.' But
I cannot depend on their observations, especially when I find one
of the chief of them, in computing the distance of the sun, to stride
from twenty eight millions to seventy-six, near fifty millions of   20
miles at once! After this, let any impartial man judge what stress is
to be laid on parallaxes!
'But Dr. Rogers supposes the parallax of the sun to be five minutes, which others cannot find to be above eleven seconds.' Why,
doctor, if this be true (namely, that the parallax which lately was   25
but eleven seconds is now increased to five minutes), 'the Earth has
approximated thirty times *nearer*' (a little harmless tautology) 'to the
sun.' That is, if both the computation of Mr. Keill and that of Dr.
Rogers be true. But who ever supposed this? If the one be true, the
other is undoubtedly false.   30
'To conclude: since there is no arguing against facts, and since the
sun's parallax is not found to exceed eleven seconds, ought you not
to give up that hypothesis as absurd and ridiculous?'
Yes, as soon as any of those facts appear. Till then, I neither espouse nor give it up. But I still look upon it as ingenious, and as   35
probable as any other.
Before I conclude, permit me, sir, to give you one piece of advice.
Be not so *positive*, especially with regard to things which are neither

---

[7] Alexander Pope, *An Essay on Man*, Epistle IV, l. 334.

[8] The reference is to Dr. John Rogers, MD, whose *Dissertation on the Knowledge of the Ancients in Astronomy* (London, 1755) Wesley had read in 1757 (*Journal*, May 12, 1757, 21:101–2 in this edn.).

easy nor necessary to be determined.[9] I ground this advice on my own experience. When I was young, I was *sure* of everything. In a few years, having been mistaken a thousand times, I was not half so sure of most things as I was before; at present I am hardly sure of anything but what God has revealed to man.

5

Upon the whole, an ingenious man may easily flourish on this head: 'How much more glorious is it for the great God to have created innumerable worlds than this little globe only!' But, after all, I would only ask this one plain question: Suppose there are more worlds than there are sands on the seashore, is not the universe finite still? It must be, unless it be God. And if it be finite, it can still bear no proportion to him that is infinite—nor more than this ball of earth does. How large soever it be, still, compared to him, it is as nothing, as the small dust of the balance. Do you ask, then, 'What is this spot to the great God?' Why, as much as millions of systems. *Great* and *little* have place with regard to us, but before him they vanish away. Enlarge the bounds of creation as much as you please, still it is as but a drop to the Creator.

10

15

20

And still the power of his almighty hand
Can form another world from every sand![10]

Yet, were this done, there would be no more proportion than there is now between him and his creatures. In this respect, one world and millions of worlds are just the same thing. Is the earth a cypher, a nothing, to the infinitely great, glorious, wise, and powerful God? So is any number of worlds which can be conceived. So is all finite being to the infinite!

25

Source: published transcription; *London Magazine* 34 (Jan. 1765), pp. 26–29.

[9] 'Philosophaster' responded to this advice, 'I do not. Those things only, where the evidence is infallible, would I be positive in, and in all others my judgement should only *incline* to where appears to be the greater probability' (*London Magazine*, March 1765, p. 128).

[10] The concluding couplet of William Broome's 'The Forty-Third Chapter of Ecclesiasticus, Paraphrased' (1727), included in *MSP* (1744), 2:99.

To the Rev. Charles Wesley

LONDON
JANUARY 11, 1765

[[Dear Brother,]]

I believe Thomas Goodwin wrote that book. Pray hasten John's
tract, and give Pine the Preface.[11]   5

Mr. [Augustus] To[plady] is not a Calvinist yet, nor Mr. [George]
Downing half an one. I have a letter from him today, and hope to be
with him at Ovington tomorrow.

I have no objection to Mr. Trail's preaching in Weavers' Hall, but
I am not rightly satisfied as to his preaching at all.[12]   10

On Monday morning I desired the preachers and the stewards to
meet me.[13] It was then inquired,

1. Can James Thwayte,[14] Benjamin Russen, Richard Perry, James
Satles,[15] John Oliver, and Thomas Bryant, who have *bought* an ordination in an unknown tongue, be received by us as clergymen?[16] No.   15

2. Can we receive them any longer as preachers? No.

3. Can we receive them as members of our society? No.

And this I ordered to be signified to each of them immediately.[17]

[[Adieu.]]

20

Address: 'To / The Revd Mr C. Wesley / in / Bristol'.
Postmark: '15/IA'. *Charge*: '4'.

---

[11] I.e., JW's *Extract* of John Goodwin's *Treatise on Justification*, with the Preface answering James Hervey, which William Pine of Bristol was printing.

[12] On Mr. Trail, see JW to Christopher Hopper, Nov. 2, 1763.

[13] The six preachers named below had been ordained by the Greek church leader Gerasimos Avlonites in Dec. 1764; an event reported in *Lloyd's Evening Post* this same Monday, Jan.
7, 1765 (p. 28). Joseph Sutcliffe records that those present at this meeting to respond to their
action included: John Wesley, John Richardson, Benjamin Colley; John Jones, John Murlin,
John Mager; and Henry Hammond, John Norton, Christian Bromley, James Ward, John Red-
hall, John Butcher, Robert Clemenson, and Thomas Lee, Stewards; see Sutcliffe, ms. History
of Methodism (MARC, MA 1977/514), 2:645.

[14] James Thwayte (1733–1803) was converted to Methodism at the age of 21 and began
to preach in 1758. He traveled at times with JW, but was never given a circuit. Five days before
this meeting in Bristol he wrote to CW, appealing for acceptance of his ordination. Thwayte's
letter shows him to have been barely literate. After this decision in Bristol, Thwayte built a chapel in which to preach, which flourished for a while then failed. See *WHS* 22 (1740): 141–43.

[15] Russen, Perry, and Satles are known primarily from this incident. Russen subsequently became an independent preacher and published a volume of sermons.

[16] Because JW had earlier requested Avlonites to ordain John Jones, the six preachers presumed that he would accept their ordinations. But JW here distinguishes their ordination from
that of Jones on two grounds: 1) they paid a fee to Avlonites; and 2) they could not understand
the words of the ordination service (unlike Jones, who knew Greek).

[17] This action was also publicly announced in a letter dated Feb. 5, 1765 to the *St. James's
Chronicle*.

Endorsement: in CW's hand, 'Jan. 11. 1765 / B. expelling his Witnesses because ordained by J. Jones's ordainer.'
Source: holograph; Emory, MARBL, Wesley Family Papers, 1/47.

To Thomas Rankin

[OVINGTON]
JANUARY 13, 1765

Dear Tommy,

    I will give you a month from this day to make a fair trial of William Darney whether he will walk according to our Rules or no; if
5 not, we must part. But if he had rather, he may go into the Wiltshire round, where a preacher is now wanting. Thomas Bryant is not now in connexion with us. I am glad you give me warning concerning Richard Austen. I trust that you will soon set them right at the Dock.[18] Gentleness, added to plainness of speech, will have influ-
10 ence upon honest brother Jones. I advise you gradually to remove all such leaders and stewards as do not cordially love the Methodist doctrine and discipline. I am, dear Tommy,
    Your affectionate friend and brother,

15   J. Wesley

Pray give my love to brother Mallon[19] of Week St. Mary[20] society. I thank him for his letter, and exhort him to stand fast in the liberty wherewith Christ has made him free.

20 *Address*: 'To / Mr T. Rankin / At Mr Wood's / At Port Isaac near Camelford / Cornwall'.
Postmark: '15/IA'. *Charge*: '4'.
Source: holograph; New York, The Pierpont Morgan Library, MA 516.2.

[18] Plymouth Dock, now Devonport.
[19] Or 'Mallow'.
[20] Orig., 'Mary Week'.

To Thomas Rankin

LONDON
JANUARY 26, 1765

Dear Tommy,

I have a fresh demand for an additional preacher in Wiltshire. Therefore the sooner William Darney goes thither, the better. I 5 hope he will have so much prudence, as not to speak against our doctrine. Then he may be of use.

Love will overcome sister Jane also.[21] But how is the house at the Dock settled? Should not this be done without delay?

If you want more, *write* receipts for Goodwin. Only keep an exact 10 list.

Speak strongly in every place concerning the yearly subscription. You saw how we were straitened last year.

Observe in the Minutes of the Conference each of the articles belonging to the office of an Assistant. Look up and receive strength! 15 I am, dear Tommy,

Your affectionate friend and brother,

J. Wesley

Address: 'To / Mr Rankin / At Mrs Blackmore's, Shopkee[pe]r / in / Plymouth Dock'.
Postmark: cut away. *Charge*: '4'.
Source: holograph; Duke, Rubenstein, Frank Baker Collection of Wesleyana, Box WF 1.

To the Printer of the *St. James's Chronicle*[22]

[LONDON] 20
[C. FEBRUARY 5, 1765]

Sir,

To the four questions proposed to me in your last week's paper, I answer:

---

[21] Perhaps the wife of Nehemiah Jane, a member of the society at Plymouth Dock; cf. JW to Thomas Rankin, Feb. 9, 1765.
[22] Replying to the letter by 'J. T.' in the *St. James's Chronicle* (Jan. 29–31, 1765), p. 4. See also the two earlier letters of 'A. P.' dated Dec. 10, 1764 and c. Jan. 8, 1765.

1. None of those six persons lately ordained by a Greek bishop were ordained with my consent or knowledge.[23]

2. I will not, cannot own or receive them as clergymen.

3. I think an ordination performed in a language not understood by the persons ordained is not valid.

4. I think it is absolutely unlawful for any one to give money to the bishop (or to any one for him) for ordaining him. I am, sir,
Your humble servant,

John Wesley

Source: published transcription; *St. James's Chronicle* (Feb. 7–9, 1765), p. 4.

To Thomas Rankin

LONDON
FEBRUARY 9, 1765

Dear Tommy,

I have little more to add to my last but that I have wrote to brother Jane[24] and the leaders at the Dock to the same effect as I wrote to James Stevens[25] and to you at St. Austell.[26]

You have only to go on steadily, and lovingly, and to overcome evil with good. I am, dear Tommy,
Yours affectionately,

J. Wesley

Address: 'To Mr Rankin / At Mr Wood's, Shopkeeper / In Port Isaac, near Camelford / Cornwall'.
Postmark: '9/FE'. *Charge*: '4'.
Source: holograph; MARC, MAM JW 4/44.

---

[23] See JW to CW, Jan. 11, 1765.

[24] Nehemiah Jane was a member of the society in Plymouth Dock and a quarterman in the dockyard; cf. JW, *Journal*, Aug. 19, 1780.

[25] James Stephens (also spelled 'Stevens') was currently serving 'on trial'; he would be admitted as an itinerant at Conference in August 1765 (see 10:303 in this edn.).

[26] Orig., 'Austle'.

To the Printer of the *St. James's Chronicle*[27]

[LONDON]
[C. FEBRUARY 10, 1765]

Sir,

In the *St. James's Chronicle* published on Saturday last there was an innocent thing wrote by a hat-maker in Southwark. It may be proper to take a little more notice of it than it deserves, lest silence should appear to be an acknowledgement of the charge.

I insert nothing in the public papers without my name. I know not the authors of what has been lately inserted; part of which I have not seen y[e]t, nor did I see any part before it was printed.

A year or two ago I found a stranger perishing for want and expecting daily to be thrown in prison. He told me he was a Greek bishop. I examined his credentials, and was fully satisfied. After much conversation (in Latin and Greek, for he spoke no English at all) I determined to relieve him effectually, which I did without delay, and promised to send him back to Amsterdam, where he had several friends of his own nation. And this I did without any farther view, merely upon motives of humanity. After this he ordained Mr. John Jones, a man well versed both in the languages and other parts of learning.

When I was gone out of town, Bishop Erasmus was prevailed upon to ordain Lawrence Coughlan, a person who had no learning at all.

Some time after, Mr. [Thomas] Maxfield, or his friends, sent for him from Amsterdam, to ordain Mr. S—t and three other persons,[28] as unlearned as any of the apostles, but I believe not so much inspired.

In December last he was sent for again, and ordained six other persons, members of our society, but every way, I think, unqualified for that office. These I judged it my duty to disclaim (to waive all other considerations) for a fault which I know not who can excuse, *buying* an ordination in an *unknown tongue*.

---

[27] Replying to an anonymous letter dated Feb. 6. published in the *St. James's Chronicle* (Feb. 7–9, 1765), p. 4; i.e., right beside JW's prior letter disavowing those ordained by Avlonites.

[28] This ordination took place in late Nov. 1764, with three of the four ordained being described as 'a cheesemonger, a tailor, and an apothecary' in the *Gazetteer and New Daily Advertiser* (Dec. 1, 1764). The fourth was identified shortly after as a 'master baker' in *Lloyd's Evening Post* (Dec. 7–10, 1764), p. 1. The 'cheesemonger' was described as an 'assistant' to Thomas Maxfield in his chapel in London, by 'J. T.' in the *St. James's Chronicle* (Jan. 29–31, 1765), p. 4. But their actual names remain unknown.

As to the other tale, 'The Bishop told me himself' (I pray in what tongue? for he speaks no English, and you no Greek, any more than your interpreter so called) 'that Mr. Wesley desired Mr. [John] Jones to know of him if he would consecrate him bishop?' Mr. Jones
5   solemnly declares that he never told the Bishop any such thing. But, be that as it may, the point does not turn on the validity of ordination by a Greek *bishop*, but on the validity of ordination procured by *money* and performed in an *unknown tongue*.

My advice to you is either be silent or procure a better defender
10   of your cause.

John Wesley

Source: published transcription; *St. James's Chronicle* (Feb. 12–14, 1765), p. 4.

To the Six Disbarred Preachers[29]

NORWICH
FEBRUARY 27, 1765

15
Mr. [Martin] Madan, Mr. [William] Romaine, and the good-natured Mr. [Walter] Shirley are almost out of patience with me for not disowning you on the housetop. In this situation of things it would be utter madness in me to do anything which they would
20   call contumacy. I am every way bound to my good behaviour, and obliged to move with all possible circumspection. Were I to allow your preaching *now*, I should be in a hotter fire than ever. That you

---

[29] The only record of this letter is in Sutcliffe's history, who was a strong sympathiser with the six preachers ordained by Avlonites (see JW to CW, Jan. 11, 1765). He characterised the removal of the men from the Wesleyan connexion in early January as 'a dreadful sentence surpassing any record in the annals of the church' (2:645). Sutcliffe insists that JW resorted to this action only because of strong pressure from Madan, Romaine, and Shirley. He introduces this letter by noting that in mid February, about a month after their expulsion, the six preachers requested to be restored to the connexion, 'and Mr. John, however rough he might be for the moment, would always bend an ear to a supplicant's voice. He wrote as follows in very cautious words' (2:646).

will preach again by-and-by I doubt not, but it is certain the time is not come yet.[30]

J. Wesley

Source: manuscript transcription; Joseph Sutcliffe, ms. History of Methodism (MARC, MA 1977/514), 2:646.

To Thomas Rankin

LONDON
MARCH 9, 1765

My Dear Brother,

Nothing can hurt you, if you are calm, mild, and gentle to all men, especially to the froward.

I think you have done all you could do at present for poor brother [Nehemiah] Jane. I will send to William Atkinson and ask him how the house is settled.[31] I know nothing about it, for I never saw the writings.

I suppose the bill intended to be brought into Parliament will never see the light.[32] The great ones find other work for one another. They are all at daggers' drawing among themselves. Our business is to go straight forward. I am, dear Tommy,

Your affectionate friend and brother,

J. Wesley

[30] Sutcliffe notes that the case of the preachers was laid before the Conference when they met in mid August. He reports (quoting John Oliver) that the ordained members of Conference thundered against readmission, but then 'the air became serene and the sun shone again, the smoke of Sodom having blown away'. As this might suggest, John Oliver was restored at the 1765 Conference as a travelling preacher and stationed in Lancashire (see 10:304–5 in this edn.). He would continue to serve for many years. By contrast, Thomas Bryant, the only other travelling preacher of the six, led a secession of members of the Sheffield society in May 1765; James Thwayte and Benjamin Russen became independent preachers; and Richard Perry and James Satles are not mentioned again in official records.

[31] William Atkinson was a native of Plymouth Dock, Devon, who had worked in the Foundery book room in London. He was now apparently back in Devon overseeing construction.

[32] This is possibly a reference to the 'Stamp Act', passed later this month by Parliament, one of the provocations leading up to the revolt of the British colonists in North America.

Address: 'To / Mr Rankin / At Mr Jos. Andrew's / In Redruth / Corn-
wall'.
Postmark: '9/MR'. *Charge*: '4'.
Source: holograph; MARC, MAM JW 4/45.

To John Newton

LIVERPOOL
APRIL 9, 1765

Dear Sir,

I have just finished your *Narrative*, a remarkable proof, as you
5   observe, that with God all things are possible.[33] The objection current here, that you talk too much of Mrs. Newton,[34] seems to me of
no force at all. I cannot apprehend that you could well have spoken
less or any otherwise than you do.

And as to what you speak concerning particular redemption and
10 the points connected therewith, you speak in so calm and dispas-
sionate a manner as cannot give offence to any reasonable man.
Nothing of this kind gives any offence to *me*, for I think and let
think. I believe every one has a right to think for himself and (in
some sense) to speak for himself. I mean, to use any mode of ex-
15 pression which appears ⟨to[35]⟩ him most agreeable to scripture. You
yourself in time past were in the same sentiment. You did not so
much enquire, 'Is a man of this or that opinion?' or 'Does he make
use of this or the other mode of expression?' but 'Is he a believer in
Jesus Christ?' and 'Is his life suitable to his profession?' Upon this
20 ground commenced ⟨the⟩ acquaintance (perhaps I might say more,
the friendship) between you and me. We both knew there was a difference in our opinions and consequently in our expressions. But,
notwithstanding this, we tasted each other's spirits, and often took
sweet counsel together. And what hinders it now? I do not know

---

[33] John Newton's *An Authentic Narrative of Some Remarkable and Interesting Particulars
in the Life of —— Communicated, in a Series of Letters, to the Reverend T. Haweiss* had been
published anonymously in 1764. It was in significant part an apology for his long efforts to
obtain ordination.

[34] His wife's maiden name was Mary Catlett (1729–90), though she went by 'Polly'.

[35] The ms. has suffered some recent fire damage. The missing portions are typically small
and can be confidently reconstructed. Only those where there might be any doubt are marked
by angle brackets.

that our opinions differ a jot more now than formerly. But a dying man has drawn a sword, and wounded, if not me, yet many others, and *you* among the rest. Poor Mr. Hervey (or Mr. Cudworth rather),[36] painting me like an hideous monster, with exquisite art both disfiguring my character and distorting my sentiments, has made even Mr. Newton afraid of me, who once thought me at least an harmless animal. A quarrel he could not make between us, neither can any one else. For *two* must go to a quarrel, and I declare to you I will not be one.[37]

But I do not think it is enough for us not to quarrel. I am persuaded we may help each other. Why not? O beware of bigotry, of an undue attachment to opinions or phrases! You of all men ought to fly from this, as you appear to be designed by divine providence for an ⟨hea⟩ler of breaches, a reconciler of honest but prejudiced men, and an uniter (happy work!) of the children of God that are needlessly divided from each other. Perhaps your very opinion and way of speaking may enable you to do this among those to whom I have no access, as my opinion and way of speaking enable me to calm those who would not give you so favourable an hearing. In the name of him that has shown *you* mercy, I beseech you show this mercy to your brethren! Soften and sweeten as far as in you lies their rugged or bitter spirits! Incite them everywhere to insist upon the one point, faith that worketh by love,[38] or (in other words) Christ enlightening, justifying, sanctifying, reigning in the believing soul.

'Oh, but Mr. Hervey says you are *half a* papist.' What if he had proved it too? What if he had proved I was a *whole* papist (though he might as easily have proved me a Mahometan)? Is not a papist a child of God? Is Thomas à Kempis, Mr. De ⟨Renty,⟩ Gregory Lopez gone to hell? Believe it who can. ⟨Yet⟩ still of such (though papists), the same is my brother and s⟨ister an⟩d mother.

---

[36] Cudworth may have played a role in the surreptitious publication in 1764 of the letters that Hervey intentionally left unpublished at his death in 1758; cf. JW to James Hervey, Nov. 29, 1758; and JW to CW, Dec. 7, 1764. But Wesley seems to imply here that the letters were actually written by Cudworth. They were not, but the 1764 publication did contain some unreliable parts, leading James Hervey's brother William to publish a corrected edition: James Hervey, *Eleven Letters from the late Rev. Mr. Hervey, to the Rev. Mr. John Wesley; containing an Answer to that Gentleman's Remarks on 'Theron and Aspasio'* (London: Charles Rivington, 1765).

[37] Newton replied to Wesley on April 18, 'Mr. Hervey's Letters have not wounded me at all. In my personal regard for you they have made no abatement, in my sentiments in other respects no alteration.' He did go on to lay out differences over the doctrine of Christian perfection.

[38] See Gal. 5:6.

I have waited a fortnight for a passage to Dublin, but am now determined to move toward Scotland first. If you should favour me with a few lines, please ‹to send› direct to Newcastle-upon-Tyne. Peace be with you both. I am, dear sir,

5   Your affectionate brother and servant,

John Wesley

Address: 'To / The Revd Mr Newton / At Oulney / Bucks'.
Postmarks: 'LIVERPOOL' '?/AP'. *Charge*: '4'.
Endorsement: 'Rev M Wesley / 9 Apr 1765'.
Source: holograph; Buffalo, New York, Karpeles Manuscript Library Museums.

To the Rev. John Erskine[39]

EDINBURGH
APRIL 24, 1765

10 Reverend Sir,

Between thirty and forty years I have had the world upon me, speaking all manner of evil. And I expected no less, as God had called me to testify that its deeds were evil.[40] But the children of God were not upon me, nor did I expect they would. I rather hoped
15 they would take knowledge that all my designs, and thought, and care, and labour were directed to this one point: to advance the kingdom of Christ upon earth. And so many of them did, however differing from me both in opinions and modes of worship. I have the pleasure to mention Dr. Doddridge, Dr. Watts, and Mr. Ward-

---

[39] About the same time that William Hervey was publishing a corrected edition of his brother's *Letters* to JW (see note 36 above), Dr. John Erskine (1721–1803), a clergyman of the Church of Scotland and pastor of the Old Greyfriars Church, Edinburgh, republished the Leeds edition (*Aspasio Vindicated* ..., Edinburgh: W. Gray, 1765), adding a preface attacking Wesley (pp. iii–x). JW replied with this personal letter, which Erskine then published in a more extended attack: *Mr. Wesley's Principles Detected: Or, A Defence of the Preface to the Edinburgh Edition of Aspasio Vindicated* (Edinburgh: W. Gray, 1765). JW responded to this second work publically, with *Some Remarks on 'A Defence of the Preface to the Edinburgh Edition of "Aspasio Vindicated"'* (1766); see 13:391–403 in this edn.

[40] See John 3:19.

robe[41] in particular. How, then, was I surprised as well as concerned that a child of the same Father, a servant of the same Lord, a member of the same family, and (as to the essence of it) a preacher of the same gospel, should, without any provocation that I know of, declare open war against me! I was the more surprised because you had told me, some months since, that you would favour me with a letter. And had this been done, I make no doubt but you would have received full satisfaction. Instead of this, you ushered into this part of the world one of the most bitter libels that was ever written against me, written by a dying man (so far as it was written by poor, well-meaning Mr. Hervey), with a trembling hand, just as he was tottering on the margin of the grave. A great warrior resigned his crown, because 'there should be some interval,' he said, 'between fighting and death.'[42] But Mr. Hervey, who had been a man of peace all his life, began a war not six months before he died. He drew his sword when he was just putting off his body. He then fell on one to whom he had the deepest obligations (as his own letters, which I have now in my hands, testify[43]), on one who had never intentionally wronged him, who had never spoken an unkind word of him or to him, and who loved him as his own child. O tell it not in Gath![44] The good Mr. Hervey (if these letters were his) died cursing his spiritual father.

And these letters another good man, Mr. [Erskine], has introduced into Scotland, and warmly recommended. Why have you done this? 'Because you have *concealed* your principles, which is palpable *dishonesty.*'[45]

When I was first invited into Scotland (about fourteen years ago), Mr. Whitefield told me: 'You have no business there, for your

---

[41] All three were Calvinist clergymen. Phillip Doddridge (1702–51) and Isaac Watts (1674–1748) were Congregationalists; Thomas Wardrobe (d. 1756) was a Presbyterian who served at the Hallbank Hexham Presbyterian church and then at the Bathgate (Scottish Presbyterian) church in Edinburgh. Wardrobe had invited JW to preach in 1746. JW reciprocated, inviting Wardrobe to preach at the Orphan House in Newcastle in 1755 (*Journal*, May 22, 1755, 21:11–12 in this edn.). JW also included an account of Wardrobe's faithful Christian death in his *Journal* (May 30, 1756, 21:56).

[42] A quotation attributed to Juan de Valdés in Izaak Walton, *The Lives of Dr. John Donne, Sir Henry Wotton, Mr. Richard Hooker, Mr. George Herbert* (London: Richard Marriott, 1670), 72.

[43] JW would later publish three of these letters from Hervey in the first volume of the *Arminian Magazine* (1:130–35).

[44] See 2 Sam. 1:20.

[45] John Erskine, Preface, in *Aspasio Vindicated, and the Scripture-Doctrine of Imputed Righteousness Defended against the Objections and Animadversions of the Rev. John Wesley, in Eleven Letters* (Edinburgh: W. Gray, 1765), ix.

principles are so well known, that if you spoke like an angel none would hear you. And if they did, you would have nothing to do but to *dispute* with one and another from morning to night.'

I answered: 'If God sends me, people will hear. And I will give
5 them no provocation to dispute, for I will studiously avoid contro- verted points, and keep to the fundamental truths of Christianity. And if any still begin to dispute, they may, but I will not dispute with them.'

I came. Hundreds and thousands flocked to hear. But I was en-
10 abled to keep my word. I avoided whatever might engender strife, and insisted upon the grand points, the religion of the heart, and salvation by faith, at all times and in all places. And by this means I have cut off all occasion of dispute from the first day to this very hour. And this you amazingly improve into a fault, construe into a
15 proof of *dishonesty.* You likewise charge me with holding *unsound principles,* and with saying, 'Right opinions are (sometimes) no part of religion.'[46]

The last charge I have answered over and over, and very lately to Bishop Warburton.[47] Certainly, had you read that single tract, you
20 would never have repeated that stale objection.

As to my principles, every one knows, or may know, that I believe the Thirty-first Article of the Church of England.[48] But can none be saved who believe this?[49] I know you will not say so. Meantime, in the main point, justification by faith, I have not wavered a mo-
25 ment for these seven-and-twenty years.[50] And I allow all which Mr. Hervey himself contends for in his entrance upon the sub- ject, 'Come to Jesus as a *needy beggar,* hang upon him as a *devoted pensioner.*'[51] And whoever does this, I will be bold to say shall not perish everlastingly.

---

[46] Ibid., iv; quoting JW, *Plain Account of the People Called Methodists,* §I.2 (9:254–55 in this edn.).

[47] See JW, *A Letter to the Right Reverend [Warburton] the Lord Bishop of Gloucester,* I.11–13, 11:477–79 in this edn.

[48] The Thirty-first Article of Religion of the Church of England asserts that Christ's one offering 'is the perfect redemption, propitiation, and satisfaction for all the sins of the whole world', as contrasted with what it claimed to be the teaching of the Church of Rome that priests offer or re-offer Christ at each celebration of the Mass. JW apparently thought that Erskine was charging him with holding the Catholic position, though this is not said explicitly in Erskine's preface.

[49] That is: Is a Catholic, or one who believes that Christ is re-offered in the Mass, ex- cluded from salvation merely for this reason?

[50] Cf. JW's 1738 sermon on *Salvation by Faith* (1:117–30 in this edn.).

[51] Cf. James Hervey, *Theron and Aspasio* (Dublin: Robert Main, 1755), 43.

As to your main objection, convince me that it is my duty to preach on controverted subjects, predestination in particular, and I will do it. At present I think it would be a sin. I think it would create still more divisions. And are there not enough already? I have seen a book written by one who styles himself *Ecclesiae Scoticae direptae* 5 *et gementis Presbyter.*[52] Shall I tear *ecclesiam direptam et gementem?*[53] God forbid! No, I will, so far as I can, heal her breaches. And if you really love her (as I doubt not you do), why should you hinder me from so doing? Has she so many friends and helpers left that you should strive to lessen their number? Would you wish to turn any 10 of her friends, even though weak and mistaken, into enemies? If you must contend, have you not Arians, Socinians, Seceders, infidels to contend with, to say nothing of whoremongers, adulterers, Sabbath-breakers, drunkards, common swearers? O *ecclesia gemens!*[54] And will you pass by all these, and single out me to fight 15 with? Nay, but I will not. I do and will fight with all these, but not with *you*. I cannot; I dare not. You are the son of my Father, my fellow labourer in the gospel of his dear Son. I love your person, I love your character, I love the work wherein you are engaged. And if you will still shoot at me (because Mr. Hervey has painted me as a 20 monster), even with arrows drawn from Bishop Warburton's quiver (how unfit for Mr. [Erskine]'s hand!), I can only say, as I always did before, the Lord Jesus bless you in your soul, in your body, in your relations, in your work, in whatever tends to his own glory! I am, dear sir, 25

Your affectionate brother,

John Wesley

Source: published transcription; [John Erskine], *Mr. Wesley's Principles Detected* (Edinburgh: William Gray, 1765), 21–24.

---

[52] 'A presbyter of the torn and wailing Scottish Church.' When JW published this letter in his collected *Works* (1773) he omitted the word '*Scoticae*' (Scottish).

[53] 'A church torn and wailing.'

[54] 'O wailing church!'

To John Newton[55]

LONDONDERRY
MAY 14, 1765

Dear Sir,

Your manner of writing needs no excuse. I hope you will always
5 write in the same manner. Love is the plainest thing in ⟨the[56]⟩world. I
know this dictates what you write, and then what need of ceremony?

You have admirably well expressed what I mean by an 'opinion',
contradistinguished from an *essential* doctrine.[57] Whatever is 'compatible with a love to Christ and a work of grace', I term an opinion.
10 And certainly the holding particular election and final perseverance
is compatible with these. 'Yet what fundamental error' (you ask)
'have you opposed with *half that frequency and vehemence* as you
have these opinions?' So doubtless you have heard. But it is not
true. I have printed near fifty sermons, and only one of these op-
15 poses them at all. I preach about eight hundred sermons in a year.
And taking one year with another, for twenty years past, I have not
preached eight sermons in a year upon the subject. But 'how many
of your best preachers have been *thrust* ⟨out⟩ because they dissented
from you in these particulars?' Not one, best or worst, good or bad,
20 was ever *thrust out* on this account. There has been no⟨t a⟩ single instance of the kind. Two or three (but far from *the best* of our preachers) voluntarily left us after they had embraced those opinions. But
it was of their own mere motion. And two I should have expelled for
immoral behaviour, but they withdrew and *pretended* 'they did not
25 hold our doct⟨rine'.⟩ Set a mark therefore on him who told you that
tale and let his word for ⟨the future⟩ go for nothing.

'Is a man a believer in Jesus Christ? And is his life suitable to his
⟨profess⟩sion?' are not only the *main* but the *sole* enquiries I make in
order to his admission into our society. If he is a Dissenter, he may
30 be a Dissenter still; if he is a Churchman, I advise him to continue
so, and that for many rea⟨sons,⟩ some of which are mentioned in the
tract upon that subject.[58]

---

[55] Replying to Newton's letter of Apr. 18, 1765.

[56] The ms. is torn and burned on the edges, requiring a number of small reconstructions.
These are generally obvious, particularly in the section that parallels his later *Plain Account of
Christian Perfection*. We have also consulted Telford's transcription in *Letters*, which appears to
have been done before the damage to the manuscript.

[57] A distinction that JW frequently drew; e.g., Sermon 39, 'Catholic Spirit', I:1–11,
2:82–87 in this edn.

[58] Wesley's *Reasons Against a Separation from the Church of England*, first published in
1758 (9:332–49 in this edn.).

When you have read what I have wrote on occasion of the letters lately published, I may say something more on that head.[59] And it will then be ti‹me› enough to show you, why some *part* of those letters *could not* be wrote by Mr. Hervey.

I think on justification just as I have done any time these seven and twenty years, and just as Mr. Calvin does. In this respect I do not differ from him an hair's breadth.

But the main point between you and me is *perfection.* 'This, you say, has no ‹prev›alence in these parts. Otherwise I should think it my duty, to oppose it with my ‹who›le strength, not as an *opinion*, but as a dangerous mistake, which appears to be ‹subv›ersive of the very foundations of Christian experience, and which has in fact given ‹occ›asion to the most grievous offences'.

Just so my brother and I reasoned thirty years ago. 'We think it our duty to oppose *predestination* with our whole strength, not as an opinion, but as a dangerous mistake, which appears to be subversive of the very foundations of Christian experience, and which has in fact given occasion to the most grievous offences'.

That it has given occasion to such offences I know. I can name time, place, and persons. But still another fact stares me in the face. Mr. [Thomas] Haweis and Mr. [John] Newton hold this, and yet I believe these have real Christian experience. But if so, this is only an *opinion*. It is not subversive (here is clear proof to the contrary) of the very foundations of Christian experience. It is 'compatible with a love to Christ and a genuine work of grace'. Yea, many hold it, at whose feet I desire to be found in the day of the Lord Jesus. If then I 'oppose this with my whole strength', I am a mere *bigot* still. I leave you, in your calm and retired moments, to make the application.

But how came this opinion into my mind? I will tell you with all simplicity.[60] In 1725 I met with Bishop Taylor's *Rules of Holy Living and Dying.*[61] I was struck particularly with the chapter upon *intention*, and felt a fixed intention to *give myself ‹wholly› up to God.* In this I was much confirmed soon after by the *Christian Pattern*,[62]

---

[59] I.e., JW's 'Answer to Hervey', 13:377–90 in this edn.

[60] What follows is a digest of a longer account JW was working on currently, which would appear the following year in *A Plain Account of Christian Perfection*, §§2–8; see 13:136–41 in this edn.

[61] Jeremy Taylor, *Rules and Exercises of Holy Living* (1650) and *Rules and Exercises of Holy Dying* (1651). Wesley included extracts of these works in *Christian Library*, vol. 9.

[62] Thomas à Kempis's *The Imitation of Christ*, which Wesley published in 1735 under the title *The Christian's Pattern* (*Bibliography*, No. 4).

and longed to *give ‹God›   all my heart*. This is just what I mean by
'perfection' now. I sought ‹after› it from that hour.

   In 1727 I read Mr. Law's *Christian Perfection*[63] and *Serious Call*,[64]
and more expli‹citly resol›ved to be *all devoted to God*, in body, soul,
5   and spirit.

   ‹In 173›0 I began to be *homo unius libri*,[65] to study (comparatively)
no ‹book› but the Bible. I then saw in a stronger light than ever before that only *‹one› thing is needful*, even *faith that worketh by the love
of God and man*, all ‹inw›ard and outward holiness. And I groaned
10   to love God with *all my heart* and ‹to serve› him with *all my strength*.

   ‹On› January 1, 1733, I preached the sermon on 'The Circumcision of the Heart' which contains all that I now teach concerning
salvation from *all sin*, and loving God with an *undivided heart*.[66] In
the same year I printed (the first time I ventured to print anything)
15   for the use of my pupils a *Collection of Forms of Prayer*.[67] And in this
I spoke explicitly of giving *the whole heart*, and *the whole life to God*.
This was then, as it is now, my idea of perfection, though I should
have started at *the word*.

   In 1735 I preached my farewell sermon at Epworth in
20   Lincoln‹shire.› In this likewise I spoke with the utmost clearness of
having *one design, one desire, one love*, and of pursuing the *one end* of
our life, in *all* our words and actions.[68]

   In January 1738 I expressed my desire in these words:

25
> O grant that nothing in my soul
>   May dwell, but thy *pure love alone!*
> O may thy love *possess me whole*,
>   My joy, my treasure, and my crown.
> Strange flames far from my heart remove!
30
> My *every* act, word, thought, be love.[69]

---

[63] William Law, *A Practical Treatise upon Christian Perfection* (1725). Wesley published an abridged version in 1743 (*Bibliography*, No. 77).

[64] William Law, *Serious Call to a Devout and Holy Life* (1729). Wesley again published an abridgement in 1744 (*Bibliography*, No. 86).

[65] 'A person of one book.' Cf. ¶ 5 of the preface to the first volume of *Sermons* (1:105 in this edn.).

[66] See Sermon 17, 1:398–414 in this edn.

[67] *Bibliography*, No. 1; in vol. 8 in this edn.

[68] Sermon 146, 'The One Thing Needful', 4:352–59 in this edn.

[69] JW's translation of a hymn in German by Paul Gerhardt, 'O Jesu Christ, mein schön-stes Licht', titled by Wesley 'Living by Christ', st. 2, *HSP* (1739), 156.

And I am still persuaded this is what the Lord Jesus hath bought for me with his own blood.

Now whether *you* desire and expect this blessing or not, is it not an astonishing thing that you or any man living should be di‹sgusted› at *me* for expecting it? Is it not more astonishing still that wellnigh all the religious world should be up in arms concerning it? And that they should persuade one another that this hope is 'subversive of the very foundations of Christian experience'? Why then whoever re‹tains it› cannot possibly have any Christian experience at all! Then my br‹other,› Mr. [John] Fletcher, and I, and twenty thousand more who *seem* both to fear and to love God, are in reality children of the devil and in the road to eternal damnation!

In God's name, I entreat you, make me sensible of th‹is! Show› me by plain, strong reasons what dishonour this hope do‹es to Christ›, wherein it opposes justification by faith, or any fundamental ‹truth› of religion. But do not wrest and wiredraw[70] and colour my words, ‹as› Mr. Hervey (or Cudworth) has done in such a manner that ‹when I› look in that glass, I do not know my own face! 'Shall I call yo‹u,' (says› Mr. Hervey) 'my father, or my friend? For you have been both to *me*.' ‹So› I was. And you have as well requited me! It is well, my rewar‹d is› with the Most High.

Wishing all happiness to you and yours, I am, dear sir,
Your affectionate brother and servant,

John Wesley

Address: 'To / The Revd Mr Newton / At[71] Mr Clunies' / Harp Lane / Thames Street / London'.
Postmarks: 'COUNTRY', 'DERRY', '27/MA', and another that has '5' at the top and is illegible at the bottom. *Charge*: multiple, illegible lines.
Endorsement: in a hand other than Wesley's: 'Rev Jno Wesley / 14 May 1765'.
Source: holograph; Bridwell Library (SMU).

---

[70] I.e., strain unwarrantably.

[71] There is a word following this ('Olney') that has been scored through by a hand other than Wesley's and all of the remaining words in the address have been added in a hand other than Wesley's.

To Darcy (Brisbane) Maxwell, Lady Maxwell of Pollok

L<small>ONDONDERRY</small>
M<small>AY</small> 25, 1765

My Dear Lady,

It is not easy for me to express the satisfaction I received in the
few hours I lately spent with you. Before I saw you I had many
fears concerning you, lest your concern for the one thing should
be abated,[72] lest your desires should be cooled or your mind a *little*
hurt by any of the things which have lately occurred.[73] So much
the greater was my joy, when all those fears were removed, when
I found the same openness and sweetness as before both in your
spirit and conversation, and the same earnestness of desire after
the only thing which deserves the whole strength of our affection.
I believe tenderness and steadiness are seldom planted by nature in
one spirit. But what is too hard for almighty grace? This can give
strength and softness together. This is able to fill your soul with all
firmness as well as with all gentleness. And hereunto are you called,
for nothing less than all the mind which was in Christ Jesus.[74]

It was with great pleasure that I observed your fixed resolution
not to rest in anything short of this. I know not why you should, why
you should be content with being *half a Christian*, devoted partly to
God and partly to the world, or more properly to the devil. Nay, but
let us be *all for God*. He has created the whole, our whole body, soul,
and spirit. He that bought us hath redeemed the whole, and let him
take the purchase of his blood![75] Let him sanctify the whole,[76] that
all we have and are may be a sacrifice of praise and thanksgiving![77]

I am not afraid of your being satisfied with less than this, but I
am afraid of your seeking it the wrong way. Here is the danger, that
you should seek it, not by faith, but as it were by the works of the
law.[78] See how exactly the apostle speaks: you do not seek it *directly*,
but *as it were* by works. I fear lest this should be your case, which

---

[72] See Luke 10:42.

[73] JW had been in Edinburgh between May 23 and 26, and he must have visited Lady
Maxwell in that period. When JW arrived in Edinburgh he learned of John Erskine's republication of the Hervey letters (see the letter above to Erskine dated Apr. 24). He was apparently
relieved to hear that Lady Maxwell had not been offended by the Edinburgh-centred controversy over the Hervey letters.

[74] See Phil. 2:5.

[75] See Acts 20:28.

[76] See 1 Thess. 5:23.

[77] In the eucharistic prayer of BCP.

[78] See Rom. 9:32.

might retard your receiving the blessing. Christ has died for *you*, he has bought pardon for *you*. Why should not you receive it *now*, while you have this paper in your hand? Because you have *not done* thus or thus? See *your own works*. Because you *are not* thus and thus, more contrite, more earnest, more sincere? See *your own righteousness*. O 5 let it all go! None but Christ! None but Christ! And if *he alone* is sufficient, if what he has *suffered* and *done*, if his blood and righteousness are enough, they are *nigh thee*, in thy mouth, and in thy heart![79] See, all things are ready![80] Do not wait for this or that *preparation*, for something to *bring* to God! Bring Christ! Rather, let him bring *you*, 10 bring you home to God! Lord Jesus, take her! Take her and all her sins! Take her *as she is*! Take her *now*! Arise, why tarriest thou? Wash away her sins! Sprinkle her with thy blood! Let her sink down into the arms of thy love and cry out, 'My Lord and my God!'[81]

Let me hear from you as soon as you can. You do not know how 15 great a satisfaction this is to, my dear Lady,

Your ever affectionate servant,

J. Wesley

Be pleased to direct to the New Room in Dublin. 20

Source: published transcription; Benson, *Works*, 16:189–90.

To James Knox[82]

SLIGO
MAY 30, 1765

Dear Sir,

Probably this is the last trouble of the kind which you will receive 25 from *me*. If you receive it in the same spirit wherein it is wrote, I

[79] See Rom. 10:8.
[80] See Matt. 22:4, Luke 14:17.
[81] See John 20:28.
[82] JW first met James Knox of Sligo on June 26, 1760, and commended his family for how they feared and served God (*Journal*, 21:265 in this edn.). JW visited Sligo again on May 1, 1762, but this time the Knox family treated him as a stranger (*Journal*, 21:364–65 in this edn.). JW returned to Sligo on May 28, 1765, and found no acceptance there (*Journal*, 22:3–4 in this edn.). The *Journal* account does not mention a meeting with James Knox on this occasion, but JW's disappointment on returning to Knox's town seems to have led to this letter.

shall be glad. If not, my record is with the Most High. I did not choose it should be delivered till I was gone, lest you should think I wanted anything from you. By the blessing of God I want nothing, only that you should be happy in time and in eternity.

5   Still I cannot but remember the clear *light* you had with regard to the nature of real scriptural Christianity. You saw what heart religion meant, and the gate of it, justification. You had earnest *desires* to be a partaker of the whole gospel blessing. And you evidenced the sincerity of those desires by the *steps* you took in your *family*, so that

10   in everything you were hastening to be not almost but altogether a Christian.

    Where is that *light* now? Do you now see that true religion is not a negative or an external thing, but the life of God in the soul of man,[83] the image of God stamped upon the heart? Do you now see

15   that, in order to this, we are justified freely through the redemption that is in Jesus Christ?[84] Where are the *desires* after this which you once felt, the hunger and thirst after righteousness?[85] And where are the outward marks of a soul groaning after God and refusing to be comforted with anything less than his love?

20   Will you say, 'But if I had gone on in that way, I should have lost my friends and my reputation'? This is partly true. You would have lost most of those friends who neither love nor fear God. Happy loss! These are the men who do you more hurt than all the world besides. These are the men whom, if ever you would be a *real Chris-*

25   *tian*, you must avoid as you would avoid hell-fire. 'But then they will censure me.' So they will. They will say you are a fool, a madman, and what not. But what are you the worse for this? Why, the Spirit of glory and of Christ shall rest upon you.[86]

    'But it will hurt me in my business.' Suppose it should, the favour

30   of God would make large amends. But very probably it would not. For the winds and the seas are in God's hands as well as the hearts of men.

    'But it is inconsistent with my duty to *the Church.*' Can a man of understanding talk so, and talk so in earnest? Is it not rather a

35   copy of his countenance? Indeed, if you can mean 'inconsistent with my pleasing this or that clergyman', I allow it. But let him be pleased or displeased, please thou God! But are these clergy-

---

[83] Evoking the title of Henry Scougal's anonymously published devotional manual, *The Life of God in the Soul of Man* (1677).

[84] See Rom. 3:24.

[85] See Matt. 5:6.

[86] See 1 Pet. 1:14.

men *the Church*? Unless they are *holy men*, earnestly loving and serving God, they are not even members of the Church, they are no part of it. And unless they preach the doctrines of the Church contained in her Articles and Liturgy, they are no true ministers of the Church, but are eating her bread and tearing out her bowels.

'But you will not leave the Church.' You never will by my advice. I advise just the contrary. I advise you to lose no opportunity of attending the services of the Church, of receiving the Lord's Supper, and of showing your regard to all her appointments. I advise you steadily to adhere to her doctrine in every branch of it, particularly with respect to the two fundamental points, justification by faith and holiness. But, above all, I cannot but earnestly entreat you not to rest till you experience what she teaches; till (to sum up all in one word) God 'cleanses the thoughts of your heart by the inspiration of his Holy Spirit, that you may perfectly love him and worthily magnify his holy name'.[87] Unless this be done, what will it profit you to increase your fortune, to preserve the fairest reputation, and to gain the favour of the most learned, the most ingenious, the most honourable clergymen in the kingdom? What shall it profit a man to gain all these and to lose his own soul?[88]

I know to God all things are possible.[89] Therefore it is possible you may take this kindly. If so, I shall hope to receive a line from you directed to Mr. Beauchamp's in Limerick. If not, let it be forgotten, till we meet at the judgement seat of Christ.

I am, dear sir,
    Your affectionate servant,

John Wesley

Endorsement: in a different hand than the letter, 'To Mr. James Knox. / He came to nothing!'
Source: Wesley's ms. proof copy; MARC, MAM JW 3/83.

---

[87] BCP, Collect for Purity.
[88] See Matt. 16:26, Mark 8:36.
[89] See Matt. 19:26, Mark 10:27.

To Margaret Dale[90]

My Dear Miss Peggy,

Certainly you not only need not sin, but you need not doubt any
5   more. Christ is yours. All is yours. You can give him all your heart,
and will he not freely give you all things? But you can only return
what he has given by continually receiving more. You have reason
to bless him who has cast your lot in a fair ground.[91] Even in this
world he does not withhold from you any manner of thing that is
10   good. Let your heart be always open to receive his whole blessing!

How far do you find power over your thoughts? Does not your
imagination sometimes wander? Do those imaginations continue
for any time? Or have you power to check them immediately?

Do you find continually the spirit of prayer? And are you always
15   happy? I trust you will be happier every day, and that you will not
forget, my dear sister,

        Your affectionate brother,

                      J. Wesley

Address: 'Miss Dale, At the Orphan House, In Newcastle-upon-Tyne'[92]
'By Portpatrick'.
Charge: '2'.[93]
Source: facsimile of holograph; Dale, *Letters*, opposite p. 7.

---

[90] Margaret ('Peggy') Dale (c. 1744–77) and her two sisters (Mary and Ann) were raised
in Kibblesworth, Durham (just outside Newcastle) by their aunt and uncle, Thomas and Sarah
Lewen, after their father died in 1755 (and their mother Eleanor, sister of Sarah [Lawrence]
Lewen sometime before that). The Lewens were active in Methodism. Their daughter Margaret Lewen took Margaret Dale along on Apr. 22, 1765, when she provided JW a ride in her
chaise to Newcastle (*Journal*, 21:504). This may have been JW's first meeting with Miss Dale.
He at least came to know her better and they struck up an extended correspondence. This is
the first letter of that interchange that survives. Margaret preserved the letters she received and
they were passed down in the family. The collection originally numbered 30, though some had
been given away by 1894 (see Dale, *Letters*, 1:7). At present, only nineteen of these are known
through surviving holographs, facsimiles, or published transcriptions. Among the letters missing is apparently JW's very first to Dale, because this letter of June 1 was numbered as the
second in the collection.

[91] See Ps. 16:7 (BCP).

[92] JW typically sent mail for society members in Newcastle to the Orphan House, where
they could collect it.

[93] The facsimile shows only the text of the letter; the full address information is found in
Telford, *Letters*, 4:306. Telford apparently had access to the holograph as some of these details
are missing from the transcription in Dale, *Letters*, 7–8.

To Thomas Rankin

LIMERICK
JUNE 9, 1765

Dear Tommy,

You see my plan on the other side.[94] Tell me of any alteration or addition which you think proper, and fix your quarterly meetings as you please, only let full notice be given.

Brother [Robert] Roberts has reunited them at the Dock; and I have a mild, loving letter from brother [Nehemiah] Jane. Nevertheless it is a doubt whether I ought to go to the Dock at all before the house is settled.

Tis pity, if a ready passage should offer, but one could exchange with George Story.[95] You know the man. If it[96] cannot be, we must be content. Peace be with your spirit. I am, dear Tommy,

Your affectionate friend and brother,

J. Wesley

⟨I[97]⟩ wrote today to have the *Select* ⟨*Hymns*⟩[98] reprinted. Tis pity but every ⟨on⟩e that is renewed had them and the ⟨*Fa*⟩*rther Thoughts.*[99]

Address: 'To / Mr Rankin / At Mr Jos. Andrew's / In Redruth / Cornwall'.

Postmarks: 'COUNTRY' and '19/IV'. Another stamp, perhaps incomplete, has 'ASHED'.

Charge: multiple markings and the notation, 'Missent'.

Source: holograph; Bridwell Library (SMU).

---

[94] The attached letter to the leaders and stewards (following).

[95] George Story (1738–1818), a native of Yorkshire, was admitted on trial in 1762 (see 10:293–94 in this edn.) and in August 1765 was appointed to East Cornwall (10:304). A printer by trade, he later became the manager of the Wesley Methodist printing office and Connexional Editor. See *EMP*, 5:218–41; and Vickers, *Dictionary*, 339.

[96] Orig., 'it it'.

[97] The postscript, written on a fold of the address, is damaged on one end, hence the reconstructed portions.

[98] JW, *Select Hymns, with Tunes Annext* was first published in 1761; an enlarged edition was published later this year. See *Bibliography*, No. 244.

[99] *Farther Thoughts upon Christian Perfection* (1762; 13:92–131).

To the Leaders and Stewards [in Cornwall]

LIMERICK
JUNE 9, 1765

My Dear Brethren,

Yours of March evening 28th I received yesterday. I shall have
5 little time to spare this autumn. Yet I will endeavour, with God's
leave, to spend a few days in Cornwall. I hope to be at Tiverton on
Tuesday, September 3, on Wednesday 4th at Bideford, on Thursday
evening 5th at Millhouse, on Friday at Port Isaac, on Saturday the
7th at St. Cubert's, on Sunday morning and afternoon at St. Agnes,
10 on Monday, 9th St. Just, Tuesday 10th St. Ives, Friday 13th St. Just,
Saturday 21st Bristol.[100] Let Mr. Rankin fix the time and place of
the quarterly meetings.

Peace be multiplied upon you. I am, my dear brethren,

Your affectionate brother,

15   John Wesley

Source: holograph; Bridwell Library (SMU), on same sheet as letter to
Thomas Rankin above.

To Margaret Dale

KILKENNY
JULY 5, 1765

My Dear Sister,

20   Although it is certain the kind of wandering thoughts which you
mention are consistent with pure love, yet it is highly desirable
to be delivered from them, because (as you observe) they hinder
profitable thoughts. And why should not you be delivered? Indeed,
in what manner this will be done we do not know. Sometimes it
25 pleases our Lord to work a great deliverance even of this kind in a
moment. Sometimes he gives the victory by degrees. And I believe
this is more common. Expect this and every good gift from him.
How wise and gracious are all his ways!

[100] The *Journal* for Sept. 3–21, 1765, shows that he observed this plan quite carefully.

Do you commonly find in yourself the witness that you are saved from sin? And is it usually clear? Or do you frequently lose it? I do not know why you should ever lose any good gift. For is not he the same yesterday, today, and forever?[101] And yet you have known but a little of him. You are to sink a thousand times deeper into him:

> That sea of light and love unknown,
> Without a bottom or a shore.[102]

I hope Miss Lewen[103] and you speak to each other, not only without disguise, but without reserve. How is your lot cast in a fair ground![104] How well are you situated for making the best of a short life!

> Secluded from the world and all its care,
> Hast thou to joy or grieve, to hope or fear?[105]

That is, with regard to present things? No, God has given you a nobler portion. You have nothing to care for but how you may most entirely and effectually present yourself a living sacrifice to God.[106] When I reflect upon your earnest desire to do this and upon your simplicity of heart, it gives an unspeakable pleasure to, my dear sister,
Your affectionate brother,

J. Wesley

I expect to be at Dublin till the end of this month. I send Miss Lewen's letter by Portpatrick to try which comes soonest.

Address: 'To / Miss Peggy Dale / At the Orphan house / Newcastle upon Tyne'.
Postmark: 'IY/9'. *Charge*: indecipherable.
Source: holograph; MARC, MAM JW 2/74.

[101] See Heb. 13:8.
[102] Isaac Watts, 'Blest be the Father, and his love', st. 4; included by JW in *CPH* (1737), 36, and *CPH* (1741), 100.
[103] As noted above (437, n. 90) Margaret Dale went to live with her aunt and uncle, Thomas and Sarah Lewen of Kibblesworth, Co. Durham (just outside Newcastle) in 1755. They and their daughter Margaret Lewen (c. 1742–66) were active in Methodism in Newcastle. Margaret Lewen was of fragile health, and partly at the advice of JW, she spent time in London in the early 1760s, where she befriended Mary Bosanquet. JW came to regard her a 'monument of divine mercy' (see *Journal*, May 2, 1764, 21:463 in this edn.), and she became a steadfast supporter and benefactress of his work, including leaving JW a bequest of £1000 at her death in 1766.
[104] See Ps. 16:7 (BCP).
[105] Matthew Prior, 'Solomon', Book II, ll. 386–87.
[106] See Heb. 12:1.

To Darcy (Brisbane) Maxwell, Lady Maxwell of Pollok

KILKENNY
JULY 5, 1765

My Dear Lady,

As yours was sent from Dublin to Cork, and then back again
5   hither, I did not receive it till yesterday. I am now setting my face
again towards England, but I expect to be in Dublin till the beginning of next month, and then to cross over, so as to be at Manchester (if it please God) about the middle of August. Either at Dublin
or at Manchester I hope to have the pleasure of hearing from you.
10   This is indeed a pleasure, as it is, to write you, though sometimes
I do this with fear, a fear lest I should give you any pain, as I know
the tenderness of your spirit. I wish I could be of some service to
you, that I could encourage you to cast yourself on him that loves
you, that is *now* waiting to pour his peace into your heart, to give
15   you an entrance into the holiest by his blood.[107] See him, see him,
full of grace and truth![108] Full of grace and truth for thee! I do not
doubt but he is gradually working in you, but I want you to experience likewise an instantaneous work. Then shall the gradual go on
swiftly. Lord, speak! Thy servant heareth![109] Say thou, 'Let there be
20   light'; and there shall be light.[110] Now let it spring up in your heart!

It may be he that does all things well[111] has wise reasons, though
not apparent to us, for working more gradually in you than he has
done of late years in most others. It may please him to give you the
consciousness of his favour,[112] the conviction that you are accepted
25   through the beloved,[113] by almost insensible degrees, like the dawn-
ing of the day. And it is all one how it began, so you do but walk in
the light.[114] Be this given in an instant or by degrees, hold it fast.
Christ is yours; he hath loved *you*; he hath given himself for *you*!
Therefore you shall be holy as he is holy, both in heart and in all
30   manner of conversation.

Give me leave, my dear friend, to add a word likewise concerning
your bodily health. You should in any wise give yourself all the air

---

[107] See Heb. 10:19.
[108] See John 1:14.
[109] See 1 Sam. 3:9 and 10.
[110] Gen. 1:3.
[111] See Mark 7:37.
[112] JW used the expression 'the consciousness of his favour' in his note on 1 John 3:21, *NT Notes.*
[113] Eph. 1:6.
[114] See 1 John 1:7.

and exercise that you can. And I should advise you (even though long custom made it difficult, if that were the case) to sleep as early as possible; never later than ten, in order to rise as early as health will permit. The having good spirits, so called, or the contrary, very much depends on this. I believe medicines will do you little service. You need only proper diet, exact regularity, and constant exercise, with the blessing of God.

Your speaking or writing was never tedious to me yet, and I am persuaded never will be. Your letters are more and more agreeable to, my very dear Lady,

> Your most affectionate servant,

> > J. Wesley

Source: published transcription; Benson, *Works*, 16:190–92.

To Thomas Rankin

KILKENNY
JULY 5, 1765[115]

Dear Tommy,

I received yours yesterday. I suppose you have now my answer to your last. The conference is to begin at Manchester on Tuesday, August 20.[116]

I have no objection to what you proposed to Mr. Hosken, only my age.[117] If he had left *that* gentleman trustee, I would not have given a groat for all his legacies. I wish he would not delay. A day ought not to be lost. I am,

> Yours affectionately,

> > J. Wesley

[115] There is a mark before the '5' that led Telford to date this letter as 'July 15'. But the mark is rubbed out, and JW was in Kilkenny on July 5, not July 15.

[116] See 10:302–14 in this edn. for the minutes of this Conference.

[117] Orig., 'Hoskins'. Joseph Hosken (1698–1780) was a wealthy farmer and supporter of Methodist work in the area of Cubert (St. Cuthberts). Wesley visited Hosken on Sept. 7 of this year (*Journal*, 22:18–19 in this edn.) and several times after.

I hope to set out for Cornwall (as I said before) immediately after the Conference. If possible, let the will be finished *before* I come. This would prevent much reproach.

You will carry Mr. Hosken's letter directly.

5

Address: 'To / Mr Rankin / At Mr John Andrews' / In Redruth / Cornwall / Per Gloucester'.[118]

Postmarks: a larger Bishop's mark 'IY/9', and a smaller Bishop's mark 'IY/15'.

Charge: various indecipherable markings.

Source: holograph; New York, The Pierpont Morgan Library, MA 516.3.

To John [or Alexander] Knox[119]

DUBLIN
JULY 20, 1765

Dear Sir,

Mr. [John] Johnson gives me a pleasing account of the state of
10   things in Derry.[120] The affection I have for the people there makes me rejoice in their prosperity. I should have been glad, had it been in my power, to have seen them once more before I left the kingdom. But as that cannot be, I am content, hoping the time will come when I shall spend a few more days with you, and that in the mean-
15   time Mrs. Knox and you and the rest of my friends will be making the best of a short life, using all the grace you have already received and waiting for the whole salvation of God.

The congregations which attend this foolishness of preaching, Mr. Johnson informs me, are still large. But what will they do as
20   the winter approaches? Perhaps it would be well to consider this now. Tis pity, but a convenient house could be built before the end

---

[118] The ms. address has 'Manchester' scored through with 'Glocester' (orig.) written underneath it. This rerouting is the likely reason for the second Bishop's mark.

[119] This letter is clearly to the father of Alexander Knox (1757–1831), of Londonderry, being the first in a bound collection passed down in the family where the remainder are to the son. This makes the address to 'John Knox' a bit puzzling, since reliable sources like Crookshank (*Ireland*, 180) report that the father's name was also Alexander (d. 1770). Either those sources are incorrect or JW had a temporary lapse of memory, substituting the name of the famous Scottish reformer. Whatever the father's name, the parents of Alexander Knox warmly received JW at Londonderry and hosted him at their home in May 1765 (see *Journal*, May 11–27, 1765, 21:507–22:2 in this edn.).

[120] John Johnson was stationed at Londonderry in 1765 (see *Minutes*, 10:306 in this edn.).

of the summer. This might be done, while so many people are well inclined, more easily than it could be afterward. It must be expected that the love of many who are now warm in affection will by and by grow cold. It would therefore be well if a convenient piece of ground can be procured to begin without delay. 5

I am much obliged to Mrs. Knox and you for your open and friendly behaviour, while I had the pleasure of staying with you, as well as for your helping me forward on my journey. I trust *your* love will not grow cold, nor your desire to make the best of a few days. You see the way: humbly to walk by faith with God,[121] to believe, 10 love, obey,[122] having received power from on high to walk in all the commandments and ordinances of God blameless.[123] May you both be steadfast and immovable therein! I am, dear sir,

> Your affectionate servant,

> > John Wesley 15

I expect to stay here ten or twelve days.

Address: 'To / Mr John Knox, in / Londonderry'.
Postmark: 'IY / 20'. *Charge*: marked, but indecipherable.
Endorsement: 'Dublin [space] 1765 / July 20, / Revd John Wesley'.
Source: holograph; Upper Room Museum, L-1.

To Sir Archibald Grant, 2nd Baronet[124]

DUBLIN
JULY 21, 1765

Sir,

A conversation which I fell into with Mr. Carr the last month oc- 20
casioned the foregoing letter. I am no judge of the contents. Only
thus far I can say, Mr. Carr, whom I have known these twenty years,

---

[121] See Micah 6:8.

[122] One of JW's favourite seals bore the inscription 'Believe, Love, Obey'.

[123] See Luke 1:6.

[124] This is a letter of introduction accompanying a long letter to Grant from John Carr, offering Carr's services as an adviser in linen manufacturing. Carr indicated that his motivation was principally religious, i.e., Carr was inclined to Wesley's vision of Christian faith and thought that Scotland would be less hostile than Ireland to his profession. Carr's letter gives Castlebar (County Mayo) as his mailing address. He is probably the same John Carr of Castlebar who later became a local preacher in that area; cf. *Journal*, May 17–18, 1778, 23:86–87 in this edn.

is a man of rigid honesty, of ⟨unwearied[125]⟩ diligence, and one that is allowed to understand the linen manufacture more than most men in this kingdom. I am, sir,
>   Your obedient servant,

5   John Wesley

Address: apparently in Carr's hand, 'To / Sir Archibald Grant, Bart / at Monimusk Near Aberdeen / Scotland'.
Postmarks: '29/IY' and 'DUBLIN'.
Source: holograph; Edinburgh, National Records of Scotland, Grant Family of Monymusk Papers, GD345/1170/1/22.

To Jane Catherine March

NEWCASTLE-UPON-TYNE
AUGUST 9, 1765

I have many fears concerning you, lest you should sink beneath the
10   dignity of your calling, or be moved to the right hand or the left from the simplicity of the gospel. Is your heart still whole with God? Do you still desire and seek no happiness but in him? Are you always or generally sensible of his presence? Do you generally, at least, find communion with him? And do you expect all that you enjoyed once,
15   and more, to be sanctified throughout before you go hence?

I hope no inward or outward reasonings are able to move you from walking exactly according to the gospel. O beware of voluntary humility, of thinking, 'Such an one is better than me, and why should I pretend to be more strict than her?' 'What is that to thee?
20   Follow thou me!'[126] You have but one pattern. Follow him inwardly and outwardly. If other believers will go step for step with you, well. But if not, follow him!

Peace be with your spirit,

[John Wesley]

25

Source: published transcription; *Methodist Magazine* 22 (1799): 200–201.

---

[125] The word 'unwearied' is questionable, the writing being obscured here.
[126] John 21:22.

To the Rev. Charles Wesley

NEWCASTLE
AUGUST 9, 1765

Dear Brother,

Yours came just to hand as I was taking my leave of Dublin. On Monday I expect to set out hence for Manchester. I wish you would write to Mr. [John] Fletcher.[127] In this case your word may go further than mine. I had engaged a young man in Dublin for the place at Bristol, but Mr. Franks[128] thinks I may save the expense, that with the help of Mr. Pine,[129] he can supply Ireland too with books, at least as well as it has been done hitherto. I will make a trial for a time. I firmly believe George Whitefield *might* recover but not till he lives like Lewis Cornaro.[130] I hope to return from Cornwall to Bristol in the latter end of September. But what is become of Lady Huntingdon? When do you see her or hear from her?

What hinders you administering the sacrament every week, or every day, to some of the poor sick? Mr. [John] Richardson can show you the way to as many as you desire. We both want more of Mr. De Renty's spirit, more of his holy love to the poor. I really believe you are a better divine than a logician, I mean, *pro hac vice*.[131] I cannot for my life see the connexion between the premises and conclusion. 'I dare not countenance John Jones, *ergo* I do not administer at Spitalfields when he is at West Street.'[132] By the same rule you ought not to administer at Kingswood when he is at London. If any of our old brethren, Robert Windsor, Richard Camp, John Riddal,[133] or any other [who] has been with us these twenty years and over and above, is alive to God, full of love to him and his children, can show me what the latter of these propositions has to

---

[127] No letter from CW to John Fletcher around this date survives.

[128] The published transcription reads 'Mrs. Franks', but this is surely Samuel Franks, JW's book steward in London.

[129] William Pine, JW's current printer in Bristol.

[130] Despite his ill health, Whitefield had left for America in 1763. He returned to England on July 7, 1765 in shattered health. Luigi Cornaro (1475–1566), was the Venetian author of a popular book translated into English as *Sure and Certain Methods of Attaining a Long and Healthful Life* (1702). JW's Oxford diary records him reading this work in Dec. 1732. Cornaro emphasised both proper diet and exercise.

[131] 'For this occasion'.

[132] CW is still questioning the legitimacy of John Jones's ordination by Gerasimos Avlonites; cf. JW to CW, Mar. 1, 1764.

[133] Robert Windsor (1703–90) was a native of London and one of the first members of the Foundery society (see JW's comment at his death, *Journal*, Feb. 7, 1790, 24:165 in this edn.). Camp and Riddal were presumably also longtime Methodists in London.

do with the former, *erit mihi magnus Apollo*.[134] 'But these men have received the sacrament from John Jones, *ergo* I dare not administer it to them.' This argument is good if their receiving from him puts them out of a state of salvation. But not else, not if they are children
5 of God still and act according to the best light they have.

Hitherto I have touched on the conclusion only, but the premise appears to me equally strange. I cannot see that the oath of supremacy affects *his* ordination anymore than it does *my* field preaching.[135] Nothing is more certain than it was never *designed* for any such thing
10 as to prevent a Greek bishop occasionally ordaining an Englishman, nor does this ordination imply that Englishman's withdrawing his allegiance in whole or in part from his sovereign, although it is sure this would be implied in his being ordained by a Romish bishop.

Undoubtedly the least inconvenience is, if you cannot get over
15 this odd scruple at which many are just now laughing in their sleeve and saying, 'Aha, so we would have it', to return to Bristol.[136] Otherwise I see nothing that can prevent an open breach between you and me. And what an occasion this would give the enemy to blaspheme!

You will never 'appease Mr. [Martin] Madan', unless you can
20 change his heart. He has a deep, cordial hatred to me, although you do not suppose he will own it. He is *mali caput et fons*.[137] The heart partly creates, partly catches hold on these occasions. I have abundantly sufficient to prove this charge under his own hand. Two of his letters, particularly his last, breathe the whole spirit of William
25 Cudworth.[138] Such exquisite bitterness I have rarely known, but it is all well. I do not know that John Jones will come to Kingswood at all. I think London is his place. I have just work and care enough. My love to Sally.

Adieu.
30

Source: published transcription; *The Christian Witness and Church Members Magazine* 18 (1861): 182–83.

[134] Virgil, *Eclogues*, iii.104; 'He will be the great Apollo to me' (Loeb).

[135] Anglican clergy were required to take the oath of supremacy to the reigning British monarch. CW had apparently objected that John Jones's ordination by Avlonites was invalid because it did not involve the oath of supremacy.

[136] CW had come to London in late May to help fill in while JW was on his extended trip to Ireland and the north of England.

[137] 'The head and fount of evil'. JW applied the same phrase to Thomas Maxfield in JW to CW, Dec. 23, 1762.

[138] Orig., 'Pudworth'; surely a misprint or misreading of JW's manuscript.

To Jane Catherine March

BRISTOL
AUGUST 31, 1765

You may be assured it is not a small degree of satisfaction to me
to hear that your soul prospers. I cannot be indifferent to anything
which concerns either your present or future welfare. As you covet,   5
so I want you to enjoy, the most excellent gifts. To your outward
walking I have no objection. But I want you to walk inwardly in
the fullness of love, and in the broad light of God's countenance.
What is requisite to this but to believe always, now to believe with
your whole heart, and to hold fast the beginning of this confidence   10
steadfast unto the end? And yet a self-complaisant thought, yea or a
blasphemous one, may steal across your spirit; but I will not say that
is your own thought. Perhaps an enemy hath done this. Neither will
I blame you for 'feeling deeply the perverseness of others', or for
'feeling your spirit tried with it'. I do not wish that you should not   15
feel it (while it remains) or that you should feel it otherwise than as
a trial. But this does not prove that there is sin in your heart or that
you are not a sacrifice to love. O my friend, do justice to the grace
of God! Hold fast whereunto you have attained.[139] And if you have
not yet uninterrupted communion with him, why not this moment,   20
and from this moment? If you have not, I incline to think it is occasioned by reasoning or by some inward or outward omission.

Source: published transcription; *Methodist Magazine* 22 (1799): 201.

To Thomas Wride[140]

REDRUTH
SEPTEMBER 9, 1765   25

My Dear Brother,
    I doubt very much whether either Jeremy Coombs or sister Wey-
worth spoke any such thing.

---

[139] See Phil. 3:16.

[140] This is the first of over thirty letters from JW to Thomas Wride (d. 1807). Wride
would be admitted on trial as an itinerant preacher in 1768 (cf. 10:366 in this edn.) and admitted into full rank in 1770 (10:380). He proved to be sharp-tongued and several of JW's letters
were attempts to discipline his language in the pulpit.

I advise you to go to Mr. Henderson and relate to him what you mentioned to me.[141] I have no objection to your speaking at those times and places which he shall think proper. On the 23rd and 24th of next month (Wednesday and Thursday) I expect, God willing, to

5 be at Salisbury myself. I am,

        Your affectionate brother,

                          J. Wesley

Address: 'To / Mr Tho. Wride, Shoemaker / Sarum'.
Postmark: illegible. *Charge*: '4'.
Source: holograph; University of Manchester, The John Rylands University Library, English Ms 343/13a.

To Thomas Rankin

                              St. John's

10   September 11, 1765

Dear Tommy,

There is a good work in Cornwall. But where the great work goes on well we should take care to be exact in little things.

I will tell you several of these just as they occur to my mind.

15 Grace Paddy at Redruth met in the select society, though she wore a large glittering necklace and met no band.[142]

They sing all over Cornwall a tune so full of repetitions and flourishes that it can scarce be sung with devotion. It is to those words, 'Praise the Lord, ye blessed ones'.[143] Away with it! Let it be heard

20 no more. They cannot sing our old common tunes. Teach these everywhere. Take pains herein.

---

[141] Richard Henderson was a native of Ireland who came to England about 1762 and soon entered the Methodist itinerancy (cf. 10:296 in this edn.). He was currently assigned as the Assistant for the Wiltshire area (see 10:304–5). Henderson ceased travelling about 1770 and settled near Bristol, where he ran an asylum for the mentally impaired. See Atmore, *Memorial*, 183–85.

[142] See JW's account of Grace Paddy (d. 1767), whom he calls a 'well bred, sensible young woman' in JW, *Journal*, Sept. 8, 1765, 22:19–20 in this edn.

[143] CW, Hymn 33, 'Thanksgiving', in *Redemption Hymns*, 43–44. While JW's comment is about the tune, not the text, it is noteworthy that he never included the text in any of his edited collections; whereas CW reproduced it in his independently published *Hymns for Those to Whom Christ is All in All* (London: n.p., 1761), 74.

The societies are not half supplied with books; not even with Jane Cooper's *Letters*,[144] or the two or three sermons which I printed last year;[145] no, not with the shilling Hymn-book,[146] or *Primitive Physick*.

They almost universally neglect fasting.

The preaching-houses are miserable, even the new ones. They 5 have neither light nor air sufficient, and they are far, far too low and too small. Look at Yarm house.

We have need to use all the common sense God has given us as well as all the grace.

I am, dear Tommy, 10
    Your affectionate friend and brother,

[John Wesley]

Recommend the *Notes on the Old Testament* in good earnest.[147] Every society as a society should subscribe. Remind them every- 15 where that two, four, or six might join together for a copy, and bring the money to their leader weekly.

Source: published transcription; Jackson, *Works* (3rd), 12:307.

To Sarah Crosby

Kingswood
October 5, 1765 20

My Dear Sister,

You oblige me much by speaking so freely. What an admirable teacher is experience! You have great reason to praise God for what he has taught you hereby and to expect that he will teach you all things. But whatever you find now, beware you do not deny what 25

[144] JW, *Letters wrote by Jane Cooper* (1764), *Bibliography*, No. 260.

[145] The only individual sermon (as a tract) that JW had printed in 1764 was a new edition of Sermon 41, *Wandering Thoughts* (2:126–37 in this edn.). He was likely including in this count Sermon 13, *On Sin in Believers* (1:317–34), published in 1763; and Sermon 43, *The Scripture Way of Salvation* (2:155–69), published in early 1765.

[146] JW (ed.), *Hymns and Spiritual Songs, Intended for the Use of Real Christians in All Denominations* (London: William Strahan, 1753); cf. *Bibliography*, No. 199.

[147] JW had just begun issuing *Explanatory Notes upon the Old Testament*, in weekly install-ments, in Aug. 1765; see *Bibliography*, No. 294.

you had once received. I do not say 'a divine assurance that you should *never sin* or sustain any *spiritual loss*'. I know not that ever you received this. But you certainly were *saved from sin*, and that as clearly and in as high a degree as ever Sally Ryan was.[148] And if you
5   have sustained any loss in this, believe and be made whole.[149]

I never doubted but ——[150] would recover her strength, though she has long walked in a thorny way.

A general temptation now is the denying what God had wrought.[151] Guard all whom you converse with from this, and from fancying
10   *great grace* can be preserved without *great watchfulness and self-denial.*

I am,

Your affectionate brother,

J. Wesley

Source: published transcription; Benson, *Works*, 16:332–33.

To Jane Catherine March[152]

A year or two ago you were pretty clear of enthusiasm. I hope you are so still. But nothing under heaven is more catching, especially when it is found in those we love, and, above all when it is in those
20   whom we cannot but believe to be sound of understanding in most instances and to have received larger measures of the grace of God than we have ourselves.

There are now about twenty persons here who believe they are saved from sin: 1) because they always love, pray, rejoice, and
25   give thanks;[153] and 2) because they have the witness of it in themselves.[154] But if these lose what they have received, nothing will be

---

[148] Cf. JW to Ann Foard, Oct. 12, 1764.

[149] See Luke 8:50.

[150] Possibly a reference to Margaret Lewen, who was in poor health and acquainted with Crosby.

[151] See Num. 23:23.

[152] Replying to her letter of Sept. 26, 1765.

[153] See 1 Thess. 5:16–18.

[154] See Rom. 8:16.

more easy than to think they never had it. There were four hundred (to speak at the lowest) in London who (unless they told me lies) had the same experience. If near half of these have lost what they had received, I do not wonder if they think they never had it. It is so ready a way of excusing themselves for throwing away the blessed gift of God.

I no more doubt of Miss ____[155] having this once than I doubt of her sister's having it now. Whether God will restore her suddenly as well as freely I know not; whether by many steps, or in one moment. But here again you halt, as Sarah Crosby did, and Sarah Ryan does. You seem to think pain, yea much pain, must go before an entire cure. In Sarah Ryan it did, and in a very few others. But it need not. Pain is no more salutary than pleasure. Saving grace is essentially such; saving pain, but accidentally. When God saves us by pain rather than pleasure, I can resolve it only into his justice or sovereign will. To use the grace we have, and now to expect all we want, is the grand secret. He whom you love will teach you this continually.

Source: published transcription; *Methodist Magazine* 22 (1799): 201–2.

To Christopher Hopper

BRISTOL
OCTOBER 16, 1765

My Dear Brother,

So honest Sander has outrode all the storms and got safe into the haven![156] The Lord does all things well.[157] I should not wish to stay here any longer than I could be useful.

You and James Kershaw are considerate men.[158] You must set your wits to work to find out ways and means. I will venture to

---

[155] Miss March had referred to a woman whose name was abbreviated in JW's published transcription to 'M. D.'. This was almost certainly either Margaret or Mary Dale; and those two are likely JW's referents here, though it is not clear in what order they should stand.

[156] The reference is to Alexander Coats (cf. JW to Coats, July 7, 1761), who died at the Orphan House in Newcastle in this month; cf. William W. Stamp, *The Orphan-House of Wesley* (London: John Mason, 1863), 112–13.

[157] See Mark 7:37.

[158] The *Minutes* of 1765 show Christopher Hopper stationed at Newcastle and James Kershaw at Yarm (10:306 in this edn.).

answer for one fifty pounds, payable next August. Let our brethren
pray in good earnest, and God will provide the rest. I am,
            Yours affectionately,

                                                    J. Wesley

5

I am returning to London.

Address: added in recent hand, 'To Christopher Hopper'.
Postmarks: '18/OC' and stylised 'BRIS/TOL'. *Charge*: no indication.
Source: holograph; Bridwell Library (SMU).

To Margaret Dale

L o n d o n
N o v e m b e r 6, 1765

10 My Dear Sister,
       By our intercourse with a beloved friend, it often pleases God to
enlighten our understanding. But this is only the second point. To
warm the heart is a greater blessing than light itself. And this effect
I frequently find from your letters. The Lord repay it sevenfold into
15 your own bosom! Do you still remain in the persuasion that you
shall not live beyond three and twenty?[159] Do you remember when
or how it began? Does it continue the same, whether your health is
worse or better? What a mercy is it that death has lost its sting![160]
Will this hinder any real or substantial happiness? Will it prevent
20 our loving one another?

            Can death's interposing tide
            Spirits one in Christ divide?[161]

25 Surely no! Whatever comes from him is eternal as himself.
       My dear sister,
            Adieu!

---

[159] JW refers to this premonition again in his letter of Dec. 31. Margaret (Dale) Avison
died in 1777 at the age of 33.
[160] See 1 Cor. 15:55.
[161] CW, 'The Communion of Saints, Pt. 6', st. 5, *HSP* (1740), 199.

Address: 'To / Miss Dale / At the Orphan House / Newcastle upon Tyne'.
Postmark: '7/NO'. *Charge*: '4'.
Source: holograph; Emory, MARBL, Wesley Family Papers, 1/48.

To William Orpe[162]

LONDON
NOVEMBER 13, 1765

My Dear Brother,
    You must in no wise return to your father's; it would be at the
price of your soul. You have already made the experiment, and you   5
made it long enough till you had wellnigh quenched the Spirit.
If you should leap into the furnace again, how would you expect
that God would bring you out? As to your temptation concerning
preaching, it is nothing uncommon. Many have had it as well as you,
and some of them for a time gave place to the devil and departed   10
from the work. So did John Catermole. So did James Morgan. But
God scourged them back again. Do not *reason* with the devil, but
pray, wrestle with God, and he will give you light. I am,
        Your affectionate brother,

J. Wesley   15

Address: in JW's hand, 'To / Mr Will. Orp / At Mr [scored through and
    illegible] / In [illegible] / Glocestershire'. This is scored through,
    and written below it in a different hand, 'Mr. Dickenson's near the
    Dolphin / in / Birmingham'.
Postmarks: 'STROUD', 'GLOUCES/TER', '12/NO', and a circular
    stamp with 'FL'.
Source: holograph; Bridwell Library (SMU).

---

[162] William Orpe was the son of a farmer at Prestwood, Staffordshire. The Minutes of
Conference show that he was admitted on trial in Aug. 1765 and assigned to the Staffordshire
circuit (10:303 and 305 in this edn.). Orpe would be admitted to regular rank the following year,
but in 1767 he married and withdrew from itinerancy; cf. JW to Orpe, Sept. 2, 1767.

To Thomas Rankin

Dear Tommy,

You have satisfied me with regard to the particulars which I men-
5 tioned in my letter from Cornwall.[163] Only one thing I desire you to
remember: never sit up later than ten o'clock; no, not for any reason
(except a watch-night), not on any pretence whatsoever. In general,
I desire you would go to bed about a quarter after nine.

Likewise be temperate in speaking—never too loud, never too
10 long, else Satan will befool you and, on pretence of being *more useful*, quite disable you from being useful at all.

Richard Henderson desired that *he* might be the book-keeper this
year in Wiltshire, and save me two shillings in the pound. But whoever you approve of, so do I. Write to Mr. [Samuel] Franks accord-
15 ingly. I am, dear Tommy,

Your affectionate friend and brother,

J. Wesley

Address: 'To / Mr Rankin / At Mr Jos. Garnet's / In Barnardcastle /
County of Durham'.
Postmark: cut away. *Charge*: '4'.
Source: holograph; Kansas City, Missouri, Kansas City Museum.

To Mary (Walsh) Leadbetter[164]

20 My Dear Sister,

Over and above that affection which arises ⟨fro⟩m[165] that general
relation which I bear to many, I ⟨ca⟩nnot but feel a particular affec-

---

[163] JW to Rankin, Sept. 11, 1765.

[164] While the address portion of this letter is missing, the recipient is Mary (Walsh) Leadbetter, to whose letter of Nov. 15 it is a reply. Mary (1733–1816) was the sister of John Walsh,
one of JW's travelling preachers. She had married Robert Leadbetter in June 1750, and been
widowed in Oct. 1758. At that point she became the governess of the children of Nathaniel
Gilbert (including Mary, mentioned in the letter), who had recently arrived in England from
Antigua. She accompanied the family on their return to Antigua in April 1759, then returned
with the children a few years later, to live with their uncle Francis Gilbert in Chester. In 1767
she married Francis Gilbert. Cf. *WHS* 55 (2005): 16–18.

[165] A small strip of the manuscript on the left-hand side of the recto and the right-hand
side of the verso is missing. The text is here reconstructed with high confidence.

tion for you and ⟨a⟩ few others. You are not only my children, but my ⟨fri⟩ends, united to me by the closest ties. I believe ⟨it⟩ is easier to experience than to describe, and much ⟨m⟩ore to account for, that strong union of spirit which ⟨I⟩ find to some, even above what we have for all the children of God. Are these not   5

> Souls which himself vouchsafes t' unite
> In fellowship divine?[166]

I have long felt this union with *you*. So I did with Miss Gilbert the   10
first moment I saw her.[167] Let us make this also, according to the design of him that gives it,

> [...] a scale
> whereby to heavenly love we may ascend.[168]   15

Not only Mr. [Alexander] Mather, when he first set out in the work, but his wife likewise spread fire wherever she went. There was in her a strength and fervour of spirit which enlivened many. But others could not bear with her infirmities, her oddness of expression, a⟨nd⟩   20
little improprieties of behaviour, so that they bore hard upon her, till her mouth was stopped a⟨nd⟩ she sunk into uselessness. I wish she could be p⟨er⟩suaded to exert herself at Chester, as she did for some months in Staffordshire. I think sever⟨al⟩ of *you* would have the skill to separate the go⟨ld⟩ from the dross.   25
    Go on, my dear friend, in that labour ⟨of⟩ love unto which God has called you. And if any opportunity offers of enlarging your sphere ⟨of⟩ action, be not afraid, but cheerfully embrace it. I trust you that are in one house are of one heart, all striving together for the hope of the gospel. But beware of thinking the promise is afar   30
off. Is it not nigh, even at the door?
    Peace be with all your spirits! I am, my dear sister,
        Your affectionate brother,

                                                                J. Wesley

                                                                                35
Source: holograph; Drew, Methodist Archives (address portion missing).

[166] CW, 'At Parting', st. 5, *HSP* (1742), 160.
[167] Mary Gilbert (1751–68), daughter of Nathaniel Gilbert. JW published *An Extract of Miss Mary Gilbert's Journal* in the year of her death, 1768 (*Bibliography*, No. 309).
[168] John Milton, *Paradise Lost*, viii.591–92; JW retained these lines in the abridgement of *Paradise Lost* that he published in 1763 (*Bibliography*, No. 253); see p. 207, ll. 505–6.

To George Gidley[169]

LONDON
NOVEMBER 25, 1765

Dear George,

I have well considered the case of Nathaniel Fenton.[170] It is cer-
5 tain we *can* have justice by moving the Court of King's Bench. But
it would probably cost forty or fifty pounds. Now, I doubt whether
this would be worthwhile, whether you had not better leave them
to themselves for the present. Only pray send Mr. Hale (as I promised) my answers to the Bishop of Exeter.[171]
10 If the justice at Exeter will grant you warrants, take them by all
means, and inform him (what probably he does not know) that I
have tried already with the whole bench of justices whether the
Conventicle Act affects the Methodists, and have cast them in
Westminster Hall. And if any, high or low, has a mind to fight with
15 me again, let them begin as soon as they please. I am,
Your affectionate friend and brother,

J. Wesley

Source: holograph; New York, The Pierpont Morgan Library, MA 7305.

To Darcy (Brisbane) Maxwell, Lady Maxwell of Pollok

LONDON,
DECEMBER 1, 1765

20 My Dear Lady,

Perhaps there is scarce any child of man that is not at some time a
little touched by prejudice, so far at least as to be troubled, though

---

[169] George Gidley was an excise officer at Port Isaac, Cornwall, who subsequently moved
to Exeter and became a leading member of the Methodist society there. See Elijah Chick, *A
History of Methodism in Exeter* (Exeter: S. Drayton, 1907).

[170] Fenton had apparently been accused of violating the Conventicle Act of 1670 (II Car.
II, c. 1), which forbade anyone over sixteen in England or Wales from being present in a religious assembly that was not conducted according to the liturgy and practices of the Church of
England. On the tenuous situation in which Methodist adherents, and particularly preachers,
stood in relationship to this Act, see 2:342, n. 8 in this edn.

[171] Hale was presumably a member of the society in Exeter. JW published (in 1750 and
1752) two open letters to George Lavington, Bishop of Exeter, in response to his book *The
Enthusiasm of Methodists and Papists Compared* in 1750 and 1752; see 11:361–429 in this edn.

not wounded. But it does not hurt unless it fixes upon the mind. It is not strength of understanding which can prevent this. The heart, which otherwise suffers most by it, makes the resistance which only is effectual. I cannot easily be prejudiced against any person whom I tenderly love till that love declines. So long, therefore, as our af- 5
fection is preserved by watchfulness and prayer to him that gave it, prejudice must stand at a distance. Another excellent defence against it is openness. I admire *you* upon this account. You dare (in spite of that strange reserve which so prevails in north Britain) speak the naked sentiments of your heart. I hope my dear friend will 10
never do otherwise. In simplicity and godly sincerity, the very reverse of worldly wisdom, have all your conversation in the world.[172]

Have you received a gleam of light from above, a spark of faith? O let it not go! Hold fast, by his grace, that token of his love, that earnest of your inheritance.[173] Come just as you are, and come boldly 15
to the throne of grace.[174] You need not delay! Even now the bowels of Jesus Christ yearn over you. What have you to do with *tomorrow*? I love you today. And how much more does he love you! He

> Pities still his wandering sheep, 20
> Longs to bring you to his fold![175]

Today hear his voice,[176] the voice of him that speaks as never man spake, the voice that raises the dead, that calls the things which are not as though they were.[177] Hark! What says he now? 'Fear not; only 25
believe!'[178] 'Woman, thy sins are forgiven thee!'[179] 'Go in peace; thy faith hath made thee whole.'[180] Indeed, I am, my dear Lady,
    Your ever affectionate servant,

John Wesley

30

Source: published transcription; Benson, *Works*, 16:192–93.

---

[172] See 2 Cor. 1:12.
[173] See Eph. 1:14.
[174] See Heb. 4:16.
[175] Cf. CW, 'At the Meeting of Christian Friends', st. 5, *HSP* (1742), 159.
[176] See Heb. 3:15.
[177] See Rom. 4:17.
[178] Mark 5:36.
[179] Luke 7:48.
[180] Mark 5:34.

To William Orpe

LONDON

DECEMBER 14, 1765

My Dear Brother,

You have a clear call to go home for a short season. But let it be as
5 short as you can. 'Let the dead bury their dead. But follow thou me.'[181]

I do not know that either getting a licence or taking the oaths
would signify a rush. These are things which the mob has little regard to. Not that there is anything in those oaths that at all entan-
gles the conscience. The very same thing which you thereby engage
10 to do every honest man must do without that engagement. We in
particular shall 'bear true allegiance to our Sovereign Lord King
George,'[182] whether we swear so to do or no.

The main point is to be all devoted to God. You might begin the
Sunday service at Birmingham as soon as the Church service ends.
15 I am,

Your affectionate brother,

J. Wesley

Address: 'To / Mr Will. Orp / At Mr Ezekiel King's / In Stroud / Gloces-
tershire'.
Postmark: '14/DE'.
Endorsement: 'Dec. 14, 1765'.
Source: holograph; MARC, MAM JW 4/31.

To Christopher Hopper

LONDON

20 DECEMBER 17, 1765

My Dear Brother,

I am glad you have been at Edinburgh, especially on so good an
errand. But I wonder Thomas Olivers ever disappointed them at

---

[181] Matt. 8:22.
[182] The Oath of Allegiance to the reigning monarch, required of all clergymen in both
the Church of England and tolerated Dissenting traditions. Since JW refused to register the
Methodists as a Dissenting tradition, his lay preachers were not required to take this oath.

Musselburgh. It is bad husbandry to neglect old places in order to preach at new. Yet I am informed he has been useful in Scotland. Whether he should now go to Glasgow or delay it a little longer I have left to Thomas Taylor's choice.[183] If you can spare Moseley[184] Cheek six or eight days, let him visit poor Dunbar. If brother Williams's affairs are not made up, he should not stay at so public a place as Edinburgh.

On one condition, that Michael[185] will make it a point of conscience to follow *your* directions in *all* things, great and small, I consent to his staying at Newcastle. If he is guideable, he may do well. O cure him of being a coxcomb![186] I am,

> Yours affectionately,

> J. Wesley

Address: 'To Mr Hopper / At the Orphanhouse / Newcastle upon Tyne'.
Postmark: '17/DE'. *Charge*: '4'.
Source: holograph; MARC, MAM JW 3/54.

[183] In 1761 Thomas Taylor (1738–1816) met JW, who invited him to become a preacher and sent him first into Wales. He went next to Ireland, and had most recently established the society in Glasgow. The question JW left to him was whether it was time for Taylor and Olivers (currently in Edinburgh) to switch places as had been adopted at the 1765 Conference (10:305 in this edn.). On Taylor, see *EMP*, 5:1–107; and Vickers, *Dictionary*, 346.

[184] Orig., 'Mosley'. Wesley had preached at the home of Nicholas Moseley Cheek in Chepstow on Aug. 31, 1763 (*Journal*, 21:427 in this edn.). Cheek was admitted as an itinerant at the 1765 Conference (10:303 in this edn.). He served in this role for three years, then became the incumbent of Salford, St. Stephen in Lancashire, in which position he published *A Collection of Psalms and Hymns to be Used in St. Stephen's Church, Salford* (Manchester: Sower and Russell, 1794). He was buried in the Church's graveyard on July 23, 1805.

[185] Michael Fenwick sought to became one of JW's helpers in 1751, but both JW and CW were doubtful of his gifts and discipline (see JW to CW, Aug. 3, 1751, 26:473 in this edn.). In 1755 JW took Fenwick as his groom for a period, commenting that he was 'upon occasion a tolerable preacher' (JW to E. Blackwell, Sept. 12, 1755). But by 1758 Fenwick had been encouraged to return to business. He was now seeking again to join the itinerancy, and would serve in this capacity between 1767 and 1774, before being again asked to step aside.

[186] I.e., cure him of being pretentious. JW repeated this advice concerning Fenwick to Hopper in a letter of Nov. 27, 1766.

To Margaret Dale

LONDON
DECEMBER 31, 1765

My Dear Peggy,

Whether that persuasion was from nature or from God a little
5 time will show.[187] It will be matter of great joy to me if God gives
you many years to glorify him in the body before he removes you to
the world of spirits. The comfort is, that life or death, all is yours,
seeing you are Christ's.[188] All is good, all is blessing! You have only
to rest upon *him* with the whole weight of your soul.

10 Temptations to pride you may have, or to anything, but these do
not sully your soul. Amidst a thousand temptations you may retain
unspotted purity. Abide in him by simple faith this moment! Live,
walk in love! The Lord increase it in you a thousandfold! Take out
of his fullness grace upon grace.[189] Tell me from time [to time] just
15 what you feel. I cannot tell you how tenderly I am, my dear sister,
      Your affectionate brother,

J. Wesley

Address: 'To / Miss Dale / At the Orphanhouse, / Newcastle upon Tyne'.
Postmark: '31/DE'. *Charge*: '4'.
Source: holograph; MARC, MAM JW 2/75.

---

[187] See the premonition of her early death mentioned in JW to Dale, Nov. 6, 1765.
[188] See 1 Cor. 3:22–23.
[189] See John 1:16.

APPENDIX

List of Wesley's Correspondence (in and out) 1756–65

This Appendix continues the project begun in the first two volumes to compile as complete a listing as possible of the letters known to have been written or received by John Wesley, whether or not the text is extant. Not included are letters that are merely inferred from the existence of a presumed reply. Similarly, references to letters from or to unnamed correspondents are not usually included. For inclusion there must be something specific, at least a clue to the correspondent or an indication of the date or contents of the letter (such as Wesley quoting extracts in his reply).

The columns list in order the date, the writer, the recipient, and details of location where either a transcription of the letter or the evidence for the letter's existence at one time can be found. For surviving letters by Wesley the last column gives where the transcription is published in this edition. For surviving letters written to Wesley, readers are generally directed to the website of The Wesley Works Editorial Project (www.wesley-works.org), where transcriptions are available (the main exception is extended rebuttals of Wesley's published volumes, which are actually books, even if cast in the title as 'letters'). The most common sources of evidence for letters that do not survive during this time period include a specific reference within another letter (abbreviated 'ref.'), quoted extracts in a surviving letter that is replying to the original, or Wesley's notation on a letter received of the date he replied.

Date	Writer	Recipient	Location
1756 Jan.	Thomas Walsh	JW	online
1756 Jan. 06	JW	William Law	Vol. 14 in this edn.
1756 Jan. 07	JW	Mary Wesley	27:1
1756 Jan. 10	JW	Joseph Cownley	27:2
1756 [c. Jan. 15]	JW	John Walsh	ref.; reply, Feb. 1
1756 Jan. 16	JW	Jonathan Pritchard	27:3
1756 Jan. 26	William Dodd	JW	ref.; JW reply, Feb. 5
1756 Feb.	'F. D.'	JW	online
1756 Feb. 01	John Walsh	JW	online
1756 Feb. 03	JW	Samuel Furly	27:4
1756 Feb. 05	JW	William Dodd	27:5–6
1756 Feb. 05	JW	Richard Tompson	27:6–10
1756 Feb. 07	JW	Burgoyne	27:11
1756 Feb. 10	JW	Sarah Ryan	ref.; reply, Feb. 17
1756 Feb. 12	Richard Tompson	JW	online
1756 Feb. 17	Sarah Ryan	JW	online
1756 Feb. 18	JW	Samuel Furly	27:11–12
1756 Feb. 18	JW	Richard Tompson	27:13
1756 Feb. 21	JW	Samuel Furly	27:13–14
1756 [c. Feb. 21]	JW	CW	ref.; JW to James West, Mar. 1
1756 Feb. 25	Richard Tompson	JW	online
1756 Feb. [late]	William Dodd	JW	ref. and extracts; reply, Mar. 12
1756 Mar. 01	JW	Ebenezer Blackwell	27:14–15
1756 Mar. 01	JW	James West	27:15–16
1756 Mar. 02	Samuel Davies	JW	online
1756 Mar. 04	JW	Ebenezer Blackwell	27:16–17
1756 Mar. 08	JW	'Sylvanus Urban'	27:18
1756 Mar. 09	Thomas Olivers	JW	ref.; JW reply, July 10
1756 Mar. 12	JW	William Dodd	27:19–25
1756 Mar. 14	JW	Samuel Furly	27:25–26
1756 Mar. 16	JW	Richard Tompson	27:26–27
1756 Mar. 27	JW	Howell Harris	27:27–28
1756 Mar./Apr.	Caleb Fleming	JW	Letter to the Reverend Mr. John Wesley, occasioned by his 'Address to the Clergy' (London: M. Cooper, 1756)

Date	Writer	Recipient	Location
1756 Apr.	unidentified	JW	online
1756 Apr. 16	JW	Samuel Furly	27:28–29
1756 Apr. 19	JW	Ebenezer Blackwell	27:30
1756 Apr. 20	Mary Wesley	JW	ref.; reply, May 7
1756 May 07	JW	Martin Madan	ref.; reply, May 18
1756 May 07	JW	Mary Wesley	27:31–32
1756 [c. May 10]	John Adams	JW	online
1756 [c. May 10]	John Gillies	JW	online
1756 May 14	JW	[Thomas Walsh?]	27:32–33
1756 [c. May 14]	Mary Wesley	JW	ref.; JW reply, May 21
1756 May 18	Martin Madan	JW	online
1756 May 21	Francis Fetherton	JW	online
1756 May 21	JW	Mary Wesley	27:33–34
1756 June [01]	clergyman in Cork	JW	online
1756 [c. June 04]	Mary Wesley	JW	ref.; JW reply, June 18
1756 June 18	JW	Mary Wesley	27:34–36
1756 [June 28]	James Clark	JW	online
1756 June 28	John Trembath	JW	online
1756 June 29	Thomas Waterhouse	JW	online
1756 July 03	JW	James Clark	27:36–40
1756 July 09	James Clark	JW	online
1756 July 10	JW	Thomas [Olivers]	27:40–41
1756 July 10	JW	Mary Wesley	27:41–42
1756 July 16	unidentified	JW	online
1756 [c. July 17]	Nicholas Norton	JW	ref. and extracts; JW reply of Sept. 3
[1756 July 18?]	JW	[Moore Booker?]	27:42–43
1756 July 19	J-B Malassis de Sulamar	JW	online
1756 Aug. 06	CW	JW	online
1756 Aug. 16	Samuel Walker	JW	online
1756 [c. Aug. 23]	William Darney	JW	ref.; JW to Norton, Sept. 3, par. 5, 16
1756 Aug. 27	Nicholas Norton	JW	ref. and extracts; JW reply of Sept. 3
1756 Aug. 31	JW	Robert Marsden	27:43–44
1756 [Sept. 03?]	JW	unidentified	27:44–45
1756 Sept. 03	JW	Nicholas Norton	27:45–50
1756 Sept. 03	JW	Samuel Walker	27:51–55
1756 Sept. 07	Judith Beresford	JW	online
1756 Sept. 09	JW	'Monthly Reviewers'	27:55–58

Date	Writer	Recipient	Location
1756 Sept. 15	JW	Martha (Wesley) Hall	27:58–59
1756 Sept. 18	JW	James Clark	27:59–63
1756 Sept. 26	CW	JW	online
1756 Sept. 30	James Clark	JW	online
1756 Oct. 01	Judith Beresford	JW	online
1756 [Oct. 05]	JW	'Monthly Reviewers'	27:63–64
1756 Oct. 11	CW	JW	online
1756 [c. Oct. 15]	unidentified	JW	online
1756 [Oct. 15]	JW	James Hervey	13:323–44 in this edn.
1756 Oct. 23	CW	JW	online
1756 Nov. 06	JW	unidentified	27:65
1756 Nov. 09	CW	JW	online
1756 Nov. 12	JW	John Gillies	27:66
1756 Nov. 16	CW	JW	online
1756 Nov. 16	JW	Capt. Richard Williams	27:66
1756 Nov. 20	JW	Samuel Furly	27:67
1756 Nov. 24	John Fletcher	JW	online
1756 Nov. 26	JW	Samuel Furly	27:68
1756 Dec.	JW	Edward Perronet	27:69
1756 Dec. 04	JW	Samuel Furly	27:69–70
1756 Dec. 13	John Fletcher	JW	online
1756 Dec. 22	JW	Dorothy Furly	27:70–71
1756 Dec. 27	J-B Malassis de Sulamar	JW	online
1757	[Richard Fawcett]	JW	*An Expostulatory Letter to the Rev. Mr. Wesley, occasioned by his 'Address to the Clergy'.* (London: J. Wilkie, 1757)
[1757 ?]	JW	Samuel Furly	27:71–72
1757 Jan. 08	JW	Matthew Errington	27:73
1757 Jan. 28	Samuel Davies	JW	online
1757 Feb. 11	JW	Samuel Furly	27:74
1757 Feb. 28	William Hitchens	JW	online
1757 Mar. 08	JW	Samuel Furly	27:74–75
1757 Mar. 24	JW	Samuel Furly	27:75–76
1757 Mar. 24	JW	Thomas Olivers	27:76–77

Date	Writer	Recipient	Location
1757 Mar. 25	JW	Proposal for *Original Sin*	27:77–79
1757 Apr. 08	J-B Malassis de Sulamar	on JW	online
1757 Apr. 22	JW	Mary Wesley	27:80–81
1757 Apr. 23	JW	Joseph Cownley	27:81–82
1757 Apr. 24	JW	Mary Wesley	27:82–83
1757 [c. Apr. 25]	JW	Mary Freeman	ref.; letter to Ebenezer Blackwell, May 28
1757 [c. Apr. 25]	JW	Thomas Walsh	ref.; reply, Apr. 30
1757 Apr. 30	J-B Malassis de Sulamar	on JW	online
1757 Apr. 30	Thomas Walsh	JW	online
1757 May 14	Sarah Crosby	JW	online
1757 May 14	Mary Wesley	JW	ref.; letter to Ebenezer Blackwell, May 28
1757 May 18	JW	Dorothy Furly	27:83–84
1757 May 26	John Fletcher	JW	online
1757 May 28	JW	Ebenezer Blackwell	27:84–86
1757 [June ?]	Mary Bosanquet	JW	ref.; JW to Dorothy Furly, June 18
1757 [June ?]	Mrs. Gaussen	JW	ref.; JW to Dorothy Furly, June 18
1757 June 14	JW	Sarah Crosby	27:86
1757 June 14	JW	Dorothy Furly	27:87
1757 June 16	JW	John Gillies	ref.; reply, Sept. 1
1757 June 18	Sarah Crosby	JW	online
1757 June 18	JW	Dorothy Furly	27:87–88
1757 July 01	JW	Sarah Crosby	27:89
1757 July [11]	JW	Dorothy Furly	27:89–90
1757 July 12	JW	Samuel Furly	27:90–91
1757 [c. July 15]	JW	Martin Madan	ref.; reply, Aug. 6
1757 July 15	J-B Malassis de Sulamar	JW	*A Short Examen of Mr. John Wesley's System: The Doctrine of Original Sin Examined … in a letter … to Mr. John Wesley* (London: J. Marshall, 1757)
1757 July 25	J-B Malassis de Sulamar	on JW	online
1757 July 27	J-B Malassis de Sulamar	on JW	online

Date	Writer	Recipient	Location
1757 July 30	J-B Malassis de Sulamar	on JW	online
1757 Aug. 03	J-B Malassis de Sulamar	on JW	online
1757 Aug. 05	J-B Malassis de Sulamar	on JW	online
1757 [c. Aug. 05]	JW	Sarah Ryan	ref.; reply, Aug. 10
1757 Aug. 06	Martin Madan	JW	online
1757 Aug. 07	Sarah Crosby	JW	online
1757 Aug. 10	Sarah Ryan	JW	online
1757 Aug. 12	J-B Malassis de Sulamar	on JW	online
1757 Aug. 23	J-B Malassis de Sulamar	on JW	online
1757 Sept. 01	John Gillies	JW	online
1757 Sept. 03	J-B Malassis de Sulamar	on JW	online
1757 Sept. 06	JW	Dorothy Furly	27:91–92
1757 [c. Sept. 10]	Samuel Walker	JW	extracts; reply, Sept. 19
1757 Sept. 15	JW	Mary Wesley	27:92
1757 Sept. 19	JW	Samuel Walker	27:93–97
1757 Sept. 20	JW	unidentified man	27:97–100
1757 Sept. 25	JW	Dorothy Furly	27:100–101
1757 Oct. 14	JW	Samuel Furly	27:101–2
1757 Oct. 21	JW	Dorothy Furly	27:102–3
1757 Nov. 01	JW	Robert Sandeman	13:347–56 in this edn.
1757 Nov. 08	JW	Sarah Ryan	27:103–4
1757 Nov. 13	Sarah Ryan	JW	online
1757 Nov. 22	JW	Sarah Ryan	27:105–6
1757 Nov. 24	J-B Malassis de Sulamar	on JW	online
1757 Nov. 25	J-B Malassis de Sulamar	on JW	online
1757 Nov. 29	Sarah Ryan	JW	online
1757 Nov. 30	JW	Sarah Ryan	27:106–7
1757 Dec. 01	Sarah Ryan	JW	online
1757 Dec. 01	JW	Walter Sellon	27:107–8
1757 Dec. 07	J-B Malassis de Sulamar	on JW	online
1757 [c. Dec. 08]	JW	Sarah Ryan	ref.; reply, Dec. 13
1757 Dec. 13	Sarah Ryan	JW	online
1757 Dec. 14	JW	Sarah Ryan	27:108–9
1757 Dec. 17	J-B Malassis de Sulamar	on JW	online
1757 Dec. 20	Sarah Ryan	JW	online
1757 [c. Dec. 23]	John Nelson	JW	online
1757 Dec. 23	J-B Malassis de Sulamar	on JW	online
1757 Dec. 30	J-B Malassis de Sulamar	on JW	online
1757 Dec. 31	Sarah Crosby	JW	online

Date	Writer	Recipient	Location
1758	John Dove	JW	*Remarks on the Rev. Mr. John Wesley's 'Sufficient Answer to the Author of the Letters of Theron and Aspasio', with a letter ...* (London: Lewis, 1758)
[c. 1758]	JW	Thomas Foulkes	27:110
1758 Jan. 06	JW	gentleman at Bristol	13:359–66 in this edn.
1758 Jan. 07	J-B Malassis de Sulamar	on JW	online
1758 Jan. 10	JW	Micaiah Towgood	Vol. 14 in this edn.
1758 Jan. 16	JW	George Merryweather	27:111
1758 Jan. 20	J-B Malassis de Sulamar	on JW	online
1758 Jan. 20	JW	Sarah Ryan	27:111–12
1758 Jan. 27	Sarah Ryan	JW	online
1758 Jan. 27	JW	Sarah Ryan	27:112–13
1758 Jan. 30	J-B Malassis de Sulamar	on JW	online
1758 Feb. 01	Sarah Ryan	JW	online
1758 Feb. 03	J-B Malassis de Sulamar	on JW	online
1758 Feb. 08	Sarah Ryan	JW	online
1758 Feb. 09	JW	Dorothy Furly	27:113–14
1758 Feb. 10	J-B Malassis de Sulamar	on JW	online
1758 Feb. 10	JW	Sarah Ryan	27:114–15
1758 Feb. 17	J-B Malassis de Sulamar	on JW	online
1758 Feb. 19	John Johnson	JW	online
1758 Feb. 20	JW	Sarah Ryan	27:115–16
1758 Feb. 24	J-B Malassis de Sulamar	on JW	online
1758 [Feb.–Mar. ?]	Elizabeth Hardy	JW	extracts; reply, Apr. 5
1758 [Feb.–Mar. ?]	Elizabeth Hardy —(2nd time)	JW	ref.; JW to Hardy, Apr. 5
1758 [c. Mar. 01]	Samuel Furly	JW	ref.; reply, Mar. 7
1758 Mar. 04	J-B Malassis de Sulamar	on JW	online
1758 Mar. 07	JW	Samuel Furly	27:116–18
1758 [c. Mar. 09]	JW	Mary Wesley	ref.; JW to Ebenezer Blackwell, July 12
1758 Mar. 10	J-B Malassis de Sulamar	on JW	online
1758 Mar. 11	Sarah Ryan	JW	online
1758 Mar. 14	Sarah Crosby	JW	online
1758 Mar. 19	JW	Sarah Ryan	ref.; reply, Mar. 20
1758 Mar. 20	Sarah Ryan	JW	online

Date	Writer	Recipient	Location
1758 Mar. 24	J-B Malassis de Sulamar	on JW	online
1758 [c. Mar 25]	JW	Martin Madan	ref.; reply, Apr. 29
1758 Mar. 25	JW	Jonathan Pritchard	27:118
1758 Mar. 30	Sarah Crosby	JW	online
1758 Apr. 03	John Newton	JW	online
1758 Apr. 04	JW	Sarah Ryan	27:119
1758 Apr. 05	JW	Elizabeth Hardy	27:119–23
1758 [c. Apr. 06]	JW	Mary Wesley	ref.; JW to E. Blackwell, July 12
1758 Apr. 08	JW	Samuel Furly	27:123–24
1758 Apr. 13	JW	Dorothy Furly	27:124–25
1758 Apr. 21	JW	John Newton	JW notation on Newton's letter of Apr. 3
1758 Apr. 25	Sarah Crosby	JW	online
1758 Apr. 29	Martin Madan	JW	online
[1758 May]	JW	Elizabeth Hardy	27:125–26
1758 May 01	JW	Samuel Furly	27:126–27
1758 [c. May 01]	JW	Sarah Ryan	ref.; JW to E. Blackwell, July 12
1758 May 02	JW	Dr. John Free	9:316–20 in this edn.
1758 May 17	Sarah Crosby	JW	online
1758 [June ?]	William Cudworth	JW	*Preservative in Perilous Times, in three letters: … II. To Mr. John Wesley …; III. To Mr. John Wesley …* (London: G. Keith, et al., 1758)
1758 June 05	JW	Ebenezer Blackwell	27:127–28
1758 June 05	JW	George Downing	ref.; JW to E. Blackwell, July 12
1758 June 21	John Walsh	JW	online
1758 June 30	Ebenezer Blackwell	JW	online
[1758 c. July 05]	JW	Peter Whitfield	ref.; John Newton to JW, Aug. 29
1758 July 12	JW	Ebenezer Blackwell	27:128–30
1758 July 21	JW	[Elizabeth Rawdon]	27:130–31
1758 July 28	JW	Samuel Furly	27:131–32
1758 [c. Aug. 20]	JW	James Deaves	ref.; reply, Aug. 25
1758 Aug. 24	JW	Dr. John Free	9:321–30 in this edn.
1758 Aug. 25	James Deaves	JW	online

Date	Writer	Recipient	Location
1758 Aug. 27 (?)	'John Wesley'	*Leedes Intelligencer*	online
1758 Aug. 29	John Newton	JW	online
1758 Sept. 02	JW	Samuel Furly	27:132–33
1758 Sept. 04	John Hodges	JW	online
1758 [c. Sept. 05]	JW	Augustus Toplady	ref.; reply, Sept. 13
1758 Sept. 13	Augustus Toplady	JW	online
1758 Sept. 13	JW	William Allwood	27:133–34
1758 Sept. 13	JW	*Leedes Intelligencer*	27:134–35
1758 Sept. 26	Sarah Ryan	JW	online
1758 Sept. 28	Sarah Ryan	JW	online
1758 [c. Oct. 01]	JW	Ruth Hall	ref.; JW to William Allwood, Oct. 15
1758 Oct. 04	JW	Francis Okeley	27:135–37
1758 Oct. 15	JW	[William] Allwood	27:138
1758 Oct. 15	JW	John Johnson	27:139
1758 Oct. 27	JW	Mary Wesley	27:139–40
1758 Oct. 28	JW	Thomas [Brisco]	27:140
1758 Nov. 04–07	JW	Robert Potter	Vol. 14 in this edn.
1758 Nov. 04	JW	[Sarah Ryan]	27:141
1758 Nov. 12	Sarah Ryan	JW	online
1758 Nov. 21	Michael Fenwick	JW	ref.; JW reply, Nov. 28
1758 Nov. 22	JW	Sarah Moore	27:141–42
1758 Nov. 28	Michael Fenwick	JW	online
1758 Nov. 29	JW	James Hervey	27:142–43
[c. Dec. 1758]	JW	Sarah Ryan	ref.; reply
[c. Dec. 1758]	Sarah Ryan	JW	online
1758 Dec. 09	JW	Augustus Toplady	27:143–44
1758 Dec. 09	JW	male lay leader in Leeds	27:144–45
1758 Dec. 23	JW	Mary Wesley	27:145–46
1758 Dec. 28	JW	Dorothy Furly	27:146–47
1758 Dec. 29	J-B Malassis de Sulamar	JW	online
[1759 c. Jan.]	Ann (Bloodworth) Furly	JW	ref.; JW to Samuel Furly, Feb. 17
1759 Jan.	JW	John Murlin	ref.; Murlin, *Experience of … Eminent Methodist Preachers* (Dublin, 1782), 1:105
1759 Jan. 06	J-B Malassis de Sulamar	JW	online

Date	Writer	Recipient	Location
1759 Jan. 10	Ruth Hall	JW	online
1759 Jan. 10	R. H.	JW	online
1759 Jan. 18	J-B Malassis de Sulamar	JW	online
1759 Jan. 19	J-B Malassis de Sulamar	JW	online
1759 Feb. 03	J-B Malassis de Sulamar	JW	online
1759 Feb. 17	JW	Samuel Furly	27:148–49
1759 Feb. 21	JW	Miss [Johnson?]	27:149–50
1759 Feb. 24	J-B Malassis de Sulamar	JW	online
[1759 Mar. ?]	JW	Samuel Furly	27:150
1759 Mar. 02	JW	Ebenezer Blackwell	27:151
1759 [c. Mar. 06]	Ebenezer Blackwell	JW	online
1759 Mar. 06	JW	William Alwood	27:152
1759 Mar. 06	JW	Dorothy Furly	27:152–53
1759 Mar. 06	JW	Matthew Lowes	27:153–54
1759 Mar. 10	JW	Lady Huntingdon	27:154–55
1759 Mar. 11	M. G.	JW	online
1759 Mar. 12	JW	Ebenezer Blackwell	27:156–57
1759 Mar. 20	JW	Miss [Johnson?]	27:157–58
1759 Mar. 21	Thomas Jones	JW	online
1759 Mar. 29	JW	William Alwood	27:158–59
1759 Apr. 09	JW	Mary Wesley	27:159–61
1759 Apr. 30	John Walsh	JW	ref.; Walsh to JW, Oct. 16, 1759
1759 [c. May 13]	James Lowther	JW	ref.; reply, May 16
1759 May 16	JW	James Lowther	27:161–63
1759 May 21	James Lowther	JW	ref.; reply, July 1
1759 [c. June 01]	J-B Malassis de Sulamar	JW	online
1759 June 08	J-B Malassis de Sulamar	on JW	online
1759 June 09	John Manners	on JW	online
1759 June 12	JW	Clayton Carthy	27:163–64
1759 June 12	JW	Mary Wesley	27:164
1759 June 19	J-B Malassis de Sulamar	on JW	online
1759 June 29	J-B Malassis de Sulamar	on JW	online
1759 July 01	JW	James Lowther	27:164–65
1759 July 03	JW	Dr. John Taylor	27:165–67
1759 July 06	JW	[Thomas Goodday]	27:167–68
1759 July 07	J-B Malassis de Sulamar	on JW	online
1759 July 07	JW	Samuel Furly	27:168–69
1759 [c. July 07]	JW	Richard Conyers	ref.; reply, July 9
1759 July 09	Richard Conyers	JW	online
1759 July 13	Thomas Goodday	JW	online

Date	Writer	Recipient	Location
1759 July 15	JW	Miss C—	27:169–70
1759 July 16	John Berridge	JW	online
1759 July 27	J-B Malassis de Sulamar	on JW	online
1759 July 29	unidentified	JW	online
1759 [Aug. ?]	JW	Walter Shirley	ref.; reply, Aug. 21
1759 [Aug. ?]	Samuel Davies	JW	ref.; Davies to JW, Aug. 06, 1760
1759 Aug. 04	J-B Malassis de Sulamar	on JW	online
1759 Aug. 06	JW	unidentified	27:170–71
1759 Aug. 10	J-B Malassis de Sulamar	on JW	online
1759 Aug. 19	JW	Dorothy Furly	27:171–72
1759 Aug. 21	Walter Shirley	JW	online
1759 Aug. 22	JW	Thomas Jones	27:172–73
1759 Aug. 22	JW	Richard Tompson	27:173
1759 Aug. 26	unidentified	JW	online
1759 [Sept. ?]	JW	Ruth Hall	ref.; reply, Sept. 9
1759 Sept. 9	Ruth Hall	JW	online
1759 [Oct. ?]	JW	Ruth Hall	ref.; reply, Oct. 12
1759 [Oct. ?]	JW	R. H.	ref.; reply, Oct. 31
1759 Oct. 12	Ruth Hall	JW	online
1759 Oct. 12	Robert Martin	JW	online
1759 Oct. 13	J-B Malassis de Sulamar	on JW	online
1759 Oct. 15	John Fisher	JW	online
1759 Oct. 16	John Walsh	JW	online
1759 Oct. 20	JW	[Editor]	27:174–75
1759 Oct. 23	JW	Mary Wesley	27:175–77
1759 Oct. 25	J-B Malassis de Sulamar	on JW	online
1759 Oct. 31	R. H.	JW	online
1759 Nov. 03	JW	Robert Martin	JW notation on Martin's letter of Oct. 12
1759 Nov. 04	JW	Editor of *London Chronicle*	27:178
1759 [c. Nov. 05]	JW	John Haughton	ref.; reply, Nov. 11
1759 Nov. 09	J-B Malassis de Sulamar	on JW	online
1759 Nov. 11	John Haughton	JW	online
1759 Nov. 17	JW	John Downes	9:351–66 in this edn.
1759 Nov. 21	JW	Samuel Furly	27:179
1759 Nov. 24	JW	Mary Wesley	27:180–81
1759 Nov. 29	A. W. P. Conradi	JW	online
1759 Dec. 11	JW	Mr. I'Ans[on?]	27:181

Date	Writer	Recipient	Location
1760 Jan. 12	Walter Shirley	JW	online
1760 [c. Jan. 20]	George Merryweather	JW	ref.; reply, Jan. 24
1760 Jan. 24	JW	George Merryweather	27:182
1760 [Feb. ?]	JW	Ruth Hall	ref.; reply, Feb. 26
1760 Feb. 06	JW	A. W. P. Conradi	JW notation on Conradi's letter of Nov. 29, 1759
1760 Feb. 18–23	JW	*Lloyd's Evening Post*	27:183–84
1760 Feb. 25	JW	Samuel Furly	27:184
1760 Feb. 26	Ruth Hall	JW	online
1760 Mar. 02	CW	JW	online
1760 Mar. 04	JW	Jane Catherine March	27:184–85
1760 [c. Mar. 06]	CW	JW	online
1760 Mar. 10	Thomas Maxfield	JW	online
1760 [c. Mar. 15]	Mary Wesley	JW	excerpts; reply, Mar. 23
1760 Mar. 17	JW	Ebenezer Blackwell	27:186
1760 Mar. 18	JW	Elizabeth Rawdon	27:186–88
1760 Mar. 23	JW	Mary Wesley	27:189
1760 Mar. 29	JW	Jane Catherine March	27:190
1760 Apr. 01	Anne (Balguy) Downes	JW	online
1760 Apr. 16	JW	Jane Catherine March	27:190–91
1760 Apr. 18	Ruth Hall	JW	online
1760 Apr. 18	JW	John Berridge	27:191–93
1760 Apr. 26	JW	Ebenezer Blackwell	27:194–95
1760 [May ?]	Dorothy Furly	JW	excerpts; reply, June 1
1760 [May ?]	Jane Catherine March	JW	ref.; reply, June 27
1760 [May ?]	JW	Ruth Hall	ref.; reply, May 30
1760 May 06	James Oddie	JW	online
1760 May 07	JW	Ebenezer Blackwell	27:195–96
1760 May 18	JW	John Rawdon	27:196–97
1760 May 27	Walter Shirley	JW	online
1760 May 30	Ruth Hall	JW	online
1760 June 01	JW	Dorothy Furly	27:197–98
1760 [c. June 10]	JW	Walter Shirley	ref.; reply, June 18
1760 June 14	JW	Mary Wesley	ref.; JW to CW, June 23
1760 June 18	Walter Shirley	JW	online
1760 June 19	JW	Samuel Furly	27:198–99
1760 June 23	JW	CW	27:199–200
1760 June 27	JW	Jane Catherine March	27:201

Date	Writer	Recipient	Location
1760 July 12	JW	Mary Wesley	27:201–3
1760 July 20	Walter Sellon	JW	online
1760 [Aug. ?]	JW	Walter Shirley	ref.; reply, Aug. 29
1760 Aug. 06	Samuel Davies	JW	online
1760 [c. Aug. 14]	JW	John Oliver	ref.; *AM* 2 (1779): 424
1760 Aug. 17	JW	John Trembath	27:203–4
1760 Aug. 29	Walter Shirley	JW	online
1760 [Aug. 30]	JW	John Oliver	27:204–5
1760 [late Aug.]	JW	William Barnard	ref.; Bernard reply, Sept.
[1760 Sept.]	William Barnard	JW	online
1760 Sept. 04	JW	Samuel Furly	27:205–6
1760 Sept. 04	JW	Walter Sellon	JW notation on Sellon's letter of July 20
1760 Sept. 09	John Newton	JW	online
1760 Sept. 17	JW	Editor	27:206–8
1760 Sept. 20	Ruth Hall	JW	online
1760 Sept. 21	JW	CW	27:208–9
1760 Sept. 28	JW	CW	27:210–11
1760 [Oct. ?]	JW	John Fletcher	quoted; Fletcher to JW, Oct. 27
1760 Oct. 03	Thomas Tobias	JW	online
1760 Oct. 27	John Fletcher	JW	online
1760 [Nov.]	JW	John Newton	ref.; reply, Nov. 14
1760 Nov. 01	Walter Shirley	JW	online
1760 Nov. 03	'Stephen Church'	JW	online
1760 Nov. 06	JW	John Fletcher	JW notation on Fletcher's letter of Oct. 27
1760 [c. Nov. 10]	'Philodemus'	JW	online
1760 Nov. 11	JW	Jane Catherine March	27:211–12
1760 Nov. 14	John Newton	JW	online
1760 Nov. 17	JW	Editor (re. 'Philodemus')	27:212–14
1760 Nov. 20	'T. H.'	JW	online
1760 [c. Nov. 20]	'Somebody'	JW	online
1760 Nov. 20	JW	voters in Durham	27:214–15
1760 Nov. 20	JW	Walter Shirley	JW notation on Shirley's letter of Nov. 1

Date	Writer	Recipient	Location
1760 Nov. 21	JW	Abigail Brown	27:215
1760 Nov. 22	John Berridge	JW	online
1760 Nov. 22	JW	Editor	27:215–18
1760 Nov. 22	JW	John Berridge	JW notation on Berridge's letter of Nov. 22.
1760 late Nov.	'R. W.'	JW	online
[1760 Dec. ?]	JW	Charles Gray, Esq.	27:218–20
[1760 Dec. ?]	unidentified	JW	extracts; JW to *Westminster Journal*, Jan. 1761
1760 Dec. 01	JW	'Philodemus', etc.	27:220–23
1760 [c. Dec. 05]	Jane Catherine March	JW	extracts; reply, Dec. 12
1760 Dec. 09	JW	Samuel Furly	27:224
1760 [c. Dec. 10]	'E. L.'	JW	online
1760 Dec. 12	JW	'Philodemus', etc.	27:225–30
1760 Dec. 12	JW	Jane Catherine March	27:230–31
1760 [c. Dec. 15?]	JW	Ruth Hall	ref.; reply, Dec. 30
1760 Dec. 17	Alexander Mather	JW	online
1760 [Dec. 20]	JW	'Mr. T. H.', etc.	27:231–33
1760 Dec. 27	Adam Milsam	JW	online
1760 Dec. 30	Ruth Hall	JW	online
1760 Dec.	'G. R.'	JW	online
1760 Dec.	'R. O.'	JW	online
1760 Dec.	J-B Malassis de Sulamar	JW	online
1761 [Jan. ?]	JW	Mary Bosanquet	ref.; reply, Feb. 1761
1761 Jan. [02]	JW	Editor	27:234–35
1761 Jan. [05–12]	JW	*Westminster Journal*	27:235–39
1761 Jan. 08	E. S.	JW	online
1761 Jan. 18	JW	Dorothy Furly	27:239–40
1761 [c. Jan. 20]	JW	John Murlin	ref.; Murlin, *Experience of … Eminent Methodist Preachers* (Dublin, 1782), 1:108
1761 Jan. 21	J-B Malassis de Sulamar	JW	online
1761 Jan. 22	Thomas Butts	JW	online
1761 Jan. 28	J-B Malassis de Sulamar	JW	online
1761 Jan.	'M. H.'	JW	online
1761 Jan.	'R. W.'	JW	online

Date	Writer	Recipient	Location
1761 Feb.	Mary Bosanquet	JW	online
1761 Feb.	John Oliver	JW	ref.; *AM* 2 (1779): 425
1761 [Feb. ?]	JW	Jane Cooper	ref.; reply, Feb. 21
1761 Feb. 02	JW	Samuel Furly	27:240–41
1761 Feb. 05	J-B Malassis de Sulamar	JW	online
1761 Feb. 11	J-B Malassis de Sulamar	JW	online
1761 Feb. 14	JW	Sarah Crosby	27:241–42
1761 Feb. 17	JW	'Mr. G. R., etc.'	27:242–44
1761 Feb. 19	JW	[Richard Challoner]	Vol. 14 in this edn.
1761 Feb. 21	Jane Cooper	JW	online
1761 Mar. 03	JW	Sarah Moore	27:245
1761 Mar. 04	JW	Jane Cooper	JW notation on Cooper's letter of Feb. 21
1761 Mar. 07	Mary Bosanquet	JW	online
1761 Mar. 13	J-B Malassis de Sulamar	JW	online
1761 Mar. 14	Elizabeth Jackson	JW	online
1761 Mar. 19	Mary Bosanquet	JW	online
1761 Mar. 24	JW	Christopher Hopper	27:245–46
1761 Mar. 30	JW	James Rouquet	27:246–47
1761 Apr. 01	Mary Bosanquet	JW	online
1761 Apr. 02	JW	Dr. John Green	27:248–49
1761 Apr. 06	George Bell	JW	online
1761 Apr. 06	Mary Bosanquet	JW	online
1761 Apr. 06	JW	George Downing	27:249–50
1761 Apr. 10	JW	William Legge	27:251–56
1761 Apr. 14	Jane Cooper	JW	online
1761 Apr. 16	Mary Bosanquet	JW	online
1761 Apr. 17	Mary Bosanquet	JW	online
1761 Apr. 18	M. W.	JW	online
1761 Apr. 23	Mrs. W.	JW	online
1761 Apr. 24	JW	Mary Wesley	27:256–57
1761 Apr. 25	JW	Thomas Olivers	27:258
1761 Apr. 30	Mrs. W.	JW	online
1761 [c. Apr. 30]	R. W.	JW	online
1761 [Apr. ?]	JW	William Green	ref.; reply, [May ?]
1761 [Apr. ?]	JW	Mrs. W.	ref.; reply, May 2
1761 [May ?]	William Green	JW	online
1761 May 01	Mary Bosanquet	JW	online
1761 May 02	Jane Cooper	JW	online

Date	Writer	Recipient	Location
1761 May 02	Jane Catherine March (?)	JW	online
1761 May 02	Mrs. W.	JW	online
1761 May 05	Mary Bosanquet	JW	online
1761 [c. May 15]	JW	Mrs. W.	ref.; reply, May 30
1761 May 29	JW	Elizabeth Booth	27:259
1761 May 30	Mrs. W.	JW	online
1761 May 30	unidentified woman	JW	online
1761 [June ?]	JW	Mary Freeman	ref.; JW to E. Blackwell, July 16
1761 June 04	unidentified man	JW	online
1761 June 07	JW	John Hosmer	27:259–60
1761 June 07	JW	George Merryweather	27:261
1761 June 14	JW	Martha (Wesley) Hall	27:261–62
1761 June 17	JW	Jane Catherine March	27:262–63
1761 June 19	JW	*London Gazette*	27:263–64
1761 June 20	Howell Harris	JW	online
1761 June 29	JW	Samuel Furly	27:264
1761 [June–July]	Alexander Coats	JW	extracts; reply, July 7
1761 July 07	JW	Alexander Coats	27:264–66
1761 July 10	H. C—k	JW	online
1761 July 14	Alexander Coats	JW	online
1761 July 15	JW	*Leedes Intelligencer*	27:266–67
1761 July 16	JW	Ebenezer Blackwell	27:268–69
1761 July 16	JW	Alexander Coats	JW notation on Coats's letter of July 14
1761 July 20	James Morgan	JW	online
1761 [c. July 20]	JW	Mrs. H. C—k	ref.; reply, July 29
1761 July 23	J. D.	JW	online
1761 July 23	William Grimshaw	JW	online
[1761 July 25?]	JW	Mary Bosanquet	27:269–70
1761 July 29	Mrs. H. C—k	JW	online
1761 July 29	JW	Henry Cantrell	27:270
1761 July 30	Mrs. W.	JW	online
1761 [July ?]	JW	Ruth Hall	ref.; reply, Aug. 04
1761 [c. Aug. 03]	'A. B.'	JW	online
1761 Aug. 04	Ruth Hall	JW	online
1761 Aug. 15	JW	Ebenezer Blackwell	27:271
1761 Sept. 01	JW	*Leedes Intelligencer*	27:272
1761 Sept. 08	JW	Samuel Furly	27:273–74
1761 Sept. 08	JW	Matthew Lowes	27:274

Date	Writer	Recipient	Location
1761 Sept. 08	JW	unidentified woman	27:275–76
1761 Sept. 08	JW	CW	27:276–77
1761 Sept. 29	Alexander Coats	JW	online
1761 Sept. 30	Hannah Harrison	JW	online
1761 [c. Oct. 03]	Thomas Rankin	JW	ref.; *MM* 34 (1811): 726–27 (2 letters)
1761 Oct. 10	JW	Alexander Coats	JW notation on Coats's letter of Sept. 29
1761 [c. Oct. 14]	JW	Thomas Rankin	27:277–78
1761 Oct. 30	JW	Matthew Lowes	27:278
1761 Nov. 11	George Whitefield	JW	online
1761 Nov. 24	JW	George Whitefield	JW notation on Whitefield letter of Nov. 11
1761 Dec. 14	JW	unidentified assistant	27:278–79
1761 Dec. 25	JW	[John Oliver?]	ref.; Sotheby's catalogue, June 9, 1909
1761 Dec. 26	JW	Elizabeth Hardy	27:279–80
1761 Dec. 26	JW	CW	27:281–82
1761 Dec. 28	Hannah Harrison	JW	online
1761 Dec. 28	Thomas Maxfield	JW	online
1761 Dec. 31	JW	unidentified	27:282
1762 [c. Jan. 12]	JW	Thomas Rankin	ref.; *Journal*, Feb. 5, 1763 (21:404 in this edn.)
1762 Jan. 14	Thomas Maxfield	JW	online
1762 Jan. 18	JW	Christopher Hopper	27:283
1762 Jan. 20	Hannah Harrison	JW	online
1762 Jan. 25	JW	Samuel Furly	27:284–85
1762 Jan. 25	JW	Matthew Lowes	27:285
1762 Jan. 26	Lawrence Coughlan	JW	online
1762 Jan. 30	JW	Jane Catherine March	27:285–86
1762 [c. Feb. 01]	Samuel Furly	JW	online
1762 Feb. 01	Ruth Hall	JW	online
1762 Feb. 13	JW	Matthew Lowes	27:286
1762 Feb. 20	JW	Thomas Rankin	27:286–87
1762 Feb. 23	JW	Samuel Furly	27:287–88
1762 Feb. 27	Erasmus Middleton	JW	online
1762 Mar. 01	JW	unidentified	27:288–89

Date	Writer	Recipient	Location
1762 Mar. 01	JW	Christopher Hopper	27:289
1762 Mar. 08	Thomas Rankin	JW	online
[1762 Mar. 10]	JW	George Horne	11:441–58 in this edn.
1762 Mar. 11	Emma Moon	JW	online
1762 Mar. 11	JW	Matthew Lowes	27:290
1762 [Mar. 12]	Mary Bosanquet	JW	online
1762 Mar. 18	Sarah Oddie	JW	online
1762 Mar. 20	JW	Samuel Furly	27:290–91
1762 Mar. 20	JW	Thomas Rankin	27:292
1762 Apr. 05	unidentified	JW	online
1762 Apr. 12	Lawrence Coughlan	JW	online
1762 Apr. 14	Emma Moon	JW	online
1762 [May ?]	JW	Thomas Rankin	JW, *Journal*, April 28, 1763, 21:410 in this edn.
1762 [c. May 01]	Samuel Furly	JW	ref.; reply, May 21
1762 [c. May 01]	Jane Catherine March	JW	ref.; reply, May 13
1762 May 04	John Manners	JW	online
1762 May 08	John Manners	JW	online
1762 May 11	Dorothea (Garrett) King	JW	online
1762 May 11	John Manners	JW	online
1762 May 12	Ruth Hall	JW	online
1762 May 12	Hannah Harrison	JW	online
1762 May 13	JW	Jane Catherine March	27:292–93
1762 May 15	John Manners	JW	online
1762 [c. May 15]	JW	Emma Moon	ref.; reply, May 24
1762 May 16	Mary Bosanquet	JW	online
1762 May 21	JW	Samuel Furly	27:293–95
1762 May 24	Emma Moon	JW	online
1762 May 28	unidentified person	JW	online
1762 May 29	John Manners	JW	online
1762 June 03	John Manners	JW	online
1762 June 04	Dorothea King	JW	online
1762 June 07	JW	Jane Lee	27:295–96
1762 June 15	Dorothea King	JW	online
1762 June 15	John Manners	JW	online
1762 June 18	JW	Christopher Hopper	27:296–97
1762 June 18	JW	Jane Lee	27:297
1762 June 19	John Manners	JW	online
1762 June 22	Ruth Hall	JW	online

Date	Writer	Recipient	Location
1762 June 26	John Manners	JW	online
1762 June 28	JW	Howell Powell	27:298
1762 [July ?]	JW	Emma Moon	ref.; reply, July 29
1762 July 03	John Manners	JW	online
1762 July 05	Dorothea King	JW	online
1762 July 07	Ruth Hall	JW	online
1762 [c. July 15]	Samuel Furly	JW	extracts; reply, July 30
1762 [c. July 15]	John Maddern	JW	ref.; JW to E. Blackwell, July 28
1762 July 20	unidentified person	JW	online
1762 [c. July 20]	unidentified person	JW	online
1762 July 25	unidentified person	JW	online
1762 July 28	JW	Ebenezer Blackwell	27:298–300
1762 July 29	Emma Moon	JW	online
1762 July 30	JW	Samuel Furly	27:300–301
1762 Aug. 01	unidentified person	JW	online
1762 [Aug.]	unidentified person	JW	online
1762 [Sept. ?]	JW	Jane Cooper	ref.; reply, Sept. 29
1762 [c. Sept 01]	Samuel Furly	JW	extracts; reply, Sept. 15
1762 Sept. 15	JW	Dorothy Furly	27:301–2
1762 Sept. 15	JW	Samuel Furly	27:302–4
1762 Sept. 22	Thomas Maxfield	JW	online
1762 Sept. 28	Benjamin Colley	JW	online
1762 Sept. 29	Jane Cooper	JW	online
1762 [Oct. ?]	Emma Moon	JW	ref.; reply, Nov. 5
1762 [c. Oct. 01]	Samuel Furly	JW	extracts; reply, Oct. 13
1762 Oct. 07	Jane Catherine March	JW	online
1762 Oct. 09	JW	Jane Catherine March	27:304–5
1762 Oct. 13	JW	Samuel Furly	27:305–6
1762 Oct. 16	Jane Catherine March	JW	online
1762 Oct. 16	Thomas Maxfield	JW	online
1762 [Nov. ?]	JW	John Fletcher	ref.; reply, Nov. 22
1762 Nov. 02	JW	Thomas Maxfield	27:306–9
1762 Nov. 05	JW	Emma Moon	27:309–10
1762 Nov. 22	John Fletcher	JW	online
1762 Nov. 26	JW	William Warburton	11:465–538 in this edn.
1762 [c. Dec. 10]	Samuel Furly	JW	ref.; reply, Dec. 20
1762 Dec. 11	JW	CW	27:311–12

Date	Writer	Recipient	Location
1762 Dec. 20	JW	Samuel Furly	27:312–13
1762 Dec. 23	JW	CW	27:313–14
[c. 1763 Jan.]	unidentified supporter	JW	online
[1763 Jan. ?]	Thomas Westell	JW	ref.; Westell to JW, Feb. 1
1763 [c. Jan. 01]	CW	JW	ref.; reply, Jan. 5
1763 Jan. 05	JW	CW	27:315–16
1763 Jan. 07	JW	*London Chronicle*	27:316–17
1763 Jan. 08	Adam Oldham	JW	online
1763 Jan. 13	JW	Jane Lee	27:317
1763 Jan. 17	John Manners	JW	online
1763 Jan. 22	James Rouquet	JW	online
1763 [c. Jan. 26]	John & Eliz. Dixon	JW	ref.; *Journal*, Jan. 28, 1763 (21:403 in this edn.)
1763 [c. Jan. 26]	John Fox	JW	ref.; *Journal*, Jan. 28, 1763 (21:403 in this edn.)
1763 Jan. 26	JW	Thomas Maxfield	27:318
1763 Feb. 01	Thomas Westell	JW	online
1763 Feb. 05	Thomas Maxfield	JW	online
1763 Feb. 08	Jane Catherine March	JW	online
1763 Feb. 08	JW	CW	27:318–19
1763 Feb. 09	JW	*London Chronicle*	27:320
1763 Feb. 26	JW	CW	27:320–21
1763 [c. Mar. 01]	'Philodemas'	JW	online
1763 Mar. 06	JW	CW	27:321–22
1763 Mar. 10	JW	Samuel Furly	27:322–23
1763 Mar. 13	Samuel Charndler	JW	*An Answer to … Wesley's Letter to William, Lord Bishop of Gloucester … in a Letter* (London: W. Nicoll, 1763)
1763 Mar. 15	Benjamin Colley	JW	online
1763 Mar. 18	JW	*Lloyd's Evening Post*	27:323–24
1763 Mar. 20	'Philodemas'	JW	ref.; 27:324 n 46
1763 Mar. 20	JW	Lady Huntingdon	27:324–25
1763 Mar. 21	JW	unidentified woman	27:326
1763 Apr. 05	JW	Editor	27:326–27
1763 Apr. 07	JW	Jane Catherine March	27:327–28

Date	Writer	Recipient	Location
1763 [May]	JW	unidentified friend	27:328–31
1763 May	JW	unidentified man	27:331
1763 May 02	Penelope Maitland	JW	online
1763 May 06	JW	John Johnson	27:332
1763 May 09	JW	Sir Archibald Grant	27:332–33
1763 May 12	JW	Penelope Maitland	27:333–34
1763 May 14	Jane Catherine March	JW	online
1763 May 16	Francis Gilbert	JW	online
1763 May 26	JW	Jane Lee	27:334
1763 [May–June ?]	Henry Venn	JW	extracts; reply, June 22
1763 [June ?]	Richard Hart	JW	ref.; reply, July 11
1763 June 03	JW	Ann Foard	27:335
1763 June 07	Richard Conyers	JW	online
1763 June 07	Samuel Meggot	JW	online
1763 June 18	Francis Gilbert	JW	online
1763 [c. June 20]	unidentified	JW	online
1763 June 22	JW	Henry Venn	27:335–39
1763 June 27	George Clark	JW	online
1763 July 11	JW	Richard Hart	27:339–40
1763 July 14	Jacob Chapman	JW	online
1763 July 16	JW	Dorothy Furly	27:340–41
1763 July 18	Benjamin Colley	JW	online
1763 July 25	Frances (Erskine) Gardiner	JW	online
1763 Aug. 02	Elizabeth Bennis	JW	online
1763 Aug. 23	JW	Elizabeth Bennis	27:341–42
1763 Sept. 03	JW	Christopher Hopper	27:342–43
1763 [Sept. 15]	George Merryweather	JW	ref.; reply, Oct. 5
1763 [c. Oct.]	unidentified	JW	online
1763 Oct. 05	JW	George Merryweather	27:343
1763 [c. Oct. 20]	Christopher Hopper	JW	extracts; reply, Nov. 2
1763 Nov. 02	JW	Frances (Erskine) Gardiner	27:344
1763 Nov. 02	JW	Christopher Hopper	27:345
1763 Dec. 15	JW	Dorothy Furly	27:345–46
1764 Jan.	JW	George Whitefield	ref.; Whitefield to JW, Sept. 25, 1764
1764 [c. Jan. 01]	Samuel Furly	JW	ref.; reply, Jan. 14

Date	Writer	Recipient	Location
1764 Jan. 08	JW	Lady Huntingdon	27:347–48
1764 Jan. 14	JW	Samuel Furly	27:348
1764 Jan. 31	JW	John Valton	27:349
1764 Feb. 10	Thomas Hanson	JW	ref.; reply, Feb. 15
1764 Feb. 15	JW	Thomas Hanson	27:350
1764 Feb. 25	JW	Thomas Hanson	27:350–51
1764 [c. Mar. 01]	Samuel Furly	JW	ref.: reply, Mar. 6
1764 Mar. 01	JW	CW	27:351–52
1764 Mar. 02	JW	Jane (Lee) Freeman	27:352–53
1764 Mar. 06	unidentified woman	JW	online
1764 Mar. 06	JW	Samuel Furly	27:353–54
1764 [Mar. 13]	John Richardson	JW	online
1764 Mar. 25	JW	unidentified woman	27:355
1764 Mar. 27	JW	Thomas Hartley	27:356–57
1764 Mar. 29	JW	unidentified man	27:357–58
1764 Apr. 05	unidentified woman	JW	online
1764 Apr. 19	JW	William Legge	27:358–61
1764 Apr. 20	JW	Lady Huntingdon	27:362
1764 Apr. 23	JW	unidentified correspondent	27:363
1764 Apr. 23	JW	Elizabeth Woodhouse	27:363–64
1764 Apr. 24	John Newton	JW	online
1764 Apr.	John Johnson	JW	online
1764 Apr.	unidentified person	JW	online
1764 [c. May 1]	Richard Hart	JW	ref.; JW to Lady Huntingdon, May 16
1764 May 04	unidentified woman	JW	online
1764 [c. May 5]	Lady Huntingdon	JW	ref.; reply, May 16
1764 May 07	JW	George Merryweather	27:364–65
1764 May 07	JW	Thomas Newall	27:365–66
1764 May 13	JW	Cradock Glascott	27:366–67
1764 May 16	JW	Lady Huntingdon	27:367–68
1764 May 22	JW	unidentified person	27:369
1764 May 23	Samuel Wells, Jnr.	JW	online
1764 May 25	JW	CW	27:369–70
1764 May 28	unidentified	JW	online
1764 May 28	JW	Dorothy Furly	27:370–71
1764 May 30	JW	Matthew Errington	27:371–72
1764 June 17	William Penington	JW	online
1764 June 18	Elizabeth Jackson	JW	online

Date	Writer	Recipient	Location
1764 June 20	JW	Darcy Maxwell	27:372–73
1764 June 24	JW	Jane Catherine March	27:374
1764 [June–July ?]	William Legge	JW	ref.; reply, July 26
1765 [c. July 1]	Darcy Maxwell	JW	ref. and extract; reply, July 10
1764 July 05	JW	Sarah Moore	27:375
1764 July 10	JW	Darcy Maxwell	27:375–77
1764 July 13	JW	unidentified man	27:377–78
1764 July 14	JW	Ebenezer Blackwell	27:379
1764 July 15	JW	Samuel Furly	27:380–82
1764 July 26	JW	William Legge	27:382–84
1764 [c. Aug. 01]	Darcy Maxwell	JW	ref.; reply, Aug. 17
1764 Aug. 17	JW	Darcy Maxwell	27:384–86
1764 [Aug.–Sept.]	Samuel Furly	JW	extracts; reply, Oct. 11
1764 [c. Sept 15]	Darcy Maxwell	JW	ref.; reply, Sept. 22
1764 Sept. 18	Nathaniel Gilbert	JW	online
1764 [c. Sept. 20]	Ann Foard	JW	ref.; reply, Sept. 29
1764 Sept. 21	JW	Thomas Rankin	27:386–87
1764 Sept. 22	JW	Darcy Maxwell	27:387–89
1764 Sept. 25	George Whitefield	JW	online
1764 Sept. 29	JW	Ann Foard	27:389–91
1764 Sept. 29	JW	Christopher Hopper	27:391–92
1764 [Oct.]	JW	Joseph Townsend	ref.; reply, Oct. 16
1764 Oct. 11	JW	Samuel Furly	27:392–93
1764 Oct. 12	JW	Ann Foard	27:394–95
1764 Oct. 13	'A Presbyterian'	JW	online
1764 Oct. 13	JW	Jane Catherine March	27:396
1764 Oct. 16	Joseph Townsend	JW	online
1764 Oct. 17	'A Presbyterian'	JW	online
1764 Oct. 24	'Solicitus'	JW	online
1764 Oct. 24	'A Presbyterian'	JW	online
1764 Oct. 25	'A Presbyterian'	JW	online
1764 Oct. 27	JW	*St. James's Chronicle*	27:397–98
1764 Oct. 29	JW	*St. James's Chronicle*	27:398–99
[1764 Nov.]	'Philosophaster'	JW	online
1764 Nov. 02	JW	Thomas Rankin	27:399
1764 Nov. 05	'A Presbyterian'	JW	online
1764 Nov. 06	JW	Thomas Rankin	27:400
1764 Nov. 08	Mary Bosanquet	JW	online
1764 Nov. 12	John Cook	JW	online

Date	Writer	Recipient	Location
1764 Nov. 20	Richard Blackwell	JW	online
1764 Nov. 28	Miss P. T.	JW	online
1764 Nov. 29	'A Presbyterian'	JW	online
1764 [Dec. ?]	JW	Miss T. H.	ref.; reply, Dec. 22
1764 [c. Dec. 1]	Mark Davis	JW	ref.; JW to CW, Dec. 07
1764 [c. Dec. 1]	Thomas Lewis	JW	ref.; JW to CW, Dec. 07
1764 [c. Dec. 1]	CW	JW	ref.; reply, Dec. 07
1764 Dec. 07	JW	CW	27:401–2
1764 Dec. 08	JW	Sarah Moore	27:403
1764 Dec. 10	Jacob Chapman	JW	online
1764 Dec. 10	'A. P.'	JW	online
1764 Dec. 15	JW	Thomas Rankin	27:403–4
1764 Dec. 20	JW	Corporation of Bristol	27:404–5
1764 Dec. 20	JW	CW	27:405
1764 Dec. 22	Miss T. H.	JW	online
1764 Dec. 23	Emma Moon	JW	online
1764 Dec. 23	James Morgan	JW	online
1764 Dec. 31	JW	CW	27:405–6
[1764 Dec. ?]	JW	Mary Leadbetter	ref.; reply, [Dec. 1764]
[1764 Dec.]	Mary (Walsh) Leadbetter	JW	online
1765 [c. Jan. 1]	Mr. Mallon	JW	ref.; JW to Thomas Rankin, Jan. 13
1765 Jan. 04	JW	'Philosophaster'	27:407–12
1765 [c. Jan. 08]	George Downing	JW	ref.; JW to CW, Jan. 11
1765 [c. Jan. 08]	'A. P.'	JW	online
1765 Jan. 11	JW	CW	27:413–14
1765 Jan. 13	JW	Thomas Rankin	27:414
1765 Jan. 26	JW	Thomas Rankin	27:415
1765 [c. Jan. 27]	'J. T.'	JW	online
1765 [c. Feb. 05]	JW	*St. James's Chronicle*	27:415–16
1765 Feb. 06	['Southwark Hatmaker']	JW	online
1765 Feb. 09	JW	Thomas Rankin	27:416
1765 [c. Feb. 10]	JW	*St. James's Chronicle*	27:417–18
1765 Feb. 15	'Southwark Hatmaker'	JW	online
1765 Feb. 27	JW	James Thwaite, etc.	27:418–19
1765 Mar.	'Philosophaster'	JW	online

Date	Writer	Recipient	Location
1765 Mar. 09	JW	Thomas Rankin	27:419–20
1765 [c. Mar. 10]	JW	William Atkinson	ref.; JW to T. Rankin, Mar. 9
1765 Mar. 28	Cornish stewards	JW	ref.; JW reply, June 9
1765 Apr.	Henry Brooke	JW	online
1765 Apr. 09	JW	John Newton	27:420–22
1765 Apr. 18	John Newton	JW	online
1765 Apr. 19	Elizabeth Jackson	JW	online
1765 Apr. 24	JW	Dr. John Erskine	27:422–25
1765 May 14	JW	John Newton	27:426–29
1765 May 25	JW	Darcy Maxwell	27:430–31
1765 May 30	JW	James Knox	27:431–33
1765 [June ?]	JW	Samuel Franks	quoted; Benjamin Colley to JW, July 20
1765 June 01	JW	Margaret (Peggy) Dale	27:434
1765 June 09	JW	Thomas Rankin	27:435
1765 June 09	JW	Cornish stewards	27:436
1765 June 13	John Dillon	JW	online
1765 June 18	Margaret Dale	JW	online
1765 [c. June 20]	Darcy Maxwell	JW	ref.; reply, July 5
1765 [June–July ?]	Martin Madan	JW	2 letters, ref.; JW to CW, Aug. 9
1765 July 05	JW	Margaret (Peggy) Dale	27:436–37
1765 July 05	JW	Margaret Lewen	ref.; JW to Margaret Dale, July 5, PS
1765 July 05	JW	Darcy Maxwell	27:438–39
1765 [c. July 10]	JW	Thomas Rankin	ref.; JW to Rankin, July 15
1765 [c. July 10]	Thomas Rankin	JW	ref.; reply, July 15
1765 July 15	JW	Thomas Rankin	27:439–40
1765 July 20	Benjamin Colley	JW	online
1765 July 20	JW	John Knox	27:440–41
1765 July 21	JW	Sir Archibald Grant	27:441–42
1765 July 22	Nathaniel Gilbert	JW	online
1765 July 27	JW	unidentified	ref.; Sotheby's catalogue, June 6, 1950
1765 [c. Aug. 01]	CW	JW	ref. and extracts; reply, Aug. 9
1765 Aug. 09	JW	Jane Catherine March	27:442
1765 Aug. 09	JW	CW	27:443–44

Date	Writer	Recipient	Location
1765 [c. Aug. 20]	Jane Catherine March	JW	extract; reply, Aug. 31
1765 Aug. 31	JW	Jane Catherine March	27:445
1765 Sept. 09	JW	Thomas Wride	27:445–46
1765 Sept. 11	JW	Thomas Rankin	27:446–47
1765 Sept. 26	Jane Catherine March	JW	online
1765 [c. Oct. 01]	Sarah Crosby	JW	extract; reply, Oct. 05
1765 Oct. 05	JW	Sarah Crosby	27:447–48
1765 Oct. 07	unidentified	JW	online
1765 Oct. 13	JW	Jane Catherine March	27:448–49
1765 Oct. 16	JW	Christopher Hopper	27:449–50
1765 Oct. 19	Damaris Perronet	JW	online
1765 Nov. 06	JW	Margaret (Peggy) Dale	27:450–51
1765 [c. Nov. 10]	Thomas Rankin	JW	ref.; reply, Nov. 18
1765 Nov. 13	JW	William Orpe	27:451
1765 Nov. 15	Mary (Walsh) Leadbetter	JW	online
1765 Nov. 18	JW	Thomas Rankin	27:452
1765 Nov. 22	JW	Mary (Walsh) Leadbetter	27:452–53
1765 Nov. 25	JW	George Gidley	27:454
1765 Dec. 01	JW	Darcy Maxwell	27:454–55
1765 Dec. 14	JW	William Orpe	27:456
1765 [c. Dec. 15]	Margaret Dale	JW	ref.; reply, Dec. 31
1765 Dec. 17	JW	Christopher Hopper	27:456–57
1765 Dec. 31	JW	Margaret (Peggy) Dale	27:458

INDEX OF RECIPIENTS OF SURVIVING LETTERS

INDEX OF PERSONS MENTIONED

Note: This index does not replicate names of recipients of surviving JW letters, unless the person is mentioned outside of the letters they received from JW.

CPSIA information can be obtained at www.ICGtesting.com
Printed in the USA
LVOW06*0858260915

455779LV00001B/1/P